THE
HISTORY
OF THE
GRAND
NATIONAL
A RACE APART

Reg Green

Foreword by
Desmond Lynam

Hodder & Stoughton
LONDON SYDNEY AUCKLAND

Many of the photographs in this book are from the author's own albums. It has not always been possible to trace copyright. The publishers apologise for any inadvertent infringement and will be happy to include an acknowledgment in any future edition.

BLACK AND WHITE PHOTOGRAPH CREDITS
W W Rouch: page 142; Sport and General Press Agency: pages 145, 248, 249, 285 (both), 307; Ossie Dale: pages 149, 170; Central Press: pages 193, 209; *Liverpool Daily Post and Echo*: pages 194, 204/5, 224, 226, 233, 234, 240 (both), 242 (both), 251, 254, 257, 271, 278, 279, 281, 288, 290, 298, 300, 311, 328, 338, 339, 357, 358, 374, 379, 382; *The Times*: pages 202 (both), 206, 216, 219, 247, 252, 266; *Illustrated London News*: page 229; Fox Photos: page 261; Press Association: pages 263, 303, 309, 323; Associated Newspapers: 268; Keystone Press Agency: pages 269, 282; Provincial Press Agency: pages 315, 320, 323, 329, 335, 341, 345 (both); John Mullen: pages 348, 365, 371; *Daily Express* (Philip Dunn): page 354; Colin Turner Photography: pages 375, 388; George Selwyn: page 384

British Library Cataloguing in Publication Data
Green, Reg
   A race apart:
   the history of the Grand National.
   1. Merseyside (Metropolitan County).
   Aintree. Racehorses. Racing. Races. Grand
   National, to 1992
   I. Title
   798.4'5

   Hodder & Stoughton trade paperback ISBN 0 340 58515 3
   Marlborough Books hardback ISBN 1 873919 11 5

THE
HISTORY
OF THE
GRAND
NATIONAL

A RACE APART

DEDICATED TO
BRENDA WITH LOVE
And to the memory
of the men and horses whose
story this is

BIBLIOGRAPHY

Heroes and Heroines of the Grand National, Finch Mason, The Biographical Press, *London, 1907*

The Grand National, David Hoadley Munroe, Huntington Press, *New York, 1931*

Grand National, Con O'Leary, Rockliff Press, *London, 1945*

The Life of Golden Miller and the Sporting Reminiscences of his Trainer, Basil Briscoe, Hutchinson & Co., *London, 1939*

One Hundred Grand Nationals, T H Bird, Country Life Ltd, *London, 1937*

Men and Horses I Have Known, The Honourable George Lambton, J. A. Allen, *London, 1924*

A Trainer to Two Kings, Richard Marsh, Cassell & Co., *London, 1925*

Famous Gentlemen Riders, Charles Adolph Voigt, Hutchinson & Co., *London, 1925*

King Edward VII As A Sportsman, Alfred E T Watson, Longmans Green & Co., *London, 1911*

Golden Miller, Gregory Blaxland, Constable, *London, 1972*

Irish Horse-Racing, John Welcome, Macmillan, *London, 1982*

The Winter Kings, Ivor Herbert & Patricia Smyly, Pelham Books, *London, 1968*

The Will to Win, Jane McIlvaine, Doubleday & Co., *New York, 1966*

The Racing Calendar – Steeplechases Past, Messrs Weatherby's, *London, 1866–1951*

Between The Flags, S J Watson, Allen Figgis & Co., *Dublin, 1969*

Gentlemen Riders Past and Present, John Maunsell Richardson & Finch Mason, Vinton & Co., *London, 1909*

My Racing Adventures, Arthur Nightingall, T Werner Laurie, *London*

FOREWORD

How grateful we are at the BBC that our forefathers had the imagination to invent The Grand National. It provides the nation with an incomparable sporting occasion. It has been my privilege to be present at Aintree for the great race for some years now; first for radio, more recently for television and I cannot think of a day that gives me more excitement, pleasure and satisfaction. But best of all the 'National always produces such wonderful stories. In my time there's been RED RUM's hat-trick of wins; the 'old crocks' race when ALDANITI and Bob Champion, who had both virtually been consigned to the scrap-heap, captured our hearts; and CORBIERE producing the first win for a woman trainer, the remarkable Jennie Pitman; and so many more.

As Reg Green recalls, in 1986 I even had a dream that I might be in a position of having to interview myself after the race if by some miracle the veteran ANOTHER DUKE could have won. I had leased the horse to run in my colours.

Like Reg, I have undying admiration for the jockeys who ride in the race and great affection for the horses that take part.

Reg has had a lifelong romance with the 'National and as you read this splendid history of it, you will understand exactly why.

DESMOND LYNAM

AUTHOR'S NOTE

When no mention is made of the conditions of the race at the head of the statistical table, it is to be understood that they had not changed significantly from the year before.

The term 'aged' where shown signifies that a horse has attained or passed the age of seven years. This is an ancient racing terminology still in use in some circles to this day.

INTRODUCTION

In the year that saw the coronation of Queen Victoria, a humble publican was taking the first steps towards the creation of a sporting event that would capture the imagination of her people – and in due course the rest of the world.

William Lynn was known as a fine host at the Waterloo Hotel in Liverpool's Ranelagh Street, and was famed locally as a great fryer of fish. But he was also something of an entrepreneur. He inaugurated and, as we would now say, sponsored a hare-coursing event, calling it the Waterloo Cup, and encouraged by the increase in trade that this produced, he turned his attention to the turf.

Horse racing had taken place in the area now known as Merseyside since the days of Elizabeth I, the contest known as the Crosby Bell having been a traditional Ascension Day entertainment for many years, attracting huge crowds to Crosby foreshore.

All these races were tests of speed over a distance of flat, uninterrupted ground and when William Lynn leased the acreage at Aintree, some seven miles from the middle of Liverpool, he intended to promote more of the same. Lord Sefton, himself a racing man, was more than happy to see his land used in this way.

With his usual energy, Lynn made plans for a grandstand at Aintree, the foundation stone of which was eventually laid on 7th February 1829 by Lord Molyneux, who placed a bottle full of sovereigns inside the footings.

The first meeting at Aintree took place on 7th July 1829, with the opening race, the one-and-a-quarter-mile Croxteth Stakes, being won by a horse called MUFTI, owned by Mr Francis. With between thirty and forty thousand people enjoying the sport, racing at Liverpool prospered, despite the competition from nearby Maghull. The owner of this adjacent race-course, John Formby by name, was a close associate of William Lynn and when the latter decided to experiment with hurdle racing, Formby looked on with great interest. Lynn held three meetings a year and in 1835 he set aside his October

Captain Becher on VIVIAN

fixture exclusively for hurdling. The idea got off to a flying start when the most celebrated cross-country rider of the day arrived to take part. Captain Martin Becher rode the sparkling hurdler VIVIAN to two successes on the same day and is known to have held a long conversation with Lynn about his friend Tom Coleman, organiser of the Great St Albans Steeplechase. For five years, this event had stood supreme as the premier contest in the comparatively new entertainment of racing 'across a country'. William Lynn now decided that what Coleman could do at St Albans, he could perfect at Aintree. His first steeplechase took place on 29th February, 1836. It was won by THE DUKE, owned by a Mr Sirdefield of the George Inn at Great Crosby and ridden by none other than Captain Becher. Still a little cautious about venturing into this new area of racing, Lynn joined forces with Formby for the renewal in 1837 and the race was run at Maghull.

With £100 donated by the Aldermen of Liverpool, the first Grand Liverpool

Henry Potts, winner of the first Grand Liverpool Chase

Steeplechase also fell to THE DUKE, though partnered this time by the outstanding Cheshire horseman Henry Potts.

In 1838, again at Maghull, Captain Becher was reunited with THE DUKE to finish third. There is some doubt, however, concerning the winner, who was either SIR HENRY or SIR WILLIAM.

If William Lynn remained undecided about the future of steeplechasing, there were plenty who needed no more convincing. Towards the end of 1838, a syndicate was formed consisting of such dignitaries as the Earls of Derby, Sefton, Eglinton and Wilton, Lord George Bentinck, Lord Stanley and Lord Robert Grosvenor and plans went ahead for the Grand Liverpool Steeplechase to be run in 1839, over a country at Aintree. Enthused by this apparent show of support, inn-keeper Lynn worked diligently to promote the event, spreading word far and wide of the spectacle in store. Within weeks of the race, though, William Lynn had resigned under mysterious circumstances and his project had passed into the hands of others.

This was perhaps the first of many controversies to be associated with the race which began as the Grand Liverpool and became the Grand National. But none could detract for long from this most enthralling of all sporting endeavours. For thrills and drama, the race has no equal on earth. But more than this, it seems to transcend mere sport in its unique power to reflect in one afternoon the whole of life. Sometimes the tragic, the evil or the cunning are seen. More often, though, it is the courageous, the humorous, the generous, the triumphantly optimistic side of life that you will find in the pages of its history.

Certainly, this severest test of man and horse against the elements is like no other. It is simply, and above all else, a race apart.

1839

At last the great day arrived, bright and clear with a chill breeze blowing across from the Mersey. Liverpool had for days been agog with talk of the contest and thousands of excited visitors flocked into the area. Parties were held at the country houses, including Croxteth and Knowsley, hotels for miles around were booked up and there were reports of some hostelries accommodating their guests four to a bed. Lynn's prediction that the City's trade would benefit from a 'Grand Steeplechase' was being proven in the best possible way. Every form of transport then known was used to get to Aintree on that historic day, from the new-fangled railway to the paddle boat on the canal; from stately carriages to the humble 'Shanks's Pony'. Then as now the talk on the way would be about just one thing. Who was going to win? With a field of at least seventeen expected, conjecture was rife.

DAXON, RUST and BARKSTON were Irish challengers all owned by Tom Ferguson, and the first two figured prominently in the betting. Ferguson was to ride DAXON. The English mare THE NUN was another with a chance, and there were claims for CHARITY. There was also LOTTERY, a nine-year-old bay gelding who was to become the most brilliant steeplechaser in the early years of the sport. Bred by a Mr Jackson at his Thirsk farm from a mare called PARTHENIA, his sire was another LOTTERY, reputedly descended from ECLIPSE. The leggy foal was at first named CHANCE and after winning two small flat races as a four-year-old, was allowed time to mature before being sent to Horncastle Horse Fair, where he was bought for £120 by no less a figure than John Elmore. It was at his new home in Harrow that CHANCE was re-named, and where the partnership with Jem Mason was formed. Mason, the son of a horse jobber, was the outstanding jump jockey of his day. He was also a most elegant dandy. A Savile

The great LOTTERY, with Jem Mason up and owner John Elmore

Row tailor made all his clothes free for him; he always wore white kid gloves when racing and his boots were made jointly by Bentley's of Oxford Street and Wren's of Knightsbridge. Despite the many successes Mason and LOTTERY enjoyed together, the horse hated the sight of the man, so that in order to mount the animal, the jockey had to resort to the subterfuge of wearing a coat over his racing colours until safely in the saddle, whereupon the partnership would perform with exemplary skill and devastating speed. Before going to Aintree the pair had carried off the Cheltenham Steeplechase in fine fashion, so it was not without good reason that LOTTERY was made favourite at 5/1.

The conditions for the race appear to have been only loosely adhered to, for instead of 'four miles across country' the distance was actually more than this and the term 'gentlemen riders' was utterly meaningless. At least nine of the jockeys were known to have ridden for hire for many seasons. 'Across country' was certainly correct, the course being set over open farm land with the only running rails from the last obstacle to the finishing line. Most of the obstacles were small two-foot banks, topped with gorse and with a ditch in front or behind. There was the odd post and rails, but apart from the four-foot-eight-inch-high stone wall near the end of the first circuit, the only really treacherous jumps were two brooks. The first of these had been specially dammed to make it eight feet wide, with a timber fence three-and-a-half feet high set back a yard on the take-off side. Running into this fence the horses would encounter the heaviest plough anywhere on the course and the landing side was fully a yard lower than the field they would be jumping out of. The second was equally formidable, again approached through ploughed country and located after a severe left-hand bend which also had a fence situated at its sharpest point. Consisting of a two-foot bank in front of a wide ditch, with a three-foot high timber fence on the far side, it was at least nine feet from the top of the bank to the top of the fence and again there was a huge drop to cope with. Both these brooks, then as now, had to be jumped twice during the course of the race. Few of the fences were level at the top, which would result in much jostling by the jockeys as they sought the lowest place to negotiate, while still taking care that they jumped the right side of the flag. With the going very heavy it was without doubt going to be a severe test of stamina, as well as jumping ability being of paramount importance.

After an exasperating delay of two hours, caused by a combination of confusion in weighing out the seventeen riders and a number of false starts, Lord Sefton's flag was lowered in earnest shortly after three o'clock. Away they went on their gallop into history, followed by a number of mounted spectators intent on getting a close-up view of the action. Mr Ferguson took DAXON into an early lead and led down to the first brook with Captain Becher in hot pursuit. The heavy going on the run across plough to the brook caused DAXON to hit the top of the rails very hard, yet somehow he managed to scramble over. CONRAD, immediately behind, committed the same error but, lacking the strength of the Irish horse, was stopped dead in his tracks. Becher was flung unceremoniously over the horse's head into the brook beyond. Diving for safety into the deepest part, the gallant Captain waited until LOTTERY, RUST, THE NUN, DICTATOR and CHARITY sped over above him, before emerging to recapture CONRAD, climb back in the saddle and continue the 'chase, leaving behind forever his name at the Brook now called Becher's. Unfortunately, his reunion with CONRAD was short-lived, for he took another soaking at the second brook and this time there was no getting back in the race. DAXON fell for the second time and an even more alarming fate befell his stable-mate RUST. His rider, Mr William McDonough, had decided to use a stretch of lane, quite legitimately, when he was deliberately hemmed in by a crowd of spectators whose interest in the event was more financial than sporting and his way was barred until the rest of the field were almost out of sight. LOTTERY could be seen at his brilliant best as they made their way into the country for the second time, but at the second brook DICTATOR toppled over, burst a blood vessel and died almost immediately. The big Aintree steeplechase had claimed its first fatality. Turning into the straight LOTTERY had his race well won barring an accident and at the last fence put the issue beyond all doubt, producing the kind of leap – said to have been all of thirty feet – for which he was to become famous in the years ahead. LOTTERY came home a worthy three length

winner from Tom Olliver on SEVENTY FOUR, with PAULINA the same distance back in third place. The only other finishers were TRUE BLUE, the remounted THE NUN, RAILROAD and PIONEER.

Despite criticism from the local press concerning the severity of the event, there was no doubt in the minds of the thousands in attendance that the Great Steeplechase was an overwhelming success. Within days the proud announcement was made by the trustees of the racecourse that 'upwards of fifty gentlemen have already subscribed to another steeplechase next year, that further subscriptions are fully expected and it is anticipated that the 'chase will be one of the most splendid ever witnessed, whether as regards the patronage it will receive or the number of horses that will be entered'.

Having stamped his mark in such an unexpected and indelible manner, Captain Becher passed from the Aintree scene. He never took part in the race again.

THE GRAND LIVERPOOL STEEPLECHASE
1839

A sweepstake of 20 sovereigns each, 5 forfeit, with 100 added; 12 stone each, gentlemen riders; four miles across country; the second to save his stake and the winner to pay 10 sovereigns towards expenses; no rider to open a gate or ride through a gateway, or more than 100 yards along any road, footpath or driftway

Date: Tuesday 26th February Starters: 17		Time: 14 mins 53 secs
1st **LOTTERY** [formerly CHANCE]	*(Mr J Elmore)*	**Jem Mason**
2nd **SEVENTY FOUR**	*(Sir George Mostyn)*	**Tom Olliver**
3rd **PAULINA**	*(Mr Theobald)*	**Mr Martin**
4th **TRUE BLUE**	*(Mr Stephenson)*	**Mr Barker**
5th **THE NUN**	*(Lord McDonald)*	**Mr Alan McDonough** [remounted]
6th **RAILROAD**	*(Capt Marshall)*	**Mr Powell**
7th **PIONEER**	*(Sir D Baird)*	**Mr T Walker**

Also Ran:
DICTATOR (Mr J S Oswell) **Carlin** *Fell*; *CONRAD* (Capt Childe) **Capt Becher** *Fell*; *CRAMP* (Mr Robertson) **Wilmot** *Fell*; *RAMBLER* (Mr H S Bowen) **Morgan** *Fell*; *DAXON* (Mr T Ferguson) **Mr Tom Ferguson** *Fell*; *BARKSTON* (Mr T Ferguson) **Byrne** *Fell*; *RUST* (Mr T Ferguson) **Mr William McDonough** *Pulled-up*; *CANNON BALL* (Mr Newcombe) **Mr Newcombe** *Fell*; *JACK* (Capt Lamb) **Wadlow** *Fell*; *CHARITY* (Mr Vevers) **Hardy** *Refused*.

Distances: *Three lengths; three lengths*

1840

The big Liverpool race came barely three weeks after the wedding of Queen Victoria to Prince Albert and again thousands made their way to Aintree despite the disappointing number of runners. With the prize money increased and extended to the second horse, it was surprising that only twelve made their way to the post. The event was deplorably recorded, with only the vaguest of details set down for future generations and many of these at variance with each other. There can be no doubt that steeplechasing was still regarded by Turf authorities as a passing fad and documentation of racing under this code was felt unessential. The owners of some runners were unknown; there was even a great doubt concerning that of JERRY, who was to play such an important part in the proceedings as will be seen. By the stallion CATTERICK, the horse was not in the General Stud Book, which was not uncommon among 'chasers in those days, but his ownership is variously attributed to John Elmore, Lord Sheffield and a Mr Villebois. Bred by Mr Marshall in Lincolnshire, JERRY was first bought by Joe Anderson, a well known Piccadilly horse-dealer, and then in quick succession by three Lords, Pembroke, Errol and Uxbridge. Just as rapidly the son of CATTERICK was returned to Anderson as being of no account. That shrewd judge of horseflesh, John Elmore, then became the owner, training the horse to win the Leamington Steeplechase at an attractive price, thus wiping the smiles off the faces of certain Peers of the Realm. It was from this point on that the ownership becomes most confusing. As a dealer, Elmore would be selling and leasing animals and often buying back those which were found unsuitable. Mr Villebois and Lord Sheffield were both customers of his and although JERRY ran in the colours of the former there is a strong possibility that the latter had at least a share in the animal. On the eve of the race, however, there were rumours that not only was the actual owner John Elmore himself, but that he had declared to win with his Leamington winner. This practice was a common one in those days when an owner was represented by more than one runner in a race and often led to moves in the betting market being taken as an indication of where the stable's confidence lay.

No less than six of the runners were Irish and two of these represented that remarkable sporting gentleman the Marquis of Waterford. He chose THE SEA, a gelding by WHALEBONE, to ride himself. Another talented Irish amateur, Alan Power, partnered his own horse VALENTINE, and had bet heavily that he would be first at the Wall, which was near enough the half-way stage of the race. The day was bright and clear and the going good. Some anger was caused when many spectators, having paid their admission charge, discovered the stands so full that they invaded Lord Derby's private stand, only to be evicted when his Lordship arrived with the Knowsley house party. Then the Start, scheduled this time for half-past one, was delayed until after three, due again to a discrepancy in weighing out the jockeys.

All the grumbling ceased when Lord Sefton lowered his flag and Power spurred VALENTINE into an immediate lead, intent on winning his bet. At Becher's, WEATHERCOCK fell and jockey Barker was so badly hurt that he was carried to the nearest farmhouse for attention. VALENTINE still led in runaway fashion down to the second brook. With his bet well on the way to being won, Mr Power was given a terrible fright. In his final strides to the obstacle, VALENTINE suddenly came to a halt, reared up on his hind legs, then amazingly corkscrewed his way over, and the partnership continued intact. Another Aintree landmark was thus christened, for in that instant the second brook became known as Valentine's. Nearing the end of the first circuit the front-running Irish outsider began showing signs of tiredness and the last few yards to the stone Wall were desperate ones for Power as he strove to maintain his lead over Jem Mason on LOTTERY. His bet was just won as his mount jumped cleanly, but the gasp that came from the crowds was for his nearest opponent. LOTTERY hit the Wall hard, coming down amid a mass of tumbling stones. Within seconds COLUMBINE, THE NUN and SEVENTY FOUR were also on the floor, so three of the best backed horses were eliminated. VALENTINE was still in front turning out into the country but JERRY and ARTHUR moved up to take issue. The latter slipped at the Brook, and turned a complete somersault. The stunned Alan McDonough bravely re-mounted and amazingly produced a re-markable turn of speed from the horse. Mr Bretherton kept JERRY well up to his work in the closing stages, fighting off a re-newed challenge from VALENTINE and then holding the late run of ARTHUR. At the post JERRY had four lengths to spare over ARTHUR, with VALENTINE the same distance back in third. Then came the only other recorded finisher THE SEA.

Over the next few days there was again criticism of the event in the press, particu-larly over the mêlée at the Wall and the fact that after almost seventy-two hours, none of the connections of WEATHERCOCK had bothered to enquire about the welfare of the jockey Barker. The poor man was still in the farmhouse he had been taken to, suffering from concussion. But there are always other races, other scandals to report on. The organisers put all behind them in their efforts to prepare the next staging of the 'Chase.

THE GRAND LIVERPOOL STEEPLECHASE
1840

A sweepstake of 20 sovereigns, 5 forfeit, with 150 sovereigns added; 12 stone each, gentlemen riders; the second horse to receive 30 sovereigns and the third to save his stake; the winner to pay 10 sovereigns towards expenses; no rider to open a gate or ride through a gateway, or more than 100 yards along any road, footpath or driftway

Date: 5th March	Starters: 12	Time: 12 mins 30 secs
1st **JERRY**	*(Mr Villebois)*	**Mr Bretherton**
2nd **ARTHUR**	*(Mr Barry)*	**Mr A McDonough** [remounted]
3rd **VALENTINE**	*(Mr A Power)*	**Mr A Power**
4th **THE SEA**	*(Marquis of Waterford)*	**Marquis of Waterford**

Also Ran:
LOTTERY (Mr J Elmore) **J Mason** *Fell*; SPOLASCO (Owner unknown) **Rose** *Fell*; THE NUN (Lord McDonald) **Mr Powell** *Fell*; COLUMBINE (Marquis of Waterford) **Mr Won** *Fell*; HASTY (Owner unknown) **Rigg** *Fell*; SEVENTY FOUR (Sir George Mostyn) **T Olliver** *Fell*; WEATHERCOCK (Owner unknown) **Barker** *Fell*; THE AUGEAN (Owner unknown) **R Christian** *Fell*.

The Betting: *3/1 The Nun; 4/1 Lottery; 7/1 Seventy Four; 8/1 Arthur; 10/1 Cruickshank [did not run]; 12/1 Jerry*

Distances: *Four lengths; four lengths*

1841

Concern had already been voiced by some Clerks of the Course that the presence of Elmore's superb gelding LOTTERY could scare away the opposition in their most prestigious 'chases, turning the betting into a farce and, most disastrously, keeping the crowds away. One official at Horncastle even went so far as to frame his race in these words, 'a sweepstake of 25 sovereigns, open to all horses, except Mr Elmore's LOTTERY'. The Liverpool executive was slightly more subtle, but no less harsh. In the conditions for their 1841 Grand Liverpool 'Chase was the proviso that the winner of the previous year's Cheltenham Steeplechase should carry an extra 18 lbs. Without even giving the horse the courtesy of naming him, for the result of this event was well known at the time the stipulation was made, they had effectively put paid to any chance LOTTERY may have had. Even with the impossible burden of 13 st 4 lbs though, Elmore sent his horse to Aintree, again in the care of Jem Mason and such was the public regard for LOTTERY he became the 5/2 favourite. At least the Wall which brought about his painful exit from last year's race, had been removed and in its place was an artificial Water Jump, ten feet wide, three feet deep, with a thick thorn fence on the take-off side.

SEVENTY FOUR took part again, but he was now considered past his best, as was the mare CHARITY. Since unexpectedly letting her supporters down at the infamous Wall two years earlier, she had completely lost her winning form, which included races on the flat, over hurdles and fences. Mr A Powell partnered her this time and he was a most experienced cross-country rider, though known to be something of a 'rough-diamond'. Again there was doubt over the ownership, for although the mare carried the colours of Lord Craven, she remained in the Cheltenham stable of William Vevers. There were strong suggestions that the trainer maintained at least a share in the horse.

As far as the bookmakers were concerned there were only two runners to threaten LOTTERY and coincidentally both were greys, CIGAR at 4/1 and PETER SIMPLE at 6s, the former having won the Horncastle race from which LOTTERY was barred.

The eleven runners were despatched on time without any early mishaps occurring. At Becher's the leader SELIM came down, as did GOBLIN, but the latter was soon remounted by Bretherton. Over the newly-built Water Jump in front of the stands the race was still wide open. OLIVER TWIST and LEGACY dropped out somewhere between the two Brooks but the rest were in a tight pack with only Elmore's champion approaching his limit and Jem Mason mercifully pulled him up. Coming back on to the racecourse for the last time a close finish was in prospect as they raced towards the final two flights of hurdles, but over the last CIGAR and PETER SIMPLE had it between them until CHARITY came with a strong run, passing both greys to win cleverly. The mare had a length to spare at the post over CIGAR, with PETER SIMPLE only half that distance back in third place. The finish was one of the closest of any race witnessed at Aintree and all present had seen an example of steeplechasing at its best.

William Vevers, in the hunting field, where most steeplechasers were to be discovered

THE GRAND LIVERPOOL STEEPLECHASE

1841

A sweepstake of 20 sovereigns, 5 forfeit, with 150 sovereigns added; 12 stone each, except for the winner of the 1840 Cheltenham Steeplechase who will carry an extra 18 lbs. Gentlemen riders; the second horse to receive 30 sovereigns and the third to save his stake; the winner to pay 10 sovereigns towards expenses; no rider to open a gate, or ride through a gateway, or more than 100 yards along any road, footpath or driftway

Date: 3rd March	Starters: 11	Time: 13 mins 25 secs
1st **CHARITY**	(Lord Craven)	**Mr Powell**
2nd **CIGAR**	(Mr Anderson)	**Mr A McDonough**
3rd **PETER SIMPLE**	(Hon F Craven)	**Walker**
4th **REVEALER**	(Mr Villebois)	**Mr Barker**
5th **THE HAWK**	(Capt Nugent)	**Saunders**
6th **SEVENTY FOUR**	(Sir George Mostyn)	**Mr Whitworth**
7th **GOBLIN**	(Lord Villiers)	**Mr Bretherton** [remounted]

Also Ran:
LEGACY (Mr Robertson) **Mr W McDonough** *Fell*; *LOTTERY* 13 st 4 lbs (Mr J Elmore) **J Mason** *Pulled-up*; *SELIM* (Capt Price) **Capt Price** *Fell*; *OLIVER TWIST* (Mr Smith) **Mr Oliver** *Fell*.

The Betting: *5/2 Lottery; 4/1 Cigar; 6/1 Peter Simple; 12/1 Legacy; 14/1 Seventy Four; 14/1 Charity; 100/6 The Hawk*

Distances: *One length; half a length*

1842

The big Liverpool steeplechase had now become the major attraction of the year for jumping enthusiasts. There was heavy betting on the event for months before, great excitement among the public and on the day the promoters were rewarded with enormous crowds. Some critics still objected that it was too severe a race but it was the people who would decide at the end of the day and they made it obvious that the Grand Liverpool was here to stay. It seems strange, therefore, that the organisers saw fit to alter the conditions for the 1842 event in a somewhat alarming manner. The entry fee was increased to 23 sovereigns, while the practice of the executive topping-up the stakes with added money was abandoned. No explanation was given for this step, nor apparently was one asked for. The result was that only the winner would receive prize money, with the second horse merely saving his stake.

The penalty concerning the Cheltenham Steeplechase was again in force, meaning that LOTTERY once more carried 13 st 4 lbs, and again he started favourite, this time at 5/1. Mason, as always, partnered the horse despite owning a runner in the race himself, SAM WELLER ridden by Barker. Last year's third, the grey PETER SIMPLE, ran again, at 6/1 joint second in the betting with another previously placed horse, SEVENTY FOUR. Apart from his renowned LOTTERY, though, Elmore was now also represented by GAY LAD, an eight-year-old bay gelding who although without experience of the tough Liverpool fences, had the undoubted advantage of Tom Olliver as his jockey.

It was Olliver who had partnered SEVENTY FOUR into second place behind Jem Mason on LOTTERY in 1839 and both riders were the greatest of friends but the greatest of opposites. 'Black Tom' Olliver, as he became known affectionately throughout the length and breadth of the country, was possibly the most brilliant cross-country rider of the nineteenth-century. Born of an impoverished family in Sussex, Tom Oliver was given the nickname 'Black' because of his swarthy looks and black hair, which he inherited from his Spanish-gypsy ancestors. There was no money in the Oliver household and the children often went barefoot. Tom it was who decided to add an extra 'l' to his surname, with the reasoning that it was 'as well to have an extra £ at hand'. From an early age Tom was a genius with horses, his talent catching the eyes of the top men in the fast-developing sport of steeplechasing. His fame spread rapidly as he rode winner after winner, but unfortunately Tom missed many rides through his frequent visits to the pokey. The debtors' prison became his second home and he was almost constantly on the verge of bankruptcy. Generous to a fault, Olliver would give hand-outs without question and his hopelessness with money rivalled his other weakness, women. They found Tom irresistible and he them and it is hard

'Black Tom' Olliver on VANGUARD, the winner of the first handicap 'National in 1843

to imagine which he missed most when behind bars, the women or the horses. He was a much liked man, full of wit, and in the saddle could work wonders with the most mediocre animal. Some cavalry officers once visited him in prison and upon asking how they could be of service to him received the typical Olliver reply, 'Send me a damned good wall-jumper'.

Despite the lack of added money, the race attracted fifteen runners and the crowds came to Aintree again in their thousands. Lord Waterford's COLUMBINE took his field over the first fence in fine style. ANONYMOUS jumped into the lead at the Brook but at the next fence SAM WELLER ran straight into the bank, catapulting Barker into the next field. The horse's owner, Jem Mason, jumped safely nearby on LOTTERY. COLUMBINE regained the lead briefly only to be passed by the impetuous grey PETER SIMPLE who was almost pulling his owner, Mr Hunter, out of the saddle. The big weight told again on LOTTERY and shortly after clearing the Brook for the second time, Mason pulled him up. SEVENTY FOUR was jumping like a stag and starting to run his opponents into the ground, with only GAY LAD looking to have a slight chance of catching him at the Canal Turn. As they came back onto the racecourse the only other with any possible chance, PETER SIMPLE, was so baulked by the crowd that he threw his jockey. As they turned into the straight SEVENTY FOUR began to slow, allowing GAY LAD to make ground on him. They raced into the last hurdle on level terms, both very tired and GAY LAD strode away to win by a comfortable four lengths. Mr Hunter somehow recovered from his late mishap on PETER SIMPLE to finish third just in front of THE RETURNED. The only other finisher was the early leader COLUMBINE.

THE GRAND LIVERPOOL STEEPLECHASE

1842

A sweepstake of 23 sovereigns. The second horse to save his stake. 12 stone each, except for the winner of the 1840 Cheltenham Steeplechase who will carry an extra 18 lbs. Gentlemen riders. No rider to open a gate, or ride through a gateway, or more than 100 yards along any road, footpath or driftway

Date: 2nd March	Starters: 15	Time: 13 mins 30 secs
1st **GAY LAD**	*(Mr J Elmore)*	**Tom Olliver**
2nd **SEVENTY FOUR**	*(Lord Mostyn)*	**Powell**
3rd **PETER SIMPLE**	*(Mr Hunter)*	**Mr Hunter** [remounted]
4th **THE RETURNED**	*(Mr W Hope-Johnstone)*	**Mr W Hope-Johnstone**
5th **COLUMBINE**	*(Lord Waterford)*	**Larry Byrne**

Also Ran:
SAM WELLER (Mr Jem Mason) **Barker** *Fell*; LOTTERY 13 st 4 lbs (Mr J Elmore) **Jem Mason** *Pulled-up*; BANATHLATH (Mr T Ferguson) **Colgan** *Fell*; LADY LANGFORD (Hon C Forester) **Abbott** *Fell*; BANGALORE (Mr Ramsey) **Capt Peel** *Failed to finish*; ANONYMOUS (Mr Moore) **Mr Moore** *Failed to finish*; SATIRIST (Lord Maidstone) **Bretherton** *Failed to finish*; LUCKS-ALL (Mr R Ekin) **Goddard** *Failed to finish*; CONSUL (Baron Rothschild) **Oldaker** *Fell*; HONESTY (Lord Clanricarde) **Mr W McDonough** *Failed to finish*.

The Betting: *5/1 Lottery; 6/1 Seventy Four & Peter Simple; 7/1 Gay Lad; 8/1 Sam Weller; 10/1 Lucks-All & Consul; 100/7 Satirist; 15/1 The Returned; 20/1 Banathlath & Bangalore*

Distances: *Four lengths; fifteen lengths*

1843

The executive of the racecourse was constantly seeking new ways to improve the spectacle for their paying spectators, a far from easy task when the controllers of flat racing condemned steeplechasing out of hand. Yet they persevered and in 1843 the most significant change seen at Aintree came when the big race was made a handicap. Edward William Topham was requested to act as handicapper, a role he had performed with great distinction at Chester since moving from his native Middleham about 1830. His skill in assessing the merits of race-horses was well known, having earned him the title of 'The Wizard' long before he became officially involved at Liverpool. In addition to framing the handicap, with a range from 11 st to 12 st 8 lbs, he also renamed the race The Liverpool and National Steeplechase and for the benefit of those attending, introduced something quite novel at that time. Race-cards, listing the runners, jockeys' names together with the colours they carried and a map of the course, were issued and greatly appreciated. The Stone Wall was re-introduced, possibly because it was felt that the sight of animals tumbling amongst a mass of masonry was something the paying customer wished to see. Certainly the change was not welcomed by owners or riders.

LOTTERY, now thirteen years old, was the sole representative of John Elmore and ridden again by Mason, benefited from the handicap in that he was no longer expected to carry in excess of 13 st. A number of wins in recent months had earned PETER SIMPLE the top weight of 13 st 1 lb, which included the 5 lbs penalty. In addition to heading the handicap he also occupied that position in the betting, being strongly fancied at 3/1.

It was unusual to see a leading flat-race owner showing an interest in the despised jumping game but perhaps Lord Chesterfield possessed more foresight than his contemporaries. His bay gelding VAN-GUARD was not registered in the General Stud Book, nor was his parentage certain, for he is shown as being by either OLD ADVANCE or BELZONI but there was no doubting his ability across country and a big factor in his favour was the man on his back, none other than Tom Olliver.

William Lynn was there, apparently bearing up well despite the 'ill-health' which brought about his resignation from the Aintree executive. Lynn was much in evidence, as he had been each year since 1839, clearing the course and enclosures and generally assisting the starter Lord Sefton.

Following the sharp overnight frost the going was hard but good, though some ice remained in the ditches. CONSUL was the first to drop out, refusing at the very first fence, while PETER SIMPLE could be seen fighting for his head. It was soon evident that the favourite was not the reformed character he had been made out to be. At the fifth VICTORIA fell leaving VANGUARD out in front. PETER SIMPLE moved up and these two led at a good pace into the Wall, which TINDERBOX hit full tilt with his chest, coming down amid a flurry of stones and rolling over his unfortunate jockey Moore, who suffered a broken collar bone. Mr Kennedy was immediately behind the falling horse on TEETO-TUM and also came down. With this tangle of bodies lying directly in the path of the already-jumping LOTTERY, a disastrous pile-up appeared inevitable. But Elmore's veteran produced the kind of leap which had so often entertained the owner's guests when the horse was asked to jump over dining tables laid out on the lawn at home. LOTTERY cleared not only the Wall, but also the sprawling mass barring his way. PETER SIMPLE took them back into the country but after Becher's, the Cheltenham-trained DRAGSMAN took over the lead and came towards the racecourse looking all over a winner. He swerved sharply at the last fence before the straight, jumped a gate at the side of the course and with his unhappy rider clinging to his neck, bolted down a lane. Crickmere eventually regained control of the horse, took him back to the fence and set off in forlorn pursuit. Incredibly by the time VANGUARD and NIMROD reached the final flight, DRAGSMAN was only a couple of lengths behind them, but Tom Olliver got a great jump out of his mount and from there the result was beyond doubt. VANGUARD had three lengths to spare over

NIMROD, who in turn held off the brave run of DRAGSMAN by half a length.

The winner provided 'Black' Tom Olliver with the distinction of being the first man to win the Liverpool 'chase in successive years. LOTTERY, sadly, had run his last Liverpool and it must have been difficult to imagine the place without him. He must surely have won the race more than once had not that unjust clause in the conditions required him to give so much weight to his rivals. LOTTERY ran his last race, fittingly a winning one, on 8th April 1844 at Windsor, whereupon he became trainer Dockeray's hack. For some reason this arrangement was short-lived and to the everlasting shame of man, the horse who 'could trot faster than most other horses could gallop', ended his days pulling a cart around the back streets of Neasden.

THE LIVERPOOL AND NATIONAL HANDICAP STEEPLECHASE
1843

A sweepstake of 23 sovereigns. The second horse to save his stake. A Handicap, the top weight to be 12 stone 8 pounds, the bottom weight 11 stone; any winner from the date of declaration to carry 5 pounds extra. No rider to open a gate, or ride through a gateway, or more than 100 yards along any road, footpath or driftway

Date: 1st March	Starters: 16	Time: Not taken
1st **VANGUARD**	**11–10** (*Lord Chesterfield*)	**Tom Olliver**
2nd **NIMROD**	**11–0** (*Mr Mare*)	**Scott**
3rd **DRAGSMAN**	**11–3** (*Mr Holman*)	**Mr Crickmere**
4th **CLAUDE DUVAL**	**11–7** (*Col Hanson*)	**Tomblin**
5th **GOBLIN**	**11–6** (*Mr Errington*)	**B Bretherton**
6th **BUCEPHALUS**	**11–5** (*Mr R Hunter*)	**Whitworth**
7th **LOTTERY**	**12–6** (*Mr J Elmore*)	**Jem Mason**
8th **PETER SIMPLE**	**13–1** (*Mr W Ekin*) [inc. 5 lbs extra]	**Frisby**
9th **THE RETURNED**	**12–0** (*Mr W Sterling Crawford*)	**Major Campbell**

Also Ran:
CONSUL 11–12 (Baron Rothschild) **Oldaker** *Refused*; REDWING 11–10 (Lord Waterford) **Doolan** *Fell*; VICTORIA 11–10 (Mr T Taylor) **Mr T Taylor** *Fell*; TINDERBOX 11–7 (Mr Hunt) **G Moore** *Fell*; TEETOTUM 11–7 (Mr Kennedy) **Mr Kennedy** *Fell*; CROXBY 11–6 (Hon F Craven) **Mr W McDonough** *Pulled-up*; THE ROMP 11–0 (Mr Lamplugh) **Holingshed** *Refused*.

The Betting: *3/1 Peter Simple; 4/1 Lottery & The Returned; 8/1 Redwing; 10/1 Dragsman & Nimrod; 12/1 Vanguard*

Distances: *Three lengths; half a length*

1844

The Liverpool Stone Wall had claimed its last victim. So decided the race organisers in 1844 and it was replaced with a post and rails.

It is surprising that although steeplechasing was proving to be such a popular spectacle, there was still no governing body to control the sport. Nor would there be for many years yet and it was to some extent this lack of supervision which earned the game a poor name in many quarters. But still the 'National went from strength to strength. It is ironic that the hero of the 1844 Aintree race should be a horse who had passed many times from dealer to dealer, each time being judged worthless. DISCOUNT was a six-year-old chestnut entire, bred by a Mr Fowler, possessing the unusual distinction for a 'chaser in those days of actually being registered in the General Stud Book. He first ran on the flat under the name of MAGNUM BONUM but was so slow that his long round of the dealers began. One of these stalwarts called Payne found himself in the frustrating position of having the horse returned to him again and again. Indeed, on one occasion he was offered fifty pounds to take the horse back, something no self-respecting trader could refuse! His last chance of getting rid of the useless chestnut seemed to be a fellow dealer named Quartermaine of Piccadilly. Each time he was approached, Quartermaine offered less for the horse rather than more, until eventually an exasperated Payne accepted his price. The deal was struck and a gleeful Mr Quartermaine announced that he would re-name the animal DISCOUNT. Crickmere took the mount at Aintree and on the basis of the horse's past form must have been shocked to find himself riding the favourite on the day. Quartermaine must have been able

J F Herring's famous picture *Steeplechase Cracks* showing DISCOUNT, SWITCHER, PETER SIMPLE, PIONEER and LOTTERY

to find something in the horse where no-one else had succeeded. PETER SIMPLE was back again with top weight, though this time completely unconsidered in the betting. CHARITY also reappeared with NIMROD and THE RETURNED. It was the newcomers who attracted most of the money with DISCOUNT and MARENGO heading the market at 5/1, HESLINGTON at 8s and the Tom Olliver-ridden WIVERTON on the same mark. For the first time John Elmore had no runner in the race, for which rain fell in torrents all day.

THE RETURNED went into an early lead but going into Becher's the hard-pulling TOM TUG, giving his jockey Rackley an uncomfortable ride, went past. CHARITY came down at the Water in front of the stands and MARENGO, LATHER, THE RETURNED and DISCOUNT followed the leader out into the country again. Little could be seen through the downpour and it wasn't until they came back towards the last two flights that the crowd could make out THE RETURNED and LATHER in front of TOM TUG, CAESAR and DISCOUNT. Crickmere brought DISCOUNT with a well-timed challenge at the last flight and left his opponents for dead, coming away to win easily by twenty lengths. THE RETURNED followed him home, a length in front of TOM TUG with the stragglers strung out down the course and all in much distress. TOM TUG's jockey Rackley was in such an exhausted state when he returned to unsaddle that he had to be lifted off the horse. This had been the most gruelling race seen at Aintree, while the horse which nobody wanted, making his only appearance in the event a winning one, provided his owner with the best DISCOUNT he was ever likely to obtain.

THE LIVERPOOL AND NATIONAL STEEPLECHASE

1844

A sweepstake of 23 sovereigns. The second horse to save his stake. A Handicap, the top weight to be 12 stone 8 pounds, the bottom weight 10 stone 7 pounds; any winner from the date of declaration to carry 5 pounds extra. No rider to open a gate, or ride through a gateway, or more than 100 yards along any road, footpath or driftway

Date: 28th February	Starters: 15	Time: Just under 14 mins
1st **DISCOUNT** [formerly MAGNUM BONUM]	6.10–12 (*Mr Quartermaine*)	**Mr Crickmere**
2nd **THE RETURNED**	12–0 (*Mr W. Sterling Crawford*)	**Scott**
3rd **TOM TUG**	10–7 (*Mr Tilbury*)	**Rackley**
4th **CAESAR**	11–10 (*Lord Maidstone*)	**Barker**
5th **LATHER**	11–2 (*Lord E Russell*)	**Ball**
6th **THE ROMP**	10–7 (*Lord S Bentinck*)	**Larry Byrne**
7th **MARENGO**	10–10 (*Mr Bretherton*)	**Sharkey**
8th **LITTLE PETER**	10–12 (*Mr Hollinshead*)	**Mr Hollinshead**
9th **LOUIS PHILIPPE**	11–0 (*Sir J Gerrard*)	**Cowell**

Also Ran:
PETER SIMPLE 12–12 (Mr W Ekin) **Frisby** *Fell*; *ROBINSON 12–7* (Mr Milbank) **Parker** *Refused*; *WIVERTON 12–4* (Lord Maidstone) **Tom Olliver** *Fell*; *HESLINGTON 12–0* (Mr W Scott) **Mr W McDonough** *Refused*; *NIMROD 10–10* (Mr Mare) **Mr A McDonough** *Fell*; *CHARITY 10–7* (Mr Vever) **Powell** *Fell*.

The Betting: *5/1 Discount & Marengo; 8/1 Heslington & Wiverton; 13/1 Charity; 14/1 Nimrod; 15/1 The Returned; 20/1 Louis Philippe; 25/1 The Romp*

Distances: *Twenty lengths; one length*

1845

In preparation for the next running of the Liverpool 'chase an attempt was made to lay turf on at least part of the course. The first field in the country after the start and the last before re-entering the racecourse were laid and although the plan was well intended, the result was less than desirable. All the other fields were fallow except the two before Becher's and it was the fact that this land was regularly farmed which ruined the treated stretches. The taking out of ploughs and other implements cut up the turf, leaving the surface badly broken and uneven.

The 1843 winner VANGUARD was brought back for this year's race, though now with a stone more to shoulder. Tom Olliver, his partner in victory, was listed as the owner but bearing in mind the constant low state of the jockey's finances, it seems most unlikely. The distaste with which the jumping sport was looked upon by many caused numerous owners to enter their horses under either assumed names or other peoples'. There were two greys in the field, coincidentally named. PETER SIMPLE was well-known to the Aintree crowds, although he always seemed to be running in the colours of a new owner. The other was Mr Milbank's gelding PETER SWIFT. Last year's runaway TOM TUG attracted much support from those who felt he would have beaten DISCOUNT if he'd had a jockey as strong as this year's, Crickmere. But the principal interest of the public was a newcomer, THE KNIGHT TEMPLAR, who was installed as 5/1 favourite.

Another making his first bid at Aintree, CURE-ALL, had been bred in Yorkshire, changing hands a number of times before arriving at Horncastle where a reserve of £260 was put on him. A would-be buyer requested he show his paces over some fences, rapidly losing interest when the horse fell heavily. Now badly lamed, there could be no question of him reaching his reserve and he was sold to William Loft for £50. Taking his crippled purchase back home, he put the animal in the care of his groom Kitty Crisp, who achieved a small miracle by restoring CURE-ALL to fitness. Loft rode his bargain buy to hounds and was so pleased that he decided to try his luck in a steeplechase at Lincoln. Despite the inexperience of both horse and rider they were beaten only a neck. Then Mr W Sterling Crawford's candidate for the Liverpool 'chase met with an accident in training and CURE-ALL picked up his nomination. In return for this concession, CURE-ALL ran in his name, even though Loft was the owner. The horse made the long journey from Grimsby to Liverpool, walking every foot of the way, led by the faithful groom Kitty Crisp.

On race day the shivering crowd, gazing at the unusual sight of the Leeds and Liverpool Canal completely frozen over, stood and waited while there was an objection by the two owners of CLANSMAN and CURE-ALL who protested to the stewards that the race should not be run. Lord Sefton and Mr George Payne eventually gathered all the owners in the weighing room and took a vote, whereupon it was agreed that the event should proceed. It was almost five o'clock when the horses moved out to the start but after the long cold delay, there was yet more anxiety, this time over the favourite THE KNIGHT TEMPLAR. No explanation was ever given as to what exactly befell the ante-post favourite, but it was said that the horse had met with an accident and he was withdrawn from the line-up. The bookies frantically re-shuffled their books, with the result that VANGUARD led the market at 4/1.

VANGUARD went straight to the front and maintained his lead over Becher's from THE EXQUISITE, PETER SIMPLE, NIMROD and BOXKEEPER, with hardly any slackening of the pace. On the second circuit the condition of the ground took its toll with VANGUARD being one of the first to be pulled-up, but between Becher's and the Canal THE EXQUISITE was still out in front. It was here that Loft on CURE-ALL noticed a narrow strip of stubble running parallel to the course and while his opponents were struggling on the plough, he saved CURE-ALL a good deal of valuable energy by galloping on the better surface. THE EXQUISITE ran himself out and for a brief instant it looked as if PETER SIMPLE was about to triumph at his fifth attempt. At the last flight though, CURE-ALL came alongside, and making good use of his seven pound weight concession, out-ran PETER SIMPLE to win by two lengths. THE EXQUISITE was the same distance back in third place with TOM TUG fourth. Apart from the exciting finish, there was little for the freezing crowds to celebrate, for CURE-ALL had been completely ignored in the betting, winning totally unquoted in the books and springing the biggest surprise result to date.

The faithful groom, Kitty Crisp, made the long walk back to Lincolnshire with CURE-ALL, where their arrival was greeted by the ringing of Healing church bells in their honour.

THE LIVERPOOL AND NATIONAL STEEPLECHASE
1845

A sweepstake of 23 sovereigns. The second horse to save his stake. A Handicap. Any winner from the date of declaration to carry 5 pounds extra. No rider to open a gate, or ride through a gateway, or more than 100 yards along any road, footpath or driftway

Date: 5th March	Starters: 15	Time: 10 mins 47 secs
1st **CURE-ALL**	11–5 *(Mr W Sterling Crawford)*	**Mr W J Loft**
2nd **PETER SIMPLE**	11–12 *(Mr Thornton)*	**Frisby**
3rd **THE EXQUISITE**	11–12 *(Capt Boyd)*	**Larry Byrne**
4th **TOM TUG**	10–2 *(Mr J T Blackburn)*	**Mr Crickmere**

Also Ran:
THE PAGE 11–10 (Mr Holman) **Mr Holman** *Refused*; *CLANSMAN 11–6* (Mr J Kelly) **Mr J Kelly** *Fell* [destroyed]; *BRENDA 11–7* (Mr Perkins & Capt France) **J Abbot** *Ran-out*; *VANGUARD 12–10* (Mr Tom Olliver) **Tom Olliver** *Pulled-up*; *BOXKEEPER 11–4* (Mr Barnett) **Bradley** *Failed to finish*; *CEREMONY 11–0* (Mr Atkinson) **T Abbot** *Failed to finish*; *PETER SWIFT 10–12* (Mr Milbank) **Mr Powell** *Failed to finish*; *THE STRANGER 10–10* (Lord Alford) **Hill** *Failed to finish*; *NIMROD 10–8* (Mr Mare) **French** *Failed to finish*; *THE ROMP 10–4* (Mr R H Jones) **Thompson** *Failed to finish*; *BRILLIANT 10–4* (Mr Wesley) **Noble** *Failed to finish*.

The Betting: *4/1 Vanguard; 5/1 Tom Tug; 6/1 Brenda; 7/1 The Page; 9/1 Peter Simple; 10/1 Brilliant*

Distances: *Two lengths; two lengths*

* Just before the start the favourite at 5/1, The Knight Templar, met with an accident and was withdrawn *

1846

The popularity of Aintree's steeple-chase and the number of nomina-tions continued to increase. For the first time, there were more than twenty runners. The top spot in the weights this time was shared at 12 st 4 lbs, by last year's victor CURE-ALL, Lord Waterford's FIREFLY and the five-year-old SWITCHER. Jem Mason was again in the saddle on the favourite VELUTI, a six-year-old half-bred owned by Mr Crawford who had been credited as owner of CURE-ALL the year before. Among the others making a re-appearance was the popular grey PETER SIMPLE, running in the race for the sixth time, though now surely past his best. The general consensus was that apart from LANCET, VELUTI and FIREFLY the rest were 'rubbish'. Two in particular came in for scathing comments, the oddly named HORNIHIHARRIHO, which the bookies in-terpreted as 'HURRY HARRY' and a bay gelding called PIONEER.

This half-brother to VANGUARD was de-scribed as being very rough and his jockey W Taylor was completely unknown. Even Adams, the owner, made it well known that under no circumstances would he risk a penny backing his horse and there can be few who have competed for the event carrying as little confidence as PIONEER.

It was bright and clear with the going good – a thorough improvement on last year, except for the fact that an error had been made in marking out the course, with the result that the actual distance was nearly five miles. As in former years, PETER SIMPLE was the one who tried to cut out the early running and after MAMELUKE and HORNIHIHARRIHO had collided, he took up a clear lead over Becher's, round the Canal bend and back over Valen-tine's. LANCET was in a good position when a mounted spectator galloped into

Alan Mcdonagh. Perhaps the finest rider of his day never to win the National. In 1840, he became the first rider to remount and gain a place in the race

The Marquis of Waterford, a great supporter of steeplechasing and a considerable benefactor in his native Ireland

him, knocking McDonough from the saddle. At Becher's next time, CULVERTHORPE jumped to the front from SWITCHER and FIREFLY, with PIONEER starting to make ground through the field and VELUTI still there with a chance. The favourite, however, broke down at the first hurdle on the return to the racecourse and Mason gently walked him back to the stables while CULVERTHORPE came into the final flight looking all over a winner. He landed in front only to be caught and passed by the rough-looking outsider PIONEER, who streaked away to win very easily by three lengths. A further three lengths away in third came SWITCHER, FIREFLY was fourth and the only other to survive the extended distance was EAGLE. PIONEER, unquoted in the betting, proved that in the Liverpool 'chase the unexpected may be expected and that jumping and stamina are more important than good looks.

THE LIVERPOOL AND NATIONAL STEEPLECHASE
1846

A sweepstake of 23 sovereigns. The second horse to save his stake. A Handicap. Any winner from the date of declaration to carry 5 pounds extra. No rider to open a gate, or ride through a gateway, or more than 100 yards along any road, footpath or driftway

Date: 4th March	Starters: 22	Time: 10 mins 46 secs
1st **PIONEER**	**6.11–12** *(Mr Adams)*	**W Taylor**
2nd **CULVERTHORPE**	**11–4** *(Mr Payne)*	**Rackley**
3rd **SWITCHER**	**5.12–4** *(Lord Howth)*	**D Wynne**
4th **FIREFLY**	**12–4** *(Lord Waterford)*	**L Byrne**
5th **EAGLE**	**11–12** *(Mr C E Brooke)*	**Capt W Peel**

Also Ran:
CURE-ALL 12–4 (Mr W J Loft) **Mr W J Loft** *Pulled-up*; *REGALIA 11–12* (Lord Waterford) **Doolan** *Fell*; *GOLDEN PIPPIN 11–12* (Mr Atkinson) **Nainby** *Ran-out*; *MAJOR A 6.11–6* (Mr Windham) **Blake** *Failed to finish*; *TROUBADOUR 11–6* (Mr Austin) **G B Rammell** *Fell*; *CARLOW 11–4* (Mr G Lambden) **Tom Olliver** *Fell*; *BRENDA 11–4* (Mr Hammond) **Mr Powell** *Fell*; *TINDERBOX 11–4* (Mr Robertson) **P Daley** *Fell*; *PETER SIMPLE 11–2* (Mr Ekin) **Frisby** *Fell*; *HORNIHIHARRIHO 11–0* (Mr H L Carter) **Parker** *Fell*; *LANCET 11–0* (Mr Hey) **Mr W McDonough** *Knocked over*; *MAMELUKE 10–12* (Capt Barnett) **Mr A McDonough** *Fell*; *PICKWICK 10–10* (Mr G Lambden) **Dally** *Failed to finish*; *PERAMBULATOR 6.10–8* (Hon F Craven) **N Stagg** *Pulled-up*; *VELUTI 6.10–8* (Mr W Sterling Crawford) **Jem Mason** *Broke down*; *THE SCAVENGER 6.10–2* (Mr Pearce) **Bradley** *Refused*; *LADY GRAY 10–0* (Sir R Brownrigg) **Thomas** *Fell*.

The Betting: *11/2 Veluti; 6/1 Eagle; 7/1 Firefly; 10/1 Lancet & Mameluke; 12/1 Culverthorpe & Golden Pippin; 16/1 Perambulator & Cure-All; 100/6 Brenda & Peter Simple; 25/1 Major A*

Distances: *Three lengths; three lengths*

* *The course was wrongly flagged by accident, causing the distance to be almost five miles* *

1847

While covering the first Aintree running of the Liverpool Steeplechase in 1839, a reporter referred to the event as the 'Grand National' and ever since, enthusiasts had affectionately dubbed it simply the 'National'. It was not until 1847, however, that the Liverpool executive realised that this unique event needed a name more fully befitting its stature. This greatest test of mount and man would henceforth be known as The Grand National Handicap Steeplechase.

As if in recognition of the illustrious new title, the 1847 race attracted twenty-six runners, the largest number yet. The post and rails which had replaced the Stone Wall was removed, making way for an artificial Water Jump again, intended to delight the customers in the stands. PIONEER returned with the same weight he had carried to victory last year and having won in the meantime the Leamington Grand Annual 'Chase he was reputed to have been purchased for £1000 by Captain Peel. Although the Captain rode him this year, he was nominated to run by a Mr O'Higgins, whose colours he carried. CULVERTHORPE was attempting to improve on his second place and apart from MARENGO there was only one other with knowledge of Aintree behind him. The 1840 winner JERRY was back, after a gap of seven years and the nearest one can tell his age is by the term 'aged' in the record books. The famous Irish mare BRUNETTE came to Liverpool having carried all before her at home. It was another from the Emerald Isle, though, who dominated the betting: the nine-year-old gelding MATTHEW, bred in Coolreagh by John Westropp. Times were at their hardest in Ireland, with the famine at its height and many thousands starving and it was suggested that with so much Irish money wagered on MATTHEW, half the population would have to emigrate should he lose. The money simply poured on the gelding, who with only 10 st 6 lbs was considered thrown in at the weights. On the day MATTHEW's position at the head of the market firmed to 4/1, his popularity no doubt strengthened by the report of a lady magician at a Liverpool theatre the night before, who, in a mesmeric state, had named him as the winner. But then, as the runners moved around at the start, the betting took a curious twist. For no apparent reason, MATTHEW drifted out to 10/1, sharing the top market position with last year's runner-up CULVERTHORPE.

BRUNETTE, who won her two prep races at Worcester and Hereford and looked the form-horse to many

When the flag fell the mare CUMBERLAND LASSIE went off in front, while Tom Olliver on ST LEGER contented himself in the mid-division alongside his old rival and friend Jem Mason on CLINKER and it wasn't until the third fence that any accidents occurred. MARENGO hit the guard rail so hard that he somersaulted into the next field, leaving poor Barker as unconscious as he had been after his 1840 fall with WEATHERCOCK. CUMBERLAND LASSIE maintained her lead, but at the fence leading on to the racecourse, she swerved away from the obstacle and fell into the lane by the canal bridge, leaving JERRY in front. He held his advantage while first one then another tried to get on terms with him and over Becher's the second time there were only a handful left in the race. Of those only CULVERTHORPE, PIONEER and the Olliver-ridden ST LEGER appeared dangerous. The Irish pair MATTHEW and BRUNETTE were so far back they seemed surely out of it. JERRY came on to the racecourse first but it could now be seen that 'Black Tom' had been biding his time, for he brought ST LEGER with a strong run, taking the final hurdle just half a length behind the leader. A great roar came from the stands as ST LEGER gained on JERRY with every stride. But it became quite deafening when a third horse joined the tussle and it was realised that the latecomer was MATTHEW. Hitting the front near the post, he won by a length from ST LEGER, who was the same distance ahead of JERRY and Captain Peel brought PIONEER home an honourable fourth. The Irish rejoiced long into the night over their first Liverpool 'Chase winner, the celebrations continuing on the seaward journey home, for what had eluded them since Tom Ferguson first tried with a trio of runners had at last been captured by Denis Wynne and MATTHEW.

THE GRAND NATIONAL HANDICAP STEEPLECHASE
1847

A sweepstake of 23 sovereigns. The second horse to save his stake. Any winner from the date of declaration to carry 5 pounds extra. No rider to open a gate, or ride through a gateway, or more than 100 yards along any road, footpath or driftway

Date: 3rd March	Starters: 26	Time: 10 mins 39 secs
1st **MATTHEW**	**9.10–6** (Mr Courtenay)	**D. Wynne**
2nd **ST LEGER**	**12–3** (Mr Watt)	**Tom Olliver**
3rd **JERRY**	**11–6** (Mr Moseley)	**Bradley**
4th **PIONEER**	**7.11–12** (Mr O'Higgins)	**Capt Peel**
5th **CULVERTHORPE**	**11–6** (Mr D'Arcey)	**H N Powell**
6th **BRUNETTE**	**13.12–6** (Mr Preston)	**Mr A McDonough**

Also Ran:
SAUCEPAN 12–6 (Mr Power) **Mr W McDonough** *Failed to finish*; BALLYBAR 11–12 (Mr Robertson) **Turner** *Failed to finish*; THE FALSE HEIR 11–4 (Mr Hall) **Wilson** *Failed to finish*; THE PLURALIST 11–4 (Mr Hall) **Denby** *Failed to finish*; FREDERICK 11–2 (Mr Preston) **Abbot** *Failed to finish*; LATTITAT 11–0 (Mr Bevill) **Mr Bevill** *Failed to finish*; MARENGO 11–0 (Capt Barnett) **Barker** *Fell*; CAVENDISH 10–10 (Mr Walter) **Scott** *Failed to finish*; AVOCA 10–10 (Capt Gambier) **Capt Broadley** *Failed to finish*; ST RUTH 11–1 (Mr R J Moore) **Canavan** *Failed to finish*; RED LANCER 10–8 (Lord Strathmore) **Lord Strathmore** *Pulled-up*; BARMAID 10–8 (Mr Lockwood) **Mr Lockwood** *Failed to finish*; GRENADE 10–8 (Mr Anderson) **Rackley** *Failed to finish*; CLINKER 10–7 (Mr Kirkpatrick) **Jem Mason** *Fell*; GAYHURST 10–7 (Mr Wesley) **Mr Wesley** *Failed to finish*; TRAMP 10–6 (Mr W Hall) **Archer** *Failed to finish*; QUICKSILVER 10–4 (Col Taylor) **Rawson** *Failed to finish*; CUMBERLAND LASSIE 10–4 (Mr Smith) **Meddock** *Ran-out*; VALERIA 5.10–3 (Mr Oakley) **Dally** *Failed to finish*; MIDNIGHT 5.10–10 (Mr H B Browne) **Gardner** *Failed to finish*.

The Betting: *10/1 Matthew & Culverthorpe; 100/8 Jerry; 15/1 St Leger, Pioneer & Avoca; 20/1 Red Lancer*

Distances: *One length; one length*

* *Matthew was at 4/1 until just before the start* *

1848

The attraction of the race to military men, begun with the famous Captain Becher in LOTTERY's year, was to provide an annual challenge to both serving and retired officers. Captain William Peel had set his sights on the 'National as early as 1842 when partnering BANGALORE and since then had combined his riding with ownership, most noticeably with PIONEER in last year's race. It was in 1848, however, that Peel became a part of one of the earliest Grand National legends. Strangely, the horse concerned was never officially given a name and was despised by the person responsible for its existence.

Sir Edward Scott of Great Bar bred from the stallion DR FAUSTUS a foal to which he took an instant dislike, referring to the animal as 'a fiddle-headed brute'. In due course he passed the horse on, in settlement of a bill, to a man named Wilkinson, engaged in the humble trade of chandler at Sutton Coldfield. The new owner worked the son of DR FAUSTUS in the shafts of his chandler's cart before selling it to Mr Garnett of Moor Hill, who could envisage no other occupation for the horse. Now known merely as 'the Chandler', the horse pulled Mr Garnett's gig regularly to the Bonehill harriers meet and it was here that Captain Peel first met 'the brute'. When his mount did not arrive for the day's sport, Peel was offered the use of CHANDLER and rather than remain a spectator, the Captain hastily unhitched the horse from the gig and saddled him. CHANDLER gave Peel such a ride, that upon returning, he bought the horse from Mr Garnett for 20 guineas plus his intended mount, which had now arrived. A few days after the deal, Garnett returned Captain Peel's horse as unwanted. So CHANDLER only cost 20 guineas, which

was quickly recouped by the shrewd Peel when he passed on the late-comer for 60 guineas. For the next five years, CHANDLER was regularly hunted before finishing second in his first steeplechase at Birmingham. Next came a twenty length victory at Warwick, where he amazed onlookers by clearing a brook with a leap alleged to measure thirty-seven feet.

One of Captain Peel's closest friends was Captain Joseph Lockhart Little, affectionately known as 'Josey' among racing's faithful and as the 'captivating Captain' in social circles. Born at Chipstead, Surrey in 1821, Little held a commission in the King's Dragoon Guards until losing everything in a bank crash. He was forced to transfer to the less fashionable 81st Regiment of Foot, but his fortunes took an immediate turn for the better when CHANDLER came his way. After riding the horse to victory at Worcester, Little collected £500 from the ring, thus beginning his climb back to solvency. After another success at Windsor, Josey Little purchased a half share in the horse from William Peel and the joint owners began to plan a try at the 'National. It would be Little's first ride in the Liverpool 'Chase but he had benefited by the expert tutelage of none other than maestro 'Black Tom' Olliver. Tom's mount this year was THE CURATE, at 6/1 just two points clear at the head of the market from MATTHEW. CHANDLER was third in the betting. Confusion was caused through two of the runners bearing the same name of PIONEER and it can only be supposed that the one quoted in the lists at 25/1 was the 1846 winner, again ridden by Captain Peel. Prizefighter Johnny Broome had chosen the toughest race of all for his initiation to the saddle, but so strong was his desire to compete that when one after another of his

Captain Josie Little on CHANDLER

chosen mounts went wrong, he begged to be given the ride on EAGLE. Broome laid a bet with Captain Alleyne that he would have reached the fourth field from home when the winner passed the post.

After a week of continuous rain, the going was exceptionally bad. One contender who had his spirits dampened even before he reached the racecourse was the Irish SIR ARTHUR, who spent almost twenty minutes in the Mersey after falling in while being unloaded from the steamer! The start was as dismal as the weather, with many of the twenty-nine runners being left behind by up to a hundred yards. ASHBERRY LASS led over the first and still led over Valentine's but groans of dismay came from the Irish contingent when it was realised that their hero MATTHEW was no longer in the contest. At the first fence on the second circuit, SAUCE-PAN caused great chaos by refusing when in front, but the pugilist-turned-jockey Johnny Broome had kept EAGLE clear of the early trouble and as they approached Becher's he was within striking distance of the leaders. BRITISH YEOMAN had opened up a twelve length lead as he cleared the Brook but the exhausted EAGLE failed to rise at the fence and the boxer hit the ground with such force that he had to be carried to a nearby farmhouse to recover his senses. The formidable Tom Olliver was biding his time on the favourite, and as they approached the racecourse for the final time THE CURATE was handily placed. THE SAILOR fell heavily at the last bank and ditch, breaking his back and seconds later COUNSELLOR and BLUE PILL tragically incurred broken legs. BRITISH YEOMAN still held the lead at the second last but the cheers of the crowds rose to the prospect of a favourite's win when THE CURATE raced into the lead on the flat. But there was another still with a finish left in him. CHANDLER drew alongside and Captain Little showed the judgment of a veteran to overhaul his mentor, getting up close to home to clinch it by half a length. BRITISH YEOMAN was a length and a half back in third place, with STANDARD GUARD the only other to finish. It is not known if the winner's co-owner, Captain Peel, got back in time to lead in his winner after parting company with PIONEER in the country. What is known is that the Captains Little and Peel collected £7,000 from the bookies through the efforts of CHANDLER. Tom Olliver proved himself a fine teacher on that soaking afternoon when the pupil turned the tables on the master.

THE GRAND NATIONAL HANDICAP STEEPLECHASE
1848

Starters: 29			Time: 11 mins 21 secs
1st **CHANDLER**	12.11–12 *(Capt J L Little)*	**Capt J L Little**
2nd **THE CURATE**	aged.11–12 *(Mr Brettle)*	**T Olliver**
3rd **BRITISH YEOMAN**	11–4 *(Mr Elmore)*	**Mr Bevill**
4th **STANDARD GUARD**	10–12 *(Mr Storey)*	**Taylor**

Also Ran:

WOLVERHAMPTON aged.11–12 (Mr R H Jones) **Bretherton** *Failed to finish; SAUCEPAN aged.11–11* (Mr W Strickland) **T Abbot** *Refused; MATTHEW 10.11–6* (Mr Courtenay) **D Wynne** *Knocked-over; JERRY aged.11–7* (Mr Moseley) **Sanders** *Pulled-up; FATHER MATTHEW 11–6* (Mr W S Crawford) **H Lamplugh** *Fell; PIONEER 8.11–6* (Mr O'Higgins) **Capt Peel** *Brought-down; THE SWITCHER aged.11–5* (Lord Strathmore) **Lord Strathmore** *Fell; ASHBERRY LASS 6.11–3* (Mr J W Haworth) **Collis** *Failed to finish; CHEROOT aged.11–2* (Mr Davies) **McGee** *Failed to finish; ARISTIDES aged.11–1* (Mr Brettle) **Rowlands** *Failed to finish; SIR ARTHUR 6.11–1* (Mr Barry) **Murphy** *Failed to finish; KHONDOOZ 11–0* (Mr J Wilson) **Rackley** *Pulled-up; SOPHIA aged.11–0* (Sir R de Burgh) **Ford** *Failed to finish; THE IRISH BARD aged.11–0* (Mr Arthur) **Freeze** *Failed to finish; EAGLE aged.11–4* (Mr C C Brooke) **John Broome** *Fell; PIONEER aged.10–13* (Mr T Harrison) **Neale** *Brought-down; PICTON aged.10–13* (Mr J N Burke) **N Burke** *Failed to finish; COUNSELLOR aged.10–12* (Mr W Coutts) **Frisby** *Fell* [destroyed]; *FORTUNE-TELLER 10–10* (Mr Kennedy) **Stagg** *Fell; THE SAILOR 6.10–8* (Mr Mason) **Holman** *Fell* [destroyed]; *THE GIPSY QUEEN 10–6* (Lord Anson) **Whitfield** *Refused; VARIETY aged.10–8* (Mr C Towneley) **Powell** *Failed to finish; BLUE PILL aged.10–3* (Mr E Cary) **Allensby** *Fell* [destroyed]; *SPARTA aged.10–0* (Mr R Brooke) **Turner** *Fell; NAWORTH aged.9–8* (Lord Strathmore) **W Archer** *Failed to finish.*

The Betting: *6/1 The Curate; 8/1 Matthew; 12/1 Chandler; 15/1 Sir Arthur; 100/6 Standard Guard; 25/1 Pioneer, Counsellor & Khondooz; 30/1 Fortune-Teller*

* *Two runners bore the same name, i.e. PIONEER, a most confusing situation and from the vague reports of the race it is impossible to determine which was the one quoted at 25/1 by the bookmakers* *

Distances: *Half a length; one and a half lengths*

Value to Winning Owner: *£1,015*

1849

An example of the lack of organised administration in steeplechasing at this time was the haphazard naming of horses. We have seen two horses bearing the same name allowed to compete as well as an unnamed animal referred to by the sire's name, and it was a frequent practice for horses to run under the names of recent 'chasing favourites. The grey PETER SIMPLE had been a regular and popular competitor in the race in the early forties, so it was confusing to say the least when, among the entries for 1849, was found a PETER SIMPLE. But unlike the former 'National stalwart whose name he bore, this 'Peter' was no grey entire. He was an eleven-year-old bay gelding by PATRON, facing Liverpool for the first time in the colours of Mr Mason Junior. Tom Olliver again carried the responsibility of partnering the favourite, PRINCE GEORGE, and the combination was thought to be unbeatable. THE CURATE was next in the market, yet curiously his conqueror CHANDLER was completely unquoted. Elmore was represented by BRITISH YEOMAN, while there was a late rush of money for THE KNIGHT OF GWYNNE, ridden by his owner Captain D'Arcy.

A huge crowd assembled at the racecourse despite the desperately cold weather. Again the going was very heavy. At the start, a section of the field shot forward, anticipating the flag fall. Starter Lord Sefton's efforts to recall them were thwarted by a portion of the crowd in the vicinity shouting encouragement to the offenders so that what was without question a false start went uncorrected. Among the few to benefit from the disorder was PETER SIMPLE, who rapidly opened up a substantial lead. By the time the second field was reached, those at the rear faced an impossible task. At the fourth fence, KILFANE fell heavily and was jumped on with such force that his thigh was broken. The unfortunate animal was put down at once. PETER SIMPLE seemed to be the only one not disturbed by the state of the ground and he was increasing his lead as he came back to the racecourse. NAPOLEON, EQUINOX and PROCEED were the nearest to the leader at this stage and Tom Olliver was in a handy position with PRINCE GEORGE. Captain D'Arcy, who had backed his mount, THE KNIGHT OF GWYNNE heavily, made a forward move early on the second circuit. Over Becher's and around the Canal Turn, the chase was on in earnest, but at the very next obstacle, which was no more than an eighteen-inch high bank of earth, PETER SIMPLE sped on leaving tragedy behind him. EQUINOX broke his back falling and JERRY and BALLYBAR were brought down. To add to the chaos, CORIANDE, CHATHAM and WOLVERHAMPTON also came to grief at this insignificant fence. At the very next fence THE CURATE came down heavily, also breaking his back. NAPOLEON and KHONDOOZ were pulled up and Tom Olliver could find nothing on the favourite PRINCE GEORGE. PETER SIMPLE entered the finishing straight with a commanding lead over THE KNIGHT OF GWYNNE, who to the dismay of his rider had given his all. It was with this realisation that Captain D'Arcy felt obliged to resort to a somewhat unusual and distinctly ungentlemanly tactic in his attempt to secure both victory and his sizeable bet. All the way to the line he called out offers of financial inducement to Cunningham in front of him, ranging from £1,000 to £4,000, if the leading rider would 'take a pull'. The fact that PETER SIMPLE passed the post with a three-length advantage indicates fully how Cunningham felt about such conduct and which prize he preferred. A long way back in third place came PRINCE GEORGE, followed at intervals by ALFRED, CHANDLER and THE BRITISH YEOMAN.

There was much indignation after the event when the details of the disasters became known. Then, as now, it was all too easy to be wise after the event, yet there was something to be learned from the observation that the obstacles which caused all the grief were of the same colour as the fields from which the horses jumped.

THE GRAND NATIONAL HANDICAP STEEPLECHASE
1849

A sweepstake of 23 sovereigns. The second horse to save his stake. Any winner from the date of declaration to carry 5 pounds extra. No rider to open a gate, or ride through a gateway, or more than 100 yards along any road, footpath or driftway

Date: 28th February	Starters: 24	Time: 10 mins 56 secs
1st **PETER SIMPLE**	11.11–0 *(Mr Mason jnr)*	**T Cunningham**
2nd **THE KNIGHT OF GWYNNE**	10–7 *(Capt D'Arcy)*	**Capt D'Arcy**
3rd **PRINCE GEORGE**	10–10 *(Mr T Mason)*	**Tom Olliver**
4th **ALFRED**	5.10–6 *(Mr Buchanan)*	**D Wynne**
5th **CHANDLER**	12–2 *(Capt Little)*	**Capt Little**
6th **BRITISH YEOMAN**	11–4 *(Mr Elmore)*	**Mr Bevill**

Also Ran:

TIPPERARY BOY 5.10–9 (Mr Terry) **Barley** *Failed to finish*; *MULLIGAN 5.11–2* (Mr Westropp) **Ford** *Failed to finish*; *KILFANE 11–0* (Mr J H Holmes) **Neale** *Fell* [destroyed]; *CORIANDER 10–6* (Mr E W Rudyard) **Bally** *Fell*; *BALLYBAR 9–12* (Mr Wesley) **H Bradley** *Fell*; *KHONDOOZ 9–10* (Mr Tillbury) **Rackley** *Pulled-up*; *THE CURATE 11–11* (Mr Brettle) **Powell** *Fell* [destroyed]; *PROCEED 11–11* (Capt Peel) **Capt Peel** *Refused*; *WOLVERHAMPTON 11–5* (Mr B Bretherton) **Mr B Bretherton** *Fell*; *ARAB ROBBER 6.11–2* (Mr Russell) **Phillips** *Failed to finish*; *THE IRON DUKE 5.11–0* (Mr C Price) **Abbot** *Failed to finish*; *THE VICTIM 10–11* (Lord Chesterfield) **Taylor** *Failed to finish*; *SIR JOHN 10–10* (Mr Sharkie) **Mr Sharkie** *Failed to finish*; *NAPOLEON 6.10–8* (Mr J Bateman) **Archer** *Pulled-up*; *CHATHAM 10–6* (Lord Strathmore) **Frisby** *Fell*; *EQUINOX 9–12* (Capt Peyton) **Moloney** *Fell* [destroyed]; *JERRY 10–4* (Mr J S Moseley) **J S Walker** *Fell*; *SPARTA 8–12* (Mr Bathurst) **Wakefield** *Fell*.

The Betting: *5/1 Prince George; 6/1 The Curate; 8/1 The Knight of Gwynne; 9/1 Proceed; 12/1 Wolverhampton; 12/1 to 15/1 The British Yeoman; 12/1 Alfred; 20/1 Chatham & Peter Simple; 50/1 Napoleon*

Distances: *Three lengths; a distance*

1850

In the twenty-five years since the first public railway opened between Stockton and Darlington, this new form of transport had all but made travel by stage-coach a thing of the past. It was in 1850, however, that the winner of the Grand National rekindled memories of what had virtually become a by-gone age, the time of the post-horn and the rattle of coach-horses' hooves. In doing this, the tiny half-bred ABD-EL-KADER acquired for himself a special place in the hearts of racegoers everywhere.

It was in 1827 that Henry Osborne, of Dardistown Castle, County Meath, was returning home by coach from London. From his position in the box seat, he observed the action of a handsome mare among the team. In reverie, Osborne pictured her winning for him the Bachelor's Plate in his native land and upon discovering that she was for sale, readily parted with the 40 guineas asking price. Naming his purchase ENGLISH LASS, he trained her for racing and in due course, not only realised his original dream but attained many other successes with the trusty 'LASS'. When sent to stud, the mare bred a total of nine foals, each of which proved most disappointing, with the single exception of her eighth. A colt, ABD-EL-KADER, by the stallion ISHMAEL, was affectionately called 'LITTLE AB' by Mr Osborne. He was sent hunting and developed into a bold, fluent jumper. Mr Osborne ventured into steeplechasing with his small but very able home-bred bay, proceeding to win races all over Ireland with him. Somewhere along this successful route the ownership of the animal changed to that of Osborne's son Joseph and it was he who foresaw in ADB-EL-KADER greater things than even his father may have dreamt of. Joe Osborne was one of the earliest contributors to *Bell's Life*, in addition to being the compiler of *The Horsebreeder's Handbook* and it was upon his insistence that the son of ISHMAEL was sent across the Irish Sea to race at Liverpool.

The race attracted thirty-two runners, the largest number so far, and the most heavily backed of these was last year's winner PETER SIMPLE at 5/1 and now owned by his partner in victory Cunningham. SIR JOHN, RAT-TRAP and THE KNIGHT OF GWYNNE were others well supported in the market and CHANDLER, again ridden by owner Captain Little, was at 16/1. For the first time an Earl of Sefton was represented, by 25/1 shot LITTLE FANNY. Apparently the one horse who escaped everyone's attention was the diminutive ABD-EL-KADER, completely unquoted in the betting and generally considered by paddock pundits to be of the wrong build to cope with the big fences. Jockey Chris Green, son of a Norfolk farmer, was like his mount 'LITTLE AB' making his first appearance in the big race.

THE OAKS went out at the first after colliding with PETER SIMPLE and the tightly bunched field went on over Becher's at a cracking pace. Another collision between CHANDLER and RAT-TRAP in the area of the Canal Turn put paid to both of their chances and as the runners entered the racecourse at the end of the first circuit THE KNIGHT OF GWYNNE and PETER SIMPLE were seen to be at the head of affairs. TIPPERARY BOY went to the front briefly early on the second circuit, but as they approached Becher's again Chris Green rushed ABD-EL-KADER up on the outside. The little horse jumped the Brook like a stag, gaining many lengths, and from there on he maintained an amazingly fast gallop. As they came towards the final fence only THE KNIGHT OF GWYNNE was in a position to offer any sort of challenge. On the run to the line Denis Wynne put in a stirring finish on the challenger but ABD-EL-KADER held on by a length and appeared fresh enough to be able to go round again. SIR JOHN finished third, followed by TIPPERARY BOY, FARNHAM, MARIA DAY and the Archer ridden VENGEANCE. It was the best possible result for the bookmakers, yet few among the vast crowd could begrudge the outsider his win after having witnessed such a foot-perfect display of fast accurate jumping. The tiny eight-year-old had also created a new time record for the course, endorsing in the finest manner Mr Osborne's faith in the mare which pulled the Shrewsbury coach.

THE GRAND NATIONAL HANDICAP STEEPLECHASE
1850

Starters: 32		Time: 9 mins 57½ secs
1st **ABD-EL-KADER**	8.9–12 *(Mr J Osborne)*	**C Green**
2nd **THE KNIGHT OF GWYNNE**	**11–8** *(Mr J Fort)*	**D Wynne**
3rd **SIR JOHN**	**11–8** *(Lord Waterford)*	**J Ryan**
4th **TIPPERARY BOY**	**6.10–0** *(Mr Hughes)*	**S Darling**
5th **FARNHAM**	**6.11–3** *(Mr Maugan)*	**T Abbot**
6th **MARIA DAY**	**10–5** *(Mr Treadgold)*	**Rackley**
7th **VENGEANCE**	**9–10** *(Mr W Vevers)*	**W Archer**

Also Ran:
PETER SIMPLE 12.12–2 (Mr Cunningham) **T Cunningham** *Failed to finish*; BRITISH YEOMAN 11–10 (Mr Elmore) **Philpot** *Failed to finish*; RAT-TRAP 11–7 (Lord Strathmore) **Frisby** *Failed to finish*; CHANDLER 14.11–3 (Capt J Little) **Capt J Little** *Failed to finish*; THE VICTIM 11–2 (Mr Hassall) **Taylor** *Failed to finish*; SPRING BUCK 10–12 (Lord G Kennedy) **Smith** *Pulled-up*; THE IRON DUKE 6.10–12 (Mr J Bell) **J Hanlon** *Failed to finish*; MEATH 10–10 (Mr Harrison) **Neale** *Failed to finish*; MULLIGAN 6.10–10 (Mr Westropp) **Mr Westropp** *Failed to finish*; ROY-DE-AISEY 5.10–10 (Lord Lurgan) **Magee** *Failed to finish*; QUADRUPED 10–8 (Mr Cunningham) **G Arran** *Failed to finish*; LAUREL 10–8 (Mr Butler) **Mr Butler** *Failed to finish*; RAINBOW 10–8 (Mr J C Ranton) **Dalby** *Fell*; EVERTON 10–8 (Mr D Lewis) **A Salt** *Failed to finish*; SHINSORE 6.10–5 (Mr Williamson) **H Bradley** *Failed to finish*; THE OAKS 5.10–5 (Mr J G Murphy) **S Canavan** *Knocked-over*; COLUMBINE 10–4 (Mr Pocket) **T Olliver** *Failed to finish*; SOBRIETY 10–4 (Mr Sandford) **J Thompson** *Failed to finish*; FISTICUFF 10–0 (Mr J Nicoll) **Parr** *Failed to finish*; HOPE 9–12 (Mr Hunter) (carried 10–1) **Mr Hunter** *Fell*; KILKENNY 9–10 (Capt Fraser) **W Holman** *Failed to finish*; LITTLE FANNY 9–0 (Lord Sefton) **Fowler** *Failed to finish*; JOHNNIE BARRIE 9–0 (Mr Laing) (carried 9–11) **Maitland** *Failed to finish*; PEGASUS 8–10 (Lord Seaham) **Tasker** *Failed to finish*; THE PONY 8–7 (Mr R Brooke) **Maney** *Failed to finish*.

The Betting: *5/1 Peter Simple; 7/1 Sir John; 9/1 Rat-Trap; 12/1 The Knight of Gwynne & Victim; 15/1 Farnham & Vengeance; 16/1 Chandler; 20/1 Columbine; 25/1 Maria Day & Little Fanny; 30/1 The Oaks*

Distances: *One length; three lengths*

Value to Winning Owner: *£950*

* Abd-El-Kader was not quoted by the bookmakers *

1851

The first dual winner, the tiny ABD-EL-KADER

Despite the manner in which ABD-EL-KADER had thrust himself on the 'National scene in 1850, the handicapper seems not to have been over-impressed. When the weights were published for the 1851 renewal, the Osborne horse received only a six pound increase for his length victory of the previous year. From the outset it was obvious that the bookmakers would not be as generous in their assessment of his chances, and so it was that on the day ABD-EL-KADER went to post at 7/1 joint favourite with fellow Irishman SIR JOHN, just one point ahead of RAT-TRAP, now ridden by Jem Mason. PETER SIMPLE was again in the field of twenty-one, with a new jockey named Tubb, but the mudlark appeared to have lost favour with punters and he lined up without a starting price. 'Black Tom' Olliver elected to ride last year's fourth-placed TIPPERARY BOY, thus causing a flood of money to firm his choice to 10/1. Another which attracted some attention in the market was the mare MARIA DAY, also a finisher last year. There was one change for ABD-EL-KADER. For some reason Chris Green stood down, the mount going to the talented Irishman T Abbot. A Mr Green was shown as being

the rider of HOPE, but there is no indication that this was the same man.

From a good start another fast pace was set, with SIR JOHN striking the front, closely followed by a cluster of horses including HALF-AND-HALF, HOPE and PETER SIMPLE. As they came to the post and rails at the end of the first stretch of plough, RAT-TRAP refused in a determined manner. Jem Mason, however, got the mulish brute over the obstacle and back in the race, though by this time they were trailing by many lengths. PETER SIMPLE, TIPPERARY BOY and MARIA DAY showed prominently just behind the leader SIR JOHN at the Canal Turn and MAURICE DALEY was jumping in fine style alongside REINDEER. At this stage ABD-EL-KADER was some way to the rear although again measuring his fences perfectly. SIR JOHN was passed by PETER SIMPLE whose rider was determined to win a bet that he would be first over the Water. A dozen strides from the jump it looked certain that he would land the bet, but he had it snatched from him when Tom Olliver brought TIPPERARY BOY with a spurt to grasp the lead. At the end of the first circuit, the outcome was wide open and as they cleared the Brook it was noticeable that ABD-EL-KADER was poised just a few lengths back in fifth place. MULLIGAN came down near the Canal Turn, followed almost immediately by FUGITIVE, while HOPE, SIR PETER LAURIE, CURRIG and MAURICE DALEY were all pulled up. Back on the racecourse, a thrilling finish was in prospect, with four horses racing almost in line abreast: SIR JOHN, TIPPERARY BOY, ABD-EL-KADER and the mare MARIA DAY who had made up a tremendous amount of ground from the rear. With no let-up in the pace, ABD-EL-KADER hit the front over the final obstacle only to be tackled immediately by MARIA DAY, the other two dropping away. Up the long run-in a truly terrific tussle developed. It was a nightmare task for the judge in the closest finish yet seen in the event, his verdict going in favour of ABD-EL-KADER by the unusual distance of 'half a neck'.

Irishmen among the spectators were cock-a-hoop at the result and with just cause. Not only had they seen a son of their soil scoring a spirited victory, but their hero had put the icing on the cake by becoming the first horse to win the great race twice and he had done it in successive years at that. There were many, and not all of them Irish, who left the course that day convinced that they had seen the greatest 'National winner since LOTTERY.

THE GRAND NATIONAL HANDICAP STEEPLECHASE
1851

Starters: 21			Time: 9 mins 59 secs
1st **ABD-EL-KADER**	9.10–4	*(Mr J Osborne)*	T Abbot
2nd **MARIA DAY**	aged.10–5	*(Mr C Higgins)*	J Frisby
3rd **SIR JOHN**	aged.11–12	*(Lord Waterford)*	J Ryan
4th **HALF-AND-HALF** [formerly SMALL-BEER]	aged.10–8	*(Mr Oakes)*	R Sly, jnr
5th **VAIN HOPE**	aged.11–8	*(Mr W Vevers)*	S Darling
6th **RAT-TRAP**	aged.10–10	*(Mr T F Mason)*	J Mason
7th **MULLIGAN**	7.10–2	*(Mr J Elmore)*	W Draper
8th **SHINSORE**	7.10–7	*(Mr King)*	Mr Gaman
9th **REINDEER** [formerly FRANK]	9–8	*(Mr May)*	C Planner
10th **TIPPERARY BOY**	7.10–3	*(Mr Tollitt)*	T Olliver

Also Ran:

SIR PETER LAURIE 11–7 (Mr W Barnett) **W Scott** *Failed to finish*; *PETER SIMPLE 13.11–7* (Mr Cunningham) **D Tubb** *Failed to finish*; *THE VICTIM 10–13* (Mr Palmer) **W Taylor** *Failed to finish*; *FUGITIVE 10–12* (Lord Lurgan) **H Bradley** *Fell*; *CURRIG 9–12* (Mr Barry) **J Debean** *Failed to finish*; *FUGLEMAN 10–0* (Col Shirley) **D Wynne** *Failed to finish*; *HOPE 9–12* (Mr S H Kemp) **Mr Green** *Pulled-up*; *VOLATILE 9–10* (Mr W Vevers) **W Fowler** *Fell*; *A Mare by GREYSTEEL 9–10* (Mr Onslow) **Thrift** *Failed to finish*; *MAURICE DALEY (formerly Flycatcher) 9–6* (Mr Cartwright) **C Boyce** *Failed to finish*; *PENRITH (formerly Charles XII) 9–4* (Mr Johnstone) **McClory** *Failed to finish*.

The Betting: *6/1 Rat-Trap; 7/1 Sir John & Abd-El-Kader; 8/1 Vain Hope; 10/1 Tipperary Boy; 15/1 Fugitive; 100/6 Maria Day; 20/1 Half-and-Half; 25/1 Sir Peter Laurie, Currig & Mulligan*

Distances: *Half a neck; two lengths*

Value to Winning Owner: £750

1852

For the third successive year, ABD-EL-KADER found himself with a new jockey, this time Denis Wynne. The handicapper was taking no chances with 'LITTLE AB' again, allotting him 11 st 4 lbs, although the horse which finished in third place behind him in 1851, SIR JOHN, was top weight with 6 lbs more. With only 9 st 12 lbs, the six-year-old LA GAZZA LADRA started favourite at 6/1, three points ahead of ABD-EL-KADER. At the other end of the market came ROYAL BLUE, Mr Harding's horse being both the first mount in the race of a youthful nineteen-year-old called George Stevens and the first runner to be officially listed at the extreme odds of 100/1. John Elmore was represented by another rank outsider EVERTON. Of the twenty-four competitors, only eight were considered good enough to be listed with a starting price.

Among those ignored by bookies and racegoers alike was a bay mare called MISS MOWBRAY, whose early life was another story of rejection. Bred by Mr Boulton in Pitmore, Bedfordshire from the stallion LANCASTRIAN, she was sent to Newmarket where various trainers declared her to be totally worthless. In due course Boulton sold the mare for 100 guineas to a drysalt merchant from Manchester who was most dissatisfied with his purchase and returned her within days. Having lost the legal wrangle which followed, Boulton frantically sought a buyer, but all agreed that MISS MOWBRAY was no good for 'chasing. Sent hunting she showed some promise, and it was thus that she was ridden one day by Mr T F Mason. He bought her from the long-suffering breeder and it was in his colours that the daughter of NORMA took her place in the line-up for the 'National. Not only was it MISS MOWBRAY's first attempt in the race but also that of her

rider, the amateur Alec Goodman.

Born in 1822, Alec grew up near Peterborough. As a boy, he spent many hours at the horse breaker's in the town, quickly acquiring a skill which was soon noticed. When barely eighteen he rode his first steeplechase, finishing second at Yaxley, and he was soon much in demand. At twenty-two, Alec began farming on his own, but still found time to hunt and 'chase. Thirty may have seemed late to be starting his bid for Aintree glory, but none of his fellow jockeys doubted his ability.

Alec Goodman pictured on SIR PETER LAURIE, who ran third with Holman aboard this year

MALEY jumped off smartly when the flag fell, but MARIA DAY, who had run so close last year, came to grief at the first, while at Becher's more casualties piled up. ABD-EL-KADER was thrilling the crowds in the country with a display of fast jumping, leading until being passed at the Canal Turn by CHIEFTAIN. At the Water, CHIEFTAIN was six lengths in front but the crowds in the stands were dismayed to see ABD-EL-KADER being pulled up. Over Becher's for the final time the leader was the same and CHIEFTAIN came back onto the racecourse five lengths in front of the beautifully ridden MISS MOWBRAY. She came upsides at the last and touching down in front, ran on to hold the late challenge of MAURICE DALEY by a length. Another who came with a late run, SIR PETER LAURIE, was a length and a half back in third, just in front of CHIEFTAIN. Not for the first time were racing's pundits put to shame by a horse they had maligned proving its worth at the severest test. It was surprising that MISS MOWBRAY had been overlooked in the betting, for she had already shown ability in winning the Warwickshire Hunt Cup and the Leamington Open Steeplechase before turning out so well at Aintree.

THE GRAND NATIONAL HANDICAP STEEPLECHASE
1852

Date: 3rd March 1852	Starters: 24	Time: 9 mins 58½ secs
1st **MISS MOWBRAY**	aged.10–4 *(Mr T F Mason)*	**Mr A Goodman**
2nd **MAURICE DALEY** [formerly FLYCATCHER]	aged.9–4 *(Mr Cartwright)* *[carried 9–6]*	**C Boyce**
3rd **SIR PETER LAURIE**	aged.11–7 *(Capt W Barnett)*	**W Holman**
4th **CHIEFTAIN**	aged.10–12 *(Mr Atkinson)*	**Harrison**
5th **LA GAZZA LADRA**	6.9–12 *(Mr Goodwin)*	**J Neale**
6th **WARNER**	aged.10–8 *(Lord Waterford)*	**W Archer**
7th **SIR JOHN**	aged.11–10 *(Lord Waterford)*	**J Ryan**

Also Ran:

BEDFORD 9–12 (Mr Chance) **A Taylor** *Fell*; *ABD-EL-KADER* 10.11–4 (Mr J Osborne) **D Wynne** *Pulled-up*; *MCIAN* 9–10 (Mr R Jones) **J Sadler** *Failed to finish*; *PETER SIMPLE* 14.11–2 (Mr G S Davenport) **Mr G S Davenport** *Fell*; *BOURTON* (formerly Upton) 10–10 (Mr Martin) **S Darling** *Fell*; *DOLLY'S BRUE* 10–0 (Mr Maugan) **McGee** *Failed to finish*; *SILENT FRIEND* 9–12 (Mr Courtenay) **Parry** *Failed to finish*; *LAMIENNE* 9–7 (Mr J G Murphy) **Meaney** *Failed to finish*; *THE VICTIM* 9–7 (Mr Gooch) **H Bradley** *Fell*; *ROYAL BLUE* 9–0 (Mr Harding) **G Stevens** *Fell*; *BEDFORD* 10–10 (Mr Barling) **Ablett** *Fell*; *AGIS* 10–10 (Capt J L Little) **T Olliver** *Refused*; *MARIA DAY* 10–6 (Mr C Higgins) **J Frisby** *Fell*; *CURRIG* 10–4 (Mr J Bourke) (inc. 10 lbs extra) **J Debean** *Pulled-up*; *EVERTON* 10–6 (Mr Elmore) (carried 9–10) **Hewitt** *Fell*; *COGIA* 9–6 (Mr J Bird) (carried 9–9) **J Tasker** *Fell*; *MALEY* 9–6 (Mr Henderson) **Connor** *Fell*.

The Betting: 6/1 La Gazza Ladra; 9/1 Abd-El-Kader; 10/1 Chieftain; 12/1 Bedford & Sir John; 30/1 Sir Peter Laurie; 50/1 McIan; 100/1 Royal Blue

Distances: *One length; five lengths*

Value to Winning Owner: *£790*

* *There were two horses named Bedford in this race. It was not specified which was the one quoted at 12/1* *

1853

After three fair-weather 'National's, the course was again in a dreadful state with slush from the thaw making a gallop extremely difficult. There were still twenty-one runners, but the severe winter had interfered with the preparation of most of these and the public chose to stick with those who had proven themselves over the course. MISS MOWBRAY was an obvious choice, yet her owner Mr Mason was in the happy position of having another top runner. This was the gelding OSCAR, the chosen mount of Alec Goodman, which fact was seen as a tip in itself and furthermore the owner declared to win with him. It was after this declaration was posted that there occurred not one but two objections to OSCAR. The owner of SIR PETER LAURIE, Capt W Barnett, lodged his on the grounds that the gelding was wrongly described. Then more seriously Mr Cartwright claimed that OSCAR was disqualified from competing, having run under a false description at Leamington. Cartwright made it clear that his one intention in entering MAURICE DALEY had been to enable him to lodge a protest. It was an unwelcome problem for the stewards with just over an hour before the race was due to start, but they ruled in favour of Mr Mason and no further reference was made to the allegations.

In spite of Mason's stated preference for OSCAR, the public went for his MISS MOWBRAY, the mare going off at 5/1. ABD-EL-KADER was here again, reunited this time with jockey Abbot, but although lowered in the handicap to 10 st 10 lbs, he found few friends at 20/1. Another old favourite was PETER SIMPLE, now running for the fifth time in the 'National and carrying the colours of his new owner Captain Little. The money which reduced his price to 9/1 was surely placed out of sentiment, for even though he was ridden by maestro Tom Olliver, PETER SIMPLE was now fifteen years old. MAURICE DALEY was the first to lead, but soon gave best to PETER SIMPLE, who cleared the third in tremendous style. He was still in front as they approached Becher's but was struck into on the offside by a loose horse. Swerving sharply to the left, the old fellow was in serious danger of going the wrong side of the flag, until knocked back on course by SIR PETER LAURIE who had moved up on the inside. Both 'PETERS' jumped the Brook safely and by the time they reached the Canal Turn PETER SIMPLE had regained the lead. After jumping Valentine's, however, 'LITTLE AB' dashed to the front with a surge of speed reminiscent of his victory days. All the way down the Canal side the dual winner increased his advantage, clearing the Water fully a hundred yards ahead of his nearest challenger, and keeping it up out into the country. Upon re-entering the racecourse, though, PETER SIMPLE was seen to be making ground rapidly and soon ABD-EL-KADER had given his all. Alec Goodman brought OSCAR with a well-timed run between the last two flights, to be joined as they levelled up for the last by stable-companion MISS MOWBRAY, but there was to be no denying the old man of the party, PETER SIMPLE landing slightly in front on the flat. Tom Olliver excelled himself on the run to the line, getting PETER SIMPLE home by three lengths from MISS MOWBRAY, with OSCAR the same distance back in third place. SIR PETER LAURIE was fourth, ABD-EL-KADER fifth. It was a third win in the race for Tom Olliver, who people now said knew Aintree like the inside of his pocket, a second win for owner Captain Little and for PETER SIMPLE, a victory which guaranteed a special place in the record books. He had become the second horse to record a double win in the race, and the first to triumph at the advanced age of fifteen.

Mr Frank Gordon, one of the most celebrated horsemen of the age. This was his only attempt at the 'National, though, as he was more dedicated to riding to hounds, where he was rated the equal of Alec Goodman, than steeplechasing. He once fell into the brook in a race at Market Harborough and in order to avoid drowning, had to bribe an onlooker with a sovereign to pull him out!

THE GRAND NATIONAL HANDICAP STEEPLECHASE

1853

Starters: 21			Time: 10 mins 37½ secs
1st **PETER SIMPLE** [by PATRON]	**15.10–10**	*(Capt J L Little)*	**T Olliver**
2nd **MISS MOWBRAY**	**aged.10–12**	*(Mr T F Mason)*	**Mr F Gordon**
3rd **OSCAR**	**aged.10–2**	*(Mr T F Mason)*	**Mr A Goodman**
4th **SIR PETER LAURIE**	**aged.11–8**	*(Capt W Barnett)*	**W Holman**
5th **ABD-EL-KADER**	**11.10–10**	*(Mr J Osborne)*	**T Abbot**
6th **THE GENERAL**	**10.4**	*(Mr B Land)*	**T Ablett**
7th **CURRIG**	**10–5**	*(Mr J Bourke)*	**D Wynne**

Also Ran:
KNIGHT OF GWYNNE 11–2 (Mr Drake) **Donaldson** *Pulled-up*; *BOURTON 11–2* (Mr Higginson) **S Darling jnr** *Fell*; *TIPPERARY BOY 10–10* (Mr S Lucy) **Butler** *Failed to finish*; *DUC AU BHURRAS 10–10* (Lord Waterford) **J Ryan** *Failed to finish*; *THE VICTIM 10–6* (Capt Scott) **J Tasker** *Pulled-up*; *FIELD MARSHAL 10–4* (Mr J Roberts) **Nelson** *Failed to finish*; *MAURICE DALEY 10–2* (Mr Cartwright) **C Boyce** *Failed to finish*; *BETSY PRIG 10–0* (Capt D Lane) **Meaney** *Fell*; *POLL 9–10* (Mr Hudson) **Debean** *Fell*; *VIEW HALLOO 9–10* (Mr Megson) **W Archer** *Failed to finish*; *MALEY 9–8* (Mr J R Henderson) **E Harrison** *Failed to finish*; *CHATTERBOX 9–8* (Mr Bretherton) **Mr McGaman** *Pulled-up*; *CRABBS 9–2* (Mr J R Henderson) **W Fowler** *Pulled-up*; *THE DWARF 9–0* (Mr Morris) **H Lamplugh** *Fell*.

The Betting: *5/1 Miss Mowbray; 6/1 Oscar & Duc au Bhurras; 7/1 Bourton; 9/1 Peter Simple; 12/1 Sir Peter Laurie & Victim; 15/1 Currig; 100/6 View Halloo; 20/1 Abd-El-Kader; 25/1 Others*

Distances: *Three lengths; three lengths*

* *Mr Mason declared to win with Oscar* *

1854

If ever the critics of steeplechasing needed reinforcement for their argument it was handed to them in 1854, when the most outrageous incident to date took place at Aintree just over an hour before the start of the race. MISS MOWBRAY had become a hot favourite for the event even before the declaration of the weights and although she then drifted, money poured on her as the big day neared, restoring her to the head of the betting. So it was with dismay that the announcement was greeted at 2.35 p.m. on 'National day that MISS MOWBRAY would not run. Her near fore-leg had been found to have 'given way' as a result of someone treacherously applying a blister to the limb sometime after the mare's arrival at the racecourse. It was a blatant case of the favourite being 'got-at' and the absence of a ruling body to investigate the affair or punish the perpetrators made it all the more scandalous. One of the most disappointed men on the course was Jem Mason, who had been persuaded to come out of retirement to ride the horse and the veteran jockey had expressed deep confidence only days before. Severe abuse was directed by angry punters at MISS MOWBRAY's connections but this was unjustified, for they had also backed the mare heavily themselves.

With but an hour to spare, the bookmakers re-shuffled their books, installing Mr Moseley's BOURTON as the 4/1 market leader, with MAURICE DALEY at 5s. This one was partnered by Tom Olliver, although he had wasted furiously to ride HALF-AND-HALF and was not at all pleased to be claimed by his retainer. ABD-EL-KADER was also unable to run, having injured himself when startled by the sliding door on the train bringing him from Dublin. Top weight was carried by ever-green PETER SIMPLE, again running for a new owner but even for him twelve stone was an horrendous burden, especially with the good going against him. Rumours of further skulduggery were rife after the shock withdrawal of MISS MOWBRAY, yet the bookies were kept busy with still more being laid on BOURTON. Mr Moseley's gelding, making his third appearance in the race, had so far failed to complete the course yet was this time carrying more weight than ever before, 11 st 12 lbs, which to many implied that someone knew a thing or two about him. Formerly named UPTON, he was ridden by the little-known jockey Tasker.

CRABBS took up the running after jumping the first, setting a decent gallop on the run down to Becher's. They all cleared the Brook but at the bank beyond there was a good deal of confusion and over the Water BURNT SIENNA was in front, with LADY ARTHUR his nearest rival, then CRABBS, BOURTON, OSCAR, HALF-AND-HALF, MALEY and SPRING. At the fence before the Brook second time, OSCAR came to grief, leaving jockey Sam Darling injured. To the relief of the crowds, the favourite BOURTON could be seen moving easily in third place and when they came back to the racecourse Tasker made his move on him. Together with CRABBS, he overtook the tiring BURNT SIENNA, racing neck-and-neck towards the final obstacles. Denis Wynne struggled desperately to keep CRABBS in touch, only to find that BOURTON had the better finishing speed and the favourite won as he liked by fifteen lengths. SPRING ran on strongly to deprive CRABBS of second spot by ten lengths. The victory of the most heavily backed horse went some way towards lessening the anger felt earlier in the day but there is no doubt that immense damage had been done to the image of the sport through the foul deed against MISS MOWBRAY.

Although no one could guess it at the time, the future of BOURTON and indeed his partner in victory Tasker, was no less dismal. Mr Moseley sold his 'National winner to a resident of Leamington for the bargain price of £50, believing that the horse would enjoy an honourable retirement. Sadly it was not to be. BOURTON was put back to racing by his new owner, fell at the Water Jump in a 'chase at Warwick the following year and had to be put down. At the same course some six weeks before this tragedy, Tasker also lost his life in a fall.

Before the year was out, a greater gloom descended with the outbreak of war in the Crimea.

THE GRAND NATIONAL HANDICAP STEEPLECHASE
1854

Starters: 20 **Time: 9 mins 59 secs**

1st **BOURTON** [formerly UPTON]	**aged.11–12**	(Mr Wm Moseley)	**J Tasker**
2nd **SPRING**	**6.9–10**	(Mr Barber)	**W Archer**
3rd **CRABBS**	**aged.9–2**	(Mr J R Henderson)	**D Wynne**
4th **MALEY**	**aged.9–10**	(Mr J R Henderson)	**Thrift**
5th **LADY ARTHUR**	**aged.9–10**	(Mr Delamarre)	**T Donaldson**
6th **HALF-AND-HALF** [formerly SMALL-BEER]	**10–8**	(Mr Bignell)	**C Green**
7th **BURNT SIENNA**	**8–12**	(Mr Slater)	**T Burrows**

Also Ran:
PETER SIMPLE 16.12–0 (Mr Bignell) **C Boyce** *Failed to finish*; *OSCAR 11–12* (Mr T F Mason) **S Darling jnr** *Knocked-over*; *PETER 10–12* (Mr Linnell) **R Sly jnr** *Failed to finish*; *BEDFORD 10–4* (Mr Barling) **Eatwell** *Broke leg* [destroyed]; *LA GAZZA LADRA 10–0* (Mr J Williams) **Mr T Abbot** *Refused*; *MAURICE DALEY 9–10* (Mr Cartwright) **T Olliver** *Failed to finish*; *STAR OF ENGLAND 9–10* (Mr Blood) **W White** *Failed to finish*; *GERALDUS 9–8* (Mr Barry) **Debean** *Refused*; *PRIDE OF THE NORTH 9–8* (Mr Olliver) **R James** *Refused*; *COCKCROW 6.9–8* (Lord Waterford) **Maher** *Failed to finish*; *TIMOTHY 9–6* (Mr A Sait) **H Lamplugh** *Refused*; *ROYALTY 5.9–4* (Capt Rhys) **Ennis** *Failed to finish*; *SHILLIBEER 6.9–0* (Lord Sefton) (carried 9–4) **E Southwell** *Failed to finish*.

The Betting: *4/1 Bourton; 5/1 Maurice Daley; 8/1 Half-and-Half; 10/1 Crabbs; 12/1 Peter Simple; 15/1 Oscar; 20/1 Spring & Peter; 25/1 Cockcrow & Burnt Sienna; 40/1 Timothy; 50/1 Others*

Distances: *Fifteen lengths; ten lengths*

1855

MISS MOWBRAY arrived at the start this year without any interference. Sam Darling took the mount on the attractive mare who started second in the betting at 4/1. The Cheltenham Steeplechase winner TROUT representing last year's winning owner Mr Moseley, was ridden by Tasker and having kept his form well through the current season started favourite at 3/1. Tom Olliver registered his 17th consecutive ride in the race astride the 15/1 shot BASTION, while Harry Lamplugh partnered the outsider JANUS, whose owner John Elmore's association with the event equalled 'Black Tom's'. At the bottom of the handicap were BURNT SIENNA and DANGEROUS, with an interesting six-year-old FREETRADER also lightly treated. The quality of the field, however, came in for much criticism, with *Bells Life* commenting that it was possibly 'the worst field ever started for the race'. Of the Irish contenders there was a good deal of speculation concerning the alleged ability of BOUNDAWAY, yet his stable-mate, WANDERER, was the better backed at 25/1, despite being described as a 'rough, undersized, common-looking hunter'. A bay horse, said to be ten years old, WANDERER, was owned by Mr Dennis and ridden by J Hanlon.

Severe frost caused the race to be postponed from the Wednesday, then a sudden thaw produced muddy conditions that demanded a degree of fitness many of the twenty runners had been prevented from attaining. In fact it was the kind of day which the now retired PETER SIMPLE would have relished. Lashed by driving rain, the crowds cheered delightedly upon seeing that TROUT showed the way into Becher's in impressive style. Upon landing over the Brook, however, he was passed by both BASTION and BOURTON, with FREETRADER and MAURICE DALEY moving up into contention. TROUT joined BASTION over the Water Jump, some two lengths in front of WANDERER and his stable mate BOUNDAWAY. BASTION was giving Tom Olliver a great ride but just when it seemed they had mastered the conditions, he slipped going into the fence before Becher's. This left WANDERER in the lead followed by FREETRADER. Sam Darling had by now brought MISS MOWBRAY into a challenging position, only for the mare to lose her footing on landing. She hit the ground on her head, with such force that her neck and back were broken on impact, a tragic end to a brave and popular race-mare. Her jockey was thrown many yards, remaining unconscious until revived by a kick on the head from a passing horse! At the Canal Turn TROUT blundered and FREETRADER and MAURICE DALEY were now the only two within striking distance of WANDERER. Hanlon, with commendable calmness, took a pull at WANDERER, allowing the others to go to the front. These two dashed at the last together, knocking it down and it was as they struggled to get back into their stride that Hanlon pounced with WANDERER, winning by two lengths from FREETRADER with four lengths further back to MAURICE DALEY.

Winning owner Mr Dennis must have had somewhat mixed feelings as he saw WANDERER so superbly ridden to victory, for he had been so certain that his horse would not stay the trip that he had invested heavily in BOUNDAWAY. His late decision to let WANDERER take his chance was but further proof that even those 'in the know' sometimes have much to learn.

THE GRAND NATIONAL HANDICAP STEEPLECHASE
1855

Starters: 20		Time: 10 mins 25 secs
1st **WANDERER**	aged.9–8 *(Mr Dennis)*	J Hanlon
2nd **FREETRADER**	6.9–4 *(Mr W Barnett)*	Meaney
3rd **MAURICE DALEY**	aged.9–6 *(Mr Cartwright)*	R James
4th **JANUS**	aged.9–10 *(Mr Elmore)*	H Lamplugh
5th **DANGEROUS**	aged.9–0 *(Mr J R Henderson)*	Fowler
6th **THE NUGGET**	10–4 *(Mr C Symonds)*	W White
7th **GARLAND**	10–2 *(Mr Minton)*	R Sly, jnr

Also Ran:
MISS MOWBRAY 11–6 (Mr T F Mason) **S Darling jnr** *Fell* [destroyed]; *PETER 11–4* (Mr S Mansell) **T Ablett** *Failed to finish*; *NEEDWOOD 11–2* (Mr B Land) **Fech** *Failed to finish*; *TROUT 10–12* (Mr Wm Moseley) **J Tasker** *Fell*; *HALF-AND-HALF (formerly Small-Beer) 10–4* (Mr Hutchinson) **Darby** *Failed to finish*; *BASTION 10–4* (Mr Roberts) **T Olliver** *Failed to finish*; *ESCAPE 10–4* (Mr Buchanan) **Knott** *Knocked-over*; *BOUNDA-WAY 6.10–0* (Mr Magee) **J Byrne** *Failed to finish*; *CUTAWAY 9–10* (Mr A Sait) **C Boyce** *Failed to finish*; *MALEY 9–6* (Mr J R Henderson) **Fulman** *Failed to finish*; *PIMPERN 9–6* (Mr H Lewis) (carried 9–8) **Weaver** *Failed to finish*; *LITTLE CHARLEY 9–4* (Mr C Capel) **D Wynne** *Knocked-over*; *BURNT SIENNA 9–0* (Mr Jenkins) **T Burrows** *Failed to finish*.

The Betting: *3/1 Trout; 4/1 Miss Mowbray; 6/1 Dangerous; 12/1 Needwood; 15/1 Bastion; 20/1 Maurice Daley, Peter & Little Charley; 25/1 Wanderer; 33/1 Janus & Garland; 50/1 Others*

Distances: *Two lengths; four lengths*

'The Wizard' Edward William Topham, who was by now firmly in control as manager of the course

1856

For the first time, there was no former winner of the event among the twenty-one starters this year, a fact which was seized upon by some detractors as a sign that the sport was losing its appeal. Yet two French horses appeared in the line-up, the first from that country to contest the Aintree 'chase and surely an indication that the 'National had 'arrived'.

Both challengers from across the English Channel were the property of Baron Lamotte, the leading 'chasing owner in France. FRANC PICARD was to become legendary among the stars of French jump racing, while on this occasion his stable companion was rated highly enough to head the betting at 9/2. The man responsible for the preparation of both horses was Harry Lamplugh, who had ridden JANUS into fourth place for John Elmore twelve months earlier. Born the son of a Yorkshire jump jockey, he began riding in France at the age of seventeen and after some success moved to Chantilly, becoming trainer/jockey to the de la Motte family. Lamplugh had the leg-up on JEAN DU QUESNE.

This was the year in which Mr Topham finally took over management of the racecourse, beginning a family association that was to last for over a century. He started by making this a two-day fixture. There was some criticism concerning the quality of the contestants, no doubt as a result of the highest weight awarded being a mere 10 st 12 lbs, jointly carried by FRANC PICARD and SIR PETER LAURIE. At the other end of the scale came second favourite HARRY LORREQUER with but 8 st 10 lbs. Many thought that off such a low mark he had only to stand up to win. Last year's runner-up, FREETRADER, was for some reason allowed to start at 25/1,

the majority of punters preferring his owner's other runner SIR PETER LAURIE.

Now a seven-year-old, FREETRADER was bred by Mr H B Powell, his sire being THE SEA, which had run fourth in 1840. He showed useful form on the flat and before turning to 'chasing won over hurdles. For just ninety guineas, the horse had become the property of Mr W Barnett, a Cheltenham man who engaged a jockey from his home town, George Stevens. Stevens had run away from home as a boy to work in a stable, and was fortunate to receive his early coaching from Tom Olliver and although of delicate health, he was to prove himself without peer over Aintree. For the first time since 1839 Tom Olliver was without a mount in the race, but could at least watch his protégé.

FREETRADER

THE FOREST QUEEN took them along followed by JEAN DU QUESNE and EMIGRANT, the jockeys appreciating the decent going and the crowds the clear visibility. At Becher's HARRY LORREQUER ran out after clearing the Brook, scattering spectators in all directions and knocking a number of them down. THE FOREST QUEEN led over

Valentine's, where Stevens moved FREE-TRADER into fourth position behind THE POTTER and JEAN DU QUESNE, but Mr Barnett's other runner SIR PETER LAURIE bolted off the course at the Canal Turn. There was a tragic accident at the second fence back in the country when BANSTEAD damaged his shoulder so severely that he had to be destroyed. THE FOREST QUEEN had so far made every yard of the running in great style, but at the fence after Becher's, the stupidity of a bystander put paid to her chances. Running across her path as she was about to take off, the foolish man collided with THE FOREST QUEEN, putting her out of the race though all concerned miraculously escaped serious injury. With the French favourite now left clear, the cheers began, but though he was first on to the racecourse, it could soon be seen that the horse was beaten. FREE-TRADER, MINERVA and the fast-finishing MINOS landed together over the last to produce a terrific race to the post with Stevens and FREETRADER prevailing by half a length.

Cheltenham residents felt so proud at the success that they presented George Stevens with a watch and Mr Barnett with a cheque to the value of £500. JEAN DU QUESNE, having been pulled up when unable to resist the challenge of the placed horses was walked back to the stables, beaten but by no means disgraced. The French experiment had proven worthwhile and not for the last time had the Tricolour flown at Aintree.

THE GRAND NATIONAL HANDICAP STEEPLECHASE
1856

Starters: 21		Time: 10 mins 9½ secs
1st **FREETRADER**	7.9–6 *(Mr W Barnett)*	**G Stevens**
2nd **MINERVA**	6.9–10 *(Mr Davenport)*	**R Sly, jnr**
3rd **MINOS**	aged.9–4 *(Mr G Hobson)*	**R James**
4th **HOPELESS STAR**	aged.10–2 *(Mr Tyler)* [inc. 6 lbs extra]	**W White**
5th **LITTLE CHARLEY**	8.9–4 *(Mr C Capel)*	**T Burrows**
6th **EMIGRANT**	10.10–2 *(Mr G Hodgman)*	**C Boyce**

Also Ran:

SIR PETER LAURIE 10–12 (Mr W Barnett) **S Darling jnr** *Baulked – Ran out*; *JEAN DU QUESNE 10–6* (Baron C de la Motte) **H Lamplugh** *Failed to finish*; *FRANC PICARD 10–12* (Baron C de la Motte) **Wakefield** *Failed to finish*; *THE PASHA 10–4* (Mr Hurley) **D Meaney** *Failed to finish*; *SEAMAN 10–2* (Mr A McDonough) (carried 10–4) **F Martin** *Failed to finish*; *THE FOREST QUEEN 10–2* (Mr Harper) **J Thrift** *Failed to finish*; *JUMPAWAY 9–10* (Mr Denison) **J Hanlon** *Failed to finish*; *THE POTTER 9–8* (Mr Barber) **Kendall** *Failed to finish*; *BRITISH YEOMAN 9–4* (Mr T F Mason) (carried 9–7) **Mr A Goodman** *Brought-down*; *DAN O'CONNELL 9–4* (Mr J Tayleure) **W Archer** *Failed to finish*; *BANSTEAD 6.9–4* (Mr Dixon) **Mr W Bevill** *Fell* [destroyed]; *VICTOR EMMANUEL 6.9–4* (Mr Pickering) **Seffert** *Fell*; *STAMFORD 9–2* (Mr Hodgman) **C Green** *Failed to finish*; *LIVERPOOL BOY 6.9–0* (Mr H King) **McLean** *Failed to finish*; *HARRY LORREQUER 5.8–10* (Mr J R Henderson) **W Fowler** *Ran-out.*

The Betting: *9/2 Jean du Quesne; 5/1 Harry Lorrequer; 7/1 Seaman; 10/1 The Potter; 12/1 Sir Peter Laurie; 15/1 The Forest Queen; 100/6 Emigrant; 25/1 Freetrader, Minerva, Hopeless Star & Jumpaway; 40/1 British Yeoman, Little Charley & The Pasha; 50/1 Banstead; Others not quoted*

Distances: *Half a length; four lengths*

1857

If past Grand National winners had anything in common, other than an abundance of courage, it was that they came from the unlikeliest of backgrounds and their paths to Aintree glory meandered through the strangest byways. Never was this better demonstrated than by EMIGRANT, the hero in 1857. An eleven-year-old bay gelding, not registered in the General Stud Book, he was owned and turned out for racing by Ben Land who knew better than most what was required in the tough world of 'chasing. Formerly a leading steeplechase jockey, Land remained in the game after a long and successful career, owning, training and dealing. Since running NEEDWOOD in the race in 1855, he had set his heart on producing the Liverpool winner and in EMIGRANT felt convinced that he had found the answer to his wish. While at Shrewsbury races, however, 'Old Ben' was unable to resist a game of cards in his hotel, soon finding himself bereft of funds. Among the onlookers was the bookmaker George Hodgman who offered to help out by buying the horse for £590, with a further £100 to be paid should the animal win at what was left of the Shrewsbury meeting. EMIGRANT duly obliged, causing his new owner no distress, for the canny Hodgman had backed the horse. Soon after this, a half share in EMIGRANT was sold to fellow bookmaker Green and the joint owners were more than pleased with the performance put up by their horse in the 1856 'National. Keeping the horse well on their side of the books for the 1857 race, they backed him heavily – Green to the tune of £5,000 – yet EMIGRANT started fourth in the betting at 10/1.

Since that day at Shrewsbury, when cards had cost him one 'National hopeful, Ben Land had come into possession of

EMIGRANT, the winner who changed hands on the turn of a card

another in the form of WEATHERCOCK, now a six-year-old carrying the minimum weight of 8 st 12 lbs. At 25/1 and with ABD-EL-KADER's old jockey Chris Green in the saddle, Land felt confident this year was his. With Alec Goodman riding last year's third MINOS, the public detected an obvious tip, installing the horse favourite at the strange odds of 100/15. French hope JEAN DU QUESNE was back, but there was none of the panic to back him as on his last appearance.

In pelting rain, it was only after seven false starts that the field of twenty-eight got away. GARRY OWEN and EMIGRANT were the most prominent in the early stages, the latter being the subject of a wager between his owners and Mr Hughes that he would be first over the Water. After the Canal Turn Charlie Boyce took EMIGRANT wide, jumping Valentine's close to the edge of the canal where he had spotted a stretch of firm going away from the ploughed land. EMIGRANT struck the front at the anchor crossing, but WESTMINSTER came upsides on the run to the Water. Hodgman's bet was safe, though, for EMIGRANT put in a wonderful leap to land a length in front. DANGEROUS appeared to be getting within striking distance of the leader, closely followed by WEATHERCOCK and JEAN DU QUESNE as they approached the racecourse for the last time. Boyce, however, was giving EMIGRANT a breather and he ran on once more coming into the last hurdle. WEATHERCOCK, though, was not done with, coming with a determined run on the flat to raise the hopes of owner Ben Land that this was indeed his year. Spectators in the stands and enclosures rose to the irony of the struggle, but at the line it was EMIGRANT by three lengths. Of Mr Hughes' four runners, TREACHERY came in third, in front of WESTMINSTER.

It was only after the race that it was made known that Boyce had ridden with the upper part of one arm strapped to his side, having suffered an injury earlier in the week. His remarkable feat of horsemanship, not to mention canny use of the towpath, was gratefully rewarded by the owners in the form of a present of £1,000. Less impressed, Aintree's management ensured that the ploy would never be used again by erecting flags at the outer extremes of the fences.

THE GRAND NATIONAL HANDICAP STEEPLECHASE
1857

Starters: 28		Time: 10 mins 6 secs
1st **EMIGRANT**	**11.9–10** *(Mr G Hodgman)*	**C Boyce**
2nd **WEATHERCOCK**	**6.8–12** *(Mr B Land)*	**C Green**
3rd **TREACHERY**	**5.9–0** *(Mr T Hughes)*	**Poole**
4th **WESTMINSTER**	**9–2** *(Mr T Hughes)* [inc. 6 lbs extra]	**Palmer**
5th **DANGEROUS**	**aged.9–8** *(Mr A Rice)*	**F Page**
6th **JEAN DU QUESNE**	**10–0** *(Count de Cunchy)*	**H Lamplugh**
7th **LADY ARTHUR**	**9–4** *(Viscomte Lauriston)*	**Weaver**
8th **THE FOREST QUEEN**	**9–8** *(Mr Harper)*	**T Donaldson**

Also Ran:
ESCAPE 11–2 (Mr J Merry) **J Thrift** *Failed to finish; MINOS 10–4* (Mr Mellish) **Mr A Goodman** *Failed to finish; CASSE CON 10–2* (Baron Monuecove) **Johnson** *Failed to finish; STAR OF THE WEST 10–0* (Mr J Colpitt) **E Jones** *Failed to finish; HOPELESS STAR 10–0* (Mr E Parr) **D Wynne** *Pulled-up; FREETRADER 8.10–0* (Mr W Barnett) **G Stevens** *Failed to finish; LITTLE CHARLEY 9.10–0* (Mr C Capel) **T Burrows** *Failed to finish; GARRY OWEN 9–12* (Col Dickson) **J Ryan** *Failed to finish; SQUIRE OF BENSHAM 9–8* (Mr W P Wrixon) **Mr Coxon** *Failed to finish; RED ROSE 9–8* (Mr T Hughes) **J Hughes** *Failed to finish; KING DAN 9–6* (Mr Jennings) **Escott** *Failed to finish; MIDGE 9–6* (Mr J Garnett) **Mr Black** *Failed to finish; ROMEO 9–6* (Mr T Hughes) **D White** *Fell; ALBATROSS 9–6* (Mr J Dennis) **D Meaney** *Failed to finish; STING 9–6* (Mr J Cassidy) **J Hanlon** *Failed to finish; MAURICE DALEY 9–2* (Mr Laurence) **R James** *Failed to finish; OMAR PASHA 9–2* (Mr W Williams) **J Kendall** *Failed to finish; TEDDESLEY 9–0* (Mr Hylton) **R Ascher** *Failed to finish; FIRST OF MAY 9–0* (Mr Raxworthy) **R Sly jnr** *Failed to finish; HORNIBLOW 9–10* (Mr T Day) **Dart** *Failed to finish.*

The Betting: *100/15 Minos; 7/1 Escape; 9/1 Hopeless Star; 10/1 Emigrant; 12/1 Teddesley; 100/7 Jean du Quesne & Little Charley; 100/6 Omar Pasha & Romeo; 20/1 The Forest Queen; 25/1 Freetrader & Weathercock; 30/1 Garry Owen; 40/1 Maurice Daley; 50/1 Dangerous & Sting; Others not quoted.*

Distances: *Three lengths; five lengths*

1858

Again the weather played a crucial part in the affairs of Aintree this year. Persistent snowfalls led to a postponement from Wednesday to Saturday. Even then it was widely suggested that the race should be cancelled. But on the day, Mr Topham and the stewards decided to go ahead. By two o'clock in the afternoon, not even the long awaited reappearance of ABD-EL-KADER had induced more than five hundred souls to venture out in such dreadful weather but the show went on. 'LITTLE AB', now under the ownership of a Mr Briscoe, carried 10 st 5 lbs and was partnered by Chris Green, reviving memories of their illustrious effort eight years before. In the absence of EMIGRANT, the majority of punters plumped for Mr Hughes's TREACHERY, for some reason preferring him to WEATHERCOCK, and last year's third became favourite at 4/1 of the sixteen while the second stood at 25/1. Perhaps this price reflected the fact that Old Ben had parted with the horse, although it was ridden by the outstanding amateur George Ede, who preferred to ride under the pseudonym of 'Mr Edwards'. Born in 1834, he and his twin brother Edward were educated at Eton, where they both distinguished themselves at cricket, a sport they were to serve greatly in later life. Upon leaving, George became friendly with Ben Land, who taught the youngster what race-riding was all about.

Tom Olliver returned to the race on professional gambler Mr Merry's ESCAPE and another competitor now well known to Liverpool racegoers was the Cheltenham-trained LITTLE CHARLEY, a bay gelding by CHARLES XII, who had made three previous attempts at the race. Owned by Christopher Capel of Prestbury House, his preparation was conducted by William Holman who, in his days as a jockey, steered SIR PETER LAURIE into third place in 1852.

The third Cheltenham man associated with LITTLE CHARLEY was William Archer, a colourful character and an excellent horseman. One of thirteen children, Archer had come up the hard way at a hard time. Having run away from home at the age of eleven, he quickly established himself as a jockey with rare ability and it was only when plagued by increasing weight that he turned to steeplechasing. No less a figure than the Emperor of Russia employed him both to manage his stud and ride his horses when Archer was only seventeen years of age, but after two years near St Petersburg the climate affected his health and he returned to the rigours of an English jump-jockey's life. By the time LITTLE CHARLEY carried him on to the snowswept Aintree course, Archer was thirty-two years old, a married man with four children, the youngest a son of fourteen months. This young Archer would in time set the racing world alight with a unique brilliance, extinguished prematurely by tragedy. The boy was christened Frederick James Archer.

With the snow-filled gale at its height, the sixteen runners were recalled from the start. In their eagerness to get on with the race, the parade had been overlooked. This formality eventually concluded, they were despatched and the casualties came thick and fast. ABD-EL-KADER came down at the second, uncharacteristically mistiming his approach. With their colours virtually indistinguishable, they surged over Valentine's, where HARRY LORREQUER gained a slight lead over CONRAD. The latter was back in front jumping Becher's the second time, though his stride was shortening. Shortly the leader dropped away beaten as Archer on LITTLE CHARLEY and Mr Edwards on WEATHER-COCK moved to the front, running neck and neck towards the final hurdles. Archer had noticed though that WEATHERCOCK was being hard ridden and, biding his time till after jumping the last, spurred LITTLE CHARLEY on for a four length victory. Fully fifty yards behind WEATHERCOCK came XANTHUS in third place, with MORGAN RATTLER fourth and the remounted CONRAD the only other to finish, a distant fifth. The man who came in from the cold of Russia had achieved glory as the conqueror of snowbound Aintree.

William Archer, father of the legendary Fred, on a horse named THERESA

LITTLE CHARLEY, winner in one of the slowest times since low-weight handicapping had become the vogue

THE GRAND NATIONAL HANDICAP STEEPLECHASE
1858

Date: 6th March 1858	Starters: 16	Time: 11 mins 5 secs
1st **LITTLE CHARLEY**	**10.10–7** *(Mr C Capel)*	**W Archer**
2nd **WEATHERCOCK**	**7.11–7** *(Viscount Talon)*	**Mr Edwards**
3rd **XANTHUS**	**aged.11–0** *(Mr Craven)*	**F Balchin**
4th **MORGAN RATTLER**	**aged.10–4** *(Sir E Hutchinson)*	**T Burrows**
5th **CONRAD**	**aged.8–4** *(Mr Tempest)*	**E Jones** [remounted]

Also Ran:
ESCAPE 10–10 (Mr J Merry) (carried 11–0) **T Olliver** *Knocked-over*; *CLAUDIUS 10–7* (Mr J C Manby) **Poole** *Fell*; *ABD-EL-KADER 10–5* (Mr Briscoe) **C Green** *Fell*; *JOE GRAHAM 9–12* (Mr Heron Maxwell) (carried 10–4) **Rutherford** *Fell*; *TREACHERY 9–8* (Mr T Hughes) **W White** *Pulled-up*; *LOUGH BAWN 9–8* (Mr Buchanan) **G Stevens** *Refused*; *BLACK BESS 9–6* (Mr T Bay) **D Wynne** *Fell*; *LITTLE TOM 9–6* (Capt Connell) **B Land jnr** *Fell*; *HARRY LORREQUER 9–0* (Mr J Henderson) **W Fowler** *Knocked-over*; *GLENAMOUR 9–0* (Mr Heron Maxwell) **Knott** *Fell*; *MOIRE ANTIQUE 9–0* (Mr J Henderson) **F Page** *Fell*.

The Betting: *4/1 Treachery; 9/2 Lough Bawn; 5/1 Little Tom; 12/1 Harry Lorrequer; 14/1 Conrad; 100/6 Little Charley & Morgan Rattler; 20/1 Escape & Black Bess; 25/1 Weathercock, Moire Antique & Abd-El-Kader; 33/1 Joe Graham & Xanthus*

Distances: *Four lengths; fifty yards*

1859

Although Liverpool was a cold place on 'National day 1859, there was thankfully no snow or heavy going to contend with this time and with beautiful clear skies over the racecourse, no shortage of racegoers either. There was a first prize of £840, the twenty runners and three invaders from France. LITTLE CHARLEY had changed hands since his victory, now running for Mr Barnett, of FREETRADER fame. For the second year in succession Mr Hughes provided the favourite, with THE BREWER at 100/30, the next in the betting being the six-year-old entire HALF CASTE on 7/1. Ben Land had discovered another promising 'chaser in the six-year-old HUNTSMAN, who figured at 100/8 and ran in the capable hands of the owner's son, Ben Land junior. Mr J L Manby's CLAUDIUS was a complete outsider, despite having the incomparable

Tommy Pickernell – alias the outstanding 'Mr Thomas'

assistance of Tom Olliver in the saddle. George Ede was without a mount but the event saw the debut of another brilliant amateur who chose to follow the practice of 'Mr Edwards'. 'Mr Thomas' weighed out to ride the mare ANATIS on behalf of Christopher Capel. In fact this gentleman rider was Thomas Pickernell, of whom much more was to be heard at Liverpool and beyond.

On the eve of the race it was brought to Lord Sefton's attention that an attempt had been made to lessen the severity of certain fences on the course. Upon whose instructions this had been done was never determined, but His Lordship countermanded them in short order.

The field got away perfectly at the second attempt when THE BREWER was soon passed by XANTHUS, GIPSY KING and FLATCATCHER. THE BREWER unseated his rider on landing at Valentine's, and although losing much ground was remounted to chase after the rest. Just before coming back onto the racecourse WEATHERCOCK broke down and THE BREWER finally went at the Water. HALF CASTE went to the front at the third fence back in the country, but Chris Green took a pull going into Becher's, allowing himself to be passed by XANTHUS. After the Canal Turn the race began in earnest with barely five lengths separating the first seven horses. FLATCATCHER was unlucky to fall and HALF CASTE held a clear lead until halfway up the straight Harry Lamplugh, riding for all he was worth, drew level on JEAN DU QUESNE. Neck and neck they raced for the line, with HALF CASTE prevailing by the narrowest of margins, a short neck, from the brave French challenger. Putting in a late spurt HUNTSMAN was but a length away third, in front of MIDGE, ANATIS, ORKONSTA, GHIKA and

ESCAPE. Nine years after his victory on ABD-EL-KADER, Chris Green had once more proved that there was no substitute for experience of Aintree's unique demands and it was widely felt that Ben Land had found a future champion in HUNTSMAN.

Almost unnoticed after a long walk back from the Canal side of the course was one who, like the winner, would never compete again over the course. Since finishing second twenty years before on SEVENTY FOUR, Tom Olliver had become a legend in his own time. His mastery in the saddle and his talent for teaching others were rare qualities in any age. After hanging up his boots he became briefly landlord of 'The Star' at Leamington but, still in love with the sport he had served so well, moved to Cheltenham, and thence to Wroughton. He became a successful and respected trainer, preparing a colt called GEORGE FREDERICK for the 1874 Derby. 'Black Tom' was never to see the Epsom triumph, for he died shortly before the 1874 classic, having been in a poor state of health for some time. His head-lad Tom Leader was credited with turning out GEORGE FREDERICK, but that fact would not have disturbed Olliver, for he was a most generous man to the last. The legacy left by 'Black Tom' Olliver would live beyond the record books. For the man who rode beside Becher and Jem Mason in that first Aintree Liverpool 'Chase set an example of bravery, daring and skill which echoes down the years with each running of the 'National.

THE GRAND NATIONAL HANDICAP STEEPLECHASE
1859

Starters: 20			Time: 10 mins 2 secs
1st **HALF CASTE**	6.9–7 (Mr Willoughby)		**C Green**
2nd **JEAN DU QUESNE**	aged.9–9 (Count F de Cunchy)		**H Lamplugh**
3rd **HUNTSMAN**	6.11–2 (Mr B Land)		**B Land, jnr**
4th **MIDGE**	aged.9–4 (Mr J Garnett)		**D Meaney**
5th **ANATIS**	9.9–4 (Mr C Capel)		**Mr Thomas**
6th **ORKONSTA**	aged.9–0 (Viscount A Talon)		**G Stevens**
7th **GHIKA**	9–10 (Mr Moreton) [carried 9–12]		**C Boyce**
8th **ESCAPE**	10–5 (Mr J Merry)		**T Donaldson**

Also Ran:

WEATHERCOCK 8.10–13 (Viscount A Talon) **Enoch** Brought-down; LITTLE CHARLEY 11.10–11 (Mr W Barnett) **T Burrows** Failed to finish; XANTHUS 10–7 (Mr Craven) **F Balchin** Fell; CLAUDIUS 10–0 (Mr J L Manby) **T Olliver** Failed to finish; ACE OF HEARTS 9–12 (Lord Waterford) **J Ryan** Fell; THE BREWER 9–10 (Mr T Hughes) **W White** Fell; BORDER CHIEF 9–10 (Mr H E Johnstone) **Watling** Failed to finish; JEALOUSY 9–8 (Mr Bayley) **J Kendall** Failed to finish; GIPSY KING 9–0 (Mr Slaney) **Edmunds** Pulled-up; GIBRALTAR 9–0 (Mr Hope) **Armstrong** Failed to finish; FLATCATCHER 8–12 (Mr Barling) (carried 9–0) **T Holmes** Knocked-over; SPRING 11.8–7 (Mr Barber) **J Nightingall** Fell.

The Betting: 100/30 The Brewer; 7/1 Half Caste; 10/1 Jealousy & Jean du Quesne; 100/8 Huntsman; 14/1 Little Charley; 20/1 Escape & Ghika; 25/1 Ace of Hearts & Anatis; 33/1 Weathercock, Midge & Orkonsta; 40/1 Spring

Distances: A short neck; one length

1860

With Britain's military involvement in the Crimean War and the Indian Mutiny concluded, no less than five of the nineteen runners in the first 'National of the 60s were the property of serving officers, with Captain Hunt's aptly named HUNTSMAN the mount of the owner's close friend and brother officer, Captain Thomas Manners Townley.

After Eton and Trinity College, Cambridge, Townley declined the clerical career planned for him by his father and took a commission in the 10th Hussars. It was with this regiment in India that Townley began his race-riding and he became the pride of his unit when he defeated an Arab sheik's thoroughbred in a desert 'match' with an Hussar charger. Having seen action at Sebastopol, Captain Townley returned to England, resigned his commission and devoted himself to riding in races. His role on HUNTSMAN was supposed to be that of pacemaker for the stable's chief hope, GOLDSMITH, ridden by Ben Land junior, and the horse started at 33/1.

The brilliant BRUNETTE was top weight with 12 st but most in demand was Christopher Capel's ANATIS. At 7/2, with 'Mr Thomas' again in the saddle, she was considered unbeatable with her 9 st 10 lbs. But there was a problem of which the public were unaware. The favourite had developed such unsound forelegs that she had received the lightest preparation imaginable, her connections not daring to risk jumping the mare over a single fence in the year since the last race.

That the sport was still suffering from an unfortunate image was illustrated by yet another rider choosing to hide behind a pseudonym. 'Mr Ekard', the pilot of BRIDEGROOM, rearranged the letters of his name, in the hope that his congregation would not notice. For the gentleman concerned was none other than the Reverend Edward Drake of Shardloes. It was no doubt to his relief that his mount was among those unquoted in the betting.

Ben Land, apparently overlooking the fact that he had a pacemaker, took the lead on GOLDSMITH, which he still held over Becher's. XANTHUS took up the running over Valentine's, and he was still in command on re-entering the racecourse. ANATIS had been in the mid-division throughout, being nursed around by 'Mr Thomas'. A forward move on the run to the Water Jump, however, took her into second place. The two leaders were still neck-and-neck at the Canal Turn, but over Valentine's ANATIS outjumped XANTHUS. HUNTSMAN was now the only other capable of issuing a challenge. Captain Townley had survived a mistake at the second Becher's in which he lost both irons and now as they approached the final hurdles, he fought his way past XANTHUS with only ANATIS in front of him. They rose at the last flight together, both jockeys flat out, with HUNTSMAN hitting the hurdle hard again causing Townley to lose an iron. Straight back into his stride, though, HUNTSMAN came with a tremendous run, drawing level with ANATIS halfway up the run-in. It seemed to be anybody's race, but Captain Townley knew he was beaten and resorted to shouting an offer of £1,000 to his rival. As on that previous occasion when a jockey had attempted to 'buy' his victory, the suggestion was ignored. ANATIS passed the post half a length to the good, with XANTHUS six lengths back in third place. It was another all-Cheltenham success with the fullest credit going to Tommy Pickernell, alias 'Mr Thomas', whose patient handling of the delicate mare brought a worthy result. When questioned later about the £1000 inducement from Captain Townley, the modest yet typical reply was that he had been too busy coaxing ANATIS home to be able to answer. The galloping parson 'Mr Ekard' received his own satisfaction in finishing sixth, yet sadly it is not known what form his sermon took the following Sunday.

ANATIS and 'Mr Thomas' from a drawing by Finch Mason

Finch Mason's sketch of Captain Townley whose anxiety to win led him to some less than sporting behaviour

THE GRAND NATIONAL HANDICAP STEEPLECHASE

1860

Starters: 19		Time: Not taken
1st **ANATIS**	**10.9–10** (Mr C Capel)	**Mr Thomas**
2nd **HUNTSMAN**	**7.11–8** (Capt G W Hunt)	**Capt T M Townley**
3rd **XANTHUS**	**aged.10–0** (Mr W G Craven)	**F Balchin**
4th **MARIA AGNES**	**6.9–8** (Mr Golby)	**G Stevens**
5th **IRISH BOY**	**aged.8–12** (Mr W Bevill)	**Mr W Bevill**
6th **BRIDEGROOM**	**aged.10–6** (Sir George Wombwell)	**Mr Ekard**
7th **BRUNETTE**	**12–0** (Mr Barrett)	**J Kendall**

Also Ran:
REDWING 10–8 (Mr Aylmer) **Rourke** Failed to finish; HORNIBLOW 10–10 (Mr H Blundell) **Enoch** Failed to finish; GOLDSMITH 10–10 (Capt G W Hunt) **B Land jnr** Failed to finish; TEASE 10–2 (Mr Francis) **W White** Brought-down; SIR ROBERT 10–2 (Mr J Courtenay) **C Boyce** Pulled-up; KILCOCK 6.10–0 (Mr Aylmer) **D Meaney** Failed to finish; TELEGRAM 9–9 (Mr Worthington) **Palmer** Failed to finish; MISS HARKAWAY 9–8 (Mr Barber) **Mr F Lotan** Refused; THE CURATE 9–4 (Mr Burling) **G Eatwell** Fell; SHYLOCK 9–2 (Maj Owen) (carried 9–5) **T Clay** Failed to finish; LEFROY 9–0 (Capt White) **C Green** Failed to finish; CONGREVE 9–0 (Capt Clifton) **Gammeridge** Refused.

The Betting: 7/2 Anatis; 7/1 Tease; 10/1 Maria Agnes & Xanthus; 12/1 Irish Boy; 100/7 Telegram; 100/6 Brunette & Goldsmith; 25/1 Shylock; 33/1 Huntsman & Sir Robert

Distances: Half a length; six lengths

1861

Edward Topham could be well pleased that his efforts as controller of Aintree were going in the right direction. 'The Wizard''s influence and energy were rising above all problems and this year there was a first prize of £985 and a record entry of eighty-nine.

It was clearly not only Cheltenham which felt confident about bringing off a double with ANATIS, for she remained at the head of the market for weeks before the event going to post at 4/1 first choice. The French were again represented, FRANC PICARD their crack 'chaser providing Harry Lamplugh with the double responsibility of trainer and jockey.

The event had already thrown up an abundance of extraordinary characters and one who was to have a profound influence in the future of the sport appeared at Aintree this year. Fothergill Rowlands was the son of a Monmouthshire doctor, who eventually took over his father's practice. Such was his prowess in the saddle, that he eventually gave up medicine in favour of riding across country. Frequently partnering his friend Lord Strathmore's horses, 'Fogo', as he was affectionately known, rivalled the leading jockeys in the paid ranks for daring and ability. It is strange that the good doctor rode in the 'National for the first time when his career as one of the leading amateurs was nearing its end. Stranger still, bearing in mind his reputation, that he secured odds of 50/1 against £100 that he would ride the winner of the race. In pursuit of this aim, 'Fogo' purchased BRUNETTE, who, despite carrying a stone less than when completing the course the previous year, was easy to back at 33/1. George Stevens had set his heart on teaming up with the mare JEALOUSY, so impressed was he with what he had seen of her in the past. Thus the Cheltenham jockey turned down thirteen other offers of rides and yet on the day found himself without a mount. One of the jockey's retainers claimed his services for his entry, but this horse was withdrawn at the last moment.

For the third year running XANTHUS broke clear from the other twenty-three at 'flag-fall', but REDWING cleared Becher's some ten lengths in front. 'Mr Edwards' was rolled on when MASTER BAGOT came down at the Canal Turn, while at Valentine's THE CONDUCTOR was so badly injured that he was put out of his misery. Back on the racecourse XANTHUS regained the lead from REDWING, but Fothergill Rowlands pulled up on BRUNETTE. The long-fought duel between the leaders continued out in the country until COCKATOO came a cropper, bringing down ANATIS. With XANTHUS beginning to run out of steam, REDWING once more struck the front, going over Becher's ahead of OLD BEN ROE, BRIDEGROOM and JEALOUSY, but when he jumped Valentine's only to stumble over the deceased form of THE CONDUCTOR, the race was thrown wide open. Approaching the final flight JEALOUSY came up to the girth of OLD BEN ROE, the rest having fallen away in defeat and from there the mare JEALOUSY raced clear, winning by two lengths. OLD BEN ROE was run out of second place on the line by a fast finishing THE DANE, who had made no show at all until after the last obstacle.

At 5/1, JEALOUSY was a most popular winner but not, one suspects, with George Stevens.

1861

Starters: 24		Time: 10 mins 14 secs
1st **JEALOUSY**	**7.9–12** *(Mr J Bennett)*	**J Kendall**
2nd **THE DANE**	**5.10–0** *(Capt Christie)*	**W White**
3rd **OLD BEN ROE**	**aged.10–7** *(Mr W Briscoe)*	**G Waddington**
4th **BRIDEGROOM**	**aged.10–7** *(Mr B J Angell)*	**Mr FitzAdam**
5th **XANTHUS**	**aged.9–8** *(Mr W G Craven)*	**C Boyce**

Also Ran:

BRUNETTE 11–0 (Mr F Rowlands) **Mr F Rowlands** *Pulled-up*; *KIBWORTH LASS 11–3 (inc. 6 lbs extra)* (Mr J L Manby) **Oliver jnr** *Refused*; *ANATIS 11.10–4* (Mr C Capel) **Mr Thomas** *Fell*; *DIAMANT 10–4* (Mr J L Manby) **Enoch** *Refused*; *BROTHER TO LADY'S MAID 10–3* (Mr J Stokes) **Harris** *Failed to finish*; *THE EMPEROR 10–2* (Mr D Briggs) **Mr A Goodman** *Failed to finish*; *FRANC PICARD 10–0* (Baron de la Motte) **H Lamplugh** *Failed to finish*; *MASTER BAGOT 10–0* (Capt J L Little) **Mr Edwards** *Fell*; *WEE NELL 9–11* (Mr Mackey) **Knott** *Failed to finish*; *LONGRANGE 9–10* (Mr C Watts) **R Sherrard** *Failed to finish*; *KILCOCK 9–10* (Mr Bowbiggins) **D Meaney** *Failed to finish*; *REDWING 9–7* (Mr E J Gannon) **J Murphy** *Fell*; *THE FRESHMAN 9–7* (Mr C Symonds) **Mr Blake** *Fell*; *THE IRISH EMIGRANT 9–0* (Mr W Owens) **R Sly jnr** *Fell*; *THE UNKNOWN 8–12* (Mr Spencer Lucy) (carried 9–0) **G Eatwell** *Failed to finish*; *THE CONDUCTOR 8–12* (Mr G Hodgman) **J Nightingall** *Fell* [destroyed]; *DR LEETE 8–8* (Marquess of Hartington) **W Mason** *Failed to finish*; *COCKATOO 8–8* (Mr S Gooderham) **C Green** *Fell*; *THE ROVER 8–8* (Mr J S Wilson) **F Page** *Failed to finish*.

The Betting: *4/1 Anatis; 5/1 Jealousy; 7/1 Cockatoo; 8/1 Master Bagot; 10/1 Old Ben Roe; 100/8 The Emperor; 14/1 Franc Picard; 100/7 The Freshman; 25/1 Redwing & Bridegroom; 33/1 Brunette & The Dane; 40/1 Kilcock & The Conductor; 50/1 Xanthus.*

Distances: *Two lengths; four lengths*

1862

A terrible accident cast the darkest of shadows over the 1862 Grand National in which year those of a superstitious disposition noted it was the first time that thirteen competitors had faced the starter. The horse carrying most money was the nine-year-old HUNTSMAN. Still an entire, HUNTSMAN was running for the third time in the race having already finished second and third and for the third time under different ownership. He now provided French nobleman Viscount de Namur with his best chance yet. Harry Lamplugh took the mount. THOMASTOWN, ANATIS and BRIDEGROOM were next in the betting and among the outsiders was the evergreen front-runner XANTHUS, also racing under new colours, this time those of the local peer Lord Sefton. BRIDEGROOM was partnered by Ben Land junior, and another son following in a successful father's footsteps was James Wynne, son of MATTHEW's rider Denny. This was to be his first encounter with the 'National. Due to ride O'CONNELL, young James received the distressing news on the morning of the race that his sister had died in Ireland. Upon hearing of the bereavement, Lord de Freyne, O'CONNELL's owner, attempted to dissuade Wynne from riding, assuring the boy that he would get him back to Ireland with the utmost speed. But declining this considerate offer, Wynne weighed out for the race he had heard so much about from his father. There was a delay of almost thirty minutes before the runners were sent on their way and as in recent years XANTHUS showed prominently straight away. THOMASTOWN the second favourite refused at the first. THE TATTLER also refused to continue at the next fence and the rest were led on to Becher's by BRIDEGROOM and XANTHUS. At the bank beyond the Brook, BUCEPHALUS met with interference which cost him considerable ground, yet gamely persevered a long way in arrears. George Stevens, back in action in the 'National after his enforced absence twelve months ago, was riding his usual patient race on HARRY, who, after jumping Valentine's, made steady headway on the outside, joining BRIDEGROOM XANTHUS and ROMEO as they turned back onto the racecourse. There appeared little to alarm the crowds in the stands as such a small number of horses approached the gorse fence before the Water, for there was more than enough room for the jockeys to pick their jumping spots. PLAYMAN, however, suddenly rushed head on into the fence, toppling heavily and bringing down WILLOUGHBY and O'CONNELL. WILLOUGHBY got up immediately, with his owner-rider Mr Lington still in the saddle. But James Wynne lay injured from his fall, when the riderless PLAYMAN stumbled and rolled over him. It was the internal injuries thus received rather than his first fall which led to young James dying later that night without regaining consciousness. Before a stunned and subdued crowd the race went on, HARRY striking the front over the Water, with BRIDEGROOM, HUNTSMAN and ROMEO in close attendance. HARRY fell at the fence before Becher's, while ROMEO jumped the wrong side of a flag. In having to retrace his steps to correct the error, owner-rider Mr Bennett must have realised he had lost too much ground to win, yet gamely went on in pursuit. From the Canal Turn there were two horses in it, BRIDEGROOM and HUNTSMAN, and Lamplugh on the latter bided his time all the way back to the final flight, racing clear on the flat to a four length victory. After a long interval the unlucky ROMEO came in third, with XANTHUS yet again completing in front of the only other to finish, BUCEPHALUS. The victory of HUNTSMAN was the first French triumph in the race and a worthy reward for jockey-trainer Harry Lamplugh who had experienced more than his share of 'National disappointments in the past. Yet somehow a spark was extinguished in the customary rejoicing for a race well won with the realisation that the Wynne family had this day suffered a double loss in the cruellest way.

The consistent BRIDEGROOM, who finished on several occasions, but never was the winner

THE GRAND NATIONAL HANDICAP STEEPLECHASE
1862

Starters: 13			Time: 9 mins 30 secs
1st **HUNTSMAN**	**9.11−0** *(Viscount de Namur)*	**H Lamplugh**
2nd **BRIDEGROOM**	**aged.10−13** *(Mr B J Angell)*	**B Land jnr**
3rd **ROMEO**	**aged.8−12** *(Mr C Bennett)*	**Mr C Bennett**
4th **XANTHUS**	**aged.9−6** *(Lord Sefton)*	**R Sherrard**
5th **BUCEPHALUS**	**10−9** *(Mr R Rowan)*	**McGrillon**

Also Ran:
ANATIS 12.10−12 (Sir E Hutchinson) **Mr Thomas** *Pulled-up*; *PLAYMAN 10−8 (inc. 10 lbs extra)* (Mr A Yates) **J. Nightingall** *Fell*; *THOMASTOWN 10−4 (Mr T Naghten)* **J Murphy** *Refused*; *WILLOUGHBY 10−0 (Mr H Lington)* **Mr H Lington** *Pulled-up*; *O'CONNELL 9−8 (Lord de Freyne)* **J Wynne** *Fell*; *THE TATTLER 9−7 (Mr W G Craven) (carried 9−8)* **C Boyce** *Pulled-up*; *HARRY 9−5 (Mr W W Baker)* **G Stevens** *Fell*; *THE POET 8−12 (Mr J Henry)* **Gatt** *Fell*.

The Betting: *3/1 Huntsman; 6/1 Thomastown; 9/1 Anatis; 10/1 Bridegroom & Harry; 100/8 Romeo & The Tattler; 100/7 Bucephalus; 20/1 Willoughby; 25/1 Xanthus & Playman; 33/1 O'Connell*

Distances: *Four lengths; twenty lengths*

1863

The 'National took place amid a welter of patriotic celebration for the wedding of The Prince of Wales and Princess Alexandra, the ceremony taking place on the day before Aintree's most important event. With the occasion being declared a National holiday, the rejoicing carried over to the steeplechase. There could have been nothing better to dispel the sad memories of last year.

The conditions for the race remained unchanged, although the distance was extended to four and a half miles, with the fences for the most part very low. Becher's and Valentine's were made more difficult, however, with the addition of a post and rail. With the low allocation of weight again giving rise to criticism of the handicapping system, it became a point of discussion that the maximum burden was 12 st for only the second time in four runnings. MEDORA had proven himself a 'chaser of the highest quality. Owned and ridden by the redoubtable 'Fogo' Rowlands, the combination had carried all before them against top class opposition. In the absence of HUNTSMAN, JEALOUSY carried the responsibility of 3/1 favouritism in addition to the steadier of 11 st 10 lbs. Second choice in the market was another mare, the seven-year-old EMBLEM, by 1851 Derby-winner TEDDINGTON out of MISS BATTY. Bred by R Swale in Wales, she won seven races on the flat. Purchased by Lord Coventry, EMBLEM was sent to be trained as a 'chaser. George William Coventry, the ninth Earl, was to become one of the most respected men of the turf, playing a leading role in sorting out the problems which for too long attached themselves to the jumping side of the sport. Devoutly religious, charming and humorous, he had his 'chasers trained at the family seat, Croome Court near Kinnersley. The Coventry colours of Brown with a Blue cap were famous the length and breadth of the country. A strong friendship between the Earl and jockey George Stevens, ensured their association in many successes together.

George Stevens on EMBLEM with trainer E Weever

Among competing riders already familiar to the Aintree crowds was Alec Goodman, riding ARBURY, 'Mr Edwards' on FRESHMAN and Nightingall partnering LIGHT OF OTHER DAYS. Making his debut in the race was George Holman on FOSCO, the second son of William who had sent out three 'National winners, FREETRADER, LITTLE CHARLEY and ANATIS. At only four years old, REAL JAM achieved the distinction of being the youngest horse so far in the season's toughest event.

Jumping Becher's the order of running was FRESHMAN, the riderless INKERMAN, MASTER BAGOT, JEALOUSY, YALLER GAL and MEDORA with Stevens on EMBLEM in his customary position towards the rear. JEALOUSY struck the front with a prodigious leap at the Canal Turn, where INKERMAN went off exploring the surrounding countryside. As the field mea-

61

sured the fence in front of them, the stands spectators must have remembered only too vividly the tragic happening here twelve months before, but happily lightning didn't strike twice. JEALOUSY leapt the Water with a six length advantage over MEDORA, and George Stevens brought EMBLEM through with a smooth run. YALLER GAL passed JEALOUSY as they rose for the Brook, and the tiring favourite was also soon overtaken by ARBURY, AVALANCHE, FOSCO and EMBLEM. There was a tremendous finish in prospect but EMBLEM was full of running. Lord Coventry's mare gave her backers a momentary fright when sliding sideways at the last, but

George Stevens, becoming as one with the mare, not only survived the error but produced from her a winning run which left the others toiling. At the post EMBLEM was twenty lengths to the good from Alec Goodman on ARBURY, with YALLER GAL two lengths back in third, and the suspect grey FOSCO giving George Holman a ride to remember in fourth place. For George Stevens, EMBLEM provided not merely a second success in the race but the acclaim of all who witnessed it.

The lost competitor, INKERMAN, caused great concern until discovered late in the night in a field some miles from the racecourse.

THE GRAND NATIONAL HANDICAP STEEPLECHASE
1863

The conditions were unchanged, but the course was lengthened by about a quarter of a mile. The fences were very low for the most part. Becher's and Valentine's were stiffened by the addition of a post-and-rail, which was put up in front of each of them; only two other fences, the Open Ditch and the Water Jump, were at all difficult

Starters: 16		Time: 11 mins 20 secs
1st **EMBLEM**	**7.10–10** *(Lord Coventry)* [inc. 10 lbs extra]	**G Stevens**
2nd **ARBURY**	**aged.11–2** *(Mr J Astley)*	**Mr A Goodman**
3rd **YALLER GAL**	**aged.10–13** *(Mr W Briscoe)*	**Mr Dixon**
4th **FOSCO**	**aged.9–11** *(Mr G Holman)*	**Mr G Holman**
5th **AVALANCHE**	**6.10–0** *(Baron de Mesnil)*	**Palmer**
6th **JEALOUSY**	**9.11–10** *(Mr Priestley)*	**J Kendall**

Also Ran:

MEDORA 12–0 (Mr F Rowlands) **Mr F Rowlands** *Pulled-up*; *THE FRESHMAN 11–13* (Mr W Meaney) **Mr Edwards** *Fell*; *THE DANE 11–6* (Capt Christie) **W White** *Pulled-up*; *MASTER BAGOT 10–4* (Mr W G Craven) **Knott** *Failed to finish*; *LIGHT OF OTHER DAYS 10–4* (Mr W W Baker) **J Nightingall** *Failed to finish*; *INKERMAN 9–11* (Mr W E Dakin) **Mr Smith** *Fell*; *THE ORPHAN 9–11* (Mr J C Tilbury) **Mr W Bevill** *Fell*; *TELEGRAPH 9–11* (Mr Campbell) **G Waddington** *Fell [destroyed]*; *BIRDBOLT 9–11* (Mr Spence) **Mr Spence** *Pulled-up*; *REAL JAM 4.9–11* (Mr T Hughes) **D Hughes** *Failed to finish*.

The Betting: *3/1 Jealousy; 4/1 Emblem; 100/12 Medora; 10/1 The Dane; 100/8 Master Bagot; 20/1 Light of Other Days, Real Jam & Yaller Gal; 25/1 Arbury; 33/1 Avalanche; 40/1 Fosco*

Distances: *Twenty lengths; two lengths*

1864

The value to the winner now exceeded £1000 and such a lavish prize for a steeplechase became the target of twenty-five competitors. A significant improvement in the allocation of weight within the handicap was another step in the right direction, with the range extending from 12 st 2 lbs at the top of the scale down to a minimum of 10 st. JERUSALEM, ridden by 'Mr Edwards', started favourite at 9/2, just half a point ahead of BANTAM which provided George Holman, now a professional with his second ride in the event. Holman's elder brother, John, was on the outsider MISS MARIA. Mr Alec Goodman preferred PORTLAND to ARBURY. Again there was no former winner taking part. Yet if Lord Coventry was unable to run the sidelined EMBLEM, he still had her

full sister EMBLEMATIC. The connection was not overlooked by punters, who backed her down to 10/1. But their enthusiasm must have suffered a blow when they saw her in the paddock, for EMBLEMATIC was far from the conventional stamp of 'chaser. With spindly legs and no quarters, she looked most unlikely to master Aintree.

In brilliant sunshine the favourite JERUSALEM and SATANELLA went sprawling early at the ditch and bank. Intent on giving the punters a run for their money, George Ede regained the saddle on JERUSALEM to follow on in the rear. Further chaos came at the next, resulting in a two hundred yard gap opening between the leaders and tail-enders with IRELEY in the lead over Becher's. Five-year-old REAL JAM came with a flurry as they re-entered the racecourse and EMBLEMATIC, belying her looks, lay third. Stumbling at the Water, though, it was Stevens yet again who nursed her through the error without losing too much ground. ARBURY led over Becher's, ahead of IRELEY with EMBLEMATIC just behind CHESTER in fourth. Over Valentine's, the pace began to tell and by the time the last fence in the country was reached there were only two left with a hope of winning. ARBURY and EMBLEMATIC raced stride for stride towards the final hurdle and upon landing, the mare raced clear to win by three lengths. CHESTER slogged on gamely to be third, a distance behind the gallant ARBURY, whose bad luck it was to come up against the two sisters in successive years.

It had been a classic case of 'handsome is as handsome does' for EMBLEMATIC who followed in the hoof-steps of her sister to

Lord Coventry, not only a great sportsman, but an expert in bone china as well

provide George Stevens with his third victory in the race, equalling the tally of his mentor Tom Olliver. Stevens had another reason to be pleased, for both he and Lord Coventry had backed EMBLEMATIC to win a substantial sum. Stevens built himself a home on top of Cleeve Hill, Cheltenham, naming it Emblem Cottage, but it is likely that memories of both sisters were shared with equal affection by the jockey.

THE GRAND NATIONAL HANDICAP STEEPLECHASE
1864

Starters: 25		Time: 11 mins 50 secs
1st **EMBLEMATIC**	6.10–6 *(Lord Coventry)*	**G Stevens**
2nd **ARBURY**	aged.11–12 *(Mr J Astley)*	**B Land jnr**
3rd **CHESTER**	aged.10–0 *(Mr Dalton)*	**W White**
4th **THOMASTOWN**	aged.12–0 *(Mr T M Naghten)*	**J Murphy**
5th **OCEAN WITCH**	5.10–2 *(Capt Lamb)*	**W Reeves**

Also Ran:

REPORTER 12–2 (Mr Fiddaman) **Mr Dixon** *Fell*; *SIR WILLIAM 11–10* (Mr T Iven) **Mr Davison** *Failed to finish*; *JERUSALEM 11–10* (Mr W Murray) **Mr Edwards** *Pulled-up*; *HARRY 11–10* (Count Cossett) **Cassidy** *Fell*; *BANTAM 11–8* (Mr Aspinall) **G Holman** *Pulled-up*; *WEE NELL 11–6* (Mr T Hunt) **Knott** *Pulled-up*; *LEONIDAS 11–4 (inc. 6 lbs extra)* (Capt J Machell) **C Boyce** *Pulled-up*; *SERIOUS CASE 11–3* (Mr T S Dawson) **G Waddington** *Fell*; *ROMEO 11–0* (Mr De Gray) **F Martin** *Fell*; *LITTLE BAB 11–0* (Mr W Murray) **P Igon** *Failed to finish*; *PORTLAND 10–12* (Mr H Matthews) **Mr A Goodman** *Fell*; *SATANELLA 10–12* (Marquess of Drogheda) **D Meaney** *Fell*; *BELL'S LIFE 10–12 (inc. 6 lbs extra)* (Maj Wombwell) **Griffiths** *Fell*; *IRELEY 10–10* (Mr B J Angell) **Mr Blake** *Knocked-over*; *NATIONAL PETITION 10–8* (Mr J Lanigan) **J Monaghan** *Failed to finish*; *REAL JAM 5.10–8* (Mr T Hughes) **D Hughes** *Failed to finish*; *BRIAN BORHOIME 10–4* (Mr Lawrence) **Poinons** *Pulled-up*; *MARTHA 10–0* (Mr T Wade) **J Land** *Fell*; *MISS MARIA 10–0* (Mr H Melville) **J Holman** *Failed to finish*; *SILK AND SATIN 10–0* (Mr Spark) (carried 10–2) **Jarvis** *Failed to finish*.

The Betting: *9/2 Jerusalem; 5/1 Bantam; 10/1 Emblematic; 11/1 Real Jam & Serious Case; 12/1 Portland & Wee Nell; 20/1 Ocean Witch; 30/1 Bell's Life; 33/1 Martha, Thomastown & Romeo; 40/1 Ireley, Arbury, Reporter & Chester; 50/1 Harry*

Distances: *Three lengths; a distance*

1865

Having achieved such deserved success with EMBLEM and EMBLEMATIC, it was characteristic of Lord Coventry that he should attempt to continue the sequence. Both sisters were entered for the 1865 event, with the younger of the pair, EMBLEMATIC, winding up favourite at 5/1 probably as a result of the owner declaring to win with this one and also because she was the preferred mount of George Stevens. Both had received harsh treatment from the handicapper, EMBLEM with top weight of 12 st 4 lbs and EMBLEMATIC 11 st 10 lbs. Not since the days of LOTTERY had a horse been required to carry as much as EMBLEM, yet she still went off at 100/8.

An article in the press this year praised the excellent work being done by Messrs Angell and Craven, along with other distinguished members of their committee, in improving steeplechasing's affairs and the day was shortly not far off when their jurisdiction would be as absolute as the Jockey Club's. It was unfortunate, therefore, when the heavily backed and brilliant 'chaser L'AFRICAINE was withdrawn at the last minute through injury, giving rise to more anger and suspicion.

Bred in France, ALCIBIADE was a chestnut horse by THE COSSACK out of AUNT PHILLIS. His career on the flat was undistinguished, to say the least, and after being claimed out of a selling race at Epsom he became the property for £400 of one of the men most concerned about steeplechasing's image, 'Cherry' Angell. He embarked upon the ambitious plan of aiming ALCIBIADE at the Grand National for his public debut over fences. It may have appeared the utmost folly when connections invested mightily on him for the big race, but what few people knew was that ALCIBIADE had left BRIDEGROOM standing in trial gallops. There could be no denying that BRIDEGROOM was the ideal

ALCIBIADE with Captain Coventry up

yardstick, having proved himself more than once around Aintree. His rider, Captain Henry Coventry, would also be facing the unknown and the twenty-three-year-old Grenadier Guards Captain did not escape derision from paddock pundits who considered him nothing but 'a swell'. The Captain was in fact a cousin of Lord Coventry and a horseman to be reckoned with.

There was another partnership almost identical to that of ALCIBIADE and Captain Coventry. The six-year-old HALL COURT was among the outsiders, though, and his partner Captain Tempest attached to a less fashionable regiment, the 11th Light Dragoons. Arthur Cecil Tempest was born in 1837 into an old Yorkshire family. At the age of twenty, Tempest obtained his commission and upon being sent to Ireland, came into contact with the legendary Alan McDonough. Under his guidance the young officer soon became a most proficient horseman, repaying McDonough by riding his horse BRYAN O'LYNN to win the Sefton 'Chase at Aintree in 1861. His loyalties would be fully tested in the 'National, though, for he owned MERRIMAC, the mount of Ben Land.

Although there was a light sprinkling of snow covering the course, the day was bright and clear. ACROBAT delayed things with a display in keeping with his name, then refused to start. So, unusually, the first casualty was registered before even the first fence was reached. ALCIBIADE, HALL COURT, TONY LUMPKIN and EMBLEM jumped Becher's in a bunch, five lengths behind MEANWOOD, at which point ARBURY and FLYFISHER began making ground. Over the Water it was ARBURY and JOE MALEY from the rest. At Becher's ARBURY came down, having looked all over a winner. Ben Land now found himself in front on MERRIMAC, opening up a twenty length lead. ALCIBIADE was seen to be going the longest way round, with Captain Coventry keeping the five-year-old to

the wide outside and this fact was already being decried by the grandstand 'jockeys'. THE CZAR came down at Valentine's, EMBLEM, JOE MALEY and PHILOSOPHER were pulled up and MERRIMAC began to fade just before reaching the racecourse. Captain Tempest seized his opportunity, sending HALL COURT to the front in determined style, but the other Captain, 'Bee' Coventry, was also quick to react. With Stevens making late headway on the

Captain Coventry, the 'swell' of the Guards

favourite EMBLEMATIC, the crowds caught the excitement. ALCIBIADE and HALL COURT rose at the final hurdle as one. Neck and neck, and stride for stride, they battled up the straight. They swept past the post inseparable as far as the spectators were concerned, but the judge declared ALCIBIADE the winner by a head. Some fifty yards back came EMBLEMATIC, with another five-year-old, MISTAKE, taking fourth. ALCIBIADE was the youngest horse to capture 'chasings richest prize, in his first ever steeplechase and Captain Coventry, 'the swell from the Guards', had made his first 'National ride a winning one. It was also his last, for he never took part in the race again.

THE GRAND NATIONAL HANDICAP STEEPLECHASE

1865

Starters: 23		Time: 11 mins 16 secs
1st **ALCIBIADE**	**5.11−4** *(Mr B J Angell)*	**Capt H Coventry**
2nd **HALL COURT**	**6.11−0** *(Capt Brown)*	**Capt A C Tempest**
3rd **EMBLEMATIC**	**7.11−10** *(Lord Coventry)*	**G Stevens**
4th **MISTAKE**	**5.10−8** *(Mr F Jacobs)*	**Jarvis**
5th **MERRIMAC**	**aged.11−4** *(Capt A C Tempest)*	**B Land, jnr**
6th **FLYFISHER**	**6.11−12** *(Mr Powell)*	**Mr J R Riddell**

Also Ran:

EMBLEM 9.12−4 (Lord Coventry) **W Walters** *Pulled-up*; *JOE MALEY 11−10* (Mr Hidson) **D Page** *Pulled-up*; *ACROBAT 11−9* (Capt J Machell) **W Mumford** *Refused*; *MEANWOOD 6.11−9* (Mr Harvey) **Knott** *Pulled-up*; *ARBURY 11−8* (Count A de Dampoerre) **C Boyce** *Fell*; *EXPRESS 11−6* (Mr D Collins) **Mr D Collins** *Pulled-up*; *LIGHTHEART 10−12* (Mr A W Clayton) **J Monaghan** *Pulled-up*; *PRINCESS DAGMAR 10−12* (Mr H Melville) **G Holman** *Pulled-up*; *PHILOSOPHER 6.10−8* (Mr Turner) **E Jones** *Pulled-up*; *STANTON 10−8* (Mr Harvey) **G Waddington** *Pulled-up*; *TUMBLER 10−6* (Capt J White) **Mr Drake** *Refused*; *TONY LUMPKIN 10−4* (Col Forster) **Mr Thomas** *Pulled-up*; *BALLYCASEY 11−0* (Mr J A Reed) **T Barton** *Fell*; *THE FRESHMAN 10−10* (Mr W H Whyte) **D Meaney** *Pulled-up*; *THE CZAR 10−0* (Mr Goodliffe) **Mr A Goodman** *Fell*; *MARKET GARDENER 10−0* (Lord Sefton) **Mr T Spence** *Refused*; *THE DWARF 10−0* (Mr Studd) **Igoe** *Pulled-up*.

The Betting: *5/1 Emblematic; 100/12 Joe Maley; 9/1 Stanton; 100/8 Princess Dagmar, Emblem & Arbury; 100/7 Tony Lumpkin & Alcibiade; 20/1 The Czar & Lightheart; 25/1 The Dwarf; 33/1 Merrimac; 40/1 The Freshman; 50/1 Meanwood, Acrobat & Hall Court*

Distances: *A head; fifty yards*

* Lord Coventry declared to win with Emblematic *

1866

1865 would be remembered as the year which saw the assassination of America's President Abraham Lincoln and the death of our own Lord Palmerston, not to mention another memorable finish to the 'National! For the supporters of steeplechasing, it also provided the welcome news that the diligent perseverance of Messrs Angell and Craven, assisted by Lord Grey de Wilton, was at last beginning to reap its reward. Their Grand National Hunt Committee successfully acquired the approval of the Jockey Club to administer and govern 'chasing's affairs. It had been a long, difficult road to form a body of responsible and respected men capable and willing not merely to improve the image of the sport

Mr B 'Cherry' Angell, one of the founder members of the National Hunt Committee

but to create and implement a set of workable rules which would ensure the integrity of steeplechasing. The committee was officially established early in 1866, the thirteen original members including such dignitaries as: B J Angell Esq, Lord Coventry, Lord Poulett, W G Craven Esq, Captain Henry Coventry, Lord Westmorland, Captain Little and Lord Grey de Wilton. A formidable body of men indeed, whose sincere allegiance to the new code of racing was beyond question and who from the first committee meeting in February 1866 set to work in setting jumping's house in order. Nothing could have been more appropriate in the inaugural year of the new governing body than that the premier event under its jurisdiction should attract what was generally accepted as the finest gathering of 'chasers yet assembled for the race.

L'AFRICAINE, reputedly the finest jumper in existence, made it to Liverpool this time without the problems encountered twelve months earlier, though the massive burden of 13 st 2 lbs was considered by most to be too much. Fellow French competitor LAURA, a five-year-old mare, was generally preferred, going off the most heavily backed at 7/1. Ben Land took the mount on former hero ALCIBIADE, at 9/1. Slightly preferred in the market was the seven-year-old CORTOLVIN, bred and owned by Lord Poulett, a member of the infant committee pledged to govern jump racing. Beside CORTOLVIN, he was represented also by REPORTER and ACE OF HEARTS, the mount of 'Mr Edwards'. REAL JAM, CREOLE and THE DOCTOR with George Stevens aboard were others well supported, but the one which had been kept well under wraps was the newcomer SALAMANDER.

The early days of this seven-year son of

SALAMANDER, rejected by his breeder because of a deformed leg

FIRE-EATER, followed a familiar pattern as far as Aintree heroes were concerned, for his breeder, Mr Bourchier, took a dislike to him on account of a crooked foreleg. He was bought in due course by Edward Studd, a wealthy retired indigo planter, and taken back to Rutland. There, the deformity seemed to correct itself as SALA-MANDER grew, developing into an attractive animal who could outgallop anything he was put against. His good looks were the subject of praise in the Aintree paddock but at the long odds of 40/1 he was almost totally neglected in the market due no doubt to the fact that L'AFRICAINE had beaten him some forty lengths at Warwick earlier in the season when conceding a stone.

A huge crowd, estimated at 30,000, turned out to watch, guaranteeing a smile on the face of Mr Topham, and even a heavy snow-storm shortly before the runners came out could not dampen the spirits of those present. Again there was an unnamed competitor among the thirty starters, this one shown on the race card as Mr Parr's gelding by TURNER and this was but another problem the newly founded

committee would soon need to eradicate. When the flag eventually fell after two false starts, SIR WILLIAM was left at the post, taking no part at all and ACE OF HEARTS took them along at a good gallop but at the second obstacle the real trouble began. The leader, ACE OF HEARTS, whipped round violently when about to take off, causing untold chaos. French crack L'AFRICAINE suffered most, being knocked over bodily when a horse collided with him broadside on. It was now CREOLE who found himself in front at the third, while KING OF HEARTS, PHILOSOPHER and STELLA fell behind him. At Becher's the crowds frantically searched for the favourite, but in vain for LAURA had gone out in the mêlée at the second. CREOLE led back onto the racecourse, his jockey George Waddington vigorously attempting to ward off the attentions of two riderless horses threatening his mount's progress. Spectators in the stands appeared oblivious to the plight of CREOLE's rider for they applauded mightily as both loose horses, HALL COURT and PHILOSOPHER, took the Water astride the leader. Ben Land had been biding his time with ALCIBIADE for the better part of the journey, bringing him into contention as they neared Becher's for the second time. Just when it seemed that Mr Angell's horse might pull it off again, however, ALCIBIADE fell at the Brook. From seemingly nowhere, Alec Goodman brought SALAMANDER with a devastating burst of speed as they re-entered the racecourse, leaving CREOLE as if he were standing still. It was all over bar a fall from that point and with Goodman's long experience there was little risk of that. SALAMANDER romped away to win easily by ten lengths from Lord Poulett's CORTOLVIN, who ran on terrifically well in the closing stages. CREOLE was a further four lengths

back, in front of LIGHTHEART and MERRIMAC. SALAMANDER's owner Mr Studd came in for the expected angry abuse when it was learned that he had backed his horse heavily, the accusations being to the effect that he had deliberately run the horse down the course before Aintree to secure longer odds. Whether or not these suggestions were justified remained a matter of conjecture but what was indisputable was the supremacy of SALAMANDER over such high-class rivals. An endorsement of his brilliance came the very next week when he romped away with the Warwick Grand Annual 'Chase and a great future was forecast for the gelding. Sadly it was not to be, though, for contesting a minor event at Crewkerne in April, SALAMANDER fell and broke his back.

THE GRAND NATIONAL HANDICAP STEEPLECHASE
1866

Starters: 30		Time: 11 mins 5 secs
1st **SALAMANDER**	**7.10–7** *(Mr Studd)*	**Mr A Goodman**
2nd **CORTOLVIN**	**7.11–6** *(Lord Poulett)*	**J Page**
3rd **CREOLE**	**aged.10–10** *(Mr Welfitt)*	**G Waddington**
4th **LIGHTHEART**	**aged.11–5** *(Mr A W Clayton)*	**E Jones**
5th **MERRIMAC**	**aged.10–7** *(Capt Shaw)*	**Capt A C Tempest**

Also Ran:

THE DOCTOR 5.10–0 (Mr Mytton) **G Stevens** *Failed to finish*; *FRANK 11–8* (Mr Cockburn) **Mr Lawrence** *Failed to finish*; *L'AFRICAINE 13–2* (Mr W R H Powell) **G Holman** *Pulled-up*; *EFFENBURG 12–8* (Count Furstenberg) **R Twiddy** *Failed to finish*; *ALCIBIADE 6.12–2* (Mr B J Angell) **B Land jnr** *Fell*; *HALL COURT 7.11–12* (Capt Brown) **W Reeves** *Fell*; *REPORTER 11–4* (Lord Poulett) **R French** *Failed to finish*; *GLENCAVIN 11–4* (Mr J Stevenson) **J Jewitt** *Failed to finish*; *THOMASTOWN 11–4* (Mr T N Naghten) **J Murphy** *Fell*; *LAURA 5.11–0* (Mr E Bourgnet) **H Lamplugh** *Fell*; *IBEX 6.10–12* (Mr Brayley) **C Boyce** *Fell*; *STANTON 10–12* (Mr J Coupland) **Welsh** *Fell*; *Gelding by TURNER 6.10–10* (Mr T Parr) **Reeves** *Failed to finish*; *MISTAKE 6.10–9* (Baron Von Grootven) **Knott** *Failed to finish*; *SIR WILLIAM 10–7* (Mr T Jones) **Ellison** *Refused & Pulled-up*; *STELLA 10–7* (Mr Spark) **Jarvis** *Fell*; *PHILOSOPHER 7.10–7* (Mr W Murray) **Wheeler** *Fell*; *GAROTTER 5.10–7* (Mr Oliver) **G Ryan** *Fell*; *ACE OF HEARTS 6.10–2* (Lord Poulett) **Mr Edwards** *Fell*; *KING OF HEARTS 10–2* (Mr W Robinson) **A Sadler** *Fell*; *MILLTOWN 5.10–2* (Mr W McGrane) (carried 10–4) **Mr Thomas** *Failed to finish*; *REAL JAM 7.10–0* (Mr F Hughes) **D Hughes** *Failed to finish*; *CUTLER 10–0* (Mr Barber) **Thorpe** *Failed to finish*; *WEST END 10–5* (Col Forester) **W White** *Failed to finish*; *COLUMBIA 10–10* (Mr Reginald Herbert) **Mr Herbert** *Failed to finish*.

The Betting: *7/1 Laura; 8/1 Cortolvin; 9/1 Alcibiade; 12/1 Real Jam; 100/7 L'Africaine; 15/1 Creole; 20/1 The Doctor; 25/1 Mistake, Merrimac & Ibex; 30/1 Hall Court & King of Hearts; 40/1 Salamander; 1000/15 Columbia; 50/1 Others*

Distances: *Ten lengths; four lengths*

1867

Now Aintree was chosen as the venue for the Grand Military Meeting. With the 'National run on the Wednesday, the Grand Military races followed giving Liverpool's spring fixture three full days of racing.

For the second year running the handicap was headed by a French invader, Baron Finot's mare ASTROLABE. Carrying 12 st 7 lbs, she found little favour with backers. HALL COURT was also thought to have too much weight, and with his owner Captain Browne now riding he was virtually ignored at 50/1. It was from the lower end of the weights that the majority looked for the winner, eventually settling for Captain Brabazon's KING ARTHUR, a five-year-old ridden by Captain Harford. At 5/1 he was two points ahead of Alec Goodman's mount SHAKSPEARE, with another five-year-old FAN the third choice.

CORTOLVIN was bred in Ireland by Lord Poulett, of apparently somewhat doubtful parentage, for his sire was shown as being either CHICKEN or CHEERFUL HORN. Lord Poulett considered CORTOLVIN soft-hearted and sold the horse to the Duke of Hamilton, commonly called either the 'Red Duke' or 'Duke Rufus'. After undergoing some financial difficulties in recent years, His Grace plunged heavily on his 'National hope which was again ridden by John Page.

Over the first fence the favourite KING ARTHUR took up the running to the delight of the spectators, only to dash their hopes by refusing at the very next. CORTOLVIN became the new leader, going on to be first

CORTOLVIN, who restored the fortunes of a colourful owner

over Becher's from SEA KING, GLOBULE, LITTLE FRANK and PLINLIMMON. LITTLE WIDEAWAKE showed briefly in front jumping Valentine's but was brought to grief at the next fence when HALL COURT bumped into him in mid-air, both horses finishing on the ground. Headstrong GLOBULE now took command, and there was little change in the order well into the second circuit. George Holman managed to restrain GLOBULE after clearing Becher's, settling behind new leader CORTOLVIN. However, GLOBULE had the stuffing knocked out of him in a collision on the flat with LIGHTHEART and was unable to quicken when FAN ranged alongside. Now there was not the slightest evidence of

CORTOLVIN's being a shirker, as he shook off FAN, running out a comfortable five length winner. Four lengths behind the second horse a terrific struggle kept the crowds on their toes as SHANGARRY pipped GLOBULE by a neck for third. Of the others, the last horse to finish belonged to the man who parted with CORTOLVIN, Lord Poulett. In addition to the substantial prize money won, the Duke of Hamilton was reported to have collected £16,000 from the bookmakers, thus restoring his fortunes, while CORTOLVIN had the distinction of carrying the biggest weight, 11 st 13 lbs, to victory since the race became a handicap.

THE GRAND NATIONAL HANDICAP STEEPLECHASE
1867

Date: 6th March 1867		Starters: 23	Time: 10 mins 42 secs
1st	**CORTOLVIN**	8.11–13 *(Duke of Hamilton)*	**J Page**
2nd	**FAN**	5.10–3 *(Mr Barber)*	**Thorpe**
3rd	**SHANGARRY**	6.10–13 *(Mr Studd)*	**Mr Thomas**
4th	**GLOBULE**	aged.11–7 *(Mr T V Morgan)*	**G Holman**
5th	**LIGHTHEART**	aged.11–1 *(Mr A W Clayton)*	**E Jones**
6th	**REVOLVER**	aged.11–1 *(Mr T Jackson)*	**Igoe**
7th	**SHAKSPEARE**	11–1 *(Mr Carew)*	**Mr A Goodman**
8th	**TENNYSON**	5.10–10 *(Lord Coventry)*	**G Stevens**
9th	**SILVER STAR**	10–9 *(Mr S J Welfitt)*	**G Waddington**
10th	**GENIEVRE**	10–3 *(Lord Poulett)* (carried 10–5)	**Mr Edwards**

Also Ran:

ASTROLABE 12–7 (Baron Finot) **Cassidy** *Knocked-over*; *HALL COURT 8.12–3* (Capt Brown) **Capt Brown** *Fell*; *BANKER 11–10* (Mr J Dally) **T Ablett** *Failed to finish*; *THOMASTOWN 11–3* (Mr T McNaghten) **J Murphy jnr** *Pulled-up*; *THE MILLER 11–1* (Mr W Smith) (carried 11–4) **Mr Lawrence** *Failed to finish*; *MARENGO 11–1* (Mr C Fermin) **Mr C Fermin** *Knocked-over*; *LITTLE FRANK 10–13* (Mr Vallender) **J Knott** *Knocked-over*; *WHITEHALL 10–13* (Mr P Herbert) **Mr Milward** *Knocked-over*; *PLINLIMMON 6.10–13* (Capt Parkinson) **J Holman** *Failed to finish*; *SEA KING 10–11* (Mr E Brayley) **G Barry** *Failed to finish*; *KING ARTHUR 5.10–3* (Capt Brabazon) **Capt Harford** *Pulled-up*; *HAVELOCK (formerly Claxton) 6.10–3* (Mr J Wood) **Jarvis** *Fell*; *LITTLE WIDEAWAKE 10–3* (Mr Schwartz) **J Rickaby** *Knocked-over*.

The Betting: *5/1 King Arthur; 7/1 Shakspeare; 9/1 Fan; 12/1 Sea King; 14/1 Globule & Shangarry; 16/1 Cortolvin; 20/1 Astrolabe, Genievre & Silver Star; 25/1 Thomastown; 30/1 Little Wideawake & Little Frank; 50/1 Tennyson & Lightheart.*

Distances: *Five lengths; four lengths*

1868

To settle the long-running argument over the exact distance of the Grand National, Mr Topham ordered the course to be properly measured and the trip was thirty yards short of four and a half miles.

With CORTOLVIN's Aintree days finished, Lord Coventry's six-year-old CHIMNEY SWEEP shared the top of the handicap with the French-bred ASTROLABE and Hungarian BUSZKE, though due to the fact that neither of these two had raced this season, both remained unfancied. But CHIMNEY SWEEP was all the rage among backers, and there were many who thought that 7/1 was generous. Next in popular demand came the pair owned by Edward Brayley, MOOSE and PEARL DIVER, the owner declaring to win with the former and the fitness of PEARL DIVER was hardly in doubt, for the gelding romped away with a handicap hurdle at Aintree barely twenty-four hours before the 'National. ALCIBIADE was back, now partnered by the colourful Colonel 'Curly' Knox. Ben Land took the mount on HALL COURT, the other horse involved in that historic struggle with ALCIBIADE in 1865 but now thought way past his best.

Both former owners of CORTOLVIN were represented, the Duke of Hamilton by GARUS and Lord Poulett with a grey called THE LAMB, the smallest horse ever to attempt Aintree's daunting fences. Standing barely 15 hands 2 inches, THE LAMB's story is the stuff of which 'National legends are made and began in County Limerick. Mr Courtenay, the owner of MATTHEW the 1847 Aintree victor, possessed a stallion called ZOUAVE which he sent to cover an unnamed mare belonging to a neighbouring farmer called Henchy. This mare was the daughter of ARTHUR, second behind JERRY in the 1840 race, and

the result of the union was a scrawny little grey foal of such a gentle nature that Henchy's son christened him THE LAMB. Treated as a pet by the delicate boy until his premature death, the small grey was sold as a three-year-old for thirty pounds, whereupon he began winning small flat races. Such was the splendid disposition of THE LAMB that he adapted readily to hunting, yet when offered to the famous Edward Studd, received the damning remark that he 'was not strong enough to carry a man's boots'. But after he had won the Kildare Hunt Plate at Punchestown, he was sold to Lord Poulett. The diminutive grey figured in the market at 10/1, ridden by 'Mr Edwards'.

A minor sensation developed before the start when a Mr Jones, with no interest in the event other than as an onlooker, objected to GARUS starting, on the grounds that he was owed a sum of money from the sale of this animal after a Hunters' race at Hereford two years earlier. A furious Duke of Hamilton reluctantly lodged the said amount under protest to enable his horse to go out and the objection was subsequently over-ruled due to it being made outside the prescribed period, and the twenty-one runners got away on heavy going, with a fierce wind blowing. Tragedy struck without a fence even being jumped, the unhappy victim being the favourite CHIMNEY SWEEP. Large boulders marked the route across the road into the country section and in accidentally brushing against one of these, Lord Coventry's horse shattered the pastern of his near foreleg. There was no alternative but to put down CHIMNEY SWEEP immediately. CAPTAIN CROSSTREE took them along, with DAISY and THE LAMB in close attendance. FAN persistently refused the second and further mayhem followed when Becher's was reached. On the approach to the Water PEARL DIVER struck the front closely attended by THE LAMB, the pair clearing the obstacle perfectly in front of CAPTAIN CROSSTREE, ALCIBIADE, HELEN and MOOSE. In the country, BUSZKE persevered further than most, but his rider Count Szapary eventually called it a day. Over Becher's ALCIBIADE made a forward move, but approaching the final obstacle PEARL DIVER hit the front, with only the tiny grey THE LAMB within striking distance. Over the last, a ding-dong tussle developed on the run to the post in which George Ede was seen at his brilliant best, riding a perfect finish more characteristic of the finest of flat race jockeys. He carried the gentle little grey across the line two lengths in front of PEARL DIVER. Ten lengths back in third came ALCIBIADE, and CAPTAIN CROSSTREE finished an honourable fourth.

A jubilant Lord Poulett graciously shared his moment of glory with Ben Land senior, who had trained THE LAMB to perfection and could also boast he had coached the courageous rider. Only weeks before the race, George Ede had been carried back to the weighing room so covered in blood as to be unrecognisable after a crashing fall in the Croydon Hurdle. But the real hero of the day was without doubt THE LAMB, a tiny mild grey 'not fit to carry a man's boots'.

Later, a near-riot developed when the high winds brought down a gambling tent reserved for 'persons of distinction'. Only the intervention of the police prevented some persons of less distinction from treating themselves to the spoils therein.

THE GRAND NATIONAL HANDICAP STEEPLECHASE
1868

Date: 4th March 1868	Starters: 21	Time: Not taken
1st **THE LAMB**	**6.10–7** *(Lord Poulett)*	**Mr Edwards**
2nd **PEARL DIVER**	aged.**10–12** *(Mr E Brayley)*	**Tomlinson**
3rd **ALCIBIADE**	**8.11–10** *(Mr B J Angell)*	**Col G W Knox**
4th **CAPTAIN CROSSTREE**	aged.**10–5** *(Mr R Herbert)*	**W Reeves**
5th **ASTROLABE**	aged.**12–0** *(M. E Bouruet)*	**A French**
6th **HELEN**	aged.**10–0** *(Mr Barber)* [carried 10–1]	**Mr A Goodman**
7th **HALL COURT**	**9.11–4** *(Capt J M Browne)*	**B Land jnr**

Also Ran:

BUSZKE 12–0 (Count Karolyi) **Count Szapary** *Pulled-up*; *CHIMNEY SWEEP 6.12–0* (Lord Coventry) **J Adams** *Broke leg* [destroyed]; *DAISY 11–7* (Mr W R H Powell) **Mr Thomas** *Pulled-up*; *THE NUN 11–6 (inc. 10 lbs extra)* (Mr E Green) **Wheeler** *Fell*; *GARUS 10–12* (Duke of Hamilton) **J Page** *Failed to finish*; *KINGSWOOD 6.10–12* (Mr W Forbes) **Gilroy** *Fell*; *HUNTSMAN'S DAUGHTER 10–12* (Mr T V Morgan) **G Holman** *Pulled-up*; *THE PLOVER 10–10* (Mr R Walker) **Mr R Walker** *Failed to finish*; *MOOSE 10–7* (Mr E Brayley) **W White** *Pulled-up*; *FAN 6.10–6* (Mr Barber) **Thorpe** *Refused*; *MENTMORE 10–4* (Mr W Forbes) **Hyland** *Fell*; *CHARMING WOMAN 10–0* (Mr J Milling) **Terratta jnr** *Failed to finish*; *SLIEVE CARNE 5.10–0* (Mr G H Moore) **Mr Pritchard** *Refused*; *THALASSIUS 6.10–0* (Lord Stamford) **Mr Crawshaw** *Fell*.

The Betting: *7/1 Chimney Sweep; 8/1 Moose; 9/1 The Lamb; 10/1 Pearl Diver & Fan; 11/1 Daisy; 12/1 Helen; 16/1 Huntsman's Daughter & Alcibiade; 20/1 The Nun; 30/1 Garus & Astrolabe; 33/1 Captain Crosstree; 40/1 Thalassius & Buszke; 50/1 Hall Court, Plover & Slieve Carne; 66/1 Charming Woman*

Distances: *Two lengths; ten lengths*

* *Mr Barber declared to win with Helen & Mr Brayley with Moose* *

1869

Great things were expected of THE LAMB, but as was to be seen so many times, the Aintree race not only took a lot of winning, it also took a good deal out of the best of winners. The condition of the grey was a cause of constant concern in the new season and it is more than likely that the wasting disease which was to keep him out of action for nearly two years had already set in. Eventually the decision was taken to aim him instead for Aintree's Sefton 'Chase the day after the big one. Mr Brayley was again doubly represented, declaring to win with his six-year-old FORTUNATUS rather than PEARL DIVER. The latter received top weight of 12 st 7 lbs from an impressed handicapper while the public made the more leniently treated FORTUNATUS a 7/2 market leader. ALCIBIADE and HALL COURT were old faithfuls trying again, Captain Tempest renewing the acquaintance with HALL COURT for the first time since that epic battle with ALCIBIADE four years earlier. This point appears to have been missed by the punters, though, for HALL COURT was ignored at 100/1. FAN's indiscretions at the second fence last year were forgiven, a flood of money making Mr Barber's mare at 4/1 the second-best backed runner.

The thousands who religiously followed the fortunes of George Stevens found themselves this time investing on an almost black entire bearing the name THE COLONEL. An impressive hurdler with a number of wins to his credit THE COLONEL was bred by John Weyman at Brampton, Shropshire. His sire, KNIGHT OF KARS, possessed the strong blood of Exmoor ponies in his pedigree, and by all accounts the training of Mr Weyman's horse was as humble as some of THE COLONEL's ancestors, being conducted by a man called

Roberts on a farm at Bishop's Castle, where the horse learned to jump through the risky process of the farm boys putting him at anything in sight. There appears to have been some sort of partnership concerning the ownership of THE COLONEL, for although most definitely the property of his breeder John Weyman, it was known for him sometimes to compete in the name of Matthew Evans.

THE COLONEL and the Cheltenham genius George Stevens

After three false starts, the field finally got under way with GLOBULE the first to show. FAN repeated her antics of last year by refusing the second, the obstacle thereafter taking on the name of the horse which showed so much dislike of it. GLOBULE stayed in front over Becher's, with HALL COURT, THE COLONEL and Q.C. all well to the rear but jumping faultlessly. Moving smoothly through the field at Becher's next time, THE COLONEL put in a terrific leap, going within four lengths of the leading pair FORTUNATUS and GARDENER. With the positions unaltered coming over Valentine's, the race was developing into a thrilling contest, with HALL COURT and ALCIBIADE moving up threateningly behind the trio in front. Excitement at the favourite heading the rest was dashed when FORTUNATUS was pulled up exhausted three from home, from which point Stevens sent THE COLONEL up to join GARDENER. There was a good battle to the last, but on landing Stevens exerted his authority, sprinting clear with THE COLONEL to a comfortable three length win. Captain Tempest rode like a demon on HALL COURT to snatch second berth by a length from GARDENER with ALCIBIADE a close up fourth. The incomparable George Stevens had chalked up a record four wins in the race, again justifying his near faultless judgement in his choice of mounts.

THE GRAND NATIONAL HANDICAP STEEPLECHASE
1869

Date: 3rd March 1869	Starters: 22	Time: 11 mins
1st **THE COLONEL**	**6.10–7** (*Mr J Weyman*)	**G Stevens**
2nd **HALL COURT**	**10.10–12** (*Capt J M Brown*)	**Capt A C Tempest**
3rd **GARDENER**	**7.10–7** (*Capt J Machell*)	**Ryan**
4th **ALCIBIADE**	**9.11–2** (*Mr B J Angell*)	**Col G W Knox**
5th **Q.C.**	**5.10–9** (*Mr Lynton*)	**Griffiths**
6th **DESPATCH**	**aged.10–8** (*Mr Studd*)	**Mr Edwards**
7th **GLOBULE**	**10–12** (*Mr T V Morgan*)	**G Holman**
8th **THE ROBBER**	**11–2** (*Mr Doncaster*)	**Mr P Merton**
9th **HARCOURT**	**8.10–10** (*Mr Eaton*)	**Capt Harford**

Also Ran:
PEARL DIVER 12–7 (Mr E Brayley) **W Reeves** *Fell*; *THE NUN 11–9* (Mr E Green) **Mr Thomas** *Fell*; *FORTUNATUS 6.11–4* (Mr E Brayley) **J Page** *Pulled-up*; *ORNE 5.11–2* (Mr T Wadlow) **W White** *Knocked-over*; *HAVELOCK 8.11–0* (Mr J Wood) **Wheeler** *Fell*; *BARBARIAN 6.10–10 (inc. 10 lbs extra)* (Mr S J Welfitt) **G Waddington** *Pulled-up*; *HUNTSMAN'S DAUGHTER 10–8* (Mr T V Morgan) **J Holman** *Pulled-up*; *FAN 7.10–6* (Mr J Barber) **Thorpe** *Refused*; *KNAVE OF TRUMPS 10–6* (Mr T Golby) **Mr F Martin** *Fell*; *BISHOPSTON 10–4* (Mr F G Hobson) **Potter** *Knocked-over*; *GUY OF WARWICK 5.10–0* (Mr Dixon) **Mr Crawshaw** *Refused*; *PLUM CAKE 6.10–0* (Mr A Yates) **Mr G Spafford** *Fell*; *DICK TURPIN 10–0* (Mr Foulkes) **J Knott** *Fell*.

The Betting: *7/2 Fortunatus; 4/1 Fan; 5/1 Despatch; 100/7 The Colonel, Guy of Warwick & Pearl Diver; 20/1 Alcibiade, Knave of Trumps & Q.C.; 25/1 Globule, The Nun & Harcourt; 33/1 Havelock; 40/1 Dick Turpin; Huntsman's Daughter & Barbarian; 50/1 Orne; 1000/15 Gardener & Plum Cake; 100/1 Hall Court & The Robber*

Distances: *Three lengths; one length*

* *Mr Brayley declared to win with Fortunatus & Mr Morgan with Globule* *

1870

There can have been few occasions in the history of the Grand National when a popular victory by a truly remarkable horse was so overshadowed by sadness and tragedy, as it was in 1870.

The first loss brought to the attention of the racing public was that of William Lynn, the man whose dream of a Grand Steeplechase at Liverpool brought about an event of such spectacle and appeal that it now rivalled the greatest of annual sporting events. Many felt Lynn had been treated shabbily by the Committee of eminent gentlemen set up to administer the race once its attraction to the public was recognised. That he lived for more than thirty years after the reason for his exclusion from Aintree's Management Committee was given as 'ill-health', gave rise to a feeling that in the eyes of certain members of the aristocracy, having served his purpose Lynn's face no longer fit. Having become Aintree's forgotten man, William Lynn fell upon hard times, dying alone and in poverty despite the efforts of some close friends. The man whose dream gave birth to a race which would become a worldwide topic of conversation forever, was laid to rest barely a ten minute walk from the hostelry in which he once entertained Captain Becher.

THE COLONEL was at the head of the betting at 7/2. His rise to 11 st 12 lbs in the handicap in no way deterred those so impressed by the manner of his win last year and with George Stevens once more in the saddle, THE COLONEL was considered unbeatable. THE DOCTOR, despite a deformity described as a club foot, was taken as the biggest danger to THE COLONEL, enjoying second favouritism at 5/1. The next in the market was the Lincolnshire-bred mare PRIMROSE on 10/1. It was suggested that the whole of this mare's home county were on her to a man, since she had won each of her four races this season making her the obvious form horse. She was ridden by her owner, the talented Mr W Rippon Brockton.

The twenty-three runners got away to a first-class start but for the third year in succession FAN refused the second fence. Ben Land jumped clear on THE ELK at the third, and kept on to be first over the Water from GARDENER, PRIMROSE, KARSLAKE and PRETENTAINE II and in this order they ran down towards Becher's for the second time. KARSLAKE took the lead but after clearing Becher's was in turn passed by PRIMROSE, CRISTAL and SURNEY. THE COLONEL began making ground rapidly after Valentine's, Stevens having adopted his usual tactics of patiently keeping to the rear for most of the journey. The topweight PEARL DIVER moved into third place behind SURNEY and PRIMROSE at the penultimate flight, only to slow right down to a stop when THE DOCTOR suddenly appeared on the scene. With THE COLONEL issuing his challenge on the outside, PRIMROSE lost her chance when bumped by the tiring SURNEY and then all eyes were on the two Georges: Stevens on THE COLONEL and Holman on THE DOCTOR. With neither jockey giving an inch, the two brave horses battled neck and neck all the way to the post in a finish more in keeping with a five furlong sprint than a four and a half mile 'chase. At the line THE COLONEL just held on by a neck from THE DOCTOR, with PRIMROSE back in third place and SURNEY fourth.

All concerned were greatly applauded for providing what was described by more than one as the finest finish to a steeplechase ever seen. George Stevens was hailed as a genius and not just for getting

George Ede, alias 'Mr Edwards' whose untimely death robbed the sport of one of its greatest characters

the favourite home by such a narrow margin. This win was his fifth in the toughest race of the year and the observation in the press that he had created a record unlikely to be equalled was indeed prophetic.

At the end of the day's racing George Ede was leaving the course with his friend Arthur Yates, intending to return home for a day's hunting at Bishop's Sutton. It was the well-known intention of 'Mr Edwards' to retire shortly from competitive race-riding as he was soon to be married. A trainer, Mr Carew, approached Ede, imploring him to partner CHIPPENHAM in the Sefton 'Chase over one circuit of the 'National course the next day. Despite the urgent advice of Arthur Yates not to ride the horse, Ede agreed, whereupon Yates made one final plea to his friend with the words; 'Don't ride the brute, George, he'll kill you'. But 'Mr Edwards' did ride CHIPPENHAM and at the fence before the Water, the same which caused the death of James Wynne eight years earlier, he lost his life in an horrendous fall. No brighter light had lit the Aintree stage with such ability, sportsmanship and cheerfulness than that bestowed by George Matthew Ede, gentleman rider in the truest sense. Together with his friend and patron Lord Poulett, he had founded the Hampshire Cricket Club and emphasising his all-round sporting prowess, scored 1,200 runs for that county in 1863. It was, however, 'Mr Edwards' astride a bold and seasoned 'chaser, leaping the ditches and brooks at Aintree who would be most remembered. And so sadly missed.

THE GRAND NATIONAL HANDICAP STEEPLECHASE
1870

Date: 9th March 1870	Starters: 23	Time: 10 mins 10 secs
1st **THE COLONEL**	7.11–12 *(Mr M Evans)*	G Stevens
2nd **THE DOCTOR**	9.11–7 *(Mr V St John)*	G Holman
3rd **PRIMROSE**	6.10–12 *(Mr W R Brockton)*	Mr W R Brockton
4th **SURNEY**	aged.10–4 *(Mr J Nightingall)*	R I'Anson
5th **KEYSTONE**	aged.10–12 *(Mr G Nelson)*	Mr R Walker
6th **GARDENER**	8.10–12 *(Capt J Machell)*	Ryan
7th **Q.C.**	6.10–10 *(Mr H May)*	Mr A Yates
8th **ALCIBIADE**	10.10–12 *(Mr B J Angell)*	Capt Harford

Also Ran:

PEARL DIVER 12–7 (Mr E Brayley) **J Page** *Failed to finish*; *MOOSE 11–7* (Mr E Brayley) **A French** *Failed to finish*; *HALL COURT 11.10–12* (Capt J M Brown) **Mr Thomas** *Failed to finish*; *TATHWELL 10–12* (Mr S J Welfitt) **G Waddington** *Failed to finish*; *SCARRINGTON 10–12* (Mr T Wilkinson) **R Wheeler** *Failed to finish*; *MIDDLETON 10–12* (Mr Yardley) **Mr T Kirk** *Failed to finish*; *PRETENTAINE II 10–8* (Mr R Hennessy) **Mumford** *Failed to finish*; *GUY OF WARWICK 6.10–8* (Mr E Weever) **Mr Edwards** *Failed to finish*; *THE ELK 10–7* (Mr Rose) **B Land jnr** *Pulled-up*; *CINNA 10–7* (Baron Finot) **Count** *Failed to finish*; *CRISTAL 5.10–6* (Lord Poulett) **Mr Crawshaw** *Pulled-up*; *TRAVELLER 5.10–4* (Lord Eglinton) **Napier** *Fell*; *CASSE TETE 5.10–0* (Mr E Brayley) **J Rudd** *Failed to finish*; *FAN 8.10–0* (Mr Lawrence) **H Taylor** *Refused*; *KARSLAKE 6.10–0* (Capt A C Tempest) **Capt A C Tempest** *Failed to finish*.

The Betting: *7/2 The Colonel; 5/1 The Doctor; 10/1 Primrose; 100/8 Surney; 100/7 Q.C.; 100/6 Pearl Diver, Guy of Warwick & Cristal; 20/1 Tathwell & Gardener; 33/1 Alcibiade & Cinna; 40/1 Hall Court; 50/1 Karslake; 1000/15 The Elk & Fan; 1000/10 Casse Tete; 1000/5 Scarrington, Middleton & Keystone*

Distances: *A neck; five lengths*

* *Mr Brayley declared to win with Pearl Diver* *

1871

In midsummer-like weather, Grand National week took on a carnival atmosphere this year, with the big race on the Tuesday coinciding with the grandest of state occasions. Queen Victoria's daughter married the Marquis of Lorne, heir to the eighth Duke of Argyle. The bells rang out, flags flew high and the nation celebrated.

Mr Topham had altered a section of the Grandstand into private boxes similar to those at Ascot and they were heavily subscribed. Notwithstanding the distractions elsewhere, a crowd well in excess of 40,000 packed the course and despite there being a considerable amount of ploughed land to cross, the going was described as excellent. Since winning last year's race, THE COLONEL had been purchased by Baron Oppenheim for £2,600 and taken back to Germany. Now, despite a lack of success there and the burden of top weight here, he made the long journey from Berlin. George Stevens once more took the mount on the 8/1 third favourite. Mr Brayley declared to win with PEARL DIVER, the 4/1 first choice in the market, while his second string CASSE TETE remained virtually unbacked at 66/1. THE DOCTOR was heavily supported, along with DESPATCH and CECIL, but the horse which everyone crowded to see after an absence of two years was the diminutive grey THE LAMB. Owner Lord Poulett had been wise in allowing THE LAMB plenty of time to recover from his disorder but in the sad absence of George Ede His Lordship's selection of a rider was curious indeed. In a letter to Tommy Pickernell, alias 'Mr Thomas', written over four months before the 'National, Lord Poulett wrote:

'*My Dear Tommy,*
Let me know for certain whether you can ride for me at Liverpool on THE LAMB. *I dreamt twice last night I saw the race run. The first dream he was last and finished among the carriages. The second dream, I should think an hour afterwards, I saw the Liverpool run. He won by four lengths and you rode him and I stood close to the winning post at the turn. I saw the cerise and blue sleeves and you, as plain as I write this. Now let me know as soon as you can and say nothing to anyone.*

Yours sincerely,
POULETT'

Lord Poulett, the successful dreamer, was a major owner and breeder with interests on the flat as well as over the jumps

That Pickernell kept the contents of this document secret until after the event should go without saying, but the fact that THE LAMB started second favourite at 5/1 suggests that it was not only the owner who invested massively on the subject of his dream. There was also a pointer for coincidence punters when on the opening day of the meeting, a lamb escaped from a railway truck in full sight of racegoers, making good its escape along the track. The decision of Ben Land to turn his attention to the flat meant finding a new trainer for THE LAMB. Chris Green, the eventual choice, was tailormade for the job having partnered ABD-EL-KADER and HALF CASTE to victory at Aintree.

John Maunsell Richardson, an amateur of outstanding ability, entered for the first time astride Captain Machell's MAGNUM BONUM and in due course this combination of owner and rider were to make their own special mark on 'National history. When the flag fell, jockey Richard Marsh on PURLBROOK suffered an alarming experience going into the first. Ahead of him and under the rail of the fence, a party of picnickers hurriedly began scampering out of the path of twenty-five galloping horses! The second fence saw THE DOCTOR refuse, but Mr Crawshaw eventually induced the Duke of Hamilton's horse to take an interest in affairs, rapidly catching up with the leaders. George Stevens dropped THE COLONEL in at the rear, content to ride his usual waiting race. RUFUS led in splendid style over Becher's, by which time the antics of SCOTS GREY were giving cause for alarm. Swerving all over the place, Major Browne's horse collided first with CECIL, knocking him over, and then turned straight into THE DOCTOR who took no further part in the race. Supporters of THE LAMB became concerned when it was seen that the grey was finding difficulty negotiating the ploughed stretches of the course but he kept on and his jumping, as

in his last 'National, was faultless. There was an anxious moment for 'Mr Thomas' at the Canal Turn when a number of fallen horses lay directly in the path of THE LAMB, yet with amazing agility the Lord Poulett's runner jumped straight over them. Upon reaching the plough out in the country again, THE LAMB once more showed his dislike of the conditions by dropping back and it was at this point that THE COLONEL began making a forward move. PURLBROOK fell and with RUFUS now taking them over Becher's, DESPATCH moved up to challenge and THE LAMB got himself back into a prominent position. After Valentine's, 'Mr Thomas' went after the leaders and THE LAMB wore them down one by one, passing RUFUS and PEARL DIVER effortlessly. At the last the grey swept past DESPATCH, going away on the flat to a terrific reception from the crowds. He had won in a new record time. DESPATCH was second, two lengths in arrears and third was the outsider SCARRINGTON.

Amid scenes of extreme jubilation, Lord Poulett proudly led in his dual winner. Horse and rider, having survived the dangers of the course, almost came to grief on the walk back to scale, the surging throngs nearly knocking them over. THE LAMB lost the best part of his white tail to souvenir hunters, while the winning owner was relieved of his pocket watch by someone desirous of a more valuable memento.

George Stevens left Aintree that March day, with rumours concerning his retirement from the saddle rife, yet the jockey returned to his home Emblem Cottage without confirming or denying them. To most people a Grand National without Stevens, biding his time at the tail end of the field, was inconceivable and anyway with the man's vast experience surely he would be seen for many years at Liverpool in the role of trainer. But it was not to be, for just three months after he had brought

THE LAMB, the third dual winner of the race, and possibly the smallest ever, with George Ede up

THE COLONEL into sixth place behind THE LAMB the unbelievable news came that George Stevens had met his death. Having daily ridden with danger a constant companion, the Cheltenham genius lost his life far from the racecourse. While out riding his hack on the Cleeve Hill he knew so well, his hat was blown off by a gust of wind, causing his steed to whip around suddenly. England's best cross-country jockey was flung from the saddle and, smashing his head against a boulder, fractured his skull. The hero of five Grand Nationals never recovered consciousness and yet again the race and the sport lost a man whose contributions to both far outweighed any of the rewards he received.

THE GRAND NATIONAL HANDICAP STEEPLECHASE
1871

Of 25 sovs., each, 15 forfeit and 5 only if declared; With 300 sovs., added. The second to receive 100 sovs., and the third to save his stake. The Winner to pay 50 sovs., towards expenses

Date: 21st March 1871	Starters: 25	Time: 9 mins 35¾ secs
1st **THE LAMB**	9.11–5 *(Lord Poulett)*	**Mr Thomas**
2nd **DESPATCH**	**aged**.10–0 *(Mr Studd)*	**G Waddington**
3rd **SCARRINGTON**	8.11–4 *(Mr T Wilkinson)*	**Cranshaw**
4th **PEARL DIVER**	**aged**.11–5 *(Mr E Brayley)*	**J Page**
5th **TUSCULANUM**	9.11–0 *(Capt W H Cooper)*	**Capt Smith**
6th **THE COLONEL**	8.12–8 *(Baron E Oppenheim)*	**G Stevens**
7th **RUFUS**	7.11–4 *(Capt J F Montgomery)*	**Ryan**
8th **SOUVENANCE**	6.11–2 *(Duke of Hamilton)*	**Rickaby**

Also Ran:
THE DOCTOR 10.11–13 (Duke of Hamilton) **Mr Crawshaw** *Refused; SNOWSTORM 8.11–7* (Mr J N Leighton) **Mr R Walker** *Fell; PHILOSOPHER aged.10–12* (Mr Gardner) **H Ellison** *Fell; WILD FOX 6.10–12* (Colonel Ainslie) **Murphy** *Fell; LORD RAGLAN 8.10–10* (Mr O Perry) **Daniels** *Broke leg* [destroyed]; *PURLBROOK 6.10–10* (Mr W Bingham) **Marsh** *Fell; MAGNUM BONUM aged.10–10* (Capt J Machell) **Mr J M Richardson** *Fell; SCALTHEEN 6.10–10* (Lord Eglinton) **G Gray** *Brought-down; CASSE TETE 6.10–10* (Mr E Brayley) **J Rudd** *Failed to finish; LADY GERALDINE 5.10–6* (Capt Haworth) **C Cunningham** *Failed to finish; CECIL 6.10–6* (Mr Etches) **R I'Anson** *Fell; SCOTS GREY aged.10–5* (Major Browne) **Welsh** *Failed to finish; ST VALENTINE 6.10–4* (Lord Anglesey) **J Adams** *Fell; BOGUE HOMA 6.10–4* (Lord Anglesey) **Tomlinson** *Failed to finish; ALCIBIADE 11.10–4* (Mr B J Angell) **Walling** *Failed to finish; INON 5.10–4* (Capt Pigott) **Capt Harford** *Failed to finish; DOG FOX aged.10–0* (Mr Mannington) **J Potter** *Broke-down*

The Betting: *4/1 Pearl Diver; 11/2 The Lamb; 8/1 The Colonel; 10/1 Despatch & Cecil; 12/1 The Doctor; 25/1 Souvenance & Purlbrook; 33/1 Dog Fox & St Valentine; 40/1 Snowstorm, Tusculanum, Bogue Homa & Wild Fox; 50/1 Magnum Bonum; 66/1 Casse Tete & Inon; 100/1 Others*

Distances: *Two lengths; four lengths; a neck*

1872

As was to be expected, THE LAMB attracted the severest attention of the handicapper when making his bid to win the race for the third time, receiving the killing weight for such a tiny horse of 12 st 7 lbs. Lord Poulett's lease on the horse having expired, Baron Oppenheim purchased the grey for £1,200, thus becoming the owner of two dual 'National winners without having the satisfaction of seeing either carry his colours to victory in the race. His first purchase, THE COLONEL, had returned to Germany to stand at stud and, later, to be used as a charger by Kaiser Wilhem I, a far more leisurely occupation than his days around Liverpool.

DESPATCH started 4/1 favourite from the newcomers NUAGE, CINDERELLA and SCHIEDAM. Making his seventh appearance, though at 66/1 now propping up the market, HALL COURT was trying for the last time, still owned by Captain J M Browne which was most unusual at a time when even famous winners changed hands regularly. The seven-year-old mare CASSE TETE stood at 20/1.

Finch Mason's picture of CASSE TETE and Mr Brayley, who had reason to look a little happier after the race

Bred by the Duke of Newcastle, by TRUMPETER out of CONSTANCE, CASSE TETE ran moderately on the flat before passing on to Mr E Brayley. He had made his money in the theatrical world, having started out as a 'Punch and Judy' operator. Brayley was greatly encouraged to hit the market when CASSE TETE ran a most promising third behind HARVESTER in Croydon's Great Metropolitan 'Chase with John Page in the saddle. Countless friends in show-business were happy to ignore *The Times* correspondent's unflattering comment that 'CASSE TETE looked as though she were in training for an anatomical museum instead of the Grand National', and connections were brimful of confidence as the race approached.

Over the first DESPATCH was overtaken by ROYAL IRISH FUSILIER and over the Canal Turn, PRIMROSE and RUFUS joined issue. PRIMROSE broke her back in a crashing fall at the second fence in the country and the owner-rider showed more concern for his mare as she was put out of her misery, than he did for his own discomfort. The accident brought about a succession of falls, but THE LAMB survived the mêlée by clearing all those blocking his path in one spectacular leap. Mr G Moore now found himself in front on SCOTS GREY, and THE LAMB ranged up alongside the leader on the run back towards the stands, the two greys being just ahead of SCARRINGTON, CASSE TETE and DESPATCH. Over the penultimate flight THE LAMB and CASSE TETE struck the front and for one glorious moment the much-loved tiny grey seemed set for a hat trick of wins. The weight, however, proved decisive on the run to the last, and the challenge which did come was from Mr Arthur Yates on his own HARVESTER. But he could not wear down CASSE TETE, slowing dramatically when twisting one of his special studded shoes. CASSE TETE ran out a comfortable six length winner from SCARRINGTON, with the favourite DESPATCH in third place. Gallantly and to a great ovation, THE LAMB kept on to be fourth, in front of FLEURISTE, ridden by Rickaby, the first generation of a famous racing family of the future. THE LAMB was sent back to Germany by his owner and sadly, broke his leg when leading the field by a distance in a race at Baden-Baden and was destroyed.

THE GRAND NATIONAL HANDICAP STEEPLECHASE
1872

Date: 21st March 1872	Starters: 25	Time: 10 mins 14½ secs
1st **CASSE TETE**	7.10–0 *(Mr E Brayley)*	**J Page**
2nd **SCARRINGTON**	9.11–2 *(Mr T Wilkinson)*	**R I'Anson**
3rd **DESPATCH**	aged.10–4 *(Mr E Studd)*	**G Waddington**
4th **THE LAMB**	10.12–7 *(Baron Oppenheim)*	**Mr Thomas**
5th **FLEURISTE**	5.10–10 *(Duke of Hamilton)*	**Rickaby**
6th **MASTER MOWBRAY**	aged.10–12 *(Mr J Goodliff)*	**G Holman**
7th **OURAGAN II**	aged.10–10 *(Mr P Merton)*	**A Holman**
8th **SCOTS GREY**	aged.10–11 *(Major Browne)*	**Mr G Moore**
9th **SCALTHEEN**	7.10–4 *(Lord Eglinton)*	**Murphy**

Also Ran:

HARVESTER 7.12–0 (Mr A Yates) **Mr A Yates** *Over-reached; MARIN 6.11–10 (Baron Finot)* **Cassidy** *Brought-down; PRIMROSE 8.11–9 (Mr W R Brockton)* **Mr W R Brockton** *Broke back* [destroyed]; *SNOWSTORM 9.11–9 (Mr Chaplin)* **Thorpe** *Fell; SCHIEDAM 7.11–4 (Lord Eglinton)* **Mr J M Richardson** *Brought-down; RUFUS 8.11–4 (Capt Montgomery)* **J Potter** *Failed to finish; NUAGE 7.11–2 (Mr Doncaster)* **Harding** *Broke leg* [destroyed]; *RYSHWORTH 6.10–12 (Mr Chaplin)* **Boxall** *Fell; FRANC LURON 6.10–7* (Capt J Machell) **J Cannon** *Fell; CINDERELLA 5.10–7 (Lord Anglesey)* **J Adams** *Fell; ACTON 6.10–7 (Mr Finchley)* **J Rudd** *Fell; PHILOSOPHER aged.10–6 (Mr W Murray)* **T Gray** *Brought-down; ROYAL IRISH FUSILIER 8.10–6 (Baron Oppenheim)* **T Andrews** *Pulled-up; SAUCEBOX (formerly THREATENER) 6.10–4* (Mr H Ellison) **Whiteley** *Fell; HALL COURT aged.10–0 (Capt J Browne)* **Mr C Browne** *Failed to finish; DERBY DAY aged.10–0 (Lord Conyngham)* **Marsh** *Fell.*

The Betting: *100/30 Despatch; 100/15 Nuage & Cinderella; 10/1 Schiedam; 100/8 The Lamb; 100/6 Scarrington, Primrose & Franc Luron; 20/1 Casse Tete; 25/1 Harvester, Marin, Master Mowbray, Derby Day & Rufus; 40/1 Acton; 50/1 Snowstorm, Scots Grey, Fleuriste & Saucebox; 66/1 Hall Court*

Distances: *Six lengths; six lengths; two lengths*

1873

From one hundred and eight original subscribers, the field on the day was twenty-eight. CASSE TETE started joint fourth in the betting at 10/1, but it was the mount of Richard Marsh, FOOTMAN, which found most favour, going off the 100/15 favourite with seven-year-old RYSHWORTH heavily backed at 15/2. Considered the class horse among those competing, RYSHWORTH had run prominently behind PRETENDER in the 1869 Derby. A bay six-year-old horse by COMMOTION out of POLLY PEACHUM, DISTURBANCE was bred by Mr Barber and owned by Captain James Machell.

Born in 1838 at Beverley, Yorkshire, Machell joined the 14th Foot, later known as the West Yorkshire Regiment, rising to the rank of Captain in 1862. One of his party-tricks in the mess was to jump on to the mantelpiece from a standing start. Resigning his commission the following year after being refused leave to attend Doncaster races, the 'retired' Captain staked everything he had on the one horse he owned, BACCHUS, in a race at Newmarket. The horse restored his owner's fortunes to the tune of £10,000, enabling Machell to set up as trainer, dealer and gambler at flat racing's headquarters. His judgment of horseflesh was much in demand and he is rumoured to have had a hand in the preparation of HERMIT the year it won the Derby. Another exploit of Machell's was the famous walking match from Newmarket to London which he won, together with the £1,000 wager. John Maunsell Richardson teamed up with Captain Machell as his regular rider, the pair sharing much success. Born in 1846 in Lincolnshire, Richardson was an equally fine athlete, both at Harrow and Cambridge. A natural horseman, Richardson was readily acknowledged as

J M Richardson – not only a fine horseman but a prominent writer on the game as well

one of the finest riders of his age.

Many improvements had taken place at Aintree since last year's race, among them a telegraph station from which twenty-word messages could be sent to any part of the country for the price of one shilling. The enterprising Mr Topham was still intent on making his meeting a very special one.

In glorious weather, RYSHWORTH took them along at a fast gallop. One of the first to exit from the race was the most recent Aintree hero, CASSE TETE, whose bridle broke, leaving Johnny Page with no alternative but to pull her up. RYSHWORTH was giving jockey Boxall an uncomfortable ride, repeatedly attempting to refuse and swerving from side to side. He was still there at the Water Jump though, just behind SOLICITOR who had taken over the lead at the previous fence and with CON-GRESS in close attendance, the survivors turned back into the country. A familiar sight was witnessed at Becher's, when a grey bearing the cerise and blue of Lord Poulett surged up to join the front runners. It was BROADLEA though, and not THE LAMB and she fell at the fence after the Brook, bringing down SOLICITOR and RED NOB. Taking advantage of these misfortunes, the mare COLUMBINE went on, turning for home some three lengths in advance of RYSHWORTH, ALICE LEE and DISTURBANCE, with the remainder some way back. Over the second last, RYSH-WORTH looked all over the winner as he passed the mare easily. But DISTURBANCE came to challenge at the final flight, and Richardson, who had once trained RYSH-WORTH for Mr Chaplin, understood that

horse's reluctance to persevere in a hard fought finish, and settled the issue decisively. Ten lengths back in third came COLUMBINE.

All competing riders agreed that it had been an extremely fast-run affair but unfortunately the time-keeper's watch stopped during the contest, making it impossible to confirm their views. Just how good a performance it was on the part of the winner was demonstrated the next day when RYSHWORTH ran away with the Sefton Steeplechase. At that evening's celebration dinner, Captain Machell added the delightful caption to the menu-card: 'DISTURBANCE but no Row'.

DISTURBANCE, who carried a big weight for his age to win

THE GRAND NATIONAL HANDICAP STEEPLECHASE
1873

Date: 27th March 1873	Starters: 28	Time: Watch stopped
1st **DISTURBANCE**	6.11–11 *(Capt J Machell)*	**Mr J M Richardson**
2nd **RYSHWORTH**	7.11–8 *(Mr H Chaplin)*	**Boxall**
3rd **COLUMBINE**	aged.10–9 *(Mr W H P Jenkins)*	**Harding**
4th **MASTER MOWBRAY**	aged.10–7 *(Mr J Goodliff)*	**G Holman**
5th **ALICE LEE**	7.10–3 *(Mr E Studd)*	**G Waddington**
6th **STAR AND GARTER**	6.10–7 *(Mr Vyner)*	**Capt Smith**

Also Ran:
REVIRESCAT 7.11–8 (Mr J S H Maxwell) **Mr W H Johnstone** *Failed to finish*; *FOOTMAN 6.11–5* (Mr Moreton) **R Marsh** *Fell*; *RED NOB 7.11–3* (Mr Sankey) **Mr J Goodwin** *Fell*; *CASSE TETE 8.11–3* (Mr E Brayley) **J Page** *Bridle broke – Knocked-over*; *CURRAGH RANGER 7.11–3* (Capt J F Montgomery) **Ryan** *Failed to finish*; *ACTON 7.11–1* (Mr Jones) **R I'Anson** *Failed to finish*; *LINGERER 6.10–13* (Mr W Burton) **Mumford** *Fell*; *REUGNY 5.10–13* (Lord Aylesford) **J Cannon** *Failed to finish*; *TRUE BLUE 7.10–13* (Lord Queensberry) **Lord Queensberry** *Fell*; *LOUSTIC 6.10–13* (Colonel Byrne) **Mr Bambridge** *Failed to finish*; *CINDERELLA 6.10–13* (Lord Anglesey) **J Adams** *Pulled-up*; *ISMAEL 7.10–13* (Mr W Wilson) **Daniels** *Refused*; *CRAWLER 6.10–10* (Mr Lynton) **Mr A Yates** *Fell*; *CONGRESS 7.10–10* (Mr H Wilson) **Mr E P Wilson** *Failed to finish*; *CECIL 8.10–9* (Mr E Etches) **R Wyatt** *Fell*; *CHARLIE aged.10–9* (Mr T Horwood) **Gregory** *Fell*; *SOLICITOR 6.10–8* (Mr Dalglish) **Mr Dalglish** *Knocked-over*; *HUNTSMAN 6.10–11* (Mr H Ellison) **Mr H Ellison** *Refused*; *NEW YORK 5.10–6* (Lord Stamford) **W Reeves** *Fell*; *BROADLEA 6.10–5* (Lord Poulett) **Mr Thomas** *Fell*; *SARCHEDON 5.10–3* (Mr W R H Powell) **Pope** *Failed to finish*; *RICHARD I 5.10–3* (Capt McCalmont) **C Gray** *Failed to finish*

The Betting: *100/15 Footman; 15/2 Ryshworth; 100/12 Cinderella; 10/1 Cecil & Casse Tete; 12/1 Master Mowbray & Broadlea; 14/1 Alice Lee; 20/1 Disturbance; 25/1 Curragh Ranger; 30/1 Sarchedon, Acton & Loustic; 40/1 Red Nob, Reugny & Congress; 50/1 Richard I, Lingerer & Crawler; 66/1 Star And Garter*

Distances: *Six lengths; ten lengths; a bad fourth*

1874

In addition to his former champion, DISTURBANCE, Captain Machell was represented this time by DEFENCE and the six-year-old French-bred REUGNY. With last year's winner seemingly weighted out of it at 12 st 9 lbs and DEFENCE in receipt of only 10 lbs from the top weight, it was REUGNY that had the best chance. But upon discovering that Lincolnshire farming friends of John Maunsell Richardson had secured the best prices about REUGNY, with 5/1 the only odds now available, Captain Machell exploded with rage. Richardson was justifiably disgusted at the accusation that he had cheated his friend, at first threatening to withdraw from the engagement to ride the horse, then relenting but with the vow that REUGNY would be his last ride in any race. The whole affair was shabby in the extreme, once more bringing into disrepute a sport still struggling to attain a modicum of respectability.

After just one false start, BRETBY, DAYBREAK, OURAGAN II and EUROTAS were disputing the lead over the first. At Valentine's OURAGAN II was pressed strongly by COLUMBINE, DAYBREAK joining in the tussle all the way back on to the racecourse and the three jumped the fences down the Canal side virtually together. Shortly before Becher's the second time, CHIMNEY SWEEP produced a burst which took him to the head of affairs, but COLUMBINE came back as they galloped to the Canal Turn and with MERLIN, MASTER MOWBRAY, DISTURBANCE and DEFENCE in close contention an exciting finish looked likely. Entering the final mile, CHIMNEY SWEEP and COLUMBINE were racing stride for stride, leaping the fences and ditches as one, while from the rear Mr Richardson quietly made ground on REUGNY. At the racecourse turn, COLUMBINE gave way to CHIMNEY SWEEP, who immediately opened up a five length lead and the result seemed assured. With most eyes on the leader, the favourite REUGNY was virtually unnoticed moving smoothly through the tired survivors. But Richardson knew REUGNY was not really a stayer and he needed the leader to make a mistake at the final hurdle. CHIMNEY SWEEP jumped true, however, and the error came from REUGNY. At precisely the moment all appeared lost, Richardson saw Jones ahead of him give his mount two frantic hits with the whip with not much response. Heartened by this, Mr Richardson sat down and rode REUGNY out in perfect style, to win by six lengths. Four lengths back came MERLIN, with Captain Machell's DEFENCE a similar distance away in fourth place.

The fiery Captain Machell, a genius at turning out a horse to win on the day

The consensus of opinion was that no-body but John Maunsell Richardson could have won on REUGNY that day. True to his word though, he never rode in another race. In 1894 Mr Richardson became the Conservative Member of Parliament for Brigg, Lincolnshire. Machell's two 'National winners, DISTURBANCE and REUGNY, together with the accomplished DEFENCE, had cost a mere £1,200. Soon after his second Aintree victory, the three were sold for £12,000, although none of them ever achieved anything of note afterwards. Captain Machell's meteoric success on the turf provided him with sufficient funds to re-acquire his family estates in Westmorland. But he lost Richardson for ever.

REUGNY, Richardson's last ride, who landed a gamble but destroyed a winning partnership

THE GRAND NATIONAL HANDICAP STEEPLECHASE		
1874		
Date: 26th March 1874	**Starters: 22**	**Time: 10 mins 4 secs**
1st **REUGNY**	**6.10−12** (*Capt J Machell*)	**Mr J M Richardson**
2nd **CHIMNEY SWEEP**	**7.10−2** (*Lord Marcus Beresford*)	**J Jones**
3rd **MERLIN**	**aged.10−7** (*Capt Thorold*)	**J Adams**
4th **DEFENCE**	**8.11−13** (*Capt J Machell*)	**Mr Rolly**
5th **MASTER MOWBRAY**	**aged.10−5** (*Mr J Goodliff*)	**A Holman**
6th **DISTURBANCE**	**7.12−9** (*Capt J Machell*)	**J Cannon**
7th **COLUMBINE**	**aged.10−6** (*Mr W H P Jenkins*)	**Harding**
8th **OURAGAN II**	**aged.10−5** (*Mr J Fearon*)	**Mr G Mulcaster**

Also Ran:
FURLEY 6.11−10 (Mr H Bruce) **Mr A Yates** *Failed to finish*; *EUROTAS 6.11−8* (Mr Chaston) **Mr Thomas** *Failed to finish*; *CONGRESS 8.11−4* (Mr H Wilson) **Mr E P Wilson** *Fell*; *CASSE TETE 9.11−0* (Mr E Brayley) **H Day** *Fell*; *DERVICHE 7.10−12* (Lord Marcus Beresford) **R I'Anson** *Failed to finish*; *DAYBREAK 8.10−11* (Mr H Houldsworth) **Holt** *Failed to finish*; *FANTOME 6.10−10* (Duke of Hamilton) **J Page** *Failed to finish*; *HERAUT D'ARMES 7.10−8* (Mr W Forbes) **Capt Smith** *Fell*; *DAINTY 8.10−7* (Mr S Davis) **Mr Hathaway** *Fell*; *VINTNER 7.10−3* (Sir R B Harvey) **Mr Crawshaw** *Fell*; *PALADIN 5.10−3* (Capt Rising) **J Rugg** *Fell*; *LAST OF THE LAMBS 5.10−0* (Mr H Houldsworth) **Mr Dalglish** *Fell*; *BRETBY 8.10−0* (Mr B J Angell) **W Daniels** *Refused*; *LORD COLNEY 5.10−0* (Capt Boynton) **Pickard** *Brought-down*

The Betting: *5/1 Reugny; 100/15 Casse Tete; 7/1 Vintner; 12/1 Furley & Columbine; 14/1 Eurotas; 16/1 Congress; 20/1 Fantome; 25/1 Chimney Sweep, Disturbance & Heraut D'Armes; 33/1 Derviche & Defence; 40/1 Merlin & Last of the Lambs; 50/1 Ouragan II & Master Mowbray; 66/1 Dainty*

Distances: *Six lengths; four lengths; four lengths*

1875

With £2,000 as bait, French nobleman and leading steeplechase owner Baron Finot sent over his good five-year-old mare LA VEINE, whose reputation preceded her to the extent that she became the best backed runner on the day at 6/1. Captain Machell relied solely on six-year-old LABURNUM this time, but denied the assistance of Mr Richardson, Machell's runner found little favour with backers.

PATHFINDER was another almost overlooked, though in his case there could have been no better partner to steer him than Tommy Pickernell, or as he preferred to be known 'Mr Thomas'. Bred near Rugby by John Cowley, PATHFINDER was sold to George Darby, a dealer specialising in good hunters. He disposed of the horse to the Master of the Quorn, John Coupland, and as his property PATHFINDER was often ridden to hounds by the famous Tom Firr. Herbert Bird became the new owner, together with Lord Huntly, popularly known as 'Cock of the North', and the horse was prepared for Liverpool by W Reeves at Epsom though rated by most as out of his depth.

At the 'off', SAILOR went into an immediate lead, jumping the first fence

PATHFINDER on his way to victory, by Finch Mason

freely despite the efforts of jockey Fleming to restrain him. The heavy going was making things difficult, but CONGRESS led over Becher's from LA VEINE, SAILOR, SPARROW and MISS HUNGERFORD. For the first time PATHFINDER became prominent at the Water, but less than half of those which started were still on their feet at the start of the second circuit. 'Mr Thomas' became anxious about PATHFINDER running through the plough towards Becher's and it was only to give the owners a reasonable run for their money that he decided to continue. VICTOIRE and CONGRESS led down the Canal side, but at the second last, Mr Hathaway pushed the mare DAINTY to the front. To the amazement of his rider, PATHFINDER then somehow found renewed energy, running on vigorously and with all but the mare done

with, 'Mr Thomas' realised he was in with a chance. DAINTY and PATHFINDER jumped the last together and at the line it was PATHFINDER by half a length from DAINTY with three lengths to Johnny Page on LA VEINE.

At the age of forty-one Tommy Pickernell, who fooled nobody with his pseudonym of 'Mr Thomas', had gained his third victory in the race and after weighing in he delightedly revealed to reporters a minor problem encountered shortly before the start. He had the habit of taking a dram before a race, but his intake that day must have been more than usual, for he found it necessary to enquire from a fellow jockey which direction he should be facing for the start. Once on his way, though, no further advice was needed!

THE GRAND NATIONAL HANDICAP STEEPLECHASE
1875

Date: 18th March 1875	Starters: 19	Time: 10 mins 22 secs
1st **PATHFINDER** [formerly THE KNIGHT]	8.10−11 (Mr H Bird)	**Mr Thomas**
2nd **DAINTY**	9.11−0 (Mr S Davis)	**Mr Hathaway**
3rd **LA VEINE**	5.11−12 (Baron Finot)	**J Page**
4th **JACKAL**	7.11−11 (Mr H Baltazzi)	**R Marsh**
5th **MARMORA**	7.11−2 (Capt R Thorold)	**J Jones**
6th **VICTOIRE**	6.10−13 (Mr G Bracher)	**Mr Barnes**
7th **SPARROW**	6.11−2 (Mr Percival)	**Gregory**
8th **CONGRESS**	9.12−4 (Mr Gomm)	**Mr E P Wilson**

Also Ran:
FURLEY 7.12−2 (Mr H Baltazzi) **Mr J Goodwin** *Refused*; *CLONAVE 7.12−1* (Sir W Nugent) **Gavin** *Fell*; *DUC DE BEAUFORT 6.11−13* (Mr Vyner) **Capt Smith** *Failed to finish*; *LABURNUM 6.11−12* (Capt J Machell) **Jewitt** *Broke-down*; *MISS HUNGERFORD 8.11−10* (Mr F Bennett) **Mr Rolly** *Fell*; *ST AUBYN 7.11−7* (Mr C A Egerton) **T Pickett** *Fell*; *SAILOR 6.11−7* (Capt S Gubbins) **Fleming** *Fell*; *MESSAGER 7.11−7* (Mr Percival) **Whiteley** *Fell*; *BAR ONE 8.11−4* (Mr L Nicholson) **Mr L Nicholson** *Fell*; *FLEURISTE 8.11−0* (Mr Grainger) **R I'Anson** *Failed to finish*; *NEW YORK 7.10−13* (Mr F Platt) **Mr Dalglish** *Fell*

The Betting: *6/1 La Veine; 7/1 Congress & Jackal; 9/1 Clonave; 100/8 Duc de Beaufort, Sailor & Marmora; 100/7 Sparrow; 100/6 Pathfinder; 20/1 Laburnum & Miss Hungerford; 25/1 Dainty; 100/3 Messager & Fleuriste; 40/1 St Aubyn*

Distances: *Half a length; three lengths; a head*

* An objection to the Winner on the grounds of insufficient description was declared to be frivolous *

1876

The crowds at Aintree on Friday, 24th March could count themselves fortunate to see a horse unanimously accepted as the most handsome 'chaser of his time. CHANDOS was a striking chestnut six-year-old entire, understandably reckoned far and away superior to anything else racing across country. His reputation owed as much to finishing fourth behind DONCASTER in the Epsom Derby three years earlier, as to the brilliance displayed over hurdles in the interim period. Owned by Lord Aylesford when competing on the flat, the horse became the property of the redoubtable James Machell and prepared for his new career by Joe Cannon, whose brother Tom had ridden CHANDOS at Epsom. A flood of money from all quarters made the horse a raging 3/1 favourite. Presumably Machell had secured attractive odds in advance this time, although with a good second string to his bow in the shape of the five-year-old REGAL, Machell took care not to ignore the possibility that the younger of his pair may in fact be better suited to the peculiarities of Liverpool foregoing the practice of declaring to win with one or other of his runners.

Unlike his stable-mate CHANDOS, REGAL had proven himself over fences as well as hurdles, carrying off Sandown's four mile Great Sandown 'Chase while still aged four and in the opinion of his trainer Joe Cannon he was a better proposition than CHANDOS. A black gelding by SAUNTERER, REGAL was not without a touch of class, his dam being the 1865 Oaks winner RE-GALIA, and all things considered, the odds of 25/1 offered against him appear generous in the extreme.

It was perhaps ironic that with Captain Machell so powerfully represented, his former trainer, rider and confidant, John Maunsell Richardson, should choose to run his ZERO in the event which had brought about his premature retirement. Entrusted with the piloting was Richardson's long time friend Viscount Melgund, whose Eton nickname of 'Mr Rolly' identified him to racegoers.

CHIMNEY SWEEP was the first to show and led over Becher's. Robert l'Anson had made steady headway on outsider SHIFNAL down the Canal side to such effect that upon reaching the racecourse he was on the heels of the leaders and he led over the Water. The loud applause was interrupted by an anxious gasp when the favourite CHANDOS blundered onto his head after jumping. Only through a miraculous feat of horsemanship was jockey James Jewitt able to bring his mount back into the race, recovering so well that they were within striking distance of the leaders again shortly before reaching the second Becher's, where ZERO, PHRYNE and GAMEBIRD rose together, with SHIFNAL, and Captain Machell's pair CHANDOS and REGAL moving up prominently. CHANDOS over-jumped the fence after Valentine's, coming down heavily and bringing a groan of despair. ZERO was the next to go, and this time the concern was of a less mercenary nature. 'Mr Rolly' was in a very badly injured state. Doctors, including Sir James Paget, rushed to attend Viscount Melgund and upon examination, they all declared that the rider's neck was broken. Miraculously, however, 'Mr Rolly's' vertebra slotted back into place on its own, the only occasion Sir James Paget had experienced such a happening in his medical career.

Meanwhile an exciting race had developed and as the final flight was reached three horses came away from the rest. Landing together in line, REGAL, SHIFNAL and CONGRESS began the excruciatingly long run to the post. When SHIFNAL gave way halfway up the straight, the riders of REGAL and CONGRESS rode for their lives, producing one of the finest finishes ever seen in the race, which REGAL won by a neck. Three lengths back came SHIFNAL, followed by CHIMNEY SWEEP, RYE, JACKAL and MASTER MOWBRAY. Captain Machell's third winner in the last four years enhanced his already famous reputation as a 'finder' of exceptional horses, while Joe Cannon had the double satisfaction of training and riding the winner.

Joe Cannon, whose brother Tom had ridden CHANDOS in the Derby and who always believed that REGAL had the better chance in the 'National. His sons, Mornington and Kempton, would later be known as two of the greatest flat-race jockeys of their day

THE GRAND NATIONAL HANDICAP STEEPLECHASE
1876

Date: 24th March 1876	Starters: 19	Time: 11 mins 14 secs
1st **REGAL**	**5.11–3** *(Capt J Machell)*	**J Cannon**
2nd **CONGRESS**	**10.11–8** *(Mr Gomm)*	**Mr E P Wilson**
3rd **SHIFNAL**	**7.10–13** *(Mr J Nightingall)*	**R I'Anson**
4th **CHIMNEY SWEEP**	**9.10–8** *(Lord Marcus Beresford)*	**J Jones**
5th **RYE**	**6.10–0** *(Mr W Weston)*	**G Waddington**
6th **JACKAL**	**8.11–0** *(Mr H Baltazzi)*	**R Marsh**
7th **MASTER MOWBRAY**	**aged.11–11** *(Mr J Goodliff)*	**G Holman**

Also Ran:
DEFENCE 10.11–11 (Mr H Baltazzi) **Mr Thomas** *Pulled-up*; *CHANDOS 6.11–7* (Capt J Machell) **Jewitt** *Fell*; *CLONAVE 8.11–5* (Sir W Nugent) **Gavin** *Refused*; *PHRYNE 8.11–3* (Mr C B Brookes) **Mr J Goodwin** *Failed to finish*; *PATHFINDER 9.11–0* (Mr H Bird) **W Reeves** *Failed to finish*; *PALM 8.11–0* (Mr G Brown) **Mr Barnes** *Refused*; *GAMEBIRD 7.10–12* (Mr Appleton) **Mr Appleton** *Fell*; *THE LIBERATOR 7.10–11* (Mr C E Hawkes) **T Ryan** *Fell*; *ZERO 6.10–10* (Mr J M Richardson) **Mr Rolly** *Fell*; *GAZELLE 5.10–9* (Mr T Smyth) **Mr Flutter** *Refused*; *THYRA 6.10–6* (Mr J Robinson) **W Daniels** *Refused*; *SPRAY 6.10–2* (Capt Bayley) **T Cunningham** *Refused*

The Betting: *3/1 Chandos; 100/8 Defence, Master Mowbray & Palm; 100/7 Jackal; 100/6 Pathfinder; 20/1 Zero, Thyra & Rye; 25/1 Congress, Clonave, Regal, Shifnal & Chimney Sweep; 33/1 Phryne; 40/1 Gazelle & Gamebird; 50/1 The Liberator*

Distances: *A neck; three lengths; three lengths*

1877

Captain Machell wasted little time in passing on those who carried his colours to victory. And always at a handsome profit. REGAL, the most recent hero, was sold to Lord Lonsdale, together with CONGRESS, which Machell had bought in time to carry off Aintree's Grand Sefton Steeplechase. It was last year's third SHIFNAL, however, which was most in demand on the day, at 100/15. Making his debut on SULTANA was the Irish amateur Mr Tommy Beasley, a man who, after this Aintree scouting mission, would stamp his mark in the most glorious manner.

Another amateur, Fred Hobson, known affectionately as 'the Squire', entered into racing ownership young. His HAMPTON won the Goodwood and Doncaster Cups, in addition to the Northumberland Plate, and in due course sired three Derby winners. Fred Hobson quickly made his mark when he took to riding over the sticks, but he had the curious and often frowned-on habit of gripping his saddle when taking a fence. The rider's explanation was that by holding onto the cantle of the saddle he eased the strain on his mount's shoulders, placing his weight as far back as possible. It was taken by most though, as a sign of nervousness. Hobson was strongly advised against partnering his own horse AUSTERLITZ in the 'National and it was only the insistence of his friend Arthur Yates which persuaded Hobson to go through with it. The horse, bred by Lord Scarborough, was a five-year-old chestnut entire by RATAPLAN out of LUFRA.

From a first-time start, AUSTERLITZ went straight to the front. Spectators at each fence down to Becher's shared mixed emotions as Hobson assumed his unorthodox grip of the saddle with each leap, some of humour but most horror and yet

the unusual style was effective. Briefly headed by ZERO, AUSTERLITZ resumed the lead as he galloped back towards the stands. Putting in a fine leap at the Water, AUSTERLITZ beat off ZERO and going back into the country first one then another issued challenges only for AUSTERLITZ to pull out a bit extra as he was reached. At the penultimate flight of hurdles, THE LIBERATOR moved past AUSTERLITZ, but it appeared that Mr Hobson was only steadying his mount for the final effort, for over the last he pushed AUSTERLITZ once more to the front, going on to win by four lengths. CONGRESS snatched second place by a neck from THE LIBERATOR with CHIMNEY SWEEP another four lengths away in fourth.

There were some embarrassed faces among those who had advised against Fred Hobson taking the mount, but it was his one and only ride in the 'National. He married the granddaughter of the famous owner and Member of Parliament, John Gully, but ten years later his wife divorced him and married Hobson's lifelong friend Arthur Yates.

Another illustrious 'National performer bowed out of the Liverpool arena after this race, though in the case of 'Mr Thomas' it was after long and legendary service. Born at Cheltenham in 1834, Tommy Pickernell benefited at an early age from the tutelage of two doyens of steeplechasing, Tom Olliver and William Holman. Upon the insistence of his family, however, young Thomas emigrated to Tasmania in search of the more respectable profession of sheep-farmer. It was in that far-off land that he rode his first steeplechase winner, a practice so often repeated that a petition was signed imploring him to desist from 'taking the bread from the mouths of professional jockeys'. Taking this hint with relish, for his heart was just not in rounding up woolly-backs, Pickernell returned to the land of his birth where in no time at all he became as much a bane to the paid riders here as he had to those down under. 'Mr Thomas' himself lost count of the number of winners he partnered both on the flat and across a country in the British Isles and on the Continent and despite allegations that he became a hard drinker towards the end of a distinguished career in the saddle, there can be no denying the wonderful contribution he made to the sport he graced so long. THE LIBERATOR, which he guided considerably into third place in the 1877 'National, was his seventeenth and final ride in the race, though certainly not by design. Retirement was forced upon him after a crashing fall at

Sandown in April of that year, which not only broke his jaw in three places but left him blind in one eye. Fully recognising the esteem in which the man was held and the abundance of experience he possessed, the National Hunt Committee appointed him as their first Inspector of Courses, a position he held until 1885 when he resigned, settling in King's Heath, Birmingham. As too often happens to the champions of the past, Tommy Pickernell spent the last years of his life in dire financial difficulties, and more than one whip-round was organised to ease his hardship. The world of sport, and steeplechasing in particular, was much the poorer when 'Mr Thomas' passed from this life in November 1912.

THE GRAND NATIONAL HANDICAP STEEPLECHASE
1877

Date: 23rd March 1877	Starters: 16	Time: 10 mins 10 secs
1st **AUSTERLITZ**	**5.10−8** (Mr F G Hobson)	**Mr F G Hobson**
2nd **CONGRESS**	**11.12−7** (Lord Lonsdale)	**J Cannon**
3rd **THE LIBERATOR**	**8.10−12** (Mr Moore)	**Mr Thomas**
4th **CHIMNEY SWEEP**	**10.10−13** (Lord Marcus Beresford)	**J Jones**
5th **DAINTY**	**11.10−4** (Mr S Davis)	**Mr J Goodwin**
6th **SHIFNAL**	**8.11−5** (Sir M Crofton)	**R I'Anson**
7th **CITIZEN**	**6.10−5** (Sir J L Kaye)	**W Reeves**

Also Ran:
REGAL 6.12−2 (Lord Lonsdale) **Jewitt** Fell; REUGNY 9.11−6 (Mr Gomm) **Mr E P Wilson** Pulled-up; PRIDE OF KILDARE 6.11−4 (Capt Bates) **D Canavan** Fell; ZERO 7.11−2 (Lord C Beresford) **Sherrington** Refused; LANCET (formerly BLUE PILL) 10.11−0 (Mr J Johnson) **S Daniels** Pulled-up; GAMEBIRD 8.10−11 (Mr Moore) **Mr Appleton** Fell; SULTANA 7.10−11 (Mr A Crofton) **Mr T Beasley** Pulled-up; EARL MARSHAL 6.10−10 (Lord Downe) **Mr Rolly** Fell; ARBITRATOR 6.10−6 (Sir C F Rushout) **Mr Crawshaw** Fell

The Betting: 100/15 Shifnal; 7/1 Chimney Sweep; 8/1 Reugny & Regal; 100/8 Pride of Kildare & Citizen; 100/7 Arbitrator; 15/1 Austerlitz; 20/1 Congress & Dainty; 25/1 The Liberator & Gamebird; 33/1 Lancet; 50/1 Zero & Sultana

Distances: Four lengths; a neck; four lengths

1878

The field of twelve was the smallest to face the starter since 1841. There came a familiar cry of foul play on the day of the race, when shortly before noon, the heavily-backed AUSTERLITZ was withdrawn with heat in a leg, but no enquiry was ordered. The five-year-old HIS LORDSHIP now carried the bulk of punters' money at 9/2. Lively interest surrounded both Irish runners, with Garrett Moore's choice PRIDE OF KILDARE being the better fancied, although Mr Tommy Beasley was confident that his mount MARTHA would belie her price of 20/1.

Tommy Beasley, whose first ride was the beginning of a remarkable family association with the race lasting almost a century. Rated as one of the finest jockeys of all time, he won the Irish Derby three times and in twelve rides in the 'National, he came to grief only twice and won three times. He also won many important races in France, including the Paris Steeplechase

Captain Machell was represented with sound jumper JACKAL. One horse which had run prominently in the last two 'Nationals was the nine-year-old SHIFNAL, this time competing under his original ownership of John Nightingall of Epsom, who first bought him out of a 'seller' at Alexandra Park.

Shortly before the parade, a panic was averted when smoke began billowing from beneath the Royal box specially erected for the visit of HRH The Prince of Wales. The straw which had caught fire was quickly extinguished, allowing attention to return to the contest about to commence.

SHIFNAL led into the first fence from MISS LIZZIE, JACKAL and MARTHA, but the fall here of NORTHFLEET, caused the downfall of favourite HIS LORDSHIP. Taking the Water Jump SHIFNAL still held a slight edge, but early on the second circuit MARTHA moved smoothly past him, with PRIDE OF KILDARE starting to make good progress. MARTHA was still at the head of affairs as they returned to the racecourse, and with Tommy Beasley holding her together well, she came into the final flight with the race at her mercy. Yet she tired rapidly after landing and Jones brought SHIFNAL to challenge and win by two lengths. PRIDE OF KILDARE came in ten lengths behind in third place and JACKAL was fourth.

Twenty-two years later DIAMOND JUBILEE won the coveted Triple Crown of the British Turf for The Prince of Wales. The young jockey in those brilliant triumphs was Herbert Jones, son of the man on the back of SHIFNAL on the day the Royal box almost went up in flames.

SHIFNAL, who won at the third attempt

THE GRAND NATIONAL HANDICAP STEEPLECHASE

1878

Date: 29th March 1878	Starters: 12	Time: 10 mins 23 secs
1st **SHIFNAL**	**9.10–12** *(Mr John Nightingall)*	**J Jones**
2nd **MARTHA**	**7.10–9** *(Capt A Crofton)*	**Mr T Beasley**
3rd **PRIDE OF KILDARE**	**7.11–7** *(Capt Bates)*	**Mr G Moore**
4th **JACKAL**	**10.10–11** *(Capt J Machell)*	**Jewitt**
5th **MISS LIZZIE**	**5.10–7** *(Capt Davison)*	**Hunt**
6th **CURATOR**	**5.10–5** *(Lord Lonsdale)*	**Mr E P Wilson**
7th **BOYNE WATER**	**6.10–12** *(Mr J Jessop)*	**J Adams**

Also Ran:

VERITY 7.10–10 (Mr J Hefford) **Gregory** *Fell; HIS LORDSHIP 5.10–7* (Mr G Brown) **R I'Anson** *Knocked-over; THE BEAR 5.10–4* (Duke of Hamilton) **R Marsh** *Knocked-over; NORTHFLEET 6.10–3* (Mr T J Clifford) *C Lawrence Fell; TATTOO 6.10–3* (Mr J G Blake) **W Canavan** *Fell*

The Betting: *9/2 His Lordship; 5/1 Boyne Water; 6/1 Pride of Kildare; 7/1 Shifnal; 10/1 The Bear; 100/8 Jackal; 14/1 Northfleet; 20/1 Verity, Martha, Miss Lizzie & Curator*

Distances: *Two lengths; ten lengths*

1879

Never far from the racing headlines during the eighteen-seventies, Captain Machell made the limelight once more when re-purchasing his former winner REGAL. Machell's activities were always closely followed by the betting public and the horse became early favourite for the race before reaching the prohibitive price of 5/2 on the day.

A powerful challenge came from across the Irish Sea, both from the horses and the riders, no less than four of whom were members of one family. These were the incredible Beasley brothers. The elder of the clan, Tommy, again partnered last year's runner-up MARTHA; Harry was on TURCO, Willie linked up with LORD MARCUS and Johnny was atop VICTOR II. It was a fellow-countryman of the Beasleys, however, who was thought to have the best chance of lifting the prize, Garrett Moore and THE LIBERATOR coming in as 5/1 second favourites. The son of DAN O'CONNELL out of a mare called MARY O'TOOLE, THE LIBERATOR, was bred by Mr Stokes in Annendale. Shortly after running in the 1876 'National, THE LIBERATOR failed to reach his reserve at auction in Dublin, whereupon Mr Garrett Moore purchased the gelding for £500. 'Garry' Moore and his brother Willie were natural horsemen, as was to be expected of sons of John Hubert Moore, the famous sportsman of Jockey Hall, The Curragh. Venturing to England while still a boy, 'Garry' grew up to be a popular and respected feature of English 'chasing.

Of the eighteen competing riders this year, no less than nine were amateurs, among them Arthur Coventry, younger

Arthur Coventry valiantly attempted to follow his brother's footsteps to victory

Garry Moore – owner and rider of THE LIBERATOR

brother of Captain Henry Coventry of ALCIBIADE fame.

Without any delay at the start, the runners set off in perfect conditions. BACCHUS, REGAL and JACKAL were the first to show, but it was two of the amateurs, Willie Beasley on LORD MARCUS and Ted Wilson with BOB RIDLEY, who led them over Becher's. Back on the racecourse, it was noticeable that Garrett Moore was giving THE LIBERATOR an easy ride in fourth place. JACKAL, MARTHA and WILD MONARCH moved nearer the leaders as the fourth from home was crossed but it was still BOB RIDLEY from LORD MARCUS in front. The latter dropped out of contention leaving BOB RIDLEY with a three length lead but Mr Moore sent THE LIBERATOR on and he cantered past the post ten lengths to the good. JACKAL moved through a cluster of tired horses to gain second place in front of Tommy Beasley on MARTHA, with WILD MONARCH fourth and BOB RIDLEY fifth.

The Beasley family day out ended most satisfactorily, with only John failing to complete the course.

THE GRAND NATIONAL HANDICAP STEEPLECHASE
1879

Date: 28th March 1879	Starters: 18	Time: 10 mins 12 secs
1st **THE LIBERATOR**	10.11–4 (Mr G Moore)	**Mr G Moore**
2nd **JACKAL**	11.11–0 (Lord Marcus Beresford)	**J Jones**
3rd **MARTHA**	8.10–13 (Mr Oeschlaeger)	**Mr T Beasley**
4th **WILD MONARCH**	8.11–7 (Marquis de St Sauveur)	**Andrews**
5th **BOB RIDLEY**	8.10–9 (Mr T D'Arcy Hoey)	**Mr E P Wilson**
6th **REGAL**	8.11–10 (Capt J Machell)	**Jewitt** [remounted]
7th **ROSSANMORE**	aged.10–7 (Mr J Connolly)	**Toole**
8th **LORD MARCUS**	7.10–9 (Mr P M V Saurin)	**Mr W Beasley**
9th **TURCO**	7.10–9 (Mr R Stackpoole)	**Mr H Beasley**
10th **BRIGAND**	aged.10–10 (Count Festetic jnr)	**Count Metternich**

Also Ran:
QUEEN OF KILDARE 6.11–5 (Mr P Doucie) **J Doucie** *Fell*; *BACCHUS 5.11–1 (Mr Dunlop)* **J Cannon** *Fell*; *HIS LORDSHIP 6.10–12 (Mr Russell)* **Levitt** *Refused*; *MARSHAL NIEL 5.10–12 (Sir J L Kaye)* **P Gavin** *Fell*; *VICTOR II 5.10–12 (Mr Denny)* **Mr J Beasley** *Pulled-up*; *THE BEAR 6.10–7 (Duke of Hamilton)* **R Marsh** *Refused*; *BELLRINGER 7.10–7 (Mr Vyner)* **Mr A Coventry** *Fell*; *CONCHA 6.10–2 (Sir T Hesketh)* **Mr W B Morris** *Pulled-up*

The Betting: *5/2 Regal; 5/1 The Liberator; 10/1 Bacchus & The Bear; 100/8 Marshal Niel; 100/7 Turco & Bellringer; 1000/65 Jackal; 20/1 His Lordship & Wild Monarch; 33/1 Bob Ridley; 40/1 Queen of Kildare; 50/1 Concha, Rossanmore, Brigand & Martha*

Distances: *Ten lengths; two lengths; half a length*

1880

Steeplechasing finally seemed to have acquired a status of legitimacy. As if to complement the enlightened attitude to its activities, the sport entered its golden age with an abundance of brilliant horses and talented men in its ranks. So popular had 'chasing become that wealthier owners sought animals capable of the highest deeds over fences, with the Aintree 'classic' always the ultimate aim. More members of the Jockey Club put aside their prejudices, with the realisation that owning a 'National winner was possibly the next best thing to leading in an Epsom Derby hero.

As was to be expected, THE LIBERATOR received harsh treatment from the handicapper. But Mr Moore's gelding had become such a celebrity to racegoers that even with 12 st 7 lbs he was made an 11/2 joint second favourite. REGAL occupied the prime spot in the market at 5/1, although he had changed hands yet again, this time running in the colours of Lord Aylesford and being reunited with his old partner in victory Joe Cannon. Quite apart from THE LIBERATOR, Ireland fielded a powerful contingent in WOODBROOK, VICTORIA and the five-year-old mare EMPRESS. Ridden respectively by Harry, John and Tommy Beasley, each attracted their own share of admirers. It was EMPRESS and Tommy Beasley though, who were considered by many to pose the biggest danger. Bred by Mr Lindesay in Ireland, the daughter of BLOOD ROYAL out of JEU DES MOTS was sold to Henry Eyre Linde. Linde was the first Irish trainer to plan regular raids on English racecourses, with such success that he became the plague of his counterparts across the Irish Sea. His establishment at Eyrefield Lodge, The Curragh, turned out winners with monotonous regularity, the trainer benefiting from the skills of his close neighbours the Beasley brothers. Setting his sights on Aintree, Linde built on his gallops a replica of the 'National course and although the methods of training adopted were harsh even by the standards of those days, there could be no denying the results they produced. EMPRESS was named after Empress Elizabeth of Austria, winning all her races over obstacles in Linde's name before being sold to Mr P Ducrot shortly before the 1880 Grand National. In Tommy Beasley, the mare had the best possible assistant. The eldest of five sons, Thomas distinguished himself as a peerless jockey on the flat before turning to 'chasing, winning three Derbys at The Curragh and defeating the immortal Fred Archer in one close-fought contest. A crack shot and skilful fisherman, Tommy could more than hold his own in the hunting field, which stood him in good stead for the rigours of the 'National.

With the Prince of Wales again in attendance, the field were despatched at the second attempt and DOWNPATRICK immediately shot to the front. A groan from those near the second obstacle signalled the fall of the favourite REGAL. There was no change over Becher's, though the outsider JUPITER TONANS, successful last year in the Irish 'National, joined them at the Canal Turn and went on at Valentine's, quickly opening up a substantial lead. An approving cheer rose from the packed stands as all but four of the original starters streamed towards the Water, the sleek looking grey DOWNPATRICK relegating JUPITER TONANS to second place. Back in the country again, though, JUPITER TONANS regained the upper hand, running at flat-race speed to open a gap of a furlong between himself and the rest. Over

Becher's, SHIFNAL, WILD MONARCH and WOODBROOK were beaten but Beasley, having overcome the loss of a stirrup earlier, was beginning to move through the field with EMPRESS. All the way back from the Canal Turn, the runaway outsider maintained his position, but round the final turn JUPITER TONANS began to falter and came back to his field. DOWNPATRICK and EMPRESS swept past and another advancing quickly from the rear was THE LIBERATOR, running on despite his burden of top weight. The issue was well and truly settled at the last hurdle, however, when EMPRESS put in a leap estimated at almost thirty feet and she won by two lengths from THE LIBERATOR. DOWNPATRICK got within a head of THE LIBERATOR, to secure third place and the brave front-runner JUPITER TONANS was a further two lengths back, an honourable fourth. EMPRESS was never able to run again, and she was retired to stud. The Grand National had entered a new, exciting era and if anything could ever be said to be certain about a race like this, it was that the Beasley boys and Linde would be an integral part of it.

THE GRAND NATIONAL HANDICAP STEEPLECHASE
1880

Date: 19th March 1880	Starters: 14	Time: 10 mins 20 secs
1st **EMPRESS**	**5.10–7** (*Mr P Ducrot*)	**Mr T Beasley**
2nd **THE LIBERATOR**	**11.12–7** (*Mr G Moore*)	**Mr G Moore**
3rd **DOWNPATRICK**	**6.10–7** (*Col Lloyd*)	**P Gavin**
4th **JUPITER TONANS**	**7.10–5** (*Mr J F Lee-Barber*)	**Mr J F Lee-Barber**
5th **WOODBROOK**	**6.11–7** (*Capt T Y L Kirkwood*)	**Mr H Beasley**
6th **WILD MONARCH**	**9.11–11** (*Count de St Sauveur*)	**R I'Anson**
7th **VICTOR II**	**6.10–7** (*Mr E Wills*)	**Mr W B Morris**
8th **VICTORIA**	**7.10–7** (*Mr J Schawel*)	**Mr J Beasley**
9th **SHIFNAL**	**11.11–11** (*Mr John Nightingall*)	**Capt Smith**
10th **DAINTY**	**14.10–2** (*Mr S Davis*)	**S Darling**

Also Ran:

REGAL 9.11–11 (Lord Aylesford) **J Cannon** *Fell*; *GUNLOCK 6.10–5* (Mr P Aaron) **H Davis** *Refused*; *SLEIGHT-OF-HAND 9.10–4* (Mr C Howard) **J Childs** *Refused*; *ST GEORGE 8.10–2* (Mr Greenall) **G Levitt** *Refused*

The Betting: *5/1 Regal; 11/2 The Liberator & Wild Monarch; 100/15 Downpatrick; 8/1 Empress; 12/1 Victoria; 20/1 Shifnal; 25/1 St George & Woodbrook; 33/1 Gunlock; 50/1 Jupiter Tonans, Sleight-of-Hand & Victor II; 66/1 Dainty*

Distances: *Two lengths; a head; two lengths*

1881

The first disappointment of Mr Topham's spring came when only thirty-four horses were subscribed to the entry list for the Aintree showpiece, which was bound to result in the smallest prize money for the race for many years. Then on the day of the race, the course resembled a quagmire and sleet and snow persisted to the discomfort of competitors and spectators alike.

The familiar figures of Tommy and Harry Beasley, Arthur Coventry, Richard Marsh and Jimmy Jewitt welcomed to their brotherhood the well-known flat race jockey Fred Webb, venturing into the unknown astride Captain Machell's promising young newcomer THE SCOT. Five-year-old THORNFIELD, trained by his jockey Richard Marsh on behalf of Leopold de Rothschild, had been the popular 'whisper' for weeks, finishing up on the day joint favourite at 11/2. Market co-leader was WOODBROOK, from Linde's famous yard and with the feared Tommy Beasley in the saddle. A seven-year-old chestnut gelding by half-bred THE LAWYER out of THE DOE, WOODBROOK was bred by Captain T Y L Kirkwood who

WOODBROOK, a winning product of the Linde academy at the Curragh

named the horse after his home in Ireland. Notwithstanding the state of the ground or the crippling weight of 12 st 7 lbs, THE LIBERATOR tried again with owner Garrett Moore up.

Such was the appeal now enjoyed by the Grand National that not even the arctic conditions could keep away the masses who packed the course, enclosures and stands on the big day, among them, if perhaps a year too late, the Empress of Austria. Sent on their way at the first time of asking, the field ran to the first headed by THE LIBERATOR and THORNFIELD. THE LIBERATOR, while still ahead of his field, came down at the fence after Valentine's, leaving Beasley and WOODBROOK in front.

Still showing the way and seemingly oblivious to the mud causing such distress to his rivals, WOODBROOK continued on the final circuit. All the way back to the racecourse frantic efforts were made by THE SCOT, MONTAUBAN, NEW GLASGOW and THORNFIELD to get back on terms but without success. Captain Machell's REGAL briefly looked a danger but over the last flight, WOODBROOK made the whole affair look easy, coming away to win unextended by four lengths. THORNFIELD was a bad third.

Soon after his win, the horse was sold for £1,300 to Mr Oeschlaeger but died at Newmarket the following year.

THE GRAND NATIONAL HANDICAP STEEPLECHASE
1881

Date: 25th March 1881	Starters: 13	Time: 11 mins 50 secs
1st **WOODBROOK**	**7.11–3** *(Capt T Y L Kirkwood)*	**Mr T Beasley**
2nd **REGAL**	**10.11–12** *(Capt J Machell)*	**J Jewitt**
3rd **THORNFIELD**	**5.10–9** *(Mr Leopold de Rothschild)*	**R Marsh**
4th **NEW GLASGOW**	**aged.10–7** *(Mr A Peel)*	**Capt A J Smith**
5th **THE SCOT**	**5.10–0** *(Capt J Machell)*	**F Webb**
6th **ABBOT OF ST MARY'S**	**5.10–9** *(Sir G Chetwynd)* [inc. 7 lbs extra]	**J Adams**
7th **CROSS QUESTION**	**6.10–0** *(Mr R Carington)*	**J Jones**
8th **MONTAUBAN**	**7.10–7** *(Mr J G Baird-Hay)*	**Mr A Coventry**
9th **THE LIBERATOR**	**12.12–7** *(Mr G Moore)*	**Mr G Moore** [remounted]

Also Ran:
FAIR WIND 10–13 (Capt P Ducrot) **Mr H Beasley** *Fell*; *LITTLE PRINCE 6.10–8* (Mr C G Way) **D Canavan** *Refused*; *FABIUS 5.10–0* (Mr H F C Vyner) **W Hunt** *Refused*; *BURIDAN 7.10–0* (Mr A Yates) (carried 10–2) **J Childs** *Refused*

The Betting: *11/2 Woodbrook & Thornfield; 6/1 The Liberator; 100/15 Cross Question; 8/1 Abbot of St Mary's; 11/1 Regal; 100/8 New Glasgow; 100/6 Montauban & Fair Wind; 25/1 Fabius & The Scot; 50/1 Buridan*

Distances: *4 lengths; a bad third*

Winner Trained By: *Mr H E Linde in Ireland*

Value to Winning Owner: *£925*

1882

Having turned out the two most recent winners of the race, Henry Linde was set fair for a hat trick of victories. In MOHICAN and CYRUS the Curragh trainer had the strongest hand possible and with two of the formidable Beasleys riding, both horses were the subjects of hefty gambles. It was Harry on the former who carried most money, going off the 100/30 favourite, while Tommy with CYRUS occupied third place in the betting at 9/2. At 4/1, THE SCOT split the Linde pair in the market, each of the remaining nine runners in another disappointingly small field being easy to back. THE LIBERATOR, now thirteen years old and with his customary top weight of 12 st 7 lbs, was considered beyond repeating his triumph of three years ago, especially with the ground no better than last year.

The six-year-old bay, SEAMAN, impressive when making a procession of a 'chase here twelve months before, stood at 10/1, largely due to money invested by his owner. Bred at Knockany, County Limerick by Captain Stainer Gubbins, SEAMAN was a small but well-proportioned animal, plagued from his earliest days by sickness. Yet despite this the horse stood up remarkably well to the harsh methods customary at Eyrefield Lodge when sent to Henry Linde. The son of XENOPHON won good races, but convinced that he had achieved the best that could be expected from SEAMAN and that the gelding would not survive a truly severe preparation, Linde persuaded the owner to accept an offer of £2,000 for the horse. The buyer was Lord John Manners, a serving officer with the Grenadier Guards. With less than four months before the next big Liverpool 'Chase, he sent the horse to James Machell to be trained. Captain Machell found himself in complete agree-

SEAMAN and Lord Manners, master of the Quorn but a novice race-rider

ment with Linde, that the horse was not robust enough to contest a race as demanding as the 'National. But the owner insisted and then announced his intention of riding SEAMAN himself at Aintree. Although Lord Manners was Master of the Quorn, his experience of race-riding was extremely limited.

The weather at Liverpool on the fateful day was just as bad as the year before. Shortly before the twelve runners came under orders, a heavier downfall of snow gave the small group an eerie spectral appearance. Among the many casting anxious eyes towards them none had more cause for misgivings than James Machell, knowing as he did that SEAMAN was only three-quarters fit. WILD MONARCH led out into the country, but EAU DE VIE swept into the lead with a mammoth leap at Becher's, and by the time the Canal Turn was reached, fifteen lengths separated her from the rest. Still with a commanding advantage, Dan Thirlwell brought the Duke of Hamilton's mare towards the Water Jump hardly able to believe the ease with which EAU DE VIE was racing. Turning away from the stands, ZOEDONE began making ground, and the long race home started in earnest. Jumping Becher's the second time in fine fashion and still full of running, EAU DE VIE veered sharply to the right, running into the scattering crowds. To the horror of his young rider, a stirrup leather had broken as they landed and their excellent chance of winning was lost. ZOEDONE was now left in front, pressed by FAY, CYRUS, SEAMAN and THE SCOT, and just three survivors came out of the blizzard towards the last two hurdles. ZOEDONE was easily overtaken by CYRUS and SEAMAN, the pair coming clear to the last. A mighty roar came from the packed stands at the prospect of Tommy Beasley scoring his third successive victory and as both horses touched down safely on the flat, it could be clearly seen

that SEAMAN was suffering some distress. The horse had in fact broken down, yet miraculously with barely three hundred yards left to run, he rallied under the powerful jockeyship of Lord Manners. Although running virtually on three legs, gallant little SEAMAN gradually drew level with CYRUS. Amazed spectators gaped in wonder as the inexperienced amateur rode the race of his life to get the better of the mighty Tommy Beasley in the very last strides. SEAMAN, the cast-off, beat CYRUS a head and though few among the crowds won money from his victory the horse was greeted a hero on his painful way to the unsaddling enclosure. Honourably retired to his owner's home, the champion no trainer wanted spent the rest of his days as Lord Manners' hack and the pet of the nobleman's children.

Just how unlucky EAU DE VIE had been in suffering that broken leather was demonstrated the day after the 'National, when Dan Thirlwell steered the mare to a fifteen length win in the Sefton Steeplechase.

THE GRAND NATIONAL HANDICAP STEEPLECHASE
1882

Date: 24th March 1882	Starters: 12	Time: 10 mins 42⅖ secs
1st **SEAMAN**	6.11–6 *(Lord Manners)*	**Lord Manners**
2nd **CYRUS**	5.10–9 *(Mr J Gubbins)*	**Mr T Beasley**
3rd **ZOEDONE**	5.10–0 *(Mr Clayton)*	**Capt A J Smith**

Also Ran:

THE LIBERATOR 13.12–7 (Mr W H Moore) **J Adams** *Fell*; *THE SCOT 6.11–8* (Mr J B Leigh) **J Jewitt** *Fell*; *WILD MONARCH aged.10–12* (Mr C Cunningham) **H Andrews** *Fell* [destroyed]; *EAU DE VIE 7.10–8* (Duke of Hamilton) **Mr D Thirlwell** *Ran-out*; *MONTAUBAN 8.10–7* (Mr J G Baird-Hay) **G Waddington** *Pulled-up*; *MOHICAN 5.10–7* (Mr Bunbury) **Mr H Beasley** *Fell*; *FAY aged.10–7* (Capt J Machell) **Mr E P Wilson** *Fell*; *IGNITION 10.10–5* (Mr H Rymill) **W Sensier** *Refused*; *BLACK PRINCE 7.10–0* (Mr P George) **F Wynne** *Fell*

The Betting: *100/30 Mohican; 4/1 The Scot; 9/2 Cyrus; 10/1 Seaman; 100/7 Fay; 15/1 Eau de Vie; 100/6 Montauban & Wild Monarch; 20/1 The Liberator; 25/1 Zoedone; 50/1 Ignition*

Distances: *A head; a bad third*

Winner Trained By: *Captain James Machell*

Value to Winning Owner: *£1,000*

1883

Through the guidance and supervision of the National Hunt Committee, steeplechasing prospered in a way undreamt of just a decade earlier. There had, however, been a drastic decline in the numbers bidding for honours in the sport's premier event, so a subcommittee was instructed to investigate. Their findings made interesting reading, the principal point emerging that Aintree's fences had suffered in recent years a reduction in size which led many owners to believe that the 'National was now more a test of extended galloping than jumping. With large areas of the course still not railed in, the problems of crowds trespassing between the obstacles during the race also gave cause for concern. An attempt was made in 1883 to remedy at least some of the faults, with the fences restored to proportions worthy of the prestige of the race. For this year, though, just ten horses paraded with their riders for the greatest steeplechase in the calendar. Tommy Beasley was on the favourite, ZITELLA, his brother Harry opting for stable-mate MOHICAN. Arthur Coventry partnered JOLLY SIR JOHN, while Dan Thirlwell took the mount on EAU DE VIE again in the colours of the Duke of Hamilton. Ted Wilson teamed up with MONTAUBAN and making his Aintree debut a certain Tom Widger was entrusted with DOWNPATRICK. Supported by a large following from his native Waterford, young Widger was the first of his family to aspire to 'National honours. He was to be by no means the last. Another having a first tilt at Liverpool was Count Charles Kinsky. A well-known huntsman, Kinsky was born in 1858 into an ancient Bohemian family renowned for their love of horses. Master of the Horse at the Kinsky household was Englishman Rowland Reynolds, who, taking the young Charles under his wing, proceeded to teach the boy everything he knew about horsemanship, the English language and a race called the Grand National. The Count's future deeds in the saddle were ample proof that Reynolds taught well. While serving in the army, the Count accompanied the Empress of Austria to England and to his intense delight, three years later in 1881 was appointed to his country's London Embassy. In that same year he saw for the first time the horse destined to fulfil his dreams, though it was a couple of years later that having just won a large sum of money from the victory of CORRIE ROY in the Cesarewitch, the sporting diplomat bought ZOEDONE for £800, with the promise of a further £200 if she won the big Aintree 'chase. She was sent to be trained by W H P Jenkins at Upton.

Prince Kinsky on his ZOEDONE brought an international flavour to the race as the first foreigner to ride the winner

The French-bred CORTOLVIN, owned by Lord Rossmore, must have raised some angry comments from the Duke of Hamilton, for the resemblance to his 1867 'National winner was in name only.

MONTAUBAN led reluctantly over the first. With a fine jump at Becher's, the favourite ZITELLA took them along at a slightly quicker gallop over the Canal Turn and Valentine's and back towards the racecourse. Stretching out over the Water hardly a length behind ZITELLA, ZOEDONE appeared to be totally at home on the heavy going. Moving to the head of affairs approaching the second Becher's, Charles Kinsky had ZOEDONE perfectly balanced, clearing Valentine's well in advance of the tiring ZITELLA. Despite knocking over the second last hurdle, she came past the winning post a comfortable ten lengths clear of BLACK PRINCE, six lengths ahead of MOHICAN.

One of the first to congratulate Kinsky was his close friend and hunting partner Captain 'Bay' Middleton, but a sour note was allegedly expressed by jockey Jimmy Adams: 'What the hell are we coming to?' he said. 'Last year it was a blooming Lord won the 'National; this year it's a furring Count and next year it'll be an old woman most likely.' Charles Kinsky, who had overheard the remark, replied immediately and typically: 'Yes, Jimmy, and I hope this old woman will be yourself.'

THE GRAND NATIONAL HANDICAP STEEPLECHASE
1883

Of 1,000 guineas; entrance 25 sovs., for starters. The second to receive 100 sovs., from the plate

Date: 30th March 1883	Starters: 10	Time: 11 mins 39 secs
1st **ZOEDONE**	**6.11−0** *(Count C Kinsky)*	**Count C Kinsky**
2nd **BLACK PRINCE**	**8.10−4** *(Mr P George)*	**D Canavan**
3rd **MOHICAN**	**6.12−1** *(Major Bunbury)*	**Mr H Beasley**
4th **DOWNPATRICK**	**9.10−7** *(Col J Lloyd)*	**Mr T Widger**
5th **ZITELLA**	**5.11−2** *(Mr J Gubbins)*	**Mr T Beasley**
6th **MONTAUBAN**	**9.10−9** *(Lord Yarborough)*	**Mr E P Wilson**
7th **EAU DE VIE**	**aged.11−10** *(Duke of Hamilton)*	**Mr D Thirlwell**

Also Ran:

ATHLACCA 8.11−4 (Mr T McDougal) **J Adams** *Pulled-up*; *CORTOLVIN 6.10−5* (Lord Rossmore) **Barker** *Fell*; *JOLLY SIR JOHN 6.10−5* (Mr Dane) **Mr A Coventry** *Fell*

The Betting: *3/1 Zitella; 9/2 Eau de Vie; 100/12 Jolly Sir John & Montauban; 9/1 Mohican & Athlacca; 100/7 Zoedone & Downpatrick; 33/1 Cortolvin & Black Prince*

Distances: *Ten lengths; six lengths*

Winner Trained By: *W Jenkins, Upton*

Value to Winning Owner: *£925*

1884

Without question, the most interesting entry for this year's race was THE SCOT, under the nomination of HRH The Prince of Wales. This royal patronage brought with it the respectability cross-country racing had been crying out for. Prince Edward officially entered the ranks of 'chasing owners in 1880, when LEONIDAS won for him the Military Hunt Steeplechase at Aldershot. He had, however, had a half-share in both CONGRESS and JACKAL in the late eighteen-seventies, although few knew of his involvement and the horses carried the colours of the registered owner, Lord Marcus Beresford. The choice of THE SCOT as a royal runner was an excellent one, for the blue-blooded gelding was the son of Derby winner BLAIR ATHOL. He had also proved he could jump the course and in a surge of patriotic fervour, the public made THE SCOT 6/1 favourite of the fifteen runners. There was a further royal connection in the shape of VOLUPTUARY, who had been bred by Queen Victoria at Hampton Court. As the property of Lord Rosebery, the son of CREMORNE raced on the flat, succeeding in Chester's Dee Stakes and finishing down the course in the 1881 Epsom Derby. VOLUPTUARY then passed into the ownership of Mr H F Boyd. The popular and talented amateur, Ted Wilson, and his brother William were entrusted with the task of preparing the horse for a jumping career but the only public experience in this field at the time of his Aintree engagement was limited to two humble hurdle events. There was support in the market from some source for VOLUPTUARY, however, since the 10/1 hardly seemed generous considering this introduction to the big fences was the sternest jumping test of all and the going was heavy.

VOLUPTUARY, the winner who brought the house down every night

A mightier roar than usual signalled the start, for THE SCOT struck the front immediately. The royal favourite was followed into heavy mist by CYRUS, REGAL, CORTOLVIN, FRIGATE, BLACK PRINCE and SATELLITE. Upon re-entering the racecourse the familiar colours of Captain Machell were seen to be to the fore, carried by REGAL, with THE SCOT going well just behind him. Turning back into the country, CORTOLVIN took up the running again with THE SCOT still fencing superbly and ideally placed. REGAL broke down and the Canal Turn saw the downfall of Prince Edward's competitor. Coming to the second last, ZOEDONE gave Count Kinsky a moment of hope but FRIGATE, VOLUPTUARY and ROQUEFORT all ran on through the mud. VOLUPTUARY flew the last perfectly, joining issue with FRIGATE on the flat and producing a better turn of foot to run out a four length winner at the post. ROQUEFORT came in third, with ZOEDONE a gallant fourth.

Almost at the moment the winner passed the post, a telegram was delivered to the Prince of Wales informing him of the sudden death of his brother, the Duke of Albany, and this sad news cast a shadow over the rest of the day.

VOLUPTUARY found his future lay far from the perils of the racecourse though the applause he won in the 'National would become a familiar sound to him. Sold to the well-known actor, Leonard Boyne, the horse became a member of the cast in *The Prodigal Daughter*, carrying his new owner over a stage Water Jump night after night at the Drury Lane Theatre.

THE GRAND NATIONAL HANDICAP STEEPLECHASE
1884

Of 1,000 guineas; by subscription of 15 sovs., 10 forfeit or 5 sov., if declared; with 545 added. The second to receive 100 sovs

Date: 28th March 1884	Starters: 15	Time: 10 mins 5 secs
1st **VOLUPTUARY**	**6.10–5** *(Mr H F Boyd)*	**Mr E P Wilson**
2nd **FRIGATE**	**6.11–3** *(Mr M A Maher)*	**Mr H Beasley**
3rd **ROQUEFORT**	**5.10–5** *(Capt Fisher)*	**J Childs**
4th **CYRUS**	**7.12–2** *(Mr J B Leigh)*	**J Jewitt**
5th **ZOEDONE**	**7.12–2** *(Count C Kinsky)*	**Count C Kinsky**
6th **BLACK PRINCE**	**9.10–11** *(Mr P George)*	**Mr T Widger**

Also Ran:
ZITELLA 6.12–0 (Mr J Gubbins) **Mr T Beasley** *Failed to finish*; *REGAL 13.11–6* (Capt J Machell) **W Hunt** *Broke down – Pulled-up*; *THE SCOT 8.11–3* (HRH The Prince of Wales) **J Jones** *Fell*; *ALBERT CECIL 6.11–2* (Mr R Sheriffe) **Mr R Sheriffe** *Failed to finish*; *IDEA 6.10–12* (Mr Oeschlaeger) **Mr W H Moore** *Failed to finish*; *SATELLITE 5.10–5* (Mr E W Tritton) **Mr J Beasley** *Failed to finish*; *TOM JONES 7.10–4* (Sir W Eden) **Capt Lee-Barber** *Fell*; *CORTOLVIN 7.10–0* (Lord Rossmore) **Capt Smith** *Fell*; *TERRIER 4.10–0* (Duke of Hamilton) **Mr D Thirlwell** *Fell*

The Betting: *6/1 The Scot; 100/12 Cortolvin & Satellite; 9/1 Cyrus; 10/1 Frigate, Voluptuary & Roquefort; 100/7 Zoedone; 100/6 Idea; 20/1 Zitella; 25/1 Tom Jones & Terrier; 50/1 Regal, Black Prince & Albert Cecil*

Distances: *Four lengths; six lengths; four lengths*

Winner Trained By: *William & Ted Wilson, Warwickshire*

Value to Winning Owner: *£1,035*

1885

This was the year when a time for celebration was turned into a day of shame. With the race due to be run for the first time over a course completely laid to turf, the executive was justly proud that Aintree and the 'National were entering into a new and exciting and respectable era. But there can never be a time for complacency when a sport generates large amounts of money. The innocent victim was the brave and noble mare, ZOEDONE, whose crime in the twisted minds of some miscreants was to be coupled in many spring doubles with the Lincoln Handicap winner BENDIGO. With the risks of an enormous amount of money being taken from the ring, ZOEDONE had to be stopped. And stopped she was, in the cruellest way. Shortly before leaving the paddock, the mare was poisoned, an evil act which was only noticed when Count Kinsky prepared to mount her. A spot of blood appeared on the Count's white sleeve where the mare had rubbed her muzzle and upon examination, a tiny puncture was found near ZOEDONE's nostril. Rather than withdraw her from the race, the sporting gentleman preferred to stay loyal to those who had backed his mount, and give them a run for their money.

ROQUEFORT, the favourite of nineteen, had been purchased by Mr Cooper on the advice of Ted Wilson and in the absence of VOLUPTUARY, on theatrical duty, Mr Wilson took the mount. Far from the easiest of rides, ROQUEFORT was bred by John Gretton in 1879 and trained by Arthur Yates at Bishops Sutton, although the licence for the yard was held by John Swatton. With favourable good ground this time, the connections had every reason to hope for the best.

Among the 50/1 outsiders was a six-year-old gelding named GAMECOCK, meriting hardly a second glance, but starting a 'National trail which would place him among the elite.

It still being the custom for a preliminary hurdle to be jumped on the way to the start, Count Kinsky had the chance to confirm his worst fears. ZOEDONE had moved onto the racecourse in a most listless manner and now fell quite heavily. Although badly shaken, the Count remounted and ZOEDONE struggled in her usual game fashion to follow BLACK PRINCE, the leader going into the first. ROQUEFORT and DOG FOX jumped up among the leading group but to the dismay of all ZOEDONE was seen to be staggering about at the rear like a drunkard. DOWNPATRICK jumped to the front with a super leap at Valentine's, and the lead changed yet again at the halfway stage, RED HUSSAR clearing the Water Jump fractionally in advance of LANG SYNE, FRIGATE, DOWNPATRICK and ROQUEFORT, but the packed stands were hushed to concerned silence when ZOEDONE reached the obstacle. Well to the rear of the others, the mare was still having great difficulty coordinating her rhythm and though she was bravely persevering, gone completely was the sparkle of former days. At the fence before Becher's ZOEDONE fell, lying for many minutes in a highly distressed state until Charles Kinsky was able to summon skilled assistance. Meanwhile DOG FOX headed them around the final bend towards the second last hurdle, after jumping which he was passed by ROQUEFORT, REDPATH and FRIGATE. Striding out well over the last, ROQUEFORT held off Harry Beasley on FRIGATE to win by two lengths. BLACK PRINCE stayed on to be third, in front of REDPATH. As a result of the treachery concerning ZOEDONE, the welcome awaiting the winner was rather subdued. Despite a determined investigation, those responsible for the outrage were never identified. ZOEDONE's racing days were over and this was also Count Kinsky's final appearance in the race. In recognition of his services to racing Kinsky was made an honorary member of the Jockey Club and the French Steeple-chase Society before also being elected to the National Hunt Committee. His world fell apart, however, with the outbreak of the Great War. Kinsky volunteered for service on the Russian Front to avoid having to fight against the British. After service with the cavalry, he returned to his ruined homeland, dying in 1919 a broken man.

THE GRAND NATIONAL HANDICAP STEEPLECHASE

1885

Of 1,000 guineas, by subscription of 15 sovs., each, 10 forfeit or 5 sovs., if declared to run; The second to receive 100 sovs

Date: 27th March 1885	Starters: 19	Time: 10 mins 10 secs
1st **ROQUEFORT**	**6.11–0** *(Mr A Cooper)*	**Mr E P Wilson**
2nd **FRIGATE**	**7.11–10** *(Mr M A Maher)*	**Mr H Beasley**
3rd **BLACK PRINCE**	**10.10–5** *(Capt J Machell)*	**T Skelton**
4th **REDPATH**	**8.10–3** *(Mr Zigomala)*	**Mr A Coventry**
5th **AXMINSTER**	**8.10–7** *(Mr J Rutherford)*	**W Sayers**
6th **ALBERT CECIL**	**7.10–9** *(Mr R Sheriffe)*	**J Childs**
7th **DOG FOX**	**6.10–3** *(Mr C Archer)*	**Capt Lee-Barber**
8th **LIONESS**	**7.11–7** *(Mr Hungerford)*	**Mr G Lambton**
9th **RED HUSSAR**	**7.10–7** *(Capt Armitage)*	**Capt Armitage**

Also Ran:

ZOEDONE 8.11–11 (Count C Kinsky) **Count C Kinsky** Fell; KILWORTH aged.11–6 (Capt E R Owen) **Capt E R Owen** Fell; CANDAHAR 6.10–12 (Mr H B Craig) **W Hunt** Refused; JOLLY SIR JOHN 8.10–12 (Mr Dane) **W Nightingall** Fell; BELMONT 8.10–11 (Mr James Daly) **W Canavan** Pulled-up; LANG SYNE 7.10–8 (Mr H de Windt) **T Hale** Fell; BEN MORE 5.10–7 (Mr H T Barclay) **Mr W H Moore** Fell; HARLEQUIN 10.10–0 (Duke of Hamilton) **D Sensier** Refused; GAMECOCK 6.10–0 (Mr E Jay) **W E Stephens** Fell; DOWNPATRICK 11.10–0 (Col J Lloyd) **Capt W B Morris** Fell

The Betting: *100/30 Roquefort; 5/1 Zoedone; 7/1 Frigate; 10/1 Kilworth; 100/8 Ben More; 100/6 Belmont; 20/1 Redpath, Downpatrick & Albert Cecil; 25/1 Candahar, Dog Fox & Axminster; 33/1 Black Prince; 50/1 Red Hussar, Harlequin, Jolly Sir John & Gamecock*

Distances: *Two lengths; four lengths; two lengths*

Winner Trained By: *Arthur Yates (licence held by John Swatton), at Bishops Sutton*

Value to Winning Owner: *£1,035*

1886

The last seven 'Nationals having seen the success of amateur riders, there seemed every likelihood that the trend would continue with eleven members of the unpaid brigade among the field of twenty-three. CORONET, a five-year-old formerly named PRINCE RUDOLPH II, enjoyed the able assistance of Captain Lee-Barber of the 3rd Dragoon Guards and started favourite. Ted Wilson again took the mount on ROQUEFORT, now top weight with 12 st 3 lbs but widely fancied at 5/1, while Harry Beasley took the pick of the Linde yard TOO GOOD. Tommy Skelton had finished third with BLACK PRINCE in the latest 'National and although always thought of as a somewhat delicate man to be engaged in the hazardous trade of jump jockey, his determination and flair had long been acknowledged. This was the first time his mount, northern hope OLD JOE, had seen Aintree.

Bred by Mr Briscoe in Cumberland from BAREFOOT out of SPOT and trained by George Mulcaster at Burgh-by-Sands, Carlisle, the gelding was kept to such a busy schedule that he won two races on the same day in 1884 at the Whitehaven and West Cumberland Hunt.

With the day clear and bright, a hectic scramble developed on the run to the first fence, ROQUEFORT reaching it in front of SINBAD, OLD JOE, FRIGATE, TOO GOOD and THE BADGER. At the third GAMECOCK took a clear lead which he maintained over Becher's. LADY TEMPEST took up the running going to Valentine's, but straightening up for the run to the Water CORONET pulled his way to the front. The favourite began the second circuit looking set to justify the odds. ROQUEFORT went in the

OLD JOE with trainer George Mulcaster and prominent amateur jockey Capt. "Wenty" Hope-Johnstone (not on board for the 'National). Owner Mr Douglas is facing us

country and CORONET cleared Becher's from OLD JOE, THE BADGER, SAVOYARD and MAGPIE, with Harry Beasley making progress from the rear on TOO GOOD. With the prospect of the market leader coming in the winner, a roar from the stands greeted CORONET as he turned towards the penultimate obstacle. The cheers were premature, however, for the horse was unable to resist the challenge of either OLD JOE or THE BADGER. Quickening in good style, OLD JOE raced away on the flat,

holding off the late run of TOO GOOD by an easy six lengths, with GAMECOCK a further five lengths back in third place.

The overjoyed owner of the winner, Mr A J Douglas displayed his delight in a positive and very generous way by rewarding the trainer with a gift of a thousand pounds and Skelton, the jockey, with the race prize money of £1,380. It can only be assumed that Mr Douglas took a sizeable slice from the ring at attractive odds.

THE GRAND NATIONAL HANDICAP STEEPLECHASE
1886

Of 15 guineas each, 10 forfeit or 5 forfeit to the fund if declared with 1,000 guineas added; The second to receive 150 sovs., and the third 100 sovs., from the stakes

Date: 26th March 1886	Starters: 23	Time: 10 mins 14⅗ secs
1st **OLD JOE**	**7.10–9** *(Mr A J Douglas)*	**T Skelton**
2nd **TOO GOOD**	**7.11–12** *(Count Erdody)*	**Mr H Beasley**
3rd **GAMECOCK**	**7.10–12** *(Mr E Jay)*	**W E Stephens**
4th **MAGPIE**	**7.10–5** *(Mr E Woodland)*	**Mr W Woodland**
5th **THE BADGER**	**9.10–3** *(Baron C de Tuyll)*	**A Nightingall**
6th **CORONET** [formerly PRINCE RUDOLPH II]	**5.10–7** *(Mr J G Muir)*	**Capt Lee-Barber**
7th **CORTOLVIN**	**9.11–7** *(Mr Abington)*	**W Dollery**
8th **LADY TEMPEST**	**6.10–5** *(Mr P M V Saurin)*	**Mr W Beasley**

Also Ran:

ROQUEFORT 7.12–3 (Mr A Cooper) **Mr E P Wilson** *Fell*; FRIGATE 8.11–13 (Mr Broadwood) **J Jones** *Fell*; REDPATH 9.11–7 (Mr P J Zigomala) **Mr G Lambton** *Failed to finish*; JOLLY SIR JOHN 9.11–6 (Mr F Gebhard) **Mr C W Waller** *Fell*; BLACK PRINCE 11.10–12 (Capt J Machell) **W Nightingall** *Brought-down*; BILLET DOUX 6.10–11 (Count Zborowski) **J Behan** *Pulled-up*; THE LIBERATOR 11.10–10 (Mr E Woodland) **Mr S J Woodland** *Fell*; BELMONT 9.10–10 (Mr James Daly) **Westlake** *Fell*; HARRISTOWN 6.10–7 (Mr J Purcell) **Mr J Purcell** *Failed to finish*; FONTENOY 9.10–4 (Mr Iquique) **J Page** *Refused*; SINBAD 5.10–3 (Mr Leopold de Rothschild) **A Hall** *Fell*; SAVOYARD 8.10–3 (Baron W Schroder) **G Kirby** *Fell*; LIMEKILN 6.10–2 (Count Zborowski) **W Brockwell** *Fell*; AMICIA 5.10–0 (Mr H Wood) **Mr F Cotton** *Failed to finish*; CONSCRIPT 5.10–0 (Capt Childe) **H Escott** *Fell*

The Betting: *3/1 Coronet; 5/1 Roquefort; 7/1 Too Good; 9/1 Frigate; 100/6 Redpath; 22/1 Lady Tempest & Savoyard; 25/1 Sinbad, Amicia, Old Joe & The Badger; 33/1 Belmont; 40/1 Jolly Sir John; 50/1 Gamecock, Black Prince & Cortolvin; 66/1 Harristown; 100/1 Billet Doux & The Liberator; 200/1 Magpie & Fontenoy*

Distances: *Six lengths; five lengths; four lengths*

Winner Trained By: *George Mulcaster, Burgh-by-Sands, Carlisle*

Value to Winning Owner: *£1,380*

1887

That Henry Linde's reputation was as powerful as ever was forcibly demonstrated when he provided the six-year-old SPAHI as favourite for the 1887 renewal. Of unquestionable ability on the flat, and with the assistance of Tommy Beasley, the money poured on him for Aintree. Yet the remarkable thing was, SPAHI had never run in either a steeplechase or hurdle race before coming to Liverpool and the huge gamble appears reckless in the extreme by today's standards. Among those trying again were OLD JOE, SAVOYARD, FRIGATE and ROQUEFORT, the latter at 7/1 the second-best backed runner, in spite of still possessing the wilful tendency to run-out during a race. A close scrutiny of the form would have revealed that the locally-owned GAMECOCK had finished well on two occasions behind ROQUEFORT and at 20/1 represented good value. Purchased as a three-year-old for £150, GAMECOCK matured into a compact, muscular jumper with boundless stamina, whose one fault was the frightening closeness to the ground with which he carried his head when galloping. Officially the property of Mr E Jay, the gelding in fact belonged to Liverpool man Mr Thornewill who, adopting the practice of many riders, hid his true identity behind an assumed name. Prepared for the big race by Jimmy Gordon near Tarporley, GAMECOCK came through a vigorous schedule with flying colours, his daily four mile gallops at nearby Oulton Park bringing him to peak fitness. Merseysiders took the horse to their hearts and most of the money riding on him came from the pockets of local residents.

SAVOYARD hit the front at a terrific pace, but GAMECOCK landed in the lead over the first and was still showing the way over the third when the all-too-familiar groan announced the departure of the favourite SPAHI, his much heralded brilliance unable to carry him over an Aintree ditch. Stretching out over the Water, outsider SPECTRUM now led from MAGPIE, JOHNNY LONGTAIL, SAVOYARD, CHANCELLOR, OLD JOE and GAMECOCK and as they made their way back into the country, the race was as wide open as at the start. Over Becher's the second time, SAVOYARD and CHANCELLOR disputed leadership, but turning for home Ted Wilson produced a spirited run from ROQUEFORT and from the stands it appeared that the former winner had secured first run on his opponents. ROQUEFORT, however, was jibbing to his right in a roguish manner and as SAVOYARD ranged alongside, swerved through the rails giving Wilson a nasty tumble. SAVOYARD led into the last, being joined by GAMECOCK as they rose to it, and was first past the post by three lengths, JOHNNY LONGTAIL staying on to be a distant third.

Locals among the crowd welcomed GAMECOCK into the winner's enclosure with an Irish-style reception and celebrations continued into the early hours in Liverpool's hotels and hostelries. Within twenty-four hours, GAMECOCK lived up to his name in the truest fashion by winning the Champion Steeplechase under 12 st 12 lbs.

GAMECOCK – a real Aintree "old faithful"

THE GRAND NATIONAL HANDICAP STEEPLECHASE
1887

Of 1,000 sovs., added to a sweepstake of 15 guineas each, 10 forfeit or 5 guineas to the fund, if declared by 1st February. The second to receive 150 sovs., and the third 100 sovs., from the stakes

Date: 25th March 1887	Starters: 16	Time: 10 mins 10⅕ secs
1st **GAMECOCK**	8.10–12 *(Mr E Jay)*	**W Daniels**
2nd **SAVOYARD**	9.10–13 *(Baron W Schroder)*	**T Skelton**
3rd **JOHNNY LONGTAIL**	9.10–6 *(Lord Wolverton)*	**J Childs**
4th **CHANCELLOR**	7.10–12 *(Capt Foster)*	**Mr W H Moore**
5th **CHANCERY**	9.11–6 *(Mr A L Popham)*	**W Dollery**
6th **TOO GOOD**	8.11–10 *(Count Erdody)*	**Mr H Beasley**

Also Ran:

MAGPIE 8.10–9 (Mr E Woodland) **Mr W Woodland** *Broke-down near winning post*; *ROQUEFORT 8.12–8* (Mr J Lee) **Mr E P Wilson** *Fell*; *OLD JOE 8.11–10* (Mr A J Douglas) **Mr C J Cunningham** *Fell*; *FRIGATE 9.11–5* (Mr F E Lawrence) **Mr F E Lawrence** *Pulled-up*; *BELLONA 5.10–10* (Mr George Lambton) **Mr G Lambton** *Fell*; *SPECTRUM 6.10–10* (Sir G Chetwynd) **R Grimes** *Fell*; *SPAHI 6.10–10* (Mr J Gubbins) **Mr T Beasley** *Fell*; *BALLOT BOX 8.10–5* (Mr P Nickalls) **Capt E R Owen** *Fell*; *SINBAD 6.10–3* (Mr J Percival) **W Nightingall** *Brought-down*; *THE HUNTER aged.10–0* (Lord Cholmondeley) **Mr W Beasley** *Fell*.

The Betting: *9/2 Spahi; 7/1 Roquefort; 100/14 Savoyard; 10/1 Magpie; 100/9 Frigate; 100/8 Old Joe & Bellona; 100/7 Too Good; 20/1 Chancellor, Sinbad & Gamecock; 33/1 Spectrum; 40/1 Ballot Box & Johnny Longtail; 100/1 The Hunter & Chancery.*

Distances: *Three lengths; a bad third*

Winner Trained By: *James Gordon, near Tarporley, Cheshire*

Value to Winning Owner: *£1,206–15 shillings*

1888

A major alteration was made to the course in time for the 'National which saw the Royal colours of the Prince of Wales appearing for the second time. Officially described as 'shortening the distance', a loop was introduced to bring the runners across the inside of the flat race course from a point just inside the Anchor crossing to a position adjacent to the distance Chair, so that instead of continuing around the outer extremity of the course after coming back from the country, a gentle left-hand curve would bring competitors on to the final two obstacles. In terms of ground saved, the distance was barely twenty-five yards, but to counter any misguided thoughts that the event was now easier, two fences replaced the flights of hurdles, before the run-in and although smaller than those in the country, they presented a far more severe finale at the end of such a demanding contest.

Undeterred by the failure of his star SPAHI in last year's race, Henry Linde insisted on the chestnut running again, though this time the mount of Terry Kavanagh was well down the betting list at 30/1. In contrast the seven-year-old USNA was all the rage for many weeks before the race. USNA was not just SPAHI's stable-mate but represented the same owner, John Gubbins. Unbeaten for three years, USNA was called the 'best 'chaser to come out of Ireland' and the handicapper had no hesitation in allotting him top weight of 12 st 7 lbs. A week before the race a rumour that USNA had suffered an injury resulted in his plummeting to 40/1 in the betting, but his position at the head of the market was restored with the news of a successful trial on the Curragh. GAME-COCK, now owned by Mr E Benzon and trained by Arthur Yates at Bishops Sut-

ton, was ridden by Captain Roddy Owen. Prince Edward's entry MAGIC, the mount of Arthur Hall, aroused little interest, 20/1 being readily available. FRIGATE was back in the ownership of her breeder Mr M A Maher but with the man who had twice steered her into second place, Harry Beasley, doing duty on the favourite, the mount fell to his brother Willie. Two other brothers taking part were William and Arthur Nightingall, the former partnering BALLOT BOX and the latter the second favourite THE BADGER. It was William's preference for BALLOT BOX which enabled the little-known George Mawson to accept the offer to ride outsider PLAYFAIR. A black seven-year-old gelding by RIPPON-DEN out of a half-bred unnamed mare, PLAYFAIR was owned by Mr E W Baird, a subaltern in the 10th Hussars. Trained by Tom Cannon, who rode the Derby winner SHOTOVER in 1882, the horse's record before coming to Aintree was hardly inspiring.

They all cleared the first fence safely, RINGLET touching down first but SPAHI refused the fourth. Spectators at Becher's were treated to a spectacular sight when BALLOT BOX produced a remarkable leap to land in the lead. ALADDIN and JOHNNY LONGTAIL gained a slight advantage as they neared the racecourse and for the first time USNA could be seen making a forward move, going second at the Water. Two fences before Becher's, Mawson found himself in trouble when PLAYFAIR slipped while taking off, straddling the fence but recovering in splendid fashion. The jockey, however, was thrown forward and for some distance was clinging precariously to his mount's neck. In true sporting spirit, Arthur Nightingall riding THE BADGER alongside, reached out and pushed Mawson back into the saddle.

Meanwhile USNA had moved smoothly into the lead, clearing Becher's with room to spare and looking all over a winner. FRIGATE moved up as they approached the Canal Turn, creating the unusual sight of two brothers riding at the head of the 'National field with just over a mile to go. They jumped on the turn almost together, but USNA dislocated his shoulder on landing and swerving to the right, ran off the course. Worse still, he carried FRIGATE out with him nearly to the point of shoving the mare into the Canal. Only the fine horse-manship of Willie Beasley got FRIGATE back into the race, though there was a tremendous amount of ground to make up. She got all the way back to new leader PLAYFAIR, but after landing first on the flat, she was unable to withstand his challenge and lost by ten lengths. Second again. Four lengths behind came BALLOT BOX. The 'National hero only ran once again and but for the helping hand of Arthur Nightingall the result in 1888 may well have been a more popular one.

THE GRAND NATIONAL HANDICAP STEEPLECHASE

1888

Of 15 guineas each, 10 forfeit or 5 forfeit to the fund if declared, with 1,000 sovs., added. The second to receive 150 sovs., and the third 100 sovs., out of the stakes

Date: 23rd March 1888	Starters: 20	Time: 10 mins 12 secs
1st **PLAYFAIR**	7.10–7 *(Mr E W Baird)*	**G Mawson**
2nd **FRIGATE**	10.11–2 *(Mr M A Maher)*	**Mr W Beasley**
3rd **BALLOT BOX**	9.12–4 *(Mr P Nickalls)*	**W Nightingall**
4th **RINGLET**	7.11–11 *(Lord Rodney)*	**T Skelton**
5th **ALADDIN**	6.11–0 *(Mr Leopold de Rothschild)*	**Mr C W Waller**
6th **JEANIE**	5.10–6 *(Mr Abington)*	**A H Barker**
7th **GAMECOCK**	9.12–4 *(Mr E Benzon)*	**Capt E R Owen**
8th **MAGIC**	aged.10–12 *(HRH The Prince of Wales)*	**A Hall**
9th **THE BADGER**	11.11–1 *(Baron C de Tuyll)*	**A Nightingall**

Also Ran:

USNA 7.12–7 (Mr J Gubbins) **Mr H Beasley** *Dislocated his shoulder & Ran-out*; *SAVOYARD 10.12–4* (Baron W Schroder) **Mr G Lambton** *Fell*; *JOHNNY LONGTAIL 10.12–0* (Mr A Yates) **W Dollery** *Failed to finish*; *BELLONA 6.11–12* (Mr T B Miller) **Mr C J Cunningham** *Fell*; *SPAHI 7.11–9* (Mr J Gubbins) **T Kavanagh** *Refused*; *OLD JOE 9.11–9* (Mr A J Douglas) **W Daniels** *Failed to finish*; *CHANCELLOR 8.11–5* (Mr Wardour) **Mr W H Moore** *Failed to finish*; *KINFAUNS 7.10–10* (Mr T Brinckman) **J Page** *Refused*; *THE FAWN 6.10–6* (Lord Cholmondeley) **Mr E P Wilson** *Fell*; *TRAP 8.10–6* (Mr Churton) **G Lowe** *Fell*; *CORK 7.10–6* (Doctor Adrian) **Mr W Woodland** *Fell*

The Betting: *15/2 Usna & Chancellor; 10/1 The Badger; 100/9 Frigate & Ringlet; 18/1 Bellona, Old Joe & The Fawn; 20/1 Gamecock, Trap & Magic; 25/1 Ballot Box & Savoyard; 30/1 Spahi; 33/1 Aladdin; 40/1 Johnny Longtail & Playfair; 100/1 Kinfauns & Cork; 200/1 Jeanie.*

Distances: *Ten lengths; four lengths; one length*

Winner Trained By: *Tom Cannon, Danebury*

Value to Winning Owner: *£1,175–5 shillings*

1889

Responding well to the increased added money of 1,500 sovereigns, owners looked to this year's 'National with greater enthusiasm and from sixty-five original subscribers, the twenty which faced the starter comprised some of the finest 'chasers in the land. Heading the handicap was BALLOT BOX. ROQUEFORT became the chosen fancy of the majority at 6/1, despite the gelding's infamous waywardness. The Prince of Wales ran MAGIC again and as a second string his recent purchase HETTIE. His theatrical career apparently at an end, the 1884 winner VOLUPTUARY found himself back in harness and GAMECOCK was another former winner trying to regain the spotlight. Of the newcomers the greatest interest was shown in the German-bred mare ET CETERA, owned by Hungarian Count Nicholas Esterhazy. WHY NOT was the mount of daredevil rider Charlie Cunningham and the Beasley brothers were back in force, Harry on BATTLE ROYAL, Willie with THE FAWN and the incomparable Tom astride everybody's favourite, FRIGATE.

The deeds of Mr Maher's bay mare had already become legendary, without her yet achieving the highest honour. But FRIGATE had captured the hearts of the Liverpool crowds. By GUNBOAT out of FAIR MAID OF KENT, her earlier pedigree read like a who's who of turf greats. GLADIATEUR, STOCKWELL and TOUCHSTONE all figured prominently in FRIGATE's ancestral lineage, yet she never raced on the level, being allowed to mature until the age of four when making her hunting debut. In FRIGATE's second outing, she won the 1883 Conyngham Cup over four miles at Punchestown, and it quickly became obvious that she was at her best when partnered by a rider bearing the surname Beasley. After two second places in Aintree's severest test, Mr Maher sold her and she achieved little in her new colours. In 1887, Willie Beasley watched her compete at Manchester in the Lancashire 'Chase and although she fell, he persuaded Mr Maher to buy her back. She immediately repaid the outlay by winning the Manchester Handicap 'Chase in the hands of none other than Willie Beasley. During the mare's preparation for Aintree, the Curragh gallops of Henry Linde were often used, leading to a general assumption that FRIGATE was trained by Linde. This was not the case, for she was in the care of her owner at his establishment in Ballinkeele, Enniscorthy, County Wexford.

After two false starts they were on their way. Closely pursued by WHY NOT, HETTIE, FRIGATE, and KILWORTH, VOLUPTUARY cleared the first fence at a fast pace.

Willie Beasley, seventh behind his brother Tommy and never a winner of the race

At the open ditch before the Water GAME-COCK held a slight advantage from WHY NOT, with THE FAWN, BATTLE ROYAL and M.P. Back out in the country THE FAWN and WHY NOT engaged in a duel, first one then the other showing in front, until turning into Valentine's the rest of the field began to close up on the two leaders. ROQUEFORT moved into third place, which was the first time the favourite had been seen with a chance, but he fell at the final ditch. WHY NOT dashed past the tiring M.P. at the penultimate fence, but on the approach to the last, FRIGATE was making rapid head-way. In a determined challenge Tommy Beasley, quietly making steady progress all the way down the Canal side, produced the mare at precisely the right moment, landing on the flat just ahead of WHY NOT. There was to be no denying FRIGATE this time and sticking to her task bravely, the mare held on for a one length victory. As FRIGATE was led back to the winner's enclosure, Aintree resounded to tumultuous cheers of appreciation for a truly great mare, whose honest persistence in the toughest race of all had finally paid off at the sixth attempt.

THE GRAND NATIONAL HANDICAP STEEPLECHASE
1889

Of 1,500 sovs., by subscription of 15 guineas each, 10 forfeit or 5 only if declared; with £791–5–0 added. The second to receive 150 sovs., and the third 100 sovs., out of the stakes

Date: 29th March 1889	Starters: 20	Time: 10 mins 1⅕ secs
1st **FRIGATE**	11.11–4 *(Mr M A Maher)*	**Mr T Beasley**
2nd **WHY NOT**	8.11–5 *(Mr D Jardine)*	**Mr C J Cunningham**
3rd **M.P.**	8.10–9 *(Mr J Rutherford)*	**A Nightingall**
4th **BELLONA**	7.11–2 *(Mr Abington)*	**Mr C W Waller**
5th **MAGIC**	aged.10–9 *(HRH The Prince of Wales)*	**J Jones**
6th **THE SIKH**	6.10–4 *(Lord Dudley)*	**Mr D Thirlwell**
7th **THE FAWN**	7.10–10 *(Lord Cholmondeley)*	**Mr W Beasley**
8th **RINGLET**	8.11–12 *(Mr Noel Fenwick)*	**J Walsh**
9th **BATTLE ROYAL**	5.10–8 *(Mr W Fulton)*	**Mr H Beasley**
10th **GAMECOCK**	10.11–12 *(Mr W Strong)*	**W Dollery**

Also Ran:

BALLOT BOX 10.12–7 (Mr P Nickalls) **W Nightingall** *Fell*; *ROQUEFORT 10.12–0* (Mr Abington) **Mr E P Wilson** *Fell*; *SAVOYARD 11.11–11* (Baron W Schroder) **Mr G Lambton** *Brought-down*; *VOLUPTUARY 11.11–3* (Mr H F Boyd) **T Skelton** *Fell*; *KILWORTH aged.10–13* (Lord Dudley) **Capt E R Owen** *Refused*; *ET CETERA 5.10–13* (Count N Esterhazy) **G Morris** *Fell*; *GLENTHORPE 5.10–10* (Mr O H Jones) **Mr W H Moore** *Fell*; *MERRY MAIDEN 7.10–7* (Capt Childe) **Capt Lee-Barber** *Fell*; *HETTIE 6.10–5* (HRH The Prince of Wales) **A Hall** *Fell*; *GREAT PAUL 7.10–0* (Mr B W J Alexander) **W Ellis** *Pulled-up*

The Betting: *6/1 Roquefort; 8/1 Frigate & Et Cetera; 10/1 The Sikh; 11/1 Why Not; 100/8 Glenthorpe; 100/6 Voluptuary; 20/1 M.P., Ballot Box, Savoyard & Bellona; 25/1 The Fawn, Battle Royal & Magic; 33/1 Gamecock; 40/1 Kilworth; 66/1 Ringlet, Merry Maiden & Hettie; 200/1 Great Paul.*

Distances: *One length; a bad third*

Winner Trained By: *Mr M A Maher, Ballinkeele, County Wexford*

Value to Winning Owner: *£1,234–5 shillings*

1890

FRIGATE's seventh appearance in the race brightened an otherwise rather sub-standard field of sixteen, but even her most fervent admirers wondered if she could be expected to win under 12 st 7 lbs at twelve years of age. Both of last year's runners-up, WHY NOT and M.P., received their share of support, as did the in-form BELLONA, but at the 'Off' it was newcomer ILEX who carried most punters' money.

The man responsible for discovering ILEX was jockey Arthur Nightingall, although his first impression of the horse had been far from favourable. Engaged to partner the then four-year-old in a selling Hunters' 'Chase at Leicester, he was confronted with a shaggy, rotund chestnut. But a display of bold jumping and a useful turn of finishing speed convinced him that ILEX's appearance was deceptive. Nightingall wasted little time in tipping off George Masterman, an owner he regularly rode for and one with a penchant for a tilt at the ring. In due course ILEX became the property of Masterman and was

ILEX, winning favourite and the first of Arthur Nightingall's three winners

sent to John Nightingall, the jockey's father, at Epsom. When ILEX was leniently treated with just 10 st 5 lbs, the owner immediately set about backing the horse heavily and never a man to conceal his confidence, he informed the racing world that barring accidents, ILEX was an absolute certainty for the Liverpool. On the strength of this tip, the public's money poured on the six-year-old, making him a 4/1 clear favourite.

GAMECOCK took a slight lead over the first, from M.P., ILEX and WHY NOT, with VOLUPTUARY and BACCY close up on the outside of the course. At the fourth WHY NOT came down, to be quickly remounted by Charlie Cunningham but way off the pace. Coming back to the racecourse M.P.

and BRACEBOROUGH disputed the lead, some eight lengths ahead of ILEX, with six lengths further back VOLUPTUARY, FIREBALL and PAN the best-placed of the rest. Back in the country the leading pair were followed by VOLUPTUARY, EMPEROR, PAN, and FETICHE, but ILEX was going far and away the best of any. Striking the front in effortless fashion at Valentine's, the favourite strode into a three length lead. When VOLUPTUARY ruined his chance at the last open ditch, ILEX and Arthur Nightingall won as they liked by twelve lengths. Great were the celebrations. The rank outsider PAN struggled into second berth a distance ahead of a weary M.P. BRUNSWICK was fourth.

THE GRAND NATIONAL HANDICAP STEEPLECHASE
1890

Of 2,000 sovs., (including a trophy value 100 sovs.) by subscription of 20 sovs. each, 15 forfeit or 5 only if declared, with 1,215 sovs. added; the second to receive 200 sovs. and the third 100 sovs. from the stakes

Date: 28th March 1890	Starters: 16	Time: 10 mins 41⅘ secs
1st **ILEX**	6.10−5 *(Mr G Masterman)*	**A Nightingall**
2nd **PAN**	7.10−5 *(Mr E Woodland)*	**W Halsey**
3rd **M.P.**	9.11−5 *(Mr J Rutherford)*	**Mr W H Moore**
4th **BRUNSWICK**	6.10−4 *(Mr Lancashire)*	**G Mawson**
5th **WHY NOT**	9.12−5 *(Mr D J Jardine)*	**Mr C J Cunningham** [remounted]
6th **EMPEROR**	5.11−1 *(Capt Machell)*	**Mr D Thirlwell** [remounted]

Also Ran:
FRIGATE 12.12–7 (Mr M A Maher) **Mr T Beasley** *Fell*; *GAMECOCK 11.12–6* (Mr Swan) **W Dollery** *Fell*; *BATTLE ROYAL 6.11–13* (Mr Fulton) **Mr Wildman** *Fell*; *BELLONA 8.11–9* (Mr Abington) **A H Barker** *Fell*; *VOLUPTUARY 12.11–7* (Mr H F Boyd) **T Skelton** *Fell*; *BRACEBOROUGH 7.10–13* (Mr F E Lawrence) **Mr F E Lawrence** *Fell*; *FETICHE aged.10–12* (M M Ephrussi) **V Baker** *Fell*; *HETTIE 7.10–11* (HRH The Prince of Wales) **Mr E P Wilson** *Fell*; *BACCY 7.10–8* (Mr E Woodland) **Mr W Woodland** *Fell*; *FIREBALL aged.10–4* (Mr H Holmes) **D Corner** *Fell*

The Betting: *4/1 Ilex; 11/2 Bellona; 8/1 M.P.; 100/9 Why Not; 10/1 Voluptuary; 100/8 Battle Royal; 100/7 Frigate; 100/6 Emperor; 20/1 Gamecock; 25/1 Fetiche & Hettie; 100/1 Baccy, Brunswick, Braceborough, Fireball & Pan.*

Distances: *Twelve lengths; a bad third*

Winner Trained By: *John Nightingall, Epsom*

Value to Winning Owner: *£1,680*

1891

There could be no grounds for complaint regarding the quality of this year's contestants, with four past winners of the race and some very bright hopefuls in the field of twenty-one. ILEX, GAMECOCK, ROQUEFORT and VOLUPTUARY were trying for the double, while such newcomers as COME AWAY, CRUISER, CHOUFLEUR and CLOISTER ensured a competitive contest. Only ILEX of the former winners aroused any interest among backers, starting at 5/1 second choice in the market. The Tommy Beasley–Henry Linde combination was felt to have an excellent chance with six-year-old CRUISER, and the Richard Marsh-trained CLOISTER, mount of Captain Roddy Owen, also attracted attention.

However, the Irish gelding COME AWAY, winner of seven of his nine starts so far, started favourite at 4/1. Some doubt existed concerning his sire, the records showing that he was by either UMPIRE or CAMBUSLANG, the dam being LARKAWAY. Now owned by Mr Willie Jameson, COME AWAY had Harry Beasley as both trainer and rider.

Harry Beasley – second of the brothers to win the great race

From a first-class break CLOISTER took command at the third, GRAPE VINE, ROQUEFORT and GAMECOCK following closely. At the Canal Turn, CLOISTER had been joined by ROQUEFORT in front, while GAMECOCK joined issue coming to the Water. ROQUEFORT was the first to crack, then at the Canal Turn GAMECOCK began to run out of steam. At Valentine's, COME AWAY swept into the lead ahead of ILEX, CLOISTER and WHY NOT, the four drawing some lengths clear. A tremendous race developed from this point, COME AWAY remaining at the head of affairs, though pressed all the way by CLOISTER and the fresh-looking WHY NOT. Charlie Cunningham brought the latter with a well-judged challenge at the second last, only to fall at

COME AWAY who overcame not just the course but an objection as well

the fence. In a terrific duel from the last, COME AWAY held on to a slender advantage as Roddy Owen attempted to squeeze CLOISTER through on the rails, but Harry Beasley refused to pull the favourite out. Perfectly within his rights in holding his position, the Irishman raced on to a half-length victory. Roddy Owen's error in going for a gap that didn't widen clearly cost CLOISTER valuable ground and probably the race. ILEX came home a distanced third. Back at the weighing room, a furious Captain Owen threatened to punish Harry Beasley in an old-fashioned manner. CLOISTER's trainer Richard Marsh endeavoured to placate him with the words: 'I don't think I should if I were you. You might be second again, you know.'

Captain Owen then lodged an objection which the stewards over-ruled, much to the relief of the multitudes waiting to be paid out on the favourite. For the fourth time the Grand National had fallen to a Beasley, but COME AWAY, who pulled up lame after the race, was never able to stand up to the demands of 'chasing again.

THE GRAND NATIONAL HANDICAP STEEPLECHASE
1891

Of 2,000 sovs., (including a trophy value 100 sovs.) by subscription of 20 sovs. each, 15 forfeit or 5 if declared, with 1,060 sovs. added; the second to receive 200 sovs. and the third 100 sovs. out of the stakes

Date: 20th March 1891	Starters: 21	Time: 9 mins 58 secs
1st **COME AWAY**	**7.11−12** *(Mr W G Jameson)*	**Mr H Beasley**
2nd **CLOISTER**	**7.11−7** *(Lord Dudley)*	**Capt E R Owen**
3rd **ILEX**	**7.12−3** *(Mr G Masterman)*	**A Nightingall**
4th **ROQUEFORT**	**12.11−13** *(Mr A Yates)*	**F Guy**
5th **CRUISER**	**6.10−8** *(Major Bunbury)*	**Mr T Beasley**
6th **GAMECOCK**	**12.12−4** *(Mr Swan)*	**W Dollery**

Also Ran:
WHY NOT 10.12−4 (Mr C Perkins) **Mr C J Cunningham** *Fell*; *ROMAN OAK 7.12−0* (Mr W Leetham) **H Escott** *Knocked-over*; *VOLUPTUARY 13.11−3* (Mr H F Boyd) **T Wilson** *Pulled-up*; *EMPEROR 6.11−3* (Capt Machell) **W Nightingall** *Pulled-up*; *CHOUFLEUR 5.11−3* (Lord Zetland) **T Kavanagh** *Fell*; *VEIL 6.10−13* (Sir James Miller) **Mr W H Moore** *Fell*; *DOMINION 6.10−13* (Mr W H Russell) **W Thornton** *Pulled-up*; *GRAPE VINE 6.10−7* (Mr G H Archer) **J Hoysted** *Fell*; *JEANIE 8.10−4* (Mr Abington) **A H Barker** *Fell*; *BRUNSWICK 7.10−4* (Mr H W Lancashire) **G Mawson** *Fell*; *FLOWER OF THE FOREST 6.10−4* (Mr Charter) **R Clark** *Fell*; *YOUNG GLASGOW 10.10−3* (Mr W Gordon-Canning) **R Mitchell** *Fell*; *FIREBALL aged.10−0* (Mr H Holmes) **W Halsey** *Pulled-up*; *ADELAIDE 7.10−0* (Mr E H Wolton) **Mr A H Ripley** *Pulled-up*; *NASR-ED-DIN 5.10−0* (Mr F Gullane) **H Brown** *Fell*

The Betting: *4/1 Come Away; 5/1 Ilex; 7/1 Cruiser; 9/1 Grape Vine; 100/9 Roman Oak & Why Not; 20/1 Cloister; 25/1 Choufleur, Emperor & Veil; 40/1 Young Glasgow, Roquefort & Brunswick; 50/1 Flower of the Forest and Nasr-ed-Din; 66/1 Voluptuary, Dominion, Jeanie & Gamecock; 100/1 Fireball; 200/1 Adelaide.*

Distances: *Half a length; a bad third*

Winner Trained By: *H Beasley*

Value to Winning Owner: *£1,680*

* An objection by the second to the winner on the grounds of a jostle was over-ruled *

1892

CLOISTER was bought by Mr Charles Duff and sent to Arthur Yates. Now ridden by amateur Mr J C Dormer, the gelding became the principal choice of gamblers, going off at 11/2 in the twenty-five runner field.

Shropshire-bred FATHER O'FLYNN, having won his two most recent contests, was partnered by last year's unhappy loser, Captain Roddy Owen. The small bay son of RETREAT was now owned by Australian-born Mr Gordon Wilson, a subaltern in the Household Cavalry.

Visibility was severely restricted by a thick fog as the runners paraded before the start. But from an even break, NAP was first away, ahead of JASON, THE MIDSHIP-MITE, ILEX, SOUTHAM, BILLEE TAYLOR and CLOISTER. By the time Becher's was reached, CLOISTER was at the head of affairs, and over Valentine's FATHER O'FLYNN had closed up with THE MIDSHIP-MITE also making a forward move. As they emerged from the fog, those on the race-course side first saw FLYING COLUMN, running on her own and a long way clear of THE MIDSHIPMITE and CLOISTER. The favourite made tremendous progress over the fences in front of the stands, seizing the lead just before the Water and racing on to the second circuit in thrilling style. CLOISTER made the sharp Canal Turn looking all over the winner, only FLYING COLUMN, THE MIDSHIPMITE, ILEX, ARDCARN and FATHER O'FLYNN being near enough to give any cause for concern. THE MIDSHIP-MITE did head CLOISTER after clearing Valentine's, only to fall at the next plain fence, leaving CLOISTER with a seemingly unassailable advantage once more. Back on the racecourse though, the unthinkable

happened. FATHER O'FLYNN appeared full of running and, benefiting from a weight concession of twenty-six pounds from CLOISTER, swept into a lead he increased with every stride. With no need this time to look for a gap, Roddy Owen passed the post twenty lengths in front of CLOISTER with ILEX a further two lengths back in third place.

For Captain Edward Roderic Owen, born at Bettws, Montgomeryshire in 1856 and educated at Eton before entering the East Devonshire Regiment, which later became known as the Lancashire Fusiliers, the win was the realisation of a lifelong ambition. But that his first love was the army was demonstrated three days after his 'National. Journeying to London, Captain Owen volunteered for active service, soon finding himself in such far off places as the Gold Coast, Uganda, India and finally Egypt. During the Dongola Expedition of 1896, he contracted cholera, dying within twelve hours. Far from the Liverpool fog which framed his greatest win, Roddy Owen was laid to rest under a sky of endless blue. The Owen Falls in Kenya are named after him.

The 1892 Grand National was the last in which the trusty ILEX took part, and also the end of the Beasley era. Almost a month to the day after the race, Willie received injuries in the Kildare Hunt Plate at Punchestown from which he never recovered, passing away on 9th May. Tommy, the elder of the brothers, died peacefully at his home in County Wicklow in 1905, while Harry survived until 1939, four years after riding his last race in Baldoyle's Corinthian Plate at 85 years young.

THE GRAND NATIONAL HANDICAP STEEPLECHASE
1892

Of 2,000 sovs., (including a trophy value 100 sovs.) by subscription of 20 sovs. each, 15 forfeit or 5 if declared, with 1,065 sovs., added; the second to receive 200 sovs. and the third 100 sovs. out of the stakes

Date: 25th March 1892		Starters: 25	Time: 9 mins 48⅕ secs
1st **FATHER O'FLYNN**	**7.10–5** *(Mr G C Wilson)*		**Capt E R Owen**
2nd **CLOISTER**	**8.12–3** *(Mr C Duff)*		**Mr J C Dormer**
3rd **ILEX**	**8.12–7** *(Mr G Masterman)*		**A Nightingall**
4th **ARDCARN**	**5.10–10** *(Major Kirkwood)*		**T Kavanagh**
5th **FLYING COLUMN**	**7.10–7** *(Capt Peel)*		**Mr W Beasley**
6th **HOLLINGTON**	**6.10–9** *(Capt A E Whitaker)*		**G Williamson**
7th **CRUISER**	**7.11–7** *(Capt J Byrom)*		**Mr W P Cullen**
8th **RELIANCE**	**10.10–8** *(Mr W Whitehead)*		**Mr J C Cheney**
9th **ULYSSES**	**8.10–10** *(Lord E Talbot)*		**Mr G B Milne**
10th **FAUST**	**7.10–5** *(General Beresford)*		**Mr Lushington**
11th **BAGMAN**	**aged.10–7** *(Capt R W Ethelstone)*		**Mr F Hassall**

Also Ran:

THE MIDSHIPMITE 6.11–6 (Mr H L Powell) **Mr Atkinson** *Fell*; *TENBY 9.11–2* (Mr A M Singer) **C Gregor** *Fell*; *PARTISAN 6.11–1* (Capt A'Court) **A H Barker** *Fell*; *LORD OF THE GLEN 7.11–0* (Mr C W Waller) **Mr C W Waller** *Fell*; *THE PRIMATE 6.10–13* (Mr F Bald) **Capt Bewicke** *Pulled-up*; *MELDRUM 7.10–12* (Mr B Goodall) **J Latham** *Fell*; *JASON aged.10–12* (Mr Abington) **G Mawson** *Fell*; *PAUL PRY 6.10–12* (Mr F E Lawrence) **T Adams** *Pulled-up*; *LORD ARTHUR 9.10–7* (Mr H T Barclay) **Capt Lee-Barber** *Pulled-up*; *NAP 7.10–7* (Mr E Woodland) **Mr H Woodland** *Fell*; *SOUTHAM 13.10–7* (Mr F Swan) **W Dollery** *Fell*; *ROLLESBY 7.10–5* (Mr P Vincent-Turner) **H Brown** *Pulled-up*; *BILLEE TAYLOR aged.10–3* (Major Kearsley) **Mr H Beasley** *Bolted*; *BRUNSWICK 8.10–2* (Mr H W Lancashire) **Mr Levison** *Fell*

The Betting: *11/2 Cloister; 100/14 The Primate; 10/1 Ardcarn; 100/9 Hollington; 100/8 Jason; 100/7 Tenby; 20/1 Ilex & Father O'Flynn; 25/1 Billee Taylor, Lord Arthur, Cruiser & The Midshipmite; 33/1 Lord of the Glen; 40/1 Partisan; 50/1 Ulysses, Southam, Flying Column & Rollesby; 100/1 Brunswick, Faust & Meldrum; 200/1 Reliance, Nap & Paul Pry.*

Distances: *Twenty lengths; two lengths*

Winner Trained By: *G C Wilson*

Value to Winning Owner: *£1,680*

1893

Not even the massive burden of 12 st 7 lbs could deter CLOISTER's army of admirers and they made Mr Duff's gelding a hotter favourite than last year at 9/2. The son of ASCETIC, CLOISTER was bred in Ireland by Lord Fingall from GRACE II, a mare so moderate that the district's postman rode her to deliver the mail. Trained on behalf of Lord Dudley by Richard Marsh, CLOISTER developed into one of the most brilliant staying 'chasers seen in years, and since becoming the property of Charles Duff and being put into the care of trainer Arthur Yates at Bishops Sutton, Hampshire, CLOISTER had improved even further. In the capable hands this year of jockey Bill Dollery, there could be little doubt that he was the one they all had to beat. WHY NOT was considered the biggest threat to the favourite due largely to the fact that he was ridden by Arthur Nightingall, and the only others in the field of fifteen to receive much support were THE MIDSHIPMITE,

Above: Arthur Yates one of the greatest riders never to win the race, but who scored twice as a trainer

Below: CLOISTER – the first horse to carry to victory the maximum weight of 12st 7lbs

AESOP, FATHER O'FLYNN and THE PRIMATE.

The sun shone and the going rode fast on the big day, attracting another huge crowd and they were not to be disappointed. AESOP went into a narrow lead from CLOISTER, THE MIDSHIPMITE, JOAN OF ARC, THE PRIMATE and CHOUFLEUR, the group leaping the first fence practically in line. By the second, CLOISTER was in front. He cleared Valentine's in classic fashion, not merely heading the field but increasing his advantage with every stride. Back on the racecourse, Dollery took a restraining hold on the favourite, allowing the others to move nearer, but even so, had four lengths to spare as he stretched out over the Water. Still the clear leader round the Canal Turn and looking full of running, CLOISTER jumped the second-last twelve lengths clear of AESOP and the cheers which had begun while they were still in the country, rose to a crescendo. Romping up the straight, CLOISTER passed the post forty lengths in front of AESOP, WHY NOT finishing a bad third in front of TIT FOR TAT.

After his runaway win, CLOISTER was acclaimed in the highest terms, being the first horse to succeed carrying 12 st 7 lbs in the fastest time yet recorded. Still only a nine-year-old Mr Duff's gelding prompted great expectations for the years ahead.

THE GRAND NATIONAL HANDICAP STEEPLECHASE
1893

Of 2,500 sovs., by subscription of 25 sovs. each, 15 forfeit or 5 if declared, with 1,510 sovs., added; the second to receive 300 sovs., and the third 200 sovs., out of the stakes

Date: 24th March 1893	Starters: 15	Time: 9 mins 32⅖ secs
1st **CLOISTER**	9.12–7 *(Mr C G Duff)*	**W Dollery**
2nd **AESOP**	7.10–4 *(Capt Michael Hughes)*	**A H Barker**
3rd **WHY NOT**	12.11–12 *(Mr C H Fenwick)*	**A Nightingall**
4th **TIT FOR TAT**	9.10–0 *(Colonel A G Lucas)*	**G Williamson**
5th **THE MIDSHIPMITE**	7.12–3 *(Mr H L Powell)*	**W T Sensier**
6th **FATHER O'FLYNN**	8.11–11 *(Mr G C Wilson)*	**Mr G B Milne**
7th **ROMAN OAK**	9.11–9 *(Sir H de Trafford)*	**Mr W P Cullen**
8th **FAUST**	8.10–6 *(General Beresford)*	**Capt Yardley**

Also Ran:

FIELD MARSHAL 7.11–4 (Mr Eustace Loder) **Capt Crawley** *Pulled-up*; *THE PRIMATE 7.11–3 (Mr F Bald)* **Capt Bewicke** *Fell*; *LADY HELEN 7.11–1 (Capt Dundas)* **R Nightingall** *Fell*; *CHOUFLEUR 7.10–13 (Mr T Toynbee)* **T Kavanagh** *Pulled-up*; *JOAN OF ARC 8.10–4 (Capt H T Fenwick)* **G Morris** *Fell*; *GOLDEN GATE 6.10–2 (Capt E W Baird)* **G Mawson** *Pulled-up*; *GOLDEN LINK 6.10–3 (Mr J Dowling)* **N Behan** *Refused*

The Betting: *9/2 Cloister; 5/1 Why Not; 7/1 The Midshipmite; 100/12 Aesop; 100/9 Father O'Flynn; 100/7 The Primate; 25/1 Tit for Tat; 28/1 Field Marshal; 30/1 Golden Gate; 40/1 Roman Oak & Faust; 50/1 Lady Helen & Joan of Arc; 100/1 Choufleur & Golden Link.*

Distances: *Forty lengths; a bad third*

Winner Trained By: *Arthur Yates (licence held by John Swatton)*

Value to Winning Owner: *£1,975*

* Time record for the race *

1894

Rumours of skulduggery were rife again this year and not allayed when CLOISTER, a 6/4 favourite for weeks before the event, was scratched after allegedly injuring himself in his final gallop. The most sinister aspect of the whole affair was that bookmakers appeared to know in advance that all was not well with the horse. Much of the race's attraction was lost through the withdrawal of the record breaker, leaving favouritism to be shared by NELLY GRAY and WHY NOT, at 5/1.

NELLY GRAY was a five-year-old mare competing for the first time in the 'National, whereas WHY NOT at thirteen was the oldest horse in the race he was making his fifth attempt to win. Bred by a Miss Nugent at Donore, County Meath, WHY NOT by CASTLEREAGH from a mare called TWITTER, developed into a fine stamp of 'chaser through a long career, changing hands many times in the process. Purchased by Captain C H Fenwick early in 1892, the gelding was sent to be trained by

W H Moore, younger brother of Garrett, trainer of WHY NOT

Willie Moore, younger brother of Garrett, at Weyhill in Hampshire, showing his well-being by rounding off 1893 with a sequence of four wins which included Liverpool's Grand Sefton.

Under a clear blue sky and on perfect going SCHOONER and AESOP set the early pace from a group including TROUVILLE, FATHER O'FLYNN, DAWN and NELLY GRAY. The latter came to grief soon after taking the lead at Valentine's, leaving AESOP in command in front of TROUVILLE, MUSICIAN, WHY NOT and LADY ELLEN II. By the narrowest of margins AESOP was first over the Water and with still all to play for, they swung out for the final circuit. Soon after jumping the Brook, AESOP gave way to LADY ELLEN II and WHY NOT, going well within himself, moved up into second place with WILD MAN FROM BORNEO. With just two fences to jump these three had drawn a long way clear. Holding the inside rail, WHY NOT saved valuable ground, striking the front at the second last but only to be passed by Joe Widger on WILD MAN FROM BORNEO. Giving more than a stone to both his rivals, WHY NOT fought back resolutely to peg back WILD MAN FROM BORNEO and then withstand the late challenge of LADY ELLEN II. The supreme artistry of Arthur Nightingall was seen to perfection as he chalked up his second win in the race, one and a half lengths ahead of LADY ELLEN II who just got the better of WILD MAN FROM BORNEO by a head. TROUVILLE was fourth.

Although blaming himself for the defeat of WILD MAN FROM BORNEO, Mr Joseph Widger vowed that he would return to Aintree, richer from the knowledge gained in his first attempt there.

Great Liverpool Steeplechase, 1839, engraved by J Harris after F C Turner.
The two mounted gentlemen on the far left of the picture are William Lynn and, on the grey, the Earl of Sefton.

Great Liverpool Steeplechase, 1839, engraved by J Harris after F C Turner.
This popular print portrays the "christening" of Becher's Brook and shows the unfortunate Captain struggling to his feet following his fall from CONRAD.

Great Liverpool Steeplechase, 1839, by Charles Hunt – ''The Stone Wall. First Round''. Powell and RAILROAD lead Mason and LOTTERY.

Great Liverpool Steeplechase, 1839 – ''Coming In'' by Charles Hunt. Mason and LOTTERY win from Olliver and SEVENTY-FOUR.

Finch Mason was a most popular writer and illustrator of the racing world and here are two of his immensely enjoyable drawings. The first, an illustration of THE LAMB jumping over the fallen horses in the 1871 Grand National, the second, one of his Sporting Nonsense Rhymes.

Said young Crœsus, "It's odd, with my Cash-an'-all,
If I can't go and win a Grand National!"
But through being Unskilled,
He got deuced near Killed,
And now he's a little more Rational.

The Grand Nationals of 1910, 1911 and 1912 portrayed by Alfred Bright, and a more modern artist Richard Joyce depicts the involvement with the race of that most popular of owners H R H the Queen Mother in ''Aintree's Queen of Hearts''.

First time round, a loose
horse and Ballyhackle
make the field swing wide

me round
lyhackle unships his jockey

Jerry M
the winner - 12 st 7 lbs

At the Canal Turn
Jerry M's
"National" - 1912

The Rip 1965

Mas-Tu-Vu 1955

Laffy 1964

evon Loch 1956

Devon Loch 1956

e Dome

Inch Arran
1973 Tophamtrophy

Two pictures of the 1920 race by Cecil Aldin. At Valentine's TROYTOWN and Jack Anthony lead the field which includes SERGEANT MURPHY, jumping in the middle of the fence, who was to win the race three years later. At the Canal turn, Captain Doyle falls from LITTLE ROVER.

LIVERPOOL SPRING MEETING, 1902,

THURSDAY, FRIDAY, and SATURDAY, MARCH 20th, 21st, and 22nd,

Under the Rules of Racing, National Hunt Rules, and the usual Conditions and Regulations at Liverpool

Before the Great War, the declarations for the whole meeting would be used as an advertising poster like this one.

A selection of race cards indicates the various companies that have sponsored the Grand National. The horses went round the course the same way as usual in 1977 even if the picture on the card seems to tell a different story!

The memorable occasion in 1985 when all the surviving jockeys who had won the Grand National were presented to H R H Princess Anne before the race. *(Kris Photography)*.

WHY NOT, the first of only two thirteen-year-olds to win the race

THE GRAND NATIONAL HANDICAP STEEPLECHASE
1894

Of 2,500 sovs., (including a trophy value 100 sovs.) by subscription of 25 sovs., each, 15 forfeit or 5 if declared, with 1,650 sovs., added; the second to receive 300 sovs., and the third 200 sovs., out of the stakes

Date: 30th March 1894	Starters: 14	Time: 9 mins 45⅖ secs
1st **WHY NOT**	13.11–13 *(Capt C H Fenwick)*	**A Nightingall**
2nd **LADY ELLEN II**	6.9–10 *(Mr J McKinlay)*	**T Kavanagh**
3rd **WILD MAN FROM BORNEO**	6.10–9 *(Mr John Widger)*	**Mr Joseph Widger**
4th **TROUVILLE**	6.10–6 *(Duke of Hamilton)*	**Mr J C Cheney**
5th **AESOP**	8.10–12 *(Capt Michael Hughes)*	**G Mawson**
6th **MUSICIAN**	8.9–10 *(Mr M Firth)*	**F Hassall**
7th **CARROLLSTOWN**	7.10–13 *(Lord Shaftesbury)*	**G Williamson**
8th **SCHOONER**	6.9–12 *(Mr M A Maher)*	**W Taylor**
9th **VARTEG HILL**	8.9–10 *(Mr Lort Phillips)*	**D Davies**

Also Ran:
FATHER O'FLYNN 9.11–3 (Mr C Grenfell) **Mr C Grenfell** *Fell*; *ARDCARN 7.10–12* (Mr G Grant) **Capt Bewicke** *Pulled-up*; *NELLY GRAY 5.9–12* (Mr F B Atkinson) **H Escott** *Bolted*; *CALCRAFT 7.9–10* (Mr J C Leslie) **Mr A H Ripley** *Fell*; *DAWN 6.9–7* (Mr E Storey) **G Morris** *Pulled-up*

The Betting: *5/1 Why Not & Nelly Gray; 11/2 Ardcarn; 6/1 Aesop; 100/7 Father O'Flynn; 25/1 Lady Ellen II, Trouville, Schooner, Dawn & Musician; 40/1 Wild Man from Borneo; 50/1 Carrollstown & Varteg Hill; 100/1 Calcraft.*

Distances: *A length and a half; a head*

Winner Trained By: *W H Moore (licence held by John Collins)*

Value to Winning Owner: £1,975

1895

CLOISTER's long-awaited return to the racecourse came appropriately at Aintree in November 1894, resulting in a convincing twenty length victory in the Grand Sefton 'Chase. Ridden by his new trainer Harry Escott, Mr Duff's champion showed every sign of his former greatness. He was again allocated top weight of 13 st 3 lbs for the forthcoming 'National, but not even this could deter his supporters who once again made him ante-post favourite. Once again, though, they were not to get a run for their money. And once again the bookies appeared to have advance knowledge of the event. Despite being surrounded by private detectives, CLOISTER rolled over in pain after a winding-up gallop at Lewes on the Monday before Aintree, and he was scratched from the race.

AESOP, second behind CLOISTER in 1893 and the mount of Arthur Nightingall, was installed favourite at 5/1 from the horse now top of the handicap, HORIZON. Former winners, WHY NOT and FATHER O'FLYNN, were back again, and newcomers attracting most attention among the nineteen runners were Bill Dollery's mount VAN DER BERG, the Terry Kavanagh-ridden MANIFESTO and a substitute ride for Harry Escott, CATHAL. True to his word, Joe Widger returned with WILD MAN FROM BORNEO. The youngest of five sons of Thomas Widger, a most respectable and prominent horse dealer in Waterford, Joe learnt to ride almost before he could walk. Remounts for most of the cavalry regiments of Europe were supplied by the Widger family and long before the youngest member of the brood made his mark in racing, their way with horses was a byword. When only fourteen, Joe ran away from school to ride a winner at Bangor in North Wales, the following year

demonstrating his extraordinary skills by taking the honours in a three mile 'chase at Cork after covering the last two miles without a bridle. From his earliest days Joe Widger had set his heart on winning the Grand National, his brother Tom having finished fourth on DOWNPATRICK in 1883. Encouraged by another brother, Mike, Joe purchased in 1893 the chestnut gelding WILD MAN FROM BORNEO, who was bred in Ireland by Mr G Keays. Joe and Mike set up headquarters at Alfriston, at the establishment of trainer Gatland who also prepared FATHER O'FLYNN for the race and with WILD MAN FROM BORNEO registered as the property of elder brother John, the scene was set for a family assault on the great Liverpool event.

On a most unpleasant day, with heavy going bedevilling the contestants and thick fog the spectators, the favourite AESOP went to the front at the start and stayed there round the Canal Turn and over Valentine's. The Water was jumped in line abreast by AESOP, DALKEITH and HORIZON, the last named encountering some interference which caused him to fall. FATHER O'FLYNN, MANIFESTO and CATHAL were going well just behind the leading pair on the run back to Becher's, where DALKEITH blundered badly. AESOP came down at the Canal Turn, so CATHAL was left in front, though only marginally, for right on his heels came MANIFESTO, WILD MAN FROM BORNEO and LADY PAT. Still in front on touching down over the last, CATHAL headed for home to the cheers of the stands crowds but Joe Widger produced a final effort from WILD MAN FROM BORNEO on the flat, gradually drawing level and then going on to win by a clever length and a half. Bill Dollery brought VAN DER BERG home a bad third, just in front of MANIFESTO.

1895

Of 2,500 sovs., (including a piece of plate value 100 sovs.), by subscription of 25 sovs., each, 15 forfeit or 5 if declared, with 1,405 sovs., added; second to receive 300 sovs., and third 200 sovs., out of the stakes

Date: 29th March 1895	Starters: 19	Time: 10 mins 32 secs
1st **WILD MAN FROM BORNEO**	7.10–11 *(Mr John Widger)*	**Mr Joseph Widger**
2nd **CATHAL**	6.10–9 *(Mr F B Atkinson)*	**H Escott**
3rd **VAN DER BERG**	9.9–13 *(Major A Crawley)*	**W A Dollery**
4th **MANIFESTO**	7.11–2 *(Mr H M Dyas)*	**T Kavanagh**
5th **WHY NOT**	14.12–0 *(Capt C H Fenwick)*	**Mr E G Fenwick**
6th **LEYBOURNE**	7.10–3 *(Capt J M Gordon)*	**G Williamson**
7th **FATHER O'FLYNN**	10.11–1 *(Mr C A Grenfell)*	**Mr C A Grenfell**
8th **LADY PAT**	8.10–13 *(Mr F D Leyland)*	**D Shanahan**
9th **DALKEITH**	aged.9–12 *(Mr W Murray-Threipland)*	**J Knox**
10th **FIN-MA-COUL II**	5.10–5 *(Mr J Arnold)*	**W Canavan**
11th **MOLLY MAGUIRE**	6.9–9 *(Mr J T Hartigan)*	**W Taylor**

Also Ran:

HORIZON 6.12–2 (Mr F W Greswolde-Williams) **G Mawson** *Fell*; *PRINCE ALBERT 7.10–12* (Mr W T Roden) **Mr W P Cullen** *Fell*; *SARAH BERNHARDT 9.10–10* (Mr C D Rose) **E Matthews** *Pulled-up*; *ARDCARN 8.10–10* (Mr E Clarke) **R Woodland** *Fell*; *AESOP 9.10–8* (Capt Michael Hughes) **A Nightingall** *Fell*; *ROYAL BUCK 8.10–4* (Mr F W Greswolde-Williams) **W Slinn** *Pulled-up*; *COCK OF THE HEATH 7.10–2* (Mr H M Dyas) **W Hoysted** *Bolted*; *CAUSTIC 6.10–1* (Mr B Benison) **Mr A Gordon** *Fell*

The Betting: *5/1 Aesop; 100/14 Horizon; 10/1 Wild Man from Borneo; 100/8 Cathal, Leybourne & Manifesto; 100/7 Father O'Flynn; 100/6 Cock of the Heath; 25/1 Lady Pat, Van der Berg & Molly Maguire; 33/1 Dalkeith; 40/1 Fin-ma-Coul II; 50/1 Prince Albert, Royal Buck, Ardcarn, Why Not & Sarah Bernhardt; 100/1 Caustic.*

Distances: *A length and a half; a bad third*

Winner Trained By: *James Gatland, Alfriston*

Value to Winning Owner: *£1,975*

1896

From sixty-three subscribers, the race this year finally drew twenty-eight competitors on a bright, cold Friday 27th March. This was the largest number to assemble for the start since 1873. Ireland was well represented, the Widgers being associated with WILD MAN FROM BORNEO, MISS BARON and their chief fancy, WATERFORD, the mount of Joe Widger. CATHAL, VAN DER BERG and MANIFESTO were back, as were WHY NOT and FATHER O'FLYNN. In a very open market, the best-backed runner RORY O'MORE was on offer at 7/1, one point shorter than ARDCARN who was trying for the fourth time to win the race.

Local interest this year was centred on the outsider THE SOARER, a seven-year-old

David Campbell – sold the winner but still rode him

bay gelding by SKYLARK out of IDALIA. Bred by Pat Doyle in Ireland, the horse first came to the attention of David Campbell of the 9th Lancers, who bought him unbroken for a modest sum. Ridden by his new owner, THE SOARER won seven times over fences as a five-year-old, but later proved difficult to train, so Mr Campbell parted company with the horse early in 1896, for the sum of £500 and the promise that he be allowed to ride the animal in the forthcoming Grand National. The new owner was Liverpool businessman William Hall-Walker, described as something of an eccentric sportsman, who became Member of Parliament for Widnes. Himself a rider of some note under Pony Club Rules, Hall-Walker was the son of the former Mayor of Liverpool responsible for the initiation of an art gallery in the city. Arriving at Aintree with but one victory from his last eleven outings, THE SOARER was easy to back at 40/1. Strange to relate, Mr Hall-Walker had some difficulty in recognising his horse before the start, finding it necessary to enquire from a bystander which one was his.

The big field spread out right across the course, headed by WHY NOT, MANIFESTO, MARCH HARE, REDHILL and DOLLAR II. Jostling for position at the first fence, REDHILL collided with MANIFESTO and both came down. ALPHEUS now went on, but last year's winner WILD MAN FROM BORNEO became a notable casualty two fences before Becher's. ALPHEUS and RORY O'MORE took them over the Water, but out in the country David Campbell was getting some fine jumps out of THE SOARER and at Becher's was almost on terms with the leader RORY O'MORE with FATHER O'FLYNN, BISCUIT and WHY NOT being also well to the fore. BISCUIT struck the front jumping Valentine's, ARDCARN failed to

Top: THE SOARER and Mr Campbell, a long-priced winner for a local owner

Left: Colonel Hall-Walker. During the war, he donated his stud in Ireland to the nation and this was the origin of the National Stud

negotiate the final ditch and with RORY O'MORE done for as they turned into the penultimate fence, THE SOARER went on smoothly. Jumping the last straight and true, THE SOARER held on, resisting the game late challenge of FATHER O'FLYNN by a length and a half, BISCUIT and BARCAL-WHEY filling the minor placings separated by a similar distance.

Mr Hall-Walker had invested £50 on his winner at the generous odds, and a large proportion of his winnings went to extend the Liverpool Art Gallery which in due course became known as the Walker Art Gallery. He was soon to turn his attention to the breeding of thorough-breds, establishing the Tully Stud in Kil-dare and subsequently became Lord Wavertree. The successful rider, David Campbell, became the first serving caval-ry officer to win the big Liverpool event. Attaining command of the 9th Lancers, Campbell took his regiment to France in 1914 and retired from the army when in command at Aldershot. General Sir David Campbell died in 1936.

1896

Of 2,500 sovs., (including a piece of plate value 100 sovs.), by subscription of 25 sovs., each, 15 forfeit, or 5 sovs., if declared, with 1,375 sovs., added; second to receive 300 sovs., and third 200 sovs., out of the stakes

Date: 27th March 1896	Starters: 28	Time: 10 mins 11⅕ secs
1st **THE SOARER**	7.9–13 *(Mr W Hall-Walker)*	**Mr D G M Campbell**
2nd **FATHER O'FLYNN**	11.10–12 *(Mr C Grenfell)*	**Mr C Grenfell**
3rd **BISCUIT**	8.10–0 *(Mr W C Keeping)*	**E Matthews**
4th **BARCALWHEY**	6.9–8 *(Capt A E Whitaker)*	**C Hogan**
5th **WHY NOT**	15.11–5 *(Mr E G Fenwick)*	**A Nightingall**
6th **RORY O'MORE**	6.10–9 *(Mr C Hibbert)*	**R Nightingall**
7th **KESTRAL**	9.9–10 *(Mr W Lawson)*	**H Smith**
8th **CATHAL**	7.11–13 *(Mr R Ward)*	**Mr Reginald Ward**
9th **VAN DER BERG**	10.10–9 *(Mr W Pritchard Gordon)*	**G Mawson**

Also Ran:

WILD MAN FROM BORNEO 8.12–0 (Mr John W Widger) **Mr T J Widger** *Fell*; *MARCH HARE 7.11–7* (Mr F C Stanley) **R Chaloner** *Fell*; *THE MIDSHIPMITE 10.11–4* (Mr H L Powell) **F Hewitt** *Fell*; *MANIFESTO 8.11–4* (Mr H M Dyas) **J Gourley** *Fell*; *MORIARTY 6.11–2* (Mr J Hale) **E Acres** *Pulled-up*; *ARDCARN 9.11–1* (Mr Egerton Clarke) **G Williamson** *Fell*; *WATERFORD 8.10–13* (Mr F E Irving) **Mr Joseph Widger** *Fell*; *SWANSHOT 6.10–13* (Capt J Orr-Ewing) **A Anthony** *Fell*; *REDHILL 8.10–12* (Capt J E Aikin) **Mr G S Davies** *Fell*; *DOLLAR II 6.10–11* (Mr J A Miller) **W Halsey** *Fell*; *ST ANTHONY 7.10–10* (Capt W F Ricardo) **Capt W F Ricardo** *Fell*; *ALPHEUS 5.10–10* (Mr R C Vyner) **Mr A Gordon** *Bolted*; *EMIN 7.10–8* (Sir S Scott) **H Brown** *Pulled-up*; *FLEETWING 6.10–6* (Mr M J Corbally) **Mr Parsons** *Broke blood vessel*; *CLAWSON 6.10–4* (Mr A Jolland) **Mr W H Bissill** *Fell*; *MISS BARON 6.10–0* (Mr M Widger) **T Kavanagh** *Fell*; *PHILACTERY 8.9–11* (Sir S Scott) **E Driscoll** *Pulled-up*; *WESTMEATH 7.9–8* (Mr F D Leyland) **G Morris** *Fell*; *CAUSTIC 7.9–7* (Mr W B Benison) **H Mason** *Fell*

The Betting: *7/1 Rory O'More; 8/1 Ardcarn; 100/12 Waterford; 100/9 Cathal; 100/7 Why Not, Manifesto & Caustic; 100/6 March Hare; 20/1 Alpheus, Swanshot & Van Der Berg; 25/1 Biscuit; 1000/30 Barcalwhey; 40/1 Moriarty, Father O'Flynn, Wild Man from Borneo & The Soarer; 50/1 Dollar II; 66/1 The Midshipmite, Clawson & Miss Baron; 100/1 Redhill, Westmeath, Kestral, Fleetwing, Philactery & St Anthony; 200/1 Emin.*

Distances: *A length and a half; the same*

Winner Trained By: *W H Moore (licence held by John Collins)*

Value to Winning Owner: *£1,975*

1897

If the suspicions associated with the unfortunate CLOISTER damaged the sport's image, then the legend created by MANIFESTO came not a moment too soon, restoring 'chasing pride and elevating the Grand National story to an undreamt of level.

Foaled in County Meath in 1888, his sire was the ferocious MAN O'WAR whose flaring nostrils and rolling eyes frequently struck fear into the bravest of men. Breeder Harry Dyas, recognising early that the raw-boned colt would require time to mature, exercised the utmost patience before allowing MANIFESTO to make his racing debut at Manchester in 1892. In the six-horse field, MANIFESTO was one of three fallers. Returning to the same course the following month though, the gelding ran away with a two-mile hurdle race. A foretaste of what lay ahead came with MANIFESTO's final race of his first season, a resounding victory in Leopardstown's Irish Champion Steeplechase, no mean feat for a four-year-old. Lightly raced in the next two seasons, the son of MAN O'WAR confounded all but his connections by carrying off the valuable Lancashire 'Chase in 1894 and from here on his actions were closely watched by handicappers. The promising introduction to Aintree when finishing fourth behind WILD MAN FROM BORNEO has been recorded, as has his early departure from the most recent 'National, but for the 1897 event, Harry Dyas wisely placed MANIFESTO in the capable hands of the Eversleigh trainer Willie McAuliffe. Terry Kavanagh had the ride again and the public duly made the gelding a 6/1 favourite.

CATHAL and NORTON were well backed, as was WILD MAN FROM BORNEO, again the mount of Joe Widger but this time carrying the colours of Miss F E Norris, of Liverpool. Later to become Mrs Joe Widger, this lady was the first of her sex officially to be represented in the 'National.

A novel idea on the part of the racecourse administrators was the provision of white cloths with the runners' names embroidered upon them, which not only provided easy identification to paddock spectators but brightened an overcast day. The field got under way at the second time of asking, TIMON immediately going to the front ahead of RED CROSS, MANIFESTO, WESTMEATH and CLAWSON. The first casualties came as late as the Canal Turn, when WILD MAN FROM BORNEO was pulled up after being cannoned into. But plenty of incident followed. Running loose, GOLDFISH preceded TIMON and MANIFESTO over the Water Jump, NELLY GRAY, GAUNTLET and CATHAL being next in line as they went back into the country. Taking Becher's almost together, TIMON and MANIFESTO were just ahead of NELLY GRAY, CATHAL and FORD OF FYNE with FAIRY QUEEN, FILBERT and THE SOARER also showing prominently although the latter was overjumping. He finally took one liberty too many, coming down heavily at Valentine's and David Campbell, on special leave from India, received a broken collar bone. Blundering badly at the second last, TIMON unseated his rider, leaving MANIFESTO with a clear advantage which was increased by the fall of CATHAL at the final obstacle. Running out the easiest of winners by twenty lengths, MANIFESTO landed the odds most convincingly, while a terrific battle was fought out by FILBERT and FORD OF FYNE for the minor honours. At the post it was the rank outsider FILBERT by a head, PRINCE ALBERT finishing fourth some way back. MANIFESTO's great victory was as popular across the Irish Sea as it was at Aintree, indeed more so, as he had been extensively coupled in ante-post doubles with Navan-trained WINKFIELD'S PRIDE, the Lincolnshire Handicap winner. For Terry Kavanagh, though, the excitement was tempered by sadness. Henry Linde, who had given Kavanagh his start in racing, was not at Aintree to witness his moment of glory. Eight days earlier the master of Eyrefield Lodge, a man well aware of the trials and tribulations of the 'National, had died of Bright's disease.

THE GRAND NATIONAL HANDICAP STEEPLECHASE
1897

Of 2,500 sovs., (including a trophy value 100 sovs.), by subscription of 25 sovs., each, 15 forfeit or 5 sovs., if declared, with 1,255 sovs., added; second to receive 300 sovs., and third 200 sovs., out of stakes

Date: 26th March 1897	Starters: 28	Time: 9 mins 49 secs
1st **MANIFESTO**	**9.11–3** *(Mr H M Dyas)*	**T Kavanagh**
2nd **FILBERT**	**7.9–7** *(Mr G R Powell)*	**Mr C Beatty**
3rd **FORD OF FYNE**	**6.10–7** *(Major J A Orr-Ewing)*	**Mr F Withington**
4th **PRINCE ALBERT**	**9.10–8** *(Mr J S Forbes)*	**Mr G S Davies**
5th **LOTUS LILY**	**7.9–7** *(Capt R W Ethelston)*	**Mr A W Wood**
6th **TIMON**	**6.9–10** *(Mr R W Brown)*	**J Tervit**
7th **FAIRY QUEEN**	**11.9–7** *(Mr G S Davies)*	**Mr E H Lord**
8th **SEAPORT II**	**8.10–7** *(Mr H M White)*	**C James**
9th **NELLY GRAY**	**8.11–3** *(Major J A Orr-Ewing)*	**G Morris**
10th **ARGONAUT**	**7.10–12** *(Mr J A Miller)*	**R Woodland**

Also Ran:

WESTMEATH 8.11–4 (Mr F D Leyland) **W Taylor** *Fell*; *CLAWSON 7.10–10* (Mr A Jolland) **Mr W H Bissill** *Pulled-up*; *NORTON aged.10–7* (Mr Spencer Gollan) **J Hickey** *Fell*; *DAIMIO aged.12–6* (Mr O Gibson) **H Escott** *Pulled-up*; *CATHAL 8.11–10* (Mr R Ward) **Mr Reginald Ward** *Fell*; *WILD MAN FROM BORNEO 9.11–5* (Miss F E Norris) **Mr Joseph Widger** *Pulled-up*; *THE SOARER 8.11–4* (Mr W Hall-Walker) **Mr D G M Campbell** *Fell*; *BALLYOHARA 8.10–3* (Lord Shrewsbury) **W G Denby** *Pulled-up*; *GOLDEN CROSS aged.10–2* (Mr C O Pemberton) **G Wilson** *Fell*; *BARCALWHEY 7.10–1* (Capt A E Whitaker) **C Hogan** *Fell*; *RED CROSS 6.10–1* (Mr J E Rogerson) **H Taylor** *Fell*; *THE CONTINENTAL 6.10–2* (Mr A H Hudson) **H Brown** *Fell*; *CHEVY CHASE 8.9–13* (Mr F F MacCabe) **A Anthony** *Pulled-up*; *GREENHILL 6.9–11* (Mr C D Rose) **E Matthews** *Knocked-over*; *MEDIATOR 8.9–8* (Lord Coventry) **W Grosvenor** *Fell*; *LITTLE JOE 8.9–10* (Mr R T Bell) **L Bland** *Fell*; *GOLDFISH 6.9–7* (Mr E C Smith) **T Fitton** *Fell*; *GAUNTLET 6.11–3* (Mr F D Leyland) **Capt W Hope-Johnstone** *Fell*

The Betting: *6/1 Manifesto; 7/1 Cathal; 9/1 Wild Man From Borneo; 10/1 Norton; 100/6 The Soarer; 20/1 Nelly Gray & Timon; 25/1 Greenhill, Ford Of Fyne, Prince Albert & Barcalwhey; 28/1 Chevy Chase; 33/1 Clawson, Argonaut & Golden Cross; 40/1 Daimio; 50/1 Fairy Queen & Seaport II; 66/1 Gauntlet & Goldfish; 100/1 Others.*

Distances: *Twenty lengths; a head*

Winner Trained By: *M McAuliffe, Eversleigh*

Value to Winning Owner: £1,975

1898

A blinding snowstorm raged throughout a 'National day already bereft of its leading attraction. Cynical observers suggested that the absence of MANIFESTO was a repeat of the CLOISTER scandals but thankfully, the reason for last year's champion missing the race was nothing more sinister than a stable lad's error. After proving his wellbeing by winning a two-mile 'chase at Gatwick in February, MANIFESTO was sold to Mr J G Bulteel for £4,000, and sent to Willie Moore. Barely a week before the Liverpool appointment MANIFESTO's box door was left open by a stable boy, who fled in terror when he returned and realised the mistake he had committed. MANIFESTO, welcoming the opportunity to explore more fully his new surroundings, strolled round the yard before jumping the gate on which he badly bruised his fetlock. So it was that the new owner, trainer and a multitude of admirers were forced to wait a further twelve months to see if Aintree could be conquered again by MANIFESTO and last year's third FORD OF FYNE and the talented Mr Fred Withington consequently found themselves favourites.

At the auction of the late Henry Linde's famous Eyrefield Lodge, the underbidder had been Richard Cecil Dawson, son of the Irish trainer and breeder and a graduate of Dublin University. His unsuccessful attempt to begin training at the Curragh brought Dawson to Whatcombe, Berkshire, accompanied by the bay gelding DROGHEDA. The son of the 1887 Irish Grand National winner, EGLANTINE, DROGHEDA was sired by CHERRY RIPE, bred by Mr G F Gradwell and named after the town near which he was born. Jointly owned by Richard Dawson and Mr G C M Adam, DROGHEDA went to

Aintree in 1898 as a six-year-old, the owners alive to the fact that a condition of the purchase from the breeder was an additional £300 should the venture achieve success. Entrusted with the ride on the 25/1 shot was John Gourley, whose only previous mount in the race had been MANIFESTO in the year he got knocked over.

An increase in the intensity of the snowfall caused a delay of some ten minutes at the start and when at last the twenty-five runners set off, GREENHILL shot to the front. By the time the runners reached the first fence, they had passed from view of the stands, into the snow. Over Becher's GREENHILL was still in command, but as the jockeys later reported, little could be seen of the obstacles till the very last moment, leading to some wild jumping. Adroitly avoiding the falling BARCAL-WHEY, Gourley sent DROGHEDA into the lead as they neared the Water Jump at which THE SOARER, now ridden by Nightingall, came down. Three from home FORD OF FYNE showed with a chance as he

DROGHEDA – not the prettiest of winners on not the finest of days

drew alongside the leader but the effort was short-lived. Coming to the final fence CATHAL, ridden by his owner Reg Ward, made a brave attempt to get on terms with DROGHEDA only to see the leader gallop on through the slush and mud to a three length victory. Four lengths back in third place came GAUNTLET.

As Gourley made his way to the winner's enclosure, he looked like a mounted snowman. A grateful and generous Mr Adams rewarded the jockey with a pension for life in recognition of a brave and determined ride through possibly the worst conditions in living memory. It was the start of a brilliant training career for Richard Dawson, who, when turning his attention to flat racing, produced three Derby winners in FIFINELLA, TRIGO and BLENHEIM.

THE GRAND NATIONAL HANDICAP STEEPLECHASE
1898

Of 2,500 sovs., (including a piece of plate value 100 sovs.), by subscription of 25 sovs., each, 15 forfeit or 5 sovs., if declared, with 1,270 sovs., added, for five-year-olds and upwards; second to receive 300 sovs., and third 200 sovs., out of the stakes

Date: 25th March 1898	Starters: 25	Time: 9 mins 43³⁄₅ secs
1st **DROGHEDA**	**6.10–12** *(Mr C G M Adams)*	**J Gourley**
2nd **CATHAL**	**9.11–5** *(Mr R Ward)*	**Mr Reginald Ward**
3rd **GAUNTLET**	**7.10–13** *(Mr F D Leyland)*	**W Taylor**
4th **FILBERT**	**8.9–12** *(Mr G R Powell)*	**Mr C Beatty**
5th **DEAD LEVEL**	**6.10–7** *(Mr G Hamilton)*	**A Anthony**
6th **FORD OF FYNE**	**7.11–0** *(Major J A Orr-Ewing)*	**Mr F Withington**
7th **GRUDON**	**8.11–5** *(Mr B Bletsoe)*	**J Hickey**
8th **BARSAC**	**6.9–12** *(Mr C A Brown)*	**Mr M B Bletsoe**
9th **PRINCE ALBERT**	**10.11–0** *(Mr J S Forbes)*	**Mr G S Davies**
10th **GREENHILL**	**7.10–3** *(Mr C D Rose)*	**C Hogan**

Also Ran:

THE SOARER *9.11–5* (Mr W Hall-Walker) **A Nightingall** *Fell*; NEPCOTE *7.10–9* (Mr Lincoln) **W Dollery** *Pulled-up*; SWANSHOT *8.10–7* (Mr H de Montmorency) **Mr H de Montmorency** *Pulled-up*; BARCALWHEY *8.10–6* (Capt A E Whitaker) **R Chaloner** *Fell*; ATHELFRITH *8.10–4* (Mr A Coats) **W Hoysted** *Fell*; SURPLICE *9.10–1* (Mr Reid Walker) **J Latham** *Fell*; KINGSWORTHY *7.10–0* (Mr F R Hunt) **E Acres** *Pulled-up*; SHERIFF HUTTON *6.10–0* (Mrs H B Singleton) **J Morrell** *Fell*; CRUISKEEN II *6.10–0* (Mrs Sadlcir-Jackson) **T Kavanagh** *Pulled-up*; ST GEORGE *8.9–11* (Mr Joseph Widger) **Mr T J Widger** *Fell*; HOBNOB *6.9–11* (Mr A Stedall) **H Box** *Fell*; ELECTRIC SPARK *7.9–11* (Mr R Wright) **A Waddington** *Pulled-up*; CUSHALEE MAVOURNEEN *7.9–11* (Mr G R Powell) **H Smith** *Pulled-up*; HALL IN *7.9–8* (Mr W Ward) **L Bland** *Fell*; LITTLE JOE *9.10–0* (Mr A Bell) **J Walsh, jnr** *Fell*

The Betting: *11/2 Ford of Fyne; 7/1 Cathal; 8/1 Prince Albert; 100/12 Gauntlet; 100/7 The Soarer & Barcalwhey; 20/1 Kingsworthy; 25/1 Grudon, Nepcote, Drogheda, Dead Level, Filbert & Barsac; 28/1 Little Joe; 40/1 Hobnob & St George; 50/1 Sheriff Hutton; 100/1 Others.*

Distances: *Three lengths; four lengths*

Winner Trained By: *Mr E Woods*

Value to Winning Owner: *£1,975*

1899

There was no stable door left open in this last year of the Empire century. MANIFESTO was set to concede fourteen pounds to the nearest to him in the handicap, his highly thought-of half-sister and former stable-companion GENTLE IDA, and three times that amount to CORNER and LITTLE NORTON. Yet such was his reputation that not even the impost of 12 st 7 lbs could blunt the public's regard for Mr Bulteel's gelding. Ridden this year by George Williamson, MANIFESTO, together with GENTLE IDA, dominated the ante-post market and on the big day the mare went off 4/1 favourite, just a point ahead of the former winner. Horatio Bottomley, of *John Bull* fame, was the new owner of GENTLE IDA although she remained in the yard of Harry Dyas, whose firm belief was that no horse living, including MANIFESTO, could possibly give her a stone. The recently purchased five-year-old AMBUSH II carried the Royal colours of the Prince of Wales and on the basis of a convincing victory in Sandown's Prince of Wales Steeplechase some weeks earlier, occupied third position in the market. Among the riders making their first 'National appearance were Liverpool born Frank Mason on DEAD LEVEL, Ernie Piggott with ELLIMAN and the popular sportsman Count de Geloes partnering his own mare PISTACHE.

There could be no complaints concerning the weather this year, while the going was perfect and at flag-fall SHERIFF HUTTON was the first of the nineteen runners to show. With the first fence safely behind them CORNER took up the running from PISTACHE, SHERIFF HUTTON and ELECTRIC SPARK and jumping Becher's there was little change in the order. As a precaution against frost, hay had been spread on the take-off and landing sides of the fences and some which had inadvertently been left on the far side of the Canal Turn brought a cry of horror from spectators in the vicinity. MANIFESTO, going well in the mid-division, cleared the obstacle in his usual flamboyant fashion only to slip on the hay as he landed. Williamson lost both irons, his feet touching the ground as the second favourite crumpled to the turf. Yet amazingly, he found himself back in the race as MANIFESTO made the most miraculous of recoveries. At the next, Valentine's, another groan from the crowd signalled the fall of GENTLE IDA and this time there was to be no reprieve. By now MUM had struck the front. Over the Water, where she maintained her advantage, there were still a surprising number of horses in with a chance although MANIFESTO was some way behind the main bunch. Early on the second circuit, however, George Williamson began making ground with the top-weight, as did Anthony on AMBUSH II and clearing Becher's for the final time both were within striking distance of the leaders. SHERIFF HUTTON and TRADE MARK were pulled up at Valentine's and at the open ditch two fences later, MANIFESTO moved effortlessly through the field, taking up the running going into the next and quickly stamping his authority on the race. Huge cheers greeted each of his last two jumps, the noise rising to a crescendo as MANIFESTO romped home five lengths in front of FORD OF FYNE, equalling the weight-carrying record. Ernie Piggott was a further two lengths away on ELLIMAN, with DEAD LEVEL fourth. The public went wild as the dual 'National hero was led in. The owner took an extremely large sum from the ring, one bet alone reputedly being of £10,000 to £800 and mindful of the role George Williamson played in the success, presented the jockey with £2,800 over and above his retained fee of £100. Aintree and the Grand National itself were also enriched by the result, for the crowds were agog at the prospect of returning in a year's time to witness the mighty MANIFES-TO attempt the impossible. Prince Edward too had reason to look forward to the next 'National, since his AMBUSH II had performed impressively enough to foster hopes of better things to come.

THE GRAND NATIONAL HANDICAP STEEPLECHASE
1899

Of 2,500 sovs., by subscription of 25 sovs., each, 15 forfeit or 5 sovs., if declared, with 1,430 sovs., added, for five-year-olds and upwards; second to receive 300 sovs., and third 200 sovs., out of the stakes

Date: 24th March 1899	Starters: 19	Time: 9 mins 49⅘ secs
1st **MANIFESTO**	**11.12–7** *(Mr J G Bulteel)*	**G Williamson**
2nd **FORD OF FYNE**	**8.10–10** *(Major J A Orr-Ewing)*	**E Matthews**
3rd **ELLIMAN**	**8.10–1** *(Mr Audley Blyth)*	**E Piggott**
4th **DEAD LEVEL**	**7.10–6** *(Mr J C Dormer)*	**F Mason**
5th **BARSAC**	**7.9–12** *(Mr C A Brown)*	**Mr H M Ripley**
6th **WHITEBOY II**	**10.9–10** *(Mr R Bourke)*	**A Banner**
7th **AMBUSH II**	**5.10–2** *(HRH The Prince of Wales)*	**A Anthony**
8th **ELECTRIC SPARK**	**8.9–11** *(Mr R Wright)*	**A Waddington**
9th **MUM**	**7.10–5** *(Mr J G Mosenthal)*	**F Hassall**
10th **FAIRY QUEEN**	**13.9–11** *(Mr Saunders Davies)*	**W Oates**
11th **CORNER**	**8.9–7** *(Mr W Harris)*	**D Read**

Also Ran:
GENTLE IDA 10.11–7 (Mr Horatio Bottomley) **W Taylor** *Fell*; *XEBEE 7.11–4* (Mr R C B Cave) **Mr A W Wood** *Fell*; *THE SAPPER 6.10–11* (Major J A Orr-Ewing) **Mr G S Davies** *Fell*; *TRADE MARK 6.10–2* (Mr A Alexander) **J Knox** *Pulled-up*; *PISTACHE 5.10–3* (Count de Geloes) **Count de Geloes** *Fell*; *LOTUS LILY 9.9–12* (Capt R W Ethelston) **J Latham** *Fell*; *SHERIFF HUTTON 7.9–11* (Mr F W Greswolde-Williams) **C Hogan** *Pulled-up*; *LITTLE NORTON aged.9–7* (Mr G R Powell) **C Clack** *Fell*

The Betting: *4/1 Gentle Ida; 5/1 Manifesto; 100/12 Ambush II; 10/1 The Sapper; 100/8 Lotus Lily; 100/7 Sheriff Hutton; 20/1 Elliman & Electric Spark; 25/1 Trade Mark & Barsac; 33/1 Xebee & Dead Level; 40/1 Ford of Fyne; 100/1 Pistache, Mum & Fairy Queen; 200/1 Little Norton, Corner & Whiteboy II.*

Distances: *Five lengths; two lengths*

Winner Trained By: *W H Moore (licence held by John Collins)*

Value to Winning Owner: *£1,975*

1900

The Grand National entered the twentieth century enjoying a new-found popularity, brought about largely by MANIFESTO's epic achievements. Not surprisingly, though still to the horror of his countless admirers, MANIFESTO received the impossible burden of 12 st 13 lbs from a handicapper in accord with the general belief that the horse was a stone better at Aintree than anywhere else. But nothing was going to deter the public from making him third favourite at 6/1. Most heavily backed of the sixteen runners was HIDDEN MYSTERY, mainly as a result of having beaten MANIFESTO at level weights at Hurst Park at the beginning of the month, while the presence of the Prince of Wales aroused a welter of patriotic backing for AMBUSH II. With the war against the Boers in South Africa at its height, many welcomed the opportunity to display support for the Crown in an event known to be of particular interest to Prince Edward. AMBUSH II, now a six-year-old, was bred by William Ashe of Narraghmore from BEN BATTLE out of MISS PLANT and it is perhaps significant that BEN BATTLE was also the grandsire of MANIFESTO. When sent to auction as a two-year-old, AMBUSH II failed to reach the modest reserve of 50 guineas.

It was Mr G W 'Tommy' Lushington who recognised possibilities in the young horse which others failed to perceive. As an officer in the 2nd Queen's Regiment stationed in Ireland, Mr Lushington became one of the leading amateur riders and then after resigning his commission, proved equally adept as a trainer. AMBUSH II never represented Lushington under National Hunt rules, for a request had come via Lord Marcus Beresford that the new trainer find a 'chaser worthy of bearing the Royal colours. Thus it was that the son of BEN BATTLE appeared in the ownership of the Prince of Wales for the first time at the age of four, justifying the faith of Tommy Lushington, retained as his trainer, by out-staying fourteen opponents in a four-mile Maiden Plate at Kildare. After a game performance which took him into seventh place behind MANIFESTO in the 'National, preparations were made for the 1900 race. Jockey Anthony, Cheltenham-born though domiciled in Ireland, was equally effective over the sticks as he was on the flat. Having ridden the winner of last year's Irish Derby, he was now striving for a unique double. Anthony was officially, but incorrectly listed as the trainer of the Royal competitor, but this task was certainly the province of Tommy Lushington.

Grand National day dawned bright and clear. An enormous crowd flocked to the course, those privileged to be in the area of the paddock enjoying the colour and grace of the contestants parading in their specially embroidered blankets, which this year became the property of the owners, by courtesy of Mr Topham. With the excitement at fever pitch, the field set off to a perfect start, BARSAC going on at a cracking rate from LEVANTER, AMBUSH II, MODEL, and EASTER OGUE. The rank outsider NOTHING bolted off the course at the first fence, where a greater shock came with the fall of Irish contender COVERT HACK, who then ran on pilotless, proving a nuisance to the leaders and an added hazard to jockeys whose main concern at this stage was keeping out of trouble. HIDDEN MYSTERY headed BARSAC coming back towards the stands, and realising that all the better fancied horses were still in the hunt, the stands spectators roared their approval as BARSAC jumped to the front again over the Water, where BARCALWHEY made a splash by falling. At the first fence second time, HIDDEN MYSTERY fell when hampered by the riderless COVERT HACK, leaving BARSAC at the head of affairs. A whoop of delight came from the furthest part of the course as AMBUSH II swept to the front over the Canal Turn, but after Valentine's a continuous volley of cheering rang out along the Canal side as MANIFESTO hit the front, jumping with a fluency that belied both his age and the weight he was carrying. First on to the racecourse, MANIFESTO looked assured of a record-breaking third victory, but between the last two fences Algy Anthony made his move on AMBUSH II, jumping the final obstacle two lengths in front. The most deafening roar ever heard on Liverpool's historic track followed the Royal champion every inch of the way to post, which AMBUSH II passed four lengths ahead of his nearest rival. BARSAC got up on the line to pip MANIFESTO a neck for second place, although George Williamson had eased the gallant old warrior when victory was beyond him. A thousand hats were tossed into the sky as

AMBUSH II with winning jockey A Anthony. This was the only horse to carry royal colours to victory in the race

the heir to the throne made his way onto the course to lead in his winner, the cheers ringing long and loud in a rapturous ovation rivalling that at Epsom four years earlier when the Prince led in his Derby winner PERSIMMON. Glorious in defeat, MANIFESTO split the loyalty of many at Aintree that day, bringing tears to the eyes of all who recognised greatness and genuine endeavour. For The Prince of Wales, this was the beginning of a season of unparalleled success, his DIAMOND JUBILEE winning the triple crown of 2,000

Guineas, Derby and St Leger, and with AMBUSH II not yet in his prime, who knew what lay ahead at Aintree? Three months later, Tommy Lushington further endorsed his outstanding talent by training and riding GALLINARIA to win the Irish Derby and Algy Anthony, another man of remarkable versatility, rode home MAY RACE to victory in the Irish Oaks. Thus, the new century began in the most memorable manner, for the nation, for Aintree and for the Grand National.

THE GRAND NATIONAL HANDICAP STEEPLECHASE
1900

Of 2,500 sovs., (including a piece of plate value 100 sovs.), by subscription of 25 sovs., each, 15 forfeit or 5 sovs., if declared, for five-year-olds and upwards; second to receive 300 sovs., and third 200 sovs., out of the stakes

Date: 30th March 1900	Starters: 16	Time: 10 mins 1⅖ secs
1st **AMBUSH II**	6.11–3 *(HRH The Prince of Wales)*	**A Anthony**
2nd **BARSAC**	8.9–12 *(Mr C A Brown)*	**W Halsey**
3rd **MANIFESTO**	12.12–13 *(Mr J G Bulteel)*	**G Williamson**
4th **BREEMOUNT'S PRIDE**	7.11–7 *(Mr G Edwardes)*	**Mr G S Davies**
5th **LEVANTER**	aged.9–8 *(Capt Scott)*	**T McGuire**
6th **GRUDON**	10.10–5 *(Mr B Bletsoe)*	**Mr M B Bletsoe**
7th **EASTER OGUE**	6.9–13 *(Lord Wm Beresford)*	**C Hogan**
8th **LOTUS LILY**	10.9–11 *(Capt R W Ethelston)*	**Mr A W Wood**
9th **SISTER ELIZABETH**	7.10–0 *(Mr Arthur James)*	**C Clack**
10th **MODEL**	7.10–7 *(Mr E Woodland)*	**P Woodland**
11th **ELLIMAN**	9.10–1 *(Mr Audley Blyth)*	**E Driscoll**

Also Ran:

HIDDEN MYSTERY 6.12–0 (Col T J Gallwey) **Mr H Nugent** *Fell*; *COVERT HACK 6.11–0* (Capt Eustace Loder) **F Mason** *Fell*; *ALPHEUS 9.10–10* (Mr R C Vyner) **A Waddington** *Fell*; *BARCALWHEY 10.10–0* (Capt A E Whitaker) **T Lane** *Fell*; *NOTHING 9.9–11* (Mr G R Powell) **W Hoysted** *Bolted*

The Betting: *75/20 Hidden Mystery; 4/1 Ambush II; 6/1 Manifesto; 100/7 Elliman; 100/6 Covert Hack; 20/1 Breemount's Pride & Barcalwhey; 25/1 Lotus Lily & Barsac; 40/1 Alpheus, Grudon & Sister Elizabeth; 50/1 Levanter; 66/1 Easter Ogue & Model; 100/1 Nothing.*

Distances: *Four lengths; a neck*

Winner Trained By: *Algy Anthony (Ireland)*

Value to Winning Owner: *£1,975*

1901

Familiar though 'chasing's loyal band of followers were to expecting the worst from Britain's weather, nothing could have prepared them for the conditions which greeted them at Liverpool on 29th March 1901. The racecourse was hidden under a deep blanket of snow while the fiercest of blizzards made the prospect of racing distinctly unlikely. Even that hardiest breed of man, the steeplechase jockey, drew the line at venturing out in such weather, almost all the twenty-four 'National riders presenting a petition to the Clerk of the course requesting that the race be postponed. Three stewards, Lord Enniskillen, Mr G Fawcett and Captain Fetherstonaugh, made a hasty examination of the racecourse before returning with the strange decision that racing was possible, and dutifully, the riders proceeded to weigh out.

Most notable of the absentees were AMBUSH II and MANIFESTO, their non-participation leaving Mr Tunstall-Moore's mare FANCIFUL at the top of the handicap with 11 st 6 lbs. LEVANTER and BARSAC, both finishers last time, occupied the leading positions in the market, the former attracting most support was the mount of the popular local jockey 'Tich' Mason. Algy Anthony took the ride on COVERT HACK, the upsetter of last year's favourite, while the promising amateur Hugh Nugent, son of Sir Charles Nugent, Bart., partnered DRUMCREE, winner of his two most recent contests. GRUDON had been considered unlucky by his connections when getting a leg through his bridle in 1900, an inconvenience which did not prevent him from finishing sixth in the hands of the owner's son, Morgan Bletsoe. This time benefiting from the services of Aintree specialist, Arthur Nightingall, the eleven-year-old was making his third attempt at the 'National, having also managed to survive the infamous blizzard three years before. Of humble origins, his sire OLD BUCK being employed as a plough horse before being bought by Bernard Bletsoe for a few sovereigns, GRUDON was an entire, bred, owned and trained by Bletsoe at Denton, Northamptonshire. With exemplary foresight Mr Bletsoe took the precaution during the preliminaries of purchasing from a local dairy two pounds of butter, which he spread into GRUDON's hooves to prevent the snow from balling there.

Conceding to the ferocity of the weather, the stewards dispensed with the parade, the runners going directly to the start where, after a delay of sixteen minutes, they were finally sent on their unen-

Arthur Nightingall – undisputedly one of the greatest jockeys ever to win the race

144

GRUDON, the bad-weather specialist who brought the 'National into the new century with tons of spirit and two pounds of butter

viable journey. With GRUDON going into an immediate lead, the runners quickly became lost from view as the snow swirled with increasing fury, but as they came back into sight at the fourteenth fence GRUDON was still in command. Clearing the Water Jump, the leader was followed by COVERT HACK, LEVANTER, BARSAC and PADISHAH, this order being maintained during the long run back into the country. When the first of the survivors at last emerged from the whirlwind of snow, immediate identification by the shivering spectators was impossible. It became apparent that GRUDON had led throughout and apart from giving his jockey a momentary fright by jumping a footpath on the run-in, his victory was clear cut. Passing the post four lengths in front of DRUMCREE, GRUDON carried Arthur Night-

ingall to a memorable if uncomfortable third success in the race. BUFFALO BILL was third, ahead of the bedraggled survivors, LEVANTER, FANCIFUL, CORAGH HILL, COVERT HACK, PRINCE TUSCAN and BARSAC. GRUDON, commonly believed to be a lazy horse, disproved that claim in the bravest way. He ran only twice more, breaking down in the Lancashire 'Chase and running unplaced at Kempton, after which he was retired to stud.

Bernard Bletsoe could well feel proud that he bred, owned and trained the game son of a plough horse to achieve victory under the worst conditions imaginable. He may also have reflected that his last-minute investment was the most valuable he ever made. Its cost: the price of two pounds of butter!

1901

Of 2,500 sovs., (including a piece of plate value 100 sovs.), by subscription of 25 sovs., each, 15 forfeit or 5 sovs., if declared: For five-year-olds & upwards; second to receive 300 sovs., and third 200 sovs., out of the stakes

Date: 29th March 1901	Starters: 24	Time: 9 mins 47⅘ secs
1st **GRUDON**	11.10–0 *(Mr B Bletsoe)*	**A Nightingall**
2nd **DRUMCREE**	7.9–12 *(Mr O J Williams)*	**Mr H Nugent**
3rd **BUFFALO BILL**	7.9–7 *(Mr J E Rogerson)*	**H Taylor**
4th **LEVANTER**	aged.9–10 *(Mr J D Edwards)*	**F Mason**
5th **FANCIFUL**	6.11–6 *(Mr H Tunstall-Moore)*	**Mr W P Cullen**
6th **CORAGH HILL**	aged.9–9 *(Mr J Lonsdale)*	**C Hogan**
7th **COVERT HACK**	7.11–4 *(Major Eustace Loder)*	**A Anthony**
8th **PRINCE TUSCAN**	8.10–6 *(Mr H Hunt)*	**Mr H Hunt, jnr**
9th **BARSAC**	9.9–13 *(Mr C A Brown)*	**Mr H M Ripley**

Also Ran:

MODEL 8.11–4 (Mr W H Pawson) **Mr W H Pawson** *Failed to finish*; *CUSHENDUN 6.11–2* (Capt H A Johnstone) **Mr G S Davies** *Failed to finish*; *SUNNY SHOWER aged.10–8* (Mrs J Widger) **Mr J W Widger** *Failed to finish*; *COOLGARDIE 7.10–6* (Mr R Davy) **A Waddington** *Failed to finish*; *THE SAPPER 8.10–5* (Mr W H Pawson) **W Halsey** *Failed to finish*; *MAYO'S PRIDE 7.10–5* (Mr W W Lewison) **J Phillips** *Failed to finish*; *HORNPOOL aged.10–5* (Mr B Wade) **E Acres** *Failed to finish*; *GREYSTONE II (formerly GREYSTONE) 8.10–1* (Mr J Herdman) **J H Stainton** *Failed to finish*; *TRUE BLUE 10.9–13* (Mr V A Parnell) **P Woodland** *Broke leg* [destroyed]; *CHIT CHAT 8.10–2* (Capt J Machell) **C Clack** *Failed to finish*; *PROSSET 6.9–13* (Mr H Barnato) **Mr F Hartigan** *Failed to finish*; *PAWNBROKER 6.9–7* (Mr R C Dawson) **J O'Brien** *Failed to finish*; *ZODIAC II 6.9–7* (Mr F Bibby) **A Banner** *Failed to finish*; *PADISHAH 8.10–1* (Mr A Gorham) **A Birch** *Failed to finish*; *GOSSIP 6.9–7* (Mr Foxhall Keene) **J Polletti** *Failed to finish*

The Betting: *5/1 Levanter; 100/14 Barsac; 9/1 Grudon; 10/1 Covert Hack & Drumcree; 100/8 Fanciful & The Sapper; 100/6 Pawnbroker; 20/1 Mayo's Pride, Cushendun & Prosset; 25/1 Chit Chat & Coragh Hill; 33/1 Prince Tuscan & Buffalo Bill; 40/1 Model & Coolgardie; 66/1 Hornpool, True Blue & Padishah; 100/1 Sunny Shower, Greystone II, Gossip & Zodiac II.*

Distances: *Four lengths; six lengths*

Winner Trained By: *B Bletsoe, Denton, Northamptonshire*

Value to Winning Owner: *£1,975*

1902

This was the year when the long-awaited rematch between AMBUSH II and the inimitable MANIFESTO looked certain to materialise, ensuring a record attendance whatever the whims of the weather. Both were entered, Mr Bulteel's double hero again receiving harsh treatment with a weight allocation of 12 st 8 lbs, but sadly AMBUSH II met with an accident which prevented his taking part.

While retaining the affection of his multitude of admirers, MANIFESTO was now fourteen years old, conceding weight to all his opponents and although ably assisted by Ernie Piggott, was considered a forlorn hope in the prevailing heavy ground. One who had shown he could jump the course and cope with poor underfoot conditions was DRUMCREE, again the mount of Mr Hugh Nugent and the horse which shared favouritism with Lord Coventry's INQUISITOR. Confusingly, the Duke of Westminster's DRUMREE was also one of the leading fancies, the six-year-old having proved his ability in winning the Stanley 'Chase over the course. BARSAC was trying for the fifth time and one newcomer to carry thoughts back to the 1890s was 50/1 shot MATTHEW, the property of John Widger. Not since 1889 had a mare succeeded in the most important 'chase of the year but this time, seven-year-old SHANNON LASS came to Liverpool as a live prospect. Her breeder, James Reidy of County Clare, sold SHANNON LASS to Mr E C Irish after she ran third in a Limerick 'chase when only three years old but she was quickly passed on to English bookmaker Ambrose Gorham. This well-known gentleman of the turf, rented gallops at Telscombe near Brighton, and it was here that SHANNON LASS was prepared for the 'National by James Hackett. It was the proud boast of all associated with the mare, that in the whole of her racing career she never once had need of the whip or spurs and with veteran jockey David Read in the saddle she looked a picture of fitness.

Setting off at a good gallop, DRUMCREE cut out the early work in front of MATTHEW, HELIUM, BARSAC, THE SAPPER and DRUMREE, who was brought down at the fourth fence. Meanwhile BARSAC assumed command, clearing Becher's at the head of the main bunch, with Ernie Piggott sensibly holding up MANIFESTO at the rear. INQUISITOR improved his position approaching the stands, showing slightly ahead of BARSAC and MATTHEW but all three were outjumped at the Water by HELIUM. The going and pace took its toll. At Becher's the race was wide open and MATTHEW jumped Valentine's perfectly in advance of TIPPERARY BOY, BARSAC, LURGAN and MANIFESTO, with DRUMCREE, DETAIL and SHANNON LASS all there. By the time the second last fence was reached, DETAIL and SHANNON LASS were challenging MATTHEW for the lead. The cheers from the stands, however, were for MANIFESTO, running on strongly in fourth place and still in with a chance. DETAIL blundered at the last fence and the issue was settled when SHANNON LASS produced the better turn of foot on the flat to run out a comfortable three length winner. The rousing applause at the finish was shared by the mare and the magnificent MANIFESTO, who battled on gamely into third place. Many observers thought this performance the finest race MANIFESTO ever ran and jockey Piggott was full of praise for the perfect ride the gallant old gentleman had given him.

This was the only 'National in which SHANNON LASS took part and although she started at 20/1 she was a most popular winner. Her name and that of her owners would long be remembered on England's south coast, for with his winnings Ambrose Gorham restored the church at Telscombe and when he died, he left the whole village, together with the parish, to Brighton Corporation. His will illustrated not merely his generosity but also the humour of the man. It included the following guidelines for a suitable future incumbent: 'I direct the Corporation shall prefer a man who is a sportsman and not a total abstainer from alcohol and tobacco.'

THE GRAND NATIONAL HANDICAP STEEPLECHASE
1902

Of 2,525 sovs., (including a trophy value 100 sovs.), by subscription of 25 sovs., each, 15 forfeit or 5 sovs., if declared: For five-year-olds & upwards; second to receive 300 sovs., and the third 200 sovs., out of the stakes

Date: 21st March 1902	Starters: 21	Time: 10 mins 3⅗ secs
1st **SHANNON LASS**	**7.10–1** *(Mr A Gorham)*	**D Read**
2nd **MATTHEW**	**6.9–12** *(Mr John Widger)*	**W Morgan**
3rd **MANIFESTO**	**14.12–8** *(Mr J G Bulteel)*	**E Piggott**
4th **DETAIL**	**6.9–9** *(Mr White-Heather)*	**A Nightingall**
5th **LURGAN**	**6.10–12** *(Lord Cadogan)*	**F Freemantle**
6th **TIPPERARY BOY**	**8.11–6** *(Mr T B Holmes)*	**T Moran**
7th **DRUMCREE**	**8.10–10** *(Mr J S Morrison)*	**Mr H Nugent**
8th **BARSAC**	**10.9–12** *(Mr C Atherton Brown)*	**F Mason**
9th **THE SAPPER**	**9.10–4** *(Mr W H Pawson)*	**H Brown**
10th **MISS CLIFDEN II**	**6.9–7** *(Mr F W Polehampton)*	**Mr H M Ripley**
11th **STEADY GLASS**	**10.9–8** *(Mr R Hardinge)*	**Mr T J Longworth**

Also Ran:
DRUMREE 6.11–4 (Duke of Westminster) **A Anthony** *Knocked-over*; *HELIUM 7.10–10* (Mr E W Tinsley) **H Caley** *Fell*; *INQUISITOR 7.10–9* (Lord Coventry) **Mr A W Wood** *Fell*; *ARNOLD 8.10–1* (Mr J A Scorror) **T Bissill** *Brought-down*; *DIRKHAMPTON 8.10–0* (Col W A W Lawson) **Mr J Sharpe** *Fell*; *AUNT MAY 6.10–0* (Mr B W Parr) **M Walsh** *Failed to finish*; *WHITEHAVEN 10.9–13* (Lord Denman) **P Woodland** *Pulled-up*; *FAIRLAND 9.9–10* (Mr T Bater) **H Taylor** *Fell*; *ZODIAC II 7.9–7* (Mr F Bibby) **A Banner** *Pulled-up*; *GOSSIP 7.9–7* (Mr Foxhall Keene) **H Hewitt** *Fell*

The Betting: *6/1 Drumree & Inquisitor; 7/1 Barsac; 10/1 Drumcree; 100/8 Lurgan & Tipperary Boy; 100/6 Manifesto; 20/1 Whitehaven, Shannon Lass & Aunt May; 25/1 Fairland & Detail; 33/1 Arnold; 40/1 The Sapper; 50/1 Matthew, Miss Clifden II, Helium & Dirkhampton; 100/1 Steady Glass; Zodiac II & Gossip.*

Distances: *Three lengths; three lengths*

Winner Trained By: *James Hackett, Telscombe, Sussex*

Value to Winning Owner: *£2,000*

1903

A perfect spring day on 27th March 1903 brought a record attendance to witness history being made when AMBUSH II became the first horse to represent a reigning monarch in the Grand National. King Edward VII's hero of 1900, shouldering 12 st 7 lbs, was set to concede weight to all his twenty-two rivals including the incomparable MANIFESTO, still going strong despite advancing years. Both DRUMCREE and DRUMREE took part again, although on this occasion the latter found far less favour, being on the 25/1 mark, whereas DRUMCREE was the overall favourite at 13/2.

Named after the home of his dam in County Westmeath, DRUMCREE was sold by breeder Mr C Hope to Sir Charles Nugent who trained the gelding at Cranborne in Dorset on behalf of Mr Owen Williams. After carrying Williams' colours into second place in 1901, DRUMCREE changed hands once more, this time for £2,500, going to the wealthy J S Morrison, who had large investments in South Africa. Having already twice completed the 'National course under the guidance of the trainer's son, Hugh Nugent, the gelding was to be partnered again by this talented amateur. Unfortunately he received a riding injury shortly before the race, whereupon twenty-one-year-old Percy Woodland became a worthy substitute. Son of the Hendon trainer, Woodland rode his first winner when thirteen years old, and was much in demand both on the flat and over jumps. His short-leathered style raised eyebrows, but the young man's rare ability to balance a horse at an obstacle soon brought its rewards. In marking the visit of His Majesty to Aintree, the City of Liverpool and the racecourse executive excelled themselves in true northern fashion. The Royal caval-cade from Knowsley to Aintree contained The King, Lord Derby and Lord and Lady Roberts. Trains from Exchange station in the city centre to the racecourse were fitted with electric lights and Mr Topham introduced a railed-off parade ring in the paddock to permit a clearer view of contestants.

DRUMCREE with handlers before the race

Straight from the off AMBUSH II jumped to the front, either in defiance of the handicapper or in an effort to delight his watching Royal owner. ORANGE PAT and EXPERT II came down at the first, FAIRLAND, KILMALLOG and INQUISITOR at the next and Horatio Bottomley's CUSHENDUN soon added to the heavy early toll. Altogether, the first circuit reduced the field to twelve runners and the catalogue of disaster continued on the second. On the way to the final fence, DRUMCREE held a fractional lead over DRUMREE, AMBUSH II, DETAIL and MANIFESTO with KIRKLAND making up ground hand over fist. Nothing appeared to be going better than DRUMREE at this stage but suddenly and inexplicably the Duke of Westminster's gelding fell on the flat as if stricken with a fit of the staggers. AMBUSH II was now the principal danger to

DRUMCREE, running on strongly under Algy Anthony and bringing a somewhat premature roar from the crowd. Hitting the fence hard, AMBUSH II toppled over with no chance of recovery, leaving DRUMCREE to run on to a three length victory from DETAIL, while twenty lengths back MANIFESTO and KIRKLAND fought out a spirited tussle for third place. The cheers which greeted MANIFESTO getting the upper hand of the younger horse by a head rivalled those for the winner, many people believing that this must surely be his last 'National. Percy Woodland celebrated his great triumph by coming out the next day to ride the winners of the Liverpool Handicap Hurdle and the Champion 'Chase. But sadly the year which began on such a high note for trainer Sir Charles Nugent ended in tragedy when his son Hugh was killed in a hurdle race at Ostend.

Winning trainer Sir Charles Nugent and son Hugh

1903

Of 2,525 sovs., (including a trophy value 105 sovs.), by subscription of 25 sovs., each, 15 forfeit or 5 sovs., if declared: For five-year-olds & upwards; second to receive 300 sovs., and the third 200 sovs., out of the stakes

Date: 27th March 1903	Starters: 23	Time: 10 mins 9²/₅ secs
1st **DRUMCREE**	**9.11–3** *(Mr J S Morrison)*	**P Woodland**
2nd **DETAIL**	**7.9–13** *(Mr White-Heather)*	**A Nightingall**
3rd **MANIFESTO**	**15.12–3** *(Mr J G Bulteel)*	**G Williamson**
4th **KIRKLAND**	**7.10–8** *(Mr F Bibby)*	**F Mason**
5th **BENVENIR**	**7.9–12** *(Mr J Meleady)*	**Mr Hayes**
6th **PAWNBROKER**	**8.9–9** *(Mr R C Dawson)*	**J O'Brien**
7th **FANCIFUL**	**8.11–7** *(Mr H Tunstall-Moore)*	**Mr W P Cullen**

Also Ran:

AMBUSH II 9.12–7 (His Majesty The King) **A Anthony** *Fell*; DRUMREE 7.11–4 (Duke of Westminster) **J Phillips** *Fell*; INQUISITOR 8.10–13 (Lord Coventry) **E Matthews** *Fell*; FAIRLAND 10.10–13 (Mr T Bater) **W Morgan** *Fell*; MARPESSA 6.10–11 (Major Eustace Loder) **Mr Persse** *Fell*; CUSHENDUN 8.10–10 (Mr Horatio Bottomley) **F E Cole** *Fell*; KILMALLOG 6.10–9 (Mr J R Cooper) **T Moran** *Fell*; DEARSLAYER 7.10–11 (Mr J G Bulteel) **E Piggott** *Fell*; THE PRIDE OF MABESTOWN 7.10–8 (Mr Owen J Williams) **W Dollery** *Fell*; MATTHEW 7.10–7 (Mr John Widger) **Mr J W Widger** *Fell*; EXPERT II 6.10–5 (Mr W Haven) **S J Woodland** *Fell*; AUNT MAY 7.10–0 (Mr B W Parr) **D Read** *Fell*; PATLANDER 7.10–7 (Mr W Nelson) **M Walsh** *Fell*; ORANGE PAT 7.9–10 (Mr B W Parr) **R Morgan** *Fell*; SAXILBY 6.9–7 (Mr G C Dobell) **G Goswell** *Fell*; GILLIE II 11.9–7 (Mr C D Barrow) **A Wilkins** *Fell*

The Betting: *13/2 Drumcree; 100/14 Detail; 10/1 Aunt May, The Pride of Mabestown & Matthew; 100/8 Kirkland; 100/6 Ambush II, Fanciful & Inquisitor; 20/1 Marpessa, Fairland & Kilmallog; 25/1 Manifesto, Drumree & Dearslayer; 40/1 Patlander, Expert II & Orange Pat; 50/1 Saxilby; 100/1 Cushendun, Pawnbroker, Benvenir & Gillie II.*

Distances: *Three lengths; twenty lengths; a head*

Winner Trained By: *Sir Charles Nugent, Cranborne, Dorset*

Value to Winning Owner: *£2,000*

1904

Happy celebrations welcomed the King to Aintree once more this year, but there was sadness in the realisation that this was most certainly the swan song of a horse who had become as much a part of the great steeplechase as Becher's Brook itself. At sixteen years of age, MANIFESTO was about to make his exit from the 'National stage he had graced so many times. Leading flat-race jockey Mornington Cannon was so impressed with MANIFESTO's appearance on the morning of the race that he persuaded the trainer to allow him to ride the legendary gelding in his final gallop, but there was another horse attracting attention in the paddock for a different reason – the ungainly giant MOIFAA had come all the way from New Zealand.

MOIFAA won nine times from thirteen starts as a four-year-old in his native New Zealand, further enhancing his reputation the following season with victory under 13 st in a three-and-a-half-mile 'chase. Subsequently despatched to England, the brown gelding was shipwrecked off the coast of Ireland, to be found some time later parading on the beach by some fishermen. Running in the colours of Mr Spencer Gollan, MOIFAA's three races before the 'National were uninspiring affairs and since his trainer Hickey of Epsom and jockey Arthur Birch were virtually unknown, his only fame in Britain was as a sort of equine Robinson Crusoe!

The King's topweight AMBUSH II was the 7/2 favourite from PATLANDER, DETAIL, INQUISITOR and KIRKLAND, MANIFESTO being at 20/1 and MOIFAA and the Widgers' representative THE GUNNER both on the 25/1 mark.

INQUISITOR set the pace and as in last year's race, the early fences exacted a heavy toll. RAILOFF came down at the first and that ominous groan from the third told its all too familiar story: the favourite AMBUSH II had fallen, together with DEARSLAYER. At the next, the leader INQUISITOR went leaving MOIFAA in front, much to the discomfort of jockey Birch, who was left with no choice but to allow the hard pulling giant to make his own way. Powering

The 'Kiwi' MOIFAA journeyed from New Zealand to find fame as a convincing 'National winner

his way through rather than over the fifth fence, the New Zealander left a tumbling mass in his wake with DETAIL the nearest challenger. SHAUN ABOO, THE PRIDE OF MABESTOWN, KIRKLAND, THE GUNNER and MANIFESTO made ground on the leading pair jumping the Water but back in the country MOIFAA was still setting a merry gallop. DETAIL drew within two lengths of the leader at Becher's, only to be knocked over by the riderless AMBUSH II at the Canal Turn and when THE PRIDE OF MABESTOWN fell two out, the issue was beyond question barring a fall, which MOIFAA avoided with perfect leaps at both jumps, coming home an easy eight length winner. KIRKLAND held on by a neck to be second from THE GUNNER and SHAUN ABOO. Then came ROBIN HOOD IV, BAND OF HOPE, NAHILLAH and finally, but to prolonged cheers, the magnificent MANIFESTO. The age-old maxim, 'handsome is as handsome does', was once more demonstrated. The awkward-looking MOIFAA was the first Colonial winner of the Grand National.

THE GRAND NATIONAL HANDICAP STEEPLECHASE

1904

Of 2,525 sovs., (including a trophy value 100 sovs.), by subscription of 25 sovs., each, 15 forfeit or 5 sovs., if declared to run: For five-year-olds & upwards; second to receive 300 sovs., and the third 200 sovs., out of the stakes

Date: 25th March 1904	Starters: 26	Time: 9 mins 58⅗ secs
1st **MOIFAA**	8.10–7 *(Mr Spencer Gollan)*	**A Birch**
2nd **KIRKLAND**	8.10–10 *(Mr F Bibby)*	**F Mason**
3rd **THE GUNNER**	7.10–4 *(Mr John Widger)*	**Mr J W Widger**
4th **SHAUN ABOO**	6.10–1 *(Major J D Edwards)*	**A Waddington**
5th **ROBIN HOOD IV**	6.10–3 *(Mr E E Lennon)*	**A Magee**
6th **BAND OF HOPE**	8.10–0 *(Capt M Hughes)*	**P Cowley**
7th **NAHILLAH**	8.9–11 *(Mr M Crowther)*	**Mr A Wood**
8th **MANIFESTO**	16.12–1 *(Mr J G Bulteel)*	**E Piggott**

Also Ran:
AMBUSH II 10.12–6 (His Majesty The King) **A Anthony** *Fell*; *THE PRIDE OF MABESTOWN 8.11–0* (Mr O J Williams) **Mr A Gordon** *Fell*; *INQUISITOR 9.10–11* (Lord Coventry) **E Acres** *Fell*; *PATLANDER 8.10–10* (Mr W E Nelson) **E Matthews** *Fell*; *DEARSLAYER 8.10–10* (Prince Hatzfeldt) **J Phillips** *Fell*; *DETAIL 8.10–7* (Mr White-Heather) **A Nightingall** *Knocked-over*; *CUSHENDUN 9.10–7* (Mr Horatio Bottomley) **D Morris** *Fell*; *KNIGHT OF ST PATRICK 7.10–6* (Mr A Buckley, jnr) **M Walsh** *Pulled-up*; *MAY KING 8.10–5* (Mr W J Compton) **W Dollery** *Pulled-up*; *COMFIT 6.10–5* (Mr F Bibby) **F Hartigan** *Fell*; *HILL OF BREE 8.10–4* (Mr Hall Walker) **G Goswell** *Fell*; *KIORA 9.10–3* (Capt Scott) **T McGuire** *Fell*; *BIOLOGY 7.10–1* (Mr Horatio Bottomley) **D Read** *Fell*; *LOCH LOMOND 6.9–10* (Mr F H Wise) **F Freemantle** *Fell*; *RAILOFF 7.9–9* (Mr H K Hamilton Wedderburn) **E Sullivan** *Fell*; *OLDTOWN 13.9–8* (Comte de Madre) **Mr H M Ripley** *Pulled-up*; *HONEYMOON II 9.9–7* (Mr Barclay Walker) **W Lynn** *Fell*; *BENVENIR 8.9–10* (Mr W N W Gape) **P Woodland** *Brought-down*

The Betting: *7/2 Ambush II; 7/1 Patlander; 100/14 Detail; 9/1 Inquisitor; 100/7 Kirkland; 20/1 Benvenir & Manifesto; 25/1 May King, Moifaa, Dearslayer, The Gunner & Comfit; 33/1 Biology, Robin Hood IV & Hill of Bree; 40/1 Band of Hope & Kiora; 50/1 Honeymoon II; 66/1 The Pride of Mabestown & Loch Lomond.*

Distances: *Eight lengths; a neck*

Winner Trained By: *Mr W Hickey, Epsom, Surrey*

Value to Winning Owner: *£2,000*

1905

AMBUSH II began his build-up to the big race with a seasonal reappearance in the Stewards' Steeplechase at Kempton Park in February. Not at all his former self, the gelding finished last of the seven runners and worse was to follow. Within weeks came the shocking news from the Curragh, that the Royal champion had died after breaking a blood vessel during training. Greatly saddened by this unexpected turn of events, the King instructed that the skeleton of AMBUSH II be presented to a museum and that a replacement be sought to represent him at Liverpool. It was MOIFAA that was finally purchased on the King's behalf by Lord Marcus Beresford, which must have caused a degree of embarrassment to His Lordship, for it was he who had described the New Zealand horse just twelve months before as having the head and shoulders of an overstuffed camel. Chosen to ride MOIFAA was former shepherd and partner of CLOISTER, Bill Dollery. Through a combination of patriotism and sympathy, the pair went off 4/1 favourites. Of the twenty-seven runners the majority were making their first appearance in the race and of these, RANUNCULUS was the most fancied, having carried big weights to victory in his last two races. Of the old brigade, AUNT MAY, DETAIL, DEARSLAYER and KIRKLAND found most favour among backers, the last named at 6/1 the nearest to MOIFAA in the market.

Bred by the Reverend E Clifford at Moneygay, County Limerick, KIRKLAND was sired by the Australian stallion KIRKHAM, from an unnamed mare. Winning first time out at Kilmallock at the age of four when owned by Mr T A Hartigan, KIRKLAND soon passed into the hands of the Liverpool manufacturer Frank Bibby, for whom he won the Grand Sefton before finishing fourth and second in the 'National. Great doubt was cast over whether KIRKLAND would get to Liverpool when he suffered an injury in training, but with careful nursing the gelding was restored to fitness. Unusual precautions were then taken to ensure that jockey Frank Mason avoided any setbacks. He was paid £300 not to ride in any races for a fortnight before the race, for fear that a fall may deny KIRKLAND of his valuable assistance. Mr Lort Phillips owned a share in the horse, in addition to preparing him for racing at Lawrenny Park, near Tenby in Pembrokeshire, where the trainer's licence was held by Mr E Thomas.

So well behaved were the assembled competitors that the starter actually despatched them at 2.59 pm, one minute before the appointed time. DETAIL rushed to the front, jumping the first ahead of MOIFAA, TIMOTHY TITUS and RANUNCULUS and although this obstacle was cleared safely by all, the next one brought the first casualties, while ASCETIC'S SILVER was a faller at the next. Becher's claimed no victims this time round, but Valentine's took its toll when DETAIL and BIOLOGY crashed there. With the riderless ASCETIC'S SILVER keeping them company, RANUNCULUS and TIMOTHY TITUS led the well-strung out field back to the stands. DEARSLAYER and MISS CLIFDEN II fell at the first fence second time, and Becher's proved too much for the favourite MOIFAA. Percy Woodland brought NAPPER TANDY with a smooth run on the outside at Valentine's, and when TIMOTHY TITUS left the contest at the next fence Captain McLaren's gelding looked the danger to RANUNCULUS. But 'Tich' Mason had been biding his time with KIRKLAND, and at the Anchor Bridge he moved into the lead. With only ASCETIC'S SILVER running loose ahead of him, the locally-owned horse completed his clear round running on strongly on the flat to resist the determined challenge of NAPPER TANDY by three lengths. Four lengths further back came 100/1 outsider BUCKAWAY II giving Alf Newey a memorable introduction to the 'National, just a neck in front of the fourth placed RANUNCULUS. Liverpool went crazy rejoicing at the success of 'their' two Franks, Bibby and Mason, and of course the chestnut gelding who made it all possible.

MOIFAA was never asked to exert himself in the race again, His Majesty eventually making a present of him to Colonel Brocklehurst, under whom he spent a well-earned retirement hunting in Leicestershire.

THE GRAND NATIONAL HANDICAP STEEPLECHASE
1905

Of 2,550 sovs., (including a trophy value 100 sovs.), by subscription of 25 sovs., each, 15 forfeit or 5 sovs. if declared; For five-year-olds & upwards; second to receive 300 sovs., and the third 200 sovs., out of the stakes

Date: 31st March 1905	Starters: 27	Time: 9 mins 48⅘ secs
1st **KIRKLAND**	**9.11–5** *(Mr F Bibby)*	**F Mason**
2nd **NAPPER TANDY**	**8.10–0** *(Capt McLaren)*	**P Woodland**
3rd **BUCKAWAY II**	**7.9–11** *(Mr P E Speakman)*	**A Newey**
4th **RANUNCULUS**	**7.9–12** *(Mr T Nolan)*	**C Hollebone**
5th **HERCULES II**	**9.9–10** *(Mr D Faber)*	**J Dillon**
6th **BAND OF HOPE**	**9.9–11** *(Mr W M G Singer)*	**W Donnelly**
7th **COTTENSHOPE**	**9.9–11** *(Mr C Levy)*	**D Morris**

Also Ran:
MOIFAA 9.11–12 (His Majesty The King) **W Dollery** *Fell*; *PHIL MAY 6.11–0* (Col H T Fenwick) **R Morgan** *Fell*; *THE ACTUARY 7.10–9* (Mr Leslie Rome) **E Matthews** *Pulled-up*; *AUNT MAY 9.10–9* (Mr B W Parr) **E Sullivan** *Fell*; *MATTHEW 9.10–9* (Mr W Bass) **W Morgan** *Pulled-up*; *DETAIL 9.10–8* (Mr White-Heather) **P Cowley** *Fell*; *DEARSLAYER 9.10–8* (Prince Hatzfeldt) **Mr A Hastings** *Fell*; *LONGTHORPE 7.10–7* (Lord Sefton) **F Freemantle** *Refused*; *SEAHORSE II 7.10–7* (Mr Cotton) **J O'Brien** *Pulled-up*; *BUCHERON 10.10–6* (Count de Songeon) **U David** *Fell*; *TIMOTHY TITUS 7.10–5* (Mr W B Partridge) **E Morgan** *Fell*; *ASCETIC'S SILVER 8.10–5* (Mr P J Dunne) **T H Dunn** *Fell*; *KIORA 10.10–5* (Mr W H Pawson) **Mr W H Pawson** *Fell*; *ROYAL DRAKE 7.10–4* (Sir P Walker) **A Waddington** *Fell*; *BIOLOGY 8.10–2* (Mr Horatio Bottomley) **P Woodland** *Fell*; *WHAT NEXT 7.10–2* (Mr H B Black) **Capt Rasbotham** *Refused*; *MISS CLIFDEN II 9.9–13* (Mr D Faber) **F Barter** *Fell*; *SAXILBY 8.9–12* (Mr G C Dobell) **P Heaney** *Pulled-up*; *NEREUS 7.9–10* (Mr C Bower Ismay) **G Goswell** *Refused*; *HALLGATE 7.9–7* (Mr Delagarde) **A Cole** *Fell*

The Betting: *4/1 Moifaa; 6/1 Kirkland; 7/1 Ranunculus; 100/8 Aunt May; 100/7 Detail; 100/6 Dearslayer & Timothy Titus; 20/1 Phil May, Seahorse II, Royal Drake & Ascetic's Silver; 25/1 Napper Tandy; 33/1 Hercules II & Longthorpe; 40/1 Biology; 50/1 What Next; 66/1 Cottenshope, The Actuary, Nereus, Matthew & Saxilby; 100/1 Kiora, Miss Clifden II, Bucheron, Buckaway II, Hallgate & Band of Hope.*

Distances: *Three lengths; four lengths*

Winner Trained By: *Mr E Thomas, Lawrenny, Pembrokeshire*

Value to Winning Owner: *£2,025*

1906

Prize-money was again increased, a novel introduction being the allocation of £50 for the horse which finished fourth. For many, however, the race lost much of its interest with the news that neither of the two most recent winners, KIRKLAND or MOIFAA would be participating. Mr Bibby found a suitable replacement in COMFIT, but to everyone's regret, His Majesty the King was not represented this time. Making a return to the scene of his 1903 triumph, DRUMCREE headed the handicap with 12 st, but not the betting at 33/1. He was partnered by the prominent amateur Walter Bulteel, whose brother enjoyed such fame as the owner of the immortal MANIFESTO. Also trained by Sir Charles Nugent and sharing the same ownership as DRUMCREE, was JOHN M.P., who was tackling the 'National for the first time. Unbeaten in five races during the current campaign, he dominated the market at 7/2, his nearest rivals in the betting being PHIL MAY, COMFIT and TIMOTHY TITUS. In preceding KIRKLAND home last year, albeit riderless, ASCETIC'S SILVER had caught the eye of no less a judge of horseflesh than the Honourable Aubrey Hastings. Upon the death of the owner and breeder of the horse, Mr J P Dunne of County Meath, Hastings bought the entire for 800 guineas, ignoring the rumour that he had gone wrong in his wind. In charge of a large string at his Wroughton yard, Aubrey Hastings' principal patron was the popular international sportsman Prince Franz Hatzfeldt and it was with this European nobleman's all-yellow colours that ASCETIC'S SILVER was henceforth adorned. The Prince's desire to win the 'National can be gauged by the fact that three of the twenty-three runners this year belonged to him. But it was ASCETIC'S SILVER, a former Irish Grand National winner and half-brother to both DRUMCREE and CLOISTER, who was considered the pick of the trio, receiving the personal assistance of trainer Aubrey Hastings from the saddle.

After early morning rain, the clouds cleared, the sun came out and a record crowd eagerly awaited the parade for the big race. COMFIT caused a false start but at the second attempt the starter got them away evenly, PHIL MAY and DATHI being the first to break line. JOHN M.P. delighted the watching crowds, jumping his way into second place behind PHIL MAY on the approach to Becher's. Racing on at a thunderous pace, PHIL MAY and JOHN M.P. came into the Canal Turn together, but the noise from onlookers so disturbed the latter that he completely lost his concentration, mistimed his leap and fell into the wings of the obstacle, turning the cheers to groans. Locally-owned COMFIT was another casualty here, so injured that he had to be put out of his misery. DEARSLAYER suffered cruel luck when just behind the leaders on re-entering the racecourse. His saddle tree broke, the stirrup irons falling uselessly to the ground leaving amateur Percy Whitaker with no alternative but to pull up. The race was still being run at a furious pace and with TIMOTHY TITUS holding the advantage over Becher's, BUCKAWAY II, ASCETIC'S SILVER and RED LAD began gaining ground. At the Canal Turn, TIMOTHY TITUS came to grief, followed at Valentine's by GLADIATOR and it was from here that ASCETIC'S SILVER assumed command and a perfect leap at the last ditch put the issue beyond doubt. With the last fence safely behind him ASCETIC'S SILVER ran out a comfortable ten length winner from RED LAD and AUNT MAY, whose amateur jockey Henry Seymour Persse, went on to become better known as 'Atty' Persse, the trainer of four classic winners and a flying machine known as THE TETRARCH.

Prince Hatzfeldt gave all the credit to Aubrey Hastings and not without reason, for the trainer had been forced to waste vigorously in order to make the weight on the horse who was first past the post in two successive 'Nationals. It was fortunate for all concerned, that on the second occasion he remembered to bring his rider with him!

THE GRAND NATIONAL HANDICAP STEEPLECHASE

1906

Of 2,750 sovs., (including a trophy value 125 sovs.), by subscription of 25 sovs., 15 forfeit or 5 sovs. if declared; For five-year-olds & upwards; second to receive 300 sovs., third 200 sovs., & the fourth 50 sovs., out of the stakes

Date: 30th March 1906	Starters: 23	Time: 9 mins 34²⁄₅ secs

1st **ASCETIC'S SILVER**	**9.10–9** *(Prince Hatzfeldt)*	**Mr A Hastings**
2nd **RED LAD**	**6.10–2** *(Mr E M Lucas)*	**C Kelly**
3rd **AUNT MAY**	**10.11–2** *(Mr B W Parr)*	**Mr H S Persse**
4th **CRAUTACAUN**	**8.10–6** *(Mr J Wynford Philipps)*	**Ivor Anthony**
5th **WOLF'S FOLLY**	**8.10–6** *(Mr A Gorham)*	**T Fitton**
6th **OATLANDS**	**6.9–13** *(Mr C T Garland)*	**H Aylin**
7th **GLADIATOR**	**6.9–9** *(Mr G Johnstone)*	**E Driscoll** [remounted]
8th **DRUMCREE**	**12.12–0** *(Mr J S Morrison)*	**Mr W Bulteel**
9th **PHIL MAY**	**7.11–5** *(Mr Cotton)*	**J Owens** [remounted]

Also Ran:
JOHN M.P. 7.11–10 (Mr J S Morrison) **W Taylor** *Fell; ROMAN LAW 8.11–5* (Mr A Buckley, jnr) **M Walsh** *Knocked-over; COMFIT 8.11–0* (Mr F Bibby) **F Mason** *Fell; TIMOTHY TITUS 8.10–12* (Mr W B Partridge) **E Morgan** *Fell; DATHI 9.10–4* (Mr T Clyde) **A Birch** *Fell; BUCKAWAY II 8.10–4* (Mr P E Speakman) **A Newey** *Fell; KIORA 11.10–4* (Mr C Bewicke) **G Clancy** *Knocked-over; DEARSLAYER 10.10–4* (Prince Hatzfeldt) **Mr P Whitaker** *Pulled-up; HILL OF BREE 10.10–3* (Mr W Hall-Walker) **R Chadwick** *Knocked-over; CANTER HOME 11.9–13* (Lord Sefton) **A Aylin** *Fell; HARD TO FIND 6.9–7* (Prince Hatzfeldt) **E R Morgan** *Fell; GLENREX 6.9–9* (Mr Barclay Walker) **Mr R Walker** *Fell; ST BOSWELLS 8.9–7* (Mr J Bell-Irving) **D Phelan** *Fell; PIERRE 8.9–7* (Mr W Paul) **J Dillon** *Pulled-up*

The Betting: *7/2 John M.P.; 10/1 Phil May, Comfit & Timothy Titus; 100/7 Roman Law; 100/6 Oatlands, Wolf's Folly, Gladiator & Crautacaun; 20/1 Ascetic's Silver & Buckaway II; 25/1 Aunt May & Dathi; 33/1 Drumcree, Kiora, Pierre & Red Lad; 50/1 Dearslayer; 66/1 Hard to Find, Hill of Bree, St Boswells & Canter Home; 100/1 Glenrex.*

Distances: *Ten lengths; two lengths*

Winner Trained By: *The Honourable Aubrey Hastings, Wroughton, Wiltshire*

Value to Winning Owner: *£2,175*

1907

In what the press were quick to describe as the most sub-standard gathering of horses ever to compete for Aintree's famous 'chase, the only real stars were top-weight ASCETIC'S SILVER and the ageing DRUMCREE. Fortunately, whatever the journalists said, the 'National had long since won the people's recognition as the high-spot of the sporting year, and with little reason to suspect that the 1907 race would lack any of the usual spectacle, attendances at Aintree on the day were greater than ever. Prize money rose to its highest level yet, with £3,000 set to be distributed between the first four home in the sunshine on 22nd March. Sharing favouritism at 7/1 were the first two home twelve months before, ASCETIC'S SILVER and RED LAD.

If there ever can be such a thing as a form horse for this, the biggest gamble on the turf, then seven-year-old EREMON at 8/1 was surely it. Bred in Ireland by James Cleary, the son of THURLES showed every indication of being thick-winded, a malady which rendered him almost unsaleable. Eventually purchased for the bargain price of £400 by Mr Stanley Howard, EREMON was sent to be trained by Tom Coulthwaite at Hednesford. A shrewd, blunt Lancastrian who was considered something of an eccentric, Coulthwaite spent the early part of his life training athletes and upon becoming a racehorse trainer used the same principles with his new charges. All his skills were required with EREMON, however, who was six years old before making his first racecourse appearance. Adapting remarkably well to 'chasing, the gelding won the first ever race over fences at Newbury in the autumn of 1906 and in the light of his two most recent victories under big weights at Warwick and Haydock, was judged to be

well in the 'National with just 10 st 1 lb.

That familiar figure, Arthur Coventry, was most insistent as starter that the line should be level before letting them go, which he perfected at the second attempt, upon which EREMON took them along at a good rate to the first fence. In the usual scrimmage over this obstacle, KILTS came down, tragically breaking his neck and two fences later Prince Hatzfeldt's second string RATHVALE crashed to the ground. Although EREMON was still standing, Alfred Newey had already run into trouble, with a broken stirrup leather causing him to relinquish the lead to TIMOTHY TITUS. Over Becher's, EREMON was back on terms with TIMOTHY TITUS, but Newey now had another problem: the unwelcome attentions of the riderless RATHVALE. As they negotiated the Canal Turn he found it necessary to use his whip on the offending loose horse. CENTRE BOARD came down here, followed by TIMOTHY TITUS, leaving EREMON at the head of affairs. EXTRAVAGANCE joined issue with the leader coming back to the stands, immediately drawing the attention of the villainous RATHVALE, who caused him to fall at the Water. All the way back into the country, RATHVALE weaved back and forth across the path of EREMON, with Newey flailing away with his whip in an attempt to keep the intruder at bay. Nevertheless, he was ten lengths clear jumping the Canal Turn, where RED LAD and DETAIL came to grief, further reducing the field by bringing down LOOP HEAD and BOUCHAL OGUE. Sensing a chance of victory in spite of all his tribulations, Alfred Newey pushed on, clearing Valentine's fully twenty lengths ahead of the rest. Over the last two fences TOM WEST made a game and determined effort, making good ground all the way on the leader but at the post, justice was done with EREMON winning by six lengths.

Incurring a 12 lbs penalty for his Aintree success, EREMON made light of it ten days later in the Lancashire 'Chase at Manchester, coming home the easiest of winners and raising expectations for the forthcoming season. Sadly it was not to be, for the gelding escaped his handlers on the gallops soon afterwards, so injuring himself in the process that he had to be put down.

THE GRAND NATIONAL HANDICAP STEEPLECHASE
1907

Of 3,000 sovs., (including a trophy value 125 sovs.), by subscription of 25 sovs., 15 forfeit or 5 sovs. if declared: For five-year-olds & upwards; second to receive 300 sovs., third 200 sovs., & the fourth 75 sovs., out of stakes

Date: 22nd March 1907	Starters: 23	Time: 9 mins 47½ secs
1st **EREMON**	**7.10–1** *(Mr S Howard)*	**A Newey**
2nd **TOM WEST**	**8.9–12** *(Mr H Hardy)*	**H Murphy**
3rd **PATLANDER**	**11.10–7** *(Mr W Nelson)*	**J Lynn**
4th **RAVENSCLIFFE**	**9.10–9** *(Mr R J Hannam)*	**F Lyall**
5th **BARABBAS II**	**6.10–7** *(Mr S J Unzue)*	**R Morgan**
6th **ASCETIC'S SILVER**	**10.12–7** *(Prince Hatzfeldt)*	**Mr A Hastings**
7th **BUCKAWAY II**	**9.10–4** *(Mr P E Speakman)*	**H Aylin** [remounted]
8th **NAPPER TANDY**	**10.10–13** *(Capt McLaren)*	**Capt R H Collis**

Also Ran:
TIMOTHY TITUS 9.11–10 (Mr W B Partridge) **C Kelly** *Fell*; *DRUMCREE 13.11–9* (Mr J S Morrison) **Mr W Bulteel** *Fell*; *ROMAN LAW 9.11–7* (Mr A Buckley, jnr) **A Anthony** *Pulled-up*; *RED LAD 7.11–3* (Mr C Hibbert) **J Dillon** *Fell*; *SEISDON PRINCE 8.11–0* (Mr T Ashton) **M Phelan** *Fell*; *RATHVALE 6.10–13* (Prince Hatzfeldt) **E Driscoll** *Fell*; *EXTRAVAGANCE 6.10–11* (Mr G Walmsley) **G Goswell** *Fell*; *CENTRE BOARD 7.10–11* (Lord Howard de Walden) **J Cain** *Refused*; *BOUCHAL OGUE 11.10–7* (Mr J Meynell-Knight) **C Graham** *Fell*; *YORK II 8.10–6* (Mr L Robinson) **T Moran** *Fell*; *KILTS 7.10–3* (Mr T Arthur) **R H Harper** *Fell*; *DETAIL 11.10–0* (Mr White-Heather) **W Payne** *Fell*; *TEDDIE III 9.9–13* (Mr W P Hanly) **Mr P O'Brien-Butler** *Fell*; *LOOP HEAD 6.9–12* (Mr F Bibby) **A Hogan** *Fell*; *THE FOREMAN 8.9–7* (Mr T Nolan) **E Lawn** *Fell*

The Betting: *7/1 Red Lad & Ascetic's Silver; 8/1 Eremon; 10/1 Extravagance; 100/8 Timothy Titus; 100/7 Ravenscliffe; 100/6 Tom West & Kilts; 20/1 Rathvale, Barabbas II & Centre Board; 25/1 Drumcree; 33/1 Napper Tandy; 40/1 Detail.*

Distances: *Six lengths; a neck*

Winner Trained By: *Mr Tom Coulthwaite, Hednesford, Staffordshire*

Value to Winning Owner: *£2,400*

1908

The Royal colours were in 'National action once more, again worn by Algy Anthony, but conveyed this time by the gelding FLAXMAN. Little was known of the King's horse, for most of FLAXMAN's racing had been in Ireland, but the general opinion was that even at 33/1 he was a more than welcome attraction. Local enthusiasm also received a boost with KIRKLAND back after a three-year absence and despite the burden of top weight, the popularity of Frank Bibby's horse ensured his place at the head of the betting. Among the other supported runners were last year's runner-up TOM WEST, and the newcomers SPRINGBOK, JOHNSTOWN LAD and PADDY MAHER. But totally ignored in the ring were three competitors who added a delightful international flavour to the proceedings, CHORUS, PROPHET III and RUBIO. Although homebred, the first two belonged to Mr Foxhall Keene, the American so instrumental in establishing 'chasing in the United States. RUBIO, on the other hand, was English owned and trained, but bred at the Rancho del Paso Stud of Mr James Ben Ali Haggin in California. His sire, the English-bred STAR RUBY, was a half-brother to the all-conquering SCEPTRE, the winner of four of the five classics in 1902.

Despatched to Newmarket sales as a yearling, RUBIO fetched only fifteen guineas, and soon afterwards was passed on to Major Frank Douglas-Pennant. Under the care of trainer Bernard Bletsoe, the immigrant gelding won three small races over fences in 1903, before breaking down badly. Then it was that a most unusual means of restoring the horse to fitness was adopted. The owner lent RUBIO to a friend who owned the Prospect Arms Hotel at Towcester, with instructions that he should be used to pull the hotel bus to and from the station each day. It apparently did the trick, for by the end of 1906 the horse was back in training, this time with Fred Withington at Danebury. When Ernie Piggott declared he would be unable to partner the stable's better fancied MATTIE MACGREGOR, William Bissill jumped at the chance of riding the mare instead of RUBIO as originally planned. The ride on the former 'bus-horse' was left to Henry Bryan Bletsoe, whose father Bernard, had first trained the American gelding and who would always be remembered as the man whose ingenious use of butter assisted GRUDON's success seven years before.

Although the going was decidedly heavy, the day was warm and sunny, a fact much appreciated by large sections of the crowd equipped with the craze of the age, the camera. Setting the early pace on ROMAN LAW, Alf Newey met with none of the problems he had on EREMON. Over the second JOHNSTOWN LAD and RUBIO took up the running, from FLAXMAN, MATTIE MACGREGOR and ROMAN LAW with KIRKLAND doing well in avoiding the blundering EXTRAVAGANCE. By the time the racecourse was reached the field was well strung out in the heavy ground although RUBIO appeared to be unhindered by the conditions. Leading over the Water by a length from THE LAWYER III, DATHI and SPRINGBOK, the American outsider took them back onto the final circuit looking as though he could stay forever. FLAXMAN momentarily revived hopes of another Royal victory but soon after the Brook, Algy Anthony lost a stirrup leather and from there on his task became increasingly difficult. Turning for home, the stable companions RUBIO and MATTIE MACGREGOR had drawn some way clear, and RUBIO put the issue beyond doubt with a splendid leap over the final obstacle, racing away to a ten length victory. KIRKLAND came down heavily at the last to be later remounted, but it was MATTIE MACGREGOR who followed the shock winner home, six lengths ahead of THE LAWYER III and FLAXMAN finishing fourth. Fred Withington had achieved what had never been done before, turning out the first two home in the toughest race of all. This was quite a start to a career which was to see him at the forefront of the trainers list until his retirement in 1930. His vast experience was recognised by his appointment, first to the National Hunt Committee and then to the Jockey Club and he became the first National Hunt trainer to serve a term as steward.

At Newmarket some weeks after the 'National, the Stars and Stripes flew high again, when NORMAN became the first American-bred winner of the Two Thousand Guineas.

THE GRAND NATIONAL HANDICAP STEEPLECHASE
1908

Of 3,000 sovs., (including a trophy value 125 sovs.), by subscription of 25 sovs., 15 forfeit or 5 sovs. if declared: For five-year-olds & upwards; second to receive 300 sovs., third 200 sovs., and the fourth 75 sovs., out of the stakes

Date: 27th March 1908	Starters: 24	Time: 10 mins 33⅕ secs
1st **RUBIO**	**10.10–5** *(Major F Douglas-Pennant)*	**H B Bletsoe**
2nd **MATTIE MACGREGOR**	**6.10–6** *(Mr W C Cooper)*	**W Bissill**
3rd **THE LAWYER III**	**11.10–3** *(Mr P Whitaker)*	**Mr P Whitaker**
4th **FLAXMAN**	**8.9–12** *(His Majesty The King)*	**A Anthony**
5th **SPRINGBOK**	**7.11–5** *(Col R L Birkin)*	**J O'Brien**
6th **RED HALL**	**11.10–8** *(Mr H G Farrant)*	**Mr H G Farrant**
7th **KIRKLAND**	**12.11–12** *(Mr F Bibby)*	**F Mason** [remounted]
8th **CHORUS**	**aged.10–5** *(Mr Foxhall Keene)*	**R Chadwick**

Also Ran:
MOUNT PROSPECT'S FORTUNE 6.11–11 (Mr P Nelke) **R Morgan** *Fell*; *ROMAN LAW 10.11–2* (Mr A Buckley, jnr) **A Newey** *Fell*; *SEISDON PRINCE 9.11–0* (Mr T Ashton) **M Phelan** *Fell*; *EXTRAVAGANCE 7.10–12* (Mr G Walmsley) **H Aylin** *Fell*; *LARA 7.10–8* (Capt J Foster) **Mr W Bulteel** *Fell*; *NANOYA 6.10–7* (Mr B W Parr) **J Lynn** *Fell*; *TOM WEST 9.10–7* (Mr H Hardy) **H Murphy** *Fell*; *JENKINSTOWN 7.10–5* (Mr S Howard) **F Morgan** *Pulled-up*; *YORK II 9.10–4* (Mr G Walmsley) **W Rollason** *Fell*; *PADDY MAHER 8.10–3* (Col Kirkwood) **Mr P O'Brien-Butler** *Fell*; *DATHI 11.10–2* (Mr J Wynford Philipps) **I Anthony** *Pulled-up*; *PROPHET III aged.10–0* (Mr Foxhall Keene) **J Dillon** *Fell*; *JOHNSTOWN LAD 7.9–12* (Mr J M Kerne) **E Driscoll** *Fell*; *WEE BUSBIE 11.9–11* (Mr J E Rogerson) **D Phelan** *Fell*; *ALERT III 8.9–11* (Mr T G Paget) **L Harland** *Fell*; *WILD FOX III 6.9–9* (Capt W A Pallin) **Capt W A Pallin** *Fell*

The Betting: *13/2 Kirkland; 8/1 Tom West & Springbok; 10/1 Johnstown Lad; 100/8 Paddy Maher; 100/7 Roman Law, Mount Prospect's Fortune, Seisdon Prince, Extravagance & The Lawyer III; 25/1 Mattie Macgregor & Lara; 33/1 Flaxman; 66/1 Rubio & Others.*

Distances: *Ten lengths; six lengths*

Winner Trained By: *Mr Fred Withington, Danebury, Hampshire*

Value to Winning Owner: £2,400

1909

Perhaps tempted by the surprise victory of RUBIO, more owners became keen to try their chances the next year, with eighty-four original entries. Of these, thirty-two stood their ground when 'National day came round, the biggest field for fifty-nine years. Prince Hatzfeldt, Major Douglas-Pennant and Mr Frank Bibby had each won and were trying again but it was a horse owned by a member of the famous Hennessy family which was the centre of attention. LUTTEUR III, a chestnut five-year-old gelding bred in France by Gaston Dreyfus, became the property of James Hennessy in 1905, whereupon he was sent to be trained by George Batchelor. Virtually useless on the flat, he was then used for a number of years as a hack. Eventually put back into training, he won at the first attempt over fences, and since jumping was clearly his forte, plans were made for a tilt at the 'National. Transferred early in 1909 to Harry Escott's yard at Lewes, the son of ST DAMIEN adapted well and put in a sterling performance to win Hurst Park's Champion Steeplechase. His partner was fellow Frenchman Georges Parfrement, a jockey with a high reputation across the Channel who made a careful study of all available maps of the course and decided that his way of dealing with the drop fences would be to lengthen his leathers. Taking the French pair to their hearts, the public gambled on LUTTEUR III to the extent that he became the 100/9 joint-favourite with the mare SHADY GIRL.

At flag-fall both going and weather were perfect. Over Becher's it was RUBIO, from SHADY GIRL, MATTIE MACGREGOR, TOM WEST and top weight ASCETIC'S SILVER, the only ones not still in the race being WICKHAM, LORD CHATHAM and PADDY MAHER. Well to the rear, but coping

"Lutteur III"
Grand National, 1909

French-bred LUTTEUR III, the last five-year-old to succeed

well with the fences, was LUTTEUR III. RUBIO approached the stands maintaining his lead, only to break down coming to the Water where he fell. The race was wide open going into Becher's, TOM WEST, CAUBEEN, SHADY GIRL and JUDAS disputing the lead with LUTTEUR III beginning to improve his position. After clearing the Canal Turn SHADY GIRL met with interference, and seizing his opportunity Georges Parfrement swept to the front with LUTTEUR III. Jumping the remaining fences swiftly and precisely, the five-year-old was always going that much better than his rivals, and despite a spirited charge by JUDAS, he won by two lengths. Mr Bibby's CAUBEEN filled third place a long way behind. To the chant of 'Vive la France', James Hennessy led in LUTTEUR III a popular and worthy winner.

Georges Parfrement displayed his talents frequently on both sides of the Channel, capturing many prizes, but shortly after winning the Imperial Cup in 1923, he was killed in a fall at Enghian.

1909

Of £3,000 (including a trophy value £125), by subscription of £25, 15 forfeit or 5 if declared to run; for 5-year-olds &
upwards. The second to receive £300, third £200 and the fourth £75 out of the stakes

Date: 26th March 1909	Starters: 32	Time: 9 mins 53⅘ secs
1st **LUTTEUR III**	**5.10−11** *(Mnsr James Hennessy)*	**G Parfrement**
2nd **JUDAS**	**8.10−10** *(Mr B W Parr)*	**R Chadwick**
3rd **CAUBEEN**	**8.11−7** *(Mr F Bibby)*	**F Mason**
4th **TOM WEST**	**10.10−9** *(Mr H Hardy)*	**H Murphy**
5th **HERCULES II**	**13.9−13** *(Mr R Faber)*	**Mr A Gordon**
6th **LEINSTER**	**11.11−7** *(Sir T Gallwey)*	**Mr J T Rogers**
7th **SHADY GIRL**	**8.10−9** *(Mr P Nelke)*	**G Clancy**
8th **ROBIN HOOD IV**	**11.9−9** *(Capt L H Jones)*	**Mr R H Walker**
9th **CARSEY**	**6.10−8** *(Mr J M Kerne)*	**Mr J M Kerne**
10th **PHAETHON**	**7.10−5** *(Col Kirkwood)*	**Mr H Ussher**
11th **WEE BUSBIE**	**12.9−13** *(Mr J E Rogerson)*	**D Phelan**
12th **LOGAN ROCK**	**9.10−0** *(Mr W L Longworth)*	**H Jackson**
13th **RATHVALE**	**8.11−7** *(Prince Hatzfeldt)*	**W Morgan**
14th **LORD RIVERS**	**7.10−6** *(Baron De Forest)*	**W Bulteel**
15th **RED HALL**	**12.10−12** *(Mr H G Farrant)*	**Mr H G Farrant** [Fell & remounted]
16th **COUNT RUFUS**	**aged.10−0** *(Mr W Charters)*	**W Payne** [Fell & remounted]

Also Ran:
ASCETIC'S SILVER 12.12–7 (Prince Hatzfeldt) **Mr A Hastings** *Failed to finish*; *RUSTIC QUEEN 7.12–0* (Mr H Hartland) **Mr A W Wood** *Fell*; *RUBIO 11.11–9* (Maj F Douglas-Pennant) **W Bissill** *Fell*; *MATTIE MACGREGOR 7.11–4* (Mr W C Cooper) **R Morgan** *Refused*; *DOMINO 7.11–1* (Mr H M Hartigan) **P Cowley** *Fell*; *LORD CHATHAM 6.11–0* (Mr G Aston) **J McKenna** *Fell*; *BLACK IVORY 9.10–12* (Mr A Scott) **Mr A Scott** *Pulled-up*; *WICKHAM 8.10–10* (Mr F Bibby) **Capt R H Collis** *Fell*; *PADDY MAHER 9.10–9* (Col Kirkwood) **Mr P O'Brien-Butler** *Fell*; *BRINEOGE 10.10–7* (Mr C F K Mainwaring) **H Smyth** *Failed to finish*; *RED MONK 11.10–6* (Mr F W Greswolde-Williams) **E Morgan** *Pulled-up*; *DAVY JONES 6.10–2* (Lord St Davids) **Ivor Anthony** *Fell*; *BUCKAWAY II 11.9–13* (Mr S F Gilbert) **R Wall** *Fell*; *YOUNG BUCK aged.9–12* (Mr F M Freake) **H B Bletsoe** *Fell*; *WILD FOX III 7.9–9* (Capt W A Pallin) **Capt W A Pallin** *Refused*; *THE LURCHER 7.9–9* (Mr T Stacey) **E Piggott** *Fell*

The Betting: *100/9 Lutteur III & Shady Girl; 100/8 Domino; 100/6 Tom West, Mattie Macgregor, Leinster & Davy Jones; 20/1 Caubeen, Rubio & Ascetic's Silver; 25/1 The Lurcher, Paddy Maher & Lord Rivers; 33/1 Judas, Hercules II & Robin Hood IV; 50/1 Wickham, Rustic Queen, Lord Chatham, Logan Rock, Count Rufus & Red Hall; 100/1 Others.*

Distances: *Two lengths; a bad third*

Winner Trained By: *H Escott, Lewes*

Value to Winning Owner: *£2,400*

1910

With no previous winner among the twenty-five runners, the build-up to this year's Grand National could have lost much of its interest, had it not been for the presence of a horse named JERRY M. Since proving himself over the course in the Becher 'Chase two years before, while still only five years old, the gelding had gone from strength to strength and his appearance in Aintree's supreme test had been eagerly awaited. For such a young horse to make his debut in the race at the top of the handicap with 12 st 7 lbs, was a measure of the esteem in which JERRY M was held and already likened to his owner's former champion CLOISTER, he started favourite at 6/1. The assistance of Algy Anthony ensured last year's second JUDAS a hefty following and Frank Bibby again selected 'Tich' Mason to accompany the main hope of his three representatives CAUBEEN. American interest lay in Mr Foxhall Keene's PRECENTOR II and the ever popular Prince Hatzfeldt had a double involvement with CARSEY and RATHVALE.

Carrying 10 st 5 lbs, JENKINSTOWN bore the EREMON colours of Stanley Howard. By HACKLER out of PLAYMATE, JENKINSTOWN was bred in County Meath by P Leonard and eventually became the property of Mr Howard for £600, to be trained by Tom Coulthwaite. There followed a series of disappointing performances, with just a solitary win in a two-mile 'chase at Wolverhampton at the end of 1909. Thirty-year-old Yorkshireman Robert Chadwick, second on JUDAS twelve months earlier, took the unpromising mount.

A snow-squall greeted the Prince of Wales, yet in true princely fashion he waved to the cheering crowds as Fred Withington accompanied him to the paddock, and as the starter lowered his flag, the sky cleared. In a rapid succession of mishaps, the first three fences eliminated half the field, but JERRY M's jockey, Driscoll, had taken an early forward position, enabling him to avoid the chaos and together with outsider ODOR, he raced in front towards Becher's, followed by FETLAR'S PRIDE, SPRINGBOK, GLENSIDE and JENKINSTOWN. ODOR assumed command coming to the Water Jump, and led just nine survivors out for the final round. That number was further reduced when WICKHAM, the least fancied of Frank Bibby's three runners, put both his stable companions on the ground, colliding with CAUBEEN, then running across GLENSIDE at the fence before Becher's, bringing that horse down as well as falling himself. SPRINGBOK landed first over Becher's but after turning at the Canal, SPRINGBOK's saddle slipped and Bill Payne was forced to pull him up. After clearing Valentine's, JERRY M forged ahead but nearing the Anchor crossing JENKINSTOWN joined him, these two drawing right away. In a terrific duel over the final two fences, JENKINSTOWN and JERRY M raced side by side, but the task of conceding thirty pounds to JENKINSTOWN was too much and JERRY M gallantly went under by three lengths. A similar distance back in third place was the rank outsider ODOR, and only two others finished.

Sadly, this was the last 'National in which that fine horseman Algy Anthony took part, but steeplechasing suffered its greatest loss on 6th May, when King Edward VII died. Some consolation was found in the fact that he had at least known the joy of victory in the race to which he gave such dignity. It would be many years before Royal colours were seen again in the Grand National.

MINORU is welcomed back to Epsom's winner's enclosure by King Edward VII after victory in the 1909 Derby

---

THE GRAND NATIONAL HANDICAP STEEPLECHASE
1910

Of £3,000, (including a trophy value £125), by subscription of £25, £15 forfeit, or £5 if declared to run; for five-year-olds and upwards. The second to receive £300, the third £200 and the fourth £75 out of the stakes

Date: 18th March 1910	Starters: 25	Time: 10 mins 44⅕ secs
1st **JENKINSTOWN**	**9.10–5** *(Mr Stanley Howard)*	**R Chadwick**
2nd **JERRY M**	**7.12–7** *(Mr C G Assheton-Smith)*	**E Driscoll**
3rd **ODOR**	**9.9–8** *(Mr R H Hall)*	**Mr R H Hall**
4th **CARSEY**	**7.10–7** *(Prince Hatzfeldt)*	**E R Morgan**
5th **FETLAR'S PRIDE**	**9.10–11** *(Mr A Law)*	**J Walsh, jnr**

Also Ran:

CAUBEEN *9.11–8* (Mr F Bibby) **F Mason** *Knocked-over*; BLOODSTONE *8.11–8* (Mr C Bower Ismay) **S Walkington** *Fell*; SPRINGBOK *9.11–5* (Col R L Birkin) **W Payne** *Pulled-up*; JUDAS *9.11–5* (Mr W W Bailey) **A Anthony** *Fell*; RATHVALE *9.11–1* (Prince Hatzfeldt) **R Morgan** *Fell*; LORD CHATHAM *7.10–12* (Mr G Aston) **J Dillon** *Fell*; ALBUERA *10.10–12* (Sir P Walker) **F Lyall** *Fell*; WICKHAM *9.10–11* (Mr F Bibby) **W Bulteel** *Fell*; PADDY MAHER *10.10–9* (Col Kirkwood) **Mr R H Walker** *Fell*; SHADY GIRL *9.10–8* (Mr P Nelke) **G Clancy** *Fell*; PRECENTOR II *aged.10–7* (Mr Foxhall Keene) **W Rollason** *Pulled-up*; GLENSIDE *8.10–4* (Mr F Bibby) **G Goswell** *Fell*; BRINEOGE *11.10–4* (Mr C F K Mainwaring) **Mr F A Brown** *Refused*; GENERAL FOX *6.10–2* (Lord Suffolk) **T Willmot** *Fell*; PHAETHON *8.10–1* (Col Kirkwood) **F Morgan** *Knocked-over*; CAPTAIN FARRELL *6.9–10* (Sir J Smiley) **G Brown** *Refused*; HERCULES II *14.9–9* (Mr David Faber) **C Hawkins** *Fell*; THE LURCHER *8.9–9* (Mr T Stacey) **F Dainty** *Fell*; LOGAN ROCK *10.9–7* (Mr W L Longworth) **H Jackson** *Knocked-over*; BUSHIDO *5.9–7* (Mr J A de Rothschild) **J Hetherington** *Knocked-over*

The Betting: *6/1 Jerry M; 13/2 Judas; 8/1 Caubeen; 100/8 Jenkinstown & Carsey; 100/7 Bloodstone & Albuera; 100/6 The Lurcher; 20/1 Logan Rock; 25/1 Glenside, Springbok & Fetlar's Pride; 33/1 Paddy Maher & Shady Girl; 66/1 Bushido, Wickham, Rathvale & General Fox.*

Distances: *Three lengths; three lengths*

Winner Trained By: *Tom Coulthwaite, Hednesford*

Value to Winning Owner: *£2,400*

1911

It had often been said that the object of the Aintree fence builder's art was one day to eliminate the entire Grand National field. If last year's event came close to realising that aim, the 1911 race was very near perfection indeed.

Although the absence of last year's uncrowned hero, JERRY M, denied the contest a degree of glamour, there could be no disputing the standard of at least a sizeable portion of the twenty-six runners. Fresh from a victory in Hurst Park's three mile Open Steeplechase, LUTTEUR III returned to the scene of his 1909 triumph with a multitude of admirers prepared to overlook the gelding's top weight of 12 st 3 lbs. Installed as clear 7/2 favourite, the Hennessy hope was spoken of as having only to stand up to win, despite the dreadfully heavy going on the day. Frank Bibby's CAUBEEN, and Mr Jones' RATHNALLY, the mount of Bob Chadwick, were joint second in the market at 8/1. GLENSIDE, the second of Mr Bibby's two runners, stood at 20/1, far from generous odds considering the horse only had one eye and was said to be wrong in his wind. By ST GRIS out of KILWINNET, GLENSIDE was bred in Ireland by Mr W G Peareth. Mr R H Harries raced the gelding in small steeplechases mainly in Wales and at Ludlow, where he was ridden by two extremely talented Welsh brothers, Ivor Anthony and the amateur Jack. Purchased by Frank Bibby, GLENSIDE made sufficient progress to be thought of as a 'National candidate, finishing second in the Grand Sefton before being put out of the big race by his stable-mate WICKHAM in 1910. Frank Mason was booked to ride GLENSIDE, but presumably the precautions taken to avoid his suffering race injuries in KIRKLAND's year were dispensed with on this occasion, for shortly

before the race he broke his leg. Trainer Captain R H Collis wisely chose as a replacement a man familiar with the horse, John Randolph Anthony, whose first ride in the race this would be.

A record crowd braved the elements on 'National day, despite torrential rain. But few could have imagined the dire effects the conditions were to have on the race. From the very first fence the contest became a story of disaster, with FLAXEN, CARDER, BRIDGE VI, CARSEY and GREAT CROSS all coming to grief, and all the way to Becher's the casualties increased. RATHNALLY and the American hope PRECENTOR II led the dwindling band over Becher's, half a length ahead of CAUBEEN, with HESPERUS MAGNUS and GLENSIDE the best placed of those still on their feet. The favourite LUTTEUR III moved up with the leaders after clearing the Brook only to misjudge the very next fence, where he became lodged across the top. Bob Chadwick made a great recovery at the Water Jump when RATHNALLY took off too soon, the pair going on into the country some four lengths in arrears of CAUBEEN and PRECENTOR II. When PRECENTOR II fell early on the second circuit, RATHNALLY moved upsides CAUBEEN, the two many lengths ahead of GLENSIDE. With Becher's safely behind them, CAUBEEN and RATHNALLY raced on to the next fence, but in

Player's Cigarettes

"Glenside"
Grand National, 1911

166

both heading for the hole in the obstacle made by LUTTEUR III, they collided, leaving the one-eyed GLENSIDE and Jack Anthony to make their solitary and exhausting way home. Two fences from the finish, Mr Bibby's horse was truly in a very distressed state and it was only the skill and sympathetic handling of the rider which brought GLENSIDE home a twenty length winner from the remounted RATHNALLY. The only others to get round were also remounted, SHADY GIRL and FOOLHARDY, who won for his owner-rider Mr Macneill a private wager that he would complete the course.

THE GRAND NATIONAL HANDICAP STEEPLECHASE
1911

Of £3,000, (including a trophy value £125), by subscription of £25, £15 forfeit or £5 if declared to run; for five-year-olds & upwards. The second to receive £300, the third £200 and the fourth £75 out of the stakes

Date: 24th March 1911	Starters: 26	Time: 10 mins 35 secs
1st **GLENSIDE**	**9.10–3** *(Mr F Bibby)*	**Mr J R Anthony**
2nd **RATHNALLY**	**6.11–0** *(Mr O H Jones)*	**R Chadwick** [remounted]
3rd **SHADY GIRL**	**10.10–5** *(Mr P Nelke)*	**G Clancy** [remounted]
4th **FOOL-HARDY**	**10.9–7** *(Mr W Macneill)*	**Mr W Macneill** [remounted]

Also Ran:

LUTTEUR III 7.12–3 (Mnsr James Hennessy) **G Parfrement** *Fell*; *TRIANON III 6.11–8* (Mnsr H de Mumm) **R Sauval** *Fell*; *JENKINSTOWN 10.11–7* (Mr S Howard) **P Woodland** *Pulled-up*; *MOUNT PROSPECT'S FORTUNE 9.11–6* (Mr P Nelke) **E Driscoll** *Fell*; *RORY O'MOORE 10.11–6* (Mr P Whitaker) **Mr P Whitaker** *Knocked-over*; *CAUBEEN 10.11–5* (Mr F Bibby) **A Newey** *Fell*; *LORD RIVERS 9.10–9* (Baron De Forest) **W Payne** *Fell*; *FETLAR'S PRIDE 10.10–7* (Mr C Pearson) **J Walsh** *Fell*; *CARSEY 8.10–6* (Mr C H Wildenburg) **P Cowley** *Fell*; *VIZ 7.10–5* (Mr G D'Arcy Edwardes) **H Bletsoe** *Fell*; *MONK V aged.10–1* (Mr J J Astor) **Mr H W Tyrwhitt-Drake** *Fell*; *SUHESCUN aged.10–1* (Mnsr Charles de Gheest) **A Chapman** *Fell*; *SCHWARMER 8.10–0* (Mr J J Astor) **F Dainty** *Fell*; *GREAT CROSS 6.9–13* (Major H M Cliff) **Mr C T Walwyn** *Fell*; *CIRCASSIAN'S PRIDE 7.9–13* (Lady Torrington) **I Morgan** *Knocked-over*; *PRECENTOR II 12.9–11* (Mr Foxhall Keene) **A Aylin** *Fell*; *BRIDGE IV 7.9–9* (Mr F S Francis) **Mr P Roberts** *Fell*; *HERCULES II 15.9–8* (Mr David Faber) **Mr R H Hall** *Pulled-up*; *CARDER 8.9–7* (Mr C Luttrell) **B Roberts** *Fell*; *FLAXEN 9.9–7* (Mr G L Pirie) **Mr A Smith** *Fell*; *ROMAN CANDLE 9.9–7* (Mr W F Stratton) **T Willmot** *Fell*; *HESPERUS MAGNUS 9.9–7* (Mr David Faber) **W Fitzgerald** *Pulled-up*

The Betting: *7/2 Lutteur III; 8/1 Caubeen & Rathnally; 100/9 Carsey; 100/7 Rory O'Moore & Jenkinstown; 20/1 Glenside; 25/1 Schwarmer, Fetlar's Pride & Circassian's Pride; 28/1 Roman Candle; 33/1 Lord Rivers, Shady Girl & Trianon III; 50/1 Flaxen, Fool-Hardy, Viz, Suhescun, Carder & Hercules II; 66/1 Mount Prospect's Fortune, Great Cross & Hesperus Magnus; 100/1 Monk V, Precentor II & Bridge IV.*

Distances: *Twenty lengths; three lengths*

Winner Trained By: *Captain R H Collis, Kinlet, Worcestershire*

Value to Winning Owner: *£2,500*

1912

Industrial action on the part of the coal miners caused chaos in 1912, disrupting rail services most severely. At one stage there was a strong possibility that the Grand National would have to be cancelled and although this threat was finally removed, the effects of the strike left large areas of the vast stands empty. Still, the smallest crowd on record gathered in excited anticipation of JERRY M's return to the scene of his honourable defeat in 1910. Now nine years old and once more burdened with 12 st 7 lbs, JERRY M was made 4/1 joint favourite with RATHNALLY, in spite of an enforced break from racing owing to an injury incurred when winning the Grande Steeplechase de Paris on 19th June 1910. But a victorious re-appearance at Hurst Park under his new jockey, Ernie Piggott, had restored the faith of his fans. Bred by Miss Kate Hartigan near Croom, County Limerick, the attractive bay gelding was by WALMSGATE out of an unnamed mare by LUMINARY. John Widger bought him as a yearling and named him after a local horse-breeder, Jerry Mulcair. After proving his worth from the word go at Clonmel, JERRY M was all set to enter into the ownership of Sir Edward Hulton when a veterinary report showing him to be thick winded led to the transaction falling through. Trainer Bob Gore was undeterred and having secured the horse for £1,200, then had to persuade his patron Charles Assheton-Smith to sign the appropriate cheque. Better known as Charles Duff, owner of the legendary CLOISTER, this staunch supporter of 'chasing had changed his name by Royal licence in 1905 in anticipation of a baronetcy. It says much for his faith in Gore that he agreed to the purchase of JERRY M. The son of WALMSGATE quickly repaid his new connections by winning Hurst Park's New Century 'Chase and gave notice of more exciting endeavours with three victories at Liverpool including the Becher and Valentine 'chases before that brave attempt in the 1910 Grand National against JENKINSTOWN, who was again among his opponents in 1912.

Ever determined to keep the 'National as the major attraction of the National Hunt season, Tophams raised the value of the race to an unprecedented £3,500, with an imaginative award of £100 going to the breeder of the winner. RATHNALLY opened up an early lead only to misjudge the third fence, as did GLENSIDE at the same obstacle. Blazing a trail in exuberant fashion, Alf Newey and CAUBEEN set a good pace from BLOODSTONE and maintained his advantage all the way back on to the final circuit. Riding to instructions, Ernie Piggott kept JERRY M tucked in just behind the leaders. JENKINSTOWN was pulled up after injuring himself at the fence after Becher's and Mr Bibby's chances of a second successive victory looked strong as CAUBEEN led the way back. Dropping out of contention before reaching the racecourse, however, CAUBEEN faded away leaving BLOODSTONE, JERRY M, CARSEY, AXLE PIN and MOUNT PROSPECT'S FORTUNE to fight out the finish. Timing his challenge to perfection, Piggott sat patiently behind BLOODSTONE until landing after the last, whereupon he allowed JERRY M to exert his authority with a six length victory. Four lengths back in third place the famous Lord Derby colours of black jacket and white cap gained their only place in the 'National frame when Ivor Anthony brought in AXLE PIN.

Not since the Royal success of AMBUSH II were such scenes of wild delight witnessed in the Aintree unsaddling enclosure as when Sir Charles Assheton-Smith led in the people's favourite JERRY M. He joined only CLOISTER and MANIFESTO, in having carried 12 st 7 lbs successfully in the race, so it was natural that comparisons were drawn between the trio. One thing neither of the other greats could match JERRY M on, though, was his victory against the French cracks in Paris and with age in his favour, expectations were high for his future. None could have known on that March afternoon that JERRY M was never to appear on a racecourse again, for he injured his back and the lay-off increased his wind problems. The horse was considerately retired and upon the death of his owner late in 1914, passed to Bob Gore. The horse who deprived JERRY M of victory in 1910, JENKINSTOWN, lived for only a brief period after the 1912 race, leaving the turf the poorer and the 'National with the task of producing new heroes.

THE GRAND NATIONAL HANDICAP STEEPLECHASE

1912

Of £3,500, (including a trophy value £125), by subscription of £30, £20 forfeit or £5 if declared to run; For five-year-olds & upwards. The second to receive £200, the third £100 and the fourth £70 out of the stakes. The breeder of the winner to receive £100

Date: 29th March 1912	Starters: 24	Time: 10 mins 13²⁄₅ secs
1st **JERRY M**	**9.12–7** *(Sir C Assheton-Smith)*	**E Piggott**
2nd **BLOODSTONE**	**10.11–6** *(Mr C Bower Ismay)*	**F Lyall**
3rd **AXLE PIN**	**8.10–4** *(Lord Derby)*	**Ivor Anthony**
4th **CARSEY**	**9.10–13** *(Mr C H Wildenburg)*	**Mr H W Tyrwhitt-Drake**
5th **MOUNT PROSPECT'S FORTUNE**	**10.11–4** *(Mr P Nelke)*	**J Kelly**
6th **SIR HALBERT**	**9.10–6** *(Capt F D Grissell)*	**Mr A Smith**
7th **WHITE LEGS II**	**aged.10–2** *(Mr E Brandon)*	**J Farrell**

Also Ran:
RATHNALLY 7.11–11 (Mr O H Jones) **R Chadwick** *Fell; JENKINSTOWN 11.11–7* (Mr G W Blundell) **W Payne** *Pulled-up; RORY O'MOORE 11.11–7* (Mr P Whitaker) **F Mason** *Failed to finish; CAUBEEN 11.11–5* (Mr F Bibby) **A Newey** *Failed to finish; GLENSIDE 10.11–0* (Mr F Bibby) **Mr H Ussher** *Fell; BRIDGE IV 8.10–8* (Mr F S Francis) **Mr G C Poole** *Failed to finish; REGENT 7.10–8* (Sir George Bullough) **F Morgan** *Failed to finish; KILKEEL 7.10–7* (Mr Hunter Moore) **R Trudgill** *Failed to finish; BALLYHACKLE 9.10–7* (Mr K F Malcolmson) **I Morgan** *Failed to finish; FETLAR'S PRIDE 11.10–7* (Mr C Pearson) **G Lyall** *Failed to finish; COVERTCOAT 6.10–5* (Sir C Assheton-Smith) **J Walsh, jnr** *Failed to finish; FOOL-HARDY 11.10–3* (Mr W Macneill) **Mr W Macneill** *Failed to finish; GREAT CROSS 7.10–1* (Major H M Cliff) **E Lawn** *Failed to finish; PRECENTOR II 13.10–0* (Mr Foxhall Keene) **A Aylin** *Failed to finish; GLENFINDER 11.10–0* (Capt H C Higgins) **J Foran** *Failed to finish; SANS PEUR 13.10–0* (Mr W Wilson) **J Kay** *Failed to finish; GOLD SEAL II 12.10–0* (Mrs R P Croft) **J Finn** *Failed to finish*

The Betting: *4/1 Rathnally & Jerry M; 9/1 Rory O'Moore; 100/9 Caubeen; 100/8 Carsey; 100/7 Jenkinstown; 20/1 Axle Pin & Ballyhackle; 25/1 Bridge IV; 33/1 Covertcoat; 40/1 Glenside, Great Cross & Bloodstone.*

Distances: *Six lengths; four lengths*

Winner Trained By: *Robert Gore, Findon, Sussex*

Value to Winning Owner: *£3,200*

1913

Having already won the 'National twice with two of the greatest horses ever to tread Aintree's turf, Sir Charles Assheton-Smith tried for a hat-trick in 1913 with the rather less illustrious COVERTCOAT. A half-brother to the 1910 Aintree hero JENKINSTOWN, COVERTCOAT was by HACKLER out of CINNAMON, and bred in Ireland by James J Maher. Purchased by Bob Gore for £1,075 at Goff's sales in Dublin, COVERTCOAT put up some undistinguished performances in the famous dark green jacket and crimson

COVERTCOAT provided his owner with a third 'National winner

cap before a workmanlike victory in a three-and-a-half mile 'chase at Sandown in December 1912 put him in the Grand National picture. The Gore-trained seven-year-old became co-second favourite with CARSEY, American-bred HIGHBRIDGE and the northern hope of Mr A H Straker, WAVELET. When Ernie Piggott broke his hand, history repeated itself for Percy Woodland, who ten years before had secured the winning ride on DRUM-CREE through a last minute injury to another. Since then the jockey had spent much of his time in France, where he won

the French Derby and the Grande Steeplechase de Paris twice each.

With no previous winner of the race among the twenty-two runners, the field, as is usual in such circumstances, was classed as sub-standard. This unfair assumption in no way damaged the appeal of the event, and with the trains back to normal, large crowds flocked to the course sending off BALLYHACKLE, ridden by the outstanding Irish amateur Harry Ussher, the 5/1 favourite. From a good start, THE REJECTED IV led over the first, where HIGHBRIDGE made an early departure. The international interest was maintained through TRIANON III, the French horse moving smoothly into a prominent position over the first ditch. Over Becher's Brook, the new leader was BLOW PIPE but it was at Valentine's that the trouble began in earnest, with TRIANON III among the fallers. The number of casualties grew and only a handful took the Water Jump at the end of the first circuit, with CARSEY now in front. More fell before Becher's, at which stage CARSEY led from IRISH MAIL and the only other serious challenger, COVERTCOAT. With only two fences left, these were the only runners on their feet, CARSEY looking all over the winner until crashing into the final obstacle. COVERTCOAT was left with the race at his mercy and Percy Woodland galloped home the winner by a distance from IRISH MAIL. The unfortunate Mr Jack Drake, a descendant of the Reverend Drake who as 'Mr Ekard' got BRIDEGROOM round in the 1860 race, remounted CARSEY to finish third, the only other survivor. As a spectacle the race was a disappointment, but in providing the owner with a third 'National and Percy Woodland with a second, COVERTCOAT more than earned his place in Aintree history.

1913

Of £3,500 (including a trophy value £125), by subscription of £30, £20 forfeit or £5 if declared to run; For five-year-olds & upwards. The second to receive £200, third £100 and the fourth £70. The breeder of the winner to receive £100

Date: 4th April 1913	Starters: 22	Time: 10 mins 19 secs
1st **COVERTCOAT**	**7.11–6** *(Sir C Assheton-Smith)* **P Woodland**	
2nd **IRISH MAIL**	**6.11–4** *(Mr W T Drake)*	**Mr Owen Anthony**
3rd **CARSEY**	**10.12–0** *(Mr C H Wildenburg)* **Mr H W Tyrwhitt-Drake** [remounted]	

Also Ran:

BLOODSTONE 11.12–7 (Mr C Bower Ismay) **F Lyall** *Fell*; *DYSART 8.12–4* (Capt H C Higgins) **Capt O'Brien Butler** *Fell*; *TRIANON III 8.12–3* (Mnsr H de Mumm) **W O'Connor** *Fell*; *HIGHBRIDGE 7.12–0* (Mr J R Fell) **F Williams** *Fell*; *BALLYHACKLE 10.11–11* (Mr K F Malcolmson) **Mr H Ussher** *Fell*; *THOWL PIN 8.11–9* (Mr F Bibby) **I Morgan** *Fell*; *REGENT 8.11–7* (Sir George Bullough) **Mr J R Anthony** *Fell*; *THE MINER 8.11–6* (Mr W A Wallis) **Mr I Brabazon** *Failed to finish*; *MELAMAR 7.11–6* (Mr W R Clarke) **W Payne** *Failed to finish*; *BLACK PLUM 9.11–5* (Mr F S Watts) **R Morgan** *Failed to finish*; *AXLE PIN 9.11–4* (Lord Derby) **Mr P Whitaker** *Fell*; *BLOW PIPE 8.11–4* (Mr M M Henderson) **W J Smith** *Fell*; *THE REJECTED IV 10.11–3* (Mr E Platt) **Mr G Cotton** *Fell*; *MERRY LAND 9.11–3* (Capt H C Higgins) **R Trudgill** *Fell*; *FETLAR'S PRIDE 12.11–2* (Mr C Pearson) **F Morgan** *Fell*; *FEARLESS VII 10.11–0* (Mr R Whitehead) **Mr G Pigot-Moodie** *Fell*; *WAVELET 6.11–0* (Mr A H Straker) **A Newey** *Fell*; *TOKAY 7.11–0* (Mr J Langley) **M Hopper** *Fell*; *FOOL-HARDY 12.11–0* (Mr W Macneill) **Mr W Macneill** *Fell*

The Betting: *5/1 Ballyhackle; 100/9 Carsey, Wavelet, Highbridge & Covertcoat; 100/8 Axle Pin & Melamar; 100/6 Bloodstone; 20/1 Thowl Pin; 25/1 Irish Mail & Blow Pipe; 33/1 Trianon III & Fetlar's Pride; 40/1 The Rejected IV; 50/1 Dysart & Tokay; 66/1 Regent & Black Plum; 100/1 The Miner, Fearless VII & Merry Land; 200/1 Fool-Hardy.*

Distances: *A distance; a distance*

Winner Trained By: *Robert Gore, Findon, Sussex*

Value to Winning Owner: *£3,170*

1914

Lady Nelson scored a first for her sex at Aintree this year, when her five-year-old ALLY SLOPER won the Stanley Steeplechase on the first day of the 'National meeting. This was the first horse owned by a woman to win a race over Liverpool fences. 7/1 favourite for the big race the next day was last year's victor COVERTCOAT, but he was heavily opposed in the market by Ivor Anthony's mount ILSTON and the French pair LUTTEUR III and TRIANON III. Now a ten-year-old, LUTTEUR III seemed back to his very best. BALLYHACKLE and JACOBUS came in for a good measure of support at 100/6, on the same mark as one from the bottom of the handicap, SUNLOCH, the mount of Cheltenham jockey Bill Smith.

This eight-year-old, set to carry a mere 9 st 7 lbs, was, like many former Aintree heroes, descended from POCAHONTAS and if this were insufficient recommendation, his grand-sire was Derby winner GEORGE FREDERICK. Bred by Mr H S Blair, SUNLOCH won prizes for him at horse shows around Leicestershire before going on to achieve modest success over fences. Trainer Thomas Tyler was so impressed with the young gelding that he gave £300 for him on behalf of a client, only to discover that the promised cheque was not forthcoming. But such was Tyler's confidence in SUNLOCH that he refused a substantial profit on his outlay from no less an Aintree 'specialist' than Sir Charles Assheton-Smith and kept the horse himself.

From a good start Smith sent SUNLOCH into a fifteen length lead, jumping the big fences as if he'd been doing it all his life,

A proud Tom Tyler leads in SUNLOCH

with falls coming thick and fast behind him. Over Becher's SUNLOCH increased the lead to twenty lengths, the riders on his closest rivals, LUTTEUR III and TRIANON III convinced that the front-runner would come back to them. No doubt those in the stands felt much the same as he cleared the Water Jump almost a fence ahead of the rest, extending his advantage to forty lengths early on the second round. Behind him lay disaster on a scale reminiscent of other recent 'Nationals, only five runners pursuing the leader after Valentine's. The collapse of the tearaway was not forthcoming, causing at least two jockeys to curse their misjudgement. TRIANON III and LUTTEUR III were sent frantically on an impossible chase after the leader and though they made much ground from the Anchor Crossing, the task proved beyond both French horses. As foot-perfect at the last as he was throughout the race, SUNLOCH was eight lengths clear at the post from TRIANON III, the same distance separating the second from LUTTEUR III. Winning owner-trainer Tom Tyler led in his family pet to the cheers of the crowd and viewed his achievement with great modesty. Surprisingly, the sale to Sir Charles Assheton-Smith, rejected so emphatically six months before the race, was accepted within a fortnight of SUNLOCH proving himself so convincingly. That the horse was of little account henceforth may possibly indicate that the vendor knew more than most would have imagined.

In June, a pistol-shot in Sarajevo signalled the end of a kind of innocence. By August, the world was at war, and would never be the same again.

THE GRAND NATIONAL HANDICAP STEEPLECHASE

1914

Of £4,000 (including a trophy value £125), by subscription of £35, £25 forfeit or £5 if declared to run; For five-year-olds & upwards. The second to receive £300 and the third £150. The breeder of the winner to receive £100

Date: 27th March 1914	Starters: 20	Time: 9 mins 58⅘ secs
1st **SUNLOCH**	**8.9–7** *(Mr T Tyler)*	**W J Smith**
2nd **TRIANON III**	**9.11–9** *(Mnsr H de Mumm)*	**C Hawkins**
3rd **LUTTEUR III**	**10.12–6** *(Mnsr James Hennessy)*	**A Carter**
4th **RORY O'MOORE**	**13.11–8** *(Mr P Whitaker)*	**Mr P Whitaker**

Also Ran:

COVERTCOAT 8.12–7 (Sir C Assheton-Smith) **P Woodland** *Failed to finish*; *BALLYHACKLE 11.12–0* (Mr K F Malcolmson) **Mr H Ussher** *Fell*; *COUVREFEU II 10.11–7* (Sir W Nelson) **Mr J R Anthony** *Failed to finish*; *BLOODSTONE 12.11–7* (Mr C Bower Ismay) **F Lyall** *Ran-out*; *ANOTHER DELIGHT 10.11–7* (Capt E H Wyndham) **G Brown** *Fell*; *JACOBUS 7.11–2* (Mr C Bower Ismay) **E Piggott** *Fell*; *GREAT CROSS 9.11–0* (Major H M Cliff) **Mr Owen Anthony** *Failed to finish*; *REGENT 9.10–12* (Sir George Bullough) **Mr H W Tyrwhitt-Drake** *Broke-down*; *ILSTON 6.10–12* (Sir George Bullough) **Ivor Anthony** *Fell*; *THOWL PIN 9.10–10* (Mr F Bibby) **I Morgan** *Fell*; *ALL GOLD II aged.10–7* (Sir J D Tichborne) **Capt Stokes** *Fell*; *DUTCH PENNANT 8.10–5* (Capt Crawshay) **A Parnham** *Fell*; *BLOW PIPE 9.10–3* (Mr A Shepherd) **H B Bletsoe** *Fell*; *FETLAR'S PRIDE 13.10–2* (Mr B C Pearson) **D Dale** *Refused*; *BAHADUR 11.9–12* (Mr G Lambarde) **Mr R H Hall** *Fell*; *DIPLOMATIST II 9.9–7* (Mr N B Davis) **Mr N B Davis** *Ran-out*

The Betting: *7/1 Covertcoat; 10/1 Lutteur III & Ilston; 100/8 Trianon III; 100/7 Ballyhackle; 100/6 Sunloch, Jacobus & Bloodstone; 20/1 Couvrefeu II & Rory O'Moore; 25/1 Blow Pipe; 33/1 Another Delight, Regent, Thowl Pin & Bahadur.*

Distances: *Eight lengths; eight lengths*

Winner Trained By: *The owner, Tom Tyler, Loughborough, Leicestershire*

Value to Winning Owner: £3,515

1915

Against the predictions of the majority, the War in Europe was not resolved by Christmas 1914, nor was it likely to be for some considerable time. Aintree's last Grand National for the duration of what was soon to become the bloodiest and costliest conflict in human history took place on a cold, clear 26th March 1915. Liverpool, as Britain's gateway to the west, took on a renewed importance as a life-line in the nation's struggle, but on that brisk spring day its famous steeplechase offered welcome relief from a frighteningly uncertain future. Military uniforms of all branches of the Empire's forces gave the city a garrison-town appearance and seldom had a smaller yet more cosmopolitan crowd attended a 'National before. This year's field of twenty was again without a previous winner and IRISH MAIL at 6/1 was just the backers' first choice from LORD MARCUS, the mount of Georges Parfrement, SILVER TOP, BALSCADDEN and FATHER CONFESSOR. The American-bred ALFRED NOBLE was an interesting newcomer.

With the importance of women in the welfare of the country at long last starting to be recognised, it was appropriate that a member of the fair sex should have an interest in the race, Lady Nelson allowing ALLY SLOPER to take his chance. Trained by Aubrey Hastings, the six-year-old had been bred in Lincolnshire by Mr C J C Hill, who got only 25 guineas for him as a yearling at Doncaster sales. Purchaser Mr Sugden Armitage sold the horse on to former jockey Herbert Randall and he in turn passed the gelding on to Lady Nelson for the more realistic price of £700. The son of TRAVELLING LAD graduated in the most promising manner by winning both the Becher and Valentine steeplechases over Liverpool's difficult fences while still but five years old. Jack Anthony was his partner in the 'National and although the going was a deal better than when he had coaxed home the one-eyed GLENSIDE, Anthony was to have a far from smooth journey.

Yet again falls were numerous throughout the race and ALLY SLOPER was fortunate on more than one occasion not to be put out through some very indifferent jumping. As early as the second fence he took off far too soon, landing on top of the obstacle. His rider was in the process of being unseated, when his brother Ivor reached across from his mount ILSTON and yanked him back in the saddle! Then another colossal error at the Canal Turn ditch left Jack Anthony hanging around ALLY SLOPER's neck and this time he had to fight his own way back into position. With JACOBUS, BALSCADDEN, FATHER CONFESSOR and ALFRED NOBLE dominating the race, ALLY SLOPER was quite a way behind the leaders as they came back to the stands. The gelding's fencing improved tremendously after jumping the Water, however, and by Becher's second time, he was within striking distance of the leading bunch. After the fall of BALSCADDEN two from home, Anthony made his effort and landing clear over the last, held off the challenge of JACOBUS for a two length victory. Eight lengths further back came FATHER CONFESSOR, with ALFRED NOBLE fourth and the remounted BALSCADDEN fifth. The result provided a double triumph in the event for trainer Aubrey Hastings and jockey Jack Anthony but the major landmark which was most toasted, was Lady Nelson becoming the first woman to lead in a Grand National winner.

Aintree's gates closed to racing. The

course was handed over to the War Office in December 1914 and it would be four long weary and costly years before those historic stands would echo to appreciative cheers again.

THE GRAND NATIONAL HANDICAP STEEPLECHASE

1915

Of £4,000 (including a trophy value £125), by subscription of £35, £25 forfeit or £5 if declared to run; For five-year-olds & upwards. The second to receive £300 and the third £150. The breeder of the winner to receive £100

Date: 26th March 1915	Starters: 20	Time: 9 mins 47⅘ secs
1st **ALLY SLOPER**	**6.10–6** *(Lady Nelson)*	**Mr J R Anthony**
2nd **JACOBUS**	**8.11–0** *(Mr C Bower Ismay)*	**A Newey**
3rd **FATHER CONFESSOR**	**6.9–10** *(Lord Suffolk)*	**A Aylin**
4th **ALFRED NOBLE**	**10.10–12** *(Mr T H Barnard)*	**T Hulme**
5th **BALSCADDEN**	**8.11–8** *(Mr C Bower Ismay)*	**F Lyall** [remounted]

Also Ran:
IRISH MAIL 8.11–12 (Mr E Platt) **Mr L Brabazon** *Pulled-up*; *BULLAWARRA 10.11–12* (Mr J M Niall) **C Hawkins** *Fell*; *ILSTON 7.11–8* (Sir George Bullough) **Ivor Anthony** *Fell*; *DISTAFF 7.10–10* (Sir George Bullough) **E Piggott** *Pulled-up*; *THOWL PIN 10.10–8* (Mr F Bibby) **W J Smith** *Failed to finish*; *BLOW PIPE 10.10–4* (Mr A Shepherd) **W Smith** *Failed to finish*; *LORD MARCUS 7.10–3* (Lord Lonsdale) **G Parfrement** *Fell*; *HACKLER'S BEY 8.10–2* (Sir T R Dewar) **Mr H S Harrison** *Failed to finish*; *SILVER TOP 8.10–0* (Mr Alex Browne) **S Walkington** *Failed to finish*; *THE BABE 7.10–0* (Mr F Bibby) **R Chadwick** *Pulled-up*; *ST MATHURIN II 10.9–10* (Mr Adam Scott) **T H Dunn** *Fell*; *BACHELOR'S FLIGHT 8.9–8* (Mr F Barbour) **H Harty** *Fell*; *DENIS AUBURN 8.9–7* (Sir George Bullough) **J Reardon** *Fell*; *BAHADUR 12.9–7* (Mr W G Lambarde) **Mr P Roberts** *Fell*; *BALLYHACKLE 12.11–9* (Mr K F Malcolmson) **S Avila** *Broke-down*

The Betting: *6/1 Irish Mail; 7/1 Lord Marcus; 9/1 Silver Top; 10/1 Balscadden & Father Confessor; 100/9 Bachelor's Flight; 100/8 Ally Sloper; 100/7 Bullawarra; 25/1 Distaff, Alfred Noble & Jacobus; 33/1 Denis Auburn, Ilston & Thowl Pin; 40/1 Hackler's Bey.*

Distances: *Two lengths; eight lengths*

Winner Trained By: *The Honourable Aubrey Hastings, Wroughton, Wiltshire*

Value to Winning Owner: *£3,515*

THE WAR YEARS
1916 1917 1918

Gatwick, scene of three wartime substitute races

As the war to end all wars dragged on remorselessly, a decision was taken to hold a race at Gatwick in place of the suspended Aintree feature. The Racecourse Association Steeplechase, over 4 miles 856 yards, took place on the 24th March 1916 but apart from the distance, this event bore no resemblance to the Liverpool spectacular. Carrying a value of 500 sovereigns, the race attracted twenty-one runners and was won by Mr P F Heybourne's six-year-old VERMOUTH, ridden by Jack Reardon at 100/8. The 9/2 favourite ALLY SLOPER could finish no better than eighth and the fact that only one horse fell during the race shows how easy the fences were in comparison to Aintree.

In 1917 the race was re-named 'The War National Steeplechase' and resulted in another triumph for Aubrey Hastings with the ten-year-old BALLYMACAD. Owned by Sir George Bullough, the winner was ridden by Edmund Driscoll, who in less troublesome times partnered JERRY M to his famous victory in Paris. ALLY SLOPER was third, with VERMOUTH fourth but the hard luck story of this race undoubtedly concerned LIMEROCK and SUNLOCH's old jockey Bill Smith. With his race well won, LIMEROCK was within yards of the winning post when he collapsed and fell.

By far the best winner of these substitute races was POETHLYN, guided to victory by Ernie Piggott in 1918. Mrs Hugh Peel's gelding was still only a young horse and although the armistice was still some eight months away, there were many who saw him win who were prepared to fancy his chances, if and when the race returned to its true home. Two who finished behind POETHLYN that day would also prove that Liverpool was more to their liking than Gatwick. Their names were SHAUN SPADAH and SERGEANT MURPHY.

1919

In an atmosphere of perhaps somewhat manic gaiety but genuine relief, the crowds flocked back to Aintree in March 1919 in greater numbers than ever before and the name on everyone's lips was POETHLYN. A short priced favourite at 11/4, in spite of incurring the severest attention of the handicapper with 12 st 7 lbs, the gelding followed the tradition of many before him in having been dismissed as almost useless at an early age. Bred by Major Hugh Peel at Bry y Pas on Deeside, from the stallion RYDAL HEAD out of a mare called FINE CHAMPAGNE, he was sold as a foal for just £7 to a Shrewsbury hotelier named Davenport. From being a weak, crooked-legged infant, POETHLYN grew into something resembling a racehorse. His breeder bought him back for £50, with the added promise of a Dee salmon as soon as he caught one! The ugly duckling proved he was on the way to becoming a swan by winning his first 'chase at Blackpool when four years old. Ernie Piggott was successful with the horse at Gatwick in the final year of the war and was again in the saddle.

The field of twenty-two was a mixed bunch, former Aintree heroes SUNLOCH and ALLY SLOPER taking their place along with the first of the substitute winners VERMOUTH. The rank outsider ALL WHITE carried some local money, as the property of Colonel Hall-Walker, always popular at this his local track. His usual jockey Chadwick was injured shortly before the race, so a replacement who could ride at 9 st 10 lbs was sought and the only one available was the Frenchman T Williams. Anxious to make the weight, Williams wasted severely for many days, only to be fatefully tempted on the day of the race

into sampling some sea food from a racecourse stall.

Falls were plentiful during the first circuit and SUNLOCH pulled up. Always well to the fore, POETHLYN matched strides over Valentine's with LOCH ALLEN, SERGEANT MURPHY and ALL WHITE with most of those behind struggling to keep their feet. Approaching Becher's again POETHLYN hit the front jumping brilliantly. ALL WHITE also moved into a challenging position jumping the Brook but before reaching the next fence was suddenly and surprisingly pulled to a halt at the side of the course. Spectators in the vicinity were amazed to see jockey Williams leaning from his mount to be violently sick. His ill-timed sea-food snack had proved costly indeed. Bravely continuing, Williams and ALL WHITE set off in hopeless pursuit of the three leaders, who by now were well clear. To a delirious reception, POETHLYN ran out the eight-length winner from BALLYBOGGAN, with POLLEN third in front of LOCH ALLEN. The fourth winner to carry 12 st 7 lbs to victory in the race, POETHLYN that day also became the shortest-priced winner of the event, and provided Ernie Piggott with his second winning ride. Harry Escott, who trained the horse at Lewes on the Sussex Downs, had also been responsible for CLOISTER and with POETHLYN's triumph enjoyed the double satisfaction of seeing his son, Anthony, come third on POLLEN. Obviously comparisons were made between the 1919 winner and the three others who shared his weight-carrying performance, but with POETHLYN likely to contend more 'Nationals there was every likelihood that the future would answer the question as to which was greatest.

The last of four horses to carry the maximum weight to victory, POETHLYN went off a short-priced favourite the next year, but made an early exit at the first fence.

THE GRAND NATIONAL HANDICAP STEEPLECHASE
1919

Of £4,000, (including a trophy value £125), by subscription of £35, £25 forfeit or £5 if declared to run: For five-year-olds & upwards: The second to receive £300 and the third £150. The trainer of the winner to receive a cup value £50 and the rider of the winner a cup value £25

Date: 28th March 1919	Starters: 22	Time: 10 mins 8²/₅ secs
1st **POETHLYN**	**9.12−7** *(Mrs Hugh Peel)*	**E Piggott**
2nd **BALLYBOGGAN**	**8.11−10** *(Mr E W Hope-Johnstone)*	**W Head**
3rd **POLLEN**	**10.11−4** *(Mr J L Dugdale)*	**A Escott**
4th **LOCH ALLEN**	**8.10−0** *(Mr V Stewart)*	**J Kelly**
5th **ALL WHITE**	**5.9−10** *(Colonel Hall-Walker)*	**T Williams**
6th **SERGEANT MURPHY**	**9.10−7** *(Mr Douglas Stuart)*	**S Walkington**
7th **PAY ONLY**	**9.11−4** *(Mr W P Hanly)*	**T Hulme**

Also Ran:

ABOU BEN ADHEM 8.12−0 (Mr J Buchanan) **A Stubbs** *Fell*; *ALLY SLOPER 10.11−3* (Lady Nelson) **Ivor Anthony** *Failed to finish*; *SHAUN SPADAH 8.11−2* (Mr T M McAlpine) **R Morgan** *Failed to finish*; *RUBINSTEIN 12.11−0* (Lt Col F Douglas-Pennant) **W Payne** *Fell*; *VERMOUTH 9.10−12* (Mr P F Heybourn) **G Parfrement** *Failed to finish*; *BALLINCARROONA 11.10−4* (Capt Ian Straker) **Capt I Straker** *Fell*; *PICTURE SAINT 7.10−0* (Col R P Croft) **F McCabe** *Fell*; *IRISH DRAGOON 5.9−13* (Mr R H Edwards) **H B Bletsoe** *Failed to finish*; *SCHOOLMONEY 10.9−10* (Mr P R L Savill) **F Cullen** *Fell*; *SUNLOCH 13.9−10* (Mr T Tyler) **E Driscoll** *Pulled-up*; *FARGUE 9.9−9* (Mr G P Sanday) **W Smith** *Failed to finish*; *CHANG 9.9−8* (Mr F S Watts) **J Reardon** *Failed to finish*; *SVETOI 9.9−8* (Mr W E Wren) **A Saxby** *Fell*; *THE TURK II 9.9−7* (Mr C L Willcox) **Mr P Roberts** *Fell*; *CHARLBURY 11.9−7* (Mr H Trimmer) **P Woodland** *Pulled-up*

The Betting: *11/4 Poethlyn; 7/1 Charlbury; 9/1 Ballyboggan; 100/7 Pollen & Pay Only; 100/6 Ally Sloper; 20/1 Ballincarroona & Vermouth; 25/1 Sunloch & Sergeant Murphy; 33/1 Loch Allen, Shaun Spadah & Schoolmoney; 40/1 Svetoi; 50/1 Rubinstein, Chang & Fargue; 66/1 All White; 100/1 Others.*

Distances: *Eight lengths; six lengths*

Winner Trained By: *Harry Escott, Lewes, Sussex*

Value to Winning Owner: *£3,590*

1920

TROYTOWN (fourth from the left) strikes the front at the very start of the race

An increase in added money brought this year's race value rising to a record £5,000, with the reward to the winning owner £4,425. Most people were of the opinion that this fortunate person would again be Mrs Peel, whose POETHLYN was returning to Liverpool with an unbeaten sequence of eleven victories behind him and not even top weight of 12 st 7 lbs nor heavy going could deter the punters. He headed the market at 3/1. Lord Wavertree, better known as Colonel Hall-Walker, again ran ALL WHITE, and of those appearing for the first time, NEUROTIC was noted as the mount of the amateur find of the season Mr F B Rees. As far as the majority were concerned, however, there was really only one danger to POETHLYN: another newcomer, the giant TROYTOWN.

Still only seven years old, TROYTOWN was bred in Ireland by his owner, Major Thomas Collins-Gerrard from ZRIA out of DIANE and on his dam's side possessed American blood from that famous stallion LEXINGTON. The day before POETHLYN's 'National in 1919, TROYTOWN was running away with the Stanley Steeplechase when his rider took the wrong course. Two days later in the Champion 'chase he made amends with a convincing win.

Later that season he made every yard of the running for a stunning victory in the Grande Steeplechase de Paris and from then on his sights were firmly set on the 'National. With race specialist Jack Anthony in the saddle and trained by Algy Anthony, the 6/1 offered about Major Gerrard's hope may well have seemed generous had it not been for the impressive record of the favourite.

The great powerhouse of a horse, TROYTOWN, who was not to live to repeat his success

The runners were set on their way in a torrential downpour and to the dismay of all, the first fence answered the book-

179

makers' prayers. POETHLYN came to grief at the very first obstacle and from that point on, the event became virtually a one-horse race. TROYTOWN proceeded to do at Aintree what he had achieved at Auteuil, cutting out all the running and powering his way over the fearsome fences. Leaving in his wake a trail of disaster as runner after runner fell in the horrible conditions, TROYTOWN was beyond the restraint of even such an accomplished horseman as Jack Anthony and the Welshman wisely resigned himself to allowing his mount to run his own race. Nothing could live with the huge Irish gelding and the only error he made, caused by the treacherous conditions, demonstrated his strength and agility. Slipping on the glue-like turf at the fence after the second Valentine's, TROYTOWN was forced to take off too soon, struck the top and gave his jockey the feeling that they had totally demolished the obstacle. Back into his stride immediately, TROYTOWN scarcely seemed to notice the mishap and romped home as he liked to a devastating twelve length victory, with Jack Anthony's main concern to prevent him going round again. THE TURK II was second in front of Mr Harry Brown on his own THE BORE and the only other finishers were SERGEANT MURPHY and NEUROTIC. Applauded all the way to the unsaddling enclosure and for long after the weighed-in signal was given, TROYTOWN received the highest praise and lavish predictions were made for his future. It was Jack Anthony's third victory in the race, endorsing the widely-held belief that the amateur was the finest horseman of the age over the demanding 'National course.

Returning to France that summer in an attempt to repeat his triumph in the Grande Steeplechase, TROYTOWN finished third behind COQ GAULOIS and the decision was made to run him again six days later in the Prix des Drags. But tragically crashing at one of the easiest obstacles on the course, the giant broke his leg and had to be destroyed.

Jack Anthony is led in on his third 'National winner and TROYTOWN looks as if he could go round again

1920

Of £5,000, (including a trophy value £150), by subscription of £50, £40 forfeit or £5 if declared to run. For five-year-olds & upwards. The second to receive £400 and the third £200. The trainer of the winner to receive a cup value £50 and the rider of the winner a cup value £25

Date: 26th March 1920	Starters: 24	Time: 10 mins 20⅖ secs
1st **TROYTOWN**	**7.11−9** *(Major T G C Gerrard)*	**Mr J R Anthony**
2nd **THE TURK II**	**10.9−8** *(Mr C L Willcox)*	**R Burford**
3rd **THE BORE**	**9.10−1** *(Mr H A Brown)*	**Mr H A Brown**
4th **SERGEANT MURPHY**	**10.10−1** *(Mr M H Benson)*	**W Smith**
5th **NEUROTIC**	**9.9−13** *(Mr T Miles)*	**Mr F B Rees**

Also Ran:

POETHLYN 10.12–7 (Mrs Hugh Peel) **E Piggott** *Fell*; *SILVER RING 8.11–4* (Sir J Buchanan) **G Duller** *Fell*; *BALLYBOGGAN 9.11–3* (Mr E W Hope-Johnstone) **Mr C Brabazon** *Fell*; *WAVERTREE 9.10–13* (Mr F Bibby) **C Kelly** *Fell*; *CLONREE 6.10–10* (Mr O Toole) **E Morgan** *Fell*; *LITTLE ROVER 14.10–3* (Mr F C Romilly) **Capt E C Doyle** *Fell*; *TURKEY BUZZARD 7.10–7* (Mrs H M Hollins) **W Payne** *Fell*; *ARDONAGH 7.10–6* (Capt C B Hanbury) **Mr P Whitaker** *Fell*; *PICTURE SAINT 8.10–1* (Col R P Croft) **Capt G H Bennet** *Fell*; *LUCY GLITTERS II 8.10–0* (Mr H J Davis) **L B Rees** *Fell*; *ALL WHITE 6.9–13* (Lord Wavertree) **R Chadwick** *Fell*; *LOCH ALLEN 9.9–12* (Mr V Samuel) **T Hulme** *Fell*; *BONNIE CHARLIE 12.9–11* (Capt Willoughby Norrie) **Mr M D Blair** *Fell*; *IRISH DRAGOON 6.9–8* (Mr R H Edwards) **A Escott** *Fell*; *SQUARE UP 7.9–8* (Mr W Read) **T Willmot** *Fell*; *DUNADRY 7.9–8* (Mrs A Blain) **S Walkington** *Fell*; *WAVEBEAM 9.9–7* (Mr H Kershaw) **A Aylin** *Fell*; *GERALD L 6.9–7* (Major F J Scott Murray) **F Dainty** *Fell*; *GENERAL SAXHAM 7.9–7* (Mrs J Putnam) **Mr P Roberts** *Fell*

The Betting: *3/1 Poethlyn; 6/1 Troytown; 10/1 Gerald L; 100/7 Ballyboggan, Sergeant Murphy, Turkey Buzzard & Silver Ring; 25/1 Clonree; 28/1 Neurotic & The Bore; 33/1 Loch Allen & All White; 40/1 Wavertree.*

Distances: *Twelve lengths; six lengths*

Winner Trained By: *Algy Anthony, The Curragh, County Kildare*

Value to Winning Owner: *£4,425*

1921

From an original entry of ninety-two, a record thirty-five held their ground in 1921 and with over fifty owners paying forfeit, first prize rose to the incredible level for a steeplechase of £7,060. There being no past winner in the race, gamblers and bookmakers alike turned to what was considered the next best thing; a bay gelding called THE BORE. Twelve months before, ridden by his owner Mr Harry Atherton Brown, THE BORE matched strides with TROYTOWN on the second circuit, until fading into third place over the last few fences. Mr Brown had come from being an unknown amateur to head the list of gentlemen riders and his expressed ambition was success in the 'National. Joe Widger's EAMON BEAG occupied second place in the betting at 10/1, with TURKEY BUZZARD, GARRYVOE and SHAUN SPADAH the best backed of the remainder.

Running in the tartan colours of Malcolm McAlpine, SHAUN SPADAH was by EASTER PRIZE out of RUSIALKA and had been bred in Ireland by Mr P McKenna. Sold as a yearling to Dick Cleary of Mullingar, SHAUN SPADAH was sent the following year to be trained at the Curragh by Algy Anthony, only to be returned as being far too slow for racing. A spell of schooling and hunting proved beneficial, for in March 1915 SHAUN SPADAH won his first race at Downpatrick, whereupon he was sold for £350 to Pat Rogers. Changing hands on a regular basis after this, he finally came to Mr McAlpine and his trainer George Poole in Lewes. Entrusted with the care of the ten-year-old in the 'National was the recent valuable addition to the paid ranks of riders, Frederick Brychan Rees. A natural horseman, with a flair for a finish, Rees was born in Tenby, South Wales and served in the Royal

Flying Corps until the end of the war.

Although the weather was brisk and clear as if to welcome King George V among the spectators, the conditions underfoot were no better than last year with the going decidedly heavy. The first fence proved the undoing of several of the leading fancies in the large field and over half had dropped out by the time the Canal Turn was reached. Jumping the Chair at the halfway stage, TURKEY BUZ-

TURKEY BUZZARD leads over the Chair

182

The spills begin early – at the very first fence, in fact – in a sensational running

ZARD led from SHAUN SPADAH, ALL WHITE and THE BORE, these four being well clear of just a handful of stragglers who failed to survive far into the country. When first TURKEY BUZZARD and then ALL WHITE came to grief, there were just SHAUN SPADAH and THE BORE left and both continued bravely with the wide expanses of the course to themselves. Rounding the turn to the second last fence THE BORE and Harry Brown appeared to be going the better but the cheers for the favourite were premature. THE BORE crashed to the ground at the penultimate fence and his rider suffered a broken collar bone. So SHAUN SPADAH came home alone, the only survivor in a carbon copy of GLENSIDE's victory ten years before. In what must have been agony, Harry Brown remounted THE BORE and with his right arm useless at his side, cleared the final obstacle to finish a remote but gallant second. Still further back came two other remounted and determined competitors, ALL WHITE and TURKEY BUZZARD, although the efforts of Captain G H Bennet were less than appreciated by TURKEY BUZZARD's affectionate owner, Mrs Hollins. She chased the Captain round the paddock with her umbrella for daring to subject the animal to further strain after falling three times. Another persistent rider was the American Morgan Blair, who fell no less than four times with his own BONNIE CHARLIE before calling it a day. His Majesty requested the winning jockey be presented to him after the formalities of weighing-in had been completed. Fred Rees was to win the jockeys' championship six times as well as the distinction of becoming the first National Hunt rider to partner over a hundred winners in one season.

1921

Of £50 each, £30 forfeit or £5 if declared, with £5,000 added (including a trophy value £200). For five-year-olds & upwards. The second to receive £500, the third £300 and the fourth £150. The trainer of the Winner to receive a cup value £50 and the rider of the Winner a cup value £25

Date: 18th March 1921	Starters: 35	Time: 10 mins 26 secs
1st **SHAUN SPADAH**	**10.11–7** *(Mr T M McAlpine)*	**F B Rees**
2nd **THE BORE**	**10.11–8** *(Mr H A Brown)*	**Mr H A Brown** [remounted]
3rd **ALL WHITE**	**7.10–13** *(Lord Wavertree)*	**R Chadwick** [remounted]
4th **TURKEY BUZZARD**	**8.12–2** *(Mrs H M Hollins)*	**Capt G H Bennet** [remounted]

Also Ran:

CLONREE 7.12–0 (Mrs A Blain) **T Hulme** *Fell*; *OLD TAY BRIDGE 7.11–8* (Mr W H Dixon) **E Piggott** *Fell*; *GENERAL SAXHAM 8.11–4* (Mrs J Putnam) **W Smith** *Fell*; *GARRYVOE 7.11–2* (Mr C Bower Ismay) **Ivor Anthony** *Fell*; *BOBBYDAZZLER 7.11–1* (Sir F Price) **A Stubbs** *Fell*; *LOCH ALLEN 10.11–0* (Mr V Samuel) **J J Kelly** *Fell*; *DAYDAWN 8.10–13* (Baron F de Tuyll) **J R Anthony** *Fell*; *PRINCE CLIFTON 8.10–13* (Mr L Pollock) **L B Rees** *Fell*; *GLENCORRIG 7.10–13* (Mr K Mackay) **H B Bletsoe** *Refused*; *WHITE SURREY 9.10–12* (Admiral Sir Hedworth Meux) **A Escott** *Fell*; *RATHER DARK 7.10–12* (Mr W H Midwood) **A Gregson** *Fell*; *SHORT KNOCK 12.10–10* (Capt E Shirley) **M Halpin** *Fell*; *HALSTON 9.10–9* (Major D Dixon) **Mr L Firth** *Fell*; *WAVEBEAM 10.10–7* (Mr H Kershaw) **Mr S C E Lloyd** *Fell*; *HILL OF CAMAS 13.10–7* (Capt W Moloney) **Capt J C Delmege** *Fell*; *ANY TIME 10.10–6* (Mr G W Hands) **F Wooton** *Fell*; *BALLYSAX 7.10–5* (Mrs J Putnam) **G Goswell** *Fell*; *PICTURE SAINT 9.10–5* (Col R P Croft) **N Hayes** *Fell*; *EAMON BRIG 8.10–4* (Mr Joseph Widger) **M Connors** *Fell*; *BLAZERS 7.10–4* (Major W T M Buller) **W Watkinson** *Fell*; *BONNIE CHARLIE 13.10–4* (Mr M D Blair) **Mr M D Blair** *Fell*; *LONG LOUGH 9.10–1* (Mr R Power) **R Trudgill** *Fell*; *RUFUS XXI 10.10–0* (Lt Col G Brooke) **Capt E C Doyle** *Fell*; *CUPID'S DART 7.10–0* (Mr James Daly) **J Hogan, jnr** *Fell*; *FOREWARNED 6.9–11* (Mr W A Bankiers) **R Burford** *Fell*; *WHITE COCKADE 8.9–10* (Mr T D Longworth) **H Wicks** *Fell*; *REDSTART V 13.9–9* (Major A W H James) **Major A W H James** *Fell*; *PROSPERITZ 7.9–8* (Major L B Holliday) **W Daly** *Fell*; *CHARLBURY 13.9–7* (Lord Denman) **B Ellis** *Fell*; *HACKAM 6.9–7* (Mr A Humphry) **G Clancy** *Fell*; *GLENEFFY 7.9–7* (Mr S Stewart) **T Willmot** *Fell*

The Betting: *9/1 The Bore; 10/1 Eamon Beag; 100/9 Shaun Spadah, Turkey Buzzard & Garryvoe; 100/8 Old Tay Bridge; 100/7 Daydawn; 30/1 Clonree, Rather Dark, All White & White Surrey; 50/1 Halston, Forewarned, Any Time & Glencorrig; 66/1 General Saxham, Hackham & Prince Clifton.*

Distances: *A distance; a bad third*

Winner Trained By: *George Poole, Lewes, Sussex*

Value to Winning Owner: *£7,060*

1922

There were again ninety-two sub-scribers for this year's event, now firmly established as by far the richest steeplechase of the season, and thirty-two took their place in the line-up on 24th March 1922. At the head of the handicap with 12 st 3 lbs, SHAUN SPADAH was fourth in the betting, representing the now Sir Malcolm McAlpine. The courageous though luckless Harry Brown was once more in charge of the favourite, Lord Woolavington's winner of his last six races, SOUTHAMPTON and the Aintree maestro Jack Anthony, partnered his brother's CLASHING ARMS. The USA had a double interest in the race, through SQUARE UP and MASTERFUL, the latter being ridden by another American, Mor-gan Blair. Barely a fortnight before the race, MUSIC HALL had clearly demon-strated his well-being as winner of the Hurst Park Trial Handicap 'Chase over four miles.

Bred in County Kildare by Mrs Freddie Blacker who owned the dam MOLLY, MUSIC HALL's sire was the Northumberland Plate winner CLIFTONHALL and with the breeder's husband, Colonel Blacker, away at war the task of breaking the colt was left to Mrs Blacker. His next owner was Mrs Molly Stokes of Great Bowden, Market Harborough and it was this excel-lent judge of horses who discovered that MUSIC HALL could gallop with the best of them. In this lady's colours the gelding won seven races during 1920 including the Scottish Grand National and it was after this victory that he went to Manchester cotton broker Hugh Kershaw who sent him to Owen Anthony, recently licensed as a trainer. Lewis Bilby Rees, elder brother of last year's victorious jockey, was the man in the saddle for the 'National.

A groan from the area of the first fence signalled disaster for the favourite SOUTH-AMPTON, and as the survivors swept on like a tide, it was seen that SHAUN SPADAH was another casualty. SERGEANT MURPHY, striding out well, avoided the chaos in what was proving to be another disastrous 'National. Half the field had gone by the time Becher's was reached and the leader came to grief at the Canal Turn taking out ALL WHITE, GENERAL SAXHAM and NORTON. It was an all too-familiar story at the Water Jump, with but a handful of runners still on their feet, A DOUBLE ESCAPE holding a slight advantage over MUSIC HALL, ARRAVALE and DRIFTER, but the loudest cheer from the stands came for the remounted SERGEANT MURPHY, way behind the leaders though trying valiantly to make up ground. TAFFYTUS, giving the young Ted Leader his first ride in the race was tailed off at this stage but plodded on gamely – and wisely – for with so few left in it there was every likelihood of a place. Amid much bumping and jostling, Valen-tine's was cleared by MUSIC HALL, DRIFTER and A DOUBLE ESCAPE, though all three failed to get through unscathed. Rees lost an iron on MUSIC HALL, DRIFTER split his coronet so badly the hoof was virtually hanging off and A DOUBLE ESCAPE was so disturbed by the fracas, that he came down at the next fence. Despite the obviously painful injury, DRIFTER stuck well to his task, but after landing over the last just half a length behind MUSIC HALL, he was unable to sustain his effort, finishing on three legs twelve lengths be-hind. TAFFYTUS battled on bravely into third place a further six lengths back, a long way ahead of the remounted SERGEANT MURPHY and A DOUBLE ESCAPE.

With recent Grand Nationals exacting such a heavy, and often fatal toll, protests began to be made from the Royal Society for the Prevention of Cruelty to Animals, causing concern to the race organisers and bringing the first suggestions that the event's conditions needed modification.

For John Crocker Bulteel, the owner of this year's third TAFFYTUS, it was the first hint of a problem he would become familiar with in his future role as Aintree's Clerk of Course.

THE GRAND NATIONAL HANDICAP STEEPLECHASE
1922

Of £50 each, £30 forfeit or £5 if declared, with £5,000 added (including a trophy value £200). For five-year-olds & upwards. The second to receive £500, the third £300 and the fourth £100. The trainer of the winner to receive a cup value £50 and the rider of the winner a cup value £25

Date: 24th March 1922	Starters: 32	Time: 9 mins 55⅘ secs
1st **MUSIC HALL**	**9.11–8** *(Mr H Kershaw)*	**L B Rees**
2nd **DRIFTER**	**8.10–0** *(Mr Joseph Widger)*	**W Watkinson**
3rd **TAFFYTUS**	**9.11–0** *(Mr J C Bulteel)*	**T E Leader**
4th **SERGEANT MURPHY**	**12.11–0** *(Mr S Sanford)*	**C Hawkins** [remounted]
5th **A DOUBLE ESCAPE**	**8.10–3** *(Mr H Adams)*	**Capt G H Bennet** [remounted]

Also Ran:

SHAUN SPADAH 11.12–3 (Sir Malcolm McAlpine) **F B Rees** *Fell*; SOUTHAMPTON 6.11–10 (Lord Woolaving-ton) **Mr H A Brown** *Fell*; WAVERTREE 11.11–10 (Mr F Bibby) **H B Bletsoe** *Fell*; NORTON 7.11–8 (Mr V T Thompson) **I Morgan** *Fell*; CLONREE 8.11–6 (Mrs A Blain) **J Mahoney** *Fell*; ST BERNARD 8.11–5 (Mrs N Brownlee) **Mr R Pulford** *Fell*; CLASHING ARMS 7.11–3 (Col W S Anthony) **J R Anthony** *Fell*; ALL WHITE 8.11–0 (Lord Wavertree) **R Chadwick** *Fell*; THE TURK II 12.10–11 (Mr T A Sutton) **Ivor Anthony** *Fell*; ARRAVALE 7.10–11 (Mr C R Baron) **Mr P Whitaker** *Fell*; SUPER MAN 7.10–9 (Mr W A Bankier) **R Burford** *Fell*; GENERAL SAXHAM 9.10–9 (Mrs J Putnam) **Mr P Dennis** *Fell*; AWBEG 11.10–9 (Mr M S Thompson) **Mr A Knowles** *Fell* [destroyed]; GAY LOCHINVAR 6.10–8 (Mr G F Godson) **F Croney** *Fell*; DUNADRY 9.10–7 (Mrs A Blain) **J Hogan, jnr** *Fell*; SQUARE UP 9.10–6 (Mr W A Read) **J Rennison** *Fell*; ANY TIME 11.10–5 (Mr G W Hands) **G Wall** *Fell*; GREY DAWN V 9.10–5 (Mr G H Edwards) **A Newey** *Fell*; MASK-ON 9.10–2 (Mr T A O'Gorman) **J Burns** *Fell*; ARABIAN KNIGHT 6.10–2 (Mr J P Westlake) **R Spares** *Fell*; MASTERFUL 9.10–1 (Mr Foxhall Keene) **Mr M D Blair** *Fell*; SUDAN II 13.10–0 (Sir Reginald Rankin) **G Calder** *Fell*; VAULX 8.10–0 (Mr E S Patterson) **A Escott** *Fell*; CONFESSOR 8.10–0 (Mr T Galletly) **R Trudgill** *Fell*; DUNSTANBURGH 10.10–0 (Mr J W Burnett) **H Watkin** *Fell*; THE INCA II 8.10–0 (Capt C W Brennand) **F Brookes** *Fell* [destroyed]; SUCH A SPORT 11.10–0 (Mr R Hardinge) **Capt J C Delmege** *Fell*

The Betting: *100/12 Southampton; 9/1 Clashing Arms; 100/9 Music Hall; 100/8 Shaun Spadah; 100/7 All White & Arravale; 100/6 Sergeant Murphy; 18/1 Drifter; 20/1 Square Up; 25/1 Wavertree, Grey Dawn & Vaulx; 33/1 The Turk II & Clonree; 40/1 A Double Escape & Norton; 50/1 Mask-On; 66/1 Taffytus, General Saxham, Dunadry, Masterful & St Bernard.*

Distances: *Twelve lengths; six lengths*

Winner Trained By: *Owen Anthony, Lambourn, Berkshire*

Value to Winning Owner: *£7,075*

1923

In an attempt to improve the quality of the competitors and stave off some of the criticism directed against the race, the cost of running a horse in the 'National rose this year from £50 to £100. Acclaimed by the experts as a much-needed step in the right direction, its only obvious effect was to swell the winner's portion of the prize money to £7,850, for of the twenty-eight finally declared to run only twelve were handicapped at eleven stone or above. Most severely treated at the weights was former hero SHAUN SPADAH with 12 st 7 lbs, conceding one pound and seven respectively to TURKEY BUZZARD and SQUARE DANCE. Clear favourite at 11/2 was Jack Anthony's mount FOREWARNED, ARRAVALE being on the 10/1 mark and both LIBRETTO and TAFFYTUS the next in demand at 100/8. Now thirteen years old and making his fifth attempt at supreme honours, although one of these had been in a substitute race at Gatwick, SERGEANT MURPHY was thought by those in the know to have left his best days behind him. From that good 'chasing mare ROSE GRAFT, the chestnut gelding was by GENERAL SYMONS, having been bred at Athboy, County Meath by Gerald Walker. Passing through the hands of various owners, SERGEANT MURPHY was bought by American carpet king John Sanford for £1,200 as a present for his son Stephen, then at Cambridge. Sanford junior found the horse too much of a handful in the hunting field and put him back into training with George Blackwell at Newmarket. After getting back into the race to finish fourth in 1922, SERGEANT MURPHY wound up that season with victory in the Scottish Grand National with Captain G H Bennet in the saddle. Geoffrey Harbord 'Tuppy' Bennet, son of a National Hunt trainer, was a qualified veterinary surgeon and one of the most prominent amateurs riding at this time and such was his relationship with the ageing SERGEANT MURPHY, he was given the mount at Aintree.

SERGEANT MURPHY leads over Becher's second time, while the Constabulary watch which way their money went

In the presence of His Majesty The King, the runners paraded before the start and due to the thick fog swirling over the racecourse, this was to be the only clear view of them those in the stands were to get. Always up with the leading quartet, SERGEANT MURPHY jumped perfectly throughout the first circuit, which yet again brought a host of casualties. FOREWARNED, LIBRETTO and TAFFYTUS all came to grief, and American hope MASTERFUL had to be destroyed. First over the Water Jump was last year's runner-up DRIFTER,

Major Wilson leads his mount over Becher's

but at Becher's second time, SERGEANT MURPHY put in a splendid leap which took him to the front. PUNT GUN moved up to challenge the leader at Valentine's with SHAUN SPADAH also in close attendance but there was to be no denying SERGEANT

MURPHY. He came home three lengths ahead of SHAUN SPADAH with gallant CONJUROR II six lengths further back, despite damage to his mouth incurred after an amazing mid-air collision with DRIFTER. SERGEANT MURPHY was welcomed back to the winner's enclosure with cheers from all who admired the old 'chaser's persistence of former years and the Americans present were delirious with joy. Stephen Sanford had become the first American owner to achieve success in the big Liverpool 'chase, a race more valued by most owners from across the Atlantic than even the Epsom Derby. The victory was also a supreme example of the versatility of trainer George Blackwell, who was better known for his success on the flat, having sent out the brilliant ROCK SAND to win the triple crown in 1903.

Captain 'Tuppy' Bennet, his greatest victory under his belt, came out the next day to do it all over again on GRACIOUS GIFT in the inaugural running of the Liverpool Foxhunters' Steeplechase, over the identical 'National course – an event soon to become known as the 'amateurs' Grand National'. The season was to see him head the gentlemen riders list with sixty-two winners, only two behind Fred Rees, the leading professional. On the crest of a wave, Captain Bennet took the mount on Sir Keith Fraser's ARDEEN in the Oteley Handicap 'Chase at Wolverhampton on the 27th December 1923. Falling at a simple fence, he received a kick on the head as he lay on the ground and seventeen days later died without regaining consciousness. If any good can ever be said to come from tragedy, this accident made the use of crash helmets compulsory. Captain Bennet's partner in 'National glory survived him by only three years, SERGEANT MURPHY having to be destroyed after breaking a leg at Bogside.

1923

*Of £100 each, £50 forfeit or £5 if declared, with £5,000 added (including a trophy value £200). For five-year-olds &
upwards. The second to receive £700, the third £400 and the fourth £150. The trainer of the Winner to receive a cup value
£50 and the rider of the Winner a cup value £25*

Date: 23rd March 1923	Starters: 28	Time: 9 mins 36 secs
1st **SERGEANT MURPHY**	**13.11–3** *(Mr S Sanford)*	**Capt G H Bennet**
2nd **SHAUN SPADAH**	**12.12–7** *(Sir M McAlpine)*	**F B Rees**
3rd **CONJUROR II**	**11.11–0** *(Major C Dewhurst)*	**Mr C P Dewhurst**
4th **PUNT GUN**	**10.11–1** *(Mrs J Putnam)*	**M Tighe**
5th **DRIFTER**	**9.10–10** *(Mr Joseph Widger)*	**W Watkinson**
6th **MAX**	**7.11–5** *(Mrs R P Croft)*	**J Hogan, jnr**
7th **CINDERS II**	**11.10–2** *(Mr J H Betts)*	**W Williams**

Also Ran:

TURKEY BUZZARD 10.12–6 (Mrs H M Hollins) **F Brookes** *Fell*; *SQUARE DANCE 11.12–0* (Mr H M Curtis)
L B Rees *Fell*; *TAFFYTUS 10.11–7* (Mr J C Bulteel) **T E Leader** *Fell*; *DUETTISTE 10.11–7* (Mr J E Widener)
A Escott *Pulled-up*; *TRENTINO 9.11–7* (Major W N Hillas) **Major J Wilson** *Fell*; *FOREWARNED 8.11–5* (Mr
W A Bankier) **J R Anthony** *Fell*; *ARRAVALE 8.11–2* (Mr C R Baron) **Mr P Whitaker** *Fell*; *EUREKA II 6.11–0*
(Lord Woolavington) **A Stubbs** *Fell*; *MADRIGAL 6.10–12* (Mr H Barry) **D Colbert** *Pulled-up*; *MY RATH
11.10–8* (Mr P Ivall) **Mr C Chapman** *Fell*; *AMMONAL 6.10–7* (Mr F M Lloyd) **I Morgan** *Fell*; *LIFFEYBANK
aged.10–7* (Major H R Cayzer) **Mr K Gibson** *Pulled-up*; *PENCOED 8.10–3* (Lt Col F Lort Phillips) **Mr D
Thomas** *Pulled-up*; *LIBRETTO 8.10–3* (Mr A S Cochrane) **G Parfrement** *Pulled-up*; *THE TURK II 13.10–2*
(Mr T A Arthur) **C Donnelly** *Fell*; *CANNY KNIGHT 9.10–0* (Mr Adam Scott) **A Vause** *Fell*; *MASTERFUL
10.10–0* (Mr Foxhall Keene) **Mr P Roberts** *Pulled-up*; *NAVANA 9.10–0* (Mr C F Kenyon) **F Mason**
Pulled-up; *PAM NUT 10.10–0* (Capt T McDougal) **S Duffy** *Pulled-up*; *GARDENRATH 8.10–0* (Mr P Layton) **J
Whelehan** *Pulled-up*; *CINZANO 6.10–0* (Mr J Kemp) **F Brown** *Refused*

The Betting: *11/2 Forewarned; 10/1 Arravale; 100/8 Libretto & Taffytus; 100/6 Sergeant Murphy,
Conjuror II & Square Dance; 20/1 Shaun Spadah, Punt Gun & Drifter; 25/1 Max; 33/1 Turkey
Buzzard; 40/1 Duettiste, Eureka II & Ammonal; 66/1 Trentino, My Rath, Gardenrath, Madrigal &
Navana.*

Distances: *Three lengths; six lengths*

Winner Trained By: *George Blackwell, Newmarket, Suffolk*

Value to Winning Owner: *£7,850*

189

1924

In 1924, the National Hunt Committee, together with the Prestbury Park executive, instituted the Cheltenham Gold Cup, to be run over three and a quarter miles less than three weeks before the Grand National. The intention that the non-handicap race should produce a championship for the cream of park fencers would take some time to materialise but from the outset the enterprise was received with encouragement and the event was a most welcome addition to the calendar. No more exciting a result could have been hoped for than that which thrilled the Cheltenham crowds in the inaugural running, when Fred Rees inched his way to victory on RED SPLASH from CONJUROR II and GERALD L. The winning distances of a head and a neck illustrate fully why CONJUROR II found such overwhelming favour, when, again ridden by Harry Brown, he took his place in the 'National line-up later that month. He started at 5/2 and was spoken of as a certainty. SERGEANT MURPHY, MUSIC HALL and SHAUN SPADAH were the three former winners bidding again, while newcomers FLY MASK and SILVO added a touch of class to the thirty-runner field. The latter had reputedly cost Liverpool cotton broker Mr W H Midwood something in the region of £4,000.

MASTER ROBERT was another making his Grand National debut, though for this gelding there was little to inspire confidence. Bred in County Donegal, by MOORSIDE II out of DODDS, the chestnut suffered throughout his career from thick-windedness. At one time a stable-mate of TROYTOWN at the Curragh, he was sent home by trainer Algy Anthony as too moderate. Breeder Robert McKinley swallowed what pride he had left and found work for the cast-off as a plough

horse in the fields of Donegal. Purchased from his humble duties for £50, in due course MASTER ROBERT became the joint property of Lord Airlie and Mr Sidney Green and was sent to Wroughton to be trained by Aubrey Hastings. He satisfied the ambition of Lord Airlie in September 1922 by carrying His Lordship to a steeplechasing success at Perth – no mean feat, as his rider was putting up 37 lbs overweight! As the 1924 'National drew close, however, MASTER ROBERT caused trainer Hastings great anxiety through a diseased bone in his foot, the need for constant poulticing continuing right up to the day of the race. Further problems arose in the selection of a jockey, as one after another of the most fashionable riders declined the ride. One man who had never been in a position to pick and

choose his mounts was the West Country freelance Robert Trudgill, who gladly accepted the offer. Just twenty-four hours before the big race, though, Trudgill received severe injuries through the crashing fall of CHARLIE WISE in the Stanley Steeplechase. Still, the jockey, with one leg stitched together like an old cushion, ignored the advice of the race-course doctor and weighed out to partner MASTER ROBERT.

CONJUROR II was well up with the leaders when a loose horse baulked him as he reached for Becher's Brook and the favourite tumbled out of the race in a frightening-looking fall. SILVO, FLY MASK, SERGEANT MURPHY and EUREKA II were the leaders at this stage but with an equal number of riderless horses accompanying them, their progress was fraught with danger. Jockey Bill O'Neill, having parted company with LIBRETTO, found a novel way to get back in the race when intercepting the loose CONJUROR II.

Scrambling into the saddle, he set off to catch up with his original conveyance and having done so switched places, where-upon the obliging CONJUROR II strolled quietly away. WINNALL hit the front when SERGEANT MURPHY blundered on landing over the Water Jump, but out in the country, the race was thrown wide open when he fell. After OLD TAY BRIDGE, SILVO, FLY MASK and SERGEANT MURPHY had rounded the Canal Turn, a whole pack of loose horses ran across the path of those following, bringing about many refusals. But MASTER ROBERT, DRIFTER, SHAUN SPA-DAH and WAVETOWN managed to get through unhindered. SILVO put in a spectacular leap at Valentine's and the cheers for him began a long way out. Amateur Hubert Hartigan received concussion when OLD TAY BRIDGE came down heavily at the second last and it was at this point

5/2 favourite CONJURER II recovered well enough from this fall to perform ferry duty for Bill O'Neill

that the danger signals first began for SILVO. With both FLY MASK and MASTER ROBERT closing, SILVO could find no extra at the last and the much-maligned MASTER ROBERT won by four lengths from FLY MASK, with SILVO six lengths back in third place. Bob Trudgill was on the verge of collapse as he dismounted, the stitches in his leg having split open, yet in true professional fashion he struggled to the scales before being taken to a doctor. Lord Airlie

and Sidney Green showed their gratitude for his courage when they gave him £2,000 as a present for bringing their horse home in front. They also considerately retired MASTER ROBERT immediately.

Two old favourites made their departure from the Grand National after this race, SHAUN SPADAH, the victor three years before, and perhaps the unluckiest man so far in the history of the event, Mr Harry Brown.

THE GRAND NATIONAL HANDICAP STEEPLECHASE

1924

Of £100 each, £50 forfeit or £5 if declared, with £5,000 added (including a trophy value £200). For five-year-olds & upwards. The second to receive £700, the third £400 and the fourth £150. The trainer of the Winner to receive a cup value £50 and the rider of the Winner a cup value £25

Date: 28th March 1924	Starters: 30	Time: 9 mins 40 secs
1st **MASTER ROBERT**	**11.10–5** *(Lord Airlie)*	**R Trudgill**
2nd **FLY MASK**	**10.10–12** *(Mr T K Laidlaw)*	**J Moylan**
3rd **SILVO**	**8.12–2** *(Mr W H Midwood)*	**G Goswell**
4th **DRIFTER**	**10.10–5** *(Mr S Sanford)*	**G Calder**
5th **SERGEANT MURPHY**	**14.11–10** *(Mr S Sanford)*	**J Hogan, jnr**
6th **WAVETOWN**	**9.10–12** *(Mr A Hood)*	**R Lyall**
7th **SHAUN SPADAH**	**13.12–5** *(Sir M McAlpine)*	**F B Rees**
8th **BALLINODE**	**8.10–4** *(Mr C J Bentley)*	**G Fitzgibbon**

Also Ran:
MUSIC HALL 11.12–7 (Mr H Kershaw) **J R Anthony** *Pulled-up*; *GERALD L 10.12–6* (Major F J Scott Murray) **I Morgan** *Pulled-up*; *OLD TAY BRIDGE 10.11–13* (Mrs W H Dixon) **Mr H M Hartigan** *Fell*; *CHIN CHIN 8.11–7* (Sir F Price) **A Stubbs** *Fell*; *EUREKA II 7.11–5* (Lord Woolavington) **A Robson** *Fell*; *ARRAVALE 9.11–3* (Mr C R Baron) **Mr P Whitaker** *Fell*; *CLONSHEEVER 9.11–2* (Mr J E Tyrrell) **F Brookes** *Fell*; *CONJUROR II 12.11–0* (Major C Dewhurst) **Mr H A Brown** *Knocked-over*; *ALL WHITE 10.10–11* (Lord Wavertree) **M Tighe** *Refused*; *WINNALL 7.10–11* (Mr H Liddell) **C Donnelly** *Fell*; *LIBRETTO 9.10–8* (Sir E Edgar) **W O'Neill** *Fell*; *PENCOED 9.10–6* (Lt Col F Lort Phillips) **Mr D Thomas** *Pulled-up*; *TAFFYTUS 11.10–6* (Mr J C Bulteel) **T E Leader** *Fell*; *A DOUBLE ESCAPE 10.10–3* (Mr H Adams) **G Smith** *Fell*; *JAMES PIGG 11.10–3* (Mr J W Corrigan) **H Morris** *Fell*; *WINTER VOYAGE 7.10–2* (Mr T D Oakshott) **J H Goswell** *Fell*; *AUCHINROSSIE 8.10–2* (Mr W G P Kincaid Lennox) **E Foster** *Pulled-up*; *MAINSAIL 8.10–1* (Mr S C Wells) **Mr D Learmouth** *Refused*; *FAIRY HILL II 8.10–0* (Major H A Wernher) **W Watkinson** *Fell*; *GAY LOCHINVAR 8.10–0* (Mr G E Godson) **S Duffy** *Fell*; *PALM OIL 8.10–0* (Mr H E Steel) **Mr P Roberts** *Fell*; *NEWLANDS 10.10–0* (Mr C Bower Ismay) **R Burford** *Pulled-up*

The Betting: *5/2 Conjuror II; 100/12 Taffytus; 100/7 Fly Mask, Silvo & Shaun Spadah; 100/6 Eureka II & Sergeant Murphy; 25/1 Master Robert, Chin Chin, Auchinrossie, Music Hall & Ballinode; 33/1 Fairy Hill II & Arravale; 40/1 All White, Winnall, Drifter, Old Tay Bridge & Pencoed; 50/1 Gerald L; 66/1 Palm Oil, Clonsheever, Winter Voyage, Newlands & Mainsail.*

Distances: *Four lengths; six lengths*

Winner Trained By: *The Honourable Aubrey Hastings, Wroughton, Wiltshire*

Value to Winning Owner: *£8,240*

1925

It was a popular belief at this time that any horse ridden in the 'National by Jack Anthony was almost certain to start favourite and although the man's ability was undeniable, it was also a curious fact that all his three victories in the race were gained before he began riding for hire. This year found him astride OLD TAY BRIDGE, who had run so well for so long last time, and their price of 9/1 was the shortest at the 'off'. The recent Cheltenham Gold Cup winner, BALLI-NODE joined the proven FLY MASK and SILVO as the next best-backed of the thirty-three runners, while other interesting contestants included a promising newcomer called SPRIG. The one with the best form in the race, though, was the 'gift-horse' DOUBLE CHANCE, whose ancestry was marred by the largest of question marks. Bred at Southcourt by Leopold de Rothschild out of a mare named KELIBIA, the *Stud Book* can only name the sire as either ROI HERODE or DAY COMET. Meeting with little success on the flat when running in the colours of Captain Anthony de Rothschild, the chestnut was, like many before him, considered of no account and given to Fred Archer, who had just started training at Malton. Nephew of the famous jockey whose name he bore and a grandson of William Archer who partnered LITTLE CHARLEY to 'National glory, there could be no doubt concerning *his* pedigree! When Archer moved his quarters to Newmarket, the gelding went with him and proceeded to win five small races. Some time before the 'National a half share in the horse was sold to David Goold, a Liverpool cotton broker, and it was his colours the gelding carried at Aintree. Entrusted with riding the 'gift-horse' was the colourful Major John Philip Wilson. The thirty-six-year-old Yorkshireman had been one of the first airmen to bomb German airfields during the recent War, and shot down a Zeppelin raider over Hull. In his more peaceful pursuits, he played cricket for Cambridge and his home county, but although recognised as an accomplished horseman, was little known away from the Northern courses.

The new-fangled starting gate was an object of great curiosity but there could be no complaint as to its effectiveness when the single strand tape despatched the runners perfectly. DRIFTER, now owned by American Stephen Sanford, cut out the early work. The Canal Turn drastically reduced the number still in the race and old stalwart SERGEANT MURPHY came down here, departing from Aintree after so many noble efforts. Jumping the Water a length in front of DOUBLE CHANCE, FLY MASK was racing well within himself but with SILVO, OLD TAY BRIDGE and SPRIG in close attendance the race was still wide open as they went on to the second circuit.

ALCAZAR heads the field at the first Becher's

As the pace increased after the Canal Turn, SPRIG and MAX became the victims of a good deal of interference, both jockeys doing well to stay in the hunt. Fred Rees also performed magnificently when SILVO slipped at the final open ditch, landing on his side at such an angle that the jockey was able to push them upright by using his left hand against the ground. By this time the dash for home was on in earnest, OLD TAY BRIDGE and FLY MASK racing on ahead of the fading DOUBLE CHANCE. The two were still in command landing over the last fence, where Jack Anthony and the favourite struck the front. Half-way up the straight OLD TAY BRIDGE was still in front and being cheered loudly, when, seemingly from nowhere, Major Jack Wilson produced a renewed effort from the flat-race reject DOUBLE CHANCE. Sprinting up on the rails, they overhauled OLD TAY BRIDGE to win, going away by a comfortable four lengths, with FLY MASK a

further six back in third place. It was to be the only appearance Fred Archer's charge made in the 'National and, well backed at 100/9, the nine-year-old received an appropriate reception.

Major Wilson's victory upheld the fine tradition of amateur riders in the event and another who, though he failed to complete the course on his own BEN CRUCHAN, would long remember his day was Mr Bill Whitbread. In the years ahead, his pioneering of race sponsorship would have an enormous effect on National Hunt racing.

Locally owned 'gift horse' DOUBLE CHANCE comes in to a hero's reception

1925

Of £100 each, £50 forfeit or £5 if declared, with £5,000 added (including a trophy value £200). For five-year-olds & upwards. The second to receive £700, the third £400 and the fourth £150. The trainer of the Winner to receive a cup value £50 and the rider of the Winner a cup value £25

Date: 27th March 1925	Starters: 33	Time: 9 mins 42⅗ secs
1st **DOUBLE CHANCE**	9.10–9 *(Mr D Goold)*	**Major J P Wilson**
2nd **OLD TAY BRIDGE**	11.11–12 *(Mrs W H Dixon)*	**J R Anthony**
3rd **FLY MASK**	11.11–11 *(Mr T K Laidlaw)*	**E Doyle**
4th **SPRIG**	8.11–2 *(Mrs M Partridge)*	**T E Leader**
5th **SILVO**	9.12–7 *(Sir E Edgar)*	**F B Rees**
6th **DWARF OF THE FOREST**	8.10–10 *(Mr H Kennard)*	**Mr H Kennard**
7th **JACK HORNER**	8.10–0 *(Mr K Mackay)*	**Mr M D Blair**
8th **MAX**	9.11–5 *(Mrs R P Croft)*	**J Hogan, jnr**
9th **DRIFTER**	11.10–3 *(Mr S Sanford)*	**W Watkinson**
10th **SERGEANT MURPHY**	15.11–7 *(Mr S Sanford)*	**A Escott** [remounted]

Also Ran:

ALCAZAR 9.12–3 (Mr R McAlpine) **Squadron-Leader C A Ridley** *Fell*; *MUSIC HALL 12.12–0* (Mr H Kershaw) **L B Rees** *Refused*; *BALLINODE 9.11–6* (Mr J C Bentley) **G Fitzgibbon** *Fell*; *WHITE SURREY 13.11–4* (Admiral Sir Hedworth Meux) **M Tighe** *Fell*; *BEN CRUCHAN 11.11–3* (Mr W H Whitbread) **Mr W H Whitbread** *Fell*; *ARDEEN 8.11–2* (Sir Keith Fraser) **A Lefebre** *Fell*; *ARRAVALE 10.11–0* (Mr C R Baron) **J Meaney** *Pulled-up*; *WINNALL 8.11–0* (Mr H Liddell) **F Gurney** *Refused*; *PATSEY V aged.10–12* (Mr B Lemon) **Mr B Lemon** *Refused*; *AMMONAL 8.10–10* (Mr J W Wood) **R Trudgill** *Pulled-up*; *HIS LUCK 9.10–10* (Capt A A Bankier) **R Burford** *Fell*; *TAFFYTUS 12.10–9* (Mr J C Bulteel) **R Lyall** *Refused*; *THROWN IN 9.10–8* (Mr David Faber) **J Goswell** *Fell*; *GRACIOUS GIFT 10.10–8* (Mr R H A Gresson) **W Parvin** *Fell*; *KEEP COOL 10.10–7* (Mr W H Midwood) **G Green** *Pulled-up*; *MAINSAIL 9.10–5* (Mr S C Wells) **R Prioleau** *Fell*; *PENCOED 10.10–3* (Lt Col F Lort Phillips) **Mr D Thomas** *Fell*; *BALLYMACRORY 8.10–3* (Mr R C Ross) **J Moylan** *Fell*; *ROUSHAM 10.10–0* (Mr H Dyke Dennis) **Mr P Dennis** *Fell*; *ALL WHITE 11.10–0* (Lord Wavertree) **J Mason** *Fell*; *PETER THE PIPER 13.10–0* (Sir E Edgar) **G Turner** *Fell*; *GARDENRATH 10.10–0* (Mr F A Waring) **T James** *Fell*; *JAMES PIGG 12.10–0* (Mr J W Corrigan) **A Robson** *Fell*

The Betting: *9/1 Old Tay Bridge; 10/1 Fly Mask, Silvo & Ballinode; 100/9 Double Chance; 20/1 Max & Drifter; 25/1 Gracious Gift & Patsey V; 28/1 Thrown In, Winnall & Ardeen; 33/1 Keep Cool, Sergeant Murphy, Pencoed, Ballymacrory & Sprig; 40/1 Peter the Piper, Ben Cruchan, Jack Horner & Taffytus; 50/1 Alcazar & His Luck; 66/1 Others.*

Distances: *Four lengths; six lengths*

Winner Trained By: *Fred Archer, Newmarket, Suffolk*

Value to Winning Owner: *£8,120*

1926

Impressed by SPRIG's performance in finishing fourth behind DOUBLE CHANCE, the public made Ted Leader's mount their main choice for the 1926 race. Both SILVO and OLD TAY BRIDGE figured prominently in the betting, together with Mr Frank Barbour's recent Gold Cup winner KOKO, who was providing Cheltenham-based jockey Tim Hamey with a first 'National ride. American interest in the race had intensified, shiploads of excited visitors arriving at Liverpool to see if Stephen Sanford's 1923 success could be repeated. Sanford was doubly represented with MOUNT ETNA and BRIGHT'S BOY and another for the American contingent to cheer was the nine-year-old JACK HORNER.

Bred by John Musker at the Melton Stud, the son of CYLLIUS and MELTON'S GUIDE had changed hands several times before being purchased by Morgan de Witt Blair in time to carry that noted American sportsman in the 1925 'National. JACK HORNER finished a remote yet creditable seventh on that occasion in the colours of his co-owner Kenneth Mackay, the future Lord Inchcape. Upon becoming the sole owner, Mr Mackay instructed trainer Harvey Leader to prepare JACK HORNER for another tilt at Aintree. Barely a fortnight before the race, however, the well-known American polo player Charles Schwartz bought JACK HORNER for £4,000, with a promise of a further £2,000 should the chestnut win the 'National. The Tasmanian-born jockey William Watkinson weighed out to ride the American hope, confident that he could better his second on DRIFTER in 1922.

As early as the first fence two of the leading fancies were eliminated when SILVO and GRECIAN WAVE fell amid a flurry of hooves. The Gold Cup winner was brought down at the Brook and LONE HAND held a fractional advantage over the Water, from SPRIG, JACK HORNER, BRIGHT'S BOY, BEN CRUCHAN, DARRACQ and OLD TAY BRIDGE. On the second circuit Fred Gurney took the blinkered DARRACQ smoothly into the lead. LONE HAND broke his neck in a crashing fall at Becher's, leaving JACK HORNER, BRIGHT'S BOY and SPRIG the closest pursuers, but after jumping Valentine's BRIGHT'S BOY struck the front. Jack Anthony joined issue on OLD TAY BRIDGE as they came onto the racecourse, only to be run out of it on the run to the post by JACK HORNER, with Mr Sanford's BRIGHT'S BOY filling third spot. A grateful Charles Schwartz suggested a sum of £4,000 as a present for the winning jockey, Watkinson, only to be persuaded into changing this to £1,000 annually for four years. Ironically, three weeks after bringing home JACK HORNER successfully in the 'National, the rider was killed in a fall at Bogside. JACK HORNER never ran in the race again. He broke down in training later that season and was shipped to America for an honourable and greatly deserved retirement.

1926

Of £100 each, £50 forfeit or £5 if declared, with £5,000 added (including a trophy value £200). For five-year-olds &
upwards. The second to receive £700, the third £400 and the fourth £150. The trainer of the Winner to receive a cup value
£50 and the rider of the Winner a cup value £25

Date: 26th March 1926	Starters: 30	Time: 9 mins 36 secs
1st **JACK HORNER**	**9.10–5** *(Mr A C Schwartz)*	**W Watkinson**
2nd **OLD TAY BRIDGE**	**12.12–2** *(Mrs W H Dixon)*	**J R Anthony**
3rd **BRIGHT'S BOY**	**7.11–8** *(Mr S Sanford)*	**E Doyle**
4th **SPRIG**	**9.11–7** *(Mrs M Partridge)*	**T E Leader**
5th **DARRACQ**	**11.10–11** *(Major F R Samson)*	**F Gurney**
6th **GERALD L**	**12.12–2** *(Mr H Kershaw)*	**F Brookes**
7th **THROWN IN**	**10.10–11** *(Lord Stalbridge)*	**Mr H Grosvenor**
8th **RED BEE**	**8.10–10** *(Major H A Wernher)*	**D Behan**
9th **DWARF OF THE FOREST**	**9.10–10** *(Mr H Kennard)*	**Mr H Kennard**
10th **MASTER BILLIE**	**7.10–0** *(Mr W Parsonage)*	**E Foster**
11th **MISCONDUCT**	**7.10–0** *(Major D M Methven)*	**W Parvin**
12th **POP AHEAD**	**8.10–0** *(Mrs Holroyd Smith)*	**S Regan**
13th **BEN CRUCHAN**	**12.11–2** *(Mr W H Whitbread)*	**Mr W H Whitbread** [remounted]

Also Ran:

SILVO 10.12–7 (Mr W H Midwood) **F B Rees** *Fell*; *ARDEEN 9.11–9* (Sir Keith Fraser) **R Trudgill** *Fell*;
MOUNT ETNA 9.11–2 (Mr S Sanford) **Mr S H Dennis** *Fell*; *KOKO 8.11–1* (Mr F Barbour) **J Hamey** *Fell*;
KNIGHT OF THE WILDERNESS 6.11–0 (Mr G White) **J Meaney** *Fell*; *PATSEY V aged.10–9* (Mr B Lemon)
Major T F Cavenagh *Fell*; *UPTON LAD 11.10–8* (Mr J C Paterson) **Mr W P Dutton** *Fell*; *GRECIAN WAVE*
8.10–8 (Mr W Hume) **Major J P Wilson** *Fell*; *WHITE SURREY 14.10–7* (Admiral Sir Hedworth Meux) **M**
Farragher *Fell*; *WALLSEND 6.10–7* (Mrs E A Cameron) **Capt H Lumsden** *Fell*; *LEE BRIDGE 9.10–5* (Mr
R G Shaw) **W Stott** *Fell*; *TEST MATCH 8.10–5* (Mr H Mosenthal) **P L'Estrange** *Fell*; *PENCOED 11.10–2*
(Lt Col F Lort Phillips) **Mr D Thomas** *Fell*; *LONE HAND 8.10–0* (Mr A W Hedges) **T Morgan** *Fell*
[destroyed]; *JOLLY GLAD 9.10–0* (Capt C B Petre) **Mr P Dennis** *Fell*; *SOLDIER BILL 10.10–0* (Mr A Hood)
Mr K Goode *Fell*; *CASH BOX 9.10–0* (Mr R Havelock-Allen) **Mr R Read** *Fell*

The Betting: *5/1 Sprig; 7/1 Silvo; 8/1 Old Tay Bridge; 100/8 Koko; 100/6 Mount Etna; 20/1 Grecian*
Wave, Lee Bridge, Knight of the Wilderness & Master Billie; 25/1 Jack Horner & Bright's Boy; 28/1
Misconduct & Dwarf of the Forest; 33/1 Ardeen & Thrown In; 40/1 Darracq & Gerald L; 50/1 Jolly
Glad & Upton Lad; 66/1 Patsey V, Ben Cruchan, Lone Hand, Pop Ahead, Cash Box, Red Bee, White
Surrey & Test Match; 100/1 Others.

Distances: *Three lengths; one length*

Winner Trained By: *Harvey 'Jack' Leader, Exning, Suffolk*

Value to Winning Owner: *£7,635*

1927

The fact that the race was to be broadcast live on the wireless has clearly not deterred a vast crowd from attending

The wonders of radio brought the most exciting race of the year to its largest audience ever in 1927, when the British Broadcasting Corporation took the thrills and spills of the event into the homes of the nation. This milestone in broadcasting history provided the sternest test for commentators Meyrick Good and George Allison, with a misty day adding to the difficulties of relaying the progress of the largest field ever to contest the event. Of the thirty-seven runners, SPRIG was again installed at the head of the betting. Owned by Mrs Partridge, the chestnut by MARCO out of SPRY had been bred by her son, Captain Richard Partridge, in 1917 while he was home on leave from the trenches. The gangly colt gave his breeder the hope that one day, when peace was restored, they could together strive for glory at Aintree. The dream was shattered just weeks before the armistice in 1918, when Richard Partridge was killed in action. SPRIG became a symbol of remembrance for the grief-stricken mother, who, determined to fulfil at least part of her son's wishes, put the horse into training with Tom Leader. From his Newmarket headquarters, Leader brought the son of MARCO along steadily, in spite of frequent leg problems. Twenty-four-year-old Ted Leader shared his father's commitment to Mrs Partridge's quest and, as in the previous two seasons, turned down large sums of money from other trainers in order to ride SPRIG. The five-year-old GRAKLE was a popular choice in the betting, at 9/1 second favourite and THROWN IN, a surprise winner of the Cheltenham Gold Cup, came in for a welter of support.

In heavy ground, however, THROWN IN got no further than the initial obstacle. GRECIAN WAVE soon took and held a long lead, going over the Water ahead of SPRIG, KEEP COOL, DWARF OF THE FOREST and BRIGHT'S BOY but before turning back into the country, GRECIAN WAVE ran out, leaving SPRIG in command. There were only ten left in it at Becher's, where the rank outsider BOVRIL III on the wide outside held a narrow lead over DWARF OF THE FOREST, KEEP COOL, MASTER BILLIE, BRIGHT'S BOY, SPRIG and AMBERWAVE. Two fences later at the Canal Turn SPRIG put in a spectacular leap, taking off in fifth place and landing in the lead. At the final open ditch, Jack Anthony pushed BRIGHT'S BOY to the front, staying there until overtaken again by SPRIG on the run to the last fence. Mr Gerald Pennington on his BOVRIL III was a good four lengths in arrears at this point, but rallied tremendously well on the flat. Stride by stride, the unknown outsider gained ground up the long run-in, pegging back BRIGHT'S BOY and then drawing closer to

the favourite. The winning post came too soon for BOVRIL III, however, who was within one length of SPRIG as they reached it, with BRIGHT'S BOY the same distance

Above: Jockey Powell leads MARSIN out of the contest at Becher's first time in what looks like hair-raising fashion

Below: 100/1 outsider BOVRIL III makes the favourite fight all the way to the line

behind. Seldom had a more popular owner received such an overwhelming and sincere reception as did Mrs Partridge when she led in SPRIG. When it was discovered that the 100/1 BOVRIL III had only one eye, the reason for his rider taking the longest way round became apparent and the appreciation of the outsider's efforts all the greater. But the moment was rightly SPRIG's, for he provided the late Richard Partridge with the memorial he would most have wished.

THE GRAND NATIONAL HANDICAP STEEPLECHASE

1927

Of £100 each, £50 forfeit or £5 if declared, with £5,000 added (including a trophy value £200). For five-year-olds & upwards. The second to receive £700, the third £400 and the fourth £150. The trainer of the Winner to receive a cup value £50 and the rider of the Winner a cup value £25

Date: 25th March 1927	Starters: 37	Time: 10 mins 20⅕ secs
1st **SPRIG**	**10.12–4** *(Mrs M Partridge)*	**T E Leader**
2nd **BOVRIL III**	**9.10–12** *(Mr G W Pennington)*	**Mr G W Pennington**
3rd **BRIGHT'S BOY**	**8.12–7** *(Mr S Sanford)*	**J R Anthony**
4th **DRINMOND**	**10.11–2** *(Mr G Balding)*	**Mr J B Balding**
5th **MASTER OF ARTS**	**10.10–10** *(Mr M D Blair)*	**Major T F Cavenagh**
6th **WHITE PARK**	**8.12–5** *(Major J T North)*	**E Foster** [remounted]
7th **BALLYSTOCKART**	**8.11–1** *(Capt R E Sassoon)*	**Capt R E Sassoon**

Also Ran:

GERALD L 13.12–5 (Mr H Kershaw) **L B Rees** *Failed to finish*; AMBERWAVE 9.12–0 (Lady Helen McCalmont) **Mr J E O'Brien** *Baulked*; GRECIAN WAVE 9.11–12 (Mr W Hume) **J Meaney** *Ran out*; MARSIN 9.11–12 (Mr S Sanford) **P Powell** *Fell*; THROWN IN 11.11–10 (Lord Stalbridge) **Mr H Grosvenor** *Fell*; KNIGHT OF THE WILDERNESS 7.11–9 (Mr W P Draper) **W Gurney** *Fell*; DWARF OF THE FOREST 10.11–4 (Mr H Kennard) **Mr H Kennard** *Fell*; SHAUN OR 8.11–3 (Lord Glanely) **W Madden** *Fell*; SILVER SOMME 10.11–3 (Mr H Liddell) **M Connors** *Refused*; KEEP COOL 12.11–3 (Mr W H Midwood) **J Goswell** *Fell*; RED BEE 9.11–3 (Major H A Wernher) **W Payne** *Fell*; HAWKER 13.11–1 (Capt A E Grant) **Capt A E Grant** *Ran-out*; TEST MATCH 9.11–1 (Mr G L Redmond) **R Lyall** *Fell*; UNCLE JACK 8.11–1 (Capt A Gollans) **T O'Sullivan** *Fell*; TRUMP CARD 9.11–1 (Mr G Newall Nairn) **Mr S H Dennis** *Fell*; MASTER BILLIE 8.10–13 (Mr W Parsonage) **F B Rees** *Fell*; POP AHEAD 9.10–13 (Mr H Fowler) **Mr H Fowler** *Fell*; MISCONDUCT 8.10–12 (Mr H G Selfridge) **W Parvin** *Fell*; SIR HUON 13.10–12 (Mr Geoffrey Gilbey) **M Rayson** *Fell*; CASH BOX 10.10–12 (Mr R Havelock-Allen) **G Green** *Fell*; SNAPPER 9.10–10 (Major T H Sebag-Montefiore) **Capt M E Dennis** *Fell*; UPTON LAD 12.10–10 (Mr J C Paterson) **Mr W P Dutton** *Fell*; EAGLE'S TAIL 8.10–9 (Mr J A Fairhurst) **F Brookes** *Fell*; GRAKLE 5.10–9 (Mr T K Laidlaw) **J Moloney** *Fell*; MR JOLLY 12.10–9 (Lt Col R W Tweedie) **J S Wight** *Fell*; CORAZON 9.10–8 (Major F W Barrett) **T Morgan** *Fell*; BLAENOR 10.10–7 (Lord Marchamley) **E Doyle** *Fell*; LISSETT III 11.10–5 (Lord Grimthorpe) **J Hamey** *Fell*; ALL WHITE 13.10–5 (Lord Wavertree) **J Mason** *Pulled-up*; MISS BALSCADDEN 8.10–5 (Mr D Thomas) **Mr D Thomas** *Fell*

The Betting: *8/1 Sprig; 9/1 Grakle; 100/8 Thrown In; 100/7 Silver Somme & Bright's Boy; 100/6 Shaun Or; 20/1 Master Billie, White Park, Misconduct, Eagle's Tail & Amberwave; 33/1 Knight of the Wilderness, Dwarf of the Forest, Trump Card, Blaenor & Keep Cool; 40/1 Pop Ahead & Snapper; 50/1 Grecian Wave, Test Match, Red Bee, Uncle Jack, Gerald L & Master of Arts; 66/1 Marsin, Drinmond, Mr Jolly, Hawker & Upton Lad; 100/1 Others.*

Distances: *One length; one length*

Winner Trained By: *Tom Leader, Newmarket, Suffolk*

Value to Winning Owner: *£8,215*

1928

Even when the entries for the 1928 Grand National were published, with one hundred and twelve subscribers ensuring a record number of runners, no-one could have foreseen the catastrophe which lay ahead. Of the forty-two which eventually faced the starter, MASTER BILLIE, ridden by Fred Rees, was just the most preferred in the market to Keith Piggott's mount TRUMP CARD. There was also money for SPRIG, EASTER HERO and AMBERWAVE but with so many unknowns taking part, the betting range extended from 5/1 to 200/1. The state of the going extremely heavy and the benefit of hindsight reveal all the ingredients for a shock result. Another large contingent of Americans arrived, brimful of confidence for the chances of their champion BILLY BARTON, who had ventured to Britain with an impressive record. Virtually unbeatable over timber in his own country, Mr Bruce's gelding could count among his victories the Maryland Hunt Cup, the Virginia Gold Cup, the Meadow Brook Cup and two wins in the Grand National Point-to-Point.

TIPPERARY TIM's odds of 100/1, on the other hand, were a fair reflection of what little chance he had on known form. The ten-year-old brown gelding was by CIPANGO out of LAST LOT, having been bred by Mr J J Ryan in County Tipperary and was named after Tim Crowe, the long distance runner of Dundrum who had won the marathon from Windsor to London. After proving useless on the flat, TIPPERARY TIM passed into the ownership of Mr C F Kenyon and thence to his brother Harold. It was in his purple and yellow striped colours that the tubed 'no-hoper' took his place in the 'National line-up. Trained in Shropshire by Joseph Dodd TIPPERARY TIM was ridden by the newly-articled Chester solicitor Mr William Parker Dutton.

From a good start, not one came down at the first obstacle and the brilliant young EASTER HERO took them along at a cracking gallop. But totally misjudging the open ditch at the Canal Turn, EASTER HERO landed squarely on top of the fence, straddling it for agonising minutes as thirty-odd horses bore down on him. Racing at full tilt, they were caught completely unawares and with horses refusing or trying to take evasive action, the pile-up was the worst ever seen on a racecourse. Only a handful were able to keep going. Subdued stands spectators gazed in amazement as so few of the big field they had witnessed at the start only minutes before made their way to the Water Jump. At the second Becher's there were only five still on their feet, BILLY

Above: BILLY BARTON makes a splash

Below: TIPPERARY TIM lets off steam

BARTON landing just in advance of MAY KING, GREAT SPAN and TIPPERARY TIM on the wide outside, with the French mare MAGUELONNE beginning to lose ground. When MAY KING fell, GREAT SPAN, ridden by seventeen-year-old Bill Payne, appeared to be going the best but at the second last his saddle slipped, giving the jockey no chance. BILLY BARTON and TIP-PERARY TIM rose at the final fence together but the former struck the top and crumpled on landing, leaving TIPPERARY TIM to come home alone to surely the quietest reception a Grand National winner ever received. Tommy Cullinan re-mounted BILLY BARTON to finish second a long way behind the winner and the American horse was subsequently immortalised by the erection of a statue at the entrance to Laurel Park Racecourse. There was to be no such tribute to TIPPER-ARY TIM, only the most searching questions as to how such a mediocre horse

could possibly succeed in racing's greatest showpiece. Before the next running, alterations would be made to both the conditions of the event and the nature of the course. TIPPERARY TIM passed back into the obscurity from which he had briefly, yet gloriously, emerged but his partner Bill Dutton gave up the law as a career in favour of the sport he had shocked to its foundations.

THE GRAND NATIONAL HANDICAP STEEPLECHASE

1928

Of £100 each, £50 forfeit or £5 if declared, with £5,000 added (including a trophy value £200). For five-year-olds & upwards. The second to receive £700, the third £400 and the fourth £150 out of the stakes. The trainer of the Winner to receive a cup value £50 and the rider of the Winner a cup value £25

Date: 30th March 1928	Starters: 42	Time: 10 mins 23²/₅ secs
1st **TIPPERARY TIM**	10.10−0 *(Mr H S Kenyon)*	**Mr W P Dutton**
2nd **BILLY BARTON**	10.10−11 *(Mr Howard Bruce)*	**T B Cullinan** [remounted]

Also Ran:

SPRIG 11.12–/ (Mrs M Partridge) **T E Leader** *Fell*; *BRIGHT'S BOY 9.12–7* (Mr S Sanford) **M Rayson** *Fell*; *EASTER HERO 8.12–5* (Capt A Lowenstein) **P Powell** *Fell*; *KOKO 10.12–2* (Capt F E Guest) **W Gurney** *Fell*; *THE COYOTE 8.11–13* (Mr V Emanuel) **J Hogan, jnr** *Failed to finish*; *AMBERWAVE 10.11–13* (Lady Helen McCalmont) **Mr J E O'Brien** *Fell*; *TRUMP CARD 10.11–10* (Mr G Newall Nairn) **K Piggott** *Fell*; *GREAT SPAN 7.11–9* (Mr W B Duckworth) **W Payne** *Saddle slipped*; *THE ACE II 6.11–6* (Mr R B Strassburger) **T Morgan** *Refused*; *GRAKLE 6.11–5* (Mr C R Taylor) **R Lyall** *Refused*; *BALLYSTOCKART 9.11–2* (Capt R E Sassoon) **Capt R E Sassoon** *Failed to finish*; *DARRACQ 13.11–2* (Mr A C Schwartz) **J Moloney** *Failed to finish*; *ARDEEN 11.11–2* (Sir Keith Fraser) **J Hamey** *Failed to finish*; *EAGLE'S TAIL 9.11–0* (Mr J A Fairhurst) **E Foster** *Failed to finish*; *RATHOWEN 8.11–0* (Mr H Deterding) **Mr H Deterding** *Failed to finish*; *FOXTROT 12.10–13* (Capt H Lumsden) **Capt H Lumsden** *Failed to finish*; *MAGUELONNE 6.10–13* (Comte P de Jumilhac) **J Bedeloup** *Fell*; *MAY KING 9.10–13* (Lord Ednam) **L B Rees** *Failed to finish*; *DRINMOND 11.10–13* (Mr J B Balding) **Mr J B Balding** *Refused*; *KEEP COOL 13.10–11* (Mr W H Midwood) **J Goswell** *Failed to finish*; *SPEAR O'WAR 7.10–10* (Lord Queenborough) **F Brookes** *Failed to finish*; *CARFAX 12.10–10* (Mr B W Ancil) **Mr B W Ancil** *Failed to finish*; *TEST MATCH 10.10–9* (Mr G L Redmond) **J M Maloney** *Refused*; *HERBERT'S CHOICE 7.10–8* (Miss D Graeme Thomson) **F Gurney** *Failed to finish*; *MASTER BILLIE 9.10–8* (Mr W Parsonage) **F B Rees** *Refused*; *SCOTCH EAGLE 12.10–8* (Mr H Fowler) **Mr H Fowler** *Failed to finish*; *BURGORIGHT 13.10–7* (Mr B L Behr) **Mr F A Bonsal** *Failed to finish*; *MASTER OF ARTS 11.10–6* (Mr M D Blair) **Major T F Cavenagh** *Failed to finish*; *RED LYNCH 7.10–5* (Mr G E Strong) **Mr W R West** *Failed to finish*; *THE GOSLING 8.10–5* (Lord Grimthorpe) **Mr S H Dennis** *Failed to finish*; *MELLERAY'S BELLE 9.10–5* (Mr W Wilson) **J P Kelly** *Pulled-up*; *COMMONSIDE 9.10–5* (Lt Col G S Brooke) **Mr C B Harvey** *Failed to finish*; *SETI THE FIRST 13.10–4* (Mr E Craig Tanner) **Mr E Craig Tanner** *Failed to finish*; *RUDDYMAN 9.10–4* (Mr H G Selfridge) **W Parvin** *Failed to finish*; *RATHORY 12.10–2* (Major H E Lyon) **D Williams** *Failed to finish*; *RATHMORE 11.10–1* (Mr Jack Hylton) **Mr L Whitfield** *Failed to finish*; *SCRAPTOFT 11.10–1* (Mr W Ross) **Mr M Barry** *Failed to finish*; *ROSSIENY 9.10–0* (Mrs J Putnam) **Mr R Everett** *Failed to finish*; *SOLDIER'S JOY 10.10–0* (Mr S G R Barratt) **D Quirke** *Failed to finish*; *DE COMBAT 11.10–0* (Mr C Mulholland) **F Croney** *Failed to finish*

The Betting: *5/1 Master Billie; 11/2 Trump Card; 10/1 Amberwave; 100/7 Easter Hero & Sprig; 20/1 Maguelonne, Bright's Boy, Darracq & Koko; 25/1 Carfax; 33/1 Billy Barton, Great Span, Grakle, Drinmond, Rathowen & Rossieny; 40/1 The Coyote, Ardeen, Seti the First & Ballystockart; 50/1 Eagle's Tail, Herbert's Choice, Spear O'War, Master of Arts & The Ace II; 66/1 Keep Cool, Rathmore, Ruddyman, Test Match & Red Lynch; 100/1 Foxtrot, De Combat, Scotch Eagle, May King, Rathory, Soldier's Joy & Tipperary Tim; 200/1 Others.*

Distances: *A distance – only two finished*

Winner Trained By: *Joseph Dodd, Whitchurch, Shropshire*

Value to Winning Owner: *£11,255*

1929

On the advice of Aintree course inspector Gilbert Cotton, who had jumped the course himself as an amateur in the 1913 'National, the notorious ditch at the Canal Turn was filled in, in an effort to prevent a recurrence of the EASTER HERO fiasco. Alterations were also made to the conditions of the race, an additional forfeit stage being introduced as a means to curtail the number of runners. The biggest lesson learned from the 1928 race, though, was that anything could happen in the Aintree spectacular and owners with a horse in any way resembling a 'chaser took comfort from the example set by TIPPERARY TIM. So it was that, to the amazement of the public and the horror of pundits, sixty-six horses went to the post for the 1929 Grand National. In spite of a top weight burden of 12 st 7 lbs and the experience of 1928, EASTER HERO was a raging favourite at the unrealistic odds of 9/1. There could be no question but that the brilliant chestnut had improved immeasurably, having won each of his five races in the present campaign, including the Cheltenham Gold Cup. Formerly owned by Captain Lowenstein, who mysteriously vanished from his private plane over the North Sea, the son of MY PRINCE now represented American millionaire 'Jock' Hay Whitney and was trained by a man with excellent Aintree credentials, Jack Anthony at Letcombe. An unusual feature in the market was to see two former winners of the race offered at long odds, SPRIG at 50/1 and TIPPERARY TIM again 100/1.

The Canal Turn as it was up to and including 1928

At the same price as last year's winner was the seven-year-old GREGALACH, a half-brother to EASTER HERO through their sire MY PRINCE. Out of the mare ST GERMAINE, he was bred in Ireland by Marriot Finlay, running first on behalf of the Right Honourable Thomas Kennedy Laidlaw, who also owned another promising 'chaser by the name of GRAKLE. In 1927 both were sold, GREGALACH becoming the property of Mrs M A Gemmell, and entering the Newmarket training establishment of Tom Leader. GREGALACH frustratingly ran up a long sequence of seconds before a lack-lustre performance at Sandown just eight days before the 'National. His rider was the Australian Robert Everett, late of the Royal Navy. A professional barely twelve months but with extensive experience in South Africa, he was partnering the least fancied of Tom Leader's five runners.

Stretching for almost half a mile in front of the stands, the sixty-six runners paraded in race-card order. EASTER HERO was sweating heavily but when the tape went up, he settled immediately, leading over the first where miraculously not one horse fell. The first ditch brought the first casualties, no less than ten runners falling or refusing but EASTER HERO was jumping like a stag and set a terrific pace. A crescendo of cheering spurred some twenty survivors over the Water and Mr Whitney's powerful chestnut continued to skip over the fences. Over Valentine's, the favourite was running them all into the ground when suddenly his stride seemed to shorten and for the first time the zest began to seep away. It was later discovered that he had spread a plate somewhere in that vicinity and from there on, every stride became agony for EASTER HERO. Battling courageously to the end, he was unable to resist the challenge of GREGALACH who overtook him between

The way it looked for every subsequent race as a plain fence

The mammoth field gets under way in two rows

the last two fences and stayed on to win by six lengths. RICHMOND II was a bad third in front of MELLERAY'S BELLE.

For the second year running the book-makers had cause to smile, for the winner was again at 100/1. And it was back to the drawing board for Tophams Limited, their plans to reduce the size of the field having clearly backfired.

THE GRAND NATIONAL HANDICAP STEEPLECHASE
1929

Of £100 each, £80 forfeit, £55 if declared by 12 March or £5 if declared by 22nd January with £5,000 added (including a trophy value £200). For five-year-olds & upwards. The second to receive £700, the third £400 and the fourth £150. The trainer of the Winner to receive a cup value £50 and the rider of the Winner a cup value £25

Date: 22nd March 1929		Starters: 66	Time: 9 mins 47²/₅ secs
1st	**GREGALACH**	**7.11–4** *(Mrs M A Gemmell)*	**R Everett**
2nd	**EASTER HERO**	**9.12–7** *(Mr J H Whitney)*	**J Moloney**
3rd	**RICHMOND II**	**6.10–6** *(Mr R McAlpine)*	**W Stott**
4th	**MELLERAY'S BELLE**	**10.10–2** *(Mr W Wilson)*	**J Mason**
5th	**MAY KING**	**10.11–2** *(Mrs H Mond)*	**F Gurney**
6th	**GRAKLE**	**7.11–9** *(Mr C R Taylor)*	**J Hamey**
7th	**DDB**	**9.10–11** *(Major A W Huntington)*	**Mr R Gubbins**
8th	**DELARUE**	**7.10–3** *(Mr J B Snow)*	**G Wilson**
9th	**KILBAIRN**	**8.10–0** *(Mr R A Parry)*	**Mr L Parry**
10th	**CAMPERDOWN**	**10.10–9** *(Mrs E Hutchinson)*	**Mr K Goode** [remounted]

Also Ran:

SPRIG 12.12–5 (Mrs M Partridge) **A Escott** *Fell*; *BRIGHT'S BOY 10.12–4* (Mr S Sanford) **E Foster** *Fell*; *KOKO 11.12–3* (Capt F E Guest) **S Duffy** *Fell*; *GREAT SPAN 8.12–0* (Mr W B Duckworth) **W Payne** *Pulled-up*; *TRUMP CARD 11.11–12* (Mr G Newall Nairn) **T Morgan** *Fell*; *MOUNT ETNA 12.11–7* (Mr S Sanford) **T E Leader** *Fell*; *KNIGHT OF THE WILDERNESS 9.11–7* (Mr F H W Cundell) **M Keogh** *Brought down*; *BILLY BARTON 11.11–7* (Mr Howard Bruce) **T B Cullinan** *Fell*; *LLOYDIE 7.11–4* (Capt R F H Norman) **F B Rees** *Fell*; *THE ACE II 7.11–3* (Mr R B Strassburger) **Mr G H Evans** *Fell*; *ARDEEN 12.11–2* (Sir Keith Fraser) **R Lyall** *Fell*; *CARFAX 13.11–1* (Mr B W Ancil) **Mr B W Ancil** *Fell*; *BALLYSTOCKART 10.11–0* (Capt R E Sassoon) **Capt R E Sassoon** *Failed to finish*; *STORT 10.11–0* (Mr R Wright) **T Chisman** *Fell – broke leg*; *LORDI 8.11–0* (Mr A M Jones) **Capt A H Weber** *Fell*; *MASTER BILLIE 10.11–0* (Mr W Parsonage) **M Rayson** *Pulled-up*; *DARRACQ 14.11–0* (Mr A C Schwartz) **Mr G S Poole** *Fell*; *MABESTOWN'S PRIDE 13.10–13* (Brig-Gen C R P Winser) **Mr D R Daly** *Knocked-over*; *LE TOUQUET 7.10–12* (M G Watinne) **J Teasdale** *Failed to finish*; *SKRUN PRINCE 8.10–12* (Col P D Stewart) **W Gurney** *Fell*; *OVERDRAFT 7.10–11* (Mrs R D Cohen) **Mr E J R Bennett** *Failed to finish*; *RAMPANT 9.10–11* (Col W S Anthony) **Major H Misa** *Failed to finish*; *TIPPERARY TIM 11.10–10* (Mr H S Kenyon) **Mr W P Dutton** *Fell*; *KCB 7.10–10* (Mr V H Smith) **J Hogan, jnr** *Brought-down*; *ARDOONS PRIDE 9.10–10* (Mrs W Mure) **R Thrale** *Fell*; *DWARF OF THE FOREST 12.10–10* (Mr H Kennard) **Mr H Kennard** *Fell*; *DRINMOND 12.10–10* (Mr J B Balding) **Mr J B Balding** *Fell*; *SANDY HOOK 8.10–9* (Mr J H Hull) **F Fish** *Fell*; *HERBERT'S CHOICE 8.10–8* (Mr J Graeme Thomson) **J Farrell** *Fell*; *UNCLE BEN 8.10–8* (Mr H B Brandt) **P Powell** *Refused*; *BEECH-MARTIN 8.10–8* (Mr David Faber) **L B Rees** *Failed to finish*; *RUDDYMAN 10.10–5* (Mr H Gordon Selfridge) **W Parvin** *Fell*; *HAWKER 15.10–5* (Capt A E Grant) **Capt A E Grant** *Pulled-up*; *FLEET PRINCE 11.10–5* (Mr G S L Whitelaw) **Mr F R Thackray** *Fell*; *KILBRAIN 9.10–4* (Mr E A Longworth) **V Piggott** *Fell*; *GAY DOG II 9.10–3* (Sir Lindsay Parkinson) **A Birch** *Failed to finish*; *DENBURGH 10.10–3* (Mr F Usher) **G Hardy** *Fell*; *SULTAN OF WICKEN 10.10–3* (Dowager Lady Penrhyn) **T James** *Fell*; *MERRIVALE II 11.10–3* (Lord Westmorland) **F Brookes** *Fell*; *BALLYHANWOOD 8.10–2* (Mr M D Blair) **J Goswell** *Refused*; *SOLDIER'S JOY 11.10–2* (Mr S G R Barratt) **Capt A F W Gossage** *Failed to finish*; *DUKE OF FLORENCE 8.10–2* (Mr A D McAlpine) **G Turner** *Failed to finish*; *BIG WONDER 9.10–2* (Mr G S L Whitelaw) **J Bisgood** *Failed to finish*; *ODD CAT 8.10–1* (Mr J B D'Ardenne) **J Sinnott** *Failed to finish*; *MORE DIN 9.10–1* (Mr H S Horne) **A Harraway** *Fell*; *IRINA 7.10–0* (Mr A Heathorn) **J Kelly** *Fell*; *HAREWOOD 7.10–0* (Mr M L Meyer) **D Williams** *Fell*; *RATHORY 13.10–0* (Major H E Lyon) **R Burford** *Fell*; *CLORINGO 8.10–0* (Mr J C Paterson) **A Wall** *Fell*; *MISS BALSCADDEN 10.10–0* (Sir David Llewellyn) **G Bowden** *Fell*; *BEST HOME 8.10–0* (Mr G Elliott) **Mr G Elliott** *Fell*; *KWANGO 8.10–0* (Mr C Goad) **A Waudby** *Brought-down*; *STAGE MANAGEMENT 9.10–0* (Major C W M Norrie) **M Doherty** *Fell*; *THEOREM 12.10–0* (Mr H M Llewellyn) **T Costello** *Fell*; *TOY BELL 7.10–0* (Mr R D Cohen) **D Morgan** *Fell*; *WILD EDGAR 9.10–0* (Mrs E A Ryan) **S Regan** *Fell*

The Betting: *9/1 Easter Hero; 100/6 Great Span; 18/1 Grakle; 20/1 Billy Barton & Master Billie; 22/1 Skrun Prince & Lloydie; 25/1 Bright's Boy & Ardeen; 28/1 Mount Etna & Lordi; 33/1 Trump Card; 40/1 Darracq, Knight of the Wilderness, Carfax, Uncle Ben, Richmond II & Harewood; 50/1 Beech-Martin, Sprig, KCB, Drinmond, Ruddyman, Duke of Florence, Big Wonder & Merrivale II; 66/1 Koko, The Ace II, May King, Ballystockart, Overdraft & DDB; 100/1 Rampant, Sandy Hook, Tipperary Tim, Ballyhanwood, Gregalach, Kilbrain, Stage Management & Toy Bell; 200/1 Others.*

Distances: *Six lengths; a bad third*

Winner Trained By: *Tom Leader, Newmarket, Suffolk*

Value to Winning Owner: *£13,000*

1930

With the beginning of the new decade, American interest in the Grand National rose to new heights with vast sums being paid for any 'chaser holding the Aintree engagement. Three representatives of the United States figured among the forty-one runners this year, with each considered lively prospects. SIR LINDSAY replaced EASTER HERO in 'Jock' Whitney's colours, Stephen Sanford ran SANDY HOOK and the attractive grey GLANGESIA carried the hopes of Mr R K Mellon.

It was GRAKLE, owned by Liverpool cotton broker Cecil R Taylor, who topped the betting, however, with Keith Piggott taking over as jockey from Tim Hamey. Always a most difficult horse to ride, this was GRAKLE's fourth attempt in the race

and on each occasion he had been partnered by a different jockey. So far only Hamey had got him round. GREGALACH was back, with top weight and a price of 100/6. By a curious coincidence the other best-backed runner was owned by another local cotton broker, Mr W H Midwood. SHAUN GOILIN was by an unknown sire. Apparently the dam, GOLDEN DAY, strayed from her paddock in County Limerick one evening to be accosted by an unbroken three-year-old colt. SHAUN GOILIN was the result and sold for a mere twenty guineas to Mrs de Sales la Terrière before Mr Midwood, Master of the Cheshire hounds, purchased him. Trained by Frank Hartigan, a nephew of Garrett Moore, at Weyhill, the gelding did not win until his seventh year but the

manner of his Grand Sefton victory in 1929 placed him on many short lists for 'National glory. Another thing in his favour was the man on board. Tommy Cullinan was on the crest of a wave after carrying off the Champion Hurdle–Gold Cup double at Cheltenham.

Straight from the start the two greys, GATE BOOK and GLANGESIA, hit the front, making a fine sight as they cleared Becher's. Both GATE BOOK and GREGALACH fell before the Anchor Crossing and clearing the Water in fine style with a two length lead, GLANGESIA preceded SHAUN GOILIN, MERRIVALE II, TOY BELL and MAY KING. With SIR LINDSAY and MELLERAY'S BELLE starting to move up, they began the final circuit. At Becher's second time round MAY KING fell spectacularly and a gasp of horror rose from onlookers. GLANGESIA kept on from TOY BELL, SHAUN GOILIN, SIR LINDSAY and MERRIVALE II but from two out the mare MELLERAY'S BELLE,

SIR LINDSAY and SHAUN GOILIN had the race between them. Cullinan lost his irons jumping the second last on SHAUN GOILIN, and it was MELLERAY'S BELLE who landed first on the flat, a length in front of SIR LINDSAY whose rider, Dudley Williams, also lost his stirrups when the horse pecked slightly. In one of the closest finishes the race had ever produced, SHAUN GOILIN got up in the final strides to win by a neck from the Scottish-owned mare MELLERAY'S BELLE, with SIR LINDSAY a somewhat unlucky third, one and a half lengths behind. Each of the first three jockeys performed tremendously, riding a flat-race finish in spite of only having one stirrup iron between them. GLANGESIA finished fourth, with BALLYHANWOOD and ROYAL ARCH II the only others to complete the course. The result was a popular one, particularly for the City of Liverpool and for jockey Tommy Cullinan, who would have partnered EASTER HERO in the race had the Gold Cup winner stayed sound and trainer Frank Hartigan, who finally joined his uncles Garrett and Willie

Above: J Mason has lost his iron on MELLERAY'S BELLE and can't quite catch SHAUN GOILIN

Left: The only time two greys have led the 'National field, with GLANGESIA touching down in front of GATE BOOK

Moore, on the 'National roll of honour. Mr Midwood had spent a small fortune trying to win this race and had every reason to feel proud of SHAUN GOILIN, who cost but a fraction of what he had paid for SILVO in 1924.

1930

Of £100 each, £85 forfeit, £60 if declared by 11th March, or £10 if declared by 28th January, with £5,000 added (including a trophy value £200). For five-year-olds & upwards. The second to receive £800, the third £500 and the fourth £200. The trainer of the Winner to receive a cup value £50 and the rider of the Winner a cup value £25

Date: 28th March 1930	Starters: 41	Time: 9 mins 40³/₅ secs
1st **SHAUN GOILIN**	10.11–7 *(Mr W H Midwood)*	**T B Cullinan**
2nd **MELLERAY'S BELLE**	11.10–0 *(Mr W Wilson)*	**J Mason**
3rd **SIR LINDSAY**	9.10–6 *(Mr J H Whitney)*	**D Williams**
4th **GLANGESIA**	10.10–4 *(Mr R K Mellon)*	**J Browne**
5th **BALLYHANWOOD**	9.10–4 *(Mr M D Blair)*	**E Foster**
6th **ROYAL ARCH II**	9.10–2 *(Mr V Emanuel)*	**Mr F R Thackray**

Also Ran:

GREGALACH 8.12–0 (Mrs M A Gemmell) **R Everett** *Fell*; GATE BOOK 9.11–8 (Marquis J de San-Miguel) **T Morgan** *Fell*; DONZELON 9.11–7 (Col G Foljambe) **R Lyall** *Fell*; GRAKLE 8.11–6 (Mr C R Taylor) **K Piggott** *Fell*; NEWSBOY 9.11–4 (Capt R E Sassoon) **Capt R E Sassoon** *Fell*; GUIDING LIGHT 9.11–3 (Mrs J B D'Ardenne) **Mr C W Langlands** *Fell*; DONEGAL 13.11–2 (Mr A Bendon) **W Speck** *Fell*; LORDI 9.11–2 (Mr A M Jones) **W Stott** *Knocked-over*; ALIKE 7.11–0 (Lady Helen McCalmont) **Mr M Barry** *Fell*; IBSTOCK 10.10–13 (Mr K Goode) **Mr K Goode** *Pulled-up*; KCB 8.10–12 (Mr V H Smith) **J Moloney** *Knocked-over*; SANDY HOOK 9.10–12 (Mr S Sanford) **T E Leader** *Knocked-over*; PEGGIE'S PRIDE 7.10–11 (Mr H B Brandt) **T McCarthy** *Fell*; BIG WONDER 10.10–11 (Mr G S L Whitelaw) **Capt H N Weber** *Fell*; SAVERNAKE 10.10–10 (Mr C Anson) **R McCarthy** *Fell*; MAY KING 11.10–9 (Mrs H Mond) **G Goswell** *Fell*; AGDEN 13.10–9 (Mr O G Moseley) **Mr D P G Moseley** *Pulled-up*; TOOTENHILL 8.10–7 (Mrs D H Boswall-Preston) **C Wenham** *Fell*; PARIS FLIGHT 10.10–7 (Mr W Harris) **E Vinall** *Pulled-up*; DELARUE 8.10–6 (Mr J B Snow) **G Wilson** *Knocked-over*; CRYPTICAL 15.10–6 (Mr F H Bowcher) **J Bisgood** *Pulled-up*; TOY BELL 8.10–5 (Mrs R D Cohen) **D Morgan** *Fell*; RUDDYMAN 11.10–2 (Mr H Gordon Selfridge) **E Brown** *Fell*; BLENNERHASSET 11.10–2 (Mr T L Parke) **Mr W P Dutton** *Fell*; MAY CRESCENT 8.10–2 (Mr David Faber) **G Hardy** *Fell*; MERRIVALE II 12.10–1 (Lord Westmorland) **F Brookes** *Fell*; ANNANDALE 8.10–0 (Lady Glenapp) **F Gurney** *Fell*; THE MONK 8.10–0 (Mr F J Honour) **W Parvin** *Pulled-up*; SOLDIER'S JOY 12.10–0 (Mr S G R Barratt) **J Farrell** *Pulled-up*; CURTAIN RAISER 7.10–0 (Mrs E W B Leake) **P Powell** *Pulled-up*; DERBY DAY II 8.10–0 (Mr C Nicholson) **Mr E V Stephenson** *Fell* [destroyed]; GAY DOG II 10.10–0 (Sir Lindsay Parkinson) **W Gurney** *Pulled-up*; THE GOSLING 10.10–0 (Major J A Coats) **A Tannock** *Pulled-up*; HAREWOOD 8.10–0 (Mr M L Meyer) **J Hamey** *Fell*; THEOREM 13.10–0 (Sir David Llewellyn) **Mr G Owen, jnr** *Fell*

The Betting: *100/12 Grakle; 100/8 Shaun Goilin; 100/7 Sir Lindsay; 100/6 Gregalach; 20/1 Melleray's Belle; 22/1 KCB; 25/1 Sandy Hook, Donegal & May Crescent; 28/1 Lordi & Alike; 33/1 Peggie's Pride, Ballyhanwood, Tootenhill & Glangesia; 40/1 May King & Merrivale II; 50/1 Gate Book, Newsboy, Big Wonder, Agden & Royal Arch II; 66/1 Toy Bell, Donzelon, Blennerhasset & Gay Dog II; 100/1 Others.*

Distances: *A neck; one and a half lengths*

Winner Trained By: *Frank Hartigan, Weyhill, Hampshire*

Value to Winning Owner: *£9,805*

1931

It was a year of change. Conditions for the Grand National were once more modified in the seemingly impossible quest to reduce the size of the field. Five-year-olds were banned from the race and the new rules stipulated that only horses placed in steeplechases of not less than three miles, or those winning a race of £500 or over, were eligible to run. The newly-instituted totalisator was bringing angry comments from bookies unaccustomed to competition and a lottery known as the Irish Hospital Sweepstakes ran its first sweep on the 'National, with the promise of huge returns should your ten-bob ticket be lifted from the 'drum'. With the Cheltenham National Hunt meeting abandoned due to frost, many runners were re-directed to Liverpool and this, despite the new conditions of entry, led to another big field of forty-three for the 'National.

EASTER HERO was back with his expected top weight of 12 st 7 lbs, yet the public still rushed to back him. With the valuable assistance of Fred Rees, the dual Cheltenham Gold Cup winner started 5/1 favourite on the day. Word had circulated that last year's winner SHAUN GOILIN had developed an enlarged joint on his off knee and his price drifted to 33/1, but MELLERAY'S BELLE was the second choice at 8s. Running in his fifth 'National GRAKLE again featured high in the betting at 100/6. The son of JACKDAW had been bought from Thomas Laidlaw by Cecil Taylor of Liverpool for 4,000 guineas. Trainer Tom Coulthwaite always considered GRAKLE superior to stable-mate GREGALACH and when both were sold, GRAKLE stayed in his care. His jockey this year was Bob Lyall, whose eldest brother Frank was narrowly beaten on BLOOD-STONE by JERRY M in the 1912 race.

The field jump the first fence at speed, with the jockeys giving a fine demonstration of the 'backward seat'

With perfect going and a summer-like day, Aintree was packed with well over two hundred thousand coming to see what was expected to be a winning return for EASTER HERO. Falls were few in the early part of the race but there was a bad incident at Becher's when SWIFT ROWLAND was jumped on by another horse and killed instantly. GREGALACH led over the Water, a length ahead of GREAT SPAN, with EASTER HERO and SOLANUM the next in line and GRAKLE, THERAS and SHAUN GOILIN well to the fore. Becher's then proved the undoing of EASTER HERO in the unluckiest of circumstances, when the riderless TAMASHA brought down SOLANUM directly in the path of the favourite. EASTER HERO could not avoid a collision and was out of the race through no fault of his own. SIR LINDSAY also came down here, as did several others, including the Czechoslovakian challenger GYI LOVAM and his owner Captain Popler. Quickly remounting, Captain Popler tried desperately to make up the lost ground, receiving the cheering encouragement of the crowds. GREAT SPAN and GREGALACH continued side by side on to the Canal Turn, but GREGALACH took the obstacle at such speed that he went wide losing valuable ground. GREAT SPAN, BALLASPORT and DRINTYRE poached a good three lengths advantage and GRAKLE also moved into the reckoning at this point. The game Czech horse fell at the final open ditch, by which time GRAKLE had moved right into contention, taking the last fence a length ahead of his former stable companion GREGALACH, with their nearest rivals a long way back. Quickening on the flat, GREGALACH made ground with every stride but Bob Lyall stuck to his instructions not to use his whip on GRAKLE until the last possible moment. The horse had shown before that he shirked when shown too much of the stick, but with a hundred yards to run, two slaps got him home a length-and-a-half in front of GREGALACH with the 100/1 shot ANNANDALE ten lengths further back in third place. The French horse RHYTICERE was fourth. At long last GRAKLE had behaved himself sufficiently to justify the judgement of trainer Tom Coulthwaite and his winning time was just two-fifths of a second outside CLOISTER's record. To the credit of owner Cecil Taylor, some weeks later he sent Tim Hamey a present of £50, 'for showing him how to get round two years ago'. The tote paid two pounds and a penny to two bob each-way on the winner and a London-domiciled Italian by the name of Emilio Scala found himself the richer by £354,544 thanks to his Irish Hospital Sweepstakes ticket and a gelding called GRAKLE.

GRAKLE pops over the last ahead of his former stablemate GREGALACH

1931

Of £100 each, £60 if declared by 17th March or £10 if declared by 27th January. With £5,000 added (including a trophy value £200). For six-year-olds & upwards. The second to receive £800, the third £500 and the fourth £200. The trainer of the Winner to receive a cup value £50 and the rider of the Winner a cup value £25

Date: 27th March 1931	Starters: 43	Time: 9 mins 32⅘ secs
1st **GRAKLE**	**9.11–7** *(Mr C R Taylor)*	**R Lyall**
2nd **GREGALACH**	**9.12–0** *(Mrs M A Gemmell)*	**J Moloney**
3rd **ANNANDALE**	**9.10–7** *(Lady Glenapp)*	**T Morgan**
4th **RHYTICERE**	**aged.10–12** *(Mr V Emanuel)*	**L Niaudot**
5th **BALLYHANWOOD**	**10.10–7** *(Mr M D Blair)*	**T Isaac**
6th **SHAUN GOILIN**	**11.12–4** *(Mr W H Midwood)*	**M Keogh**
7th **GLANGESIA**	**11.10–10** *(Mr R K Mellon)*	**J Browne**
8th **MELLERAY'S BELLE**	**12.10–10** *(Mr W Wilson)*	**J Mason**
9th **GREAT SPAN**	**10.11–0** *(Mr M D Blair)*	**G Hardy**

Also Ran:

EASTER HERO 11.12–7 (Mr J H Whitney) **F B Rees** *Fell*; *GIB 8.12–5* (Mr B D Davies) **E Foster** *Fell*; *KAKUSHIN 8.11–13* (Mr W M G Singer) **R Everett** *Fell*; *DRINTYRE 8.11–7* (Capt C N Brownhill) **Capt C N Brownhill** *Refused*; *SIR LINDSAY 10.11–6* (Mr J H Whitney) **Mr F R Thackray** *Fell*; *KILBUCK aged.11–6* (Mr E R Hartley) **T Chisman** *Fell*; *TRUMP CARD 13.11–5* (Lord Stalbridge) **W Gurney** *Refused*; *GYI LOVAM aged.11–3* (Capt R Popler) **Capt R Popler** *Fell*; *THERAS 6.11–2* (Mr Holford Harrison) **J Walsh** *Fell*; *SWIFT ROWLAND 10.11–2* (Mrs Chester Beatty) **T E Leader** *Fell*; *DRIN 7.11–2* (Mr A Bendon) **W Speck** *Fell*; *GUIDING LIGHT 10.11–0* (Mr O M Smith) **Mr F E McKeever** *Pulled-up*; *BALLASPORT 7.11–0* (Sir Harold A Wernher) **D Williams** *Fell*; *SANDY HOOK 10.10–12* (Mr S Sanford) **F Fish** *Fell*; *GEORGINATOWN 10.10–12* (Mr J H Wallace) **F Maxwell** *Fell*; *EASY VIRTUE 8.10–12* (Mr W P Tyser) **P Powell** *Fell*; *BIG BLACK BOY 9.10–12* (Major C H Stevens) **W Payne** *Fell*; *APOSTASY 10.10–12* (Lady Lindsay) **F Brookes** *Fell*; *SOUTH HILL 9.10–12* (Mr H G Blagrave) **T B Cullinan** *Fell*; *STARBOX 8.10–10* (Major J B Walker) **Mr K Urquhart** *Fell*; *MAY KING 12.10–10* (Lady Melchett) **Capt R G Fanshawe** *Fell*; *ALIKE 8.10–10* (Mr R K Mellon) **Mr F R Sclater** *Fell*; *OXCLOSE 7.10–10* (Mr A Hall Watt) **F Gurney** *Fell*; *ASPIRANT 8.10–10* (Mr C S Green) **W Parvin** *Fell*; *MOREKEEN 10.10–10* (Miss D Robinson) **J Cooke** *Fell*; *SOLANUM 6.10–8* (Miss Dorothy Paget) **J Hamey** *Fell*; *RUDDYMAN 12.10–8* (Mr H Gordon Selfridge) **E Brown** *Refused*; *TAMASHA 10.10–7* (Mr G Elliott) **Mr G Elliott** *Fell*; *PIXIE 6.10–7* (Mrs D FitzGerald) **Capt R E Sassoon** *Refused*; *MALLARD aged.10–7* (Mr James Harrison) **Mr W P Dutton** *Brought-down*; *HAREWOOD 9.10–7* (Mr M L Meyer) **Mr K Goode** *Fell*; *ROYAL ARCH II 10.10–7* (Mr V Emanuel) **J Bedeloup** *Brought-down*; *TOY BELL 9.10–7* (Mrs R D Cohen) **D Morgan** *Brought-down*; *SLIEVE GRIEN 10.10–7* (Capt R B Moseley) **Capt R B Moseley** *Brought-down*

The Betting: *5/1 Easter Hero; 8/1 Melleray's Belle; 100/6 Grakle & Ballasport; 20/1 Drintyre, Drin & Georginatown; 22/1 Kakushin; 25/1 Sir Lindsay & Gregalach; 28/1 Swift Rowland & Alike; 33/1 Gib, Shaun Goilin & Oxclose; 40/1 Glangesia, Tamasha, Ballyhanwood, Sandy Hook & Apostasy; 50/1 Great Span, Kilbuck, Rhyticere, Solanum, Ruddyman, South Hill & Harewood; 66/1 Trump Card, Big Black Boy, Slieve Grien & Aspirant; 100/1 Others.*

Distances: *One and a half lengths; ten lengths*

Winner Trained By: *Tom Coulthwaite, Rugeley, Staffordshire*

Value to Winning Owner: *£9,385*

1932

The Grand National had stood supreme as a thrilling spectacle and the severest test of horse and rider for over half a century, yet even its staunchest supporters could not deny that the very nature of the event often deprived the best horse of success. Anything could and usually did happen. The Cheltenham Gold Cup, on the other hand, was considered a far fairer test of the jumper and when a five-year-old called GOLDEN MILLER defeated the odds-on GRAKLE in that race on 1st March 1932, the manner of his victory set the whole racing world alight. At last the grace and beauty of jumpers at speed, giving their all for the most modest prize money, brought enlightenment to those who had hitherto thought of the sport as unworthy of their attention. Disqualified by age from contesting the 'National this year, GOLDEN MILLER's activities had to remain confined to racing over park fences for the time being but the question of how he would cope with Aintree was a most intriguing one.

Mr Goode parts company with REDLYNCH but Mr Wilson wobbles back on board to complete the course with SEA SOLDIER

Three former winners topped the handicap, GREGALACH, SHAUN GOILIN and GRAKLE, and it was the last named who shared favouritism at 100/12 with the brilliant Irish mare HEARTBREAK HILL. Unbeaten since before winning the Grand Sefton the previous November, HEARTBREAK HILL's chances were obvious.

FORBRA may have looked as though he was merely making the numbers up at 50/1 and with hardly any form, but his trainer, Tom Rimell of Kinnersley, gave the seven-year-old the label of 'the horse that could not fall' and with the seasoned professional Tim Hamey riding, he was thought by some to be capable of running into a place. Owned by retired bookmaker William Parsonage of Ludlow, FORBRA was by FORESIGHT out of THYMBRA and by

winning a 'chase at Taunton rendered himself ineligible for Aintree's Stanley Steeplechase, which had been his original target.

Once again the field enjoyed an almost incident-free journey until reaching Becher's where EVOLUTION, FORBRA and EGREMONT were setting the pace but INVERSE, QUITE CALM and REDLYNCH fell. EGREMONT cleared Valentine's with a great leap, in front of FORBRA, NEAR EAST, HEARTBREAK HILL, GREGALACH and DUSTY FOOT, with COUP DE CHAPEAU falling heavily in the centre of the course. At the last ditch before rejoining the racecourse the riderless PELORUS JACK put two-thirds of the runners out of the race when running across the fence. GREGALACH was caught broadside-on as he was in the act of

taking off and fell through the obstacle, trapping his amateur rider Fred Thackray beneath him. So badly injured was the highly talented Mr Thackray that he was never able to ride in a race again. HEARTBREAK HILL was pushed into the wing and Willie O'Grady was forced to put her back at the fence in order to continue. In the meantime, the four lucky enough to have avoided the pile-up, KCB, FORBRA, NEAR EAST and EGREMONT raced on to the Water Jump where KCB came down. From then on the race became a duel between FORBRA and EGREMONT, the pair drawing even further ahead of the remainder as they

FORBRA strikes the front at the first fence

215

jumped fence after fence together. Although EGREMONT was partnered by an amateur, Edward Paget, there was a tremendous financial inducement for him to get the horse home in front. Mr Paget, a stockbroker, had included his mount in a £1 spring double with JEROME FANDOR, the 40/1 winner of the Lincoln Handicap and stood to collect £4,000 if he could be first home in the 'National. He was still well there at the last, but FORBRA beat him for speed on the flat to record a three length victory. The ever faithful SHAUN GOILIN finished a bad third. Sadly Mr Parsonage died in 1934 and FORBRA, the horse who had given him his greatest racing triumph broke a leg at Newbury early the following January.

At the mighty Becher's, the race has developed into a classic duel between FORBRA nearest the camera and EGREMONT

1932

Of £100 each, £60 if declared by 8th March or £10 if declared by 26th January. With £5,000 added (including a trophy value £200). For six-year-olds & upwards. The second to receive £800, the third £500 and the fourth £200. The trainer of the Winner to receive a cup value £50 and the rider of the Winner a cup value £25

Date: 18th March 1932	Starters: 36	Time: 9 mins 44⅗ secs
1st **FORBRA**	**7.10–7** *(Mr W Parsonage)*	**J Hamey**
2nd **EGREMONT**	**8.10–7** *(Mrs Ireland)*	**Mr E C Paget**
3rd **SHAUN GOILIN**	**12.12–4** *(Mr W H Midwood)*	**D Williams**
4th **NEAR EAST**	**7.10–10** *(Mr H B Brandt)*	**T McCarthy**
5th **ASPIRANT**	**9.10–10** *(Sir Peter Grant Lawson)*	**Sir Peter Grant Lawson**
6th **HEARTBREAK HILL**	**7.11–6** *(Mrs C S Bird, Jnr)*	**W O'Grady**
7th **ANNANDALE**	**10.10–10** *(Lord Glenapp)*	**W Stott** [remounted]
8th **SEA SOLDIER**	**aged.11–7** *(Mr A H Niblack)*	**Mr A G Wilson** [remounted]

Also Ran:

GREGALACH 10.12–7 (Mrs M A Gemmell) **Mr F R Thackray** *Fell*; *GRAKLE 10.12–3* (Mr C R Taylor) **Mr J Fawcus** *Refused*; *COUP DE CHAPEAU aged.11–10* (Mr J Drake) **G Wilson** *Fell*; *INVERSE 6.11–7* (Lady Lindsay) **R Lyall** *Fell*; *VINICOLE 8.11–3* (Capt J W Bridges) **D Morgan** *Fell*; *APOSTASY 11.11–0* (Lady Lindsay) **W Parvin** *Fell*; *HOLMES 12.11–0* (Mr E T Tyrwhitt-Drake) **Mr C C Beechener** *Refused*; *THERAS 7.10–12* (Mr J Metcalf) **Mr G Owen, jnr** *Baulked*; *ALIKE 9.10–11* (Mr K Mellon) **G Turner** *Fell*; *MERRIMENT IV aged.10–10* (Lord Haddington) **Lord Haddington** *Fell*; *GLANGESIA 12.10–9* (Mr R K Mellon) **Mr J Ryan** *Fell*; *OTTAWA 8.10–8* (Mr N Alvarez) **T E Leader** *Refused*; *HANK aged.10–8* (Mr H D Cherry-Downes) **Mr F E McKeever** *Fell*; *ARUNTIUS 11.10–7* (Mr M D Blair) **F Mason** *Refused*; *EVOLUTION aged.10–7* (Mr W C Langley) **T B Cullinan** *Fell*; *GIBUS 11.10–7* (Major Keith Menzies) **W Redmond** *Fell*; *PELORUS JACK aged.10–7* (Mr C Phillips Brocklehurst) **Mr R G Fanshawe** *Fell*; *THE ACE II 10.10–7* (Marquis de San-Miguel) **F Maxwell** *Pulled-up*; *QUITE CALM 8.10–7* (Mr R E Morel) **F Gurney** *Fell*; *REDLYNCH 11.10–7* (Mr J Pendarves) **Mr K Goode** *Unseated rider*; *DUSTY FOOT 8.10–7* (Mr J H Whitney) **W Speck** *Refused*; *KCB 10.10–7* (Mr V H Smith) **J Mason** *Fell*; *DELARUE 10.10–7* (Mr J B Snow) **W Kidney** *Refused*; *HAREWOOD 10.10–7* (Mr R H Warden) **Mr R H Warden** *Pulled-up*; *TOOTENHILL 10.10–7* (Mrs Boswall-Preston) **R McCarthy** *Refused*; *GREAT SPAN 11.10–7* (Mr M D Blair) **G Hardy** *Fell*; *PRINCE CHERRY 8.10–7* (Mr M D Blair) **J Geary** *Refused*; *RUDDYMAN 13.10–7* (Mr H Gordon Selfridge) **E Brown** *Refused*

The Betting: *100/12 Heartbreak Hill & Grakle; 100/9 Gregalach; 100/7 Annandale; 20/1 Great Span, Holmes & Quite Calm; 22/1 Pelorus Jack; 25/1 Dusty Foot; 28/1 Coup de Chapeau; 33/1 Vinicole, Inverse, Glangesia, Hank & Egremont; 40/1 Shaun Goilin & Ottawa; 45/1 Merriment IV; 50/1 Sea Soldier, Alike, Near East, Forbra, KCB & Evolution; 66/1 Apostasy, Theras, Aspirant, Harewood & Tootenhill; 100/1 Others.*

Distances: *Three lengths; a bad third*

Winner Trained By: *T R Rimell, Kinnersley, Worcestershire*

Value to Winning Owner: *£8,165*

1933

KELLSBORO' JACK at the second Becher's on his way to victory in record time

There could have been no finer setting for the first 'National appearance of the 'horse of the century' than Aintree on that glorious spring day, 24th March 1933. Miss Dorothy Paget's outstanding gelding arrived fresh from a convincing second Cheltenham Gold Cup victory and with an unbeaten record of five wins from as many races in the current campaign. Trained to the minute by Basil Briscoe, the six-year-old fired the imagination of the public to the degree that not even his high handicap mark of 12 st 2 lbs, nor his lack of knowledge of Aintree could prevent his being backed down to 9/1 favourite. GREGALACH, again with the maximum burden, was the second choice of punters with HEARTBREAK HILL, EGREMONT, REMUS and PELORUS JACK also supported. SHAUN GOILIN was back, this time partnered by the promising amateur Peter

Cazalet, who entrusted his own YOUTELL to the care of his lanky and frail-looking friend, the twenty-four-year-old Anthony Mildmay. Almost half of the thirty-four runners were ridden by members of the unpaid brigade, among them CHADD'S FORD, owned by American sewing-machine millionaire F Ambrose Clark and the mount of Mr Evan Williams. Mr Clark's wife, Florence, also had a runner, seven-year-old KELLSBORO' JACK, and the man on board was another, though unrelated, Williams, Dudley of that name and a professional. Bred by Mr H Hutchinson of Kellsboro', near Kells in County Kilkenny, KELLSBORO' JACK was by JACKDAW out of KELLSBORO' LASS. After being bought by Mr Clark, the gelding was sent to be trained by Ivor Anthony at Wroughton and it was during a lean spell that the trainer suggested a change of ownership may alter the horse's luck. Ambrose Clark duly asked his wife for a one pound note and announced that she was the new owner of KELLSBORO' JACK. The gelding duly won the Stanley 'Chase over one circuit of the 'National course in 1932.

YOUTELL with Mr Anthony Mildmay was a faller at the first but in general falls were thankfully few and COLLIERY BAND led over Becher's in front of KELLSBORO' JACK, REMUS, GREGALACH, DELANEIGE and SLATER, with GOLDEN MILLER going well in ninth place. Back on the racecourse, no less than twenty-four horses cleared the fences in front of the stands, but by the time Becher's was reached again, those left in the race were stretched over a wide area. KELLSBORO' JACK struck the front at the Brook, out-jumping REMUS and landing half a length in front with SLATER jumping superbly three lengths further back. It took all of Ted Leader's skill to

survive a colossal mistake by GOLDEN MILLER here, when the favourite clipped the top of the fence, but they were still well in touch at the next fence. It was a short-lived reprieve, however, for when moving into a challenging fourth place at the Canal Turn, GOLDEN MILLER angled his jump too sharply and deposited his jockey on the ground. At the last open ditch REMUS began to fade, leaving the improving PELORUS JACK to take on free-running KELLSBORO' JACK and from this point the two 'JACKS' raced side by side, only for PELORUS JACK to mistime his take-off at the last and fall with all to play for. The only challenge left was from outsider REALLY TRUE, but there was no catching the bargain-buy of the race and KELLSBORO' JACK held on for a three length win. The blinkered SLATER finished like an express train to capture third place. DELANEIGE was fourth in front of a very high number of finishers. When the winner's time of 9

The two 'Jacks' at the last fence. PELORUS JACK, nearest the camera is about to fall. KELLSBORO JACK went on to win

minutes 28 seconds was announced as a record for the event, the Americans present went wild. The grateful owner had her own special reward for KELLSBORO' JACK: she vowed he would never again be asked to face the Aintree fences.

THE GRAND NATIONAL HANDICAP STEEPLECHASE

1933

Of £100 each, £60 if declared by 14th March or £10 if declared by 31st January. With £4,000 added (including a trophy value £200). For six-year-olds & upwards. The second to receive £800, the third £500 and the fourth £200. The trainer of the Winner to receive a cup value £50 and the rider of the Winner a cup value £25

Date: 24th March 1933	Starters: 34	Time: 9 mins 28 secs
1st **KELLSBORO' JACK**	**7.11–9** *(Mrs F Ambrose Clark)*	**D Williams**
2nd **REALLY TRUE**	**9.10–12** *(Major Noel Furlong)*	**Mr F Furlong**
3rd **SLATER**	**8.10–7** *(Mr G S L Whitelaw)*	**Mr M Barry**
4th **DELANEIGE**	**8.11–3** *(Mr J B Snow)*	**J Moloney**
5th **ALPINE HUT**	**8.11–6** *(Sir Alfred Butt)*	**Mr R Harding**
6th **FORBRA**	**8.11–9** *(Mr W Parsonage)*	**J Hamey**

The following completed the course, though it is not recorded in what order:
SHAUN GOILIN 13.12–1 (Mr W H Midwood) **Mr P Cazalet**; *REMUS 8.11–12* (Mr A E Berry) **T Morgan**; *COLLIERY BAND 9.11–9* (Mrs H M Hollins) **G Hardy**; *TROUBLE MAKER aged.11–6* (Mrs T H Somerville) **Mr N Laing**; *TROCADERO aged.11–2* (Vicomte Max de Rivaud) **M Thery**; *EGREMONT 9.11–1* (Mr S A Maxwell) **Mr E C Paget**; *SOUTHERN HERO 8.10–12* (Mr J V Rank) **T Isaac**; *MASTER ORANGE 8.10–7* (Mrs D'Oyly-Mann) **Capt O Prior-Palmer**; *NEAR EAST 8.10–7* (Mr H B Brandt) **A Robson**; *CHADD'S FORD aged.10–7* (Mr F Ambrose Clark) **Mr E Williams**; *RUIN 8.10–7* (Mrs R Fellowes) **Major H Misa**; *MERRIMENT IV aged.11–4* (Lord Haddington) **Lord Haddington** [remounted]; *BALLYBRACK 9.11–0* (Lt Col R W Tweedie) **Mr G Elliott** [remounted].

Also Ran:
COUP DE CHAPEAU aged.12–2 (Mr J Drake) **G Wilson** *Fell*; *GOLDEN MILLER 6.12–2* (Miss Dorothy Paget) **T E Leader** *Fell*; *HEARTBREAK HILL 8.11–9* (Mrs C S Bird, jnr) **W O'Grady** *Fell*; *ANNANDALE 11.10–10* (Lord Inchcape) **D Morgan** *Fell*; *THERAS 8.10–10* (Mr J Metcalf) **G Owen** *Fell*; *SOCIETY 7.10–8* (Mr G P Shakerley) **Mr G P Shakerley** *Fell*; *PELORUS JACK aged.10–7* (Mrs B D Davis) **W Stott** *Fell*; *YOUTELL 8.10–7* (Mr P V F Cazalet) **Mr A Mildmay** *Fell*; *BALLYHANWOOD 12.10–7* (Mr M D Blair) **J Goswell** *Fell*; *DUSTY FOOT 9.10–7* (Mr J H Whitney) **Mr G Bostwick** *Fell*; *GUIDING LIGHT 12.10–7* (Lord Somerton) **Lord Somerton** *Fell*; *APOSTASY 12.10–9* (Lady Lindsay) **R Lyall** *Brought-down*; *GREGALACH 11.12–7* (Mrs M A Gemmell) **W Parvin** *Pulled-up*; *HUIC HOLLOA 8.11–11* (Mr W Waddington) **Mr W Ransom** *Slipped-up*; *HOLMES 13.10–13* (Mr E T Tyrwhitt-Drake) **C Beechener** *Ran-out*

The Betting: *9/1 Golden Miller; 10/1 Gregalach; 100/8 Heartbreak Hill; 100/7 Egremont; 100/6 Remus & Pelorus Jack; 20/1 Merriment IV, Delaneige, Annandale & Society; 25/1 Kellsboro' Jack; 28/1 Coup de Chapeau; 33/1 Forbra; 40/1 Shaun Goilin, Colliery Band & Theras; 45/1 Near East; 50/1 Huic Holloa, Alpine Hut, Southern Hero, Slater, Ballybrack, Chadd's Ford, Ruin, Holmes, Ballyhanwood & Dusty Foot; 66/1 Really True; 100/1 Others.*

Distances: *Three lengths; a neck*

Winner Trained By: *Ivor Anthony, Wroughton, Wiltshire*

Value to Winning Owner: *£7,345*

1934

With KELLSBORO' JACK excused duty in future Grand Nationals, the public looked with hope to the runner-up of a year before. Ridden by owner Major Noel Furlong's twenty-four-year-old son, Frank, REALLY TRUE was favourite of the thirty runners at 7/1, relegating all-powerful GOLDEN MILLER to second choice, despite Miss Paget's champion having just won his third successive Cheltenham Gold Cup. By GOLDCOURT out of MILLER'S PRIDE, GOLDEN MILLER was bred in County Meath by Laurence Geraghty and was bought at Dublin Sales as a yearling for one hundred guineas by Mr Paddy Quinn. As an unbroken three-year-old, GOLDEN MILLER was spotted grazing in a field by Captain Farmer who persuaded trainer Basil Briscoe to purchase the horse unseen for £500. When the purchase arrived at the Longstowe establishment of his new owner, however, Mr Briscoe was far from delighted with the appearance of the son of GOLDCOURT, whom he described as looking like a 'wet bear, with his long coat sticking up in places like a porcupine'. More impressed by the stable's newcomer, however, was Philip Carr, a patron of Briscoe's, who duly paid £1,000 for 'the MILLER' and was rewarded by the horse winning three times and being placed on four occasions from his next seven outings. GRAKLE's old partner in Aintree glory, Bob Lyall, declared GOLDEN MILLER the best three-year-old he had ever ridden and upon Mr Carr falling into the illness from which he was never to recover, 'the MILLER', together with his stable companion INSURANCE, was sold to Lord Queenborough's daughter Miss Dorothy Paget for £12,000 the pair. The purchase price was subsequently seen to be far from extravagant when GOLDEN MILLER proceeded to carry everything before him over fences and INSURANCE won two Champion Hurdles. Miss Paget's introduction to the winter sport was at the prompting of her cousin, Mr 'Jock' Hay Whitney and like him, the

The first leg of the unique double for GOLDEN MILLER in 1934 as he takes his third Cheltenham Gold Cup before making a second 'National attempt

eccentric lady was soon smitten with the desire to win the 'National.

On another perfect day for jumping, GOLDEN MILLER looked a picture in the paddock at Aintree, with Gerry Wilson up. Among his principal rivals were former winners FORBRA and GREGALACH, DELANEIGE, PELORUS JACK and Mr Whitney's Becher 'Chase winner THOMOND II. The field charged across Melling Road to the first fence, where GREGALACH was the first to touch down safely. Third from last as they streamed on to the next was GOLDEN MILLER but Wilson was content to let him settle himself. SOUTHERN HUE led over Becher's from the blinkered grey UNCLE BATT. The pace was incredibly fast and with all the most fancied horses still in contention as they approached the Water, the stands crowds gave them appreciative applause. On the long run back to the seventeenth fence GOLDEN MILLER surged to the front, landing level with DELANEIGE, just in front of GREGALACH and FORBRA

and with THOMOND II, UNCLE BATT and the improving REALLY TRUE well in touch. GREGALACH was pulled up shortly after the Canal Turn, but with no let-up in the pace DELANEIGE, GOLDEN MILLER, FORBRA and THOMOND II cleared Valentine's almost in line. SOUTHERN HUE came down here and at the next fence REALLY TRUE tumbled out of the race. Re-entering the racecourse with a slight lead over GOLDEN MILLER, DELANEIGE was full of running and with Gerry Wilson riding a waiting race on Miss Paget's gelding, the cheering began in anticipation of an exciting finish. GOLDEN MILLER ranged up on the outside of DELANEIGE as they came at the final obstacle, both horses almost level as they touched down, but once on the flat there was only one horse in it. GOLDEN MILLER

GREGALACH (far side) holds a fractional lead at the water from DELANEIGE and FORBRA with GOLDEN MILLER poised to strike in fourth place ahead of THOMOND II

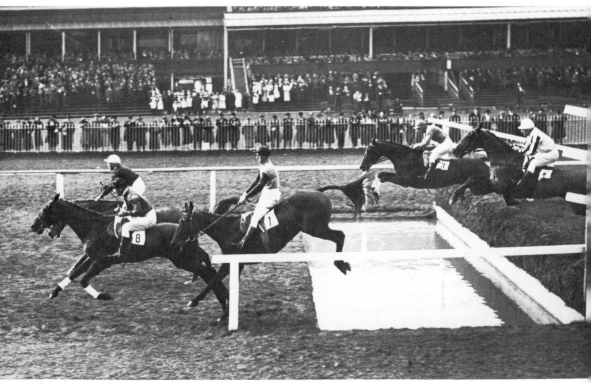

surged away with an electrifying burst, reaching the winning post five lengths ahead, with THOMOND II the same distance back in third place. In fourth place came FORBRA.

Surrounded by a protective cordon of policemen, the winner was escorted back to scale amid scenes of wild excitement. GOLDEN MILLER's time was eight seconds faster than the record created last year by KELLSBORO' JACK and it was achieved under a seven pounds heavier burden. Miss Dorothy Paget proudly led in her hero, accompanied by her father Lord Queenborough, and that night she held a celebration dinner at Liverpool's Adelphi Hotel attended by well over a hundred guests.

THE GRAND NATIONAL HANDICAP STEEPLECHASE

1934

Of £100 each, £60 if declared by 13th March or £10 if declared by 30th January. With £4,000 added (including a trophy value £200). For six-year-olds & upwards. The second to receive £800, the third £500 and the fourth £200. The trainer of the Winner to receive a cup value £50 and the rider of the Winner a cup value £25

Date: 23rd March 1934	Starters: 30	Time: 9 mins 20⅖ secs
1st **GOLDEN MILLER**	**7.12–2** *(Miss Dorothy Paget)*	**G Wilson**
2nd **DELANEIGE**	**9.11–6** *(Mr J B Snow)*	**J Moloney**
3rd **THOMOND II**	**8.12–4** *(Mr J H Whitney)*	**W Speck**
4th **FORBRA**	**9.11–7** *(Mr W Parsonage)*	**G Hardy**
5th **UNCLE BATT**	**8.10–13** *(Mr H B Brandt)*	**A Robson**
6th **APOSTASY**	**13.10–7** *(Lady Lindsay)*	**E Brown**
7th **REMUS**	**9.11–9** *(Mr A E Berry)*	**T Morgan**
8th **BLUE PETER III**	**11.10–7** *(Commander A V Courage)*	**Mr F Cundell**

Also Ran:
GREGALACH 12.12–7 (Mrs M A Gemmell) **W Parvin** *Broke-down – pulled-up*; ANNANDALE 12.10–9 (Lord Inchcape) **Mr P Payne-Gallwey** *Fell*; READY CASH 7.11–9 (Capt C A Cartwright) **Mr F Walwyn** *Fell*; PARSON'S WELL 10.11–8 (Mr G Bates) **W Hollick** *Fell*; ALPINE HUT 9.11–6 (Sir Alfred Butt) **Mr R Harding** *Fell*; SOUTHERN HERO 9.11–5 (Mr J V Rank) **J Fawcus** *Fell*; REALLY TRUE 10.11–4 (Major Noel Furlong) **Mr F Furlong** *Fell*; FLAMBENT 9.11–3 (Mrs Gilbert Robinson) **T Duggan** *Fell*; DESTINY BAY aged.11–2 (Mr H Lloyd Thomas) **Mr H Lloyd Thomas** *Fell*; PELORUS JACK aged.11–2 (Mrs B D Davis) **W Stott** *Fell*; SORLEY BOY 8.11–1 (Mr F Ambrose Clark) **D Morgan** *Fell*; TROCADERO aged.10–13 (Vicomte Max de Rivaud) **M Thery** *Fell*; KILBUCK aged.10–8 (Miss R M Harrison) **T B Cullinan** *Fell*; FORTNUM 9.10–7 (Commander A V Courage) **F Sclater** *Fell*; THE ACE II 12.10–11 (Lady Mary Dunn) **Capt A Head** *Fell*; CANTILLIUS II 8.10–7 (Mr V H Smith) **J Mason** *Fell*; MASTER ORANGE 9.10–7 (Mrs D'Oyly-Mann) **Mr P Cazalet** *Fell*; EGREMONT 10.10–12 (Mr S A Maxwell) **Mr E C Paget** *Refused*; PRINCE CHERRY 10.10–11 (Mr M D Blair) **J Goswell** *Refused*; LONE EAGLE II 8.10–13 (Mr J H Whitney) **J Hamey** *Pulled-up*; SLATER 9.10–12 (Mr G S Whitelaw) **K Piggott** *Pulled-up*; SOUTHERN HUE 10.10–7 (Mr A R Smith) **T F Carey** *Pulled-up*

The Betting: *7/1 Really True; 8/1 Golden Miller; 100/8 Forbra; 100/7 Delaneige, Sorley Boy & Trocadero; 18/1 Thomond II; 20/1 Ready Cash & Alpine Hut; 22/1 Cantillius II; 25/1 Gregalach, Southern Hero & Pelorus Jack; 33/1 Fortnum & Slater; 40/1 Remus & Destiny Bay; 45/1 Uncle Batt; 50/1 Lone Eagle II; 66/1 Others.*

Distances: *Five lengths; five lengths*

Winner Trained By: *Basil Briscoe, Exning, Suffolk*

Value to Winning Owner: *£7,265*

1935

Giving The Chair the once-over before the 1935 race

I f ever in the history of steeplechasing a horse appeared unbeatable then GOLDEN MILLER was he in 1935. After winning the race he had made virtually his own, the Cheltenham Gold Cup, for a fourth consecutive time, Aintree was again his destination. The winner of all his five races before the 'National, Miss Paget's champion topped the handicap with 12 st 7 lbs, yet such was his reputation that he started for the big Liverpool 'Chase at 2/1 – the shortest priced favourite in the history of the event. People everywhere went GOLDEN MILLER mad, investing large and small amounts on him becoming the most popular dual winner ever. The cautionary words of the few who pointed out that 'the MILLER' had needed to pull out all the stops to

defeat THOMOND II at Cheltenham, were dismissed as rubbish. It was 'Jock' Whitney's horse who was the closest to him in the Liverpool betting and with a pull of eight pounds, last year's third certainly bore consideration.

This year the efforts of the executive in attempting to reduce the number of runners at last appeared to be having an effect, for the field of twenty-seven was the smallest since 1923. Among the owners represented were the circus king Bertram Mills with JIMMY JAMES and Lieutenant-Colonel R W Tweedie attempting to provide Scotland's first winner of the race with BALLYBRACK, ridden by his son.

Mr Frank Furlong, REALLY TRUE's rider last year, was on this occasion astride his father's second string, the eight-year-old near-black gelding REYNOLDSTOWN. Named after the place of his birth near Naul, County Dublin, REYNOLDSTOWN was by MY PRINCE out of FROMAGE and was bred by Mr Richard Ball. He had been offered for sale to Mr J H Whitney, but the American was unable to travel to see the horse and the opportunity of a lifetime was missed. Major Noel Furlong was more fortunate, purchasing the son of MY PRINCE and taking him back to Leicestershire to train him. Major Furlong's son Frank was a subaltern in the 9th Lancers and a most accomplished horseman. He had already ridden REYNOLDSTOWN to three victories in the current season.

Escorted by four attendants, two of whom were rumoured to be private detectives, GOLDEN MILLER led the parade in front of the stands and when he turned and cantered back to the start, the cheers which washed over him were an indication not only of 'the MILLER''s popularity, but also of the huge amount of money riding with him. A tremendous roar came as the tape rose and the field began their journey, all eyes centred on GOLDEN MILLER racing close to the inside rail. HUIC HOLLOA and BRAVE CRY came down at the first, SLATER following suit at the next and with THERAS leading from THOMOND II, EMANCIPATOR and GOLDEN MILLER, they made their way on towards Becher's, which REALLY TRUE failed to survive. Jumping Valentine's in a clear lead, CASTLE IRWELL maintained the strong gallop set from the start, with the favourite tucked in nicely on the rails just to his rear. Two jumps later, one of the most grievous groans ever heard on a racecourse rang its unbelievable news from those in the area. Incredibly, GOLDEN MILLER was out of the race, having unseated Wilson jumping the fence. The stunned spectators in the stands stared

The same obstacle later the same day with the grey UNCLE BATT leading the field

dumbly at the leaders taking the Water Jump in front of them, unable to comprehend GOLDEN MILLER's absence from their number. Mr Whitney's pair, THOMOND II and ROYAL RANSOM now held the lead, closely attended by BLUE PRINCE, REYNOLDSTOWN and UNCLE BATT but for many thousands all interest had gone with the favourite. Surviving a bumping from THOMOND II, REYNOLDSTOWN hit the front with a brilliant jump at Becher's and from that point on these two steadily drew further away from the rest. Over the final fence THOMOND II veered to the right, against Mr Furlong and REYNOLDSTOWN but the latter shrugged off the contact and raced up the straight to a three length victory. Billy Parvin put in a spirited challenge from the last fence on BLUE PRINCE, overtaking THOMOND II but unable to get in a blow at the winner. It was a great riding performance on the part of Parvin for he was contending with a slipped saddle on the runner-up. LAZY BOOTS was fourth, UNCLE BATT fifth and BACHELOR PRINCE the only other to get round.

The result proved ideal copy for newspaper reporters, many rejoicing in the family triumph with the headline, 'Grand National won by three Furlongs'. Winning rider Frank became the second Old

Harrovian to partner a 'National winner, repeating the feat of John Maunsell Richardson and at a time one fifth of a second faster than 'the MILLER's'!

The unfortunate sequel to the GOLDEN MILLER mishap was a bitter and fiery argument between Miss Paget and her trainer Basil Briscoe in the County Stand after the race. After consultations with veterinary surgeons, the decision was taken to run the horse the next day in the Champion 'Chase and this time an even-money favourite, GOLDEN MILLER blotted his copy book for the second time in twenty-four hours, unseating Gerry Wilson at the very first fence. The furious owner laid the blame for such reversals in form squarely at the trainer's door. Anger had taken precedence over common sense and reason, with the result that Miss Paget removed all her horses from Briscoe's yard and the whole unhappy series of events cast a shadow over racing and the 'National.

Winning jockey Frank Furlong's parents proudly bring in their champions

1935

Of £100 each, £60 if declared by 19th March or £10 if declared by 29th January. With £4,000 added (including a trophy value £200). For six-year-olds & upwards. The second to receive £800, the third £500 and the fourth £200. The trainer of the Winner to receive a cup value £50 and the rider of the Winner a cup value £25

Date: 29th March 1935	Starters: 27	Time: 9 mins 20⅕ secs
1st **REYNOLDSTOWN**	8.11−4 *(Major Noel Furlong)*	**Mr F Furlong**
2nd **BLUE PRINCE**	7.10−7 *(Lady Lindsay)*	**W Parvin**
3rd **THOMOND II**	9.11−13 *(Mr J H Whitney)*	**W Speck**
4th **LAZY BOOTS**	9.10−7 *(Sir Geoffrey Congreve)*	**G Owen**
5th **UNCLE BATT**	9.10−7 *(Mr H B Brandt)*	**T Isaac**
6th **BACHELOR PRINCE**	8.10−10 *(Miss M Lark)*	**W O'Grady**

Also Ran:

GOLDEN MILLER 8.12–7 (Miss Dorothy Paget) **G Wilson** *Unseated rider*; *ROYAL RANSOM 8.11–8* (Mr J H Whitney) **J Hamey** *Fell*; *SOUTHERN HERO 10.11–0* (Mr J V Rank) **J Fawcus** *Fell*; *BRIENZ 9.11–0* (Mr G Beeby) **W Kidney** *Fell*; *REALLY TRUE 11.10–13* (Major Noel Furlong) **D Morgan** *Fell*; *CASTLE IRWELL 7.10–10* (Mr G H Bostwick) **Mr G H Bostwick** *Fell*; *BALLYBRACK 11.10–8* (Lt Col R W Tweedie) **Mr R R Tweedie** *Fell*; *BRAVE CRY 13.10–7* (Mr J C W Lewis) **Mr J C W Lewis** *Fell*; *EMANCIPATOR 7.10–7* (Mr P V F Cazalet) **Mr P Cazalet** *Fell*; *HUIC HOLLOA 10.10–7* (Mr W Waddington) **Mr A Marsh** *Fell*; *JIMMY JAMES 8.10–7* (Mr Bertram Mills) **H Nicholson** *Fell*; *MASTER ORANGE 10.10–7* (Mrs R C D'Oyly-Mann) **Mr A Mildmay** *Fell*; *PRINCESS MIR 10.10–7* (Mr D A Jackson) **Mr D A Jackson** *Fell*; *SLATER 10.10–7* (Mr G S L Whitelaw) **F Maxwell** *Fell*; *SOUTHERN HUE 11.10–7* (Mr Joseph McGrath) **P Powell** *Fell*; *TAPINOIS 7.10–7* (Mr F E Peek) **F Gurney** *Fell*; *TROCADERO aged.10–8* (Mr G F Perry) **T B Cullinan** *Fell*; *ALEXENA 9.10–7* (Mr J A Redman) **Mr P Payne-Gallwey** *Refused*; *FOUQUET 8.10–7* (Mr M D Blair) **E Brown** *Refused*; *THERAS 10.10–7* (Mr J Metcalf) **T F Carey** *Refused*; *RED PARK 9.10–7* (Lady Houston) **P Fitzgerald** *Pulled-up*

The Betting: *2/1 Golden Miller; 9/2 Thomond II; 8/1 Tapinois; 100/7 Castle Irwell; 18/1 Really True; 20/1 Southern Hero; 22/1 Brienz & Reynoldstown; 25/1 Bachelor Prince; 28/1 Royal Ransom & Alexena; 40/1 Blue Prince & Uncle Batt; 50/1 Ballybrack, Slater, Princess Mir & Trocadero; 66/1 Emancipator; 100/1 Others.*

Distances: *Three lengths; eight lengths*

Winner Trained By: *Major Noel Furlong, Skeffington, Leicestershire*

Value to Winning Owner: *£6,545*

1936

After winning his fifth Cheltenham Gold Cup on 12th March 1936, GOLDEN MILLER was again heavily backed to rectify his lapse of the previous year in the 'National. Now trained by Owen Anthony, Miss Paget's wonder horse appeared better than ever at Cheltenham and not even the 12 st 7 lbs allocated to him by the Aintree handicapper could prevent him being backed to 5/1 second favourite. Tom Rimell turned out the market leader, the sparkling seven-year-old AVENGER, winner of the National Hunt Handicap 'Chase and the mount of the trainer's son, twenty-three-year-old Fred Rimell. Lord Rosebery's KEEN BLADE and Lord Derby's HILLS-BROOK were two capable contenders in a good field and another Peer of the Realm doubly involved in the race was Lord Mildmay of Flete, whose 100/1 outsider DAVY JONES had been purchased to provide a mount for his son Anthony. A seven-year-old chestnut standing almost seventeen hands high, DAVY JONES was a tubed entire, trained by Harry Whiteman at Fairlawne in Kent and his current form justified his market position. Notable absentees among those riding were Gerry Wilson, whose place on GOLDEN MILLER was taken by Evan Williams and Mr Frank Furlong, replaced by his brother officer from the 9th Lancers Fulke Walwyn in the saddle of REYNOLDSTOWN.

From a perfect first time start, the long raking stride of DAVY JONES took him to the front where he led over the first by a couple of lengths. In a nasty-looking series of falls, CASTLE VIEW, LAZY BOOTS, BUCK-THORN and OEIL DE BOEUF all exited at this fence and GOLDEN MILLER, directly behind the last named, was brought down. Williams held on to him and was back in the saddle in seconds but Miss Paget's horse had lost so much ground that whatever chance he may have had was surely gone. DAVY JONES, his forelegs heavily bandaged, was really stretching them, jumping the fences with ease and a precision seldom seen from a horse encountering Aintree for the first time. These front-running tactics were no cause for alarm to the more experienced professionals riding behind Mr Mildmay for his mount was a confirmed hard puller and over an extended distance of country, they expected him to fade soon after halfway. A long way behind the leaders, GOLDEN MILLER dug his toes in at the open ditch after Valentine's, refusing again and again to go any further. DAVY JONES proceeded to take them along and cleared the Water Jump in front of EMANCIPATOR, DOUBLE CROSSED, AVENGER and REYNOLDSTOWN. Back in the country, the favourite issued his challenge going into the seventeenth, but with disastrous results. Crashing heavily at what is one of the smallest fences on the course, AVENGER was killed. The task of catching the runaway outsider was now left to Mr Walwyn and REYNOLDSTOWN, who moved up to within a length of DAVY JONES as they soared over Becher's. With REYNOLDS-TOWN testing the horsemanship of Fulke Walwyn with mistakes at each of the last three fences before the racecourse, Mr Mildmay seemed assured of victory on his father's outsider. But though he was still in the lead over the penultimate fence, DAVY JONES pecked slightly on landing, causing the buckle of the reins to come apart. Unable to steer his mount, Mildmay was powerless to prevent DAVY JONES veering left at the final obstacle and scattering the crowds alongside it as he threw away his chance by running out. Left with the easiest of tasks, REYNOLDSTOWN romped home twelve lengths ahead of his

THE DRAMATIC GRAND NATIONAL OF 1936:
A TWO-YEARS-IN-SUCCESSION WINNER; FAVOURITES WHO FAILED; DAVY JONES.

THE GREAT DISAPPOINTMENT AT THE FIRST FENCE IN A GRAND NATIONAL MARKED BY A SUCCESSION OF DRAMATIC INCIDENTS: GOLDEN MILLER (CENTRE) FALLS AND LOSES HIS JOCKEY; TO GET UP AGAIN AND REFUSE SHORTLY AFTERWARDS.

TRAGEDY OVERTAKES THE FAVOURITE: AVENGER ON THE GROUND AFTER THE FALL IN THE SECOND ROUND WHICH BROKE HIS NECK—WITH PENCRAIK NEARLY ON TOP OF HIM.

THE MOST EXTRAORDINARY EVENT IN A REMARKABLE RACE: DAVY JONES RUNS OUT, HIS REINS HAVING BROKEN (RIGHT), WHILE REYNOLDSTOWN, WHOM HE APPEARED TO BE BEATING, WENT ON TO WIN.—(Photograph by Courtesy of British Movietone News.)

WINNER OF THE GRAND NATIONAL FOR TWO YEARS IN SUCCESSION—A FEAT NOT EQUALLED SINCE 1870: REYNOLDSTOWN, WITH HIS OWNER, MAJOR FURLONG, AND (LEFT) MR. FRANK FURLONG, WHO RODE HIM LAST YEAR.

VICTORIOUS REYNOLDSTOWN—MR. F. WALWYN UP: THE WINNER TAKING THE LAST FENCE MANY LENGTHS AHEAD OF EGO—DAVY JONES HAVING RUN OUT.

THE GRAND NATIONAL WINNER: REYNOLDSTOWN LED IN BY HIS OWNER-TRAINER, MAJOR FURLONG—MR. F. WALWYN, WHO WAS AT SANDHURST WITH MR. FRANK FURLONG, UP.

This year's Grand National was remarkable for a series of dramatic incidents. That famous horse, Golden Miller, had been a pronounced favourite, but the odds against him went to five to one before the start. Golden Miller disappointed his backers by coming down at the first fence. Avenger had moved up to favourite just before the off. He was going well, but fell at the first fence "in the country" during the second round and broke his neck. Happily, his rider was not injured. By the time that the Canal Turn had been reached on the second time round Davy Jones and Reynoldstown had drawn well ahead. Reynoldstown was ridden by that great rider, Mr. Walwyn. None the less, it seemed to many that Mr. Mildmay (son of the owner, Lord Mildmay of Flete) was the more likely winner of the duel on Davy Jones—a horse quoted at a hundred to one! Just before he reached the last fence but one the buckle of Davy Jones's reins came undone and the horse ran out. Thus Reynoldstown won the Grand National for the second year in succession, a feat not equalled for sixty-six years. Reynoldstown is owned by Major Noel Furlong. Last year, our readers will recall, Reynoldstown was ridden to victory by Major Furlong's son, Mr. Frank Furlong.

The Race in pictures from *The Illustrated London News*

nearest rival to what was regarded as the luckiest victory in the annals of racing. 50/1 shot EGO, ridden for his father by Mr Harry Llewellyn, was second six lengths in front of BACHELOR PRINCE, with CROWN PRINCE fourth. Despite the last fence drama of DAVY JONES, REYNOLDSTOWN was quite rightly welcomed back as a worthy winner, the first horse to win the race at Aintree in successive years since THE COLONEL in 1870.

THE GRAND NATIONAL HANDICAP STEEPLECHASE
1936

Of £100 each, £60 if declared by 17th March or £10 if declared by 4th February. With £4,000 added (including a trophy value £200). For six-year-olds & upwards. The second to receive £800, the third £500 and the fourth £200. The trainer of the Winner to receive a cup value £50 and the rider of the Winner a cup value £25

Date: 27th March 1936		Starters: 35	Time: 9 mins 37⅘ secs
1st	**REYNOLDSTOWN**	9.12–2 *(Major Noel Furlong)*	**Mr F Walwyn**
2nd	**EGO**	9.10–8 *(Sir David Llewellyn)*	**Mr H Llewellyn**
3rd	**BACHELOR PRINCE**	9.10–9 *(Mr J V Rank)*	**J Fawcus**
4th	**CROWN PRINCE**	11.10–7 *(Mr R Strutt)*	**Mr R Strutt**
5th	**INVERSIBLE**	8.10–9 *(Lt Col W E Peel)*	**S McGrath**
6th	**PROVOCATIVE**	6.10–9 *(Mrs J de Selincourt)*	**E Brown**
7th	**CASTLE IRWELL**	8.11–3 *(Mr G H Bostwick)*	**Mr G H Bostwick**
8th	**DOUBLE CROSSED**	8.11–4 *(Mr J H Whitney)*	**D Morgan**
9th	**MOORLAND VIEW**	10.10–7 *(Mr A F Nicholson)*	**Mr E C Paget**
10th	**COMEDIAN**	8.10–7 *(Mr R E Morel)*	**G Turner** [remounted]

Also Ran:
GOLDEN MILLER 9.12–7 (Miss Dorothy Paget) **E Williams** *Fell, remounted & refused*; *AVENGER 7.11–8* (Mrs Violet Mundy) **T F Rimell** *Fell*; *ROYAL RANSOM 9.11–7* (Mr J H Whitney) **H Jones** *Fell*; *DELANEIGE 11.11–2* (Mr J B Snow) **H Nicholson** *Fell*; *BRIENZ 10.11–0* (Mr G Beeby) **J Hamey** *Fell*; *BLUE PRINCE 8.11–0* (Lady Lindsay) **W Parvin** *Unseated rider*; *OEIL DE BOEUF 9.11–0* (Marquis de San-Miguel) **M Feakes** *Fell*; *PERSIAN SUN 10.10–12* (Mr H B Brandt) **E Vinall** *Fell*; *BUCKTHORN 8.10–9* (Mr C M Clements) **Capt R Harding** *Fell*; *THE BOY IN BLUE 7.10–8* (Mr N Dixon) **Mr P Vaux** *Fell*; *HILLSBROOK 10.10–8* (Lord Derby) **W O'Grady** *Fell*; *KILTOI 7.10–8* (Mr J Metcalf) **T F Carey** *Fell*; *DAVY JONES 7.10–7* (Lord Mildmay of Flete) **Mr A Mildmay** *Ran out at last*; *UNCLE BATT 10.10–7* (Mr H B Brandt) **T McNeill** *Fell*; *EMANCIPATOR 8.10–7* (Mr P V F Cazalet) **Mr P Cazalet** *Fell*; *PENCRAIK 9.10–7* (Mrs I Strang) **J Lynn, jnr** *Refused*; *CASTLE VIEW 9.10–7* (Mr H Dyke Dennis) **G Owen** *Fell*; *D'EYNCOURT 8.10–7* (Mr F W Dennis) **P Carey** *Fell*; *ROD AND GUN 9.10–7* (Mr J H Whitney) **Mr L Stoddard** *Fell*; *KEEN BLADE 9.10–7* (Lord Rosebery) **T Elder** *Fell*; *EVASIO MON 10.10–11* (Mr T Holland-Martin) **Mr T Holland-Martin** *Fell*; *LYNTON 9.10–7* (Mr M D Blair) **C Hook** *Baulked – refused*; *ZAG 11.10–11* (Major O L Prior-Palmer) **Major Prior-Palmer** *Fell*; *BLAZE 7.10–7* (Sir Ernest Wills) **K Piggott** *Fell*

The Betting: *100/30 Avenger; 5/1 Golden Miller; 8/1 Castle Irwell; 10/1 Reynoldstown; 100/7 Keen Blade; 20/1 Double Crossed, Blue Prince & Emancipator; 25/1 Delaneige & Lazy Boots; 33/1 Royal Ransom & Provocative; 40/1 Brienz, Buckthorn, Inversible & Hillsbrook; 50/1 Ego & D'Eyncourt; 66/1 Persian Sun, Bachelor Prince, Kiltoi, Uncle Batt, Moorland View & Crown Prince; 100/1 Others.*

Distances: *Twelve lengths; six lengths*

Winner Trained By: *Major Noel Furlong, Skeffington, Leicestershire*

Value to Winning Owner: *£7,095*

1937

Celebrated as the centenary of the great race by the Liverpool Racecourse Executive, the 1937 Grand National was graced with the presence of King George VI and Queen Elizabeth, and the City of Liverpool was lavish in its welcome on their first visit to the provinces since the accession. A decision to lower the minimum weight to 10 stone brought forth protests, including a letter from George Lambton. 'The Grand National,' he wrote, 'is not meant to be won by moderate horses. If the authorities encourage owners to enter them, the race will lose its high tone and quality and revert to the farcical scramble it became some years ago.'

GOLDEN MILLER'S sequence of Cheltenham Gold Cup victories could not be continued this season due to the loss of the race through flooding, but he took his place in the 'National line-up, again with 12 st 7 lbs and at 8/1 the principal selection of the public. EGO, DIDORIC and DON BRADMAN were the next best backed of the thirty-three runners, a notable absentee being dual winner REYNOLDSTOWN whose owner considerately decided had done enough to be excused further efforts. DAVY JONES was also absent through injury but one who had lost favour in recent weeks after being an early ante-post favourite was backed again on the day of the race. This was the all black half-brother to REYNOLDSTOWN, ROYAL MAIL, who on only his second outing of the season had beaten GOLDEN MILLER in the Becher 'Chase over the course. Bred by Charlie Rogers from MY PRINCE and FLYING MAY, ROYAL MAIL was sold as an unbroken three-year-old to Hubert Hartigan, who passed him on to the former assistant secretary to The Prince of Wales, Mr Hugh Lloyd Thomas. Trained by Ivor Anthony and

ridden by Evan Williams, the gelding looked a picture of health as he took his place in the parade directly behind GOLDEN MILLER. Further down the line, a special cheer of encouragement was given to sixteen-year-old Bruce Hobbs, going out for his 'National debut on Mrs Ambrose Clark's FLYING MINUTES.

MISDEMEANOUR II was left badly at the start, and PASSING FANCY, DRIM and DON BRADMAN all came down at the first, although amateur Alec Marsh was soon back in the saddle on DON BRADMAN and continued a long way behind the rest. The falls came thick and fast from then on, although Becher's Brook claimed no casualties this time, TAPINOIS, READY CASH, GOLDEN MILLER and DELACHANCE clearing it in fine style at the head of the field. Going into the last open ditch before the racecourse, GOLDEN MILLER'S stride began to shorten and ignoring the urgings of Danny Morgan, the favourite once more called it a day. Meeting the obstacle side on, GOLDEN MILLER dropped into the ditch, then as quickly jumped back out again but no persuasion on earth could induce him to continue. ROYAL MAIL had jumped perfectly throughout, continuing to do so on the way back to Becher's where he took up the running again from FLYING MINUTES, with COOLEEN making ground despite the savage attentions of the loose horse DRIM. All the way back from the Canal Turn Jack Fawcus on COOLEEN had a nightmare of a journey, his mount being continually attacked by the villainous DRIM and it speaks volumes for the jockey's ability that he was able to bring his mare to within two lengths of the leader at the last fence. Once on the flat, though, ROYAL MAIL produced the better speed to hold on for a three length win. Ten lengths further behind came another mare, PUCKA BELLE, with EGO a close up fourth. ROYAL MAIL's delighted owner, an amateur rider of some distinction, gave notice after the race of his intention to ride the horse in next year's 'National, fitting in race-riding with his duties as a member of the British Diplomatic Service. Sadly it was not to be, for just a month before the 1938 Aintree event, Mr Hugh Lloyd Thomas was killed in a fall in a steeplechase at Derby.

THE GRAND NATIONAL HANDICAP STEEPLECHASE
1937

Of £100 each, £60 if declared by 9th March or £10 if declared by 2nd February. With £4,000 added (including a trophy value £200). For six-year-olds & upwards. The second to receive £800, the third £500 and the fourth £200. The trainer of the Winner to receive a cup value £50 and the rider of the Winner a cup value £25

Date: 19th March 1937	Starters: 33	Time: 9 mins 59⅘ secs
1st **ROYAL MAIL**	**8.11–13** *(Mr H Lloyd Thomas)*	**E Williams**
2nd **COOLEEN**	**9.11–4** *(Mr J V Rank)*	**J Fawcus**
3rd **PUCKA BELLE**	**11.10–7** *(Mr E W W Bailey)*	**Mr E W W Bailey**
4th **EGO**	**10.10–9** *(Sir David Llewellyn)*	**Mr H Llewellyn**
5th **CROWN PRINCE**	**12.10–6** *(Mr R Strutt)*	**Mr R Strutt**
6th **PENCRAIK**	**10.10–3** *(Mr Alan Pilkington)*	**G Archibald**
7th **DON BRADMAN**	**11.10–8** *(Mr S Wilkinson)*	**Mr A Marsh** [remounted]

Also Ran:

GOLDEN MILLER 10.12–7 (Miss Dorothy Paget) **D Morgan** *Refused*; WHAT HAVE YOU 9.11–5 (Mr F M Gould) **Mr W Streett** *Fell*; READY CASH 10.11–3 (Mr V H Smith) **T F Carey** *Refused*; DELANEIGE 12.11–2 (Mr J B Snow) **J Hamey** *Fell*; DAWMAR 7.10–13 (Mr W S Murphy) **J Richardson** *Fell*; DIDORIC 8.10–10 (Mr R Lehman) **H Nicholson** *Fell*; TAPINOIS 9.10–10 (Mr W Hutchinson) **F Maxwell** *Fell*; BUCKTHORN 9.10–9 (Capt C M L Clements) **K Piggott** *Fell*; DELACHANCE 8.10–9 (Mr J B Snow) **T F Rimell** *Fell*; KEEN BLADE 10.10–7 (Lord Rosebery) **Mr E C Paget** *Refused*; SUNSPOT II 7.10–5 (Mrs M Burke) **R Everett** *Fell*; EMANCIPATOR 9.10–5 (Mr P V F Cazalet) **Mr P Cazalet** *Pulled-up*; MISDEMEANOUR II 8.10–4 (Sir Peter Grant Lawson) **S Magee** *Fell*; FLYING MINUTES 7.10–2 (Mrs F Ambrose Clark) **B Hobbs** *Fell*; KILTOI 8.10–1 (Mr J Metcalf) **Capt R Harding** *Fell*; MILK PUNCH 13.10–0 (Mr G S L Whitelaw) **G Wilson** *Fell*; DRYBURGH 8.10–0 (Mr R B Vick) **B Carter** *Fell*; DRIM 10.10–9 (Mr B K Tighe) **Mr B K Tighe** *Fell*; IRVINE 8.10–4 (Mr A P Parker) **Mr A P Parker** *Fell*; BLAZE 8.10–0 (Sir Ernest Wills) **W Parvin** *Fell*; FIELD MASTER 9.10–3 (Mr L Densham) **Mr L Densham** *Fell*; UNCLE BATT 11.10–0 (Mr H B Brandt) **D McCarthy** *Brought-down*; SUGAR LOAF 10.10–0 (Mrs H H Stubbs) **E Carr** *Fell*; TRUE BLUE 9.10–0 (Mr P R Eliot-Cohen) **Mr P R Eliot-Cohen** *Fell*; PASSING FANCY 9.10–5 (Lord Berner) **D Holland** *Fell*; SPIONAUD 9.10–0 (Mr D A Jackson) **E Brown** *Baulked & fell*

The Betting: *8/1 Golden Miller; 10/1 Ego; 100/8 Didoric & Don Bradman; 100/6 Royal Mail, Pucka Belle & Delachance; 18/1 Spionaud; 20/1 Misdemeanour II & Delaneige; 22/1 Ready Cash; 25/1 Pencraik; 28/1 Keen Blade & Dryburgh; 33/1 Cooleen, Emancipator & Milk Punch; 40/1 What Have You, Dawmar, Tapinois, Buckthorn & Irvine; 50/1 Crown Prince & Blaze; 66/1 Flying Minutes; 100/1 Others.*

Distances: *Three lengths; ten lengths*

Winner Trained By: *Ivor Anthony, Wroughton, Wiltshire*

Value to Winning Owner: *£6,645*

1938

For the first time in five years the Grand National was without GOLDEN MILLER, Miss Paget's brilliant yet controversial 'chaser finally having got the message across that his aversion to Aintree was incurable. His stubborn and frustrating displays in the race since that record-breaking victory of 1934 were to remain mysteries, although one strongly-held view was that GOLDEN MILLER was too clever to exert himself fully more than once over such hazardous country. Mr Rank's COOLEEN, the luckless runner-up in the most recent running and the consistent BLUE SHIRT, winner of his last three long-distance races went off joint favourites at 8/1. There were many unknown quantities in the field of thirty-six, including the Duchess of Norfolk's HURDY GURDY MAN, ridden by the up-and-coming amateur John Hislop, and twenty-five-year-old Fred Rimell's mount PROVOCATIVE.

Overlooked by most was 40/1-shot BATTLESHIP, an American owned and bred entire, who at 15.2 hands was the smallest competitor since THE LAMB in the last century. Owned by Mrs Marion du Pont Scott, wife of the famous cowboy film-star Randolph Scott, BATTLESHIP had been bred at the Mereworth Stud in Kentucky by Walker J Salmon from MAN O'WAR out of QUARANTINE. Developing in his native land into a first-class jumper, he won the 1934 American Grand National before being sent to the Lambourn yard of trainer Reg Hobbs to be coached for English 'chasing. It was trainer Hobbs' seventeen-year-old son Bruce who took the leg-up on the tiny American horse and the young jockey's confidence could hardly have been given a boost when his father commented that BATTLESHIP would be unable to see over The Chair. Hobbs senior also refused to bet on the horse until shortly before the 'off', when he relented, taking £10 each-way at the 100/1 offered by London bookmaker Percy Thompson. Of most concern to the trainer was that the drop fences would cause such a small horse to land on his nose and, as an aid against this, he had the reins lengthened eighteen inches.

A somewhat ragged start caused several horses to dwell, with Reg Hobbs' second string WHAT HAVE YOU coming off worst, being left many lengths but the noted front-runner AIRGEAD SIOS was well away and led them into the country. At Becher's ROYAL DANIELI joined AIRGEAD SIOS in the lead with a perfect leap. The only two who failed to survive the Brook were HURDY GURDY MAN and, a long way behind the rest, the straggler WHAT HAVE YOU. At the next plain fence, BATTLESHIP gauged his jump well, turning in mid-air to line up for the Canal Turn, but the manoeuvre took his young jockey by surprise. Losing his balance, Bruce Hobbs and the little horse were on the way to parting company when Fred Rimell,

Randolph Scott and his wife Marion bring a touch of Hollywood to Aintree

233

The youngest and the smallest: Bruce Hobbs going to post on BATTLESHIP

seeing the difficulty and riding alongside, reached out and pulled him back into the plate. After AIRGEAD SIOS had come down at the one after Valentine's, ROYAL DANIELI took command and led them past the stands. The tiny BATTLESHIP was close up and going well but as his trainer had feared he was coming down so steeply at the drop fences that his nose was actually touching the ground. Moving up on the inside, BATTLESHIP jumped Becher's a length to the good over ROYAL DANIELI. These two disputed the lead from here on, another Irish horse WORKMAN, joining them as they approached the fourth from home. At the third last, the American horse made a shocking mistake and it was only the superb horsemanship of Bruce Hobbs which kept the partnership intact, although they lost a considerable amount of ground. Displaying a jockey's wisdom way beyond his years, the young rider sensibly allowed his mount time to recover and, appreciating the breather, BATTLESHIP overhauled the tiring WORKMAN and jumped the last fence at speed two lengths behind ROYAL DANIELI. The riderless TAKVOR PACHA came between the two leaders on the long run to the post, forcing BATTLESHIP to switch under the stand rails as yard by blistering yard the diminutive entire drew closer to the Irish champion. In what was decidedly a judge's nightmare, both horses raced on opposite sides of the course almost in line. After an agonising delay the announcement came that BATTLESHIP had won by a head, with WORKMAN a bad third and COOLEEN fourth. Upon returning to the weigh-in, it could clearly be seen that the winner's nose was smeared with blood. At first it was thought to be a broken blood vessel, but examination showed BATTLESHIP's nose to have been cut through repeated contact with the ground. Never before had a blinkered runner succeeded in the Grand National and as the smallest competitor, carrying the youngest jockey, BATTLESHIP was a most popular winner despite being an outsider. Sent back to a hero's welcome in America, BATTLESHIP

became a very successful stallion, living until 1958.

Reg Hobbs received a pleasing return for his £10 each way, but it emerged that even on the morning of the race, the trainer had attempted to persuade Mrs Scott to withdraw the horse, so convinced was he that the little fellow had no chance. Bruce Hobbs, at an age when most boys were still at school, capped an outstanding season in the saddle by adding the Welsh Grand National and the Cedarhurst Grand National at Lond Island, to that unforgettable Aintree victory. Before the year was out, however, he broke his back in a race fall and although he became fit enough to ride home winners again, the most promising of futures was interrupted by the Second World War.

The field takes Becher's first time

1938

Of £100 each, £60 if declared by 15th March or £10 if declared by 1st February. With £4,000 added (including a trophy value £200). For six-year-olds & upwards. The second to receive 10% (£924), the third 5% (£462) and the fourth 2½% (£231). The trainer of the Winner to receive a cup value £50 and the rider of the Winner a cup value £25

Date: 25th March 1938		Starters: 36	Time: 9 mins 27 secs
1st	**BATTLESHIP**	11.11–6 *(Mrs Marion Scott)*	**B Hobbs**
2nd	**ROYAL DANIELI**	7.11–3 *(Mr H C McNally)*	**D Moore**
3rd	**WORKMAN**	8.10–2 *(Sir Alexander Maguire)*	**J Brogan**
4th	**COOLEEN**	10.11–8 *(Mr J V Rank)*	**J Fawcus**
5th	**DELACHANCE**	9.10–9 *(Mr J B Snow)*	**J Moloney**
6th	**RED KNIGHT II**	9.10–0 *(Mr E T Hunt)*	**D Jones**
7th	**BLUE SHIRT**	7.10–3 *(Mr Arthur Sainsbury)*	**R Smyth**
8th	**HOPEFUL HERO**	10.10–9 *(Mr H A J Silley)*	**Mr W Dawes**
9th	**UNDER BID**	6.10–2 *(Lord Derby)*	**M Pringle**
10th	**BACHELOR PRINCE**	11.10–6 *(Mr J V Rank)*	**D Morgan**
11th	**LOUGH COTTAGE**	11.10–7 *(Mrs S H Creagh)*	**Mr R Black**
12th	**PROVOCATIVE**	8.10–7 *(Mrs J de Selincourt)*	**T F Rimell**
13th	**DRIM**	11.11–3 *(Mr B K Tighe)*	**Mr B K Tighe**

Also Ran:

ROYAL MAIL 9.12–7 (Mrs C Evans) **E Williams** *Pulled-up*; *AIRGEAD SIOS* 8.12–0 (Sir Francis Towle) **T McNeill** *Fell*; *PONTET* 8.11–7 (Mr G V Malcolmson) **J Parkinson** *Fell*; *DOMINICK'S CROSS* 7.11–0 (Mr A Donn) **R Everett** *Fell*; *DUNHILL CASTLE* 8.10–12 (Sir Warden Chilcott) **H Nicholson** *Fell*; *INVERSIBLE* 10.10–10 (Lt Col W E Peel) **M Hogan** *Fell*; *TAKVOR PACHA* 6.10–9 (Marquis de San-Miguel) **A Kalley** *Fell*; *ROCKQUILLA* 8.10–8 (Mr V H Smith) **T F Carey** *Fell*; *WHAT HAVE YOU* 10.10–7 (Mr F M Gould) **S Magee** *Fell*; *FROBISHER* 7.10–6 (Miss M F Cohen) **Capt R Harding** *Fell*; *BLUE PRINCE* 10.10–5 (Lady Lindsay) **W Parvin** *Fell*; *CABIN FIRE* 7.10–4 (Mrs P Kiely) **T Hyde** *Fell*; *ROCK LAD* 8.10–4 (Mr H R Bain) **J Bissill** *Fell*; *BRIGHTER COTTAGE* 8.10–2 (Capt D W Daly) **W O'Grady** *Fell*; *DIDORIC* 9.10–2 (Mr R Lehman) **D Butchers** *Fell*; *STALBRIDGE PARK* 7.10–2 (Mr C Hennecart) **G Wilson** *Fell*; *PROMINENT LAD* 7.10–2 (Mrs E Tozer) **H Jones** *Fell*; *HURDY GURDY MAN* 10.10–0 (Duchess of Norfolk) **Mr J Hislop** *Fell*; *LAZY BOOTS* 12.10–4 (Sir Geoffrey Congreve) **Sir G Congreve** *Fell*; *EMANCIPATOR* 10.10–3 (Mr C R D Gray) **Mr C R D Gray** *Fell*; *KDH* 7.10–0 (Mrs J Metcalf) **G Archibald** *Fell*; *DAWMAR* 8.10–7 (Mr W S Murphy) **R Burford** *Pulled-up*; *TAPINOIS* 10.10–1 (Mr W Hutchinson) **A Scratchley** *Pulled-up*

The Betting: 8/1 Blue Shirt & Cooleen; 100/9 Delachance; 100/8 Royal Mail; 100/7 Takvor Pacha; 100/6 Stalbridge Park; 18/1 Royal Danieli; 20/1 Dunhill Castle; 22/1 Provocative & Dominick's Cross; 25/1 Airgead Sios & Bachelor Prince; 28/1 Rockquilla, Red Knight II & Workman; 33/1 Inversible & Cabin Fire; 40/1 Battleship, Lough Cottage, Under Bid & Brighter Cottage; 50/1 Didoric & Blue Prince; 66/1 Pontet, Frobisher & Rock Lad; 100/1 Others.

Distances: *A head; a bad third*

Winner Trained By: *Reg Hobbs, Lambourn, Berkshire*

Value to Winning Owner: *£7,598*

1939

Rumours of war were again in the air as the masses made their way to Aintree on 24th March 1939. KILSTAR, owned by Miss Dorothy Paget, started 8/1 favourite, the word being that he was the perfect successor to GOLDEN MILLER and partnered by the talented American-born jockey George Archibald was expected to make his first 'National appearance a winning one. Of the thirty-seven runners, ROYAL MAIL was once more top weight with 12 st 7 lbs and Danny Morgan replaced his usual jockey Williams. Scotland, still without a success in the race, staked their hopes on Captain Scott Briggs' seven-year-old MACMOFFAT and although his form was little to rave about, northern support brought his price down to 25/1. Mrs Scott was represented this time with the Billy Parvin-ridden WAR VESSEL, a half-brother to her BATTLESHIP. The loudest whisper was for Ireland's WORKMAN. Bred by Mr P J O'Leary at Charleville, County Cork, from COTTAGE and CARIELLA, WORKMAN first drew attention to himself when winning the La Touche Memorial Cup at Punchestown in the hands of his owner Mr R de L Stedman. Shortly afterwards he was bought by Sir Alexander Maguire, the Liverpool-born industrialist who had interests on both sides of the Irish Sea and who placed the gelding in the care of trainer Jack Ruttle. It was the trainer who persuaded Tim Hyde to forsake his success in the show jumping world in favour of steeplechasing, believing that only Hyde would be able to bring out the best in WORKMAN.

ROCKQUILLA took them across Melling Road, to be out-jumped at the first fence by BIRTHGIFT, while TEME WILLOW, MESMERIST, DRIM, WAR VESSEL and BRENDAN'S COTTAGE all made an early exit. ROYAL DANIELI mistimed his take-off at the Brook, coming down in a nasty looking fall and, racing back in front of the stands, KILSTAR headed the leading bunch, closely attended by Lord Derby's UNDER BID, WEST POINT and the steadily improving WORKMAN. KILSTAR was still dominating proceedings over Becher's, but both BLACK HAWK and MACMOFFAT had made up a tremendous amount of ground to be well in contention. Tim Hyde was riding an intelligent race on WORKMAN, bringing him to the front after clearing Valentine's, and in a collision with BLACK HAWK at the last fence before the racecourse, his strength proved the greater. BLACK HAWK came down and WORKMAN now had the race won barring a fall. Resisting the strong challenge of MACMOFFAT, he held on for a three length win with the favourite KILSTAR fifteen lengths further back in third. Mr J V Rank's COOLEEN was again fourth. At 100/8 WORKMAN was a popular winner, particularly with his owner's local connections, but the performance of the Scottish runner-up MACMOFFAT prompted many to mark him down as a future contender. The prospect of this, however, depended upon political and diplomatic affairs in Europe and as the crowds departed from the racecourse, more than a few thoughts were given to whether or not there would be a 'National to attend in twelve months' time.

1939

Of £100 each, £60 if declared by 14th March or £10 if declared by 31st January. With £4,000 added (including a trophy value £200). For six-year-olds & upwards. The second to receive 10% (£886), the third 5% (£443) and the fourth 2½% (£221). The trainer of the Winner to receive a cup value £50 and the rider of the Winner a cup value £25

Date: 24th March 1939	Starters: 37	Time: 9 mins 42⅕ secs
1st **WORKMAN**	9.10–6 *(Sir Alexander Maguire)*	**T Hyde**
2nd **MACMOFFAT**	7.10–3 *(Capt L Scott Briggs)*	**I Alder**
3rd **KILSTAR**	8.10–3 *(Miss Dorothy Paget)*	**G Archibald**
4th **COOLEEN**	11.11–8 *(Mr J V Rank)*	**J Fawcus**
5th **SYMAETHIS**	7.10–0 *(Mr Arthur Sainsbury)*	**M Feakes**
6th **DOMINICK'S CROSS**	8.11–1 *(Mr A Donn)*	**R Everett**
7th **WEST POINT**	6.10–2 *(Mr P Dunne Cullinan)*	**J Brogan**
8th **PENCRAIK**	12.10–0 *(Mr A Pilkington)*	**A Scratchley**
9th **ROYAL MAIL**	10.12–7 *(Mrs C Evans)*	**D Morgan**
10th **BACHELOR PRINCE**	12.10–2 *(Mr J V Rank)*	**T Isaac**
11th **UNDER BID**	7.10–0 *(Lord Derby)*	**G Wilson** [remounted]

Also Ran:

ROYAL DANIELI 8.11–13 (Mr H C McNally) **D Moore** *Fell*; *DUNHILL CASTLE 9.11–9* (Sir Warden Chilcott) **F Walwyn** *Fell*; *ROCKQUILLA 9.11–7* (Lord Bicester) **T F Carey** *Fell*; *BRENDAN'S COTTAGE 9.11–2* (Mrs A Smith-Bingham) **G Owen** *Fell*; *TEME WILLOW 8.10–13* (Sir Edward Hanmer) **T F Rimell** *Fell*; *PERFECT PART 9.10–13* (Mrs Violet Fitzgerald) **J Ward** *Fell*; *RED HILLMAN 11.10–12* (Lord Latymer) **E Foley** *Fell*; *BLACK HAWK 8.10–8* (Mrs C Jones) **J Moloney** *Fell*; *INVERSIBLE 11.10–7* (Lt Col W E Peel) **M Hogan** *Fell*; *WAR VESSEL 6.10–7* (Mrs Marion Scott) **W Parvin** *Fell*; *RED FREEMAN 8.10–5* (Mr W U Goodbody) **W Redmond** *Fell*; *SECOND ACT 8.10–5* (Mrs A A Sidney Villar) **J Dowdeswell** *Fell*; *BLUE SHIRT 8.10–4* (Mr Arthur Sainsbury) **R Smyth** *Fell*; *MONTREJEAU II 9.10–5* (Lady Granard) **H Nicholson** *Fell*; *MILANO 8.10–10* (Mrs L E Stoddard) **Mr L Stoddard** *Fell*; *DESLYS 10.10–1* (Mrs Ackerley) **Mr A Marsh** *Fell*; *SPORTING PIPER 8.10–0* (Mr R Strutt) **Mr J Hislop** *Fell*; *SCOTCH WOOD 9.10–0* (Mr A Gillson) **Capt P Herbert** *Fell*; *DRIM 12.10–6* (Mr J Morris) **Mr J Morris** *Fell*; *MESMERIST 8.10–0* (Mr A E Berry) **Capt R Harding** *Fell*; *EPIPHANES 7.10–0* (Mr J B Rolls) **Mr H Applin** *Fell*; *ST GEORGE II 8.10–11* (Mr A J G Leveson Gower) **Mr R Petre** *Refused*; *BIRTHGIFT 8.10–0* (Mr N E Dixon) **T McNeill** *Refused*; *LUCKY PATCH 9.10–0* (Mr N E Dixon) **T Elder** *Refused*; *TUCKMILL 9.10–0* (Mr G W Roll) **G Kelly** *Ran-out*; *LUCKPENNY 10.10–12* (Mrs H M Hollins) **Major R Moseley** *Broke-down*

The Betting: *8/1 Kilstar; 10/1 Blue Shirt; 100/9 Teme Willow; 100/8 Royal Mail, Royal Danieli & Workman; 100/6 Rockquilla; 22/1 Cooleen, Inversible & Under Bid; 25/1 Macmoffat & Brendan's Cottage; 28/1 Dunhill Castle; 33/1 Dominick's Cross, Perfect Part & St George II; 40/1 Black Hawk & Montrejeau II; 50/1 War Vessel, Sporting Piper, Red Freeman & Milano; 66/1 West Point, Red Hillman, Bachelor Prince, Symaethis & Lucky Patch; 100/1 Others.*

Distances: *Three lengths; fifteen lengths*

Winner Trained By: *Jack Ruttle, Celbridge, County Dublin, Ireland*

Value to Winning Owner: *£7,284*

1940

By the time the thirty runners for the Grand National made their way to the start on 5th April 1940, the Second World War was almost seven months old. Liverpool was once again elevated to a position of importance, its port a vital link in Britain's chain against the enemy. The city resembled a garrison town, with uniforms from every corner of the Empire converging in answer to the call to arms and in preparation for a long, bitter struggle. At Aintree too, the crowds assembled might well have been mistaken as a gathering for a military tattoo instead of spectators at a race-meeting. Even the jockeys arrived unrecognisable in uniform, to emerge from the weighing room in their more familiar garb of silks and breeches to take their places among owners in the paddock who were attired as if about to inspect the troops. The sports pages of newspapers featured air raid instructions for those attending the race.

ROYAL DANIELI was top weight with 11 st 13 lbs and was just preferred in the market at 4/1 to Miss Paget's KILSTAR. Scotland's hope, MACMOFFAT, came next in demand, with MILANO, THE PROFESSOR II and BLACK HAWK also receiving a fair amount of attention from those anxious to bet on what was likely to be the last Grand National for a long time. Both local Earls were represented this year, Lord Derby with UNDER BID and Lord Sefton with BOYO. Another Peer trying his luck, with a horse he trained as well as owned, was Lord Stalbridge. His seven-year-old gelding BOGSKAR, by WERWOLF out of IRISH SPRING, was bred in County Dublin by Mr C Roche and was purchased as a three-year-old from Sydney McGregor of Leamington. Running without success for three seasons, the gelding came good in Gatwick's National Trial 'Chase a little

over a month before the real thing at Aintree, but fell in his final race before the 'National. Taking the mount was Flight Sergeant Mervyn Jones, the nephew of Ivor Anthony, and joining him on leave for the day from the Royal Air Force was his brother Hywel, doing duty on 'Jock' Whitney's NATIONAL NIGHT.

From the start a hot pace was set by ROYAL DANIELI, who led over Becher's from ROCKQUILLA, GOLD ARROW, THE PROFESSOR II, MACMOFFAT and NATIONAL NIGHT and a remarkable feature of the race, considering the speed at which they were travelling, was that only CORN LAW and BACHELOR PRINCE had so far fallen. At the fourteenth NATIONAL NIGHT fell when lying sixth, racing on riderless while his jockey Hywel Jones rushed back to watch the finish. MACMOFFAT was in front jumping the Water. Back in the country, the fast gallop began taking its toll. Clearing Becher's side by side, ROYAL DANIELI and MACMOFFAT were just in front of GOLD ARROW, AWAY, VENTURESOME KNIGHT and BOGSKAR. Lord Sefton's BOYO was involved in a nasty looking fall at the Canal Turn, though some way off the pace at the time and from this point MACMOFFAT looked like improving on his second place of twelve months before. Accompanied by the riderless NATIONAL NIGHT, Alder rode the Scottish horse boldly back towards the stands, ahead of ROYAL DANIELI, GOLD ARROW, KILSTAR and the improving BOGSKAR. When ROYAL DANIELI fell heavily at the second last, MACMOFFAT appeared to have the prize in his pocket. He was still receiving the unwelcome attentions of the loose NATIONAL NIGHT, though, and rising to the last fence was joined also by BOGSKAR. The latter made a slight mistake on landing, was held together well by Mervyn Jones and then produced the better turn of foot to draw away to win by four lengths. First horse past the post by one length, however, was NATIONAL NIGHT. His jockey, standing near the finishing line, had the consolation of seeing his brother Mervyn Jones take the honours, behind the horse which dumped him on the first circuit. GOLD ARROW was six lengths behind MACMOFFAT in third, with SYMAETHIS fourth.

Aintree racecourse was again turned over to the War Department for the duration of hostilities, jockeys returned to their regiments and within two months of BOGSKAR's win, the evacuation from Dunkirk took place. Britain and the Empire stood alone against a powerful and resolute enemy.

Right: A famous stable on the course gets put to new use for the Duration

Below: Air raid wardens study plans of the course where previously so many had studied the Form

1940

Of £100, £60 if declared by 26th March or £10 if declared by 30th January. With £5,000 added (including a trophy value £200). For six-year-olds & upwards. The second to receive £500 and the third £250. The trainer of the Winner to receive a cup value £50 and the rider of the Winner a cup value £25

Date: 5th April 1940	Starters: 30	Time: 9 mins 20³/₅ secs
1st **BOGSKAR**	7.10–4 *(Lord Stalbridge)*	**M A Jones**
2nd **MACMOFFAT**	8.10–10 *(Capt L Scott Briggs)*	**I Alder**
3rd **GOLD ARROW**	8.10–3 *(Mr J R Neill)*	**P Lay**
4th **SYMAETHIS**	8.10–7 *(Mr T Westhead)*	**M Feakes**
5th **VENTURESOME KNIGHT**	10.10–8 *(Lt Col H E Joicey)*	**Mr R Tweedie**
6th **THE PROFESSOR II**	9.11–8 *(Mrs I Strang)*	**G Owen**
7th **TAKVOR PACHA**	8.10–4 *(Major H P Rushton)*	**Major O Prior-Palmer**
8th **AWAY**	9.11–2 *(Mr I K Muir)*	**Mr I K Muir**
9th **INVERSIBLE**	12.10–6 *(Lt Col W E Peel)*	**M Hogan**
10th **DOMINICK'S CROSS**	9.11–1 *(Mr A Donn)*	**C Mitchell**
11th **LUXBOROUGH**	6.10–3 *(Mr J A de Rothschild)*	**E Brown**
12th **KILSTAR**	9.11–0 *(Miss Dorothy Paget)*	**G Archibald**
13th **ROCKQUILLA**	10.11–5 *(Lord Bicester)*	**T F Carey**
14th **DOWNRIGHT**	11.10–6 *(Capt J Seely)*	**Capt J Seely**
15th **LAZY BOOTS**	14.10–10 *(Sir Geoffrey Congreve)*	**Sir G Congreve**
16th **RED EAGLE**	9.11–2 *(Mr H B Brandt)*	**T Elder**
17th **TUCKMILL**	10.10–3 *(Mr G W Roll)*	**G Kelly**

Also Ran:
ROYAL DANIELI 9.11–13 (Mr H C McNally) **D Moore** *Fell*; *LITIGANT 9.10–7* (Major Noel Furlong) **Mr R Black** *Fell*; *CORN LAW 8.10–3* (Mr W Hutchinson) **T McNeill** *Fell*; *DUNHILL CASTLE 10.11–5* (Sir Warden Chilcott) **G Wilson** *Fell*; *BLACK HAWK 9.11–0* (Mrs C Jones) **T F Rimell** *Fell*; *NATIONAL NIGHT 8.10–5* (Mr J H Whitney) **H A Jones** *Fell*; *RED FREEMAN 9.10–3* (Mr W U Goodbody) **W Redmond** *Fell*; *UNDER BID 8.10–3* (Lord Derby) **H Nicholson** *Fell*; *MILANO 9.10–9* (Mrs L E Stoddard) **D Morgan** *Pulled-up*; *BOYO 9.10–4* (Lord Sefton) **R Morgan** *Fell*; *BACHELOR PRINCE 13.10–9* (Mr R Loewenstein) **Mr R Loewenstein** *Fell*; *STERLING DUKE 9.10–3* (Sir Alexander Maguire) **T Hyde** *Pulled-up*; *SECOND ACT 9.10–3* (Mrs A A Sidney Villar) **J Dowdeswell** *Broke-down*

The Betting: *4/1 Royal Danieli; 5/1 Kilstar; 8/1 MacMoffat; 100/9 Milano; 100/8 The Professor II; 100/6 Black Hawk, Symaethis & Sterling Duke; 20/1 Rockquilla; 25/1 Inversible & Bogskar; 28/1 Venturesome Knight; 33/1 Under Bid & Takvor Pacha; 40/1 Dominick's Cross; 50/1 Red Eagle, Dunhill Castle, Litigant, Red Freeman & Gold Arrow; 66/1 Boyo; 100/1 Others.*

Distances: *Four lengths; six lengths*

Winner Trained By: *Lord Stalbridge, Eastbury, Berkshire*

Value to Winning Owner: *£4,225*

1941–1945

This war was the first in which the civilian population found itself in the front line of the action. Together with other major cities in Britain, Liverpool suffered a continuous pounding during the blitz. A new spirit emerged from the ruins of shattered homes, a will to endure and the indefatigable resolve to fight on, come what may. If all too briefly, class became a thing of the past, the people united in the belief that their cause was just and that the horrors endured would mould a better land and a truly free world. Immense sacrifices were made, at home and abroad and the injustices of the past were laid aside in the quest for victory and nobody suffered the illusion that victory would come cheaply. Aintree racecourse played its own part in the war effort, housing many thousands of American troops in the build-up to the allied invasion of Europe.

Among the multitude who paid the supreme sacrifice in the fight for freedom were Frank Furlong of the Fleet Air Arm, Bobby Everett of the Royal Navy, Mervyn Jones, sergeant pilot Royal Air Force, and Tommy Cullinan serving with an anti-aircraft unit. Their names live among countless thousands upon memorials of stone, and together they share a revered place on the Grand National Roll of Honour.

When next the crowds would make their way to Aintree, the world would have to be prepared to start anew. In the meantime, jockeys who in 1940 were on the threshold of sparkling careers had passed into anonymity, and horses fresh with the bloom of promise had lost the best years through enforced inactivity.

Left: The condition of the finishing straight left a lot to be desired by the end of the war. Here the Stars and Stripes can be seen flying above the stands

Right: American military vehicles parked in the enclosures

1946

With speed and planning worthy of a military operation, Aintree was prepared for racing by Tophams Ltd within days of the last army personnel vacating the premises. Driving force behind the enormous task was Mrs Mirabel Dorothy Topham, who had taken over chairmanship of the Company through the illness of her husband Ronald. Her influence and dynamism was to place the Grand National, and indeed the racecourse itself, in a far greater position of importance than ever before.

PRINCE REGENT, by MY PRINCE out of NEMAEA, had enjoyed a good war racing in his native Ireland where the sport suffered far less than on the mainland. He came to Aintree the winner of fourteen races, the most recent being the Cheltenham Gold Cup, shouldered top weight of 12 st 5 lbs and of the thirty-four runners, he started a roaring favourite at 3/1. Owned by Mr J V Rank, the gelding was trained in Ireland by Tom Dreaper and ridden by Tim Hyde. Little regard was paid to the fact that PRINCE REGENT would be tackling the Aintree fences for the first time, or that he was now eleven years old.

Of four amateurs riding in the race, Captain Robert Charles Petre of the Scots Guards appealed to many ex-servicemen, while the homely name of his mount, LOVELY COTTAGE, caught the attention of housewives. The nine-year-old was bred in County Cork by Mr M J Hyde from COTTAGE and THE NUN III, the dam having been a first-class point-to-point performer. Following in his mother's hoofsteps, LOVELY COTTAGE adapted well to steeplechasing, winning three times in 1944. He was then offered for sale by his owner Mrs Hyde, wife of the breeder, the asking price being £2,000 with a contingency of another £1,000 'when he should win the Grand National at Aintree'. This expression of confidence attracted the attention of Mr John Morant, who agreed to the conditions of sale and bought the horse, to be trained by Tommy Rayson at Winchester. The racecourse was bursting at the seams with an estimated three hundred thousand spectators celebrating the hard won peace and the return of the race which was so much a part of the British way of life. The field were led over Melling Road by Mr Cousins on his own GYPPO and the runners took the fence almost in line. LARGO came down on his head at Becher's in a fall which seemed certain to be fatal, yet fortunately both horse and rider escaped injury. PRINCE REGENT was finding difficulty in coping with the big fences, making mistakes which would have floored a lesser horse. Yet despite his errors, he was in close touch approaching the Water Jump and powered his way to the front early on the second circuit. Now PRINCE REGENT was surrounded by a posse of loose horses, which increased rather than lessened the further they went and coming back from the Canal Turn, Tim Hyde was forced to ride a series of finishes in an effort to shake them off. At the last fence the favourite was still clear, with only five weary rivals chasing him, but before reaching the elbow in the straight the danger signs were showing. Struggling on gamely under his massive burden, Mr Rank's gelding had given his all and was unable to fight back when challenged and overtaken by first LOVELY COTTAGE and then outsider JACK FINLAY. LOVELY COTTAGE won by four lengths from JACK FINLAY with the brave PRINCE REGENT three lengths back in third place. The sympathy heaped on the beaten favourite tended to overshadow the performance of LOVELY COTTAGE who won on merit. Captain

Petre, who had topped the amateur riders' list in 1938, had ridden a well-judged race and it was a great loss when his career in the saddle was cut short soon afterwards. Having survived the perils of the race-course and the horrors of war, he slipped on a breakwater, fracturing his leg so badly that it had to be amputated.

There has been a popular suggestion that the defeat of PRINCE REGENT in this 'National led owners of class staying 'chasers to steer clear of the event. But these views are the result of hindsight and for a time yet, there was to be no doubt in anyone's mind that the greatest test of a jumper was the Grand National.

THE GRAND NATIONAL HANDICAP STEEPLECHASE
1946

Of £100 each, £60 if declared by 26th March or £10 if declared by 5th February. With £4,000 added (including a trophy value £200). For six-year-olds & upwards. The second to receive £800, the third £500 and the fourth £200. The trainer of the Winner to receive a cup value £50 and the rider of the Winner a cup value £25

Date: 5th April 1946	Starters: 34	Time: 9 mins 38⅕ secs
1st **LOVELY COTTAGE**	9.10–8 *(Mr J Morant)*	**Capt R Petre**
2nd **JACK FINLAY**	7.10–2 *(Mr L S Elwell)*	**W Kidney**
3rd **PRINCE REGENT**	11.12–5 *(Mr J V Rank)*	**T Hyde**
4th **HOUSEWARMER**	9.10–2 *(Miss Dorothy Paget)*	**A Brabazon**
5th **SCHUBERT**	12.11–0 *(Mrs K Cameron)*	**C Beechener**
6th **LIMESTONE EDWARD**	12.10–2 *(Mr C Nicholson)*	**D Doyle**

Also Ran:
SYMBOLE aged.11–11 (Mr R Saint) **W Redmond** *Fell*; *LARGO 7.10–13* (Mrs I Strang) **J Cooke** *Fell*; *HEIRDOM 14.10–10* (Mr H Quinn) **P Cahalin** *Fell*; *BOGSKAR 13.10–9* (Lord Stalbridge) **R Mathews** *Fell*; *KAMI 9.10–9* (M. André Adele) **H Bonneau** *Fell*; *MACMOFFAT 14.10–8* (Capt L Scott Briggs) **I Alder** *Fell*; *ASTROMETER 8.10–3* (Miss Dorothy Paget) **M Gordon** *Fell*; *KNIGHT'S CREST 9.10–3* (Mr F E Benner) **P Murphy** *Fell*; *SUZERAIN II 8.10–3* (Mr Ben Davis) **G Archibald** *Fell*; *VAIN KNIGHT 13.10–2* (Mr H C Falconer) **R Curran** *Fell*; *SILVER FAME 7.10–0* (Lord Bicester) **D Ruttle** *Fell*; *HISTORICAL REVUE 8.10–0* (Mr J R Porter) **S Ryan** *Fell*; *TULYRA 10.10–0* (Mr D A Jackson) **Mr D A Jackson** *Fell*; *DUNSHAUGHLIN 8.10–0* (Miss Dorothy Paget) **R J O'Ryan** *Fell*; *DOUBLE FLUSH 10.10–0* (Mr L Michaelson) **E Newman** *Fell*; *YUNG-YAT 10.10–0* (Mr F W E Gradwell) **T Cullen, jnr** *Fell*; *LOUGH CONN 10.10–0* (Mrs M Rowe) **D McCann** *Fell*; *JOCK 8.10–2* (Lord Rosebery) **F Gurney** *Fell*; *MUSICAL LAD 9.10–0* (Mr L Michaelson) **M Browne** *Fell*; *BRICETT 9.10–2* (Mr H Linsley) **J Brogan** *Fell*; *GYPPO 12.10–0* (Mr J Cousins) **Mr J Cousins** *Fell*; *ALACRITY 13.10–0* (Mr J Bowden) **G Bowden** *Fell*; *CLOSURE 9.10–0* (Mr J D Norris) **Mr H Applin** *Fell*; *ELSICH 10.10–0* (Mr K Edwards) **W Balfe** *Fell*; *RED POWER 12.11–7* (Lord Stalbridge) **G Kelly** *Pulled-up*; *EP 11.10–2* (Mr J Ismay) **M Molony** *Pulled-up*; *NEWARK HILL 12.10–1* (Mr T A Spiers) **P Lay** *Brought-down*; *KING GESSON 10.10–0* (Mrs G Coles) **R Burford** *Refused*

The Betting: *3/1 Prince Regent; 13/2 Limestone Edward; 100/8 Dunshaughlin; 100/7 Schubert; 22/1 Red Power & Knight's Crest; 25/1 Lovely Cottage; 28/1 Bricett; 33/1 Kami, Symbole, Suzerain II & Lough Conn; 40/1 Gyppo & Silver Fame; 50/1 Jock, MacMoffat, Astrometer, Newark Hill & EP; 66/1 Largo, Heirdom, Bogskar & Historical Revue; 100/1 Others.*

Distances: *Four lengths; three lengths*

Winner Trained By: *Tommy Rayson, Headbourne Worthy, Hampshire*

Value to Winning Owner: *£8,805*

1947

A break with tradition was made this year, when the race was run on a Saturday at the request of the Prime Minister, Clement Attlee, who suggested to Mrs Topham that the new date for the event would be, 'in the interests of British industry'. Mainland Britain suffered its worst winter in living memory, resulting in the loss of all racing fixtures between 22nd January and 15th March and the National Hunt Meeting at Cheltenham being postponed until April. When the thaw at last set in, flooding followed. With so many opportunities to pick up prize money lost, an abundance of runners were sent to Liverpool, producing a field of fifty-seven for the 'National, the second largest in the history of the race. The second and perhaps most important result of that long winter was that the preparations of most horses had been severely interrupted and only a fraction of the huge field were anywhere near race-fit. PRINCE REGENT, once more top weight with 12 st 7 lbs, was again favourite though this time at the more realistic odds of 8/1. With LOVELY COTTAGE absent through injury, Captain Petre took the mount on Lord Bicester's promising newcomer SILVER FAME. Another amateur with a military background went to unusual lengths to be able to partner his own MARTIN M in the race. Major Skrine received injuries during the Italian campaign which caused one leg to be shorter than the other and in order to be able to ride in this 'National, underwent an operation to bring his good leg into line with the damaged one. Among the twenty-six bracketed at 100/1 was an eight-year-old named CAUGHOO. Being by WITHIN-THE-LAW out of SILVERDALE, he had not a drop of jumping blood in him. His breeder, Mr Patrick Power of Fethard-on-Sea, County Wexford, sent CAUGHOO to Ballsbridge Sales in 1941 where for fifty guineas he became the property of John McDowell, a Dublin jeweller. The new owner's brother Herbert, a veterinary surgeon, was entrusted with training the horse, which he did well enough for CAUGHOO to win successive Ulster Nationals at Downpatrick in 1945 and 1946. Even so, the McDowell brothers' gelding still looked well short of Aintree-winning ability. Jockey Eddie Dempsey, making his first visit to England, had the consolation that CAUGHOO would at least be fully fit, for throughout the winter, Herbert McDowell had kept the gelding active on the beach of Sutton Strand near Dublin.

That conditions at Aintree were more exacting this year than for a long time was shown on the opening day of the meeting when all sixteen runners in the Stanley 'Chase fell, the race eventually being won by Tim Molony on the remounted BILLY-KIN. A heavy mist lay over the rain-soaked course on 'National day but the miserable weather did not affect attendances and another huge crowd braved the elements to watch the cavalry-charge the big field was certain to produce. From the start it was obvious that little would be seen of the action out in the country and with visibility difficult for spectators and radio commentators, only a scant report of the race was possible. REVELRY, EP, DAY DREAMS, BULLINGTON, MICHAEL'S PEARL and WICKLOW WOLF were all put out before Becher's, where LUAN CASCA joined their number. At this stage LOUGH CONN led from the grey KILNAGLORY, followed by BRICETT, GORMANSTOWN, DOMINO, PRINCE REGENT, TULYRA and SILVER FAME, the remainder already well strung out behind. Over the Water Jump and back out again, LOUGH CONN still held his advantage from

MUSICAL LAD, the pair accompanied by half a dozen loose horses. Over Becher's LOUGH CONN had increased his lead to ten lengths, with CAUGHOO making progress into second place. Coming out of the mist back on to the racecourse, CAUGHOO was way out on his own, causing a frantic search of their racecards by those in the stands trying to identify the unfamiliar colours. A last fence blunder brought a gasp from the crowds, but Dempsey was quickly back in control, riding his shock winner home to a twenty length victory from the tired early leader and fellow Irishman LOUGH CONN. Four lengths back

in third place came Mr John Hislop on the French bred KAMI, in front of PRINCE REGENT. The stragglers came home at their own pace, including Major Skrine with MARTIN M.

An interesting sequel to this surprise success came some years later, when Eddie Dempsey encountered second jockey Daniel McCann, who accused Dempsey of having cheated in the 'National by taking a short cut in the fog. In true Irish fashion, the dispute led to fisticuffs and the story was repeated in court. The ridiculous claim was dismissed as sour grapes – and the drink talking!

THE GRAND NATIONAL HANDICAP STEEPLECHASE

1947

Of £100 each, £60 if declared by 18th March or £10 if declared by 4th February. With £5,000 added (including a trophy value £200). For six-year-olds & upwards. The second to receive £1,216, the third £608 and the fourth £304. The trainer of the Winner to receive a cup value £50 and the rider of the Winner a cup value £25

Date: 29th March 1947	Starters: 57	Time: 10 mins 3⅘ secs
1st **CAUGHOO**	8.10−0 *(Mr J J McDowell)*	**E Dempsey**
2nd **LOUGH CONN**	11.10−1 *(Mrs M Rowe)*	**D McCann**
3rd **KAMI**	10.10−13 *(Sir Allan Gordon Smith)*	**Mr J Hislop**
4th **PRINCE REGENT**	12.12−7 *(Mr J V Rank)*	**T Hyde**
5th **SOME CHICKEN**	10.10−2 *(Mr J J Cleaver)*	**R Turnell**
6th **HOUSEWARMER**	10.10−6 *(Miss D Paget)*	**R J O'Ryan**
7th **REFUGIO**	9.11−0 *(Mrs F Adams)*	**F Adams**
8th **KILNAGLORY**	12.11−1 *(Miss D Paget)*	**B Marshall**
9th **OCULTOR**	12.11−0 *(Mr G R E Owen)*	**Mr D Owen**
10th **HALCYON HOURS**	7.11−2 *(Mr F More O'Ferrall)*	**M Gordon** [remounted]
11th **BRICK BAT**	8.10−0 *(Mr J V Rank)*	**E Newman**
12th **MARTIN M**	7.10−0 *(Major W H Skrine)*	**Major Skrine** [remounted]
13th **SCHUBERT**	13.10−11 *(Mrs K Cameron)*	**C Beechener**
14th **REARMAMENT**	10.11−1 *(Mrs C D Wilson)*	**G Kelly**
15th **ROWLAND ROY**	8.10−3 *(Mr A G Boley)*	**Mr R Black** [remounted]
16th **TOYETTE**	10.10−6 *(Major R Waugh Harris)*	**Major R Waugh Harris**

The following also completed the course:

CLYDUFFE 12.10–0 (Mr N P Donaldson) **M Hogan**; *LEAP MAN 10.11–0* (Mr A W Fletcher) **T F Rimell**; *BRIGHTER SANDY 9.10–7* (Mr M Barker) **Capt J Eustace-Smith**; *HANDY LAD 12.10–0* (Mrs F G Knight) **Capt W Williams**; *JUBILEE FLIGHT 12.10–0* (Mr W F Ransom) **E Hannigan**.

Also Ran:

BRICETT 10.11–1 (Mr H Linsley) **M C Prendergast** *Fell*; *REVELRY 7.10–12* (Mr J T Doyle) **D Moore** *Fell*; *SILVER FAME 8.10–12* (Lord Bicester) **R Petre** *Fell*; *JACK FINLAY 8.10–8* (Mr L S Elwell) **W Kidney** *Fell*; *LUAN CASCA 7.10–7* (Mr F More O'Ferrall) **A Brabazon** *Fell*; *BULLINGTON 11.10–6* (Major W W Higgins) **J Bissill** *Fell*; *EP 12.10–5* (Mr J Ismay) **M Molony** *Fell*; *KLAXTON 7.10–5* (Mr T Radmall) **J Maguire** *Fell*; *MUSICAL LAD 10.10–4* (Mr L Michaelson) **M J Prendergast** *Fell*; *BOGSKAR 14.10–4* (Lord Stalbridge) **R Burford** *Fell*; *FIRST OF THE DANDIES 10.10–3* (Mr G Wilson) **J Moloney** *Fell*; *MACMOFFAT 15.10–4* (Capt L Scott Briggs) **I Alder** *Fell*; *SHEILA'S COTTAGE 8.10–1* (Sir Hervey Bruce) **A P Thompson** *Fell*; *MICHAEL'S PEARL 8.10–0* (Mr W Seward) **E Reavey** *Fell*; *BOMBER COMMAND 8.10–0* (Mr A B Askew) **A Jarvis** *Fell*; *PARTHENON 8.10–0* (Lord Bicester) **P Murray** *Fell*; *SODA II 6.10–2* (Mr G Clover) **F Gurney** *Fell*; *PRATTLER 12.10–0* (Mr E Manners) **P Conlon** *Fell*; *BLACK JENNIFER 7.10–0* (Mr M Uglow) **J Sheehan** *Fell*; *DOUBLE SAM 12.10–0* (Mr S D Clark) **H Haley** *Fell*; *GYPPO 13.10–0* (Mr J Cousins) **Mr J Cousins** *Fell*; *GOOD DATE 9.10–0* (Mrs H Heywood-Jones) **J Dowdeswell** *Fell*; *BORDER BOB 9.10–0* (Mr J R Bower) **J Neely** *Fell*; *TRIBUNE 13.10–0* (Mrs Guy Janson) **K Gilsenan** *Fell*; *OH JOE 7.10–0* (Mrs E P Moss) **E Vinall** *Fell*; *SHANAKILL 9.10–0* (Mr R I Sainsbury) **W Denson** *Fell*; *GRECIAN VICTORY 10.10–0* (Mr G Cheney) **P Lay** *Brought-down*; *TULYRA 11.10–0* (Mr D A Jackson) **Mr D A Jackson** *Refused*; *GRANITZA 8.10–0* (Mr C B Rendall) **N Dixon** *Refused*; *DAY DREAMS 8.10–0* (Mr L Michaelson) **M Browne** *Pulled-up*; *LINTHILL 11.10–0* (Mr J Martin Sanderson) **P Taylor** *Pulled-up*; *WICKLOW WOLF 7.10–0* (Mr H Lane) **M J Hogan** *Pulled-up*; *YUNG-YAT 11.10–1* (Mr F W E Gradwell) **J Brogan** *Pulled-up*; *GORMANSTOWN 7.10–9* (Mr C Nicholson) **T Molony** *Pulled-up*; *DOMINO 7.10–0* (Major W H MacKenzie) **D Morgan** *Pulled-up*; *PATRICKSWELL 9.10–0* (Mr J Smurfit) **P Cahalin** *Carried out*

The Betting: *8/1 Prince Regent; 100/6 Revelry; 22/1 Bricett & Luan Casca; 25/1 Housewarmer; 28/1 Domino; 33/1 Rearmament, Silver Fame, Kami, Lough Conn, Musical Lad & Jack Finlay; 40/1 Kilnaglory, Gormanstown, Sheila's Cottage, Parthenon & Some Chicken; 50/1 Halcyon Hours, Leap Man, Clyduffe, Prattler, Soda II & Black Jennifer; 66/1 Schubert, Brighter Sandy, Klaxton, Bullington, Rowland Roy, First of the Dandies, Brick Bat & Martin M; 100/1 Others.*

Distances: *Twenty lengths; four lengths*

Winner Trained By: *Herbert McDowell, Malahide, County Dublin, Ireland*

Value to Winning Owner: *£10,007*

CAUGHOO passes the post so fresh his achievement is questioned

1948

In the twelve years since coming so close to winning the 'National on DAVY JONES, Anthony Mildmay had succeeded his father as Lord Mildmay of Flete, served with distinction in the Welsh Guards and the Guards Armoured Division and dominated the amateur division of 'chase riding in the immediate post-war period. Together with his close friend Peter Cazalet, now training at Fairlawne, he put together a formidable team of top-class jumpers but uppermost in both their minds was the dream of triumph in Aintree's great 'Chase. Their representatives in this year's race were CROMWELL and ULTRA BENE, both owned by Mildmay and the former ridden by him. PRINCE REGENT was making a final attempt, once more burdened with top weight but now at thirteen years old his chances were reflected in the starting price of 25/1. It was in Lord Bicester's unbeaten SILVER FAME, a half-brother to BOGSKAR, that the public placed their faith, backing him down to 9/1 first choice and with the brilliant Martin Molony riding even these odds appeared generous to many. Miss Dorothy Paget ran HOUSEWARMER and HAPPY HOME, both trained by former winning jockey Fulke Walwyn and another of that elite band, Bruce Hobbs, saddled the great WAR RISK, partnered by Bob Turnell. Gerry Wilson, GOLDEN MILLER's old jockey, was also now among the ranks of trainers and in FIRST OF THE DANDIES had more than an outside chance of starting with a big winner.

A half-sister to LOVELY COTTAGE through her sire COTTAGE, SHEILA'S COTTAGE was like her dam SHEILA II endowed with the fiercest of tempers which made her a nightmare ride. Bred by Mrs P Daly in County Limerick, the mare was bought by Sir Hervey Bruce of the Royal Scots Greys, who was at the time adjutant at Catterick Camp. Former cavalry officer Neville Crump trained the horse at Middleham in Yorkshire, finding his Irish-born stable jockey Arthur Thompson the only one capable of controlling the wayward lady. Two good wins over Haydock's drop fences proved the mare had ability but she fell at the twelfth fence in the 1947 'National and, after losing a good deal when SHEILA'S COTTAGE could finish no better than third at Cheltenham, her owner decided to sell. For the sum of £3,500 she passed into the ownership of John Procter, a Grimsby trawler-owner who also owned the Lord Nelson pub in Brigg, Lincolnshire. He kept the mare with Crump.

Under bright sunshine, of the forty-three runners only MUSICAL LAD dwelt at the start. LOUGH CONN and CLONCARRIG made the running in the early part of the race, but those in the vicinity of the Brook saw the downfall of the favourite SILVER FAME. CLONCARRIG blundered the Chair, allowing FIRST OF THE DANDIES to go on in front over the Water. As they came back into the country LOUGH CONN burst a

ZAHIA leads over the Water Jump from HAPPY HOME, LE DAIM and SHEILA'S COTTAGE

blood vessel, leaving Jimmy Fitzgerald with no alternative but to pull him up and at the fence after Becher's PRINCE REGENT was carried out by a loose horse. FIRST OF THE DANDIES was still going strongly in front, chased by his nearest rivals ZAHIA, HAPPY HOME, SHEILA'S COTTAGE and CROMWELL who by now was going better than any. It was somewhere about this point that Mildmay's Aintree jinx struck again. Many months before, Lord Mildmay had broken his neck in a fall at Folkestone, since when he had often been afflicted with sudden crippling cramp in his neck muscles and at the worst possible moment the painful problem occurred again. His head fell forward, and with his chin resting on his chest CROMWELL's rider became nothing more than a passenger. Coming to the second last FIRST OF THE DANDIES was joined by ZAHIA, seemingly full of running and looking like providing another 100/1 shock result. Eddie Reavey, however, mistook the course after landing safely and to everyone's amazement took ZAHIA wide of the final fence. Over the last with a clear lead FIRST OF THE DANDIES set

course for home, but Arthur Thompson timed his run on SHEILA'S COTTAGE to perfection, drawing level a hundred yards from the post and staying on the stronger to win by one length. Six lengths away in third place CROMWELL ran on, a most unlucky loser, with HAPPY HOME fourth and PLATYPUS fifth. The vile-tempered mare had become the first of her sex to win the 'National since SHANNON LASS in 1902. She provided her trainer Neville Crump with the recognition he richly deserved and to her equally brilliant jockey, Arthur Thompson, she presented a souvenir of their victory he would never forget. During a photographic session at Middleham the Monday after the race, SHEILA'S COTTAGE bit the top off one of Arthur's fingers, confirming the trainer's belief that she was 'an ornery old cow'. Strangely though, after an unsuccessful period at stud, SHEILA'S COTTAGE was given to Arthur Thompson and her final resting place is at the bottom of his garden in Wexford.

SHEILA'S COTTAGE and HAPPY HOME in hot pursuit of the leader at the last fence

1948

Of £100 each, £60 if declared by 9th March or £10 if declared by 3rd February. With £5,000 added (including a trophy value £200). For six-year-olds & upwards. The second to receive £1,106, the third £553 and the fourth £276. The trainer of the Winner to receive a cup value £50 and the rider of the Winner a cup value £25

Date: 20th March 1948	Starters: 43	Time: 9 mins 25⅖ secs
1st **SHEILA'S COTTAGE**	**9.10–7** *(Mr J Procter)*	**A P Thompson**
2nd **FIRST OF THE DANDIES**	**11.10–4** *(Major D J Vaughan)*	**J Brogan**
3rd **CROMWELL**	**7.10–11** *(Lord Mildmay)*	**Lord Mildmay**
4th **HAPPY HOME**	**9.11–10** *(Miss D Paget)*	**G Kelly**
5th **PLATYPUS**	**7.10–6** *(Mr R I Sainsbury)*	**A Jack**
6th **ROWLAND ROY**	**9.11–8** *(Mr A G Boley)*	**B Marshall**
7th **PARTHENON**	**9.10–0** *(Lord Bicester)*	**P Murray**
8th **MALTESE WANDERER**	**9.10–0** *(Mr G J Wells)*	**K Gilsenan**
9th **OFFALY PRINCE**	**9.10–5** *(Mr G C Judd)*	**Mr A Parker**
10th **KLAXTON**	**8.11–8** *(Mr T Radmall)*	**R Smyth**
11th **WAR RISK**	**9.11–1** *(Mrs J Rogerson)*	**R Turnell**
12th **REVELRY**	**8.11–6** *(Mr J D Clark)*	**D Moore**
13th **SCHUBERT**	**14.10–2** *(Mrs K Cameron)*	**L McMorrow**
14th **LOVELY COTTAGE**	**11.11–4** *(Mr J Morant)*	**C Hook** [remounted]

Also Ran:

ROIMOND 7.11–7 (Lord Bicester) **R Black** *Fell*; *CADDIE II 10.11–7* (Mr P Mellon) **J Maguire** *Fell*; *SILVER FAME 9.11–6* (Lord Bicester) **M Molony** *Fell*; *BRICETT 11.11–3* (Mr H Linsley) **T Molony** *Fell*; *REARMAMENT 11.11–2* (Mrs C D Wilson) **D Ruttle** *Fell*; *CLONCARRIG 8.10–13* (Sir Allan Gordon-Smith) **Mr J Hislop** *Fell*; *CLONABOY 10.10–10* (Mr A H Wood) **E Hannigan** *Fell*; *GORMANSTOWN 8.10–9* (Mr C Nicholson) **M Hogan** *Fell*; *HOUSEWARMER 11.10–6* (Miss D Paget) **H Nicholson** *Fell*; *SIR JOHN 7.10–3* (Mr F Dyson) **Major C Blacker** *Fell*; *TUDOR CLOSE 11.10–3* (Mr P D Turner) **T Maher** *Fell*; *LOYAL ANTRIM 11.10–3* (Mr S Martin) **E Newman** *Fell*; *ULSTER MONARCH 9.10–1* (Mr N P Donaldson) **Capt J Eustace-Smith** *Fell*; *MUSICAL LAD 11.10–1* (Mr L Michaelson) **M Browne** *Fell*; *ULTRA BENE 9.10–1* (Lord Mildmay) **A Grantham** *Fell*; *LE DAIM 9.10–1* (Mrs G I Osborne) **S Pinch** *Fell*; *SODA II 7.10–0* (Mrs V M Pulham) **H Bonneau** *Fell*; *HIGHLAND LAD 9.10–0* (Mrs A H Watts) **E Kennedy** *Fell*; *SOME CHICKEN 11.10–0* (Mr J J Cleaver) **W Redmond** *Fell*; *SERPENTINE 10.10–0* (Mr D P O'Brien) **C Mitchell** *Fell*; *BORA'S COTTAGE 10.10–0* (Mr F L Vickerman) **E Vinall** *Fell*; *TOMMY TRADDLES 7.10–0* (Mr J S Schilizzi) **C Harrison** *Unseated rider*; *WEEVIL 9.10–11* (Mr D Morris) **V Mooney** *Brought-down*; *HALCYON HOURS 8.11–5* (Mr F More O'Ferrall) **M C Prendergast** *Refused*; *CAUGHOO 9.11–1* (Mr J J McDowell) **E Dempsey** *Pulled-up*; *LOUGH CONN 12.10–5* (Mrs M Rowe) **J Fitzgerald** *Pulled-up*; *SKOURAS 8.10–0* (Mr R Collen) **A Power** *Pulled-up*; *PRINCE REGENT 13.12–2* (Mr J V Rank) **T Hyde** *Carried out*; *ZAHIA 8.10–2* (Mr F N Gee) **E Reavey** *Took wrong course*

The Betting: *9/1 Silver Fame; 100/9 Rowland Roy; 22/1 Roimond, Cloncarrig, Loyal Antrim & Lough Conn; 25/1 Prince Regent, Housewarmer & First of the Dandies; 28/1 Caughoo; 33/1 Revelry, War Risk, Cromwell, Weevil & Happy Home; 40/1 Klaxton & Soda II; 50/1 Caddie II, Some Chicken, Halcyon Hours, Sheila's Cottage & Highland Lad; 66/1 Rearmament, Lovely Cottage, Schubert, Platypus, Clonaboy & Gormanstown; 100/1 Others.*

Distances: *One length; six lengths*

Winner Trained By: *Neville Crump, Middleham, Yorkshire*

Value to Winning Owner: *£9,103*

1949

Lord Sefton sold Aintree racecourse to Tophams Limited in 1949 for a figure reputed to be in the region of £275,000, thus enabling the family who had been associated with Aintree for over a century to become outright owners instead of lessees. The enterprising Mirabel Topham celebrated the occasion by not only enlarging the spring meeting to a four-day affair but by instituting a new steeplechase over one circuit of the 'National course. This new race was called The Topham Trophy Steeplechase and provided some consolation for Jimmy Brogan's narrow defeat in last year's big race, for he took the prize on 20/1 shot CADAMSTOWN. The Champion 'Chase provided an excellent curtain-raiser on the second day with an eight-year-old named FREEBOOTER giving a flawless display over the big fences, prompting many to believe they had seen a Grand National winner in the making.

Mrs Mirabel Topham who was to become synonymous with the great race that her family had served for so many years

In a field of the same number as last year, CROMWELL was a popular favourite at 6/1, the conviction and hope being that Lord Mildmay would this time find that essential element of luck without which no 'National victory is possible. Miss Paget's HAPPY HOME came next in the market, with CAVALIERO, ROYAL MOUNT, CLONCARRIG and BRICETT also well supported. Top weight with 11 st 12 lbs was Lord Bicester's stylish young chestnut ROIMOND, a 22/1 chance providing Dick Francis with a first ride in the race.

Along with twenty-two others listed at 66/1 was a nine-year-old gelding called RUSSIAN HERO who had made the short journey from Malpas in Cheshire as the hope of his owner-breeder Fernie Williamson and trainer George Owen, the former jump jockey. By PETER THE GREAT out of LOGIQUE, RUSSIAN HERO was a very chancy jumper, considered unable to stay beyond two and a half miles and few apart from his connections gave him a second thought. Irishman Leo McMorrow, virtually unknown in England, took the mount.

MONAVEEN was prominent over the first fence but Irish challenger SAGACITY slipped on the run to the next fence. REPLICA went out at the fourth followed at the next by CAUGHOO, whose bridle came so badly adrift that the former winner ran-out. ACTHON MAJOR was in front over Becher's, but there were a great number of fallers on the way back to the racecourse. With ROIMOND in command from WOT NO SUN, ROYAL MOUNT, CROMWELL and MONAVEEN at the Water, RUSSIAN HERO came into the reckoning. ROYAL MOUNT held a slight advantage over ROIMOND jumping Becher's for the final time, though WOT NO SUN fell and ROYAL COTTAGE refused, shooting his jockey Dick Black over and into the Brook. ROYAL MOUNT was jumping beautifully some three lengths in front of ROIMOND over the Canal Turn where McMorrow began making ground on the leaders with RUSSIAN HERO. A bad mistake at the fence after Valentine's cost ROYAL MOUNT the lead, and RUSSIAN HERO and ROIMOND dashed past, duelling all the way back to the racecourse. Confounding the experts, RUSSIAN HERO stayed the better, jumping the last fence clear and running out a convincing eight length winner from ROIMOND, who was just a length in front of ROYAL MOUNT. CROMWELL was fourth. The owner, a tenant farmer of the Duke of Westminster, had backed his long-shot for £10 at 300/1. He probably didn't mind that the horse never won another race.

Mention must be made of the Liverpool Foxhunters' Steeplechase, which was run for the last time this year over the identical 'National course and distance. The winner was BALLYHARTFIELD, ridden by Mr John Straker. Another member of this old Northumbrian sporting family was to figure prominently some thirty years later in the 'National's moment of truth.

The field swings away from the Canal Turn

RUSSIAN HERO passes the Post

1949

Of £100 each, £60 if declared by 8th March or £10 if declared by 1st February. With £5,000 added (including a trophy value £300). For six-year-olds & upwards. The second to receive £1,158, the third £579 and the fourth £289. The trainer of the Winner to receive a cup value £50 and the rider of the Winner a cup value £25

Date: 26th March 1949	Starters: 43	Time: 9 mins 24⅕ secs
1st **RUSSIAN HERO**	**9.10–8** *(Mr W F Williamson)*	**L McMorrow**
2nd **ROIMOND**	**8.11–12** *(Lord Bicester)*	**R Francis**
3rd **ROYAL MOUNT**	**10.10–12** *(Mrs May Harvey)*	**P J Doyle**
4th **CROMWELL**	**8.11–3** *(Lord Mildmay)*	**Lord Mildmay**
5th **FLAMING STEEL**	**8.10–9** *(Mr A D Wimbush)*	**Mr J Spencer**
6th **HAPPY HOME**	**10.11–10** *(Miss D Paget)*	**B Marshall**
7th **TONDERMAN**	**12.10–4** *(Mr J Bloom)*	**Mr J Bloom**
8th **LUCKY PURCHASE**	**11.10–2** *(Mrs S C Banks)*	**A Jack**
9th **BRICETT**	**12.10–9** *(Mr H Linsley)*	**T Molony** [remounted]
10th **CLYDUFFE**	**14.10–0** *(Mr A A Stuart Black)*	**J Power**
11th **PERFECT NIGHT**	**11.10–0** *(Mr A F M Wright)*	**Mr D Ancil** [remounted]

Also Ran:

CLONCARRIG 9.11–7 (Sir Allan Gordon-Smith) **K Gilsenan** *Fell*; *ULSTER MONARCH 10.11–2* (Mr N P Donaldson) **R Curran** *Fell*; *CAVALIERO 8.11–1* (Mr W R Porter) **J Brogan** *Fell*; *ACTHON MAJOR 9.10–11* (Mrs J S Gorman) **R J O'Ryan** *Fell*; *CADDIE II 11.10–10* (Mr P Mellon) **J Maguire** *Fell*; *LEAP MAN 12.10–10* (Mr A W Fletcher) **E Vinall** *Fell*; *BRUNO II 9.10–9* (Major W J Anstruther-Gray) **M Pringle** *Fell*; *GALLERY 11.10–8* (Mr J Davey) **G Slack** *Brought-down*; *SAN MICHELE 9.10–5* (Mr H W Metcalf) **Mr J Boddy** *Fell*; *ASTRA 8.10–4* (Mr J W Ellis) **A P Thompson** *Fell*; *MAGNETIC FIN 10.10–4* (Mr N Willis) **L Vick** *Fell*; *LOYAL ANTRIM 12.10–4* (Mr S Martin) **Mr A Scannell** *Fell*; *BORA'S COTTAGE 11.10–3* (Mr F L Vickerman) **E Kennedy** *Fell*; *MONAVEEN 8.10–3* (Mr D Hawkesley) **A Grantham** *Fell*; *WOT NO SUN 7.10–3* (Major T D Wilson) **G Kelly** *Fell*; *REPLICA 11.10–3* (Mr R K Mellon) **E Reavey** *Fell*; *ARRANBEG 12.10–2* (Mrs V H Parr) **R McCarthy** *Fell*; *MARTIN M 9.10–1* (Major W H Skrine) **Major W H Skrine** *Fell*; *SOUTHBOROUGH 11.10–1* (Contessa di Sant Elia) **P Murray** *Fell*; *STONE COTTAGE 8.10–1* (Mr C Nicholson) **M Hogan** *Fell*; *CELTIC CROSS 11.10–0* (Mr T Southern) **J Parkin** *Fell*; *MORNING STAR II 10.10–0* (Major J F Gresham) **G Bowden** *Fell*; *SHIP'S BELL 9.10–0* (Mrs M Parker) **M O'Dwyer** *Fell*; *OFFALY PRINCE 10.10–4* (Mr G C Judd) **Mr A Parker** *Fell*; *BARN DANCE 10.10–0* (Mrs E G Williams) **E Newman** *Fell*; *PARTHENON 10.10–5* (Lord Bicester) **R Bates** *Fell*; *SAGACITY 11.10–0* (Mr J McCann) **A Power** *Fell*; *BRIGHTER SANDY 11.11–2* (Mr T M Barker) **R Turnell** *Brought-down*; *ARDNACASSA 11.10–5* (Mr S H Martin) **M Connors** *Brought-down*; *SEN TOI 14.10–5* (Mr J J Cleaver) **T Cusack** *Brought-down*; *ROYAL COTTAGE 9.10–12* (Mr H E Prettyman) **R Black** *Refused*; *CAUGHOO 10.11–0* (Mr J J McDowell) **D McCann** *Ran-out*

The Betting: *6/1 Cromwell; 10/1 Happy Home; 100/8 Cavaliero; 18/1 Cloncarrig & Royal Mount; 20/1 Bricett; 22/1 Roimond; 28/1 Ulster Monarch; 33/1 Flaming Steel & Royal Cottage; 40/1 Brighter Sandy, Gallery & Wot No Sun; 50/1 Acthon Major, Astra, Magnetic Fin, Loyal Antrim, Bora's Cottage, Monaveen, Barn Dance & Lucky Purchase; 66/1 Others.*

Distances: *Eight lengths; one length*

Winner Trained By: *George Owen, Malpas, Cheshire*

Value to Winning Owner: *£9,528*

1950

Through his brilliant example, boundless energy and obvious devotion to steeplechasing, Lord Mildmay had become the finest ambassador the sport could ever have wished for. Perhaps the crowning achievement of his countless contributions to racing over the sticks came when, towards the end of the 1949 season, Her Majesty Queen Elizabeth allowed Mildmay's intense enthusiasm to persuade her into becoming a National Hunt owner. Set with the difficult task of finding a horse worthy of carrying the Royal colours, Lord Mildmay and Peter Cazalet finally and with

some difficulty managed to secure the Irish-bred MONAVEEN, which had run well for a long way in the most recent 'National. Thus Her Majesty became the first British Queen since Queen Anne to be involved in racing as an owner and as if conscious of the fact, MONAVEEN won first time out at Fontwell in the colours of HRH Princess Elizabeth who was the joint owner with her mother. Making their future plans obvious, trainer Peter Cazalet next aimed the Royal runner at the Aintree's Grand Sefton 'Chase, where MONAVEEN was only outpaced in the closing stages by the Yorkshire-trained

A vast crowd assembled for a Royal occasion

FREEBOOTER, who was becoming something of a Liverpool specialist. Reversing the placings in Hurst Park's valuable Queen Elizabeth Steeplechase, MONAVEEN approached the 1950 'National the winner of his last three races with a high position in the market. The presence of The King and Queen, accompanied by their two daughters, was an added attraction to the huge crowds cramming into the racecourse on a perfect spring day, and the fact that it was forty-two years since a Royal competitor last ran in the race was not lost on the press. Joint favourites at 10/1 of the forty-nine runners were ROIMOND and FREEBOOTER.

The King and Queen inspect the fences before the race

Bred in County Waterford by Mr W F Phelan, by STEEL POINT out of PROUD FURY, FREEBOOTER was sold as a three-year-old for 620 guineas to Dan Moore, who two years later passed him onto Mrs Lurline Brotherton for almost five times that amount. In the hands of trainer Bobby Renton the powerful gelding went from strength to strength. FREEBOOTER's regular partner, twenty-six-year-old Jimmy Power, also hailed from Waterford.

After a good start the action came thick and fast, RUSSIAN HERO falling at the first when trying to match strides with the leader MONAVEEN, who went on in front of ROIMOND, FREEBOOTER, STOCKMAN and INCHMORE. Four fell at the Brook, five went out at the next fence, two at the Canal Turn, another five lost interest at Valentine's and at the next ditch CROMWELL and Lord Mildmay fell. The course was by now littered with riderless horses, but still out in front and going strongly was MONAVEEN from CLONCARRIG, ACTHON MAJOR, SAINTFIELD, FREEBOOTER and SHAGREEN. At the fence before the Chair the Royal runner hit the obstacle, but with incredible skill Tony Grantham held on as his mount dropped back several places. It was FREEBOOTER's turn next when he struck the Chair with his chest, a mistake which would have turned most horses over. The recovery the horse made was equalled by the brilliance of jockey Jimmy Power who was left clinging to FREEBOOTER's neck for agonising moments before regaining his place in the saddle. After allowing him time to recover, Jimmy Power was steadily making up his ground on FREEBOOTER and with a superb leap over the Brook landed in third place. SHAGREEN fell at the next fence followed by the leader ANGEL HILL at the Canal Turn and from here on it became a virtual match between FREEBOOTER and CLONCARRIG. Some way behind came WOT NO SUN, ACTHON MAJOR and MONAVEEN but as they crossed the Melling Road all eyes were on the two out in front. At the second last Bob Turnell on CLONCARRIG held a slight lead, only to clip the top of the fence and come down in a diving fall. FREEBOOTER came home a most convincing winner by fifteen lengths. WOT NO SUN ran on to take second place, a further ten lengths ahead of ACTHON MAJOR, who was followed in by ROWLAND ROY, MONAVEEN, SHIP'S BELL and INCHMORE. The first three home were all Yorkshire-trained. Receiving a hero's welcome, FREEBOOTER was hailed as the best winner of the race since GOLDEN MILLER.

THE GRAND NATIONAL HANDICAP STEEPLECHASE
1950

Of £100 each, £60 if declared by 7th March or £10 if declared by 31st January. With £5,000 added (including a trophy value £200). For six-year-olds & upwards. The second to receive £1,132, the third £566 and the fourth £283. The trainer of the Winner to receive a cup value £50 and the rider of the Winner a cup value £25

Date: 25th March 1950	Starters: 49	Time: 9 mins 24⅕ secs
1st **FREEBOOTER**	9.11–11 *(Mrs L Brotherton)*	**J Power**
2nd **WOT NO SUN**	8.11–8 *(Major T D Wilson)*	**A P Thompson**
3rd **ACTHON MAJOR**	10.11–2 *(Mrs J S Gorman)*	**R J O'Ryan**
4th **ROWLAND ROY**	11.11–7 *(Mr A G Boley)*	**R Black**
5th **MONAVEEN**	9.10–13 *(HRH Princess Elizabeth)*	**A Grantham**
6th **SHIP'S BELL**	10.10–0 *(Mrs M Parker)*	**M O'Dwyer**
7th **INCHMORE**	13.10–0 *(Mr H C Falconer)*	**R Curran**

Also Ran:

GARDE TOI 9.12–1 (Marquis de Portago) **Marquis de Portago** *Fell*; *ROIMOND 9.12–1* (Lord Bicester) **R Francis** *Fell*; *KLAXTON 10.11–13* (Mr W D Gibson) **J Maguire** *Fell*; *CLONCARRIG 10.11–9* (Sir Allan Gordon-Smith) **R Turnell** *Fell*; *SHAGREEN 9.11–8* (Mr J V Rank) **G Kelly** *Fell*; *CAVALIERO 9.11–6* (Mr W R Porter) **J A Bullock** *Fell*; *RUSSIAN HERO 10.11–4* (Mr W F Williamson) **L McMorrow** *Fell*; *CROMWELL 9.11–4* (Lord Mildmay) **Lord Mildmay** *Fell*; *STOCKMAN 8.11–1* (Mr R G Patton) **D Thomas** *Fell*; *ROYAL MOUNT 11.11–0* (Mr T Goodall) **Mr A Corbett** *Fell*; *MERMAID IV 11.11–0* (Mr T B Palmer) **Mr T B Palmer** *Fell*; *BATTLING PEDULAS 11.10–11* (Mr J Lipton) **D Marzani** *Fell*; *CASTLEDERMOT 8.10–9* (Mrs M H Keogh) **T Molony** *Fell*; *GALLERY 12.10–8* (Sir Arthur Pilkington) **G Slack** *Fell*; *CADAMSTOWN 10.10–8* (Mr R McIlhagga) **E Dempsey** *Fell*; *ARDNACASSA 12.10–5* (Mr S H Martin) **Mr T Brookshaw** *Fell*; *SODA II 9.10–5* (Mrs V M Pulham) **K Mullins** *Fell*; *KNOCKIRR 10.10–4* (Mrs V Taylor) **T Cusack** *Fell*; *ANGEL HILL 10.10–3* (Capt T R Colville) **T Shone** *Fell*; *COTTAGE WELCOME 11.10–3* (Mr E Dobson) **C Hook** *Fell*; *INVERLOCHY 11.10–3* (Mr F S Dyson) **P J Doyle** *Fell*; *BARNEY VI 12.10–2* (Mr W Quirke) **T P Burns** *Fell*; *SKOURAS 10.10–2* (Mr A G Delahooke) **M Browne** *Unseated rider*; *COLUMN 10.10–2* (Mr A Sainsbury) **A Mullins** *Brought-down*; *POSSIBLE 10.10–1* (Duchess of Norfolk) **P Conlon** *Fell*; *TOMMY TRADDLES 9.10–1* (Mr J S Schilizzi) **F O'Connor** *Fell*; *CONFUCIUS 9.10–0* (Mr J P Frost) **C O'Connor** *Pulled-up*; *SAN MICHELE 10.10–0* (Mrs E Metcalfe) **J Boddy** *Fell*; *HIGHLAND COTTAGE 10.10–0* (Mr C Nicholson) **M Hogan** *Fell*; *LIMESTONE COTTAGE 10.10–0* (Mr A Cooper) **J Dowdeswell** *Fell*; *PASTIME 9.10–0* (Brig R O Critchley) **C Sleator** *Fell*; *SOUTHBOROUGH 12.10–0* (Contessa di Sant Elia) **E Reavey** *Fell*; *IVAN'S CHOICE 9.10–0* (Mr H J Jones) **P J O'Brien** *Fell*; *OLE MAN RIVER 8.10–0* (Mr A Dickinson) **G Bonas** *Fell*; *COMERAGH 9.11–0* (Major Noel Furlong) **P J Kelly** *Fell*; *ZARTER 10.10–0* (Capt I A Henderson) **Mr J Straker** *Fell*; *DYNOVI 9.10–0* (Mr G Coxon) **A Jack** *Brought-down*; *FIGHTING LINE 11.10–8* (Mrs C A Hall-Hall) **Mr E Greenway** *Refused*; *SAINTFIELD 13.10–0* (Lt Col N M H Wall) **Mr M Gosling** *Refused*; *HAPPY RIVER 7.10–12* (Mrs P P Hogan) **D McCann** *Pulled-up*; *BINGHAMSTOWN 11.10–7* (Mr L Furman) **Mr L Furman** *Pulled-up*; *SAFETY LOCH 9.10–0* (Mrs J H Thursby) **Mr D Punshon** *Pulled-up*

The Betting: *10/1 Roimond & Freebooter; 100/7 Wot No Sun & Monaveen; 18/1 Cromwell; 20/1 Shagreen & Castledermot; 22/1 Russian Hero; 25/1 Cloncarrig; 28/1 Gallery; 33/1 Acthon Major, Soda II & Angel Hill; 40/1 Klaxton, Rowland Roy, Royal Mount, Happy River & Confucius; 50/1 Battling Pedulas, Fighting Line, Inverlochy, Possible & Comeragh; 66/1 Cavaliero, Cadamstown, Knockirr, Tommy Traddles, Ship's Bell, Highland Cottage, Pastime & Zarter; 100/1 Others.*

Distances: *Fifteen lengths; ten lengths*

Winner Trained By: *Robert Renton, Ripon, Yorkshire*

Value to Winning Owner: *£9,314*

Mr P O'Connor joins P Double for a worm's-eye view of the race in 1983. They have departed from O'ER THE BORDER and SYDNEY QUINN respectively. *(Kris Photography)*.

A bird's-eye view of the course photographed in 1976. The stands are at the top of the picture. *(Kris Photography).*

Below left: After the victory of LAST SUSPECT, a delighted Duchess of Westminster receives the winner's trophy in 1985 from Mrs Bronfman, wife of the Canadian chairman of Seagram. On the left is Mr Ivan Straker, Chairman of Seagrams UK.

Bottom left: The immensely popular CORBIERE parading with Ben de Haan up.

Below right; Geraldine Rees who became the first woman to complete the course in 1982. *(John Mullen).*

The agony . . . Mr R Beggan leaves CARL'S WAGER by the side door at the Chair in 1984 . . . The ecstacy . . . at Becher's first time in the same year EARTHSTOPPER touches down just in front of the grey TWO SWALLOWS. *(Kris Photography)*.

Two of the great horsemen of the post-war period, neither of whom had the luck to win the Grand National but both of whom have turned their enormous talent to writing marvellous thrillers with a racing background. Dick Francis and John Francome. *(John Mullen).*
Below: The story they wouldn't have dared to write as fiction! Bob Champion brings home Aldaniti to win the race in 1981. *(Sport and General).*

Two views of Aintree hero RED RUM. He is photographed *(above)* with another legendary character Mrs Mirabel Topham and *(below)* at Haydock Park making the very last public jump of his racing career. *(Ossie Dale; Kris Photography).*

HALLO DANDY and Neal Doughty clear the last in front of the popular Irish Challenger GREASEPAINT in 1984, *(above)* while at the half-way point of the race in 1985, LAST SUSPECT and Hywel Davies, on the left of the picture in yellow, are well placed to provide a shock result. *(Kris Photography).*

Richard Dunwoody, regarded by many as a future champion, brings the eventual winner WEST TIP upsides CLASSIFIED at the fourteenth fence in 1986, *(above)*. The famous Joel colours of the black jacket and red cap can be spotted as Steve Knight heads for home on MAORI VENTURE in 1987. *(Kris Photography; John Green).*

All the glory of Aintree captured in Mike Powel's photograph of the 1983 race. FORTINA'S EXPRESS is nearest the camera with HALLO DANDY visible beyond. *(All-Sport)*.

1951

The tragic and untimely death by drowning of Lord Mildmay, shortly after his last 'National ride on CROMWELL, left not only the darkest of shadows over racing but the deepest sense of loss to all who admire bravery, enthusiasm and genuine sportsmanship. Wherever he rode, Anthony Mildmay added a dignity yet a sense of excitement to the occasion and the cries from the Silver Ring of 'C'mon M'Lord' were an indication of the affectionate esteem in which he was held.

Lord Mildmay, on the right of the picture, in characteristic pose with the King and Queen in the Aintree paddock in 1950

American 'Jock' Whitney was back with a vengeance in 1951, providing the favourite ARCTIC GOLD, a six-year-old chestnut unbeaten in his last three races. At 8/1 he was two points clear of FREE-BOOTER, SHAGREEN and CLONCARRIG. Since winning last year's race FREEBOO-TER had won only one small three-mile affair at Haydock, giving credence to the view that success in the 'National ruined the future careers of horses. Now he had to concede weight to all in the thirty-six runner field. The former owner of Aintree, Lord Sefton, ran IRISH LIZARD ridden by Irishman Pat Taaffe, whose first mount in the race this was and other up-and-coming riders making their 'National debuts were Fred Winter with GLEN FIRE, Dave Dick on ROWLAND ROY and Mr Michael Scudamore on EAST A'CALLING. Ireland sent over a smaller contingent than usual, three in all, SHAGREEN, DER-RINSTOWN and ROYAL TAN. Trained by Vincent O'Brien, a man rapidly making his mark on the jumping scene, this young chestnut was ridden by Mr 'Phonsie' O'Brien, the trainer's brother.

It was probably the poor record of mares in the race which allowed NICKEL COIN to be available in the betting at 40/1, for she was the winner of six races to date, was an out-and-out stayer and was not without a touch of class. Her sire PAY UP won the 1936 Two Thousand Guineas as well as finishing fourth in The Derby. Bred by Richard Corbett, NICKEL COIN cost Mr Jeffrey Royle 50 guineas as a yearling but with a good deal of regret he parted with her after a couple of years. Using a portion of his army gratuity, Frank Royle bought the mare back for his father upon demobilisation and after time as a successful show-jumper, NICKEL COIN was put into training with Jack O'Donaghue at Reigate. Her partner in the 'National was John Bullock, an ex-paratrooper and prisoner-of-war, who had fallen at Becher's last year with CAVALIERO.

As the field came under starter's orders at least half the runners were still milling around, their riders deciding which position to take in the line-up, when to the amazement of everyone the starter Mr Leslie Firth pressed the lever releasing the barrier. Even more astonishingly there was no false-start recall signal given and one of the maddest scrambles ever witnessed on a racecourse began as jockeys tried desperately to make up lost ground. Melling Road was crossed in a mad dash and no less than twelve, a third of the field, came to grief before even half a mile was covered. Among those caught up in the chaos at the first fence were FINNURE, LAND FORT, STALBRIDGE ROCK, EAST A'CALLING and Lord Sefton's IRISH LIZARD and for many all interest went from the race when at the next fence FREEBOOTER was brought down by the falling GALLERY. ARCTIC GOLD, in his usual front-running style, avoided the shambles to lead over Becher's from ROWLAND ROY, CAESAR'S WIFE, RUSSIAN HERO, ROIMOND and NICKEL COIN but the catalogue of disaster continued. Three more went out at the seventh and a further five at the Canal

Turn, and the field was soon whittled down to just seven runners. RUSSIAN HERO led his stable mate DOG WATCH back onto the racecourse, their efforts coming to naught when both came down at the Chair and the dumbstruck crowds in the stands watched Dick Curran on GAY HEATHER lead NICKEL COIN, DERRINSTOWN, ROYAL TAN and BROOMFIELD over the Water. GAY HEATHER crumpled on landing at Becher's bringing down DERRINSTOWN. BROOMFIELD went at the next, leaving just NICKEL COIN and ROYAL TAN to make their lonely way home. Holding a narrow advantage coming into the last fence, ROYAL TAN ruined his chance with a bad mistake and Johnny Bullock swept to the front on NICKEL COIN, bringing the mare home six lengths clear. A long way behind came the remounted DERRINSTOWN to collect third place prize money.

The press were understandably vociferous in their condemnation of 'The Grand Crashional', and while Mr Royle and his considerate son Frank celebrated their wisdom in buying back NICKEL COIN, for many people the Grand National had lost a little of its magic through one man's momentary error.

THE GRAND NATIONAL HANDICAP STEEPLECHASE
1951

Of £100 each, £60 if declared by 20th March or £10 if declared by 6th February. With £5,000 added (including a trophy value £300). For six-year-olds & upwards. The second to receive £1,040, the third £520 and the fourth 2½% of the whole stakes. The trainer of the Winner to receive a cup value £50 and the rider of the Winner a cup value £25

Date: 7th April 1951	Starters: 36	Time: 9 mins 48⅘ secs
1st **NICKEL COIN**	**9.10–1** *(Mr J Royle)*	**J A Bullock**
2nd **ROYAL TAN**	**7.10–13** *(Mrs M H Keogh)*	**Mr A S O'Brien**
3rd **DERRINSTOWN**	**11.10–0** *(Mr P Digney)*	**A Power** [remounted]

Also Ran:

FREEBOOTER 10.12–7 (Mrs L Brotherton) **J Power** *Brought-down*; *SHAGREEN 10.12–2* (Mr J V Rank) **G Kelly** *Fell*; *CLONCARRIG 11.12–0* (Mr J Olding) **R Turnell** *Fell*; *ROIMOND 10.12–0* (Lord Bicester) **A Jarvis** *Fell*; *FINNURE 10.12–0* (Lord Bicester) **R Francis** *Fell*; *LAND FORT 7.11–3* (Mr H Oliver) **B Marshall** *Fell*; *RUSSIAN HERO 11.11–1* (Mr W F Williamson) **L McMorrow** *Fell*; *ARCTIC GOLD 6.10–13* (Mr J H Whitney) **T Molony** *Fell*; *SERGEANT KELLY 10.10–12* (Mr F C Brambleby) **R De'Ath** *Brought-down*; *ROWLAND ROY 12.10–12* (Mr A G Boley) **D V Dick** *Fell*; *PRINCE BROWNIE 9.10–9* (Lady Carew-Pole) **A Grantham** *Fell*; *ARMOURED KNIGHT 7.10–8* (Mr G H Dowty) **T Cusack** *Brought-down*; *STALBRIDGE ROCK 8.10–5* (Mr R Bazell) **Mr R McCreery** *Fell*; *CADAMSTOWN 11.10–4* (Mr A E Bullen) **J Dowdeswell** *Fell*; *GALLERY 13.10–4* (Sir Arthur Pilkington) **A Mullins** *Fell*; *DOG WATCH 10.10–2* (Mr A Lloyd) **T Brookshaw** *Fell*; *EAST A'CALLING 10.10–2* (Mr C F Knipe) **Mr M J Scudamore** *Brought-down*; *PARTPOINT 9.10–5* (Major A C Straker) **A P Thompson** *Fell*; *STOCKMAN 9.10–2* (Mrs E D Thacker) **G Vergette** *Brought-down*; *BROOMFIELD 10.10–4* (Mr W P Westhead) **R Emery** *Fell*; *IRISH LIZARD 8.10–1* (Lord Sefton) **P Taaffe** *Brought-down*; *GLEN FIRE 8.10–1* (Mr S Mercer) **F T Winter** *Fell*; *TEXAS DAN 9.10–1* (Mr H Riddell) **P Fitzgerald** *Brought-down*; *CONFUCIUS 10.10–0* (Mr J Mayson) **M O'Dwyer** *Fell*; *QUEEN OF THE DANDIES 10.10–0* (Mrs R Fowler) **R Carter** *Fell*; *TASMAN 11.10–0* (Mr G Varnavas) **C Hook** *Refused*; *COLUMN 11.10–1* (Sir Arthur Pilkington) **Mr A Corbett** *Fell*; *GAY HEATHER 10.10–0* (Mr J D Paisley) **R Curran** *Fell*; *MORNING COVER 10.10–0* (Mrs E G Williams) **G Slack** *Fell*; *REVEALED 11.10–0* (Mr W Francis) **Mr W Beynon-Brown** *Fell*; *CAESAR'S WIFE 9.10–8* (Mr G B Rogers) **Mr G B Rogers** *Fell*; *BINGHAMSTOWN 12.10–0* (Mr L Furman) **Mr L Furman** *Fell*; *PARSONSHILL 12.10–2* (Mr J Seely) **Mr J Seely** *Fell*

The Betting: *8/1 Arctic Gold; 10/1 Cloncarrig, Shagreen & Freebooter; 100/7 Roimond; 20/1 Land Fort; 22/1 Finnure & Royal Tan; 33/1 Prince Brownie, Dog Watch, Partpoint, Broomfield & Glen Fire; 40/1 Russian Hero, Sergeant Kelly, Nickel Coin & Morning Cover; 50/1 Gallery, Rowland Roy, Cadamstown, East A'Calling & Irish Lizard; 66/1 Armoured Knight, Stalbridge Rock, Texas Dan, Derrinstown & Gay Heather; 100/1 Others.*

Distances: *Six lengths; a bad third*

Winner Trained By: *Jack O'Donaghue, Reigate, Surrey*

Value to Winning Owner: *£8,815*

1952

Nothing could have been more ill-timed, following the calamitous events of 1951, than the dispute between Tophams Limited and the British Broadcasting Corporation over copyright of the race commentary. That Mrs Topham might well have had a justifiable claim in her arguments meant little to the majority who found themselves being denied radio coverage of the most exciting race of the year. At the last minute Tophams compromised to a degree by enlisting their own team of commentators but this was a disappointing alternative to the excellence the public had enjoyed from the BBC.

FREEBOOTER was back in favour after winning his first four races of the season, and not even his fall when favourite for the Cheltenham Gold Cup could deter punters from making the top weight their first choice in the betting at 10/1. Miss Paget ran LEGAL JOY, trained by Fulke Walwyn and ridden by Michael Scudamore. Nineteen-year-old Mr Gene Weymouth from Delaware, standing six-feet-three-inches rode his own twelve-year-old POSSIBLE, listed among the 100/1 others.

Representing the powerful Neville Crump stable were WOT NO SUN, SKYRE-HOLME and TEAL, the latter being the pick of the bunch with three wins under his belt in the current term. Bred by Gerald Carroll near Clonmel, TEAL was by BIMCO out of MILTOWN QUEEN and after being sold to Richard Gough of Tipperary for £35 was sent to England where for the same sum he was sold again. Under the ownership of Mr Ridley Lamb, the horse developed into a reliable jumper. Mr Harry Lane, a twenty-two-stone construction magnate from South Shields, paid a reputed £2,000 for TEAL and brimful of confidence, he chartered a train to bring six hundred of his employees to watch Arthur Thompson ride the gelding in the 'National.

On a cold, damp and misty day, the forty-seven runners were kept on their toes at the start by riders conscious of last year's trouble and mindful of the senior steward's cautionary advice to them about taking it easy into the first fence. Still a section of the field rushed the tape, breaking it and causing a delay of some twelve minutes. Then yet again the first fence took a terrific toll with ten horses, including EARLY MIST, RUSSIAN HERO and IRISH

LIZARD, coming down. TEAL and FREE-BOOTER led the way to Becher's in front of BROWN JACK III who was ridden by his owner, the Spanish Duke of Alburquerque. At the Water Jump, where only eighteen were still in the race, TEAL was still at the head of affairs. He gave Arthur Thompson an anxious moment at Becher's second time round when he came down on his nose, but the jockey's supreme horsemanship saved the day, although the error cost him the lead to FREEBOOTER. Bryan Marshall was on the top weight and still going well, but at the Canal Turn, he fell. The race now lay between TEAL, LEGAL JOY and ROYAL TAN, and an exciting finish looked likely. ROYAL TAN crashed at the last fence and with LEGAL JOY unable to quicken, TEAL passed the post five lengths in front of him. WOT NO SUN was a bad third. The victory provided both Neville Crump and Arthur Thompson with a second success in the race, but for the second year running, the 'National was tainted in the eyes of the public. So many fallers in the early stages led to more pontificating about the severity of the course. Worse still, to those unable to watch the race, was the amateur attempt to replace the BBC's commentary. The unhappy exercise had given TEAL as a faller at the first fence.

FREEBOOTER leads over the third fence from the Duke of Alburquerque on BROWN JACK III as R Morrow takes a spectacular tumble from WHISPERING STEEL

Date: 5th April 1952	Starters: 47	Time: 9 mins 21½ secs
1st **TEAL**	**10.10–12** *(Mr H Lane)*	**A P Thompson**
2nd **LEGAL JOY**	**9.10–4** *(Miss Dorothy Paget)*	**M Scudamore**
3rd **WOT NO SUN**	**10.11–7** *(Capt T D Wilson)*	**D V Dick**
4th **UNCLE BARNEY**	**9.10–4** *(Mr L Michaelson)*	**J Boddy**
5th **OVERSHADOW**	**12.10–5** *(Mrs J A Wood)*	**E Newman**
6th **PRINTERS PIE**	**8.10–0** *(Lt Col J Harrison)*	**G Slack**
7th **HIERBA**	**7.10–0** *(Mrs A Warman)*	**A Mullins**
8th **COLUMN**	**12.10–0** *(Sir Arthur Pilkington)*	**P Pickford**
9th **PARSONSHILL**	**13.10–1** *(Mr J Seely)*	**Mr J Seely**
10th **SERGEANT KELLY**	**11.10–9** *(Mr F C Brambleby)*	**R Cross** [remounted]

Also Ran:

FREEBOOTER 11.12–7 (Mrs L Brotherton) **B Marshall** *Fell*; *ROIMOND 11.11–13* (⸀ ord Bicester) **T Molony** *Fell*; *CLONCARRIG 12.11–13* (Mr W Dugdale) **Mr W Dugdale** *Fell*; *CARDINAL ERROR 8.11–8* (Lady Joicey) **J Power** *Brought-down*; *NAGARA 10.11–7* (Mr J P Phillips) **P Hieronimus** *Fell*; *ROYAL TAN 8.11–6* (Mr J H Griffin) **Mr A S O'Brien** *Fell*; *SKYREHOLME 9.11–3* (Mr C Booth) **R Francis** *Fell*; *KELEK 8.10–13* (Lady Hague) **C Hook** *Refused*; *SKOURAS 12.10–13* (Mr R Keith) **Mr R Keith** *Fell*; *DOMINICK'S BAR 8.10–13* (Mrs P Kiely) **A Prendergast** *Fell*; *TANTIVY 11.11–1* (Mr C Burns) **Mr M Westwick** *Fell*; *BORDER LUCK 7.10–12* (Mr J R Bower) **T Shone** *Unseated rider*; *RUSSIAN HERO 12.10–11* (Mr W F Williamson) **L McMorrow** *Fell*; *WHISPERING STEEL 7.10–11* (Mr F Dyson) **R Morrow** *Fell*; *EARLY MIST 7.10–11* (Mrs J V Rank) **P Taaffe** *Fell*; *ANOTHER DELIGHT 9.10–10* (Lord Lewes) **G Kelly** *Fell*; *POSSIBLE 12.11–0* (Mr E Weymouth) **Mr E Weymouth** *Fell*; *HAL'S VENTURE 7.10–8* (Mr C Olliff-Lee) **J Foster** *Fell*; *PEARLY PRINCE 9.10–5* (Mr A Leigh Boulter) **D Leslie** *Fell*; *MENZIES 10.10–4* (Mr J Gilman) **M O'Dwyer** *Brought-down*; *STARLIT BAY 8.10–3* (Lady Grimthorpe) **Mr C Straker** *Fell*; *IRISH LIZARD 9.10–3* (Lord Sefton) **R J Hamey** *Brought-down*; *INTER ALIA 9.10–3* (Mr G Barry) **C Sleator** *Fell*; *WOLFSCHMIDT 12.10–3* (Mr G Clark) **F O'Connor** *Fell*; *ICY CALM 9.11–0* (Marquis de Portago) **Marquis de Portago** *Pulled-up*; *BRONZE ARROW 10.10–2* (Mr J Straker) **Mr J Straker** *Fell*; *ST KATHLEEN II 9.10–2* (Mr S Small) **P J Doyle** *Fell*; *ROYAL STUART 9.10–3* (Lord Leverhulme) **T Brookshaw** *Refused*; *ROCKET VI 8.10–1* (Mr C Robinson) **V Speck** *Fell*; *TRAVELLER'S PRIDE 9.10–1* (Mr S Pickles) **L Stephens** *Fell*; *CAESAR'S WIFE 10.10–6* (Mr G Rogers) **Mr G Rogers** *Unseated rider*; *COURT PAINTER 12.10–0* (Lt Col E Harris-St John) **F Carroll** *Refused*; *GOLDEN SURPRISE 7.10–3* (Mr T Clarke) **Mr T Clarke** *Fell*; *CREAM OF THE BORDER 7.10–0* (Mr G Mackie) **A Kelly** *Refused*; *BROWN JACK III 8.10–10* (Duke of Alburquerque) **Duque de Alburquerque** *Fell*; *TAVOY 9.10–0* (Mr T Johnson) **D McCann** *Pulled-up*; *DERRINSTOWN 12.10–0* (Mr P Digney) **A Power** *Pulled-up*

The Betting: *10/1 Freebooter; 100/7 Teal; 100/6 Legal Joy; 18/1 Early Mist; 20/1 Border Luck; 22/1 Royal Tan & Overshadow; 25/1 Another Delight & Pearly Prince; 33/1 Icy Calm, Irish Lizard, Menzies, Roimond, Wot No Sun & Cardinal Error; 40/1 Skyreholme, Kelek, Brown Jack III & Whispering Steel; 45/1 Hal's Venture; 50/1 Caesar's Wife, Nagara, St Kathleen II, Starlit Bay, Cloncarrig, Cream of the Border, Royal Stuart, Russian Hero & Tantivy; 66/1 Dominick's Bar, Hierba, Inter Alia & Skouras; 100/1 Others.*

Distances: *Five lengths; a bad third*

Winner Trained By: *Neville Crump, Middleham, Yorkshire*

Value to Winning Owner: *£9,268*

1953

Frost blighted the first fixture scheduled to be run over the newly-built Mildmay Course in December 1952, the abandonment spoiling the plans of Tophams to celebrate its opening in a manner befitting the gallant gentleman whose name it bore. The November meeting at Liverpool, however, had thrown up some useful pointers for the next Grand National, LITTLE YID winning the Molyneux 'Chase and LARRY FINN capturing the Becher Steeplechase. Like FREEBOOTER before him, LITTLE YID came from the stable of Bobby Renton, was partnered by Jimmy Power and in a field devoid of obvious stars became the punters' first choice at 7/1. Last year's winner TEAL, the long-time ante-post favourite, sadly died after rupturing a gut during the Cheltenham Gold Cup. Lord Sefton's IRISH LIZARD was being asked to work overtime in the 'National, having two days before won the Topham Trophy 'Chase over one circuit of the course, and the task looked all the harder with jockey Bob Turnell putting up five pounds overweight.

ROYAL TAN missed this year's race through injury although his stable mate EARLY MIST was considered a more than useful substitute. By BRUMEUX out of SUDDEN DAWN, EARLY MIST was bred by Mr D J Wrinch and although a product of the mainland, most of his racing was conducted in Ireland in the colours of Mr J V Rank. Upon the death of that most popular of owners, EARLY MIST was sold at the dispersal to Vincent O'Brien for 5,300 guineas on behalf of Mr Joe Griffin, with Lord Bicester, like Mr Rank a man whose dream was to win the 'National, the underbidder. This year saw the smallest crowds for a long time, an indication perhaps that the events of recent 'Nationals had lessened its appeal. Nonetheless, the old thrill was there when the starter mounted his rostrum and Michael Scudamore took ORDNANCE straight to the front. There were plenty of fallers on the way to Becher's and skipping over the Canal Turn with a ten length lead, ORDNANCE was really stretching those that were left. EARLY MIST moved up to the girths of ORDNANCE as they jumped the nineteenth just ahead of LITTLE YID and MONT TREMBLANT with the remainder a good way back. After setting such a cracking pace and making all the running ORDNANCE fell at the next fence, leaving EARLY MIST the leader going into Becher's. Over and round the Canal Turn, EARLY MIST went further away and not even a slight mistake at the second last

The legendary Vincent O'Brien pictured in his more recent glory days on the Flat

fence could halt his progress. He passed the post twenty lengths clear of MONT TREMBLANT, and looked fit enough to go round again. IRISH LIZARD was a further four lengths back in third. Pat Taaffe on OVERSHADOW and Dick Francis with SENLAC HILL were the only others to finish. Trainer Vincent O'Brien received much praise for producing EARLY MIST in such all-conquering form just three weeks after saddling KNOCK HARD to win the Cheltenham Gold Cup. Bryan Marshall, who had survived a sniper's bullet in the closing days of the War, had given the gelding a superb ride and the team deserved the civic reception which awaited them in Dublin.

THE GRAND NATIONAL HANDICAP STEEPLECHASE

1953

With £6,000 added (including a trophy value £500). For six-year-olds & upwards. The second to receive 10%, the third 5% and the fourth 2½% of the whole stakes. The trainer of the Winner to receive a cup value £50 and the rider of the Winner a cup value £25

Date: 28th March 1953	Starters: 31	Time: 9 mins 22⅘ secs
1st **EARLY MIST**	8.11–2 *(Mr J H Griffin)*	**B Marshall**
2nd **MONT TREMBLANT**	7.12–5 *(Miss D Paget)*	**D V Dick**
3rd **IRISH LIZARD**	10.10–6 *(Lord Sefton)*	**R Turnell**
4th **OVERSHADOW**	13.10–4 *(Mrs J A Wood)*	**P Taaffe**
5th **SENLAC HILL**	8.10–10 *(Lord Bicester)*	**R Francis**

Also Ran:

CARDINAL ERROR 9.11–5 (Lady Joicey) **R Curran** *Fell*; CLONCARRIG 13.11–5 (Mr W S Dugdale) **Mr R McCreery** *Fell*; WHISPERING STEEL 8.10–13 (Mr F H Curnick) **R Morrow** *Brought-down*; LAND FORT 9.10–13 (Mr H Oliver) **Mr H Oliver, jnr** *Fell*; QUITE NATURALLY 9.10–8 (Mrs G Kohn) **T Molony** *Fell*; GLEN FIRE 10.10–8 (Mr S Mercer) **M Lynn** *Refused*; KNUCKLEDUSTER 9.11–0 (Mr P B Browne) **Mr P B Browne** *Pulled-up*; WITTY 8.10–5 (Mr C Nicholson) **G Slack** *Unseated rider*; PARASOL II 8.10–4 (Mr A A Walton) **Mr A Oughton** *Fell*; ORDNANCE 7.10–3 (Mr W J Rimell) **M Scudamore** *Fell*; LARRY FINN 9.10–11 (Mr B Bealby) **A P Thompson** *Brought-down*; LITTLE YID 11.10–1 (Mrs E Truelove) **J Power** *Refused*; WAIT AND SEE 8.10–5 (Mrs E Taylor) **A Freeman** *Brought-down*; ARMOURED KNIGHT 9.10–1 (Mr G H Dowty) **T Mabbutt** *Fell*; PEARLY PRINCE 10.10–0 (Mr A E Leigh Boulter) **R E Jenkins** *Fell*; BAIRE 7.10–0 (Mr M L Marsh) **J Foster** *Fell*; CREAM OF THE BORDER 8.10–0 (Mr G Mackie) **B Wilkinson** *Brought-down*; HEAD CREST 7.10–0 (Mr G H Dowty) **S Barnes** *Fell*; LUCKY DOME 7.10–0 (Mr J A Wood) **P J Doyle** *Pulled-up*; UNCLE BARNEY 10.10–4 (Mr H Bannister) **J Boddy** *Fell*; GRAND TRUCE 9.10–0 (Mr J D Pickering) **D Leslie** *Fell*; STEEL LOCK 9.10–0 (Mr E Maggs) **Mr E Maggs** *Refused*; DESIRE 12.10–0 (Mr C C Cameron) **T Cullen** *Pulled-up*; HIERBA 8.10–0 (Mrs A Warman) **A Mullins** *Fell*; HAPPY DAYS 13.10–0 (Mr J S Kirkham) **A Benson** *Fell*; PUNCHESTOWN STAR 9.10–0 (Mr J G Greenaway) **S McComb** *Refused*

The Betting: *7/1 Little Yid; 9/1 Whispering Steel; 10/1 Glen Fire & Lucky Dome; 100/7 Cardinal Error; 18/1 Mont Tremblant & Quite Naturally; 20/1 Early Mist; 22/1 Witty; 25/1 Parasol II, Knuckleduster & Ordnance; 33/1 Irish Lizard & Overshadow; 40/1 Larry Finn, Baire, Uncle Barney & Head Crest; 50/1 Wait and See, Hierba & Land Fort; 66/1 Others.*

Distances: *Twenty lengths; four lengths*

Winner Trained By: *Vincent O'Brien, Cashel, County Tipperary, Ireland*

Value to Winning Owner: *£9,330*

1954

To the delight of jumping enthusiasts everywhere, Liverpool staged its first all-National Hunt fixture in the first week of December 1953, with the long-awaited opening of the Mildmay Steeplechase Course. In the company of the late Lord Mildmay's sister, Mrs Helen White, Mrs Mirabel Topham and Major J C Bulteel, Lord Sefton performed the opening ceremony by untying the ribbon stretched across the course. That the garland was in the famous pale blue and white colours of Lord Mildmay was a most thoughtful touch on the part of the executive.

A little over four months later, however, it was seen as a sad reflection on the quality of the 'National runners that only two of the twenty-nine starters were handicapped above eleven stone, ROYAL TAN and LEGAL JOY. As the convincing winner of the Grand Sefton 'Chase, the giant CONEYBURROW was talked of as a champion in the making and with Pat Taaffe as jockey, found many admirers among the betting public. Favourite at 15/2, though, was Lord Sefton's IRISH LIZARD, the mount of Michael Scudamore, and 8/1 joint second favourite was ROYAL TAN. The Tipperary-born chestnut with the prominent white blaze was bred by Mr J Topping from TARTAN and the mare PRINCESS OF BIRDS and was first owned by Mr P Bell. After becoming the property of Mrs M H Keogh, ROYAL TAN came under the care of trainer Vincent O'Brien whose genius produced the gelding fit enough to finish second in both the Irish and Aintree Grand Nationals of 1951. At the end of that year the Dublin businessman Joe Griffin, known to his friends as 'Mincemeat Joe', purchased ROYAL TAN and the horse made a bold showing until coming down at the last fence in the 1952 'National. Three weeks after a terrible fall at Kempton, regular jockey Bryan Marshall pronounced himself fit enough to take the ride.

Even with a smaller field than usual the first fence caused problems, ALBERONI, WHISPERING STEEL and GENTLE MOYA getting no further than this point. Another three went at the second, with three more dropping out before Becher's. CONEYBURROW, in the hands of Pat Taaffe, was making the running, with SANPERION, ROYAL STUART, CHURCHTOWN and PUNCHESTOWN STAR in close attendance round the Canal Turn. At this point ROYAL TAN was some way off the pace, bringing up the rear with only one behind him. At the Water, CONEYBURROW totally misjudged his take-off, giving his hind legs a thorough soaking. SANPERION, CHURCHTOWN and TUDOR LINE were at the head of affairs over the second Becher's, with CONEYBURROW running on again and ROYAL TAN starting to make progress from the rear. At Valentine's Bryan Marshall took ROYAL TAN into a half-length lead from TUDOR LINE with CHURCHTOWN hard on their heels. CONEYBURROW crashed fatally at the final ditch and when shortly after CHURCHTOWN broke a blood vessel, the only threat to ROYAL TAN was TUDOR LINE. The latter, showing signs of tiredness by jumping to the right, was losing ground at each remaining fence and landed at the last three lengths behind ROYAL TAN. IRISH LIZARD came with a flurry in the closing stages but at the elbow Marshall appeared to have the race sewn up. Suddenly, though, TUDOR LINE began to run on and was getting up with every stride. Marshall and George Slack, excellent horsemen both, were seen at their best in the closest finish for many years. ROYAL TAN prevailed by a neck from TUDOR LINE,

IRISH LIZARD staying on to be third, ten lengths behind. In fourth place came CHURCHTOWN.

The congratulations for owner, trainer and jockey in returning to the winner's enclosure for the second year running were overshadowed by the tragic news that four horses, DOMINICK'S BAR, PARIS NEW YORK, LEGAL JOY and CONEYBURROW, had lost their lives in the race. Amid a nationwide outcry for changes to the fences came a mood of antipathy towards the great race. For the Grand National the fifties had brought very little to celebrate.

ROYAL TAN withholds the strong late challenge of TUDOR LINE

1954

With £6,000 added (including a trophy value £500). For six-year-olds & upwards. The second to receive 10%, the third 5% and the fourth 2½% of the whole stakes. The trainer of the Winner to receive a cup value £50 and the rider of the Winner a cup value £25

Date: 27th March 1954	Starters: 29	Time: 9 mins 32⅘ secs
1st **ROYAL TAN**	10.11–7 *(Mr J H Griffin)*	**B Marshall**
2nd **TUDOR LINE**	9.10–7 *(Mrs E Truelove)*	**G Slack**
3rd **IRISH LIZARD**	11.10–5 *(Lord Sefton)*	**M Scudamore**
4th **CHURCHTOWN**	9.10–3 *(Mrs M V O'Brien)*	**T Taaffe**
5th **SANPERION**	9.10–2 *(Mr J H Burgess)*	**D Leslie**
6th **MARTINIQUE**	8.10–1 *(Mr A Greenberg)*	**Mr E Greenway**
7th **UNCLE BARNEY**	11.10–0 *(Mr H Bannister)*	**L McMorrow**
8th **SOUTHERN COUP**	12.10–10 *(Capt E A Gargan)*	**A P Thompson**
9th **ONTRAY**	6.10–8 *(Capt L Scott Briggs)*	**Mr R Brewis**

Also Ran:

LEGAL JOY 11.11–3 (Miss D Paget) **D V Dick** *Fell & destroyed*; *WHISPERING STEEL 9.10–12* (Mr F H Curnick) **R Morrow** *Fell*; *ALBERONI 11.10–12* (Mr J Crowe) **Mr E Cousins** *Fell*; *CONEYBURROW 8.10–11* (Mr I E Levy) **P Taaffe** *Fell & destroyed*; *DOMINICK'S BAR 10.10–7* (Mrs P Kiely) **T Molony** *Dropped dead*; *SWINTON HERO 10.10–6* (Mr D Fowler) **Mr C Harty** *Fell*; *PRINCE OF ARRAGON 13.10–2* (Mr T A Connolly) **J Gorey** *Fell*; *ICY CALM 11.10–5* (Mrs O Martin-Montis) **R Francis** *Pulled-up*; *GAY MONARCH II 8.10–4* (Mr J R Roberts) **T Brookshaw** *Fell*; *ORDNANCE 8.10–1* (Sir Ronald Gunter) **J Dowdeswell** *Fell*; *BAIRE 8.10–0* (Mr M L Marsh) **J Foster** *Fell*; *HIERBA 9.10–0* (Mrs A Warman) **R J Hamey** *Fell*; *BORDER LUCK 9.10–0* (Mr J R Bower) **T Shone** *Fell*; *PARIS NEW YORK 7.10–0* (Mr R E Ansell) **M Roberts** *Fell & destroyed*; *STATESMAN 8.10–0* (Mrs C Magnier) **E Newman** *Fell*; *GENTLE MOYA 8.10–0* (Mr J J Straker) **Mr J Straker** *Fell*; *ROYAL STUART 11.10–0* (Lord Leverhulme) **J Power** *Refused*; *TRIPLE TORCH 8.10–0* (Major J I Medlicott) **D Ancil** *Unseated rider*; *MINIMAX 10.10–0* (Mr A J Sellar) **Capt M MacEwan** *Refused*; *PUNCHESTOWN STAR 10.10–0* (Mr J G Greenaway) **S McComb** *Refused*

The Betting: *15/2 Irish Lizard; 8/1 Royal Tan & Coneyburrow; 10/1 Churchtown & Tudor Line; 100/6 Gentle Moya; 18/1 Ordnance; 20/1 Sanperion; 33/1 Legal Joy & Dominick's Bar; 40/1 Southern Coup, Whispering Steel & Icy Calm; 50/1 Statesman, Gay Monarch II & Uncle Barney; 66/1 Others.*

Distances: *A neck; ten lengths*

Winner Trained By: *Vincent O'Brien, Cashel, County Tipperary, Ireland*

Value to Winning Owner: *£8,571*

1955

Aintree's misfortunes continued when three days of incessant rain put the race in danger of abandonment. After a stewards' inspection at 11 a.m., the go-ahead was given, but with the most badly waterlogged part of the course to be dolled-off. Thus the Water Jump was omitted for the first time in the history of the race. Despite the weather, it was a right Royal 'National, graced by the presence of Her Majesty The Queen, Queen Elizabeth the Queen Mother and HRH Princess Margaret. The Queen Mother was represented in the race by M'AS TU VU, ridden by Arthur Freeman.

Since the collapse of his business empire, Mr Joe Griffin's two 'National winners had been sold, EARLY MIST to Mr John Dunlop and ROYAL TAN to Prince Aly Khan. Bryan Marshall chose the former. Ireland fielded a strong hand, having no less than eight of the thirty runners. From the County Wicklow yard of Paddy Sleator the Tim Molony-ridden COPP was made 7/1 favourite on the strength of his unbeaten run of three wins, which included a victory over SUNDEW in the Leopardstown 'Chase. EARLY MIST came second in the betting at 9s and TUDOR LINE attracted his share of support.

Of Vincent O'Brien's quartet, the nine-year-old QUARE TIMES made his Aintree debut with a reputation as a versatile 'chaser who would have no difficulty staying the trip. By ARTIST'S SON out of LAVENCO, he was bred by Mr P P Sweeney of Thurles and purchased as a yearling by Mrs Robert Smyth for three hundred guineas. After giving him a number of years out at grass, Vincent O'Brien began training the gelding seriously and in his second season QUARE TIMES displayed his potential by winning two 'chases. Mrs

By-passing the Water Jump, SUNDEW leads from M'AS TU VU and STEEL LOCH

W H E Welman became his new owner the next season. In Pat Taaffe, QUARE TIMES had the ideal partner. Son of trainer Tom Taaffe, Pat progressed from the hunting field, point-to-points and the show-ring, to being first jockey to the powerful Tom Dreaper stable.

In the deep going, MARINER'S LOG and BLUE ENVOY came down at the first and SUNDEW ran on in front. There was a shocking crash at Becher's when the falling ESB brought down ROMAN FIRE, whose rider Jack Dowdeswell was buried in a flurry of hooves. Jockey Pat Doyle did well to take evasive action when a riderless horse jumped across SUNDEW's path at the Chair, and by-passing the Water, he led from M'AS TU VU, STEEL LOCK, CAREY'S COTTAGE, GENTLE MOYA and IRISH LIZARD. The latter blundered badly at Becher's, M'AS TU VU began to tire and Pat Taaffe brought QUARE TIMES smoothly through into second place behind SUNDEW. At the Canal Turn QUARE TIMES was in command, closely attended by SUNDEW, GIGOLO, TUDOR LINE and CAREY'S COTTAGE, the remainder being almost out on

their feet. SUNDEW fell at the last open ditch where STEEL LOCK was knocked over and 'Tosse' Taaffe briefly showed in front with CAREY'S COTTAGE from his brother Pat on QUARE TIMES. Back on the racecourse, though QUARE TIMES came to the final fence full of running and out-pacing TUDOR LINE on the run-in he won by twelve lengths. CAREY'S COTTAGE was third, four lengths behind. For the third year in succession Vincent O'Brien had saddled the winner and no praise could be too high for the achievement of Ireland's proudest son.

Mercifully, in spite of the dreadful conditions, there were no serious injuries to horses or riders. Yet disregarding the weather, the press emphasised the fact that the attendance was the smallest in living memory.

Some five weeks later, QUARE TIMES proved his continued well-being by winning a two-mile hurdle race at Leopardstown.

Pat Taaffe and QUARE TIMES storm over the last

1955

With £6,000 added (including a trophy value £500). For six-year-olds & upwards. The second to receive 10%, the third 5% and the fourth 2½% of the whole stakes. The trainer of the Winner to receive a cup value £50 and the rider of the Winner a cup value £25

Date: 26th March 1955		Starters: 30	Time: 10 mins 19⅕ secs
1st	**QUARE TIMES**	**9.11–0** *(Mrs W H E Welman)*	**P Taaffe**
2nd	**TUDOR LINE**	**10.11–3** *(Mrs E Truelove)*	**G Slack**
3rd	**CAREY'S COTTAGE**	**8.10–11** *(Mr D J Coughlan)*	**T Taaffe**
4th	**GIGOLO**	**10.11–3** *(Mrs M Milne Green)*	**R Curran**
5th	**ONTRAY**	**7.10–8** *(Capt L Scott Briggs)*	**Mr R Brewis**
6th	**GENTLE MOYA**	**9.10–0** *(Mr J J Straker)*	**Mr J Straker**
7th	**CLEARING**	**8.10–2** *(Mr M Kingsley)*	**R J Hamey**
8th	**WILD WISDOM**	**10.10–0** *(Mr G R Marsh)*	**Lt Col W Holman**
9th	**EARLY MIST**	**10.12–3** *(Mr J Dunlop)*	**B Marshall**
10th	**RED RUBE**	**8.10–3** *(Sir John Carew-Pole)*	**A Oughton**
11th	**IRISH LIZARD**	**12.10–9** *(Lord Sefton)*	**M Scudamore**
12th	**ROYAL TAN**	**11.12–4** *(Prince Aly Khan)*	**D V Dick**
13th	**UNCLE BARNEY**	**12.10–0** *(Mr H Bannister)*	**L McMorrow**

Also Ran:

MARINER'S LOG 8.11–12 (Lord Bicester) **R Francis** *Fell*; *MR LINNETT* 7.11–5 (Mr Leo Partridge) **Mr J R Cox** *Pulled-up*; *SUNDEW* 9.11–3 (Mrs G Kohn) **P J Doyle** *Fell*; *ESB* 9.11–1 (Mrs L Carver) **T Cusack** *Fell*; *ORIENTAL WAY* 7.10–12 (Mr L Abrahamson) **F T Winter** *Fell*; *LITTLE YID* 13.10–10 (Mrs E Truelove) **R Emery** *Pulled-up*; *COPP* 11.10–8 (Mr C C Allan) **T Molony** *Fell*; *M'AS TU VU* 9.10–7 (HM Queen Elizabeth The Queen Mother) **A Freeman** *Fell*; *NO RESPONSE* 9.10–2 (Sir Thomas Ainsworth) **D Ancil** *Fell*; *DARK STRANGER* 10.10–5 (Mr L A Coville) **Mr J Bosley** *Fell*; *BLUE ENVOY* 10.10–1 (Mrs E M Halahan) **Mr E Greenway** *Fell*; *ANOTHER RAKE* 10.10–1 (Mr F H Gilman) **D Leslie** *Fell*; *MOOGIE* 12.10–0 (Mrs M Westwood) **J Neely** *Fell*; *STEEL LOCK* 11.10–0 (Mrs D M Harris) **J A Bullock** *Knocked-over*; *ROMAN FIRE* 12.10–0 (Mrs H R Marsh) **J Dowdeswell** *Brought-down*; *MUNSTER KING II* 8.10–0 (Mrs A T Hodgson) **V Speck** *Fell*; *SUN CLASP* 7.10–0 (Mr E D Boardman) **J Power** *Fell*

The Betting: *7/1 Copp; 9/1 Early Mist; 10/1 Tudor Line; 100/9 Quare Times; 100/8 Irish Lizard & Mariner's Log; 100/6 Gigolo; 20/1 Mr Linnett & Carey's Cottage; 22/1 M'As Tu Vu; 28/1 Royal Tan & Sundew; 33/1 Oriental Way; 40/1 Dark Stranger; 45/1 Another Rake & No Response; 50/1 Gentle Moya, Clearing, Little Yid & Uncle Barney; 66/1 Others.*

Distances: *Twelve lengths; four lengths*

Winner Trained By: *Vincent O'Brien, Cashel, County Tipperary, Ireland*

Value to Winning Owner: *£8,934*

* The Water Jump was omitted due to the waterlogged state of the course in this area *

1956

The ever imaginative Mrs Topham brought a new dimension to the racecourse with the construction of a motor racetrack, which was first used shortly after the 1955 Grand National. Hailed by motor sport enthusiasts as the finest of its kind in Europe, it was subsequently to host both the British and European Grand Prix and attract such internationally famous drivers as Stirling Moss, Juan Fangio and Mike Hawthorne.

But exciting as the new venture undoubtedly was, all the talk was of steeplechasing as the 1956 race drew near. Interest was heightened by The Queen Mother this time having two runners entered. M'AS TU VU, making a second bid, was joined by stable-mate DEVON LOCH, a ten-year-old son of DEVONIAN, with proven ability over park fences. The mount of former champion jockey Dick Francis, DEVON LOCH was a popular selection of the countless thousands who admired the owner's valuable contribution to racing.

Favourite of the twenty-nine runners at 7/1 was MUST, with SUNDEW, now trained in England and ridden by Fred Winter, the second choice. QUARE TIMES was unable to take part, Vincent O'Brien relying on ROYAL TAN, while his first 'National hero EARLY MIST was once more in the line-up and ridden by Bryan Marshall who now trained him. That grand old gentleman of National Hunt racing, Lord Bicester, had recently died without realising his life's ambition of winning the great race, but as a final mark of respect his colours were again carried in the race by MARINER'S LOG.

On the same price of 100/7 as DEVON LOCH and PIPPYKIN was ten-year-old E.S.B., the mount of tall and cheerful Dave Dick. Bred in County Kildare by Miss Sheila Bourke, E.S.B. was by BIDAR out of a mare called ENGLISH SUMMER. After passing through various hands he became the property of Mrs Leonard Carver, whose husband trained him for the 1955 race in which he got no further than Becher's. Now prepared by Fred Rimell at Kinnersley, Worcestershire, the gelding was considered cherry ripe after winning his two most recent engagements at Haydock and Manchester.

Over the Water. DEVON LOCH is on the extreme left

ARMORIAL III led at the first fence, where REVEREND PRINCE, EARLY MIST, HIGH GUARD and the favourite MUST all fell, and still led at the Water Jump, from M'AS TU VU, SUNDEW, EAGLE LODGE and MUCH OBLIGED, with E.S.B., and DEVON LOCH taking closer order. The nineteenth put paid to the chances of M'AS TU VU, WITTY and DUNBOY II and SUNDEW came down at Becher's. Moving into contention on the outside at the Canal Turn, DEVON LOCH appeared to be merely coasting while his rivals were being hard ridden to hold their places for the last mile home. At the fence after Valentine's, front-runner ARMORIAL III and MUCH OBLIGED both fell and with DEVON LOCH left in front, EAGLE LODGE, ONTRAY, E.S.B., and GENTLE MOYA rushed

up to challenge. Galloping strongly, DE-
VON LOCH came over the last fence one and
a half lengths in front of E.S.B., lengthen-
ing his stride easily on touching down to
increase his advantage. From the stands
and enclosures came the loudest cheering
ever heard on a racecourse as the crowds
gave vent to their joy at the first Royal
Grand National winner for fifty-six years.
The roar of applause increased with every
stride DEVON LOCH took, for it brought him
nearer victory and further away from his
weary pursuer. But with less than fifty
yards to run, the impossible happened.
DEVON LOCH lifted his forelegs as if to take
off at a non-existent obstacle, then realising his error, slithered along the turf on his
belly. Dave Dick, reconciled to finishing
second, now drove E.S.B. on past the sta-
tionary DEVON LOCH to pass the post the
luckiest winner in the annals of racing. A
devastated Dick Francis dismounted and
led DEVON LOCH back to the paddock,
through an eerily silent and mystified
crowd. GENTLE MOYA finished second, ten
lengths behind the winner, with ROYAL
TAN the same distance away in third place
and EAGLE LODGE fourth.

There was much sympathy for all concerned with DEVON LOCH. A cruel twist of
fate had denied them a richly-deserved
victory and trainer Peter Cazalet must
have been reminded of his late friend Lord
Mildmay's anguish twenty years before
with DAVY JONES. Her Majesty The Queen
Mother won the hearts of everyone for the
manner in which she hid her disappointment, first consoling jockey Dick Francis
and then congratulating the winning
owner Mrs Leonard Carver.

A dejected Dick Francis retrieves his whip as the inquest begins on the unluckiest loser of them all.
The DEVON LOCH mystery is still debated whenever the 'National is discussed

1956

With £6,000 added, (including a trophy value £500). For six-year-olds & upwards. The second to receive 10%, the third 5% and the fourth 2½% of the whole stakes. The trainer of the Winner to receive a cup value £50 and the rider of the Winner a cup value £25

Date: 24th March 1956	Starters: 29	Time: 9 mins 21⅖ secs
1st **E.S.B.**	**10.11–3** *(Mrs L Carver)*	**D V Dick**
2nd **GENTLE MOYA**	**10.10–2** *(Mr J J Straker)*	**G Milburn**
3rd **ROYAL TAN**	**12.12–1** *(Prince Aly Khan)*	**T Taaffe**
4th **EAGLE LODGE**	**7.10–1** *(Mr N A Mardon)*	**A Oughton**
5th **KEY ROYAL**	**8.10–8** *(Mr A H Birtwhistle)*	**T Molony**
6th **MARTINIQUE**	**10.10–0** *(Mr A Greenberg)*	**S Mellor**
7th **CAREY'S COTTAGE**	**9.10–13** *(Colonel W H Whitbread)*	**R Turnell**
8th **CLEARING**	**9.10–1** *(Mr M Kingsley)*	**J A Bullock**
9th **WILD WISDOM**	**11.10–1** *(Mr E Foster)*	**Mr L Bridge**

Also Ran:

EARLY MIST 11.12–2 (Mr J Dunlop) **B Marshall** *Fell*; *MARINER'S LOG* 9.11–11 (The late Lord Bicester) **R Emery** *Fell*; *DEVON LOCH* 10.11–4 (HM Queen Elizabeth The Queen Mother) **R Francis** *Slipped in lead near the post*; *SUNDEW* 10.11–4 (Mrs G Kohn) **F T Winter** *Fell*; *HIGH GUARD* 9.11–1 (Mr J A Keith) **A P Thompson** *Fell*; *MUCH OBLIGED* 8.11–0 (Mr H Draper) **M Scudamore** *Fell*; *DUNBOY II* 12.11–0 (Mrs M Bruce) **Mr R Brewis** *Fell*; *ARMORIAL III* 7.10–10 (Mme K. Hennessy) **J. Dowdeswell**; *MERRY WINDSOR* 8.10–10 (Mr I Holliday) **L McMorrow** *Fell*; *MUST* 8.10–10 (Mrs W L Pilkington) **R Morrow** *Fell*; *M'AS TU VU* 10.10–6 (HM Queen Elizabeth The Queen Mother) **A Freeman** *Fell*; *REVEREND PRINCE* 10.10–5 (Mr P Dufosee) **Mr C Pocock** *Fell*; *WITTY* 11.10–4 (Mr C Nicholson) **P A Farrell** *Fell*; *DOMATA* 10.10–4 (Mr E Stanning) **D Ancil** *Fell*; *POLONIUS* 10.10–3 (Mrs D Hailstone) **E F Kelly** *Refused*; *ATHENIAN* 7.10–3 (Col W H Whitbread) **R J Hamey** *Fell*; *NO RESPONSE* 10.10–1 (Sir Thomas Ainsworth) **C Finnegan** *Fell*; *ONTRAY* 8.10–0 (Capt L Scott Briggs) **R Curran** *Fell*; *BORDER LUCK* 11.10–0 (Mr J R Bower) **M O'Dwyer** *Refused*; *PIPPYKIN* 8.10–0 (Mr R D Darragh) **J Power** *Refused*

The Betting: *7/1 Must; 8/1 Sundew; 10/1 Carey's Cottage; 100/7 E.S.B., Devon Loch & Pippykin; 100/6 Ontray; 20/1 Armorial III; 22/1 Gentle Moya, High Guard & Mariner's Log; 25/1 Early Mist; 28/1 Merry Windsor, Key Royal & Royal Tan; 40/1 M'as Tu Vu, Reverend Prince & Martinique; 50/1 No Response & Much Obliged; 66/1 Others.*

Distances: *Ten lengths; ten lengths*

Winner Trained By: *Fred Rimell, Kinnersley, Worcestershire*

Value to Winning Owner: *£8,695*

1957

In an effort to improve falling attendances, it was decided to restore the race to its traditional Friday, an experiment less than successful, due in part, yet again, to the weather. But if the day was dismal, there could be few complaints about the quality of the thirty-five runner field, which contained former winners E.S.B. and ROYAL TAN. The 1954 Cheltenham Gold Cup winner FOUR TEN, together with the Peter Cazalet trained ROSE PARK provided a welcome touch of class and Mr H J Joel's striking grey GLORIOUS TWELFTH was a lively tip on the day. The Fulke Walwyn trained FELIAS, ridden by Bill Rees, the son of MUSIC HALL's winning jockey, was owned by Mrs P Saunders who won the horse in a daily newspaper competition. Local interest centred around the smallest competitor, the mare RED MENACE owned by Wirral businessman Gerry McParland and trained by Bill Dutton, the one-time solicitor whose ride to glory on TIPPERARY TIM gave him a new career. A late rush of money made Neville Crump trained GOOSANDER the 5/1 favourite.

Trying for the third time was the giant-sized chestnut SUNDEW, a gelding standing seventeen and a half hands and said to have feet like floats. Mr J McArdle bred SUNDEW from a pairing of SUN KING with PARSONSTOWN GEM in County Meath, and after passing through the hands of a couple of Irish owners the horse was purchased for £3,000 by Mrs Geoffrey Kohn on the eve of the 1955 Grand National. SUNDEW was the only 'chaser in Frank Hudson's small yard at Henley-in-Arden, Warwickshire, but as in the previous year was partnered by the brilliant Fred Winter. ARMORIAL III again dashed to the front, but at the fourth fence over-jumped, coming down in a sprawl and leaving SUNDEW in front of CHERRY ABBOT, ATHENIAN and GENTLE MOYA. From here on it became a procession, SUNDEW bowling along in front, stumbling at Becher's yet surviving and taking chunks out of a number of other fences but always being brought through by his great strength. Four lengths clear at the Water, SUNDEW began the second circuit ahead of ATHENIAN, E.S.B. and THE CROFTER, with TIBERETTA, GOOSANDER, WYNDBURGH and SYDNEY JONES improving from the rear. Over Becher's again it was still SUNDEW. E.S.B. and THE CROFTER challenged between the last two fences but on the flat the biggest danger came from WYNDBURGH, for whom the winning post came too soon. SUNDEW won by eight lengths with TIBERETTA six lengths back in third and GLORIOUS TWELFTH running on well to finish fourth. The victory owed as much to the jockey as to the horse, for few besides Fred Winter could have coped with the numerous errors made by SUNDEW. His success was greeted with genuine delight by the multitude who so admired a champion jockey and a marvellous man.

Some eight months after the 'National, SUNDEW broke his shoulder at the Water Jump in a 'chase at Haydock Park and was destroyed. He is buried on the course where he met his end.

1957

With £6,000 added, (including a trophy value £500). For six-year-olds & upwards. The second to receive 10%, the third 5% and the fourth 2½% of the whole stakes. The trainer of the Winner to receive a cup value £50 and the rider of the Winner a cup value £25

Date: 29th March 1957	Starters: 35	Time: 9 mins 42⅖ secs
1st **SUNDEW**	**11.11–7** *(Mrs G Kohn)*	**F T Winter**
2nd **WYNDBURGH**	**7.10–7** *(Miss R M P Wilkinson)*	**M Batchelor**
3rd **TIBERETTA**	**9.10–0** *(Mr E. R. Courage)*	**A. Oughton**
4th **GLORIOUS TWELFTH**	**8.11–1** *(Mr H J Joel)*	**B Wilkinson**
5th **THE CROFTER**	**9.10–0** *(Lt Col D M Baird)*	**J Power**
6th **GOOSANDER**	**9.11–7** *(Mrs Bache Hay)*	**H J East**
7th **SYDNEY JONES**	**10.10–12** *(Mr P S Tory)*	**Mr M Tory**
8th **E.S.B.**	**11.11–13** *(Mrs L Carver)*	**D V Dick**
9th **MERRY THROW**	**9.10–12** *(Major A C Straker)*	**T Brookshaw**
10th **SANDY JANE II**	**10.10–2** *(Mrs P M Lamb)*	**H R Beasley**
11th **GENTLE MOYA**	**11.10–6** *(Mr J J Straker)*	**G Milburn**

Also Ran:

ROSE PARK 11.11–13 (Mr G G Lawrence) **G Nicholls** *Pulled-up; ROYAL TAN 13.11–12* (Prince Aly Khan) **T Taaffe** *Carried out; FOUR TEN 11.11–11* (Mr A Strange) **R Morrow** *Fell; MUCH OBLIGED 9.11–4* (Mr H Draper) **M Scudamore** *Fell; ICELOUGH 11.11–3* (Mr R H Usher) **P Taaffe** *Brought-down; ARMORIAL III 8.11–1* (Mme K Hennessy) **J A Bullock** *Fell; VIRGINIUS 8.10–12* (Mr R R Guest) **Mr A Lillingston** *Brought-down; HART ROYAL 9.10–10* (Mr L C Denton) **P Pickford** *Fell; ATHENIAN 8.10–7* (Col W H Whitbread) **D Ancil** *Fell; CAREY'S COTTAGE 10.10–6* (Col W H Whitbread) **T Shone** *Refused; TUTTO 10.10–6* (Miss E R Armitage) **J Lehane** *Fell; RENDEZVOUS III 9.10–6* (Major H S Cayzer) **A Freeman** *Brought-down; FELIAS 9.10–5* (Mrs P Saunders) **W Rees** *Brought-down; CHINA CLIPPER II 10.10–3* (Major W D Gibson) **Major W D Gibson** *Fell; IRISH LIZARD 14.10–2* (Lord Sefton) **D Nicholson** *Fell; CLEARING 10.10–1* (Mr M Kingsley) **R Curson** *Fell; MORRCATOR 10.10–0* (Mr P M Jones) **L McMorrow** *Fell; RED MENACE 8.10–0* (Mr G McParland) **L Wigham** *Fell; GO-WELL 9.10–9* (Mr S C Wagstaffe) **Capt P Bengough** *Fell; WILD WISDOM 12.10–1* (Mr L Bridge) **Mr L Bridge** *Pulled-up; FAHRENHEIT 10.10–0* (Miss P Edwards) **T O'Brien** *Fell; MONKEY WRENCH 12.10–0* (Mrs J F C Bryce) **R J Hamey** *Pulled-up; WAKING 13.10–5* (Capt A W C Pearn) **Capt A W C Pearn** *Fell; CHERRY ABBOT 12.10–0* (Mr C Ferrie) **G Underwood** *Fell*

The Betting: *5/1 Goosander; 10/1 Much Obliged; 100/8 Glorious Twelfth; 100/7 Hart Royal; 100/6 Tutto; 20/1 E.S.B., Sundew & Rendezvous III; 25/1 Sydney Jones & Wyndburgh; 28/1 Gentle Moya, Rose Park, Icelough & Royal Tan; 33/1 Red Menace; 40/1 Merry Throw & Sandy Jane II; 45/1 Felias & Clearing; 50/1 Carey's Cottage, Four Ten, Virginius, Armorial III & Morrcator; 66/1 Others.*

Distances: *Eight lengths; six lengths*

Winner Trained By: *Frank Hudson, Henley-in-Arden, Warwickshire*

Value to Winning Owner: *£8,868*

1958

Steeplechasing received a shot in the arm in 1957 through the imaginative sponsorship of the Whitbread Gold Cup at Sandown Park and other companies were quick to appreciate the value of the idea. The Irish Hospital Sweepstakes became the first to invest money in Aintree's great race when in 1958 they put up £5,000 towards the prize and with Messrs Tophams' added money of £7,000. The value to the winning owner reached its highest yet, £13,719.

E.S.B., the only previous winner among the thirty-one runners, was now twelve years old and with top weight was considered to have only a slender chance. It was the game little WYNDBURGH, trained in Scotland, that the betting public made clear 6/1 favourite, with the nearest to him in the betting GOOSANDER at 100/7. Last season's Liverpool Foxhunter 'Chase winner COLLEDGE MASTER was one of the promising newcomers and the Duchess of Westminster's SENTINA was sent over from Ireland as the mount of Pat Taaffe. Despite having beaten SENTINA in Navan's Troytown 'Chase, eight-year-old MR WHAT was thought of as little more than a novice who would do well even to get round at Aintree. Bred in County Westmeath by Mrs Barbara O'Neill, he was by GRAND INQUISITOR out of the mare DUCHESS OF PEDULAS and was bought when five years old for £500 by trainer Tom Taaffe, the father of Pat and 'Tosse'. Passed on to Mr D J Coughlan, a Dublin businessman, MR WHAT remained in the Taaffe yard and it was only a week before the 'National when jockey Arthur Freeman was booked to partner the horse in the big race.

The field approached the first fence at a more sensible rate than in recent 'Nationals, the heavy going making the riders cautious. All thirty-one negotiated the first safely, but LONGMEAD went at the next, the jump before Becher's claimed VALIANT SPARK, RENDEZVOUS III and PRINCESS GARTER, Becher's itself eliminated another four, and when the remainder came out of the mist back to the stands they were stretched over a wide expanse of ground. GOOSANDER was giving Tim Molony a great ride at the head of the pack, closely tracked by ATHENIAN and the improving MR WHAT. COLLEDGE MASTER went at the seventeenth and jumping into the lead at Becher's, MR WHAT went on from GOOSANDER, TIBERETTA, EAGLE LODGE, E.S.B., GREEN DRILL and WYNDBURGH. After rounding the Canal Turn, MR WHAT began drawing away from his weary rivals, jumping splendidly and revelling in the mud. The little Irish 'novice' came to the final fence with an unassailable lead, but with Arthur Freeman taking a quick glance behind him, the horse became unbalanced and he hit the fence. Happily, the jockey rectified the error immediately, bringing MR WHAT home the easiest of winners by thirty lengths from TIBERETTA, GREEN DRILL and WYNDBURGH. MR WHAT was a most popular winner, and all the more creditable for Freeman having to put up six pounds overweight. In thirty-three subsequent outings MR WHAT never again entered the winners enclosure.

THE GRAND NATIONAL HANDICAP STEEPLECHASE
1958

With £12,000 added, being £5,000 given by The Irish Hospital Sweepstakes and £7,000 by Messrs Tophams Limited, (including a gold trophy value £500). For six-year-olds & upwards. The second to receive 10%, the third 5% and the fourth 2½% of the whole stakes. The trainer of the Winner to receive a cup value £50 and the rider of the Winner a cup value £25

Date: 29th March 1958	Starters: 31	Time: 9 mins 59⅘ secs
1st **MR WHAT**	**8.10−6** *(Mr D J Coughlan)*	**A Freeman**
2nd **TIBERETTA**	**10.10−6** *(Mr E R Courage)*	**G Slack**
3rd **GREEN DRILL**	**8.10−10** *(Lord Cadogan)*	**G Milburn**
4th **WYNDBURGH**	**8.11−3** *(Miss R M P Wilkinson)*	**M Batchelor**
5th **GOOSANDER**	**10.11−7** *(Mrs Bache Hay)*	**T Molony**
6th **E.S.B.**	**12.11−12** *(Mrs L Carver)*	**D V Dick**
7th **HOLLY BANK**	**11.10−13** *(Mr S H Brookshaw)*	**Mr P Brookshaw**

Also Ran:

WISE CHILD 10.11−6 (Wing Commander R E Stephenson) **S Hayhurst** *Pulled-up*; *GLORIOUS TWELFTH 9.11−3* (Mr H J Joel) **B Wilkinson** *Refused*; *COLLEDGE MASTER 8.11−2* (Mr L R Morgan) **W Rees** *Pulled-up*; *LONGMEAD 8.11−1* (Mr F Rea) **G W Robinson** *Fell*; *ACE OF TRUMPS 10.10−12* (Mr C Nicholson) **P A Farrell** *Pulled-up*; *ATHENIAN 9.10−11* (Col W H Whitbread) **D Ancil** *Fell*; *SENTINA 8.10−11* (Duchess of Westminster) **P Taaffe** *Brought-down*; *HART ROYAL 10.10−11* (Mr L C Denton) **P Pickford** *Refused*; *SYDNEY JONES 11.10−12* (Mr P S Tory) **Mr M Tory** *Brought-down*; *VALIANT SPARK 9.10−7* (Mr O H Gilbey) **M Scudamore** *Fell*; *RENDEZVOUS III 10.10−3* (Major H S Cayzer) **J A Bullock** *Fell*; *BROOKLING 9.10−3* (Mr C Rooney) **T Taaffe** *Fell*; *SPRINGSILVER 8.10−4* (Mrs M F Magnier) **F T Winter** *Refused*; *NEVER SAY WHEN 9.10−2* (Mr A H Wood) **S Mellor** *Fell*; *PIPPYKIN 10.10−5* (Mr K R Redfern) **T Brookshaw** *Fell*; *PRINCESS GARTER 11.10−3* (Mr E Davies) **Mr W Roberts** *Fell*; *MUST 10.10−1* (Mrs W L Pilkington) **R Morrow** *Fell*; *SOUTHERNTOWN 12.10−1* (Mr P J M Place) **P Cowley** *Unseated rider*; *THE CROFTER 10.10−0* (Lt Col D M Baird) **J Power** *Fell*; *MOSTON LANE 9.10−0* (Mr F Bramwell) **R E Jenkins** *Refused*; *RICHARDSTOWN 10.10−0* (Mr J Neville) **J Morrissey** *Fell*; *EAGLE LODGE 9.10−0* (Mr N A Mardon) **A Oughton** *Pulled-up*; *COMEDIAN'S FOLLY 10.10−0* (Mr L G Scott) **Mr D Scott** *Refused*; *FROZEN CREDIT 12.10−12* (Mr W F Ransom) **Mr P Ransom** *Refused*

The Betting: *6/1 Wyndburgh; 100/7 Goosander; 18/1 Mr What, Hart Royal, Sentina, Eagle Lodge & Springsilver; 20/1 Valiant Spark; 22/1 Pippykin & Athenian; 25/1 Colledge Master; 28/1 E.S.B., Green Drill, Glorious Twelfth, Tiberetta, Brookling, Longmead & Sydney Jones; 40/1 The Crofter, Ace of Trumps & Richardstown; 45/1 Rendezvous III & Wise Child; 50/1 Must, Never Say When & Holly Bank; 66/1 Others.*

Distances: *Thirty lengths; fifteen lengths*

Winner Trained By: *Tom Taaffe, Rathcoole, County Dublin, Ireland*

Value to Winning Owner: *£13,719*

1959

KERSTIN became one of the few mares ever to top the Grand National handicap and although without a win this term, as winner of last season's Cheltenham Gold Cup, she was entitled to the utmost respect. Receiving five pounds from the mare, MR WHAT had jumped a colossal twenty-three pounds in the weights, yet such was the ease with which he had won the last running in the mud that he was an emphatic favourite at 6/1. Only once out of the first four in the current campaign, WYNDBURGH returned to the course he knew so well with a new partner, the jovial and highly-talented Tim Brookshaw.

Royston trainer Willie Stephenson was already famous as the man responsible for turning out triple Champion Hurdle winner SIR KEN and the 1951 Epsom Derby victor ARCTIC PRINCE. He caused something of a surprise when going to 3,200 guineas to acquire a robust-looking point-to-point horse called OXO at the Newmarket October Sales of 1957. Now the supreme test of his judgement became the 1959 Grand National. By BOBSLEIGH out of PATUM, OXO was bred in Dorset by Mr A C Wyatt. In the colours of trainer Stephenson's patron Mr J E Bigg, OXO won four 'chases before making his bid for the 'National, in which he was providing Michael Scudamore with his ninth ride in the race.

SURPRISE PACKET with Gerry Scott in the saddle was the first to show, soon to be joined by TIBERETTA. The two front-runners took the Brook perfectly, but no less than eight fell behind them. Rounding the Canal Turn the positions up front remained the same, and at this point MR WHAT and WYNDBURGH were some distance in arrears. ROYAL TOURNAMENT refused at the seventeenth when some way

behind the leaders and from here WYNDBURGH and OXO began making ground. The long-time leader SURPRISE PACKET fell at the second Becher's in a pile-up which left OXO and WYNDBURGH disputing the lead some six lengths in front of the improving MR WHAT, GREEN DRILL, VIGOR, CANNOBIE LEE, TIBERETTA and JOHN JACQUES but for Tim Brookshaw Becher's had created a major problem: the steep drop had caused his off-side stirrup to break. So to even things up, Brookshaw slipped his other foot from the remaining iron and continued in the hunt abreast of OXO. Fence after fence they jumped together, first one gaining a slight advantage, then the other, while behind them GREEN DRILL, CANNOBIE LEE, TURMOIL and PINTAIL fell by the wayside. Producing the better speed between the last two fences, OXO reached for the final obstacle four lengths in front of WYNDBURGH but misjudged his jump and hit it hard. His strength and the supreme jockeyship of Michael Scudamore allowed him to sur-

Tim Brookshaw riding without irons cannot quite get up to OXO on the line

THE CROFTER gives Stan Mellor no chance of staying on board at Becher's first time and is about to be joined on the ground by ETERNAL

vive the error and at the elbow he maintained his advantage by three lengths. But to the delight of the crowds, WYNDBURGH and Tim Brookshaw were not yet done with, and running on under their great handicap they began eating up the ground in pursuit of the leader. But for once that long run-in was not long enough and at the post OXO was one-and-a-half lengths in front. Beaten by the weight, MR WHAT was a further eight lengths away in third place, the only other to complete being TIBERETTA.

Both first and second had been superbly ridden, but despite the drama, courage and immense skill the race produced, the fact that only four survived the full distance and HENRY PURCELL was killed yet again led to demands for stringent alterations both to the conditions of the event and to the conformation of the fences.

1959

With £12,000 added, being £5,000 given by The Irish Hospital Sweepstakes and £7,000, (including a gold trophy value £600), by Messrs Tophams Limited. For six-year-olds & upwards. The second to receive 10%, the third 5% and the fourth 2½% of the whole stakes. The trainer of the Winner to receive a cup value £100 and the rider of the Winner a cup value £50

Date: 21st March 1959	Starters: 34	Time: 9 mins 37⅘ secs
1st **OXO**	**8.10–13** *(Mr J E Bigg)*	**M Scudamore**
2nd **WYNDBURGH**	**9.10–12** *(Mrs J K M Oliver)*	**T Brookshaw**
3rd **MR WHAT**	**9.11–9** *(Mr D J Coughlan)*	**T Taaffe**
4th **TIBERETTA**	**11.10–9** *(Mr E R Courage)*	**A Oughton**

Also Ran:

KERSTIN 9.12–0 (Mr G H Moore) **S Hayhurst** *Fell*; *DONE UP 9.11–3* (Mr J U Baillie) **F T Winter** *Brought-down*; *JOHN JACQUES 10.11–0* (Mrs D G Wares) **H J East** *Fell*; *SLIPPERY SERPENT 8.10–11* (Mr B Sunley) **P Taaffe** *Fell*; *MAINSTOWN 9.10–10* (Mrs M Milne Green) **M Batchelor** *Fell*; *CANNOBIE LEE 8.10–10* (Miss D Paget) **D Nicholson** *Fell*; *MR GAY 12.10–9* (Mr P Thrale) **D Ancil** *Brought-down*; *DONDROSA 7.10–11* (Mr C B Taylor) **Mr C B Taylor** *Refused*; *GLORIOUS TWELFTH 10.10–7* (Mr H J Joel) **G Slack** *Brought-down*; *GREEN DRILL 9.10–6* (Lord Cadogan) **G Milburn** *Fell*; *IRISH COFFEE 9.10–5* (Mr J A Hale) **C Finnegan** *Fell*; *ETERNAL 8.10–4* (Lt Col R Fenwick-Palmer) **P Major** *Fell*; *VIGOR 11.10–5* (Mrs A R B Owen) **W Rees** *Refused*; *PINTAIL 10.10–4* (Mr J P Bissill) **B Wilkinson** *Pulled-up*; *OSCAR WILDE 9.10–4* (Mr T T Jasper) **R E Jenkins** *Fell*; *SURPRISE PACKET 10.10–5* (Mrs S Richards) **G Scott** *Fell*; *VALIANT SPARK 10.10–3* (Mr O H Gilbey) **J Lehane** *Fell*; *SOLTOWN 7.10–3* (Mr G Garratt) **W Brennan** *Fell*; *KILBALLYOWN 12.10–2* (Mrs M A Lynch) **E McKenzie** *Brought-down*; *RICHARDSTOWN 11.10–1* (Mr R Neville) **F Carroll** *Pulled-up*; *STOP LIST 10.10–1* (Mr A Watson) **T Shone** *Fell*; *TURMOIL 9.10–1* (Mrs G Kohn) **J Hudson** *Pulled-up*; *NIC ATKINS 8.10–1* (Mrs P M Lamb) **F Shortt** *Fell*; *SUNDAWN III 10.10–0* (Mr L Skelton) **J Power** *Brought-down*; *BELSIZE II 10.10–0* (Mr W G Boomer) **Mr G Rooney** *Fell*; *EAGLE LODGE 10.10–0* (Mr N A Mardon) **J A Bullock** *Refused*; *SOUTHERNTOWN 13.10–0* (Mr P J M Place) **P Cowley** *Fell*; *ROYAL TOURNAMENT 9.10–0* (Lt Col M Gilliat) **R Morrow** *Refused*; *THE CROFTER 11.10–0* (Lt Col D M Baird) **S Mellor** *Fell*; *HENRY PURCELL 12.10–0* (Mrs E C Smith) **A C Keen** *Fell*

The Betting: *6/1 Mr What; 8/1 Oxo; 9/1 Slippery Serpent; 10/1 Wyndburgh; 100/7 Done Up; 20/1 Nic Atkins, Tiberetta & Turmoil; 22/1 Green Drill; 25/1 Soltown & Kerstin; 28/1 Mr Gay, Oscar Wilde & Belsize II; 33/1 Irish Coffee, John Jacques, Glorious Twelfth & Kilballyown; 40/1 Valiant Spark & Mainstown; 45/1 Cannobie Lee & Eagle Lodge; 50/1 Eternal; 66/1 Stop List, Dondrosa, Vigor & Richardstown; 100/1 Others.*

Distances: *One and a half lengths; eight lengths*

Winner Trained By: *Willie Stephenson, Royston, Hertfordshire*

Value to Winning Owner: *£13,646*

1960

At long last the whole nation was able to watch the thrills and spills of the Grand National this year, thanks to an agreement between Mrs Topham and the BBC. The BBC had sought permission to cover the race with cameras for years and when finally given the go-ahead, they were faced with as mammoth a task as their first radio commentary of the event, thirty-three years before. As always though, they had first-class professionals to tackle the pioneering enterprise, with Peter O'Sullevan, Clive Graham and Peter Bromley as commentators, Dennis Monger, Ray Lakeland and John Vernon the producers and Derek Hart with Peter Montague Evans making up the team. A most innovative feature of the transmission was to be a mobile camera, travelling alongside the runners, made possible by use of the motor racetrack on the inside of the course.

MR WHAT was top weight, from WYND-BURGH and Fred Winter's mount DANDY

BBC TV men (from left) Peter Dimmock, Peter O'Sullevan and Ray Lakeland survey the course from the main camera position

SCOT but in the smallest field since 1920, the public went wild about the chances of another from the formidable stable of Neville Crump. At 13/2 MERRYMAN II was returning to the scene of his triumph in last year's Foxhunters 'Chase. By CARNIVAL BOY out of MAID MARION, he was bred by the Marquess of Linlithgow from whose executors he was purchased when five years old by Miss Winifred Wallace of Edinburgh. It was this lady who broke him, and rode him in point-to-points before sending him to Neville Crump at Middleham. Heavily coupled in doubles with the Lincolnshire Handicap winner, MUSTAVON, MERRYMAN II would really hurt the bookies if he landed the odds in the 'National, but the path to Aintree had been far from smooth for Miss Wallace's horse. He had developed an inflamed bone in a foot after a race at Chepstow some months earlier and only the genius of his trainer made it possible for him to be fit enough for the big race. Furthermore, just a week before the 'National, regular jockey Gerry Scott broke his collar bone for the second time in five days. With replacement jockey Johnny East standing by, however, Scott defied the advice of his physiotherapist, got himself strapped up and duly weighed out for the favourite.

Home Secretary Rab Butler was a guest of Mrs Topham's, intent on seeing for himself the race which had aroused such condemnation in the wake of recent tragedies. Also mindful that once more the event was under the microscope, Lord Sefton gathered the competing riders to warn them that the going was riding fast and that the usual mad dash to the first fence must be avoided. Heeding this advice, the field went off at a more reasonable pace than usual, with only LOTORAY falling at the first. GREEN DRILL, TEA FIEND,

281

The television cameras which can be seen in the background could now relay this kind of drama live. Here, MR WHAT and GREEN DRILL come to earth at Becher's on the second circuit

Grand National was won by the first clear favourite to win the race since SPRIG in 1927, the occasion of the first radio commentary on the event and as on that day, the victor was owned by a lady.

All in all the events of the day were an overwhelming success, not just for those associated with MERRYMAN II or all who backed him, but for the countless thousands who enjoyed the excitement of the race from the comfort of their armchairs and for the racecourse executive as well. For the latter came a congratulatory telegram from the Home Secretary, giving hope that the criticism of recent times, if well intentioned, was without foundation.

ARLES and SABARIA led them along without further incident, with MR WHAT and MERRYMAN II nicely placed just behind the leading quartet. Uncharacteristically WYNDBURGH fell at Becher's, the first time he had ever failed to survive an Aintree obstacle and MERRYMAN II almost added to the casualties at the next, but he rectified the mistake to continue some lengths behind TEA FIEND, still dominating the proceedings. There were twenty left going back out into the country. TEA FIEND, MERRYMAN II and BADANLOCH were some lengths clear coming into Becher's again but at the fence after Valentine's the former began to fade as GREEN DRILL and CLEAR PROFIT tried to improve their positions. Striding out confidently, MERRYMAN II took up the running at the last open ditch, leaving Stan Mellor on BADANLOCH unable to cope with their acceleration. Drawing ever farther ahead, the favourite came to the final fence with his race safe bar a fall, landed in full stride and romped home fifteen lengths clear of BADANLOCH, with CLEAR PROFIT third and TEA FIEND fourth. By coincidence the first televised

MERRYMAN II comes home a comfortable winner under G Scott. Mr Scott can be found these days at the other end of the course as one of our most experienced Starters

282

1960

With £12,000 added, being £5,000 given by The Irish Hospital Sweepstakes and £7,000 (including a gold trophy value £600), by Messrs Tophams Ltd. For six-year-olds & upwards. The second to receive 10%, the third 5% and the fourth 2½% of the whole stakes. The trainer & rider of the Winner receive a cup value £100

Date: 26th March 1960	Starters: 26	Time: 9 mins 26⅕ secs
1st **MERRYMAN II**	**9.10−12** (*Miss W H S Wallace*)	**G Scott**
2nd **BADANLOCH**	**9.10−9** (*Lord Leverhulme*)	**S Mellor**
3rd **CLEAR PROFIT**	**10.10−1** (*Mr B Sunley*)	**B Wilkinson**
4th **TEA FIEND**	**11.10−0** (*Mr J D Pickering*)	**P G Madden**
5th **SABARIA**	**9.10−3** (*Mr A R Turnell*)	**M Roberts**
6th **GREEN DRILL**	**10.10−3** (*Lord Cadogan*)	**G Milburn**
7th **ARLES**	**8.10−4** (*Mr H K Jones*)	**Mr A Moule**
8th **SKATEALONG**	**12.10−0** (*Mr H Thomson Jones*)	**R R Harrison**

Also Ran:

MR WHAT 10.11–11 (Mr D J Coughlan) **A Freeman** *Fell*; *WYNDBURGH 10.11–7* (Mrs J K M Oliver) **M Scudamore** *Fell*; *DANDY SCOT 10.11–7* (Mr S C Banks) **F T Winter** *Fell*; *HOLLY BANK 13.10–12* (Mr S H Brookshaw) **Mr P Brookshaw** *Fell*; *TEAM SPIRIT 8.10–12* (Mrs D R Brand) **G W Robinson** *Fell*; *IRISH COFFEE 10.10–11* (Mr W St George Burke) **Mr W St George Burke** *Pulled-up*; *CLANYON 12.10–8* (Mr W N Johns-Powell) **R E Jenkins** *Fell*; *CANNOBIE LEE 9.10–7* (The Late Miss D Paget) **D Nicholson** *Refused*; *KNOXTOWN 10.10–5* (Mr M Cowley) **Mr E P Harty** *Fell*; *SKIPPER JACK 8.10–4* (Mr R A Keith) **D O'Donovan** *Fell*; *PENDLE LADY 10.10–4* (Mr A Watson) **M Towers** *Fell*; *JONJO 10.10–4* (Mr J L O'Hagen) **P Taaffe** *Fell*; *UNCLE WHISKERS 8.10–1* (Mr W St George Burke) **C Finnegan** *Fell*; *CLOVER BUD 10.10–1* (Mr G G Llewellin) **T Taaffe** *Pulled-up*; *EAGLE LODGE 11.10–1* (Mr N A Mardon) **W Rees** *Pulled-up*; *BELSIZE II 11.10–0* (Mr W G Boomer) **P Shortt** *Fell*; *LOTORAY 10.10–6* (Mr W Miller) **M Batchelor** *Fell*; *ALIFORM 8.10–0* (Mr A Summers) **T W Biddlecombe** *Fell*

The Betting: *13/2 Merryman II; 8/1 Wyndburgh; 9/1 Team Spirit; 10/1 Dandy Scot; 100/9 Cannobie Lee; 100/7 Badanloch; 18/1 Mr What; 20/1 Clear Profit & Clover Bud; 33/1 Tea Fiend & Green Drill; 40/1 Pendle Lady; 45/1 Arles, Aliform, Knoxtown & Eagle Lodge; 50/1 Holly Bank, Jonjo, Uncle Whiskers & Clanyon; 66/1 Others.*

Distances: *Fifteen lengths; twelve lengths*

Winner Trained By: *Neville Crump, Middleham, Yorkshire*

Value to Winning Owner: *£13,134*

1961

No doubt inspired by the report of Mr Georgi Malenkov, the former Russian Premier, who had been the guest of Mrs Topham for the 1956 race, the Soviet Union set their sights on the 'National in 1961. Three wiry-looking horses, EPIGRAF II, GRIFEL and RELJEF, made a 2,000 mile journey from Russia, finishing their preparation at Haydock Park, in a sporting invasion which for an all too brief period eased the tension of relations between East and West. Due to the conditions of the handicapping system in this country, the Soviet trio were placed at the head of the weights with the now maximum 12 st but shortly before race day, EPIGRAF, reputedly their brightest prospect, was declared unfit to run.

The Irish Hospital Sweepstakes were joined in their sponsorship of the event by Messrs Schweppes Limited, so this became the richest Grand National ever. In an imaginative and novel attempt to extend rewards to those involved in the finish, cash prizes ranging from £12 to £1,000 were set aside for the trainers, jockeys and stable employees of the first four horses. Welcomed by many critics was the long called-for modification of the obstacles, which without affecting their size, did away with their daunting upright appearance through the provision of a sloping 'apron' on the take-off side.

Leopardstown 'Chase winner JONJO, ridden by Pat Taaffe, replaced last year's hero MERRYMAN II shortly before the off as

Russian invader RELJEF and his jockey part company at the first brook

7/1 favourite. OXO, MR WHAT and WYND-BURGH were also in the field of thirty-five, making this one of the most interesting contests for many years.

On looks alone, the super-fit grey NICO-LAUS SILVER, drew much interest although his single success since moving to the Kinnersley yard of Fred Rimell was hardly earth-shattering. A product of County Tipperary, by NICOLAUS out of RAYS OF MONTROSE, the grey was bred by James Heffernan and after an indifferent career in Ireland, was purchased on be-half of Mr Charles Vaughan at Balls-bridge in November 1960 for £2,600. Partnered by Bobby Beasley, grandson of Harry who had won with COME AWAY seventy years earlier, the nine-year-old was easy to back at 28/1.

FLOATER, APRIL QUEEN and CLOVER BUD came down at the first, leaving the Liver-pool-owned FRESH WINDS blazing a trail to Becher's. CARRASCO, BRIAN OGE, TAXIDER-MIST and GRIFEL were fallers here, though Soviet Master Sportsman Vladimir Prakhov gamely remounted, continuing a long way in arrears. The second Russian horse, RELJEF, unseated his rider Boris Ponomarenko after jumping Valentine's and GRIFEL was pulled-up after taking the Water. Coming to the end of his tether, FRESH WINDS tumbled at the first open ditch back in the country, leaving NICO-LAUS SILVER in front of JONJO, WYND-BURGH, IMPOSANT, MR WHAT, MERRYMAN II

and KILMORE and in this order they gal-loped to Becher's again. IMPOSANT and OXO pulled up here and DOUBLE CREST refused, the fourteen survivors now being taken along by MERRYMAN II closely pressed by NICOLAUS SILVER. Taking the lead at the second last, the grey cleared the final fence to race away on the run-in and win by five lengths from MERRYMAN II, who held off the late spurt of O'MALLEY POINT by a neck. SCOTTISH FLIGHT II was fourth. Despite his price, NICOLAUS SILVER had apparently been the selection of many smaller backers and unlike Fred Rimell's first winner E.S.B., he was a most worthy victor. As the first grey to win the 'Nation-al in ninety years and only the second of that colour in the history of the race, NICOLAUS SILVER had more than repaid the purchase price paid by Mr Vaughan. He had also revived, through his jockey Bobby Beasley, memories of the mighty Beasley brothers of the last century.

Above: At the last fence the grey has established a lead which he will keep over last year's winner

Left: MERRYMAN II and Nicolaus Silver touch down together over Becher's second time round

1961

With £17,000 added, being £5,000 given by Messrs Schweppes Limited; £5,000 by The Irish Hospitals Sweepstakes and £7,000, (including a gold trophy value £600), by Messrs Tophams Limited. The second to receive 10%, the third 5% and the fourth 2½% of the whole stakes. For six-year-olds & upwards. The trainer of the Winner to receive a cup value £100 and the rider of the Winner a cup value £50

		Date: 25th March 1961	Starters: 35	Time: 9 mins 22⅗ secs
1st	**NICOLAUS SILVER**	9.10–1 *(Mr C Vaughan)*	**H R Beasley**
2nd	**MERRYMAN II**	10.11–12 *(Miss W H S Wallace)*	**D Ancil**
3rd	**O'MALLEY POINT**	10.11–4 *(Mr A Elliott)*	**P A Farrell**
4th	**SCOTTISH FLIGHT II**	9.10–6 *(Mrs A T Hodgson)*	**W Rees**
5th	**KILMORE**	11.11–0 *(Mr N Cohen)*	**F T Winter**
6th	**WYNDBURGH**	11.11–5 *(Mrs J K M Oliver)*	**T Brookshaw**
7th	**JONJO**	11.10–7 *(Mr J L O'Hagen)*	**P Taaffe**
8th	**BADANLOCH**	10.10–11 *(Lord Leverhulme)*	**S Mellor**
9th	**TEAM SPIRIT**	9.10–13 *(Mrs D R Brand)*	**G W Robinson**
10th	**SIRACUSA**	8.10–1 *(Mrs E Truelove)*	**B Wilkinson**
11th	**MR WHAT**	11.11–9 *(Mr D J Coughlan)*	**D V Dick**
12th	**ERNEST**	9.10–1 *(Mrs L Brotherton)*	**H J East**
13th	**SABARIA**	10.10–2 *(Mr A R Turnell)*	**M Roberts**
14th	**IRISH COFFEE**	11.10–6 *(Mr W St George Burke)*	**J Magee**

Also Ran:

RELJEF 7.12–0 (USSR) (B Alexiev) **B Ponomarenko** *Unseated rider*; *GRIFEL 8.12–0* (USSR) (B Alexiev) **V Prakhov** *Pulled-up*; *OXO 10.11–8* (Mr J E Bigg) **M Scudamore** *Pulled-up*; *TAXIDERMIST 9.11–4* (Mrs P Hastings) **Mr J Lawrence** *Fell*; *HUNTER'S BREEZE 10.10–13* (Mrs L H Brown) **F Carroll** *Fell*; *IMPOSANT 9.10–13* (Mr R Couetil) **Mr R Couetil** *Pulled-up*; *FLOATER 8.10–11* (Mr C Hambro) **E P Harty** *Fell*; *FRESH WINDS 10.10–10* (Mr A Maiden) **R Edwards** *Fell*; *BRIAN OGE 10.10–10* (Mr F R Pullen) **J Guest** *Fell*; *CLOVER BUD 11.10–10* (Mr G G Llewellin) **D Mould** *Brought-down*; *DOUBLE CREST 9.10–7* (Mrs R M Byers) **A Irvine** *Refused*; *BANTRY BAY 10.10–7* (Mr H W Dufosee) **Sir Wm Pigott-Brown** *Fell*; *WILY ORIENTAL 9.10–6* (Mr E H Mount) **P G Madden** *Fell*; *OSCAR WILDE 11.10–4* (Mr T T Jasper) **R E Jenkins** *Fell*; *JIMURU 10.10–4* (Lady Leigh) **Mr J Leigh** *Fell*; *CARRASCO 9.10–3* (Mr D J W Jackson) **P Pickford** *Fell*; *PENNY FEATHER 8.10–1* (Mr N Hall) **J Lehane** *Pulled-up*; *KINGSTEL 9.10–0* (Mr C Hornby) **G Slack** *Fell*; *VIVANT 8.10–6* (Mrs T W Parker) **D Nicholson** *Fell*; *TEA FIEND 12.10–0* (Mr J D Pickering) **R R Harrison** *Fell*; *APRIL QUEEN 10.10–2* (Mr M P Fear) **A Biddlecombe** *Fell*

The Betting: *7/1 Jonjo; 8/1 Merryman II; 100/7 Siracusa & Hunter's Breeze; 100/6 O'Malley Point & Scottish Flight II; 20/1 Badanloch, Team Spirit, Mr What & Oxo; 28/1 Nicolaus Silver; 33/1 Kilmore, Wyndburgh, Ernest & Jimuru; 40/1 Bantry Bay, Carrasco, Taxidermist, Tea Fiend & Wily Oriental; 45/1 Oscar Wilde; 50/1 Vivant, Clover Bud, Floater, Irish Coffee, Kingstel & Double Crest; 66/1 Penny Feather & Fresh Winds; 100/1 Others.*

Distances: *Five lengths; a neck*

Winner Trained By: *Fred Rimell, Kinnersley, Worcestershire*

Value to Winning Owner: *£20,020*

1962

Frost and heavy rain had turned the track into a quagmire and on 'National day itself the elements varied from brief spells of sunshine to snow, hail and sleet. Extremes existed among the competitors too, in both age and experience of what lay ahead. The brilliant young FRENCHMAN'S COVE, a son of Derby winner AIRBORNE, was tackling the big fences for the first time, yet such was his reputation over Park courses that he headed the betting at 7/1.

After becoming a leading flat race apprentice, increasing weight had forced Josh Gifford to turn his attention to the winter sport and he was rapidly emerging as a rising star in this field. His debut 'National ride was the Renton-trained SIRACUSA. For the third successive year MERRYMAN II had a new partner, once more as a result of an injury to Gerry Scott, but without a victory in the current season and despite the valuable assistance of Dave Dick as jockey, the top weight was allowed to start at 20/1. NICOLAUS SILVER, meanwhile, was the object of stringent security procedures after his rider Bobby Beasley received threatening letters warning him not to win and memories of the days of GOLDEN MILLER were revived. Since his victory last year the grey had won the Grand Sefton and Great Yorkshire 'Chases in tremendous style and even with nine pounds more than last time was the subject of many hefty gambles. Of the old brigade, WYNDBURGH, MR WHAT, TEAM SPIRIT and KILMORE renewed rivalry, although they were now felt to be past their best.

KILMORE, trained by hurdle race specialist Ryan Price, was bred by George Webb at Corolanty, County Offaly, being by ZALOPHUS out of BROWN IMAGE and through the dam was related to the legen-dary BROWN JACK. Through a series of owners and trainers KILMORE performed doggedly over both hurdles and fences, without ever giving the impression he was destined for great things. Late in 1960 he was purchased for 3,000 guineas by film magnate Nat Cohen who ran the horse in partnership with Ben Rosenfield, a Hatton Garden jeweller. Again partnered by Fred Winter, KILMORE went off at 28/1. In what was to be one of the grimmest tests of stamina ever, the thirty-two runners set off, only the strongly fancied SPRINGBOK failing to survive the first fence and considering the conditions the first circuit was surprisingly trouble-free. SIRA-CUSA coming down at the eleventh and DANDY TIM falling at the Water left twenty-nine gamely slogging on into the country for the final time. FREDITH'S SON, an Irish long-shot, had thus far made all the running, ahead of CANNOBIE LEE, MR WHAT, FRENCHMAN'S COVE and DUPLICA-TOR but the further they went, the more strung out they became. Pat Taaffe took KERFORO up to challenge the leader, only to fall at the fence before Becher's where FREDITH'S SON held a ten-length lead over another outsider from Ireland GAY NAVARREE. Then came MR WHAT, WYND-BURGH, NICOLAUS SILVER, CLEAR PROFIT and the improving KILMORE and at this stage it seemed certain the winner would come from these seven. With FREDITH'S SON tiring, amateur Mr Cameron sent GAY NAVARREE to the front. Coming into the last fence there were four almost in line, WYNDBURGH, MR WHAT, GAY NAVARREE and KILMORE, but touching down first, Fred Winter quickly opened up a decisive lead on KILMORE. Chased home by WYND-BURGH and MR WHAT, KILMORE passed the post ten lengths and the same in front of his veteran pursuers, with GAY NAVARREE staying on to finish fourth. KILMORE became at twelve the oldest horse to win the race since SERGEANT MURPHY in 1923 and with WYNDBURGH and MR WHAT the same age, it was a day of celebration for the tried and tested ones. Fred Winter's second 'National success was the more rewarding for him with KILMORE trained by his retained stable and prepared by the man associated with so many of his other race-course triumphs, Ryan Price. For WYNDBURGH, this was the end of his gallant attempts at Grand National glory. Retired to his owner's home, with nothing more vigorous than an occasional run to hounds ahead of him, WYNDBURGH, placed second three times, would be remembered with affection longer than some winners.

The great Fred Winter and KILMORE splash their way to a ten length victory

1962

With £17,000 added, being £5,000 given by Messrs Schweppes Limited; £5,000 by The Irish Hospital Sweepstakes and £7,000, (including a gold trophy value £600), by Messrs Tophams Limited. The second to receive 10%, the third 5% and the fourth 2½% of the whole stakes. For six-year-olds & upwards. The trainer of the Winner to receive a cup value £100 and the rider of the Winner a cup value £50

Date: 31st March 1962	Starters: 32	Time: 9 mins 50 secs
1st **KILMORE**	12.10–4 *(Mr N Cohen)*	F T Winter
2nd **WYNDBURGH**	12.10–9 *(Mrs J K M Oliver)*	T A Barnes
3rd **MR WHAT**	12.10–9 *(Mr G V Keeling)*	J Lehane
4th **GAY NAVARREE**	10.10–0 *(Mr J F Hoey)*	Mr A Cameron
5th **FREDITH'S SON**	11.10–11 *(Mr M P Keogh)*	F Shortt
6th **DARK VENETIAN**	7.10–0 *(Mrs T M Stuck)*	P Cowley
7th **NICOLAUS SILVER**	10.10–10 *(Mr C Vaughan)*	H R Beasley
8th **CANNOBIE LEE**	11.10–1 *(Mrs A M Bancroft)*	E P Harty
9th **ERNEST**	10.10–0 *(Mr R B Woodard)*	A Dufton
10th **CLOVER BUD**	12.10–4 *(Mr G G Llewellin)*	D Nicholson
11th **BLONDE WARRIOR**	10.10–6 *(Mr A H East)*	T W Biddlecombe
12th **SOLFEN**	10.11–2 *(Mr B Naughton)*	P Taaffe
13th **MERRYMAN II**	11.11–8 *(Miss W H S Wallace)*	D V Dick
14th **COLLEDGE MASTER**	12.10–13 *(Mr L R Morgan)*	Mr L R Morgan
15th **FORTRON**	9.10–0 *(Mr J D Pickering)*	R Langley
16th **POLITICS**	10.10–0 *(Mrs T M Stuck)*	D Bassett
17th **CLEAR PROFIT**	12.10–0 *(Mr B Sunley)*	T J Ryan

Also Ran:

FRENCHMAN'S COVE 7.11–5 (Mr Stanhope Joel) **S Mellor** *Brought-down*; *TAXIDERMIST 10.10–10* (Mrs P Hastings) **Mr J Lawrence** *Pulled-up*; *CHAVARA 9.10–7* (Mrs I Evans) **M Scudamore** *Pulled-up*; *SUPERFINE 9.10–6* (Miss B Kerwood) **Sir Wm Pigott-Brown** *Fell*; *TEAM SPIRIT 10.10–6* (Mr R B Woodard) **G W Robinson** *Fell*; *SPRINGBOK 8.10–6* (Col Lord Joicey) **P Buckley** *Fell*; *CLIPADOR 11.10–4* (Mr F L Vickerman) **P A Farrell** *Pulled-up*; *KERFORO 8.10–3* (Mr F J Stafford) **P Taaffe** *Fell*; *DUPLICATOR 9.10–2* (Miss A H Robertson) **G Milburn** *Fell*; *DANDY TIM 9.10–0* (Mr C J Baines) **R Carter** *Fell*; *VIVANT 9.10–0* (Mrs T W Parker) **R J Hamey** *Pulled-up*; *SIRACUSA 9.10–0* (Mrs E Truelove) **J Gifford** *Fell*; *CARRAROE 10.10–0* (Mrs Miles Valentine) **Mr W McLernon** *Fell*; *MELILLA 8.10–0* (Mr D H Ellison) **G Cramp** *Pulled-up*; *SEAS END 10.10–5* (Mrs M D Kempton) **J H Kempton** *Pulled-up*

The Betting: *7/1 Frenchman's Cove; 9/1 Solfen; 100/9 Nicolaus Silver & Kerforo; 100/8 Springbok; 100/6 Superfine & Vivant; 20/1 Merryman II & Taxidermist; 22/1 Mr What & Team Spirit; 28/1 Kilmore & Duplicator; 33/1 Colledge Master & Siracusa; 40/1 Cannobie Lee; 45/1 Wyndburgh; 50/1 Chavara & Dandy Tim; 66/1 Blonde Warrior, Clear Profit, Fredith's Son, Carraroe, Clipador & Ernest; 100/1 Others.*

Distances: *Ten lengths; ten lengths*

Winner Trained By: *Ryan Price, Findon, Sussex*

Value to Winning Owner: *£20,238*

1963

One of the co-sponsors, Schweppes, withdrew their support of the 'National in 1963, preferring to inaugurate an event on the opening day of the Liverpool meeting. It received widespread publicity as the richest race of its kind in Britain, a most auspicious launch for the Schweppes Gold Trophy Handicap Hurdle. Stepping into the breach in place of Schweppes came another company in the liquid refreshment business, Messrs Vaux Limited and in recognition of their sponsorship, the Grand National Steeplechase carried the sub-title, 'for the Vaux Gold Tankard'.

Gregory Peck and his wife Veronique, with Pat Taaffe, rider of Mr Peck's OWEN'S SEDGE

There was more than a touch of glamour in the shapely form of Hollywood actress Kim Novak making her first visit to Aintree and Gregory Peck was another visitor, though in his case there was a far more personal reason for attending. He was the owner of a striking grey called OWEN'S SEDGE, the mount of Pat Taaffe. As the housewives' choice, Mr Peck's runner figured prominently in the market. Favourite at 10/1 was last year's first fence faller SPRINGBOK, this time ridden by Gerry Scott and with MERRYMAN II absent, Neville Crump's only representative. Former winners KILMORE, NICOLAUS SILVER and MR WHAT were trying to repeat their moment of glory and for MR WHAT it was a sixth appearance in the race. Now trained by former jockey Jack Dowdeswell the thirteen-year-old was a first 'National ride for promising Irish jockey Tommy Carberry. It was eleven years since the Duke of Alburquerque took part in the race, but the experience must have left an impression on the tall Spanish nobleman for he was back again to ride his own horse JONJO. TEAM SPIRIT, LOVING RECORD, DAGMAR GITTELL and CARRICKBEG were well supported in the betting, the last-named running in the colours of Mr Gay Kindersley, a leading amateur rider. A half share in CARRICKBEG was owned by that most descriptive of racing journalists, Mr John Lawrence, who also took the mount on the seven-year-old.

Eighteen of the forty-seven runners were listed as 66/1 others, among them a chestnut gelding by the name of AYALA. By SUPERTELLO out of ADMIRAL'S BLISS, he was bred by Mr J P Phillips and after an unsuccessful spell on the flat was switched to National Hunt racing. Considered of no account also in this branch of the sport, AYALA was sold at Epsom for just £200 in 1960 to trainer Keith Piggott, father of the outstanding Lester, and a man whose own career in the saddle had brought him into contact more than once with the 'National. Piggott sold a half share in his purchase to well-known hairdresser Mr P B Raymond, to whom the media attached the nickname 'Teazy-Weazy'. A most difficult horse to train, AYALA had only three races in his preparation for Aintree. Pat Buckley took the mount, no doubt reflecting on the turnabout in his fortunes, for last year he had partnered the strongly-fancied SPRINGBOK.

OUT AND ABOUT led them all a merry chase, striding out a long way ahead of the bunch, which after the falls of CONNIE II and AVENUE NEUILLY at the fence after Valentine's still consisted of thirty-eight runners. As they ran back down to Becher's Josh Gifford and OUT AND ABOUT were still running away with the race and the top weights were having difficulty reducing his lead. There were no fallers at the Brook, but OUT AND ABOUT began to come back to his field. FRENCH LAWYER, SPRINGBOK, OWEN'S SEDGE and CARRICK-BEG all closed on the leader and Pat Buckley moved AYALA quietly into a challenging position. Four from home, OUT AND ABOUT fell and Mr Lawrence was forced to take evasive action on CARRICK-BEG, but as they made the turn to the second last fence, CARRICKBEG was right back in the hunt and with HAWA'S SONG, SPRINGBOK, AYALA, KILMORE and OWEN'S SEDGE close up, a good finish looked likely. As CARRICKBEG ran to the final fence in front, Pat Buckley shouted a word of encouragement to John Lawrence, convinced that the race was theirs. Passing the elbow with a lead of a couple of lengths, Mr Lawrence looked certain to become the first amateur to succeed since 1946, but with less than a hundred yards to run, he felt the horse change legs and knew his mount had broken down. John Lawrence gave CARRICKBEG every assistance to last the trip through yet with Pat Buckley finishing powerfully on AYALA the struggle was an unequal one. Caught in the final fifty yards, CARRICKBEG went under by three parts of a length and AYALA became the longest-priced winner since RUSSIAN HERO in 1949. HAWA'S SONG finished five lengths back in third place, in front of TEAM SPIRIT, SPRINGBOK, KILMORE and Gregory Peck's runner OWEN'S SEDGE. In all, twenty-two completed the course, an overwhelming justification for the recent modification of the fences and an encouragement for owners of top-class animals to enter their horses in the 'National. As trainer and co-owner of AYALA, Keith Piggott joined his famous father Ernie on the Aintree's Roll of Honour and with son Lester being compared with the immortal Fred Archer as the maestro of flat racing, the talents of this incredible family became a source of wonder. The worthy winner on the day, AYALA failed to finish in the first four in ten subsequent outings.

1963

With £17,000 added, being £5,000 given by Messrs Vaux Limited, £5,000 by The Irish Hospitals Sweepstakes and £7,000 by Messrs Tophams Limited. The second to receive 10%, the third 5% and the fourth 2½% of the whole stakes. For six-year-olds & upwards. The trainer of the Winner to receive a cup value £100 and the rider of the Winner a cup value £50

Date: 30th March 1963	Starters: 47	Time: 9 mins 35⅘ secs
1st **AYALA**	**9.10–0** *(Mr P B Raymond)*	**P Buckley**
2nd **CARRICKBEG**	**7.10–3** *(Mr G Kindersley)*	**Mr J Lawrence**
3rd **HAWA'S SONG**	**10.10–0** *(Mr W Stephenson)*	**P Broderick**
4th **TEAM SPIRIT**	**11.10–3** *(Mr R B Woodard)*	**G W Robinson**
5th **SPRINGBOK**	**9.10–12** *(Col Lord Joicey)*	**G Scott**
6th **KILMORE**	**13.11–0** *(Mr N Cohen)*	**F T Winter**
7th **OWEN'S SEDGE**	**10.11–6** *(Mr Gregory Peck)*	**P Taaffe**
8th **FRENCH LAWYER**	**9.10–0** *(Mr R L Newton)*	**T Ryan**
9th **DARK VENETIAN**	**8.10–2** *(Mrs T M Stuck)*	**D Bassett**
10th **NICOLAUS SILVER**	**11.11–0** *(Mr B Sunley)*	**H R Beasley**
11th **ETERNAL**	**12.10–10** *(Lt Col R Fenwick-Palmer)*	**T Brookshaw**
12th **CHAVARA**	**10.10–2** *(Mrs I Evans)*	**R Edwards**
13th **CARRAROE**	**11.10–1** *(Mrs Miles Valentine)*	**Mr W McLernon**
14th **SIRACUSA**	**10.10–0** *(Mrs E Truelove)*	**D Mould**
15th **SHAM FIGHT**	**11.10–1** *(Mr R M C Jeffreys)*	**J Fitzgerald**
16th **BLONDE WARRIOR**	**11.10–9** *(Mr M Naylor-Leyland)*	**B Lawrence**
17th **LOYAL TAN**	**8.10–5** *(Mrs G Kohn)*	**T Biddlecombe**
18th **WOODBROWN**	**9.10–0** *(Mr P Brown)*	**J Kenneally**
19th **O'MALLEY POINT**	**12.11–1** *(Major L S Marler)*	**M Scudamore**
20th **FRENCHMAN'S COVE**	**8.12–0** *(Mr Stanhope Joel)*	**D V Dick**
21st **FORTY SECRETS**	**9.10–7** *(Mr A D Clark)*	**C Chapman**
22nd **DANDY TIM**	**10.10–0** *(Mr C J Baines)*	**L Major**

Also Ran:

LOVING RECORD 9.10–12 (Mr J L Young) **T Taaffe** *Pulled-up*; *MR JONES 8.10–10* (Major J G Lyon) **P A Farrell** *Fell*; *MR WHAT 13.10–8* (Mr G V Keeling) **T Carberry** *Brought-down*; *OUT AND ABOUT 8.10–7* (Mr B Sunley) **J Gifford** *Fell*; *GOOD GRACIOUS 9.10–7* (Mr J F Smith) **P Connors** *Fell*; *DAGMAR GITTELL 8.10–5* (Mrs L Brotherton) **H J East** *Pulled-up*; *JONJO 13.10–6* (Duque de Alburquerque) **Duke of Alburquerque** *Fell*; *PEACETOWN 9.10–4* (Mrs F Williams) **R Langley** *Fell*; *MOYRATH 10.10–2* (Mrs R L Johnson) **F Carroll** *Pulled-up*; *GAY NAVARREE 11.10–1* (Mr G Wright) **P Cowley** *Fell*; *SEAS END 11.10–3* (Mrs M D Kempton) **J H Kempton** *Pulled-up*; *COLLEGE DON 11.10–0* (Mrs I Watts) **B Wilkinson** *Pulled-up*; *WINGLESS 8.10–3* (Mr O H Gilbey) **A Biddlecombe** *Fell*; *AVENUE NEUILLY 8.10–4* (Major Derek Hague) **D Nicholson** *Fell*; *REPRIEVED 10.10–1* (Mrs S Nossell) **P Pickford** *Pulled-up*; *VIVANT 10.10–0* (Mrs T W Parker) **R J Hamey** *Brought-down*; *CONNIE II 11.10–0* (Mr P W Hicks) **J Guest** *Fell*; *HOLM STAR 9.10–0* (Mr J F Smith) **E F Kelly** *Pulled-up*; *WARTOWN 12.10–1* (Col R L Crouch) **J Gamble** *Fell*; *LOOK HAPPY 10.10–0* (Mrs J C M Roberts) **J Haine** *Fell*; *MERGANSER 10.10–4* (Mrs W Archdale) **Mr J Mansfield** *Fell*; *CAPRICORN 10.10–0* (Mr R A Phelps) **A Major** *Pulled-up*; *MAGIC TRICKS 9.10–0* (Mr J H Boyes) **O McNally** *Fell*; *MELILLA 9.10–0* (Mr D H Ellison) **G Cramp** *Pulled-up*; *SOLONACE 12.10–0* (Mr S C Warner) **K B White** *Fell*

The Betting: *10/1 Springbok; 100/8 Kilmore; 13/1 Team Spirit; 100/7 Loving Record & Dagmar Gittell; 100/6 Frenchman's Cove; 20/1 Carrickbeg & Owen's Sedge; 25/1 Eternal & Out and About; 28/1 Hawa's Song, Nicolaus Silver & Mr Jones; 33/1 Carraroe, Moyrath, Dark Venetian, O'Malley Point & Siracusa; 40/1 Look Happy, Vivant & Chavara; 50/1 Forty Secrets, Sham Fight, Peacetown, Gay Navarree, French Lawyer, Reprieved, Dandy Tim & Connie II: 66/1 Ayala and Others.*

Distances: *Three-quarters of a length; five lengths*

Winner Trained By: *Keith Piggott, Lambourn, Berkshire*

Value to Winning Owner: *£21,315*

1964

At just the time when the dangers of Aintree had to all intents and purposes been reduced to a level acceptable to all, there occurred an accident which once more opened up the age-old argument of safety at the Liverpool venue. That the tragic incident took place away from the Grand National course, and might well have been on any jump course in the country, held little sway with those ever ready to point the damning finger. Tim Brookshaw, that most genial and talented of jockeys ever to grace the National Hunt scene, incurred horrific injuries in a fall during the running of the Holly Handicap Hurdle at Aintree's Yuletide meeting in December 1963. When the news came through that this brave thirty-four-year-old rider had suffered a broken back which would deny him amongst many other things his livelihood, the critics in their fury missed the obvious point most in need of urgent appraisal: What compensation or welfare provision existed for those at the business end of the Sport of Kings and Queens? It was a question left unanswered by those best able to answer and, as will sadly be seen, the problem remained.

Once more under the microscope, Aintree prepared for the 1964 Grand National with little attention paid to the fact that this year the race was without commercial sponsorship, its prize money made up from the added money provided by Tophams and a contribution of £10,000 from the Horserace Betting Levy Board. There were thirty-three runners, of which four shared favouritism at 100/7. These were Pat Taaffe's mount PAPPAGENO'S COTTAGE, the grey FLYING WILD, the Michael Scudamore-ridden TIME and Her Majesty the Queen Mother's eight-year-old LAFFY. Giving weight to all was the 1960 Cheltenham Gold Cup winner PAS SEUL, trained by Bob Turnell and ridden by Dave Dick, and the inclusion of such a class horse was an indication that the recent alterations to the fences were having the desired effect. AYALA and KILMORE were back, together with SPRINGBOK, OUT AND ABOUT and GAY NAVARREE, although the latter having been bought by holiday camp king Mr Fred Pontin now carried the name PONTIN-GO. Another making a reappearance, for the fifth successive time, was twelve-year-old TEAM SPIRIT and as the winner of the most recent Grand Sefton 'Chase he figured well in the betting despite his age. Small in stature but with enormous heart, he was bred by Mr P J Coonan in County Kildare and was by that prolific sire of jumpers VULGAN, out of LADY WALEWSKA. Purchased at Ballsbridge for 250 guineas by Dan Moore, he eventually ended up as the property of a syndicate of owners, Americans Ronald B Woodard and John K Goodman and Englishman Gamble North. He was also transferred to the highly successful stable of Fulke Walwyn, a man with more than a passing knowledge of Aintree and its requirements. Irishman Willie Robinson was in the saddle again.

Before the day's racing, yet more tragedy was to attach itself to the event. A plane crashed near the Canal Turn and cast a shadow over the afternoon's activities, for the five occupants of the aircraft had all perished. Among them was television personality, author and journalist Nancy Spain, on her way to Aintree as the guest of Mrs Topham.

Racing at a sensible pace, the field came over the first fence headed by the notorious front-runner OUT AND ABOUT, the only faller here being the grey mare FLYING WILD. LAFFY was the next to go at the fourth, by which time OUT AND ABOUT and locally-trained PEACETOWN had opened up a big lead. Becher's was crossed without incident and there were surprisingly few casualties as the leaders turned to come back to the racecourse, although PAS SEUL was missing. With PEACETOWN and OUT AND ABOUT well in advance as they came to the Chair, the main group of runners crowded into the narrow approach, some horses became unsighted and there were some nasty falls. BORDER FLIGHT turned over in an awful-looking somersault and it was obvious that his jockey Paddy Farrell was seriously injured. PEACETOWN led OUT AND ABOUT by three lengths over the Water, with TEAM SPIRIT twelve lengths back in third place, then came TIME, REPRODUCTION, MERGANSER, PAPPAGENO'S COTTAGE, PURPLE SILK and KILMORE. On the run back to Becher's OUT AND ABOUT began to flag, and round the Canal Turn it was still PEACETOWN with a commanding lead, with PURPLE SILK, SPRINGBOK, ETERNAL, PONTIN-GO and TEAM SPIRIT all ready to pounce. At the last fence, John Kenneally brought PURPLE SILK to the front with a well-timed run. PURPLE SILK had his five pursuers stretched across the course and hugging the far rail, he passed the elbow two lengths to the good. He was still in front and going strongly two hundred yards from the post, when Willie Robinson found an extra gear with little TEAM SPIRIT and sprinting up the centre of the course began reducing the deficit stride by stride. It was only in the final yards that TEAM SPIRIT edged in front, to pass the post a half-length winner in one of the most exciting finishes seen for a long time. PEACETOWN was six lengths back in third place, ahead of ETERNAL, who was admirably ridden by nineteen-year-old Cheshire amateur Stephen Davenport taking part in his first 'National. It was a triumphant return to Aintree for co-owner Ronald Woodard, who in 1943 had been stationed here as a member of the American forces. Fulke Walwyn joined the elite band of men to have both ridden and then trained a Grand National winner and the reward for game little TEAM SPIRIT was honourable retirement in the United States.

The tragic accident to thirty-four-year-old Paddy Farrell, coming so soon after that to Tim Brookshaw, revealed a dreadfully inadequate state of affairs on the question of compensation to jockeys injured in races. For such as Paddy Farrell, the father of four children under the age of seven, the future was a bleak and painful one. The reaction of many of those at the top of the sport was disappointingly negative, to say the least, and it was left to humanitarians such as Mr Edward Courage and Mr Clifford Nicholson to lay the foundations of the Injured Jockeys Fund, which thanks to the generosity of the public now provides the support so deserved by those who daily risk life and limb. In the meantime, the hardship suffered by the courageous Paddy Farrell and his family was an indictment of a system of unthinking administration.

1964

With £17,000 added, being £10,000 given by The Horserace Betting Levy Board and £7,000, (including a gold trophy value £600), by Messrs Tophams Limited. For six-year-olds & upwards. The second to receive 10%, the third 5% and the fourth 2½% of the whole stakes. The trainer of the Winner to receive a cup value £100 and the rider of the Winner a cup value £50.

Date: 21st March 1964	Starters: 33	Time: 9 mins 46⅘ secs
1st **TEAM SPIRIT**	12.10−3 *(Mr J K Goodman)*	**G W Robinson**
2nd **PURPLE SILK**	9.10−4 *(Mr T Beattie)*	**J Kenneally**
3rd **PEACETOWN**	10.10−1 *(Mrs F Williams)*	**R Edwards**
4th **ETERNAL**	13.10−2 *(Lt Col R Fenwick-Palmer)*	**Mr S Davenport**
5th **PONTIN-GO** (formerly GAY NAVARREE)	12.10−0 *(Mr F W Pontin)*	**P Jones**
6th **SPRINGBOK**	10.10−11 *(Col Lord Joicey)*	**G Scott**
7th **APRIL ROSE**	9.10−0 *(Mrs M Cowley)*	**E P Harty**
8th **BAXIER**	8.10−0 *(Lord Fermoy)*	**Mr W McLernon**
9th **CROBEG**	11.10−4 *(Mr M J Richardson)*	**Mr J Lawrence**
10th **PAPPAGENO'S COTTAGE**	9.11−0 *(Mr W G King)*	**P Taaffe**
11th **JOHN O'GROATS**	10.10−3 *(Mr F Clay)*	**P Kelleway**
12th **SUPERSWEET**	7.10−1 *(Miss M Britton)*	**P Broderick**
13th **CLAYMORE**	11.10−0 *(Mr C Davies)*	**Mr C Davies**
14th **OUT AND ABOUT**	9.10−1 *(Mr B Sunley)*	**B Gregory**
15th **SEA KNIGHT**	9.11−0 *(Mr F D Nicholson)*	**Mr P Nicholson**

Also Ran:

PAS SEUL 11.12−0 (Mr John Rogerson) **D V Dick** *Fell*; FLYING WILD 8.11−3 (Mr R R Guest) **D Mould** *Fell*; BEAU NORMAND 8.10−10 (Mr H J Joel) **J King** *Refused*; LAFFY 8.10−8 (Her Majesty The Queen Mother) **W Rees** *Fell*; AYALA 10.10−7 (Mr P B Raymond) **D Nicholson** *Fell*; KILMORE 14.10−7 (Mr N Cohen) **F T Winter** *Fell*; L'EMPEREUR 10.10−5 (Comte L de Kerouara) **J Daumas** *Refused*; BORDER FLIGHT 9.10−3 (Mr E R Courage) **P A Farrell** *Fell*; RED THORN 8.10−3 (Mrs L H Brown) **T Biddlecombe** *Pulled-up*; LIZAWAKE 11.10−4 (Mr G C Hartigan) **H R Beasley** *Fell*; DANCING RAIN 9.10−0 (Capt P T Fenwick) **O McNally** *Fell*; CENTRE CIRCLE 9.10−0 (Mr W L Pilkington) **J Haine** *Fell*; REPRIEVED 11.10−0 (Mr C S Gardener) **P Harvey** *Pulled-up*; TIME 9.10−4 (Mr J Cheatle) **M Scudamore** *Fell*; REPRODUCTION 11.10−0 (Mr K R Ashton) **R Langley** *Fell*; MERGANSER 11.10−0 (Mr W Archdale) **J Lehane** *Fell*; GALE FORCE X 7.10−0 (Mr F Warrington-Gillet) **R Coonan** *Fell*; GROOMSMAN 9.10−0 (Mr J F Cleary) **F Shortt** *Fell*

The Betting: *100/7 Time, Pappageno's Cottage, Laffy & Flying Wild; 100/6 Beau Normand, Kilmore, Springbok, Border Flight & Purple Silk; 18/1 Team Spirit & Lizawake; 22/1 Pas Seul, April Rose & John O'Groats; 33/1 Out and About, Ayala & Red Thorn; 40/1 Supersweet, Baxier, Centre Circle, L'Empereur & Peacetown; 50/1 Crobeg, Gale Force X & Claymore; 66/1 Others.*

Distances: *Half a length; six lengths*

Winner Trained By: *Fulke Walwyn, Lambourn, Berkshire*

Value to Winning Owner: *£20,280*

1965

An announcement by Mrs Mirabel Topham on 1st July 1964, that she was selling Aintree racecourse to Capital and Counties Property Limited for building development, brought a gasp of astonishment from public and press alike. The intervention of Lord Sefton in seeking an injunction from the High Court to forbid the sale was based on his claim that the transaction was in breach of a covenant contained in the contract of sale when Tophams Limited purchased the racecourse from him fifteen years earlier. That carefully worded and crucial codicil, restricting the use of the land at Aintree to racing and agriculture during the lifetime of Lord and Lady Sefton, did at first glance appear to secure the future of the racecourse and with it the Grand National. Heard before Mr Justice Stamp, the court case in October 1964 received wide media coverage. Lord Sefton insisted that his actions did not seek damages, merely the right to preserve the great steeplechase. Great emphasis was made during the case, by eminent members of the National Hunt Committee, supported unanimously by leading trainers, that contrary to Mrs Topham's suggestions a Grand National run anywhere else but at Aintree was not only unthinkable but totally impractical. It was also made to appear somewhat sinister that shortly before her intention to sell the racecourse was made known, Mrs Topham had secured the copyright of the event's name, Grand National Steeplechase. That Lord Sefton won his injunction was hardly cause for applause, for as had correctly been determined during the case nothing and nobody could force Tophams Limited to continue promoting and financing horse racing at Aintree. It was with this most unsatisfactory state of affairs that Mirabel Dorothy Topham prepared for what, in her words, was to be the Last Grand National in March 1965.

It is interesting to note that, despite her pronounced intentions and with public opinion solidly, if unfairly against her, the forceful first lady of Aintree still provided four race meetings between October 1964 and March 1965. All without the assistance of sponsorship.

There was much excitement when the brilliant MILL HOUSE appeared among the one hundred and twelve entries for the 'last' 'National but with his subsequent withdrawal, the work of the handicapper was thrown into complete disarray. In accordance with Rule 50 of the National Hunt Committee all the weights were raised, resulting in all at the bottom of the handicap carrying 10 st 13 lbs. Top weight with 11 st 10 lbs was Scottish hope FREDDIE, owned and trained by Reg Tweedie. As winner of last season's Cheltenham Foxhunters' Challenge Cup and his two most recent races, FREDDIE was made favourite at 7/2, a most ungenerous price in a field of forty-seven. RONDETTO, KAPENO, VULTRIX and The Queen Mother's THE RIP were the next best supported in the betting, with American bred JAY TRUMP also attracting the attention of backers and the press.

Bred in Pennsylvania by Mr Jay Sessenich, JAY TRUMP was by TONGA PRINCE out of BE TRUMP and after failing to win on the flat, was purchased by leading American amateur rider Crompton Smith, on behalf of Mrs Mary Stephenson of Ohio who was anxious to find a horse to win the Maryland Hunt Cup. Crompton Smith's faith in JAY TRUMP was rewarded when the gelding twice carried him to victory in the premier American event over timber, after which horse and rider came to

Britain to prepare for the 'National. Both received rigorous coaching from the newest addition to the ranks of trainers, Fred Winter, who sent the horse and twenty-six-year-old rider out to win three times before they took their place at Aintree. FREDDIE was well up with the leaders over the first fence of the 'last' 'National, where AYALA was the only faller. Disputing the lead with FREDDIE over Becher's were DARK VENETIAN, PEACETOWN and PHEBU, while immediately behind them a pile-up further reduced the field. JAY TRUMP, moving well on the inside of the mid-division, avoided the chaos. Over Valentine's, the Duque de Alburquerque took a heavy fall with GROOMSMAN and the riderless RED TIDE was giving Pat McCarron on FREDDIE some anxious moments, before swerving across the path of PHEBU and bringing him down at the thirteenth. Approaching Becher's again it was PEACETOWN and RONDETTO, from L'EMPEREUR, FREDDIE, THE RIP, KAPENO and PONTIN-GO and for the first time JAY TRUMP appeared in a favourable position. Nimbly avoiding the fallen PONTIN-GO at the Canal Turn, JAY TRUMP moved through smoothly on the inside and with PEACETOWN tiring and RONDETTO falling at the twenty-sixth, the closing stages became a match between FREDDIE and JAY TRUMP. Neck and neck they raced to the last, the American champion crashing through it, yet surviving to come away a length in front. Switching to the far rail at the elbow, JAY TRUMP was set fair for a clear run to the line but Pat McCarron produced a brave last effort from the Scottish horse. With his tongue flopping from the side of his mouth, FREDDIE kept coming and when JAY TRUMP's rider struck him with the whip the race was almost thrown away. The horse

The Queen Mother and Princess Margaret in the Paddock before the big race. With them is Mr Peter Cazalet who trained the Queen Mother's Grand National entrant THE RIP

299

swerved, swished his tail in apparent anger and was within a second of being overtaken. But Crompton Smith realised his error immediately and putting down the stick, rode out with hands and heels to pass the post three-quarters of a length in front of FREDDIE. Twenty lengths further back came Mr Christopher Collins on his recent purchase MR JONES and RAINBOW BATTLE was fourth.

In training the winner of the race he had twice triumphed in as a jockey Fred Winter also deserved credit for his preparation of the rider. And all this in his first season as a licence-holder. After such an epic contest, the suggestion that there should be no more Grand Nationals seemed all the more inconceivable. But what could be done?

A victorious Crompton Smith is led in on the popular JAY TRUMP

THE GRAND NATIONAL HANDICAP STEEPLECHASE

1965

With £17,000 added, being £10,000 given by The Horserace Betting Levy Board and £7,000, (including a gold trophy value £600), by Messrs Tophams Limited. For six-year-olds & upwards. The second to receive 10%, the third 5% and the fourth 2½% of the whole stakes. The trainer of the Winner to receive a cup value £100 and the rider of the Winner a cup value £50

Date: 27th March 1965	Starters: 47	Time: 9 mins 30⅗ secs
1st **JAY TRUMP**	8.11−5 *(Mrs M Stephenson)*	**Mr T C Smith**
2nd **FREDDIE**	8.11−10 *(Mr R R Tweedie)*	**P McCarron**
3rd **MR JONES**	10.11−5 *(Mr C D Collins)*	**Mr C D Collins**
4th **RAINBOW BATTLE**	9.10−13 *(Mr W Shand-Kydd)*	**G Milburn**
5th **VULTRIX**	7.11−1 *(Mr H Dare)*	**D Nicholson**
6th **L'EMPEREUR**	11.10−13 *(Mr J Ciechanowski)*	**Mr J Ciechanowski**
7th **THE RIP**	10.11−5 *(Her Majesty The Queen Mother)*	**W Rees**
8th **LOVING RECORD**	11.11−0 *(Mr J J McDowell)*	**B Hannon**
9th **TANT PIS**	10.10−13 *(Mr J Alder)*	**Mr J Alder**
10th **BROWN DIAMOND**	10.10−13 *(Mrs P M Lamb)*	**Mr W McLernon**
11th **APRIL ROSE**	10.10−13 *(Major P Bengough)*	**Major P Bengough**
12th **CULLEENHOUSE**	11.10−13 *(Mrs L Carver)*	**T W Biddlecombe**
13th **PEACETOWN**	11.11−0 *(Mrs F Williams)*	**P Pickford**
14th **MOYRATH**	12.10−13 *(Mrs G Simpson)*	**B Richmond**

Also Ran:

RONDETTO 9.11–6 (Mr A B Mitchell) **J King** *Fell*; *FORGOTTEN DREAMS 11.11–0* (Mrs P Meehan) **R Coonan** *Fell*; *KAPENO 8.11–6* (Mrs A T Hodgson) **D V Dick** *Fell*; *AYALA 11.10–13* (Mr P B Raymond) **S Mellor** *Fell*; *BARLEYCROFT 10.10–13* (Mr A J Moore) **P Harvey** *Brought-down*; *LIZAWAKE 12.10–13* (Mrs E M Marshall) **Mr G Hartigan** *Pulled-up*; *TIME 10.10–13* (Capt M H Scott) **Mr B Scott** *Fell*; *PHEBU 8.10–13* (Mr N Brereton) **J Morrissey** *Brought-down*; *DARK VENETIAN 10.10–13* (Mr F Vincent) **J Renfree** *Fell*; *RED TIDE 8.10–13* (Mr Paul Mellon) **J Haine** *Fell*; *RUBY GLEN 10.10–13* (Mrs N H Le Mare) **S Davenport** *Brought-down*; *COLEEN STAR 11.10–13* (Mr P Milner) **J Leech** *Refused*; *PONTIN-GO* (formerly GAY NAVARREE) *13.10–13* (Mr F W Pontin) **J Lehane** *Fell*; *LEEDSY 7.10–13* (Mrs C Levy) **G W Robinson** *Fell*; *RONALD'S BOY 8.11–1* (Mr G Kindersley) **Mr G Kindersley** *Fell*; *BALLYGOWAN 11.10–13* (Mrs W L Pilkington) **A Redmond** *Refused*; *BOLD BIRI 9.10–13* (Mr J E Bigg) **M Scudamore** *Fell*; *REPRODUCTION 12.10–13* (Mr K R Ashton) **R Langley** *Pulled-up*; *SIZZLE-ON 9.10–13* (Mrs I D Jordan) **P Hurley** *Brought-down*; *LESLIE 9.10–13* (Lord Sherborne) **P Jones** *Baulked*; *SWORD FLASH 12.10–13* (Mr H T Smith) **T Ryan** *Pulled-up*; *VULCANO 7.10–13* (Miss Enid Chanelle) **T Carberry** *Pulled-up*; *GROOMSMAN 10.10–13* (Duque de Alburquerque) **Duque de Alburquerque** *Fell*; *QUINTIN BAY 9.10–13* (Mr S Martin) **P Taaffe** *Pulled-up*; *SOLONACE 14.10–13* (Mr W Clay) **R W Jones** *Baulked*; *FEARLESS CAVALIER 14.10–13* (Mr J K Hooton) **R West** *Refused*; *BLONDE WARRIOR 13.10–13* (Mrs K B Nicoll) **Mr D Crossley-Cooke** *Fell*; *CUTLETTE 8.10–13* (Mr B Parker) **M Roberts** *Pulled-up*; *NEDSMAR 11.10–13* (Mrs E E Graham) **J Hudson** *Fell*; *MR MCTAFFY 13.10–13* (Mrs P Barnett) **T Jackson** *Pulled-up*; *BLACK SPOT 8.10–13* (Mrs V M McGregor) **J Gamble** *Fell*; *CROBEG 12.10–13* (Mrs H J Rice Stringer) **Mr M C Gifford** *Brought-down*; *FRENCH COTTAGE 13.10–13* (Mr W A Tellwright) **Mr W A Tellwright** *Refused*

The Betting: *7/2 Freddie; 9/1 The Rip; 100/8 Rondetto & Kapeno; 100/6 Jay Trump & Vultrix; 18/1 Leedsy; 22/1 Forgotten Dreams; 25/1 Culleenhouse, Peacetown & Quintin Bay; 33/1 Red Tide, Loving Record, Leslie, Phebu & Ruby Glen; 40/1 Time, Tant Pis & Reproduction; 50/1 Brown Diamond, Vulcano, Cutlette, Pontin-Go, Rainbow Battle, Ayala, Mr Jones; 66/1 Ballygowan; 100/1 Others.*

Distances: *Three-quarters of a length; twenty lengths*

Winner Trained By: *Fred Winter, Lambourn, Berkshire*

Value to Winning Owner: *£22,041*

1966

Somehow, Aintree's fixtures continued, the Grand Sefton 'Chase being run in the autumn and the New Year meeting over the Mildmay course again taking place. The reprieve for the 'National was welcomed, but Mrs Topham was insistent that the 1966 renewal would be positively the last to be held at Liverpool.

One-hundred-and-nine entries ensured another large field for the second of the 'last Grand Nationals', the eventual number facing the starter being forty-seven. Top weight was a seven-year-old gelding from Japan, FUJINO-O, trained whilst in this country by Fulke Walwyn and ridden by Jeff King. The Irish-trained grey mare FLYING WILD, represented Mr Raymond Guest, the American Ambassador to Ireland whose colours had been carried successfully by LARKSPUR in the 1962 Derby. A fellow countryman of Mr Guest's bidding to become the oldest rider to win the race was sixty-six-year-old Tim Durant, riding his daughter's horse KING PIN, though their starting price of 100/1 was hardly encouraging. With his heroic effort behind JAY TRUMP fresh in the public's mind, FREDDIE dominated the ante-post lists from the day the weights were published, firming on the day of the race to become at 11/4 the shortest priced 'National runner since GOLDEN MILLER in 1935.

Fred Winter's new career as a trainer, begun so auspiciously in his very first season with JAY TRUMP, had progressed favourably since, although there was nothing of the calibre of the American horse in his yard this time. Now he relied on the eight-year-old outsider ANGLO, whose best performance to date was a win in a three mile Windsor 'Chase against moderate opposition. Bred near Down-

patrick by William Kennedy, the chestnut was by GREEK STAR out of MISS ALLIGATOR and he changed hands with frightening regularity. As a two-year-old he raced on the flat in the colours of General Sir Randle Feilden under the name of FLAG OF CONVENIENCE but his performances were far from impressive. Eventually, he was bought by trainer Ryan Price for a sum in the region of £1,000. The transaction was conducted on behalf of Mr Stuart Levy, a partner with Nat Cohen in Anglo-Amalgamated Films and FLAG OF CONVENIENCE was renamed ANGLO. Upon the withdrawal of Ryan Price's licence, Fred Winter took on ANGLO and feeling that the horse may be suited to a distance of ground aimed him at the 'National. There was a last-minute hitch when ANGLO's jockey received injuries in a car crash near Aintree racecourse but with stitches in his face, twenty-two-year-old Tim Norman was passed fit.

Less than an hour before the runners came out for the parade, DRAKE'S DRUM stole the Aintree limelight by winning the six furlong Hulton Plate and was led in by Beatle Paul McCartney, who had bought the horse for his father and was attending Liverpool races for the first time.

The 'National field were headed into the first fence by WILLOW KING, FOREST PRINCE, L'EMPEREUR, IRISH DAY, PACKED HOME and FREDDIE. ROUGH TWEED was the only casualty before Becher's, and coming back across Melling Road, FOREST PRINCE led a field reduced by only four. His colours had a familiar touch about them, since owner Mrs Thompson was the daughter of Frank Bibby whose GLENSIDE and KIRKLAND had made them famous in the race so many years before. KAPENO came down at Becher's second time when lying second, joined on the ground by

WHAT A MYTH, LESLIE, VALOUIS, GREEK SCHOLAR and SUPERSWEET and with HIGHLAND WEDDING, FREDDIE, ANGLO and THE FOSSA moving up close behind FOREST PRINCE they came round the Canal Turn on the run for home. At the second-last, ANGLO joined leader FOREST PRINCE, and on the flat, Tim Norman brought ANGLO right away from the opposition, running out a decisive twenty length winner from FREDDIE and an exhausted FOREST PRINCE. Terry Biddlecombe was fourth on THE FOSSA, followed by amateur Nick Gaselee with JIM'S TAVERN. Having given Fred Winter his second successive 'National victory since his retirement from the saddle, ANGLO was led in to the usual hero's welcome. For jockey Tim Norman, dame fortune had turned full circle in the forty-eight hours since he was lifted from the wreckage of a car. But as the throngs left the course, the major question was whether they would be returning in twelve months' time.

Sandwiched between two fallen horses, VALOUIS joins the casualties. But Pat McCarron steers FREDDIE (no 2) safely through the mayhem

1966

With £17,000 added, being £10,000 given by The Horserace Betting Levy Board and £7,000, (including a gold trophy value £600), by Messrs Tophams Limited. For six-year-olds & upwards. The second to receive 10%, the third 5% and the fourth 2½% of the whole stakes. The trainer of the Winner to receive a cup value £100 and the rider of the Winner a cup value £50

Date: 26th March 1966	Starters: 47	Time: 9 mins 52⅘ secs

1st **ANGLO** [formerly FLAG OF CONVENIENCE]	**8.10–0** *(Mr S Levy)*	**T Norman**
2nd **FREDDIE**	**9.11–7** *(Mr R R Tweedie)*	**P McCarron**
3rd **FOREST PRINCE**	**8.10–8** *(Mrs D Thompson)*	**G Scott**
4th **THE FOSSA**	**9.10–8** *(Mr R Greatbach)*	**T W Biddlecombe**
5th **JIM'S TAVERN**	**9.10–0** *(Mrs P F J Colvin)*	**Mr N Gaselee**
6th **QUINTIN BAY**	**10.10–0** *(Mr S Martin)*	**J Cullen**
7th **NORTHER**	**9.10–0** *(Mr J G Jones)*	**P Jones**
8th **HIGHLAND WEDDING**	**9.10–0** *(Mr C F W Burns)*	**O McNally**
9th **VULCANO**	**8.10–1** *(Miss Enid Chanelle)*	**J Gifford**
10th **GALE FORCE X**	**9.10–0** *(Capt F Warrington-Gillet)*	**R Coonan**
11th **BIG GEORGE**	**11.10–0** *(Mrs R J McAlpine)*	**J Morrissey**
12th **LOVING RECORD**	**12.10–0** *(Mr J J McDowell)*	**B Hannon**

Also Ran:

FUJINO-O 7.12–0 (Japan) (Mr Kazuo Fujii) **J King** *Refused*; *WHAT A MYTH 9.11–4* (Lady Weir) **P Kelleway** *Fell*; *FLYING WILD 10.11–0* (Mr R R Guest) **P Taaffe** *Pulled-up*; *STIRLING 10.10–11* (Mr W J Ingram) **H R Beasley** *Pulled-up*; *VULTRIX 8.10–7* (Mr H Dare) **S Mellor** *Pulled-up*; *ROUGH TWEED 12.10–7* (Mr S L Green) **P Buckley** *Fell*; *KAPENO 9.10–6* (Mr W H Whitbread) **D Mould** *Fell*; *PACKED HOME 11.10–3* (Mr R R Guest) **T Carberry** *Fell*; *GREEK SCHOLAR 7.10–4* (Mr J Thornton, jnr) **M Scudamore** *Fell*; *SOLIMYTH 10.10–1* (Lt Col J R E Benson) **Mr J Lawrence** *Pulled-up*; *BROWN DIAMOND 11.10–0* (Mrs P M Lamb) **F Shortt** *Fell*; *DORIMONT 12.10–0* (Mr W Shand-Kydd) **Mr W Shand-Kydd** *Unseated rider*; *POPHAM DOWN 9.10–0* (Mrs C Turriff) **G W Robinson** *Fell*; *PONTIN-GO* (formerly GAY NAVARREE) *14.10–0* (Mr F W Pontin) **T M Jones** *Fell*; *APRIL ROSE 11.10–7* (Major P Bengough) **Major P Bengough** *Pulled-up*; *GAME PURSTON 8.10–0* (Mr J P Yeomans) **P Cowley** *Fell*; *L'EMPEREUR 12.10–2* (Duque de Alburquerque) **Duque de Alburquerque** *Pulled-up*; *SUPERSWEET 9.10–6* (Miss M Britton) **Mr D Crossley-Cooke** *Fell*; *WILLOW KING 11.10–0* (Capt C A G Perry) **L McLoughlin** *Pulled-up*; *MONARCH'S THOUGHT 12.10–0* (Mr D H Ellison) **G Cramp** *Refused*; *VALOUIS 7.10–0* (Mr Prendergast) **E Prendergast** *Brought-down*; *MAJOR HITCH 8.10–1* (Mr W Noddings) **P Broderick** *Fell*; *ROYAL RUSE 8.10–0* (Mr R B Woodard) **T Hyde** *Pulled-up*; *GROOMSMAN 11.11–0* (Mrs S Roberts) **Mr S Roberts** *Refused*; *IRISH DAY 10.10–0* (Mr A Pownall) **J Magee** *Fell*; *LESLIE 10.10–5* (Mr J M Opperman) **Mr J M Opperman** *Brought-down*; *SCOTTISH FINAL 9.10–0* (Mr B W Meaden) **J Gamble** *Fell*; *MAC'S FLARE 10.10–0* (Capt J Wilson) **R Langley** *Pulled-up*; *FLAMECAP 9.10–0* (Mr C Ronaldson) **F Carroll** *Fell*; *BLACK SPOT 9.10–0* (Mrs O M Lusty) **J Speid-Soote** *Fell*; *KING PIN 10.10–11* (Mrs D Dye) **Mr T Durant** *Pulled-up*; *IN HASTE 8.10–3* (Lord Chelsea) **J Leech** *Pulled-up*; *HARRY BLACK 9.10–0* (Mr H Lane) **R Court** *Fell*; *MY GIFT 10.10–0* (Mr P Rooney) **A Redmond** *Pulled-up*; *BOLD BIRI 10.10–0* (Mr J E Bigg) **J Lehane** *Pulled-up*

The Betting: *11/4 Freddie; 11/2 What a Myth; 15/2 Highland Wedding; 100/7 Forest Prince, Vuitrix & Kapeno; 20/1 The Fossa & Flying Wild; 22/1 Popham Down & Rough Tweed; 25/1 Vulcano; 28/1 Stirling; 33/1 Packed Home & Big George; 40/1 Irish Day; 50/1 Anglo, Greek Scholar, Major Hitch, Loving Record, Gale Force X, Dorimont & Valouis; 100/1 Others.*

Distances: *Twenty lengths; five lengths*

Winner Trained By: *Fred Winter, Lambourn, Berkshire*

Value to Winning Owner: *£22,334*

1967

The long drawn-out legal battle over Aintree's future eventually reached the House of Lords, where the original decision allowing Lord Sefton's injunction was reversed and costs were awarded in favour of Tophams Ltd. This news, coupled with the fact that there was to be no autumn meeting at the racecourse in 1966, yet again created an air of uncertainty and a hardening of attitude towards Mrs Mirabel Topham. Meetings between the local councils took place in an effort to discover a means of developing a sports complex on the site centred around the annual running of the great 'Chase and rumours were rife that plans were being made for a consortium of wealthy businessmen to take control of the racecourse. Meanwhile, to general relief the 'National appeared in the solitary fixture set for Liverpool in the spring of 1967 and if the portents were ominous, there could be no denying that the forty-four runners which lined up for the start on 8th April comprised one of the finest fields ever assembled for the 'National.

Form horse and obvious favourite on the day was HONEY END, from the stable of the now reinstated Ryan Price and a gelding who for some time had seemed tailor made for the worst that Aintree had to offer. Ridden by Josh Gifford, well on his way to a record-breaking jockey's championship, HONEY END was the subject of a hefty gamble shortly before the 'off' which firmed his odds to 15/2. BASSNET, FREDDIE and Gregory Peck's sparkling park 'chaser DIFFERENT CLASS were others in constant demand in the betting, while THE FOSSA, ANGLO and KILBURN commanded their own share of the public's money.

Among the thirteen 100/1 others was a nine-year-old gelding called FOINAVON who had interested the press during his time in the Aintree stables solely because of his constant companion, a white goat named Susie. A half brother to TEAM SPIRIT, through his sire VULGAN, FOINAVON was bred from the mare ECILACE in County Limerick by Mr Timothy Ryan. FOINAVON's blood lines attracted the attention of Tom Dreaper, who bought him on behalf of the Duchess of Westminster. Passed on after winning only one of twenty-two contests, he was eventually bought for 2,000 guineas at Doncaster Sales by trainer John Kempton and after first running in the name of Mr M Bennellick, took his place in the 'National line-up in the colours of Cyril Watkins. Ridden by his trainer John Kempton, FOINAVON had finished a remote last behind WOODLAND VENTURE in the Cheltenham Gold Cup and there was little to inspire confidence that he would fare any better at Aintree. So dismal did his chances appear, that neither owner nor trainer was with him at Aintree. John Kempton was riding THREE DONS to win a novice hurdle at Worcester. The blinkered no-hoper was ridden by twenty-seven-year-old John Buckingham, whose first Grand National ride he was and who had served his apprenticeship at Mr Edward Courage's Oxfordshire yard.

Locally-trained PENVULGO was the early leader, but there was the tell-tale groan when second favourite BASSNET crashed at the first obstacle. MEON VALLEY also came down here, bringing down, fatefully as it turned out, POPHAM DOWN. Approaching Becher's for the final time CASTLE FALLS held a narrow lead from PRINCEFUL, KAPENO, RONDETTO and RUTHERFORDS, with a larger number still in contention than is usual at such a late stage in the race. Led by two loose horses the well strung-out survivors all cleared the Brook safely, FREDDIE, LIMEKING,

NORTHER and DIFFERENT CLASS each moving into challenging positions just behind the leaders. The next fence is the smallest on the course and as so many runners bore down on it there was not the slightest reason to suspect that it would cause any trouble to those who had just negotiated the most fearsome obstacle in the world. Riderless POPHAM DOWN was the joker in the pack however, for at the very last instant he cut from the inside right across the front of the fence, causing a pile-up unprecedented in modern-day racing. In a scene reminiscent of the chaos brought about by EASTER HERO in the 1928 race, the entire field were brought to a standstill, with horses and riders falling, crashing into each other and piling into the fence. Racing from the rear after jumping Becher's, John Buckingham sized up the dreadful situation in an instant and taking FOINAVON to the wide outside, steered a clear course through the bedlam. Coming away from the carnage of the twenty-third fence with a lead of a hundred yards, FOINAVON proceeded to make the best of his lonely way home and with HONEY END, GREEK SCHOLAR and RED ALLIGATOR each giving their all in an effort to catch him, he stuck to his task in the most commendable fashion. At the post FOINAVON held on by fifteen lengths from HONEY END, RED ALLIGATOR being a further three lengths back after putting in a most determined run. GREEK SCHOLAR was fourth.

Having braved a day of constant rain to witness what was expected to be a classic contest, racegoers felt cheated by what to most was an anticlimax and terms such as farce and fiasco did much harm to the already tarnished image of the race, in addition to detracting from the achievement of FOINAVON and the diligent John Buckingham, for whom victory was the high-spot of his career. At such long odds (and the Tote paid 444/1), there were few with reason to celebrate his surprising

though worthy victory. The stewards of the meeting took the unusual step of issuing the following statement as an explanation to the shocked and somewhat angry crowds.

'As a result of the leading loose horse running across the fence after Becher's (23rd) on the second circuit, there was a pile-up and FOINAVON was the only horse

to jump the fence first time. The remainder of the finishers were either remounted or put to the fence a second time.' That two such bland sentences could sum up what only hours before had promised to be the most exciting jumping spectacle of the year, boded ill for the race.

What nobody could have foreseen was that the two-year-old dead-heating winner of a Selling Plate at Aintree, some twenty-four hours before this catastrophic 'National, was destined to restore the event to its rightful glory. The horse's name was RED RUM.

FOINAVON is the sensational winner a long way in front of the unlucky favourite HONEY END

1967

With £17,000 added, being £10,000 from The Horserace Betting Levy Board and £7,000 (including a gold trophy value £1,000) from Messrs Tophams Limited. For six-year-olds & upwards. The second to receive 20%, the third 10% and the fourth 5% of the whole stakes. The trainer of the Winner to receive a cup value £100 and the rider of the Winner a cup value £50

Date: 8th April 1967	Starters: 44	Time: 9 mins 49⅗ secs
1st **FOINAVON**	**9.10–0** *(Mr C P T Watkins)*	**J Buckingham**
2nd **HONEY END**	**10.10–4** *(Mr C Pugh)*	**J Gifford**
3rd **RED ALLIGATOR**	**8.10–0** *(Mr J Manners)*	**B Fletcher**
4th **GREEK SCHOLAR**	**8.10–9** *(Mr J Thornton, jnr)*	**T W Biddlecombe**
5th **PACKED HOME**	**12.10–0** *(Mr R R Guest)*	**T Carberry**
6th **SOLBINA**	**10.11–2** *(Mrs M Sobell)*	**E P Harty**
7th **AUSSIE**	**10.10–0** *(Mrs R H Preston)*	**F Shortt**
8th **SCOTTISH FINAL**	**10.10–0** *(Mr B Howard)*	**Mr B Howard**
9th **WHAT A MYTH**	**10.12–0** *(Lady Weir)*	**P Kelleway**
10th **KAPENO**	**10.11–1** *(Mr W H Whitbread)*	**Mr N Gaselee**
11th **QUINTIN BAY**	**11.10–0** *(Mr S Martin)*	**J Cullen**
12th **BOB-A-JOB**	**13.10–0** *(Mr T D Hudson)*	**C Young**
13th **STEEL BRIDGE**	**9.10–0** *(Mrs W Macauley)*	**E Prendergast**
14th **CASTLE FALLS**	**10.10–3** *(Mr C Nicholson)*	**S Hayhurst**
15th **ROSS SEA**	**11.10–3** *(Mrs J Jones)*	**J Cook**
16th **RUTHERFORDS**	**7.10–11** *(Mr R S Reynolds, jnr)*	**J Leech**
17th **FREDDIE**	**10.11–13** *(Mr R R Tweedie)*	**P McCarron**
18th **GAME PURSTON**	**9.10–0** *(Mr J P Yeomans)*	**K B White**

Also Ran:

RONDETTO 11.11–7 (Mr A B Mitchell) **J Haine** *Refused*; *DIFFERENT CLASS 7.11–2* (Mr Gregory Peck) **D Mould** *Brought-down*; *ANGLO 9.11–1* (Mr J R Gaines) **H R Beasley** *Pulled-up*; *KILBURN 9.11–0* (Mme Borel de Bitche) **T Norman** *Fell*; *LIMEKING 10.10–13* (Mr A Chester Beatty) **P Buckley** *Brought-down*; *BASSNET 8.10–11* (Mr W A Silvester) **D Nicholson** *Fell*; *FORECASTLE 9.10–10* (Mr J A Wood) **N Wilkinson** *Pulled-up*; *MEON VALLEY 12.10–7* (Mr A R Turnell) **A Turnell** *Fell*; *LUCKY DOMINO 10.10–5* (Mr G F Waring) **J Kenneally** *Fell*; *THE FOSSA 10.10–2* (Mr R Greatbach) **S Mellor** *Pulled-up*; *NORTHER 10.10–0* (Mr J G Jones) **Mr J Lawrence** *Pulled-up*; *DORIMONT 13.10–0* (Mr W Shand-Kydd) **R Pitman** *Fell*; *KIRTLE-LAD 8.10–3* (Mr R F Tinning) **P Broderick** *Refused*; *POPHAM DOWN 10.10–0* (Mrs C Turriff) **M C Gifford** *Brought-down*; *APRIL ROSE 12.10–8* (Major P Bengough) **Major P Bengough** *Fell*; *VULCANO 9.10–0* (Miss E Chanelle) **J Speid-Soote** *Fell*; *DUN WIDDY 11.10–10* (Mr J A C Edwards) **Mr J Edwards** *Pulled-up*; *PENVULGO 8.10–0* (Mr J D McKechnie) **J Lehane** *Pulled-up*; *LEEDSY 9.10–5* (Mrs C Lee Levy) **T S Murphy** *Brought-down*; *PRINCEFUL 9.10–2* (Mr R R Hitchins) **R Edwards** *Brought-down*; *RONALD'S BOY 10.10–13* (Mr E F Robins) **Mr P Irby** *Fell*; *BORDER FURY 8.10–2* (Mr D Crossley Cooke) **Mr D Crossley Cooke** *Fell*; *HARRY BLACK 10.10–0* (Mr H Lane) **R Reid** *Pulled-up*; *AERIAL III 11.10–9* (Mr T Durant) **Mr T Durant** *Fell*; *TOWER ROAD 9.10–0* (Mrs D Dallimore) **R Williams** *Fell*; *BARBERYN 12.10–1* (Mr P Milner) **N Mullins** *Refused*

The Betting: *15/2 Honey End; 10/1 Bassnet; 100/9 Freddie; 100/8 Different Class, The Fossa, Anglo & Kilburn; 20/1 Greek Scholar & What a Myth; 25/1 Kapeno & Solbina; 28/1 Rutherfords & Kirtle Lad; 30/1 Red Alligator; 33/1 Limeking & Rondetto; 40/1 Vulcano & Tower Road; 50/1 Forecastle, Quintin Bay, Leedsy, Norther, Aussie, Castle Falls & Penvulgo; 66/1 Game Purston, Meon Valley, Ross Sea, Lucky Domino, April Rose & Popham Down; 100/1 Foinavon and Others.*

Distances: *Fifteen lengths; three lengths*

Winner Trained By: *John Kempton, Compton, Berkshire*

Value to Winning Owner: *£17,630*

* As a result of a leading loose horse running across the fence after Becher's on the second circuit (the 23rd), there was a pile-up and Foinavon was the only horse to jump the fence first time. The remainder of the finishers were either remounted or put to the fence a second time. *

Josh Gifford, another great jockey who didn't score in the 'National, but who made up for it by training the fairy-tale winner ALDANITI

1968

A fine day, forty-five runners of brilliant and not so brilliant ability and the assurance again that this was indeed to be positively the last Aintree Grand National brought a huge crowd to the racecourse and among them a large contingent from America. Gregory Peck, as owner of the favourite DIFFERENT CLASS, was once more greeted enthusiastically and his well-timed pronouncement that the race was the finest sporting spectacle in the world made a nonsense of the British racing authorities' apparent disregard for its future.

RUTHERFORDS, the mount of Pat Buckley, FRENCH KILT, MASTER OF ART and the Josh Gifford-ridden REGAL JOHN were all well backed and last year's winner FOINAVON, without a win since his surprise victory, started at 66/1 this time. At the same long odds was the mare POLARIS MISSILE, trained by John Thorne and partnered by his fifth-form seventeen-year-old son Nigel. Three years older than Master Thorne, the professional Brian Fletcher was encountering the perils of the 'National for the second time on the horse he had determinedly guided through the mayhem a year before, RED ALLIGATOR. A half-brother to ANGLO through their dam MISS ALLIGATOR, the attractive chestnut was by the stallion MAGIC RED and was bred by William Kennedy in County Down. Bought as a yearling at Ballsbridge by Messrs Kerr & Co for 340 guineas, RED ALLIGATOR won a solitary hurdle race from twenty-seven attempts in his first three seasons. Passing into the ownership of Mr John Manners, a farmer and butcher based in County Durham, the son of MAGIC RED was placed in the care of trainer Denys Smith at Bishop Auckland. Racing mainly in the North of England and in Scotland, RED ALLIGATOR showed

remarkable improvement when put over fences, displaying a fluent, reliable jumping style and an abundance of stamina. His performance in finishing third behind FOINAVON was, under the circumstances, no mean feat, for his rider had found it necessary to put him at the notorious twenty-third fence three times before getting over safely.

VALOUIS, PRINCEFUL, RUTHERFORDS, THE FOSSA and MOIDORE'S TOKEN headed the closely-bunched field into Becher's, with only FORT ORD and BEECHAM missing. The Brook claimed six victims and Valentine's five more. Racing back to the stands, the pack was narrowly headed over the Chair by THE FOSSA, RONDETTO, RUTHERFORDS, DIFFERENT CLASS and MOIDORE'S TOKEN. THE FOSSA was giving Roy Edwards a great ride up front, taking Becher's again in tremendous style, but moving nicely just off the pace and being given a clear view of the fences by Brian Fletcher was RED ALLIGATOR. RONDETTO came down at the fence forever to be known as FOINAVON's, bringing down the David Elsworth-ridden CHAMORETTA and the cheers prematurely rang out as DIFFERENT CLASS struck the front going into Valentine's. Galloping smoothly on the outside, RED ALLIGATOR moved into contention over the last open ditch, and after the last fence, he left them all for dead. The expected challenge from DIFFERENT CLASS was not forthcoming, MOIDORE'S TOKEN passing him on the run-in to gain second place by a neck, twenty lengths behind RED ALLIGATOR.

After the tribulations of recent years, this 'National brought heart back to the race and the hint of a tear in the eye of winning jockey Fletcher reminded us of what it means for a moment to stand on top of the world. Even the bookies wore a

Galloping grandfather Mr Tim Durant, who came over from America to partner AERIAL III, meets up with Tich Mason, who rode KIRKLAND to victory in 1905

smile despite sixty-eight-year-old American grandfather Tim Durant remounting to collect a case of champagne from them, together with £500 generously donated to the Injured Jockeys Fund. So as the sun finally set on another Grand National day there remained hope yet that the heart and spirit of Aintree could still survive.

THE GRAND NATIONAL HANDICAP STEEPLECHASE
1968

With £17,000 added, being £10,000 from The Horserace Betting Levy Board and £7,000 (including a gold trophy value £1,000), from Messrs Tophams Limited. For six-year-olds & upwards. The second to receive 20%, the third 10% and the fourth 5% of the whole stakes. The trainer of the Winner to receive a cup value £100 and the rider of the Winner a cup value £50

Date: 30th March 1968		Starters: 45	Time: 9 mins 28⅘ secs
1st	**RED ALLIGATOR**	**9.10–0** *(Mr J Manners)*	**B Fletcher**
2nd	**MOIDORE'S TOKEN**	**11.10–8** *(Miss P Harrower)*	**B Brogan**
• 3rd	**DIFFERENT CLASS**	**8.11–5** *(Mr Gregory Peck)*	**D Mould**
4th	**RUTHERFORDS**	**8.10–6** *(Mr J Bonnier)*	**P Buckley**
5th	**THE FOSSA**	**11.10–4** *(Mr R Greatbatch)*	**R Edwards**
6th	**VALBUS**	**10.10–0** *(Mr T H Shepherd)*	**R Langley**
7th	**HIGHLAND WEDDING**	**11.11–0** *(Mr C F W Burns)*	**O McNally**
8th	**REYNARD'S HEIR**	**8.10–4** *(Mr R Buckley)*	**T Kinane**
9th	**PRINCEFUL**	**10.10–4** *(Mr R R Hitchens)*	**J Leech**
10th	**STEEL BRIDGE**	**10.10–4** *(Mrs W Macauley)*	**E P Harty**
11th	**MANIFEST**	**10.10–0** *(Mr J Filmer Wilson)*	**R Pitman**
12th	**SAN ANGELO**	**8.10–10** *(Mr E R Courage)*	**W Rees**
13th	**SOME SLIPPER**	**11.10–0** *(Mrs B S L Trafford)*	**R Atkins**
14th	**FRENCH KILT**	**8.10–0** *(Major C H Nathan)*	**S Mellor**
15th	**HIGHLANDIE**	**11.10–12** *(Mr T Durant)*	**Mr T Durant** [remounted]
16th	**DUN WIDDY**	**12.10–2** *(Mr A P Moore)*	**Mr A P Moore**
17th	**QUINTIN BAY**	**12.10–0** *(Mr S Martin)*	**G W Robinson**

Also Ran:

WHAT A MYTH 11.12–0 (Lady Weir) **P Kelleway** *Fell*; *RONDETTO 12.10–12* (Mr A B Mitchell) **J King** *Fell*; *BASSNET 9.10–12* (Mr W A Silvester) **D Nicholson** *Brought-down*; *FORT ORD 8.10–9* (Mr P B Spanoghe) **T Norman** *Fell*; *VULTRIX 10.10–8* (Mr H Dare) **T Biddlecombe** *Fell*; *PHEMIUS 10.10–8* (Mrs D Bannister) **G Scott** *Pulled-up*; *QUITTE OU DOUBLE L 8.10–8* (Mrs A Besnouin) **Mr J Ciechanowski** *Fell*; *REGAL JOHN 10.10–8* (Mr H L Vickery) **J Gifford** *Refused*; *FORECASTLE 10.10–8* (Mr J A Wood) **Mr W McLernon** *Pulled-up*; *GREAT LARK 9.10–6* (Mr R R Guest) **T Carberry** *Refused*; *MASTER MARCUS 9.10–6* (Mr J Bairstow) **Mr J Lawrence** *Fell*; *MASTER OF ART 8.10–2* (Dr M L Slotover) **Mr B Hanbury** *Fell*; *FOINAVON 10.10–5* (Mr M Bennellick) **P Harvey** *Brought-down*; *GO-PONTINENTAL 8.10–0* (Mr F W Pontin) **M C Gifford** *Fell*; *RONALDS BOY 11.10–0* (Mr E F Robbins) **J P Harty** *Brought-down*; *ROSS FOUR 7.10–0* (Mr W T Organ) **P Jones** *Fell*; *CHAMPION PRINCE 9.10–12* (Mr R W Wates) **Mr A Wates** *Brought-down*; *FORT KNIGHT 9.10–0* (Mr W J Bebbington) **R Reid** *Fell*; *MIXED FRENCH 9.10–0* (Mrs N L Durdy) **G Holmes** *Fell*; *CHU-TEH 9.10–0* (Mrs M McMeekin) **Mr N Gaselee** *Brought-down*; *KIRTLE-LAD 9.10–0* (Mr R F Tinning) **J Enright** *Fell*; *POLARIS MISSILE 9.10–0* (Mr M J Thorne) **Mr N Thorne** *Fell*; *GAME PURSTON 10.10–0* (Mr J P Yeomans) **D Cartwright** *Pulled-up*; *BEECHAM 9.10–0* (Mr P S Williams) **B R Davies** *Fell*; *CHAMORETTA 8.10–1* (Major A W C Pearn) **D Elsworth** *Brought-down*; *VALOUIS 9.10–1* (Mr J J Prendergast) **E Prendergast** *Fell*; *WILLING SLAVE 8.10–2* (Mr A Maiden) **M B James** *Pulled-up*; *PORTATION 10.10–0* (Mr D H Ellison) **G Cramp** *Refused*

The Betting: *17/2 Different Class; 100/9 Rutherfords; 100/7 Red Alligator, French Kilt, Master of Art & Regal John; 100/6 Moidore's Token & Great Lark; 18/1 Highland Wedding & Bassnet; 25/1 San Angelo & Go-Pontinental; 28/1 Reynard's Heir, The Fossa, Vultrix & What a Myth; 33/1 Rondetto & Chu-Teh; 35/1 Ford Ord; 40/1 Fort Knight & Valouis; 50/1 Forecastle, Phemius & Kirtle-Lad; 66/1 Champion Prince, Manifest, Master Marcus, Quintin Bay, Quitte ou Double L, Some Slipper, Foinavon, Polaris Miss & Princeful; 100/1 Others.*

Distances: *Twenty lengths; a neck*

Winner Trained By: *Denys Smith, Bishop Auckland, County Durham*

Value to Winning Owner: *£17,848*

1969

As the tumultuous sixties drew towards a close, there appeared a glimmer of hope for the future of the 'National. Liverpool Corporation's alleged interest in the racecourse for a sum said to be in the region of £1 million, revived the belief that the event was once and for all safe. It was, however, unfortunate that the reason given for delay in the Council making a final decision was given as 'illnesses'. Who was ill and how seriously was never determined but it was a sad thought shared by many that the proud City of Liverpool survived the might of the Luftwaffe without a council official's bout of flu interrupting its resolve.

That the number of runners was reduced this year to thirty was considered a welcome step by most, since the unmanageable fields of recent times had contributed greatly to the hazards of the race. Last-minute betting on the event centred mainly around proven Aintree campaigner RED ALLIGATOR and Terry Biddlecombe's promising young mount FEARLESS FRED, with the former slightly preferred, while there was a strong tip for Paul Mellon's attractive grey gelding THE BEECHES. Further American interest was provided by brothers Paul and George Sloan, amateur riders of TEROSSIAN and PECCARD respectively. In a late flurry by those wishing to have a runner in the race, bookmaker John Banks bought GAME PURSTON and THE INVENTOR became the property of Mrs Sangster, the wife of Vernons Pools chief Robert. Another with local connections, elderly Liverpool businessman Noel Le Mare ran FURORE II in an attempt to capture the prize he had dreamed of winning for almost sixty years.

Making his third appearance in the race the twelve-year-old HIGHLAND WEDDING was thought by many to have missed his 'National chance but to students of form, Toby Balding's charge was on the crest of a wave having won his last three races. Bred at Prestwick, Ayrshire by Mr John Caldwell, he was by QUESTION out of the mare PRINCESS. Jointly owned by American Thomas McKoy and Canadian Charles Burns, HIGHLAND WEDDING lost his usual partner Owen McNally when that jockey broke his elbow, but thirty-one-year-old Eddie Harty was a more than adequate substitute. The question of HIGHLAND WEDDING's staying power was beyond doubt, as had been recently demonstrated when the gelding won Newcastle's Eider 'Chase for the third time and DOZO's victory under Eddie Harty in the Topham Trophy Steeplechase on the opening day of the Liverpool meeting gave the best possible hint that the Balding stable was in form.

All thirty runners cleared the first fence safely but TUDOR FORT went out at the first open ditch, followed by FEARLESS FRED at the next and the grey PECCARD brought George Sloan's Aintree adventure to an end at Becher's. FLOSUEBARB fell two before Becher's, leaving STEEL BRIDGE to go on in front over the Brook, closely attended by HIGHLAND WEDDING, THE FOSSA, RONDETTO and the spectre-like form of the grey THE BEECHES. KILBURN failed to survive the Brook, bringing down TAM KISS with his owner-rider Jeremy Hindley. The fall of KILBURN led to an uncharacteristic error on the part of the commentator stationed at Becher's who became confused by the similarity of their colours and announced that it was HIGHLAND WEDDING who had fallen. This case of mistaken identity was corrected when HIGHLAND WEDDING jumped to the front at the Canal Turn, hard pressed by STEEL

BRIDGE, RONDETTO and BASSNET with RED ALLIGATOR and MOIDORE'S TOKEN no longer in the hunt. Staying on resolutely, the twelve-year-old jumped the last fence three lengths in advance of STEEL BRIDGE and RONDETTO, increasing the margin to twelve at the winning post. HIGHLAND WEDDING's reward was a well earned retirement in his owner's homeland of Canada.

Eddie Harty and HIGHLAND WEDDING come home unchallenged to record a decisive victory for Toby Balding

1969

With £17,500 added, being £10,000 from The Horserace Betting Levy Board and £7,500 (including a gold trophy value £1,500), from Messrs Tophams Limited. For six-year-olds & upwards. The second to receive 20%, the third 10% and the fourth 5% of the whole stakes. The trainer of the Winner to receive a cup value £200 and the rider of the Winner a cup value £100

Date: 29th March 1969		Starters: 30	Time: 9 mins 30⅘ secs
1st	**HIGHLAND WEDDING**	**12.10–4** *(Mr T H McCoy, jnr)*	**E P Harty**
2nd	**STEEL BRIDGE**	**11.10–0** *(Mr J L Drabble)*	**R Pitman**
3rd	**RONDETTO**	**13.10–6** *(Mr A B Mitchell)*	**J King**
4th	**THE BEECHES**	**9.10–1** *(Mr Paul Mellon)*	**W Rees**
5th	**BASSNET**	**10.10–12** *(Mr W A Silvester)*	**J Gifford**
6th	**ARCTURUS**	**8.11–4** *(Lady Hay)*	**P Buckley**
7th	**FORT SUN**	**8.10–4** *(Mr W J Pilsworth)*	**J Crowley**
8th	**KELLSBORO' WOOD**	**9.10–10** *(Mrs L M Prior)*	**A Turnell**
9th	**FURORE II**	**8.10–0** *(Mr N H Le Mare)*	**M C Gifford**
10th	**MISS HUNTER**	**8.10–0** *(Mrs W Macauley)*	**F Shortt**
11th	**THE FOSSA**	**12.10–9** *(Capt A H Parker Bowles)*	**Capt A H Parker Bowles**
12th	**LIMEBURNER**	**8.10–0** *(Mrs S N J Embericos)*	**J Buckingham**
13th	**CASTLE FALLS**	**12.10–0** *(Mr C Nicholson)*	**S Hayhurst**
14th	**LIMETRA**	**11.10–9** *(Mr H Lane)*	**P Broderick**

Also Ran:

FEARLESS FRED 7.11–3 (Mr B P Jenks) **T Biddlecombe** *Fell*; *RED ALLIGATOR 10.10–13* (Mr J Manners) **B Fletcher** *Fell*; *KILBURN 11.10–9* (Mme Borel de Bitche) **T Carberry** *Fell*; *HOVE 8.10–9* (Mr F Parker) **D Nicholson** *Fell*; *TEROSSIAN 9.11–3* (Mr H Hooker) **Mr P Sloan** *Refused*; *MOIDORE'S TOKEN 12.10–9* (Miss P Harrower) **B Brogan** *Pulled-up*; *TUDOR FORT 9.10–4* (Lord Joicey) **J Haldane** *Fell*; *PECCARD 8.10–4* (Mr G Sloan) **Mr G Sloan** *Fell*; *THE INVENTOR 8.10–0* (Mrs R E Sangster) **T Hyde** *Saddle slipped – fell*; *VILLAY 11.10–3* (Mr D D Scott) **Mr D Scott** *Pulled-up*; *TAM KISS 10.10–13* (Mr J R Hindley) **Mr J R Hindley** *Brought-down*; *ROSINVER BAY 9.10–5* (Mr A W Riddell Martin) **P Taaffe** *Refused*; *JUAN 13.10–9* (Mr P J H Wills) **Mr P J H Wills** *Refused*; *FLOSUEBARB 9.10–0* (Mrs E F Old) **J Guest** *Fell*; *GAME PURSTON 11.10–0* (Mr J Banks) **S Mellor** *Pulled-up*; *BALLINABOINTRA 10.10–1* (Mr L Sachs) **P Kelleway** *Fell*

The Betting: *13/2 Red Alligator; 15/2 Fearless Fred; 100/9 Highland Wedding; 100/8 Bassnet; 100/6 Hove, Moidore's Token, Arcturus & The Beeches; 20/1 Furore II; 22/1 Kilburn; 25/1 Rondetto; 28/1 Fort Sun; 33/1 Game Purston, The Inventor & The Fossa; 50/1 Steel Bridge, Limetra, Rosinver Bay, Tam Kiss, Terossian, Tudor Fort, Peccard & Miss Hunter; 66/1 Limeburner, Kellsboro' Wood & Castle Falls; 100/1 Others.*

Distances: *Twelve lengths; one length*

Winner Trained By: *Toby Balding, Weyhill, Hampshire*

Value to Winning Owner: *£17,849*

1970

It was a year of farewells at Aintree in 1970, with two likeable and highly talented jockeys in Pat Taaffe and Josh Gifford both having their final rides in the race. For Gilbert Cotton, that cheerful, sprightly ninety-year-old inspector of National Hunt courses it was also a melancholy moment as he made his fiftieth and last examination of the 'National course he had competed over in 1913. Marking the occasion, Mrs Topham presented Major Cotton with an inscribed silver cigarette box after his walk of the course had brought the usual expression of satisfaction.

That the Fred Rimell-trained eight-year-old GAY TRIP was the only one of twenty-eight runners set to carry a weight in excess of eleven stone, could have suggested that the field was lacking in quality, but with such good horses as RED ALLIGATOR, TWO SPRINGS, FRENCH EXCUSE, DOZO and PRIDE OF KENTUCKY in the line-up, public interest was as intense as ever. Guy Harwood's runner ASSAD was the last ride Josh Gifford would have on a racecourse, the former champion being set to take over the new role of trainer from his previous guvnor Ryan Price.

When the usual jockey Terry Biddlecombe received an injury which ruled him out of the race and the ride on GAY TRIP, he advised Fred Rimell to engage the forty-year-old Pat Taaffe. A small yet well-proportioned gelding, GAY TRIP was by that outstanding sire of steeplechasers VULGAN, from the mare TURKISH TOURIST and was bred by Mr F D Farmer. The winner of one flat race, and sixth on his most recent outing, the Cheltenham Gold Cup, he came to Aintree with the dubious distinction of never having won beyond two-and-a-half miles.

When PERRY HILL fell and brought down QUEEN'S GUIDE at the first, the pattern of the race was set at an early stage. TWO SPRINGS, the favourite, came down at the first open ditch, joined almost immediately by THE BEECHES, RACOON, ON THE MOVE, GAME PURSTON, PERMIT, BATTLEDORE and RONDETTO and the Irish mare PERSIAN HELEN was so disturbed by events at the third that she refused the next fence. Sticking close to the inside, Josh Gifford had ASSAD in a handy position over Becher's, alongside NO JUSTICE and VULTURE, FORT ORD being close but RED ALLIGATOR last of all at this stage. Valentine's saw the end of FORT ORD, BOWGEENO went at the next and RED ALLIGATOR crashed out at the last open ditch before the racecourse. Taking up the running crossing Melling Road, Mr Derek Scott with his own VILLAY led his twelve rivals towards the stands. VILLAY continued in front on the way back to Becher's, where THE OTTER and SPECIFY fell and THE FOSSA and NO JUSTICE refused. There were only seven left in it when VILLAY fell four from home and as they returned to the racecourse, Pat Taaffe sent GAY TRIP upsides with DOZO, while VULTURE, GINGER NUT and MISS HUNTER struggled to keep in touch. Touching down in front at the second last, GAY TRIP drew steadily ahead, clearing the final fence with a decisive lead and running away for a twenty length win on the flat. DOZO faded on the run-in, being passed by VULTURE and MISS HUNTER and with GINGER NUT fifth, the only others to finish were PRIDE OF KENTUCKY and Josh Gifford on ASSAD.

It was a most fitting end to the magnificent career of Pat Taaffe, fifteen years after his first 'National victory with QUARE TIMES, and for trainer Fred Rimell GAY TRIP provided a third visit to the most coveted winner's enclosure in steeplechasing. Both first and second were half-brothers by VULGAN and the army of Irish visitors enjoyed seeing the first five horses home partnered by sons of the Emerald Isle.

THE GRAND NATIONAL HANDICAP STEEPLECHASE
1970

With £17,500 added, being £10,000 from The Horserace Betting Levy Board and £7,500 (including a gold trophy value £1,500), from Messrs Tophams Limited. For six-year-olds & upwards. The second to receive 20%, the third 10% and the fourth 5% of the whole stakes. The trainer of the Winner to receive a cup value £200 and the rider of the Winner a cup value £100

Date: 4th April 1970	Starters: 28	Time: 9 mins 38 secs
1st **GAY TRIP**	**8.11−5** *(Mr A J Chambers)*	**P Taaffe**
2nd **VULTURE**	**8.10−0** *(General R K Mellon)*	**S Barker**
3rd **MISS HUNTER**	**9.10−0** *(Mrs W Macauley)*	**F Shortt**
4th **DOZO**	**9.10−4** *(Mrs E W Wetherill)*	**E P Harty**
5th **GINGER NUT**	**8.10−0** *(Mr B P Jenks)*	**J Bourke**
6th **PRIDE OF KENTUCKY**	**8.10−0** *(Mr E R Courage)*	**J Buckingham**
7th **ASSAD**	**10.10−1** *(Mrs E A Clarke)*	**J Gifford**

Also Ran:
BOWGEENO 10.10–13 (Mr H J Joel) **J Haine** *Fell*; RED ALLIGATOR 11.10–12 (Mr J Manners) **B Fletcher** *Fell*; SPECIFY 8.10–7 (Mr F W Pontin) **J Cook** *Brought-down*; TWO SPRINGS 8.10–7 (Mr D H Barnes) **R Edwards** *Fell*; BATTLEDORE 9.10–5 (Mr W E Morton) **T S Murphy** *Brought-down*; RONDETTO 14.10–5 (Mr A B Mitchell) **J King** *Unseated rider*; FORT ORD 10.10–5 (Dr R Ehnbom) **A Turnell** *Fell*; PERMIT 7.10–3 (Mr T T Lennon) **P Buckley** *Brought-down*; FRENCH EXCUSE 8.10–2 (Mr J Jennings) **K B White** *Fell*; THE OTTER 9.10–1 (Mrs J Dening) **T M Jones** *Fell*; ALL GLORY 9.10–0 (Mr A S Robinson) **A L T Moore** *Fell*; THE BEECHES 10.10–0 (Mrs R Lomer) **S Mellor** *Fell*; THE FOSSA 13.10–0 (Capt A H Parker Bowles) **G W Robinson** *Refused*; GAME PURSTON 12.11–5 (Mr M C Lloyd) **Mr M C Lloyd** *Unseated rider*; NO JUSTICE 9.10–0 (Mr A S Neaves) **J Guest** *Refused*; ON THE MOVE 8.10–1 (Mr Gordon Jarvis) **G Dartnall** *Fell*; PERRY HILL 11.10–0 (Mr J U Baillie) **P Kelleway** *Fell*; PERSIAN HELEN 7.10–0 (Mr P E Smith) **D T Hughes** *Refused*; QUEEN'S GUIDE 9.10–0 (Mr W Wade) **Mr G Wade** *Brought-down*; RACOON 8.10–3 (Mr R H Kieckhefer) **D Mould** *Fell*; VILLAY 12.10–0 (Mr D D Scott) **Mr D Scott** *Fell*

The Betting: *13/2 Two Springs; 100/8 French Excuse & Dozo; 13/1 Pride of Kentucky & Red Alligator; 100/7 Specify; 15/1 Gay Trip & Vulture; 20/1 The Otter; 22/1 The Beeches, Bowgeeno & Rondetto; 25/1 Battledore; 28/1 Ginger Nut, Perry Hill & Assad; 33/1 Miss Hunter & Racoon; 35/1 Permit & Persian Helen; 40/1 Queen's Guide; 50/1 The Fossa, All Glory, Fort Ord & No Justice; 100/1 Others.*

Distances: *Twenty lengths; half a length*

Winner Trained By: *Fred Rimell, Kinnersley, Worcestershire*

Value to Winning Owner: *£14,804*

1971

FOR ONE HUNDRED AND THIRTY·FOUR YEARS....

THE GRAND NATIONAL
1837   1971

....HOLDERS OF THE BLUE RIBAND OF THE STEEPLECHASING WORLD

Even without a win to his credit since his 'National feat, GAY TRIP was an obvious choice to head the weights and re-united with the ever popular Terry Biddlecombe, he carried the added responsibility of being 8/1 favourite. Receiving just two pounds from the former winner at 11 st 12 lbs, THE LAIRD brought to the race that element of class so lacking in recent times. Owned by that staunch supporter of British racing, Mr H J Joel, and trained by Bob Turnell, THE LAIRD had proved himself to be one of the most exciting park jumpers in training and had been beaten only a neck by FORT LENEY in the 1968 Cheltenham Gold Cup. The winner of his last three races before Liverpool, the Jeff King-ridden gelding became the subject of some hefty gambles. The Irish, meanwhile, fielded one of their strongest teams for some time. A case could be made out for MONEY BOAT, KING VULGAN, CNOC DUBH and last year's runner-up VULTURE but BLACK SECRET, by St Leger winner

Many of the racing fraternity started the New Year with best wishes for "all good going" in 1971 from the Topham's Christmas card

BLACK TARQUIN, was strongly fancied to give his trainer's son Jim Dreaper a victorious first ride in the Grand National.

One thought to be severely in need of a race was Epsom-trained SPECIFY, the property of jovial holiday camp magnate Fred Pontin. By SPECIFIC out of ORA LAMAE, the nine-year-old was bred in Norwich by Mr Alan Parker. After many races on the flat, SPECIFY won over hurdles in the colours of Denis Rayson but his turf career almost came to an abrupt end when he broke a bone in his face through a fall in the Schweppes Gold Trophy of 1968. Ever after something of a nervous character, SPECIFY began showing some ability over fences and in due course was bought by Mr Pontin and entered the yard of John Sutcliffe. The combination of owner, trainer and jockey John Cook was

319

attempting a unique double. Since earlier in the season their CALA MESQUIDA had won a close contest in the Schweppes Gold Trophy.

The thirty-eight runners were sent off to a great roar but the favourite GAY TRIP was among five fallers at the first fence. More shocks followed just two jumps later when THE LAIRD found the open ditch too much for him. At the Canal Turn a loose horse carried GAY BUCCANEER wide, relegating him from first to last and leaving SMOOTH DEALER in front of MISS HUNTER, VICHYSOISE, SPECIFY and BOWGEENO with a whole cluster of runners close on their heels. Falls came thick and fast and after jumping Becher's for the second time with a clear advantage, BEAU BOB unseated his rider on the run to the next fence. Turning at the Canal, Bob Turnell's third string LIMEBURNER, ridden by John Buckingham, held a narrow lead over SANDY SPRITE, ASTBURY, BLACK SECRET, THE INVENTOR, SPECIFY, BOWGEENO, TWO SPRINGS and REGIMENTAL, and crossing Melling Road for the last time, there were six horses almost in line. LIMEBURNER fell at the second-last, fortunately rolling away from the following SPECIFY, who raced to the final fence in fifth place behind SANDY SPRITE, BOWGEENO, BLACK SECRET and ASTBURY. With less than four hundred yards to run it was still anybody's race, the closest and most exciting climax the 'National had produced in modern times. In one of the coolest examples of jockeyship ever seen, John Cook brought SPECIFY with a last-second run up the inside rails to pip BLACK SECRET virtually on the line by a neck. Two-and-a-half lengths back in third place was ASTBURY, a length-and-a-half in front of BOWGEENO, a rewarding first 'National ride for rising star Graham Thorner.

For once, and in spite of the winner's long odds, the press applauded the race for producing such a dramatic and nail-biting finish and echoed the sentiments of all who watched it. How could the future of such a thrilling event as this ever be questioned?

SPECIFY survives an untidy jump at the last with ASTBURY on his right

1971

With £17,500 added, being £10,000 from The Horserace Betting Levy Board and £7,500 (including a gold trophy value £1,500), from Messrs Tophams Limited. For six-year-olds & upwards. The second to receive 20%, the third 10% and the fourth 5% of the whole stakes. The trainer of the Winner to receive a cup value £200 and the rider of the Winner a cup value £100

Date: 3rd April 1971	Starters: 38	Time: 9 mins 34⅕ secs
1st **SPECIFY**	**9.10–13** (*Mr F W Pontin*)	**J Cook**
2nd **BLACK SECRET**	**7.11–5** (*Mrs J Watney*)	**Mr J Dreaper**
3rd **ASTBURY**	**8.10–0** (*Mr B P Jenks*)	**J Bourke**
4th **BOWGEENO**	**11.10–5** (*Mr V T Holt*)	**G Thorner**
5th **SANDY SPRITE**	**7.10–3** (*Mrs G M Sandiford*)	**R Barry**
6th **TWO SPRINGS**	**9.11–4** (*Mr D H Barnes*)	**R Edwards**
7th **VICHYSOISE**	**9.10–3** (*Lord Chelsea*)	**P Blacker**
8th **KING VULGAN**	**10.11–0** (*Mr J P Costelloe*)	**J Crowley**
9th **REGIMENTAL**	**8.10–6** (*Major D Wigan*)	**Mr J Lawrence**
10th **GAY BUCANEER**	**10.10–0** (*Mr R W McKeever*)	**P Black**
11th **FINAL MOVE**	**11.10–0** (*Mr J Liddle*)	**T Stack**
12th **LIMEBURNER**	**10.10–0** (*Mrs S N J Embiricos*)	**J Buckingham** [remounted]
13th **COMMON ENTRANCE**	**10.10–0** (*Mr A J Maxwell*)	**Mr M Morris** [remounted]

Also Ran:

GAY TRIP 9.12–0 (Mr A J Chambers) **T Biddlecombe** *Fell*; *THE LAIRD 10.11–12* (Mr H J Joel) **J King** *Fell*; *CHARTER FLIGHT 9.11–8* (Mr J Rogerson) **W Rees** *Pulled-up*; *BRIAN'S BEST 11.10–11* (Lord Leverhulme) **R Evans** *Brought-down*; *CNOC DUBH 8.10–11* (Mr R R Guest) **T Carberry** *Fell*; *LORD JIM 10.10–9* (Mr G Dudley, jnr) **S Mellor** *Fell*; *THE INVENTOR 10.10–7* (Mrs R E Sangster) **B Fletcher** *Refused*; *MONEY BOAT 7.10–7* (Mr P Doyle) **R Coonan** *Fell*; *SOLDO 10.10–7* (Mrs B Moresby) **D Mould** *Fell*; *BATTLEDORE 10.10–6* (Mr W E Morton) **J Enright** *Refused*; *TWIGAIRY 8.10–6* (Mr V C Matthews) **E P Harty** *Brought-down*; *BEAU BOB 8.10–3* (Mr W H Whitbread) **R Dennard** *Unseated rider*; *SMOOTH DEALER 9.10–3* (Mr R R Guest) **A L T Moore** *Refused*; *THE OTTER 10.10–1* (Mrs J Dening) **T M Jones** *Fell*; *COPPERLESS 10.10–1* (Mr A S Neaves) **M Gibson** *Fell*; *COUNTRY WEDDING 9.10–0* (Mr H Billington) **R Champion** *Brought-down*; *FLOSUEBARB 11.10–1* (Mrs E F Old) **J Guest** *Pulled-up*; *CRAIGBROCK 12.10–1* (Sir Archibald Edmonstone) **P Ennis** *Fell*; *HIGHWORTH 12.10–5* (Mr R H Woodhouse) **Mr R H Woodhouse** *Pulled-up*; *INDAMELIA 8.10–5* (Mr M J Thorne) **Mr P Hobbs** *Fell*; *KELLSBORO' WOOD 11.10–0* (Mrs L M Prior) **A Turnell** *Fell*; *MISS HUNTER 10.10–0* (Mrs W Macauley) **Mr J Fowler** *Fell*; *PRIDE OF KENTUCKY 9.10–0* (Mr E R Courage) **A Mawson** *Brought-down*; *VULTURE 9.10–0* (Mrs R K Mellon) **S Barker** *Fell*; *ZARA'S GROVE 8.10–0* (Mr N H Le Mare) **G Holmes** *Fell*

The Betting: *8/1 Gay Trip; 9/1 Lord Jim; 12/1 The Laird & The Otter; 13/1 Two Springs; 16/1 Money Boat, Vulture & King Vulgan; 20/1 Black Secret, Cnoc Dubh & The Inventor; 25/1 Charter Flight & Twigairy; 28/1 Specify; 33/1 Astbury, Brian's Best, Flosuebarb, Miss Hunter, Sandy Sprite & Smooth Dealer; 40/1 Beau Bob; 45/1 Battledore; 50/1 Country Wedding, Pride of Kentucky; 66/1 Gay Buccaneer, Bowgeeno, Regimental, Final Move, Zara's Grove & Soldo; 80/1 Craigbrock; 100/1 Others.*

Distances: *A neck; two-and-a-half lengths*

Winner Trained By: *John Sutcliffe, snr, Epsom, Surrey*

Value to Winning Owner: *£15,500*

1972

For the first time since 1963, the race received the aid of a sponsor, Messrs BP Limited, whose support raised the winning owner's prize money to its highest level yet, £25,765. Any hopes, however, that the doubts surrounding the future of Aintree were at an end were promptly destroyed with the announcement that talks between Tophams Limited, Lancashire County and Liverpool City Councils had broken down. Once again the future of the great steeplechase looked bleak and once again the 1972 renewal was emphatically described as the last. The difference this time, though, was that the announcement was greeted by the public with an overwhelming display of apathy.

Still, interest picked up, as ever, when the weights for this 'last' running were published and it was seen that at the head of the handicap was dual Cheltenham Gold Cup winner L'ESCARGOT. Owned by Mr Raymond Guest and trained in Ireland by Dan Moore, the gelding's reputation preceded him to such effect that not even the burden of 12 st could prevent his starting the clear 17/2 favourite. GAY TRIP and CARDINAL ERROR were the next best backed of the forty-two runners. Among the riders new to the event was John Francome, destined to make his own distinctive mark on the sport in the years ahead.

Backed down from 33/1 to 14s almost overnight, WELL TO DO, the mount of reigning champion jockey Graham Thorner, was caught in one of those extraordinary twists of fate which for so long have been the lifeblood of the 'National. Bred by Mrs Lloyd Thomas, widow of the owner of 1937 hero ROYAL MAIL, he was by the French stallion PHEBUS, from the unraced mare PRINCESS PUZZLEMENT and was purchased as a three-year-old by Captain Tim Forster on behalf of Mrs Heather Sumner. WELL TO DO won six times for his owner before her untimely death from cancer in June 1971. In Mrs Sumner's will the gelding was left to the man who knew him best, Tim Forster. It was with only a quarter of an hour to spare that the trainer sent a telegram confirming WELL TO DO's entry for the race, so uncertain was he about risking the horse in the greatest test of all.

In driving rain and against a biting wind FAIR VULGAN took them along, closely attended by MISS HUNTER, BLACK SECRET, GAY BUCCANEER and L'ESCARGOT. GYLEBURN and SAGGART'S CHOICE both fell at the first and a despairing gasp signalled the exit of the favourite L'ESCARGOT who was baulked and knocked over at the third. The riderless GAY BUCCANEER interfered with FAIR VULGAN at the Water, Macer Gifford doing well to keep the leader on his feet, but he was never going quite so well after this. BLACK SECRET led over Becher's for the second time and from the Canal Turn all the way back, it was apparent that the winner would come from the four matching strides with each other at the front. Outsider of the quartet GENERAL SYMONS took up the running at the second-last from the hard-ridden BLACK SECRET, with GAY TRIP and WELL TO DO coasting smoothly on the inside rails. Landing first by the narrowest of margins on the flat, Graham Thorner and WELL TO DO began that longest run to the post and though Terry Biddlecombe found better ground in the centre of the course for GAY TRIP, his twenty-two pounds weight concession to WELL TO DO proved too much. Staying the distance in tremendous fashion, WELL TO DO passed the winning post two lengths in front of GAY TRIP, with a dead-heat declared for third place between BLACK SECRET and GENERAL SYMONS, three lengths further back. Welcoming his gift-horse winner into the unsaddling enclosure, Tim Forster displayed a modest and refreshing pride in WELL TO DO and the following January a three-mile 'chase at Towcester was named after Captain Forster's champion. Most appropriately, it was won by the top-weight, WELL TO DO.

Right: The popular Terry Biddlecome, second on GAY TRIP, a great champion jockey who never won the race

WELL TO DO and Graham Thorner jumping in good style with outsider GENERAL SYMONS (no 25) staying on bravely

THE GRAND NATIONAL HANDICAP STEEPLECHASE
1972

With £30,000 added, being £10,000 from The Horserace Betting Levy Board, £10,000 from Messrs BP and £10,000 (including a gold trophy value £1,500), from Messrs Tophams Limited. For six-year-olds & upwards. The second to receive 20%, the third 10% and the fourth 5% of the whole stakes. The trainer of the Winner to receive a cup value £200 and the rider of the Winner a cup value £100

Date: 8th April 1972	Starters: 42		Time: 10 mins 8⅖ secs
1st **WELL TO DO**	9.10–1	*(Capt T Forster)*	**G Thorner**
2nd **GAY TRIP**	10.11–9	*(Mr A J Chambers)*	**T W Biddlecombe**
3rd **BLACK SECRET**	8.11–2	*(Mrs J Watney)*	**S Barker**
3rd **GENERAL SYMONS**	9.10–0	*(Mrs E N Newman)*	**P Kiely**
5th **ASTBURY**	9.10–0	*(Mr B P Jenks)*	**J Bourke**
6th **SPECIFY**	10.10–11	*(Mr F W Pontin)*	**B Brogan**
7th **BRIGHT WILLOW**	11.10–1	*(Mr A Cure)*	**W Smith**
8th **MONEY BOAT**	8.10–3	*(Mr P Doyle)*	**F Berry**
9th **ROUGH SILK**	9.10–6	*(Major C H Nathan)*	**D Nicholson**

Also Ran:

L'ESCARGOT 9.12–0 (Mr R R Guest) **T Carberry** *Knocked over*; *ALASKA FORT 7.10–13* (Mrs G Mulholland) **H R Beasley** *Brought-down*; *RIGTON PRINCE 11.10–9* (Major E M W Cliff-McCulloch) **J Enright** *Pulled-up*; *TWIGAIRY 9.10–9* (Mr V C Matthews) **T G Davies** *Pulled-up*; *FORTINA'S PALACE 9.10–7* (Mr J Nesbitt Davis) **J King** *Fell*; *THE PANTHEON 9.10–4* (Mr J A Dillon) **K B White** *Fell*; *PEARL OF MONTREAL 9.10–4* (Mr G F F Fasenfield) **R Coonan** *Pulled-up*; *SWAN-SHOT 9.10–3* (Mr C Freestone & Mr J R Craig) **P McCarron** *Fell*; *GYLEBURN 9.10–4* (Mrs C Berry) **R Barry** *Fell*; *THE INVENTOR 11.10–2* (Mrs R E Sangster) **W Shoemark** *Refused*; *CARDINAL ERROR 8.10–4* (Mrs Juan M Ceballos) **J Francome** *Refused*; *SAGGART'S CHOICE 9.10–1* (Mr V E Foy) **T Stack** *Fell*; *DEBLINS GREEN 9.10–0* (Mr G H Yardley) **D Cartwright** *Pulled-up*; *NEPHIN BEG 10.10–0* (Lady Mostyn) **P Morris** *Pulled-up*; *CLOUDSMERE 8.10–4* (Mr W H Whitbread) **D Mould** *Fell*; *KELLSBORO' WOOD 12.10–0* (Mrs L M Prior) **A Turnell** *Fell*; *PERMIT 9.10–0* (Mr J Pickavance) **R R Evans** *Fell*; *LIME STREET 8.10–1* (Mr P Buckenham & Mr E P Hickling) **R Pitman** *Fell*; *JUST A GAMBLE 10.10–1* (Capt & Mrs F Tyrwhitt-Drake) **P Buckley** *Fell*; *LISNAREE 9.10–0* (Mrs Ornella Mancinelli) **Mr F Turner** *Fell*; *NOM DE GUERRE 10.10–0* (Mrs T D Pilkington) **J Haine** *Fell*; *GAY BUCCANEER 11.10–0* (Mrs P G McCrea) **T Hyde** *Fell*; *MISS HUNTER 11.10–0* (Mrs W MacCauley) **A L Moore** *Pulled-up*; *VICHYSOISE 10.10–3* (Lord Chelsea) **P Blacker** *Refused*; *THE OTTER 11.10–0* (Mrs J Dening) **T M Jones** *Fell*; *BULLOCKS HORN 9.10–0* (Mrs E P Barker) **Mr R Smith** *Refused*; *THE POOKA 10.10–5* (Mr Cecil Ross) **Mr C Ross** *Fell*; *FAIR VULGAN 8.10–0* (Mr F Pullen) **M C Gifford** *Fell*; *BEAU PARC 9.11–2* (Mrs C Gordon-Creed) **Mr A Nicholson** *Fell*; *EVEN DELIGHT 7.10–2* (Mr J McClorey) **R Dennard** *Pulled-up*; *LIMEBURNER 11.10–0* (Mrs S N J Embiricos) **W Rees** *Pulled-up*; *VULTURE 10.10–2* (Sir Hugh Fraser) **P Brogan** *Refused*; *COUNTRY WEDDING 10.10–4* (Mr H Billington) **R Champion** *Fell*

The Betting: *17/2 L'Escargot; 12/1 Gay Trip & Cardinal Error; 14/1 Well to Do, Black Street & Fair Vulgan; 16/1 Fortina's Palace & Money Boat; 18/1 Cloudsmere; 20/1 Gyleburn; 22/1 Specify; 25/1 Rigton Prince, Rough Silk, Lime Street, The Otter & Astbury; 28/1 Bright Willow, Saggart's Choice, Twigairy & Bullocks Horn; 33/1 Nom de Guerre, Swan-Shot, The Inventor, The Pantheon, Alaska Fort, Gay Buccaneer & Deblin's Green; 40/1 Even Delight & General Symons; 50/1 Miss Hunter, Beau Parc, The Pooka & Country Wedding; 55/1 Pearl of Montreal; 100/1 Nephin Beg, Kellsboro' Wood, Permit, Just a Gamble, Lisnaree, Vichysoise, Limeburner & Vulture.*

Distances: *Two lengths; three lengths*

Winner Trained By: *Capt Tim Forster, Letcombe Bassett, Berkshire*

Value to Winning Owner: *£25,765*

1973

When just weeks before this year's race, Mrs Topham revealed to Julian Wilson in an exclusive interview for BBC Grandstand that she had a buyer for the racecourse, the cynics gave knowing winks and predictable chuckles. Her professed deep hope that the sale would allow the 'National to remain at Aintree was also treated flippantly, though not by those familiar with the lady's energetic managerial involvement with racing's greatest showpiece over a period of forty years. If indeed this was to be the final act of the Tophams' Aintree story, then the cast for the show could hardly be better.

Topping the weights was L'ESCARGOT again, this time, though, sharing the position with the brightest jumping star yet to come from the land of the Southern Cross, CRISP. Owned by Sir Chester Manifold, ten-year-old CRISP had carried everything before him in his native Australia before arriving at Fred Winter's Lambourn yard, in much the same way that JAY TRUMP had journeyed across the oceans for preparation by the maestro. In receipt of just one pound from the joint-top-weights was SPANISH STEPS, owned and trained by Mr Edward Courage, who for more years than he would care to admit had tried in vain to realise his dream of winning the 'National. That ambition had been narrowly thwarted on three occasions when his TIBERETTA ran second, third and fourth in the race and it did not go unnoticed that this gallant mare was the dam of his present contender SPANISH STEPS. BLACK SECRET was trying again in the race which seemed to bring out the best in him and PROUD TARQUIN was the mount of Lord Oaksey, who ten years earlier, when known as John Lawrence, had suffered the heartbreak of being beaten in the final strides on CARRICKBEG.

But the horse who had really caught the imagination of the majority of the public, inside and out of racing, was the eight-year-old RED RUM and it was as much the fairytale background of the gelding and his connections as his ability over fences which led to his being 9/1 joint favourite with CRISP. Bred by Martin McKenery in Ireland, by QUORUM out of MARED, RED RUM won three times on the flat in the colours of Maurice Kingsley when trained by former champion jump-jockey Tim Molony. When switched to National Hunt racing, RED RUM was successful five times over fences and three times over the minor obstacles in the ownership of Mrs Lurline Brotherton, but was considered somewhat lacking in determination and in August 1972 was put up for sale at Doncaster. Southport garage-owner and recent addition to the ranks of trainers, Donald McCain acquired the son of QUORUM for six thousand guineas on behalf of octogenarian Noel le Mare, but the purchase price was looked upon by the 'experts' as too much for too little. From his stables behind that humble car showroom in sleepy Birkdale, McCain set about putting new life into the over-raced, under-interested gelding, who he now discovered had at some time suffered an attack of the dreaded pedalostitis. In what proved to be the greatest advertisement any British seaside resort could ever have wished for, the balmy breezes and cooling spray of Southport's sands totally revitalised RED RUM, to such effect that within little more than six weeks he vindicated McCain's judgement by winning all five steeplechases he contested. He was then put aside from early November until the end of January 1973, and it became apparent to even his sternest critics that the astute, if rather unorthodox trainer had a real chance of lifting 'chasing's most famous prize. His senior patron, Mr Le Mare, had built his Liverpool-based Norwest Construction Company into a major force in civil engineering while cherishing a lifelong ambition to own a 'National winner. Now he found himself with two powerful contenders, for GLENKILN, his second string in the Birkdale yard, held one important advantage over his better-known stable-mate and that was experience of the course. GLENKILN had proved that the big fences held no terror for him when a one-day version of the lost autumn meeting was re-introduced the previous October. Partnering GLENKILN in the 'National was the ebullient Irishman Jonjo O'Neill, whose first encounter with the race this was to be, while the task of steering RED RUM was laid on the shoulders of Brian Fletcher. Since his moment of glory five years earlier on RED ALLIGATOR, the north-eastern jockey had suffered more than most, a near fatal fall at Stockton making his struggle back to the top a monumental task, but in RED RUM he was to find the perfect Aintree conveyance.

CRISP survived his only blunder at the first to quickly open up a substantial lead. With falls few and far between, the race became a procession, CRISP forging well clear of his rivals and treating onlookers and television viewers to the most perfect demonstration of how the frightening fences should be jumped. At breathtaking speed, CRISP increased his advantage all round the first circuit and back into the country. It was at the nineteenth that Brian Fletcher realised that the Australian runaway would soon be too far ahead for any of them to catch and drawing away from the main group, he set off in lone pursuit. RED RUM cleared Becher's really well, but jumping with an equal fluency,

CRISP maintained his twenty length lead all the way back to the racecourse. Richard Pitman detected a slight change in CRISP's rhythm as they crossed Melling Road but they were still a long way clear and he jumped the second last as perfectly as he had the rest. Suddenly terribly tired over the final fence, CRISP was still all of fifteen lengths in front of RED RUM, but as the leader moved out to by-pass the elbow, it was obvious that he was continuing now on instinct and guts alone. The most pitiful scene ever enacted on that punishing run-in brought the 1973 'National to its awful yet glorious end, as CRISP bravely staggered towards the victory he had truly earned but was not to gain. It was only in the final strides that RED RUM, receiving no less than twenty-three pounds from his rival, got up to win by three-quarters of a length. A long way back in third place came L'ESCARGOT, in front of SPANISH STEPS. The nightmare final yards of the race brought CRISP and Richard Pitman only sympathy, yet there was some small consolation in the fact that the race time of 9 minutes 1.9 seconds shattered the previous record.

RED RUM made the short journey back to Southport, the hero of a 'National which had produced all the finest qualities of racing and which more than ever made a nonsense of the doubt hanging over the future of the race. As was the Topham custom, RED RUM's name took its honoured place on the County Stand Roll of Honour within days of that moment of joy and heartbreak. Ominously, though, beneath the name was inscribed the following words:

'THE END OF AN ERA.'

On 19th November 1973, Mrs Topham sold Aintree racecourse to Liverpool property developer Mr Bill Davies for £3 million.

1973

With £30,000 added, being £10,000 from The Horserace Betting Levy Board, £10,000 from Messrs BP and £10,000 (including a gold trophy value £2,000), from Messrs Tophams Limited. For six-year-olds & upwards. The second to receive 20%, the third 10% and the fourth 5% of the whole stakes. The trainer of the Winner to receive a cup value £200 and the rider of the Winner a cup value £100

Date: 31st March 1973	Starters: 38	Time: 9 mins 1.9 secs
		* A Record *

1st	**RED RUM**	8.10–5	*(Mr N H Le Mare)*	**B Fletcher**
2nd	**CRISP**	10.12–0	*(Sir Chester Manifold)*	**R Pitman**
3rd	**L'ESCARGOT**	10.12–0	*(Mr R R Guest)*	**T Carberry**
4th	**SPANISH STEPS**	10.11–13	*(Mr E R Courage)*	**P Blacker**
5th	**ROUGE AUTUMN**	9.10–0	*(Mr B P Jenks)*	**K B White**
6th	**HURRICANE ROCK**	9.10–0	*(Mr D J Proctor)*	**R Champion**
7th	**PROUD TARQUIN**	10.10–11	*(Sir John Thompson)*	**Lord Oaksey**
8th	**PROPHECY**	10.10–3	*(Mrs C M Richards)*	**B R Davies**
9th	**ENDLESS FOLLY**	11.10–0	*(Mrs V Vanden Bergh)*	**J Guest**
10th	**BLACK SECRET**	9.11–2	*(Mrs J Watney)*	**S Barker**
11th	**PETRUCHIO'S SON**	10.10–5	*(Mr P Blackburn)*	**D Mould**
12th	**THE POOKA**	11.10–0	*(Mrs J Bowes-Lyon)*	**A L Moore**
13th	**GREAT NOISE**	9.10–2	*(Mr J W Rowles)*	**D Cartwright**
14th	**GREEN PLOVER**	13.10–0	*(Mr A M Darlington)*	**Mr M F Morris**
15th	**SUNNY LAD**	9.10–3	*(Mrs R E Sangster)*	**W Smith**
16th	**GO-PONTINENTAL**	13.10–4	*(Mrs H O'Neill)*	**J McNaught**
17th	**MILL DOOR**	11.10–5	*(Mr E F Birchall)*	**P Cullis**

Also Ran:

GREY SOMBRERO 9.10–9 (Mr W F Caudwell) **W Shoemark** *Fell*; *GLENKILN 10.10–7* (Mr N H Le Mare) **J J O'Neill** *Fell*; *BEGGAR'S WAY 9.10–1* (Mr D W Samuel) **T Kinane** *Fell*; *CANHARIS 8.10–1* (Lord Zetland) **P Buckley** *Brought down*; *GENERAL SYMONS 10.10–0* (Mrs E N Newman) **P Kiely** *Pulled-up*; *HIGHLAND SEAL 10.10–6* (Mrs J Dening) **D Nicholson** *Pulled-up*; *MR VIMY 10.10–2* (Mrs F Harvey) **J Haine** *Pulled-up*; *ASTBURY 10.10–2* (Mr B P Jenks) **J Bourke** *Pulled-up*; *SWAN-SHOT 10.10–0* (Mr C Freestone & Mr J R Craig) **M Blackshaw** *Refused*; *BEAU PARC 10.10–1* (Mr D Ancil) **A Turnell** *Pulled-up*; *ASHVILLE 8.10–4* (Mr R R Guest) **J King** *Fell*; *TARQUIN BID 9.10–0* (Mrs J H Weekes) **J Bracken** *Fell*; *ROUGH SILK 10.10–0* (Major C H Nathan) **T Norman** *Pulled-up*; *RICHELEAU 9.10–0* (Mrs E J Taplin) **N Kernick** *Fell*; *PRINCESS CAMILLA 8.10–4* (Mr J E Bigg) **R Barry** *Refused*; *RAMPSMAN 9.10–0* (Mr J Rose) **D Munro** *Pulled-up*; *FORTUNE BAY II 9.10–3* (Mr G A Sloan) **Mr G Sloan** *Fell*; *CHARLEY WINKING 8.10–0* (Mr L G Scott) **Mr D Scott** *Fell*; *PROUD PERCY 10.10–0* (Mr R F Fisher) **R R Evans** *Fell*; *NEREO 7.10–3* (Duke of Alburquerque) **Duke of Alburquerque** *Pulled-up*; *CULLA HILL 9.10–7* (Mr B J Brookes) **Mr N Brookes** *Fell*

The Betting: *9/1 Red Rum & Crisp; 11/1 L'Escargot; 14/1 Ashville; 16/1 Princess Camilla, Spanish Steps & Canharis; 20/1 Prophecy & Highland Seal; 22/1 Proud Tarquin & Black Secret; 25/1 Sunny Lad & Grey Sombrero; 33/1 Beggar's Way, General Symons & Glenkiln; 40/1 Rouge Autumn; 50/1 Astbury, Great Noise, Petruchio's Son & Richeleau; 66/1 Nereo, Fortune Bay II & Rough Silk; 100/1 Others.*

Distances: *Three-quarters of a length; twenty-five lengths*

Winner Trained By: *Donald McCain, Southport, Lancashire*

Value to Winning Owner: *£25,186*

1974

Mrs Topham and Bill Davies share a joke in 1973

Throwing himself completely into the complex and, for him, unknown business of staging the greatest racing spectacle in the calendar, Bill Davies, through his company the Walton Group, doubled the Levy Board's contribution of £10,000 towards the prize money. He also reintroduced the once very popular Jump Sunday, defunct since 1960 as a result of vandalism, and as an indication of his commitment to the event, he purchased the improving 'chaser WOLVERHAMPTON to represent him in the race. The fact that Tophams still regarded the Grand National with deep affection was demonstrated by their presentation of an Historic Challenge Trophy to the winning owner, an excellent gesture which regrettably went almost unnoticed by the general public.

Of the seventy-seven original subscribers, forty-two elected to run and with RED RUM receiving the maximum twelve stone, an increase of twenty-three pounds since last year, the public preferred to look elsewhere for a favourite. The obvious choice was SCOUT, ridden by Tommy Stack and winner of his last three races and on the lenient mark of 10 stone, four points clear of the Southport champion at 7/1. L'ESCARGOT, again high in the handicap, was also in heavy demand at 17/2. Making a more determined assault on the race than ever before, Mr Edward Courage weighed out three runners, SPANISH STEPS, ROYAL RELIEF and QUINTUS, while that most persistent of all amateurs the Duke of Alburquerque took the leg-up again on eight-year-old NEREO. Female vocalist Dorothy Squires ran NORWEGIAN FLAG, a half-brother to L'ESCARGOT.

Jockey Martin Blackshaw was caused some embarrassment and a deal of discomfort when his mount, the mare PRINCESS CAMILLA, gave a display of bucking more suited to a rodeo, causing the start to be delayed. Once on their way though, she settled down well in the mid-division. The only casualty at the first was Lord Oaksey with ROYAL RELIEF and as the big field thundered on, falls were few until the Canal Turn where four dropped out. PEARL OF MONTREAL showed the way back onto the racecourse, in front of a group consisting of ROUGH SILK, STRAIGHT VULGAN, CHARLES DICKENS, SUNNY LAD and L'ESCARGOT and in this order they began the second circuit. The strong pace quickly took its toll back in the country and at Becher's RED RUM had struck the front, rather earlier than his rider would have wished. But with CHARLES DICKENS, SCOUT, L'ESCARGOT and SPANISH STEPS hard on his heels, Brian Fletcher accepted the situation. Jumping brilliantly despite his top weight, RED RUM set them all the task of catching him. After Valentine's, SCOUT moved up into a challenging position and there was a moment's anxiety as

RED RUM pitched badly on landing at the twenty-sixth. In the style of a truly great horse, however, the pride of Merseyside recovered immediately without losing so much as a foot of ground and, coming back onto the racecourse in front, he had the crowds cheering a long way from home. Seven lengths clear of L'ESCARGOT at the post, RED RUM received an ovation befitting the first dual winner of the race since 1936 and the delight on the face of Brian Fletcher as he reined in his third 'National winner said all there was to say about the glory of the race. Amid scenes of wild rejoicing, RED RUM was led in, this time without the spectre of CRISP's col-lapse hanging over him, a most worthy and brilliant winner and a great credit to his trainer Donald McCain. In defying his increased weight burden, RED RUM emphatically placed himself among the all-time Aintree greats and his partner in triumph Brian Fletcher became only the second rider this century to ride three Liverpool 'National winners.

Out of the frame and this time also out of hospital, was the gallant Duke of Albur-querque who had every reason to be proud of guiding NEREO round into eighth place and on a day when not even the increased admission charges could keep the sun and smiles away from Aintree.

The incomparable RED RUM and Brian Fletcher clear the last on their way to their second successive victory

1974

With £30,000 added, being £10,000 from The Horserace Betting Levy Board. The Walton Group of Liverpool have given £20,000, (including a gold trophy value £2,000). For six-year-olds & upwards. The second to receive 20%, the third 10% and the fourth 5% of the whole stakes. The trainer of the Winner to receive a cup value £200 and the rider of the Winner a cup value £100

Date: 30th March 1974	Starters: 42	Time: 9 mins 20.3 secs
1st **RED RUM**	9.12–0 *(Mr N H Le Mare)*	**B Fletcher**
2nd **L'ESCARGOT**	11.11–13 *(Mr R R Guest)*	**T Carberry**
3rd **CHARLES DICKENS**	10.10–0 *(Lt Col P Bengough)*	**A Turnell**
4th **SPANISH STEPS**	11.11–9 *(Mr E R Courage)*	**W Smith**
5th **ROUGH SILK**	11.10–0 *(Mrs P G McCrea)*	**M F Morris**
6th **VULGAN TOWN**	8.10–8 *(Brig Gen W P Gilbride)*	**J Haine**
7th **ROUGE AUTUMN**	10.10–0 *(Mr B P Jenks)*	**K B White**
8th **NEREO**	8.10–6 *(Duke of Alburquerque)*	**Duke of Alburquerque**
9th **SAN-FELIU**	11.10–3 *(Lady Hay)*	**P Buckley**
10th **NORWEGIAN FLAG**	8.10–0 *(Miss Dorothy Squires)*	**J Bourke**
11th **SCOUT**	8.10–0 *(Mr A D W Allen)*	**T Stack**
12th **QUINTUS**	8.10–0 *(Mr E R Courage)*	**G Thorner**
13th **DUNNO**	10.10–1 *(Mrs E Mitchell)*	**Mr N Mitchell**
14th **TUBS VI**	11.10–6 *(Mr T V O'Brien)*	**V O'Brien**
15th **ESCARI**	8.10–2 *(Mr J J McDowell)*	**P Black**
16th **SUNNY LAD**	10.10–4 *(Mrs R E Sangster)*	**D Cartwright**
17th **PRINCESS CAMILLA**	9.11–4 *(Miss C H Bartholomew)*	**M Blackshaw**

Also Ran:

ARGENT 10.11–10 (Mr J J Byrne) **R Coonan** *Brought-down*; *ROYAL RELIEF 10.11–6* (Mr E R Courage) **Lord Oaksey** *Fell*; *HUPERADE 10.10–12* (Mr J Carden) **Mr J Carden** *Fell*; *STRAIGHT VULGAN 8.10–8* (Mrs G M Sandiford) **R Barry** *Fell*; *ROMAN HOLIDAY 10.10–7* (Lord Chelsea) **J King** *Pulled-up*; *ROUGH HOUSE 8.10–6* (Mr R P Brown) **Mr J Burke** *Fell*; *BAHIA DORADA 9.10–2* (Mr J R F Pullen) **J Guest** *Pulled-up*; *GLENKILN 11.10–2* (Mr N H Le Mare) **R Crank** *Fell*; *SHANEMAN 9.10–2* (Mr T J Lawlor) **B Hannon** *Unseated rider*; *THE TUNKU 8.10–1* (Mr D W Rimmer) **R R Evans** *Pulled-up*; *STEPHEN'S SOCIETY 8.11–5* (Mr C D Collins) **Mr C D Collins** *Pulled-up*; *CLOUDSMERE 10.10–4* (Mr W H Whitbread) **P Kelleway** *Carried-out*; *FRANCOPHILE 9.10–5* (Mr & Mrs S Powell) **R Pitman** *Refused*; *PEARL OF MONTREAL 11.10–0* (Mr G F F Fasenfield) **T Kinane** *Pulled-up*; *DEBLIN'S GREEN 11.10–0* (Mr G H Yardley) **N Wakley** *Brought-down*; *BEAU BOB 11.10–0* (Mr W H Whitbread) **J Glover** *Fell*; *SIXER 10.10–0* (Mr G Clay) **M Salaman** *Brought-down*; *CULLA HILL 10.10–8* (Mr B J Brookes & Mr N H Brookes) **Mr N Brookes** *Fell*; *BEGGAR'S WAY 10.10–2* (Mr H Jackson) **V Soane** *Refused*; *ASTBURY 11.10–0* (Mr B P Jenks) **Mr W Jenks** *Pulled-up*; *WOLVERHAMPTON 7.10–0* (Mr Bill Davies) **R Quinn** *Pulled-up*; *ESTOILE 10.10–0* (Mr H Burt) **R Hyett** *Fell*; *KARACOLA 9.10–0* (Mr D M Adams) **C Astbury** *Brought-down*; *MILL DOOR 12.10–2* (Mr W E Lipka) **J McNaught** *Fell*; *GO-PONTINENTAL 14.10–0* (Mr R Armstrong) **J Suthern** *Fell*

The Betting: *7/1 Scout; 17/2 L'Escargot; 11/1 Red Rum; 14/1 Rough House; 15/1 Spanish Steps & Straight Vulgan; 16/1 Francophile; 18/1 Royal Relief; 20/1 Sunny Lad; 22/1 San Feliu & Tubs VI; 25/1 Deblin's Green & Wolverhampton; 28/1 Princess Camilla & Rouge Autumn; 33/1 Quintus; 35/1 Vulgan Town; 40/1 Stephen's Society; 50/1 Argent, Glenkiln, Norwegian Flag, Shaneman & Pearl of Montreal; 66/1 Roman Holiday, Sixer, Astbury, Estoile, Escari, Beggar's Way & Rough Silk; 100/1 Huperade, Nereo, Bahia Dorade, The Tunku, Beau Bob, Cloudsmere, Culla Hill, Karacola, Mill Door, Dunno & Go-Pontinental.*

Distances: *Seven lengths; a short head*

Winner Trained By: *Donald McCain, Southport, Lancashire*

Value to Winning Owner: *£25,102*

1975

That well-known Sunday newspaper the *News of the World* entered into a sponsorship agreement this year which guaranteed winning prize money in excess of £38,000 and at first this encouraging development in the affairs of Aintree gave rise to a sense of well-being. This was premature for in only his second year as owner of the racecourse Bill Davies was encountering the same difficulties with racing's hierarchy as the former owner had experienced. Forced again to increase admission charges, the new administration came in for the fiercest criticism and this year's race took place before one of the smallest attendances in the history of the event. There was additional anxiety for Mr Davies on the eve of the race, when his entry WOLVERHAMPTON dropped dead in his final gallops with trainer Don McCain's string and with values plummeting in the property market, the would-be saviour of the 'National was one way and another finding 1975 a very trying year.

Of the thirty-one runners RED RUM was the overwhelming favourite at the unrealistic odds of 7/2. His performance last year, followed so quickly by an equally impressive display when taking the Scottish Grand National at Ayr, had established him as the outstanding long distance 'chaser of the age and at still only ten years old, it was deemed inconceivable that he could be beaten in the 'National. In general, the field could hardly be described as vintage and the market reflected the fact, with only seven horses at less than 20/1. There was a huge tip on the day for Lord Chelsea's consistent MONEY MARKET and of the long-shots, former Cheltenham Gold Cup winner THE DIKLER, and Lord Oaksey's mount ROYAL RELIEF, came in for each-way support.

In what was expected to be his last race, L'ESCARGOT was the main hope of the Irish, and although now a twelve-year-old, Raymond Guest's dual Gold Cup winner went off the 13/2 second favourite. A strong chestnut gelding by ESCART III out of WHAT A DAISY, L'ESCARGOT was bred by Mrs B O'Neill and after winning on the flat, became a top-class hurdler. But it was in the demanding world of 'chasing that L'ESCARGOT hit the headlines and after finishing third and second in the race and now receiving eleven pounds from RED RUM, his American owner and connections were brimful of confidence.

To the frustration of all, not least the riders, the start was delayed when JUNIOR PARTNER was found to have spread a plate and some fifteen minutes late, the field eventually set off led by ZIMULATOR. That most able of amateurs, Peter Greenall, had the briefest of encounters with his first 'National when SHANEMAN fell at the first and at the next JUNIOR PARTNER was another faller. Hitting the smallest fence on the course very hard at the seventh, L'ESCARGOT shot Tommy Carberry forward onto his neck but the Irishman made a superb recovery to continue just off the pace, leaving Lord Oaksey rolling on the turf behind from his fall with ROYAL RELIEF. As they approached the Chair, possibly the most feared of all obstacles, the leading jockeys were faced with the horrible prospect of measuring the big ditch in the wake of four unpredictable riderless horses. Fortunately the wayward ones jumped the Chair straight and true but LAND LARK actually died in mid-air and falling sideways on the landing side, brought anxious moments for GLANFORD BRIGG, BEAU BOB and L'ESCARGOT. Back out in the country, GLANFORD BRIGG, SOUTHERN QUEST and BEAU BOB shared the lead closely followed by HIGH KEN, then a group including L'ESCARGOT, SPANISH STEPS, RED RUM, THE DIKLER, MANICOU BAY and MONEY MARKET. Becher's brought the second tragedy of the race when BEAU BOB fell and broke his neck. From here RED RUM and SOUTHERN QUEST dictated affairs with THE DIKLER poised just behind and L'ESCARGOT also in close attendance. Tiring soon after Valentine's, GLANFORD BRIGG dropped back and when RED RUM struck the front over the next fence the cheering began for what looked certain to be a record-breaking third victory for the best loved 'chaser in the annals of the sport. Brian Fletcher, however, knew that his mount had little in reserve on going unsuited to him. At the third-last, he shouted across to Carberry on L'ESCARGOT, 'Well done, Tommy, you've got me beat,' and although the two came over the last fence together, L'ESCARGOT was always going that little bit better. Racing

away on the flat, L'ESCARGOT won by fifteen lengths from RED RUM, with SPANISH STEPS a further eight back in third place. MONEY MARKET was fourth.

Winning owner Raymond Guest led in his winner with justifiable pride, having succeeded after twenty years of trying to win the race. It would be impossible to guess if this victory provided him with as much or more pleasure than the Derby wins of his LARKSPUR and SIR IVOR. Trainer Dan Moore, at last took his place in the Aintree winner's enclosure which he so narrowly missed riding into when pipped on the line by BATTLESHIP in 1938, and the generous announcement by Mr Guest that L'ESCARGOT, his racing days now over, was to be given to the trainer's wife ensured that Dan would have a constant reminder of their memorable

Two of the modern greats: Gold Cup winner L'ESCARGOT and RED RUM together over the last

achievement. The ever-cheerful Tommy Carberry had, in five short weeks of toil, skill and courage, steered home the winners of the Cheltenham Gold Cup, the Irish National, the Topham Trophy 'Chase and the most sought after prize of all the Aintree Grand National. RED RUM, glorious in defeat, returned quietly to Birkdale with the promise that when the eyes of the world again centred on Aintree, he would again grace that hallowed turf with his presence.

THE GRAND NATIONAL HANDICAP STEEPLECHASE
1975

With £50,000 added, being £10,000 given by The Horserace Betting Levy Board and £40,000 by The News of the World, the latter amount including a trophy value £2,000. For six-year-olds & upwards. The second to receive £11,740, the third £5,870 and the fourth £2,935. The trainer of the Winner to receive a trophy value £250 and the rider of the Winner a trophy value £250

Date: 5th April 1975		Starters: 31	Time: 9 mins 31.1 secs
1st	**L'ESCARGOT**	12.11–3 *(Mr R R Guest)*	**T Carberry**
2nd	**RED RUM**	10.12–0 *(Mr N H Le Mare)*	**B Fletcher**
3rd	**SPANISH STEPS**	12.10–3 *(Mr E R Courage)*	**W Smith**
4th	**MONEY MARKET**	8.10–13 *(Lord Chelsea)*	**J King**
5th	**THE DIKLER**	12.11–13 *(Mrs D August)*	**R Barry**
6th	**MANICOU BAY**	9.10–7 *(Mr D Bunn)*	**R Champion**
7th	**SOUTHERN QUEST**	8.10–6 *(Mr W Fletcher)*	**S Shields**
8th	**GLANFORD BRIGG**	9.11–4 *(Mr P Harper)*	**M Blackshaw**
9th	**HALLY PERCY**	11.10–0 *(Mr D Badham)*	**M C Gifford**
10th	**RAG TRADE**	9.10–4 *(Mr P B Raymond)*	**J Francome**

Also Ran:

CLEAR CUT *11.11–1* (Mr J Hemingway) **T Stack** *Fell*; HIGH KEN *9.11–1* (Mr R Hickman) **B Brogan** *Fell*; ROYAL RELIEF *11.11–1* (Mr E R Courage) **Lord Oaksey** *Fell*; APRIL SEVENTH *9.11–0* (Mrs B Meehan) **A Turnell** *Brought-down*; ROUGH HOUSE *9.10–12* (Mrs W Brown) **J Burke** *Fell*; BARONA *9.10–8* (Mr W H Whitbread) **P Kelleway** *Fell*; EVEN DAWN *8.10–4* (Mr S Wainwright) **D Mould** *Pulled-up*; BALLYRICHARD AGAIN *10.10–1* (Mr J Webber) **A Webber** *Unseated rider*; LAND LARK *10.10–1* (Mr T Pocock) **G Thorner** *Fell*; CASTLERUDDERY *9.10–4* (Mrs K Harper) **Mr T Walsh** *Refused*; SHANEMAN *10.10–8* (Mr P Greenall) **Mr P Greenall** *Pulled-up*; ZIMULATOR *8.10–0* (Mrs N Swan) **Capt D Swan** *Fell*; FEEL FREE *9.10–0* (Mr G Syvret) **M Salaman** *Fell*; GLEN OWEN *8.10–0* (Lord Cadogan) **D Atkins** *Fell*; JUNIOR PARTNER *8.10–0* (Mrs F Wheatley) **K B White** *Fell*; ROUGH SILK *12.10–8* (Brig Gen W Gilbride) **Mr L Urbano** *Refused*; TUDOR VIEW *9.10–0* (Mr P Upton) **G McNally** *Brought-down*; BEAU BOB *12.10–1* (Mr W H Whitbread) **J Glover** *Fell*; KILMORE BOY *9.10–2* (Mr A Grogan) **P Blacker** *Fell*; BALLYATH *9.10–0* (Mr N H Le Mare) **J Bourke** *Pulled-up*; SPITTIN IMAGE *9.10–0* (Mrs J Welch, jnr) **M Cummins** *Fell*

The Betting: *7/2 Red Rum; 13/2 L'Escargot; 12/1 Rough House; 14/1 Land Lark & Money Market; 18/1 Junior Partner & Rag Trade; 20/1 Clear Cut, Glanford Brigg, Spanish Steps & The Dikler; 22/1 Royal Relief & Glen Owen; 28/1 April Seventh, High Ken & Rough Silk; 33/1 Southern Quest & Castleruddery; 40/1 Kilmore Boy, Ballyrichard Again, Manicou Bay & Barona; 50/1 Even Dawn & Spittin Image; 66/1 Hally Percy & Feel Free; 100/1 Shaneman, Zimulator, Tudor View, Beau Bob & Ballyath.*

Distances: *Fifteen lengths; eight lengths*

Winner Trained By: *Dan Moore, The Curragh, County Kildare, Ireland*

Value to Winning Owner: *£38,005*

1976

Following the row over increased admission charges, a dispute between Bill Davies and the Jockey Club placed the bearded Liverpudlian once more in the spotlight while reviving serious doubts about the future of the Grand National. His request for a £75,000 grant from racing's governing body fell on deaf ears, as did his proposal to stage an Aintree Derby, and in May 1975 Mr Davies announced that he was selling the racecourse to Irish property developer Patrick McCrea. By August the deal had fallen through, the Levy Board had offered a derisory £400,000 for the course and bookmaking giants Ladbrokes entered the market with a bid of £1.5 million. In December the Jockey Club gave Aintree's owner a deadline of less than a month in which to reach some sort of agreement, failing which they would transfer the race to Doncaster. This was indeed an about-turn on the part of those who just twelve years before had poured scorn on Mrs Topham's suggestion that the 'National could be staged away from its traditional home. On 22nd December 1975 Bill Davies secured an arrangement with Ladbrokes who guaranteed to manage the race until 1978, with an option to renew which would effectively put them in charge of the 'National till the year 1982. Working with commendable speed and efficiency, Ladbrokes got on with the enormous task in hand and the result, in little over three months, was an example to all who had wallowed in apathy. A new Clerk of the Course was appointed, the professional expertise of Ladbrokes marketing executives, in particular Nigel Payne and Mike Dillon, swept into full gear and as the public passed through the turnstiles on the first day of the 1976 meeting they encountered a refreshing mood of optimism and purpose. With greater emphasis on jumping, only four races at the fixture were run on the level. Valuable sponsorship improved not only the quantity of the competitors but also their quality and, creating her own milestone in racing history, Miss Charlotte Brew became the first of her sex to ride over the big fences when piloting BARONY FORT into fourth place in the Foxhunters' Chase.

Of the thirty-two-strong 'National field, Paul Kelleway was placed in the hot-seat on Mr W H Whitbread's 7/1 favourite BARONA, when a flood of late betting relegated RED RUM to second place in the market. RAG TRADE was backed down from 20/1 to 14s shortly before the 'off'. Bred in Ireland by Ian Williams, son of the 1937 winning jockey Evan Williams, RAG TRADE was by MENELEK out of THE RAGE and was the winner of but a single race before 1974. After carrying John Francome into tenth place in last year's 'National, the gelding came under the care of Fred Rimell, was aimed at a second Aintree attempt and in his final outing before the big one, gained a lucky victory in Chepstow's Joe Coral Welsh Grand National.

Becher's brought the downfall of TREGARRON, TUDOR VIEW and GLANFORD BRIGG and only a skilful piece of horsemanship prevented the Duke of Alburquerque from parting company with NEREO when squeezed for room at the seventh. Back on the racecourse, he was actually at the head of the twenty-four survivors but he gave his fifty-seven-year-old Spanish rider a heavy fall two before the Chair. Jonjo O'Neill was also a casualty here through the fall of RED RUM's stable companion MERIDIAN II. Under his new jockey, Tommy Stack, RED RUM himself was giving his usual foot-perfect display turning back into the country in twelfth position. At Becher's leader GOLDEN RAPPER nosedived into the ground giving John Francome a crushing fall. The excitement rose as the race entered its final stages and five horses were almost in line at the penultimate fence, RED RUM, EYECATCHER ridden by the former's old jockey Brian Fletcher, RAG TRADE, CEOLNA-MARA and THE DIKLER, but landing in front after the final fence, RED RUM seemed to have put the matter beyond issue. The customary Lancastrian roar rang out in anticipation of a record-breaking third victory for the Southport battler, but in the space of a few yards RAG TRADE suddenly picked up so well that he had opened up a four length gap between himself and the dual winner by the time the elbow was reached. Responding in the manner of a truly great racehorse, RED RUM battled all the way to the line and although RAG TRADE held on gamely, his advantage had been reduced to two lengths by the time the post was reached. Eight lengths away, the mare EYECATCHER held off a late burst from BARONA to secure third place.

RAG TRADE provided owner Mr P B Raymond with his second success in the race, trainer Fred Rimell with a record-breaking fourth 'National victory and for Irish jockey John Burke it was a rapid elevation to the top flight of jockeyship, following so closely his winning ride on ROYAL FROLIC in the Cheltenham Gold Cup. RED RUM increased his army of admirers with another peerless performance under top weight and although that elusive third win now seemed a forlorn dream, the horse's charisma was beyond comparison in racing history. In the nine short but highly eventful years since his first encounter with the Grand National, Brian Fletcher had emerged as the possessor of the finest riding record in the race since the days of Jack Anthony. With three wins, one second and two thirds to his credit, Brian went home to County Durham safe in the knowledge that his 'National tally was the envy of many a more fashionable jockey.

RED RUM and Tommy Stack are just beaten again, this time by RAG TRADE and John Burke

1976

With £50,000 added, being £10,000 given by The Horserace Betting Levy Board and £40,000, (including a trophy value £2,000), given by The News of the World. A historic challenge trophy will be presented by Messrs Tophams Limited to the Winning owner, to be held until 1st March 1977. For six-year-olds & upwards. The second to receive £11,410, the third £5,630 and the fourth £2,740. The trainer of the Winner to receive a trophy value £250 and the rider of the Winner a trophy value £250

Date: 3rd April 1976	Starters: 32	Time: 9 mins 20.9 secs
1st **RAG TRADE**	**10.10–12** *(Mr P B Raymond)*	**J Burke**
2nd **RED RUM**	**11.11–10** *(Mr N H Le Mare)*	**T Stack**
3rd **EYECATCHER**	**10.10–7** *(Mr J R Bosley)*	**B Fletcher**
4th **BARONA**	**10.10–6** *(Mr W H Whitbread)*	**P Kelleway**
5th **CEOL-NA-MARA**	**7.10–6** *(Mrs M Seddon-Brown & Mrs D Warnes)*	**J Glover**
6th **THE DIKLER**	**13.11–7** *(Mrs M A Boddington)*	**R Barry**
7th **SANDWILAN**	**8.10–0** *(Mr M C Spedding)*	**R Hyett**
8th **SPITTIN IMAGE**	**10.10–0** *(exors of the late Mrs M J Welch)*	**A Turnell**
9th **SPANISH STEPS**	**13.10–2** *(Mr E R Courage)*	**J King**
10th **BLACK TUDOR**	**8.10–0** *(Mr F D Chapman)*	**G Thorner**
11th **CHURCHTOWN BOY**	**9.10–6** *(Mr J Lovell)*	**M Salaman**
12th **HIGHWAY VIEW**	**11.10–10** *(Mr C Carr)*	**P Black**
13th **JOLLY'S CLUMP**	**10.10–3** *(Mr R Hutchinson)*	**I Watkinson**
14th **MONEY MARKET**	**9.11–0** *(Lord Chelsea)*	**R Champion**
15th **COLONDINE**	**9.10–0** *(Mrs E K Dudgeon)*	**B Forsey**
16th **INDIAN DIVA**	**9.10–3** *(Miss A J Thorne)*	**Mr N Henderson**

Also Ran:
GLANFORD BRIGG 10.11–3 (Mr P J Harper) **M Blackshaw** *Fell*; *HIGH KEN 10.10–12* (Mr R Hickman) **M Dickinson** *Fell*; *ROMAN BAR 7.10–10* (Mrs D I O'Sullivan) **G Newman** *Fell*; *GOLDEN RAPPER 10.10–8* (Mr G N Clarke) **J Francome** *Fell*; *PERPOL 10.10–6* (Mr O J Henley) **K B White** *Pulled-up*; *PROLAN 7.10–3* (Mr M Cuddy) **M F Morris** *Brought-down*; *MERRY MAKER 11.10–2* (Mr A Mildmay-White) **Mr A Mildmay-White** *Fell*; *TREGARRON 9.10–1* (Mr H W Blyth) **C Tinkler** *Fell*; *NEREO 10.10–1* (Duke of Alburquerque) **Duke of Alburquerque** *Fell*; *HUPERADE 12.10–4* (Mr J Carden) **Mr J Carden** *Fell*; *MERIDIAN II 9.10–0* (Mr B Aughton) **J J O'Neill** *Fell*; *TUDOR VIEW 10.10–0* (Mr P J Upton) **C Read** *Fell*; *BALLYBRIGHT 9.10–0* (Mrs B A Waller) **Mr S Morshead** *Fell*; *THOMOND 11.10–3* (Miss T Pearson) **Mr A J Wilson** *Brought-down*; *BOOM DOCKER 9.10–0* (Mr R G Pilkington) **J Williams** *Brought-down*; *ORMONDE TUDOR 7.10–0* (Mr W A Hickling & Mr J A Kelly) **K Bamfield** *Fell*

The Betting: *7/1 Barona; 10/1 Red Rum; 12/1 Jolly's Clump, Money Market & Tregarron; 13/1 Prolan; 14/1 Rag Trade; 22/1 Spanish Steps & Ceol-Na-Mara; 25/1 The Dikler; 28/1 Golden Rapper, Glanford Brigg & Eyecatcher; 33/1 Churchtown Boy, High Ken, Highway View, Meridian II & Roman Bar; 50/1 Black Tudor, Boom Docker, Nereo & Merry Maker; 60/1 Colondine; 66/1 Spittin Image & Perpol; 80/1 Ballybright; 100/1 Others.*

Distances: *Two lengths; eight lengths*

Winner Trained By: *Fred Rimell, Kinnersley, Worcestershire*

Value to Winning Owner: *£37,420*

1977

Ladbrokes surpassed even their own high standards in 1977 by totally re-framing the entire spring meeting. Flat racing became a thing of the past and each richly-sponsored race, over hurdles or fences, was designed to attract the finest jumpers in the kingdom. The result was a festival of jumping approaching the excellence of Cheltenham.

Champion hurdle victor NIGHT NURSE and Cheltenham Gold Cup winner DAVY LAD headed the star-studded list of competitors at the fixture, the latter widely tipped as a 'National snip with only 10 st 13 lbs to carry. However, a late rush of money for Fred Rimell's eight-year-old ANDY PANDY made him 15/2 favourite of the forty-two runners and the confidence of the Kinnersley contingent was obvious. Last year's winning jockey John Burke took the leg-up. RED RUM, now twelve years old and as usual top weight, was at 9/1 supported largely out of sentiment for his only success all season had been a three-runner affair almost six months before. Nonetheless trainer McCain was adamant that 'Rummy' would win provided the ground was in his favour. He was also outspoken in his views on the presence in the field of twenty-one-year-old Miss Charlotte Brew, declaring that the 'National was no place for lady riders. Partnering her own horse BARONY FORT, on which she completed one circuit of the course in the 1976 Foxhunters' 'Chase, the young lady from Essex received intense media attention as the first of her sex to pit her skill and strength against the perils of the race. No matter how sporting her intention, the odds of 200/1 offered against her were a true reflection of her chances. One rider thought to have a much better chance was Michael Dickinson on WINTER RAIN. The Duke of Albur-

querque was ruled medically unfit to take part on NEREO by the Jockey Club, while French-based Martin Blackshaw picked up a late booking to pilot CHURCHTOWN BOY, who two days before the race carried off the Topham Trophy 'Chase in the most convincing manner.

RED RUM and Tommy Stack during the parade

With record first prize money of £41,140 and a magnificent Aynsley China Trophy, value £1,000, all that was required after two days of rain was some kindness from the weather. The day duly dawned clear and sunny, tempting the crowds to the course in numbers greater than for many years. A demonstration of some half dozen sympathisers of a convicted armed robber delayed the start but once the police moved them on, the starter effected a level break. The first fence brought a premature end to the efforts of seven runners and the first open ditch accounted for another four, including the Cheltenham champion DAVY LAD. At the head of affairs from the start SEBASTIAN V held a three length lead over BOOM DOCKER going into Becher's, but the drop proved the undoing of the leaders, CASTLERUDDERY and WINTER RAIN, the latter being fatally injured in his fall. Left in front, BOOM DOCKER went on strongly and the fall of SAGE MERLIN at the Chair further increased his lead. But when still a long way in front, he decided his day's work was over by refusing at the seventeenth. Taking up the running, ANDY PANDY thrilled spectators on the railway embankment with a succession of perfect leaps, quickly widening the gap between himself and his pursuers. Tailed off by now but persevering, Charlotte Brew raised a cheer at each fence as she pushed BARONY FORT along, in the hope of completing the course. Striding along twelve lengths ahead of the rest, ANDY PANDY met Becher's well only to overbalance on landing, leaving RED RUM in front. All eyes were now on RED RUM, making the running a long way from home and certainly earlier than Tommy Stack would have wished. Chased by WHAT A BUCK, CHURCHTOWN BOY, HAPPY RANGER, SIR GARNET and THE PILGARLIC, RED RUM stepped up the pace after jumping the Canal Turn, taking each subsequent fence in faultless style. Re-crossing Melling Road, now four lengths to the good, RED RUM ran into a crescendo of cheering unsurpassed on any racecourse, from crowds

aware they were witnessing history in the making. At the second last Martin Blackshaw brought CHURCHTOWN BOY with a well-timed challenge which got him to within two lengths of the leader but a mistake at the fence interrupted his run. Another immaculate leap at the final obstacle brought an even greater roar from the stands and with just two loose horses keeping him company, RED RUM strode majestically up the straight, drawing even further away from those in his wake. A third victory in the Grand National and in the most convincing manner imaginable, by twenty-five lengths, put RED RUM rightfully in a class all his own. CHURCHTOWN BOY was second, six lengths ahead of EYECATCHER, then came THE PILGARLIC. BARONY FORT struggled on bravely until the fourth from home, where he refused, bringing Miss Brew's 'National quest to an end.

Indisputably the King of Aintree, RED RUM gave new meaning to all that the Grand National had for so long stood for and in so doing, enriched the lives of all who were privileged to witness his incredible performance on that bright spring afternoon.

Owner Noel Le Mare thanks his great champion. 'Rummy' is arguably the most popular horse of all time and has enjoyed a busy retirement opening supermarkets and making celebrity appearances. Apart from his great heart, it was probably his economy of effort – he was never an outlandish jumper – that made him such a superb performer at Aintree

1977

With £50,000 added, being £10,000 given by The Horserace Betting Levy Board and £40,000, (including a trophy value £1,000), given by The News of the World. A historic challenge trophy will be presented by Messrs Tophams Limited to the Winning owner, to be held until 1st March 1978. For six-year-olds & upwards. The second to receive £10,612, the third £5,206 and the fourth £2,503. The trainer of the Winner to receive a trophy value £250 and the rider of the Winner a trophy value £250

Date: 2nd April 1977	Starters: 42	Time: 9 mins 30.3 secs
1st **RED RUM**	12.11–8 *(Mr N H Le Mare)*	**T Stack**
2nd **CHURCHTOWN BOY**	10.10–0 *(Mr B Arnold & Mr J Watkins)*	**M Blackshaw**
3rd **EYECATCHER**	11.10–1 *(Mr J R Bosley)*	**C Read**
4th **THE PILGARLIC**	9.10–4 *(Mrs G Poole & Mr A Poole)*	**R R Evans**
5th **FOREST KING**	8.10–12 *(Mr K W Hogg)*	**R Crank**
6th **WHAT A BUCK**	10.11–4 *(Lord Vestey)*	**J King**
7th **HAPPY RANGER**	10.10–5 *(Mr N Devonport)*	**P Blacker**
8th **CARROLL STREET**	10.10–0 *(Mr B H McGrath)*	**R Linley**
9th **COLLINGWOOD**	11.10–1 *(Mrs J D Tombs & Mr R L Chapman)*	**C Hawkins**
10th **HIDDEN VALUE**	9.10–4 *(Mr S G Norton)*	**J Bourke** [remounted]
11th **SAUCY BELLE**	11.10–0 *(Mr G D Smith)*	**R F Davies** [remounted]

Also Ran:

ZETA'S SON 8.11–4 (Mr M Buckley) **M F Morris** *Fell*; *DAVY LAD 7.10–13* (Mrs J B McGowan) **D T Hughes** *Fell*; *ROMAN BAR 8.10–10* (Mrs D I O'Sullivan) **P Kiely** *Fell*; *GAY VULGAN 9.10–8* (Mrs W L Pilkington) **W Smith** *Pulled-up*; *PENGRAIL 9.10–8* (Mrs G T Morton & Mrs C E Thornton) **R Atkins** *Fell*; *ANDY PANDY 8.10–7* (Mrs S D Mulligan) **J Burke** *Fell*; *PRINCE ROCK 9.10–6* (Mr M Buckley) **G Thorner** *Fell*; *WAR BONNET 9.10–6* (Mr R K Agnew) **T Carberry** *Fell*; *WINTER RAIN 9.10–6* (Mr F Tyldesley) **M Dickinson** *Fell*; *HIGH KEN 11.11–3* (Mr R Hickman) **Mr J Edwards** *Brought down*; *SIR GARNET 8.10–3* (Mr A Kay) **J J O'Neill** *Unseated rider*; *BROWN ADMIRAL 8.10–1* (Mr H R K Zeisel) **S Morshead** *Fell*; *DUFFLE COAT 9.10–4* (Mr G A Hubbard) **B R Davies** *Fell*; *LORD OF THE HILLS 10.10–1* (Mrs M A Berry) **D Goulding** *Pulled-up*; *NEREO 11.10–0* (Duke of Alburquerque) **R Kington** *Fell*; *SAGE MERLIN 9.10–5* (Mr J D Bingham) **I Watkinson** *Fell*; *BOOM DOCKER 10.10–0* (Mr R G Pilkington) **J Williams** *Refused*; *CASTLERUDDERY 11.10–0* (Mrs K Harper) **L O'Donnell** *Fell*; *HARBAN 8.10–0* (Mr J W Ashmore) **F Berry** *Fell*; *SEBASTIAN V 9.10–1* (Mr R M C Jeffreys) **R Lamb** *Fell*; *ROYAL THRUST 8.10–0* (Mrs J Greenhalgh) **C Tinkler** *Fell*; *BURRATOR 8.10–0* (Mrs B Ward) **Mr J Docker** *Fell*; *SANDWILAN 9.10–0* (Mr M C Spedding) **R Hyett** *Refused*; *FORESAIL 10.10–0* (Mr W Nolan) **G Holmes** *Refused*; *INYCARRA 10.10–0* (Mr C W R Fryer) **S Jobar** *Fell*; *SPITTIN IMAGE 11.10–5* (Mr J Welch, jnr) **R Champion** *Fell*; *WILLY WHAT 8.10–0* (Mr M D R Williams) **J Glover** *Fell*; *FORT VULGAN 9.10–0* (Mr A J Jacobs & Mr H R K Zeisel) **N Tinkler** *Brought down*; *BARONY FORT 12.10–1* (Mrs R Brew) **Miss Charlotte Brew** *Refused*; *HUPERADE 13.10–7* (Mr J Carden) **Mr J Carden** *Fell*; *THE SONGWRITER 8.10–0* (Mr P R Callander) **B Smart** *Pulled-up*

The Betting: *15/2 Andy Pandy; 9/1 Red Rum & Gay Vulgan; 10/1 Davy Lad; 15/1 Pengrail; 16/1 War Bonnet & Winter Rain; 18/1 Prince Rock, Zeta's Son & Eyecatcher; 20/1 What a Buck, Sir Garnet, Sage Merlin & Churchtown Boy; 22/1 Sebastian V; 25/1 Roman Bar; 28/1 Brown Admiral; 33/1 Forest King; 40/1 Hidden Value, The Pilgarlic & Castleruddery; 50/1 High Ken, Collingwood, Carroll Street, Burrator, Sandwilan, Spittin Image, Willy What & Fort Vulgan; 66/1 Boom Docker, Happy Ranger & Harban; 100/1 Duffle Coat, Foresail, Lord of the Hills, Royal Thrust, Inycarra & Nereo; 200/1 Others.*

Distances: *Twenty-five lengths; six lengths*

Winner Trained By: *Donald McCain, Southport, Lancashire*

Value to Winning Owner: *£41,140*

1978

The last-minute withdrawal of RED RUM deprived the race of much of its interest and the subsequent announcement that the nation's best-loved racehorse had been retired was looked upon as a terrific loss to the race, the history of which he had re-written. 'Rummy' had been clear ante-post favourite for weeks and the news that he had injured a foot whilst galloping on the beach the Monday before the race brought a hurried re-shuffling of the odds. Locally-owned MASTER H and Irish-trained TIED COTTAGE were heavily backed, yet it was RED RUM's former conqueror who wound up favourite at 8/1. Beset by injuries since his victory two years earlier, RAG TRADE had caused his trainer endless problems, but now under the care of George Fairbairn and ridden by Jonjo O'Neill, his chance was obvious.

Late money for LUCIUS brought his odds down from 20s to 14/1 and although inclined to make the occasional error, he had been brought along by trainer Gordon W Richards with this race as his main objective. By the stallion PERHAPS-BURG out of MATCHES, he was bred by Dr Margaret Lloyd and purchased at Doncaster Sales as an unbroken three-year-old by Penrith trainer Richards for 1,800 guineas. Remaining in the yard after being passed on to Mrs D A Whittaker, LUCIUS won five hurdle races before graduating to fences, at which he proved equally adept. In his nine races before the 'National, he only once failed to finish in the first two and although injury prevented his regular jockey from partnering him, he had a first class substitute in three-time champion Bob Davies.

Proving a headstrong handful for jockey Tommy Carberry, TIED COTTAGE dashed to the front the moment the barrier rose to lead over the first, where OTTER WAY, CORNISH PRINCESS and TEDDY BEAR II exited. In a clear lead at the Brook, TIED

'RUMMY' leads the parade and, despite the rain and his injured foot, wishes he was still running

COTTAGE attempted to take it at an angle and crashed to the ground as the unfamiliar drop took him by surprise. SEBASTIAN V led over the Water from DRUMROAN, HARBAN, LUCIUS, ROMAN BAR, BROWN ADMIRAL and LEAN FORWARD but going back into the country former leader LUCIUS moved up again to challenge. Ridley Lamb was enjoying a perfect ride on SEBASTIAN V, at this stage, the ten-year-old gaining ground with precision jumping. Becher's Brook, safely jumped by the two leaders, caught out HARBAN and Graham Thorner made a most spectacular recovery when TAMALIN came down on his belly. In the closing stages of the race the excitement grew as SEBASTIAN V and LUCIUS were strongly challenged by LORD BROWNDODD, THE PILGARLIC, MICKLEY SEABRIGHT, COOLISHALL, DRUMROAN and THE SONGWRITER. Martin O'Halloran looked the biggest danger as he jumped the last fence in second place on COOLISHALL, just a length and a half behind SEBASTIAN V. But in one of the closest and most thrilling climaxes the race has ever produced, LUCIUS came from behind to overhaul SEBASTIAN V in the last hundred yards and then resist the late sprint of the Irish outsider DRUMROAN. The winning margin at the post was half a length with fast-finishing DRUMROAN a neck away in third place and COOLISHALL running on again a close up fourth just a head in front of THE PILGARLIC. More even than the foot-perfect display of LUCIUS, the thrill of such a close-fought finish helped to ease the passing of the RED RUM era, and as so many times before, the Grand National itself proved supreme as a spectacle, whoever the participants may be.

THE GRAND NATIONAL HANDICAP STEEPLECHASE
1978

With £50,000 added, being £10,000 given by The Horserace Betting Levy Board and £40,000 by The Sun Newspaper, the latter amount including a trophy value £1,000. A historic challenge trophy will be presented by Messrs Tophams Limited to the Winning owner, to be held until 1st March 1979. For six-year-olds & upwards. The second to receive £10,076, the third £4,938 and the fourth £2,369. The trainer of the Winner to receive a trophy value £250 and the rider of the Winner a trophy value £250

Date: 1st April 1978	Starters: 37	Time: 9 mins 33.9 secs
1st **LUCIUS**	9.10−9 *(Mrs D A Whitaker)*	**B R Davies**
2nd **SEBASTIAN V**	10.10−1 *(Mr R M C Jeffreys)*	**R Lamb**
3rd **DRUMROAN**	10.10−0 *(Mrs G St John Nolan)*	**G Newman**
4th **COOLISHALL**	9.10−0 *(Mr & Mrs P W Harris)*	**M O'Halloran**
5th **THE PILGARLIC**	10.10−1 *(Mrs G Poole & Mr A Poole)*	**R R Evans**
6th **MICKLEY SEABRIGHT**	10.10−3 *(Mr P T Brookshaw)*	**Mr P Brookshaw**
7th **LORD BROWNDODD**	10.10−7 *(Mr J Brazil)*	**J Francome**
8th **THE SONGWRITER**	9.10−0 *(Mr P R Callander)*	**B Smart**

9th	**ROMAN BAR**	**9.10−8** *(Mrs D O'Sullivan)*	**P Kiely**
10th	**BROWN ADMIRAL**	**9.10−0** *(Mr H R K Zeisel)*	**J Burke**
11th	**GOLDEN WHIN**	**8.10−4** *(Mrs G L Taylor)*	**S Holland**
12th	**TAMALIN**	**11.11−2** *(Mr T A Metcalfe)*	**G Thorner**
13th	**LEAN FORWARD**	**12.10−0** *(Sir John Thompson)*	**H J Evans**
14th	**NEREO**	**12.10−0** *(Duke of Alburquerque)*	**M Floyd**
15th	**NEVER ROCK**	**9.10−0** *(Mr G Barley)*	**K Mooney**

Also Ran:

SHIFTING GOLD 9.11–6 (Mr R H Russell) **R Champion** *Fell*; *TIED COTTAGE 10.11–4* (Mr A S Robinson) **T Carberry** *Fell*; *RAG TRADE 12.11–3* (Mr P B Raymond) **J J O'Neill** *Pulled-up*; *MASTER H 9.11–2* (Mr S P Marsh) **R Crank** *Saddle slipped – unseated rider*; *APRIL SEVENTH 12.10–11* (Mrs B Meehan) **A Turnell** *Refused*; *OTTER WAY 10.10–10* (Mr O J Carter) **J King** *Fell*; *WAR BONNET 10.10–8* (Mr S Flynn) **D T Hughes** *Fell*; *SO 9.10–4* (Mr R De Vere Hunt) **Mr N Madden** *Fell*; *HIDDEN VALUE 10.10–0* (Mr F Mitchell) **T Stack** *Fell*; *MASTER UPHAM 10.10–0* (Mr R E Brinkworth) **P Barton** *Fell*; *IRISH TONY 10.10–0* (Cocked Hat Farm Foods) **D Atkins** *Fell*; *DOUBLE NEGATIVE 8.10–0* (Mrs M Wood Power) **C Tinkler** *Fell*; *CHURCHTOWN BOY 11.10–0* (Mr B Arnold) **M Blackshaw** *Fell*; *CORNISH PRINCESS 10.10–1* (Mr W G Turner) **R Hoare** *Fell*; *HARBAN 9.10–0* (Mr J W Ashmore) **J P Byrne** *Unseated rider*; *HENRY HALL 9.10–0* (Mr St J G O'Connell) **F Berry** *Fell*; *BURRATOR 9.10–0* (Mrs M A Berry) **J Suthern** *Fell*; *DOUBLE BRIDAL 7.10–1* (Maj Gen Sir James d'Avigdor-Goldsmid) **W Smith** *Fell*; *TEDDY BEAR II 11.10–4* (Mr G D Smith) **P Blacker** *Fell*; *SILKSTONE 10.10–0* (Mr K C Kelsall) **G Graham** *Fell*; *GLEAMING RAIN 10.10–0* (Mrs J R Mullion) **S Treacy** *Fell*; *SADALE VI 11.10–1* (Mrs J A George) **C Candy** *Fell*

The Betting: *8/1 Rag Trade; 9/1 Tied Cottage; 10/1 Master H; 14/1 Lucius, Churchtown Boy & So; 16/1 Shifting Gold, Otter Way, Lord Browndodd & Coolishall; 20/1 April Seventh; 25/1 Gleaming Rain, Sebastian V, Master Upham, Tamalin & Hidden Value; 33/1 Roman Bar, Brown Admiral, Double Negative, Irish Tony, Lean Forward, Mickley Seabright & The Pilgarlic; 40/1 Nereo; 50/1 War Bonnet, Drumroan, Golden Whin, Double Bridal, Never Rock, The Songwriter & Teddy Bear II; 66/1 Others.*

Distances: *Half a length; a neck; two lengths; a head*

Winner Trained By: *Gordon W Richards, Greystoke, Cumbria*

Value to Winning Owner: *£39,092*

1979

A victim of the cough, LUCIUS was missing from the race which was sponsored this year by the Colt Car Company. But the Cheltenham Gold Cup winner ALVERTON was among the thirty-four runners, along with the 1976 Gold Cup victor ROYAL FROLIC, one of four representing Fred Rimell and bearing top weight. Another trainer with a powerful hand was Captain Tim Forster. Both his charges, Lord Leverhulme's MR SNOWMAN and the American-owned BEN NEVIS, were heavily backed and the rider of the latter, Baltimore banker Mr Charlie Fenwick, had made frequent visits to this country to partner his mount in preliminary events. In ALVERTON, though, Jonjo O'Neill was considered to have his best chance yet of winning Aintree's great test and with less than 11 stone to carry, the chestnut was thought to be such a blot on the handicap that he became clear favourite at 13/2. That popular Liverpool football star Emlyn Hughes had his colours carried by WAYWARD SCOT, from the RED RUM yard of Donald McCain, but was unable to be present as he was appearing for his club at Maine Road, Manchester in an FA Cup semi-final.

A first runner in the race for both his trainer John Leadbetter and jockey Maurice Barnes was ten-year-old RUB-STIC. Bred by Mrs Robert Digby from I SAY and the mare LEUZE, RUBSTIC cost 500 guineas as a yearling and after spells with trainers Bell and Gordon W Richards, entered the small Roxburghshire yard of Leadbetter. Owned by former British Lion rugby international John Douglas, he came to Aintree with the reputation of never having fallen and there were no doubts concerning his stamina. In Maurice Barnes he had a capable if little-known jockey whose father could advise

him on the best route to take at Aintree, having ridden WYNDBURGH into second place in 1962. Perhaps the fact that no runner trained north of the Border had ever won was why RUBSTIC was allowed to start at the generous odds of 25/1.

Bob Champion was the first to show on PURDO, taking the field over the first where the three outsiders, WAYWARD SCOT, VINDICATE and SANDWILAN fell. There were no further casualties until Becher's, which saw the departure of front-running PURDO and another of the long-shots OSKARD, leaving ZONGALERO in control. The leaders swept round the Canal Turn, at which point SANDPIT dropped out and two fences later DRUMROAN failed to get high enough. Back on the racecourse, ALVERTON was going very easily just behind ZONGALERO and with RUBSTIC well to the fore, they came on to the Chair preceded by two riderless horses. In the space of seconds the area around the biggest obstacle on the course resembled a battlefield, as the loose horses veered across the path of the main body of runners. The worst pile-up since FOINAVON's year resulted in no less than nine runners being put out of the race, among them RAMBLING ARTIST, THE CHAMP and GODFREY SECUNDUS, and although BEN NEVIS was remounted by his American rider, he was sensibly pulled up at the next. The three leaders having escaped the chaos at the Chair, continued out on to the final circuit, now tracked by the improving WAGNER and John Francome on ROUGH AND TUMBLE, but as they lined up for Becher's, the favourite ALVERTON appeared to be merely cantering. Altering his stride shortly before reaching the fence, however, he struck it hard with his chest, crashing to the ground with his neck broken. With ARTISTIC PRINCE a faller at the twenty-sixth and FLITGROVE, COOLISHALL and RED EARL dropping out soon after, the race over the last two fences was confined to ROUGH AND TUMBLE, ZONGALERO, RUBSTIC and THE PILGARLIC with WAGNER beginning to fade. Clearing the last fence almost in line, ROUGH AND TUMBLE, ZONGALERO and RUBSTIC on the wide

RUBSTIC (*left*) takes the last upsides ZANGALERO and ROUGH AND TUMBLE

outside began the exhausting run up the straight and it was RUBSTIC who stayed on the most tenaciously. At the post the verdict was RUBSTIC by a length and a half from ZONGALERO with ROUGH AND TUMBLE five lengths back in third, just ahead of THE PILGARLIC. The only others to get round were WAGNER, ROYAL FROLIC and the 200/1 shot PRIME JUSTICE.

Scotland could well feel pride in her first 'National winner, and RUBSTIC's victory march back to the tiny hamlet of Denholm was led by a kilted piper. The deaths of ALVERTON and KINTAI left a cloud over the event and as expected tremendous criticism in the press, together with a call for action to be taken which would prevent loose horses causing the kind of havoc which occurred at the Chair.

Proud owner Mr J Douglas with his winner RUBSTIC

1979

With £50,000 added, being £10,000 given by The Horserace Betting Levy Board and £40,000 by The Colt Car Company Limited, the latter amount including a trophy value £1,200. A historic challenge trophy will be presented by Tophams Limited to the Winning owner, to be kept until 1st March 1980. For six-year-olds & upwards. The trainer of the Winner to receive a trophy value £300 and the rider of the Winner a trophy value £300

Date: 31st March 1979	Starters: 34	Time: 9 mins 52.9 secs
1st **RUBSTIC**	10.10–0 *(Mr J Douglas)*	**M Barnes**
2nd **ZONGALERO**	9.10–5 *(Mr D Montagu & Sir James Goldsmith)*	**B R Davies**
3rd **ROUGH AND TUMBLE**	9.10–7 *(Mr L Dormer)*	**J Francome**
4th **THE PILGARLIC**	11.10–1 *(Mrs G Poole & Mr A Poole)*	**R R Evans**
5th **WAGNER**	9.10–0 *(Mr P Piller)*	**R Lamb**
6th **ROYAL FROLIC**	10.11–10 *(Sir John Hanmer)*	**J Burke**
7th **PRIME JUSTICE**	9.10–0 *(Mr D A Mallam)*	**A K Taylor**

Also Ran:

BEN NEVIS 11.11–2 (Mr R C Stewart, jnr) **Mr C Fenwick** Brought-down; ALVERTON 9.10–13 (Snailwell Stud Co) **J J O'Neill** Fell; THE CHAMP 11.10–12 (Miss Leila Smith) **W Smith** Fell; PURDO 8.10–12 (Mr D W Samuel) **R Champion** Fell; MR SNOWMAN 10.10–9 (Lord Leverhulme) **G Thorner** Fell; SANDPIT 9.10–7 (Mrs B D Flood) **T Carmody** Fell; WAYWARD SCOT 10.10–7 (Mr Emlyn Hughes & Mr D McCain) **R F Davies** Fell; RAMBLING ARTIST 9.10–6 (Mr E F Robbins) **D Goulding** Brought-down; DRUMROAN 11.10–4 (Mrs G St John Nolan) **G Newman** Fell; GODFREY SECUNDUS 9.10–3 (Mrs G L Taylor) **C Tinkler** Brought-down; COOLISHALL 10.10–2 (Mr & Mrs P W Harris) **A Webber** Fell; DOUBLE NEGATIVE 9.10–5 (Mrs M Wood Power) **Mr E Woods** Fell; ARTISTIC PRINCE 8.10–3 (Mr R Stigwood) **P Blacker** Fell; LORD BROWNDODD 11.10–3 (Mr J Brazil) **A Turnell** Pulled-up; RED EARL 10.10–0 (Mr Henry Ford) **H J Evans** Pulled-up; KINTAI 10.10–0 (Mr H Jackson) **B Smart** Brought-down; NO GYPSY 10.10–1 (Mr C H Bennion) **J Suthern** Brought-down; CHURCHTOWN BOY 12.10–0 (Mr B Arnold) **M Salaman** Brought-down; DROMORE 11.10–10 (Mr P Duggan) **Mr P Duggan** Pulled-up; KICK ON 12.10–0 (Mr K Lewis) **R Hyett** Brought-down; FLITGROVE 8.10–1 (Lord Vestey) **R Linley** Pulled-up; OSKARD 10.10–0 (Mr W W Smith & Mr C M Wilson) **M Blackshaw** Fell; ALPENSTOCK 12.10–0 (Mr H Thomson) **Mr D Gray** Brought-down; BROWN ADMIRAL 10.10–0 (Mr T A Rathbone) **S Morshead** Unseated rider; SANDWILAN 11.10–0 (Mr G A Ham) **Mrs J Hembrow** Fell; VINDICATE 12.11–8 (Mr P J Doyle) **Mr A O'Connell** Fell; CARTWRIGHT 10.10–0 (Mr R F Fisher) **A Phillips** Brought-down

The Betting: *13/2 Alverton; 10/1 Mr Snowman; 12/1 Coolishall; 14/1 Ben Nevis & Rough And Tumble; 16/1 Rambling Artist & The Pilgarlic; 20/1 Drumroan & Zongalero; 22/1 Sandpit; 25/1 The Champ, Artistic Prince, Purdo, Rubstic, Godfrey Secundus, Churchtown Boy, Lord Browndodd & Royal Frolic; 50/1 Dromore, Kick On, Red Earl, Flitgrove & Wagner; 66/1 Double Negative & No Gypsy; 100/1 Alpenstock, Brown Admiral, Kintai, Oskard, Sandwilan & Wayward Scot; 200/1 Vindicate, Cartwright & Prime Justice.*

Distances: *One and a half lengths; five lengths*

Winner Trained By: *John Leadbetter, Denholm, Roxburghshire*

Value to Winning Owner: £40,506

1980

With constant rain producing the worst conditions underfoot since 1972, the race looked set to be a test of stamina which few would survive. Trainer Gordon Richards took one look at the going on the morning of the race and withdrew his dashing grey, top weight MAN ALIVE, and WAGNER was also pulled out at this late stage, leaving thirty runners to face the starter. The winner of his two most recent races, RUBSTIC was made 8/1 favourite to repeat last year's victory, while JER, ROUGH AND TUMBLE and ZONGALERO figured most prominently of the rest in the market.

Unlike last year, American hope BEN NEVIS was virtually ignored in the betting at 40/1, for the state of the going was thought to be totally against him and he was without a single victory in twelve races in Europe. By the unfashionable stallion CASMIRI out of BEN TRUMISS, BEN NEVIS was bred in England by A S Pattenden Limited and began racing in point-to-points. Sold to Mr Redmond C Stewart jnr, he was taken to his owner's native United States, where he was unbeaten in twelve races, seven over timber. After winning his second successive Maryland Hunt Cup in 1978, BEN NEVIS was sent back to England to be trained by Captain Tim Forster with the Grand National as his principal objective. Caught up in the trouble at the Chair in his first attempt, he was now trying again at the age of twelve, ridden once more by merchant banker Charlie Fenwick, also yet to score his first victory this side of the Atlantic. Mr Fenwick was the son-in-law of the gelding's owner and the grandson of Mr Howard Bruce, the American whose BILLY BARTON came so close to winning the race in 1928. Advised by the recently-retired Graham Thorner, Mr Fenwick studied the contours of the course earnestly, watched countless films of past 'Nationals and left the paddock with the less than encouraging instructions to 'keep on remounting'.

The field set off at a sensible pace, yet even so MANNY BOY and SALKELD failed to get further than the first fence. Two more went out at the third, and amateur Broderick Munro-Wilson was unseated from COOLISHALL at the fourth when a stirrup iron broke. SO AND SO gave his rider Richard Linley a hefty fall at Becher's, where Jonjo O'Neill was also deposited when ANOTHER DOLLY fell. In an effort to prevent interference on the approach to the Chair, gaps had been left in the inner running rail to allow pilotless horses to run out, yet one ignored the invitation and ran dangerously in front of leader DELMOSS as he measured up for the big ditch. Jumping straight the riderless horse in fact caused no problem but as RUBSTIC moved up to challenge the leader, he misjudged his take-off and for the first time in his life fell. Leaving the Water Jump behind him with a ten length lead, DELMOSS went back out into the country. As BEN NEVIS moved up quickly into second place, the nineteenth, an open ditch, took its toll by adding seven fallers to the mounting list of casualties. Looking very tired, ZONGALERO only just managed to scramble over, getting no further than the next fence where Steve Smith-Eccles decided to call it a day in his first 'National. A mistake by THREE TO ONE now left DELMOSS racing side by side with BEN NEVIS well clear. At Becher's BEN NEVIS landed safely as DELMOSS fell, leaving the American horse a dozen lengths clear of the rest. From this point, the race became a procession, and although John Francome moved ROUGH AND TUMBLE closer between the last two fences, he was never a serious danger.

Striding out well to the line, BEN NEVIS pulled clear again to win by twenty lengths from ROUGH AND TUMBLE and the only others to finish, THE PILGARLIC and ROYAL STUART, who both passed the post at walking pace. Captain Forster's second 'National training triumph in eight years came as a most delightful surprise for him, as only days before the race BEN NEVIS had shown signs of falling victim to the dreaded cough. The decision to race was taken only in consideration of the fact that so many people had crossed the Atlantic to see the horse perform and in the greatest slogging match for years, the courage of BEN NEVIS and Charlie Fenwick made the journey worthwhile.

Mrs Mirabel Dorothy Topham passed away at the age of eighty-eight just two months after the 1980 Grand National. For at least forty-five years, since her appointment as Director to Tophams Limited, this forceful, imaginative and sometimes abrasive personality had proved herself a woman of principle and incredible vision. Often misunderstood and frequently misquoted, Mrs Topham nurtured Aintree and the Grand National with the care and affection only a woman can provide. Whatever else may be said, the First Lady of Aintree built her life around the Grand National with such effect and purpose that its importance as an international event was never allowed to diminish. Her contribution and example as an administrator would be impossible to measure, as would be the loss felt by those who admired her.

Jonjo O'Neill, a faller on ANOTHER DOLLY and one of the great champion jockeys never to win the great Aintree showpiece. Like Bob Champion before him, Jonjo has staged an enormously courageous fightback against cancer. Now that he has turned his great talent to training, there could be no more popular in the as yet unwritten future history of the race than Jonjo greeting a winner prepared at his Cumbrian yard. Until that happy day – and probably long after it as well – Jonjo will be remembered as the man who partnered the fantastic mare DAWN RUN to a wonderfully thrilling Cheltenham Gold Cup victory in 1986

1980

With £60,000 added, being £10,000 given by The Horserace Betting Levy Board and £50,000 by Sun Newspapers, the latter amount including a trophy value £1,250. A historic challenge trophy will be presented by Messrs Tophams Limited to the winning owner, to be kept until 1st March 1981. For six-year-olds & upwards. The second to receive £23,740, the third £11,755 and the fourth £5,762. The trainer of the Winner to receive a trophy value £300 and the rider of the Winner a trophy value £300

Date: 29th March 1980	Starters: 30	Time: 10 mins 17.4 secs
1st **BEN NEVIS**	**12.10–12** *(Mr R C Stewart, jnr)*	**Mr C Fenwick**
2nd **ROUGH AND TUMBLE**	**10.10–11** *(Mr L Dormer)*	**J Francome**
3rd **THE PILGARLIC**	**12.10–4** *(Mrs G Poole & Mr A Poole)*	**R Hyett**
4th **ROYAL STUART**	**9.10–10** *(Mr & Mrs J Murray Begg)*	**P Blacker**

Also Ran:

ROYAL FROLIC 11.11–4 (Sir John Hanmer & Mr F R Watts) **J Burke** *Refused*; *PRINCE ROCK 12.11–0* (Mr M Buckley & Mr F R Watts) **T Carmody** *Refused*; *ZONGALERO 10.10–13* (Mr D Montagu & Sir James Goldsmith) **S Smith Eccles** *Refused*; *CASAMAYOR 10.10–12* (Mr R R Guest) **J King** *Fell*; *RUBSTIC 11.10–11* (Mr J Douglas) **M Barnes** *Fell*; *ANOTHER DOLLY 10.10–10* (Mr Ian Urquhart) **J J O'Neill** *Fell*; *SO AND SO 11.10–10* (Mr D W Samuel) **R Linley** *Fell*; *FLASHY BOY 12.10–8* (Mrs A Bayley & Mr Denys Smith) **C Grant** *Fell*; *THE VINTNER 9.10–8* (Westwood Garages Ltd) **B R Davies** *Pulled-up*; *COOLISHALL 11.10–10* (Mr B Munro-Wilson) **Mr B Munro-Wilson** *Unseated rider*; *EVEN UP 13.10–6* (Mr N Whitcomb) **A Webber** *Refused*; *OUR GREENWOOD 12.11–6* (Mr M J Russell) **Mr A O'Connell** *Fell*; *JIMMY MIFF 8.10–5* (Mr G Tanner) **A Brown** *Fell*; *DRUMROAN 12.10–5* (Mrs G St John Nolan) **T McGivern** *Fell*; *JER 9.10–4* (Mr G D Wyse) **P Tuck** *Fell*; *LEVANKA 11.10–4* (Mr P C Heron) **F Berry** *Pulled-up*; *DELMOSS 10.10–2* (Mrs F Vessels) **G Newman** *Fell*; *MANNYBOY 10.10–2* (Mr F H Pullen) **R Rowe** *Unseated rider*; *SALKELD 8.10–0* (Mr E Bell) **C Hawkins** *Fell*; *DROMORE 12.10–8* (Mr P Duggan) **Mr P Duggan** *Pulled-up*; *CHURCHTOWN BOY 13.10–0* (Mr B Arnold) **A Turnell** *Brought-down*; *GODFREY SECUNDUS 10.10–0* (Mrs G L Taylor) **S Morshead** *Pulled-up*; *THREE TO ONE 9.10–2* (Mr J C Manners & Mrs J K M Oliver) **Mr T G Dun** *Fell*; *SANDWILAN 12.10–0* (Mr G A Ham) **Mrs J Hembrow** *Pulled-up*; *KININVIE 11.10–0* (Mr S Sarsfield & Mr A J K Dunn) **J Williams** *Pulled-up*; *RATHLEK 10.10–0* (Mr D R Greig) **P Barton** *Refused*

The Betting: *8/1 Rubstic; 10/1 Jer; 11/1 Zongalero & Rough and Tumble; 12/1 Another Dolly & Prince Rock; 16/1 The Vintner & Royal Frolic; 20/1 Royal Stuart, Salkeld & Godfrey Secundus; 22/1 Drumroan; 25/1 Three to One & Delmoss; 28/1 So and So; 33/1 Mannyboy & The Pilgarlic; 35/1 Rathlek; 40/1 Ben Nevis & Coolishall; 50/1 Casamayor, Flashy Boy, Even Up, Jimmy Miff & Churchtown Boy; 100/1 Sandwilan, Our Greenwood, Levanka, Dromore & Kininvie.*

Distances: *Twenty lengths; ten lengths*

Winner Trained By: *Captain Tim Forster, Letcombe Bassett, Oxfordshire*

Value to Winning Owner: *£45,595*

1981

Never before in the annals of the turf did a race contain more ingredients to tug at the heart-strings of the nation than the 1981 Grand National. Like every other jump jockey who ever put a horse at a fence, Bob Champion was no stranger to adversity, yet the news given to him in July 1979 that he had cancer was a far more shattering blow than he could ever have expected even in the course of his hazardous profession. Faced with the probability that his life would be over in just months, Bob Champion's only hope lay in chemotherapy, a treatment so unbelievably severe that his spirit would be tested as never before. Through the long painful hospitalisation and the endless months of convalescence, his courageous fight back to fitness was inspired by one simple thought: riding ALDANITI in the Grand National.

Since finishing third under Champion in the 1979 Cheltenham Gold Cup, ALDANITI had broken down with leg trouble at Sandown the following November and to trainer Josh Gifford this latest recurrence of a problem which had plagued the horse for most of his career looked like the end of the line. Taken back to his owner's home at Barkfold Manor, Sussex, ALDANITI was nursed back to health through the loving care of head stable girl Beryl Millam. When the horse was returned to the Findon yard of Josh Gifford, the former jockey performed wonders in getting him gently back to race fitness and against all the odds ALDANITI was reunited with a recovered Bob Champion to win the Whitbread Trial 'Chase at Ascot in February 1981. By now the story of both horse and rider's tremendous battle against the worst that life could throw at them had been spread far and wide and the public money which now made them 10/1 second favourite for the 'National came more from the heart than the form-book. Was a single race after such a long lay-off sufficient preparation for the hardest test of all? Would ALDANITI's legs stand up to the pounding they would suffer at Aintree's notorious drop fences? And would Bob Champion have the necessary strength, after such a long and harrowing course of treatment, to pilot the horse through the most exacting contest on earth? Only the 'National itself could answer these questions, but the mere inclusion of Bob Champion and ALDANITI among the thirty-nine runners generated more interest in the race than there had been for many years.

The 8/1 favourite SPARTAN MISSILE was also competing with a large measure of sentiment behind him. Bred, owned, trained and ridden by fifty-four-year-old grandfather John Thorne, the gelding's dam was POLARIS MISSILE, a faller in the 1968 'National when partnered by Mr Thorne's talented teenage son Nigel. A very promising amateur rider, Nigel had shortly afterwards been tragically killed in a motoring accident when returning from a race meeting. Twice a winner of Liverpool's Foxhunters' 'Chase, SPARTAN MISSILE had proven ability over the course and if proof were needed of John Thorne's prowess, one had only to remember his incredible feat of winning one of these contests without irons from Becher's.

In a better than average field, RUBSTIC, ZONGALERO, ROYAL MAIL, ROYAL EXILE and ROYAL STUART each commanded serious attention in the market. The Irish staked all on SENATOR MACLACURY and a late gamble brought CHEERS, the mount of Peter Scudamore, in to 20/1. Mother of twins, Mrs Linda Sheedy flew the flag for the ladies this time, on the 100/1 chance

DEIOPEA and the persistent solicitor John Carden tried yet again with his ten-year-old BRYAN BORU.

KININVIE took an early lead as they cleared the first. A slight mistake here by ALDANITI brought a gasp from the crowd as he landed on his nose, but picking him up well, Champion was able to continue towards the rear. Leaving BRYAN BORU among the casualties, KININVIE and CHORAL FESTIVAL jumped Becher's in front, followed by CARROW BOY, ZONGA-LERO, PACIFY and TENECOON and for once the Brook was accident-free. At this point SPARTAN MISSILE was lying in the mid-division about twelfth and much further back on the wide outside came ALDANITI. ANOTHER PROSPECT went out at the Canal Turn, DRUMROAN and NO GYPSY at Valentine's and CARROW BOY at the tenth, where KININVIE was also a victim. Having pulled his way to the front, ALDANITI landed first over the eleventh, where TENECOON dropped out and, running freely, he disputed the lead over the Chair with SEBASTIAN V, ROYAL STUART and ZONGALERO. Bowling along in front, ALDANITI was six lengths clear at the first fence back in the country, while SPARTAN MISSILE was starting to make ground from the rear. An error at the eighteenth, however, appeared to have put paid to the winning chance of the favourite, as John Thorne had to allow him time to recover. A broken leather put ROYAL STUART out of the race at the twentieth and the tiring ZONGALERO came down at Becher's, together with PACIFY. The leap by ALDANITI at Becher's Brook was clean, bold and confident and as he rounded the Canal Turn still in front, the only dangers seemed to be RUBSTIC and ROYAL MAIL. A rare mistake at the last fence before the racecourse cost ALDANITI some of his momentum, allowing ROYAL MAIL to get into a challenging position, but with RUBSTIC fading rapidly, only the last two fences stood between ALDANITI and the victory everyone most wished. When ROYAL MAIL clouted the penultimate fence hard, victory for the pair of 'champion crocks' looked assured as THREE TO ONE, SENATOR MACLACURY and SPARTAN MISSILE were fully fifteen lengths in arrears. Safe on the flat, Bob Champion sat down to ride into the realisation of the dream which had sustained him in his darkest hours, but coming from nowhere with a tremendous turn of foot, SPARTAN MISSILE suddenly raced into the picture. At the elbow the result looked uncertain, with John Thorne riding the race of his life on the favourite and gaining stride by stride, yard by yard. But, as if the gods who govern that punishing final stretch of Aintree turf were conscious of all that was at stake, ALDANITI and his jockey found enough to resist SPARTAN MISSILE's brave late run, holding on for a four length victory, to rapturous applause from all. ROYAL MAIL was two lengths behind SPARTAN MISSILE in third place, just a neck ahead of THREE TO ONE.

That the 'National, so often a race of heartbreak, should be conquered by a horse and jockey both written off as has-beens was the finest result possible. All was well with the world on that fine spring Aintree day and through the freely-flowing tears, everybody smiled. Tributes to the winning pair came from all over the world, while owner Nick Embericos and trainer Josh Gifford shared their own memories of what it had taken to arrive at the winner's enclosure. Their loyalty and devotion to a wreck of a horse and a stricken jockey was in the highest tradition of the Grand National, contributing enormously to the latest and possibly greatest story to emerge from the race.

1981

With £65,000 added, being £15,000 given by The Horserace Betting Levy Board and £50,000 by Sun Newspapers, the latter amount including a trophy value £1,500. A historic challenge trophy will be presented by Messrs Tophams Limited to the Winning owner, to be held until 1st March 1982. For six-year-olds & upwards. The second to receive £13,491, the third £6,745 and the fourth £3,372. The trainer of the Winner to receive a trophy value £300 and the rider of the Winner a trophy value £300

Date: 4th April 1981	Starters: 39	Time: 9 mins 47.2 secs
1st **ALDANITI**	**11.10–13** *(Mr S N J Embiricos)*	**R Champion**
2nd **SPARTAN MISSILE**	**9.11–5** *(Mr M J Thorne)*	**Mr M J Thorne**
3rd **ROYAL MAIL**	**11.11–7** *(Mr & Mrs J Murray Begg)*	**P Blacker**
4th **THREE TO ONE**	**10.10–3** *(Mr J C Manners & Mrs J K M Oliver)*	**Mr T G Dun**
5th **SENATOR MACLACURY**	**7.10–2** *(Mr F D Cullen)*	**J P Harty**
6th **ROYAL EXILE**	**12.10–0** *(Mr W C Rigg)*	**B De Haan**
7th **RUBSTIC**	**12.10–7** *(Mr J Douglas)*	**M Barnes**
8th **COOLISHALL**	**12.10–3** *(Mr B Munro-Wilson)*	**W Smith**
9th **RATHLEK**	**11.10–1** *(Mr D R Greig)*	**P Barton**
10th **SO**	**12.10–8** *(Mr De Vere Hunt)*	**J Francome**
11th **SEBASTIAN V**	**13.10–2** *(Mr R M C Jeffreys)*	**R Lamb**
12th **CHEERS**	**9.10–0** *(Mr J W Evans & Mr M R Evans)*	**P Scudamore**

Also Ran:

CARROW BOY 9.11–6 (Mr W Durkan) **G Newman** *Fell*; CHUMSON 10.11–7 (Mr J E Beirne) **Mr A O'Connell** *Fell*; ZONGALERO 11.10–11 (The Hon David Montagu & Sir James Goldsmith) **S Smith Eccles** *Fell*; BARNEY MACLYVIE 10.10–8 (Mr M Malone) **M Lynch** *Fell*; THE VINTNER 10.10–8 (Westwood Garages Ltd) **C Grant** *Refused*; MARTINSTOWN 9.10–7 (Mrs M Easton) **Mr M Batters** *Fell*; CASAMAYOR 11.10–6 (Mr R R Guest) **Mr P Webber** *Refused*; KILKILWELL 9.10–6 (Mr P Hamilford) **N Madden** *Fell*; ANOTHER PROSPECT 9.10–8 (Mr H M Thursfield & Mr P J Corbett) **Mr A J Wilson** *Fell*; ROYAL STUART 10.10–2 (Mr & Mrs J Murray Begg) **H Davies** *Unseated rider*; DELMOSS 11.10–1 (Mrs F Vessels) **F Berry** *Fell*; DRUMROAN 13.10–6 (Mrs G St John Nolan) **Mr M Graffe** *Fell*; KYLOGUE LADY 9.10–0 (Mr D English) **T Quinn** *Fell*; LORD GULLIVER 8.10–0 (Mr P R Callender) **C Brown** *Fell*; MIGHT BE 10.10–0 (Mr H J Knott) **A Webber** *Fell*; BRYAN BORU 10.10–0 (Mr J Carden) **Mr J Carden** *Refused*; PACIFY 11.10–0 (Mr C R Glyn & Mr B G Norman) **S Jobar** *Fell*; ANOTHER CAPTAIN 9.10–0 (Mr A Scott) **C Hawkins** *Fell*; TENECOON 12.10–0 (Mr F A Smith) **C Mann** *Fell*; MY FRIENDLY COUSIN 11.10–2 (Mr R Scott) **A Brown** *Pulled-up*; SON AND HEIR 11.10–0 (Mr R J Scandrett) **S Morshead** *Refused*; DROMORE 13.10–8 (Mr P Duggan) **Mr P Duggan** *Refused*; CHORAL FESTIVAL 10.10–2 (Mr M J Low) **Mr M J Low** *Fell*; NO GYPSY 12.10–0 (Mr E Treacy & Mr J J Bridger) **J Suthern** *Fell*; THREE OF DIAMONDS 9.10–4 (Mr C Barnes) **P Leach** *Fell*; KININVIE 12.10–0 (Lady Dunn) **P Hobbs** *Fell*; DEIOPEA 10.10–0 (Mr W R Sheedy) **Mrs L Sheedy** *Refused*

The Betting: *8/1 Spartan Missile; 10/1 Aldaniti; 11/1 Rubstic; 14/1 Zongalero; 16/1 Royal Mail, Royal Exile & Royal Stuart; 20/1 Senator Maclacury, Cheers & The Vintner; 25/1 Coolishall; 33/1 Three to One, Sebastian V, Carrow Boy, Barney Maclyvie, Martinstown & Kilkilwell; 40/1 So, Another Prospect & Another Captain; 50/1 Rathlek, Chumson, Delmoss, Drumroan, Lord Gulliver, Might Be & Pacify; 66/1 Choral Festival; 100/1 Casamayor, Kylogue Lady, Bryan Boru, Tenecoon, My Friendly Cousin, Son and Heir, Dromore, No Gypsy, Three of Diamonds, Kininvie & Deiopea.*

Distances: *Four lengths; two lengths*

Winner Trained By: *Josh Gifford, Findon, Sussex.* **Value to Winning Owner:** £51,324

1982

Dark clouds hung over Britain and Aintree on the morning of the 1982 Grand National. Argentina's invasion of the Falkland Islands had brought prompt action from the British government with the raising of a task force bound for the South Atlantic. By comparison, the troubles at Aintree may well have appeared trivial, particularly as they involved the old weary argument of who would take on responsibility for the racecourse, for this was the final year of Ladbrokes' administration. Bill Davies' asking price was now £7 million, a sizeable leap from the sum required less than a decade before and this fact alone demonstrated how complacency and inertia can compound an already difficult situation. A long campaign by the racing press for positive action to be taken by the sport's controllers at long last bore fruit with the Jockey Club's decision that, through its subsidiary Racecourse Holdings Trust, a legal agreement was to be entered into with the Walton Group at this most recent figure. The racing public's first sigh of relief was halted in mid-breath when the details were revealed as to how this colossal sum was to be raised. The Jockey Club reasoned that if the man in the street sincerely wanted racing's greatest showpiece to remain at Aintree, then he must pay for it. Thus began what many considered the final degradation for an event unequalled in international sport. The Aintree Grand National Appeal was instituted with a plethora of fine sounding proclamations, which, when it came down to it, meant that the very survival of the race depended in the main on a begging bowl. A begging bowl, furthermore, being held out by an organisation that consisted of some of the wealthiest men in the world. A deadline of just seven months to raise the required sum looked distinctly optimistic to those who argued that if the seven years' breathing space allowed by Ladbrokes' leasing of the course had failed to facilitate a solution, what chance was there of raising £7 million in as many months? Those doubters were understandably branded as cynics at least, for with the governing body of racing now directly involved in preserving this 'vital part of our sporting heritage', it was reasonable to assume that the security of the 'National was at last in the right hands. Only time would tell, but as the crowds gathered for the annual test of horse and horseman, it was noticeable that not one solitary collecting box was anywhere to be seen on the vast expanse of the 'National course. Racing for the richest prize ever in the history of the race, £52,507, thirty-nine runners again paraded before the start, with ROYAL MAIL top weight just one pound above ALDANITI. Absent through injury was the runner-up to ALDANITI, SPARTAN MISSILE, whose gallant partner John Thorne had been tragically killed in a point-to-point just weeks before. The bravest of horsemen and an inspiration to all, he had been the first to congratulate Bob Champion after last year's race and he would be most missed, not only by his family but many friends in racing and farming circles.

A close friend and fellow-amateur Dick Saunders, at forty-eight years of age, was partnering the hunter-chaser GRITTAR in the race he had never even seen except on television, although the pair had proved their ability over the course when winning the 1981 Liverpool Foxhunters' Chase. Bred by his owner, Mr Frank Gilman of Leicestershire from a mating of his mare TARAMA with the grey stallion GRISAILLE, GRITTAR progressed from the flat, through hurdling on to the major obstacles and in the 1980/81 season established himself as one of the leading staying jumpers in the country. After a favourable showing in sixth place in the Cheltenham Gold Cup, GRITTAR appealed to the betting public who duly installed him as 7/1 favourite. They didn't have as much confidence in either Charlotte Brew, partnering her mother's MARTINSTOWN, or the local lass from Tarleton near Preston, Geraldine Rees, on the newly-purchased CHEERS.

DELMOSS was the first to show when the barrier rose and his usual front-running tactics paved the way for disaster at the first fence. Reaching it far too fast, almost a quarter of the field, including ALDANITI, failed to survive. After the third obstacle, the field was starting to look decidedly ragged as another four exited, but for DELMOSS the chaos behind was of no consequence, as he raced on at a cracking pace. Jumping Becher's he led by three lengths from CARROW BOY, GRITTAR and SAINT FILLANS, while four more, including ROYAL MAIL, joined the growing list of casualties. DELMOSS was finally overtaken at the second fence on the final circuit, while at the second Becher's SAINT FILLANS pecked badly and the confidently-ridden GRITTAR assumed command. Drawing steadily away from the remainder, GRITTAR came back from the Canal Turn the assured winner if he could keep his feet and a mix-up behind him at the fourth from home made it all the easier. SAINT FILLANS and CARROW BOY fell at this, the final open ditch, so badly hampering the grey LOVING WORDS that jockey Richard Hoare was dislodged in an untidy heap. It was at the last fence that the favourite made his only mistake, but

Owner Mr Frank Gilman, in the hat, leads the celebrations at a local hostelry when his winner Grittar comes home. With him is jockey Dick Saunders, relishing his superb achievement no doubt, but not tempted to try again!

once on the flat, GRITTAR pulled away to a fifteen length victory from HARD OUTLOOK, a distance ahead of the remounted LOVING WORDS and DELMOSS. As the first woman to complete the Grand National course, Geraldine Rees received a great ovation as she brought home CHEERS, one of only four other survivors. GRITTAR was the first clear favourite to win since MERRYMAN II in 1960.

Having become only the fourth amateur to win the race since the Second World War, Dick Saunders, also the oldest man ever to win it and a member of the Jockey Club, announced that he had ridden his last race. Retiring in the proudest possible manner, after one solitary yet unforgettable attempt, Dick Saunders received the warmest congratulations later in the month from his fellow Jockey Club members and there was increased hope that their plans to save Aintree might yet succeed.

1982

With £66,000 added, being £15,000 given by The Horserace Betting Levy Board and £51,000 by Sun Newspapers, the latter amount including a trophy value £1,500. For six-year-olds & upwards. The second to receive £13,540, the third £6,640 and the fourth £3,190. The trainer of the Winner to receive a trophy value £300 and the rider of the Winner a trophy value £300

Date: 3rd April 1982	Starters: 39	Time: 9 mins 12.6 secs
1st **GRITTAR**	**9.11–5** *(Mr F H Gilman)*	**Mr C Saunders**
2nd **HARD OUTLOOK**	**11.10–1** *(Lady Wates)*	**A Webber**
3rd **LOVING WORDS**	**9.10–11** *(Mr A Netley)*	**R Hoare** [remounted]
4th **DELMOSS**	**12.10–3** *(Mr J Goodman)*	**W Smith**
5th **CURRENT GOLD**	**11.10–8** *(Mr A Picke)*	**N Doughty**
6th **TRAGUS**	**10.11–4** *(Lord Hartington)*	**P Scudamore**
7th **THREE OF DIAMONDS**	**10.10–7** *(Mr H Harpur-Crewe)*	**Mr P O'Connor**
8th **CHEERS**	**10.10–0** *(Mr C Mackenzie)*	**Mrs Geraldine Rees**

Also Ran:

ROYAL MAIL 12.11–10 (Mr J Begg) **B R Davies** *Fell*; *ALDANITI 12.11–9* (Mr S Embiricos) **R Champion** *Fell*; *AGAIN THE SAME 9.11–8* (Mr D McLaughlin) **J J O'Neill** *Pulled-up*; *CARROW BOY 10.11–7* (Mr W Durkan) **G Newman** *Fell*; *PETER SCOT 11.11–5* (Mr G Amey) **P Barton** *Fell*; *DEEP GALE 9.11–2* (Mr J McManus) **T J Ryan** *Fell*; *RAMBLING JACK 11.11–1* (Mr G Adam) **T G Dun** *Fell*; *MAN ALIVE 11.11–0* (Jim Ennis Construction Ltd) **A Turnell** *Fell*; *MULLACURRY 10.10–12* (Mr J Shannon) **Mr T J Taaffe** *Fell*; *ROLLS RAMBLER 11.10–12* (Mr B Brazier) **Mr A J Wilson** *Refused*; *SAINT FILLANS 8.10–11* (Mr R Wilson) **P Tuck** *Fell*; *GOOD PROSPECT 13.10–12* (Mr C Moorsom) **R Linley** *Refused*; *GANDY VI 13.10–8* (Mrs E White-Spunner) **N Madden** *Fell*; *OLD SOCIETY 8.10–8* (Mrs D Fortune) **P Walsh** *Fell*; *ROUGH AND TUMBLE 12.10–8* (Mr L Dormer) **J Francome** *Refused*; *THE VINTNER 11.10–7* (Westwood Garages Ltd) **Mr D Browne** *Unseated rider*; *ROYAL STUART 11.10–4* (Mr J Begg) **Mr D Gray** *Brought down*; *MARTINSTOWN 10.10–3* (Mrs R Brew) **Miss C Brew** *Unseated rider*; *THREE TO ONE 11.10–3* (Mr J Manners) **R Lamb** *Fell*; *SUN LION 12.10–3* (Mr R Waley-Cohen) **S Smith Eccles** *Fell*; *TIEPOLINO 10.10–4* (Mrs B House) **H Davies** *Refused*; *COOLISHALL 13.10–3* (Mr B Munro-Wilson) **R Barry** *Fell*; *SENATOR MACLACURY 8.10–0* (Mr M Lanigan) **P Kiely** *Fell*; *ARTISTIC PRINCE 11.10–0* (Mr R Stigwood) **C Brown** *Fell*; *JIMMY MIFF 10.10–1* (Mr B Davies) **Mr M Williams** *Fell*; *MONTY PYTHON 10.10–0* (Mr W Gaff) **B De Haan** *Refused*; *COLD SPELL 10.10–0* (Lord Leverhulme) **S Jobar** *Brought down*; *THIS WAY 11.10–2* (Mrs J George) **C Candy** *Fell*; *CHORAL FESTIVAL 11.10–4* (Mr M Low) **Mr M Low** *Unseated rider*; *DEERMOUNT 8.10–0* (Mrs M Babbage) **J P Byrne** *Fell*; *RATHLEK 12.10–12* (Mr J Carden) **Mr J Carden** *Fell*.

The Betting: *7/1 Grittar; 17/2 Royal Mail; 12/1 Aldaniti & Three To One; 14/1 Tragus; 16/1 Loving Words, Again the Same, Mullacurry, Rough and Tumble & Rambling Jack; 20/1 Rolls Rambler & Senator Maclacury; 22/1 Deep Gale; 25/1 Current Gold; 33/1 Man Alive, Coolishall & Old Society; 40/1 Royal Stuart, Carrow Boy & Cold Spell; 50/1 Hard Outlook, Delmoss, Artistic Prince, Gandy VI, Good Prospect, Jimmy Miff, Sun Lion, The Vintner & Tiepolino; 66/1 Cheers & Monty Python; 100/1 Martinstown, This Way, Choral Festival, Deermount, Rathlek & Three of Diamonds.*

Distances: *Fifteen lengths; a distance*

Winner Trained By: *Frank Gilman, Morcott, Leicestershire*

Value to Winning Owner: *£52,507*

1983

Little was heard of the Aintree Grand National Appeal after its well-publicised launch on GRIT-TAR's day of glory. Admittedly the more serious matter of freeing the Falkland Islands took precedence over most things and the subsequent South Atlantic Appeal became a far worthier cause than that of racing's administrators. Even so, the news on that fateful deadline of 1st November 1982, that the sum required to purchase the racecourse had not been raised, came as a blow to all those who had allowed themselves to believe that the intervention of the Jockey Club was a sure-fire solution to the problem of protecting the Grand National. In truth, the Aintree Grand National Appeal never got off the ground, which fact would not be forgotten by the general public in the months ahead.

Having recruited a firm of professional fund raisers, the Jockey Club presented Aintree's owner Bill Davies with their assessment that the most which they could hope to raise through public subscription was £4 million. A new contract was drawn up, after more threats that the 'National would be transferred to another venue, leaving Mr Davies little choice but to comply with the latest proposals, and the same boring rigmarole of fund raising began again. This time the day of reckoning was scheduled for the 1st May 1983, the County Council of Merseyside threw in its support and Lord Vestey was appointed Chairman of the Appeal. Thus another breathing space was granted, during which agreement was reached to permit the would-be purchasers to organise the running of the 1983 Grand National. Following the tremendous seven-year demonstration by Ladbrokes of just what could be done, the 1983 Ain-tree Festival of Jumping was prepared most efficiently and with Nigel Payne retained to market proceedings, the bill of fare proved excellent.

As interesting as the forthcoming big race were the efforts of fund raisers in their attempts to secure the future of the event. For a lesson in enterprise, the campaign organisers needed to look no further than the racecourse itself ten days before 'National day. Sixty-six-year-old course foreman, Mr Ossie Dale, the oldest member of the racecourse staff, set out on a two-hour sponsored bicycle ride around the motor race-track, accompanied by the youngest employee, his twenty-year-old grandson Jimmy Stevenson. Pedalling their way through a raging blizzard, the pair made a valuable contribution to the efforts to save the race, through donations from local men, women and school children. A member of the Aintree staff since his appointment as a ploughman in 1953, Ossie Dale had through the years become as colourful and well-known a character as any in the long history of the race and through his period as stable manager, displayed a friendly and efficient countenance to the countless trainers who left their horses in his dedicated care.

Most heavily backed of the forty-one runners was the most recent winner GRIT-TAR, now partnered by Paul Barton and firm in the market at 6/1 in spite of topping the handicap with 11 st 12 lbs. Back after a period of leg trouble, SPARTAN MIS-SILE was the mount of Hywel Davies and running under the ownership of John Thorne's widow, was trained by her son-in-law Nicky Henderson, formerly assistant to Fred Winter. There were two lady riders competing, Geraldine Rees with newly-purchased MIDDAY WELCOME and American Mrs Joy Carrier on her hus-

band's Irish-trained KING SPRUCE. Women were also well represented as trainers, four of them saddling no less than six of the runners. Making a three-pronged attack on 'chasing's greatest prize with ARTISTIC PRINCE, MONTY PYTHON and eight-year-old CORBIERE, Mrs Jenny Pitman had every reason to feel confident that the winner would come from the Upper Lambourn yard that she had built up from nothing into a stable to be feared. Best supported of the three at 13/1, CORBIERE was bred by M Parkhill from the stallion HARWELL and the mare BALLY CASHEN and beginning his racing career with Mrs Pitman in his fourth year, proved successful over hurdles. Equally adept over fences, CORBIERE soon established a reputation as a first-rate staying chaser and a resounding victory in the Welsh 'National at Chepstow set him right on course for the real thing at Aintree. Ridden by twenty-three-year-old

Ben de Haan, CORBIERE was owned by Mr Bryan Burrough who was the same age as his jockey.

DELMOSS and CORBIERE led over the first, where MID DAY GUN, MIDDAY WELCOME and the grey TOWER MOSS came down, and at Becher's, where for the second year running ROYAL MAIL crashed, along with Mrs Carrier and KING SPRUCE. A length in front of CORBIERE at Valentine's, DELMOSS maintained his advantage on the run back to the stands with the outsider HALLO DANDY moving up handily. Hampered by a riderless horse at the thirteenth, Bill Smith and DELMOSS were still in front at the Chair, which once more took a heavy toll. Racing on the wide outside, HALLO DANDY took up the running at the seventeenth, closely tracked by CORBIERE, COLONEL CHRISTY and the rapidly improving Irish hope GREASEPAINT. SPARTAN MISSILE added to the growing list of casualties when unseating his rider at Becher's, and GREASEPAINT hit the next fence hard, but came back into the contest after jumping Valentine's, which CORBIERE and HALLO DANDY took together. Unsuited by the going, HALLO DANDY began to fade between the final fences and CORBIERE took the last two lengths in front of GREASEPAINT, increasing the margin to twice that by the time he passed the elbow. But GREASEPAINT rallied on the flat, gaining ground rapidly on the long run to the post. In a nail-biting finish, which must have revived memories for Jenny Pitman of CRISP's narrow defeat when ridden by her then husband ten years before, CORBIERE held on to win by three-quarters of a length. Twenty lengths back in third was YER MAN, outstaying HALLO DANDY. For the second year in succession history had been made by the ladies, Jenny Pitman becoming the first woman to saddle the 'National winner. With tears in her eyes she gave the go-ahead for celebrations to begin at Upper Lambourn, via the David Coleman post-race television interview.

Shortly before the race Lord Vestey had informed the popular television presenter that the Appeal Fund was well on target to reach the amount required to save the race, with barely one million pounds left to collect. It was therefore the more bewildering, if not infuriating, when on 1st May 1983 the announcement was made that the Jockey Club's Aintree campaign had not merely failed, but failed miserably. No statements of amounts raised were ever published, nor were reasons forthcoming why pledges from abroad were withdrawn. The size of the bill paid to the professional fund-raisers was another closely guarded secret and although each of these points was now purely academic, the Aintree purchase shambles would not easily be forgotten. If the fund-raisers are criticised, though, it must also be pointed out that the British public had not, at the end of the day, shown themselves desperate to save the 'National.

Ben De Haan just holds off the late flourish of Mr Colin Magnier, putting up a couple of pounds overweight on GREASEPAINT

THE GRAND NATIONAL HANDICAP STEEPLECHASE
1983

With £66,000 added, being £15,000 given by The Horserace Betting Levy Board and £51,000 by Sun Newspapers, the latter amount including a trophy value £1,600. For six-year-olds & upwards. The second to receive £13,656, the third £6,698 and the fourth £3,219. The trainer of the Winner to receive a trophy value £400 and the rider of the Winner a trophy value £400

Date: 9th April 1983	Starters: 41	Time: 9 mins 47.4 secs
1st **CORBIERE**	**8.11–4** *(Mr B R H Burrough)*	**B De Haan**
2nd **GREASEPAINT**	**8.10–7** *(Mrs N Todd)*	**Mr C Magnier**
3rd **YER MAN**	**8.10–0** *(Mr N Keane)*	**T V O'Connell**
4th **HALLO DANDY**	**9.10–1** *(Mr R Shaw)*	**N Doughty**
5th **GRITTAR**	**10.11–12** *(Mr F H Gilman)*	**P Barton**
6th **PEATY SANDY**	**9.11–3** *(exors of the late Mrs I Hamilton)*	**T G Dun**
7th **POLITICAL POP**	**9.11–3** *(Mrs A Starkie)*	**G Bradley**
8th **VENTURE TO COGNAC**	**10.11–12** *(Mr N E C Sherwood)*	**Mr O Sherwood**
9th **COLONEL CHRISTY**	**8.10–0** *(Mrs H R McLaughlin)*	**P Hobbs**
10th **DELMOSS**	**13.10–3** *(Mr R Q Sutherland)*	**W Smith**

Also Ran:

TACROY 9.11–9 (Mr A J Duffield) **F Berry** *Pulled-up*; *SPARTAN MISSILE 11.11–7* (Mrs M W Thorne) **H Davies** *Unseated rider*; *KING SPRUCE 9.11–4* (Mr R N Carrier) **Mrs J Carrier** *Fell*; *ROYAL MAIL 13.11–4* (Mr & Mrs J Murray Begg) **Mr T Thomson Jones** *Fell*; *THE LADY'S MASTER 12.11–2* (Mr M C Duggan) **Mr W P Mullins** *Ran-out*; *CARROW BOY 11.10–12* (Mr W Durkan) **G Newman** *Fell*; *BONUM OMEN 9.10–9* (Mr L B Thwaites) **K Mooney** *Refused*; *MID DAY GUN 9.10–8* (Mr R Gibbons) **G McCourt** *Fell*; *PILOT OFFICER 8.10–7* (Mr R A Padmore) **S Morshead** *Fell*; *BEACON TIME 9.10–6* (Mr F S Markland) **J J O'Neill** *Pulled-up*; *BEECH KING 9.10–8* (Mrs J J Jones) **Mr P Duggan** *Fell*; *FORTINA'S EXPRESS 9.10–3* (Mr P Piller) **P Scudamore** *Pulled-up*; *HOT TOMATO 11.10–2* (Mr H A Insley) **J Burke** *Fell*; *THREE TO ONE 12.10–2* (Mr D H Cavendish-Pell) **P Tuck** *Fell*; *DUNCREGGAN 10.10–0* (Mr B Desmond, jnr) **G McGlinchey** *Fell*; *KEENGADDY 10.10–0* (Mr I Single) **S Smith Eccles** *Fell*; *MENDER 12.10–1* (Miss N Carroll) **A Webber** *Fell*; *MENFORD 8.10–0* (Shirlstar Container Tpt Ltd & Mr P Richardson) **M Perrett** *Refused*; *OAKPRIME 8.10–5* (Mrs D Nicholson) **R Linley** *Pulled-up*; *THE VINTNER 12.10–0* (Mr D O Williams) **C Grant** *Refused*; *ARRIGLE BOY 11.10–1* (Mr D Eddy) **C Pimlott** *Refused*; *ARTISTIC PRINCE 12.10–0* (Mr R Stigwood) **C Brown** *Refused*; *O'ER THE BORDER 9.10–12* (Mr H F Harpur-Crewe) **Mr P O'Connor** *Refused*; *CANFORD GINGER 8.10–0* (Mr A W H Sykes) **J H Davies** *Pulled-up*; *MONTY PYTHON 11.10–2* (Rank Organisation PLC) **P O'Brien** *Refused*; *WILLIAMSON 9.10–0* (Hillfields Farming Co) **C Mann** *Brought down*; *MIDDAY WELCOME 12.10–0* (Mr V Burke) **Mrs G Rees** *Fell*; *SYDNEY QUINN 11.10–0* (Mr W J Kelly & Mr J A Taylor) **P Double** *Fell*; *THAT'S IT 9.10–0* (Mr L A White) **G Holmes** *Fell*; *TOWER MOSS 10.10–1* (Mr A S Neaves) **R Rowe** *Fell*; *NEVER TAMPER 8.10–0* (J J Saunders Ltd) **J Williams** *Refused*

The Betting: *6/1 Grittar; 15/2 Bonum Omen; 9/1 Spartan Missile; 12/1 Peaty Sandy; 13/1 Corbiere; 14/1 Greasepaint & Mid Day Gun; 15/1 Keengaddy; 20/1 Fortina's Express; 22/1 Pilot Officer; 25/1 Beacon Time & Three To One; 28/1 Political Pop, King Spruce & Venture To Cognac; 33/1 Canford Ginger, Carrow Boy & Tacroy; 50/1 Delmoss, Mender & Royal Mail; 60/1 Beech King & Hallo Dandy; 66/1 Artistic Prince, Colonel Christy, Oakprime & The Vintner; 75/1 Duncreggan; 80/1 Yer Man; 100/1 Arrigle Boy, Hot Tomato, Menford & Williamson; 150/1 Monty Python; 200/1 O'er The Border, That's It & The Lady's Master; 300/1 Sydney Quinn & Tower Moss; 500/1 Midday Welcome & Never Tamper.*

Distances: *Three quarters of a length; twenty lengths*

Winner Trained By: *Mrs Jenny Pitman, Upper Lambourn, Berkshire*

Value to Winning Owner: *£52,949*

1984

Too much of the shabby wrangling over the purchase of Aintree is still fresh in people's minds to warrant repeating it. Suffice it to say that thanks solely to the last-minute intervention of Canadian whisky firm Seagram and its far-sighted British chairman Major Ivan Straker, the Grand National was saved from extinction in a closer run thing than any ever witnessed on Aintree's turf. Mr Bill Davies was eventually left with little alternative but to accept £3.4 million for the racecourse. All responsibility for the Grand National passed into the hands of the Jockey Club and for the first time in almost twenty years the Grand National of 1984 was enjoyed completely free of doubt as to its future. Bowing out gracefully, after sponsoring the race since 1975, News International made way for Seagram, who at great expense provided the prize money for all six races on Grand National day. The newly-formed Aintree Racecourse Company made a monumental step towards improving safety by limiting the number of runners for the big race to forty, but scrapped most of the conditions of entry. This year any horse above the age of six years who had won a steeplechase of any description between 1st July 1981 and 15th January 1984 was eligible to run and this resulted in 141 horses being entered. Captain Christopher Mordaunt, the handicapper, came in for severe criticism from the trainers of both CORBIERE and GREASEPAINT but there could be no denying that his assessment produced a vastly improved quality among those on the minimum mark of 10 stone.

CORBIERE, ASHLEY HOUSE and GRITTAR headed the weights, above such worthies as SPARTAN MISSILE, MIDNIGHT LOVE and the two powerful Irish challengers GREASEPAINT and ELIOGARTY. Having changed ownership, GREASEPAINT was trained this time by Dermot Weld, who had sent out SAVING MERCY to win the Lincoln Handicap at a big price a week before Aintree and now found himself in charge of the 'National favourite at 9/1. Shrewd racegoers, however, bore well in mind the brilliance of HALLO DANDY's jumping last year and noted that the ground was now in his favour. By MENELEK out of DANDY HALL, the gelding had been bred by Mr J P Frost, fetching 10,000 guineas as an unbroken three-year-old before being put into training with the man forever associated with RED RUM, Donald McCain. Demonstrating only modest ability over hurdles, HALLO DANDY improved tremendously when put over fences and in due course came under the care of the master of Greystoke, Gordon Richards. London insurance broker Richard Shaw bought HALLO DANDY shortly before the 1983 'National and with talented Neale Doughty again in the saddle, the Cumbrian runner found the approval of many members of the racing press.

Entrusted for the first time with the responsibility of despatching the Grand National field, Captain Michael Sayers set them off to the most perfect of breaks at the first time of asking. It was unusual and encouraging to see the entire field negotiate the first two obstacles without incident and the first to fall was GOLDEN TRIX at the third. BURNT OAK jumped Becher's some twelve lengths clear of the pack. Upon returning to the racecourse, the leader began tiring, his lead being cut to six lengths as they approached the Chair, where both the Michael Dickinson-trained runners ASHLEY HOUSE and CARL'S WAGER unshipped their riders. Going back to the country, GRITTAR, EARTH-STOPPER and GREASEPAINT took command, chased now by LUCKY VANE, TWO SWALLOWS, TACROY, CORBIERE, SPARTAN MISSILE, YER MAN and ELIOGARTY and for the first time HALLO DANDY could be seen improving his position. Keeping the same position he had throughout, on the outside, HALLO DANDY put in a spectacular leap at Becher's which gained him so much ground that he landed in sixth place and full of running. At the fence after Valentine's he and GREASEPAINT moved clear of the remainder. Back on the racecourse GREASEPAINT was still in command, until another fine jump at the second last took HALLO DANDY into the lead and, repeating the process at the last, he landed on the flat with a two length advantage. As HALLO DANDY veered sharply over to the stands rails, GREASEPAINT rallied as he had the year before, but running on again determinedly HALLO DANDY pulled away in the final furlong for a four length win. Only a length and a half behind the runner-up came CORBIERE, having made up a tremendous amount of late ground, and in fourth place was LUCKY VANE. The gallant EARTHSTOPPER dropped dead after passing the post in fifth, the only sad note of a race which provided the largest number of finishers ever, twenty-three in all.

CORBIERE superbly caught in flight at Becher's Brook

THE GRAND NATIONAL HANDICAP STEEPLECHASE
1984

With £66,000 added, being £15,000 given by The Horserace Betting Levy Board and £51,000 by Seagram, the latter amount including a trophy value £1,600. For six-year-olds & upwards. The second to receive £14,132, the third £6,936 and the fourth £3,338. The trainer of the Winner to receive a trophy value £400 and the rider of the Winner a trophy value £400

Date: 31st March 1984	Starters: 40	Time: 9 mins 21.4 secs
1st **HALLO DANDY**	10.10–2 *(Mr R Shaw)*	**N Doughty**
2nd **GREASEPAINT**	9.11–2 *(Mr M J Smurfit)*	**T Carmody**
3rd **CORBIERE**	9.12–0 *(Mr B R H Burrough)*	**B de Haan**
4th **LUCKY VANE**	9.10–13 *(Miss B Swire)*	**J Burke**
5th **EARTHSTOPPER**	10.11–1 *(Mrs C Wright)*	**R Rowe**
6th **TWO SWALLOWS**	11.10–0 *(Mr & Mrs G Steinberg)*	**A Webber**
7th **FETHARD FRIEND**	9.10–12 *(H H Kais Al-Said & Y Idliby)*	**G Newman**
8th **BROOMY BANK**	9.10–12 *(Capt J M G Lumsden & Viscountess Boyne)*	**Mr A J Wilson**
9th **JIVAGO DE NEUVY**	9.11–0 *(Mr Roger Grand)*	**Mr R Grand**
10th **GRITTAR**	11.11–10 *(Mr F H Gilman)*	**J Francome**
11th **HILL OF SLANE**	8.10–2 *(Mrs M A Jarvis & Mrs R J Kaplan)*	**S Smith Eccles**
12th **TACROY**	10.10–7 *(Mr A J Duffield)*	**F Berry**
13th **DOUBLEUAGAIN**	10.10–5 *(Mr P J McBennett)*	**T Morgan**
14th **BEECH KING**	10.10–1 *(Mr J J Jones)*	**P Kiely**
15th **ELIOGARTY**	9.11–5 *(Miss C J Beasley)*	**Mr D Hassett**
16th **SPARTAN MISSILE**	12.11–4 *(Mrs M W Thorne)*	**Mr J White**
17th **YER MAN**	9.10–2 *(Mr N Keane)*	**T V O'Connell**
18th **FAULOON**	9.10–13 *(Mr R K Kieckhefer)*	**W Smith**
19th **ANOTHER CAPTAIN**	12.10–1 *(Mr A Scott, jnr)*	**A Stringer**
20th **MID DAY GUN**	10.10–3 *(Mr R Gibbons)*	**G McCourt**
21st **POYNTZ PASS**	9.10–5 *(Mr T F Harty)*	**H Rogers**
22nd **JACKO**	12.10–4 *(Mr H B Shouler)*	**S Morshead**
23rd **CANFORD GINGER**	9.10–1 *(Mr A W H Sykes)*	**C Brown**

Also Ran:

ASHLEY HOUSE 10.11–13 (Mr J McLoughlin) **G Bradley** *Fell*; *MIDNIGHT LOVE* 9.11–4 (Carpenters Paints Ltd) **C Grant** *Fell*; *SILENT VALLEY* 11.10–8 (Mr J Walby) **T G Dun** *Pulled-up*; *HAZY DAWN* 9.10–9 (Mr R E Daniels) **Mr W P Mullins** *Fell*; *BURNT OAK* 8.10–7 (Brig C B Harvey) **P Scudamore** *Pulled-up*; *IMPERIAL BLACK* 8.10–7 (Mr T Webster) **C Hawkins** *Fell*; *BUSH GUIDE* 8.10–5 (Miss Valerie Alder) **Miss V Alder** *Fell*; *THE DRUNKEN DUCK* 11.10–3 (Mr B Munro-Wilson) **A Brown** *Pulled-up*; *DOORSTEP* 8.10–2 (Mr J Horgan) **Mr J Queally** *Fell*; *PILOT OFFICER* 9.10–2 (Mr R A Padmore) **Mr A Sharpe** *Refused*; *CARL'S WAGER* 9.10–2 (Leisure Racing Ltd) **Mr R J Beggan** *Fell*; *THREE TO ONE* 13.10–2 (Mr D H Cavendish-Pell) **P Tuck** *Fell*; *ROMAN GENERAL* 11.10–3 (Mr B Munro-Wilson) **Major M Wallace** *Unseated rider*; *FORTUNE SEEKER* 9.10–0 (Mrs G T McKey) **P Barton** *Fell*; *GOLDEN TRIX* 9.10–1 (Mr B L Chinn) **K Mooney** *Fell*; *CLONTHTURTIN* 10.10–0 (Mr F Conroy) **T J Taaffe** *Fell*; *KUMBI* 9.10–0 (Mr D A Lunt & Mr T Webster) **K Doolan** *Fell*

The Betting: *9/1 Greasepaint; 12/1 Lucky Vane, Broomy Bank & Grittar; 13/1 Hallo Dandy; 16/1 Corbiere & Eliogarty; 18/1 Spartan Missile; 20/1 Ashley House; 22/1 Fethard Friend; 25/1 Burnt Oak & Yer Man; 28/1 Carl's Wager, Midnight Love, Tacroy & Two Swallows; 33/1 Bush Guide, Earthstopper, Hill of Slane, Pilot Officer & Silent Valley; 40/1 Mid Day Gun; 50/1 Fauloon, Golden Trix, Imperial Black & Jivago de Neuvy; 66/1 Another Captain, Beech King, Jacko & Three to One; 100/1 Hazy Dawn, Poyntz Pass, Doubleuagain, The Drunken Duck, Door Step, Roman General, Fortune Seeker, Canford Ginger, Clonthturtin & Kumbi.*

Distances: *Four lengths; one and a half lengths*

Winner Trained By: *Gordon W Richards, Greystoke, Cumbria*

Value to Winning Owner: *£54,769*

1985

Grand National day this year revived memories of past glories when some two hours before the main event, a reunion of former winning jockeys received Aynsley china trophies from HRH Princess Anne. From Neale Doughty, the most recent hero, back through the years to the oldest member of the party, eighty-two-year-old Tim Hamey, the giants of steeplechasing past and present took their places on the rostrum in a moving and enjoyable ceremony.

The peril faced by jump jockeys was forcibly demonstrated when the injured Neale Doughty and Ben de Haan were ruled unfit to partner HALLO DANDY and CORBIERE. Deputising for them, Graham Bradley and Peter Scudamore were presented with outstanding chances of achieving a first win in the big race. Joint favourites at 13/2 were the ever-popular GREASEPAINT and impressive rising star WEST TIP, ridden by the find of the season, Richard Dunwoody. Yorkshire-trained MR SNUGFIT had come to hand well since publication of the weights, winning a succession of long distance 'chases, which prompted a flood of money for him in the 'National, in which he seemed a blot on the handicap with only 10 stone.

Twenty years before, the mighty ARKLE had thrilled racegoers everywhere with his brilliance, yet his owner the Duchess of Westminster had been emphatic that the wonder-horse would never run at Aintree. But her famous colours were at last seen in the 'National, carried by one who on all known form could not be mentioned in the same breath as ARKLE. On breeding, LAST SUSPECT could hardly be faulted. His sire was ABOVE SUSPICION and his dam, LAST LINK. Yet on the only proving ground that matters, the racecourse, LAST SUSPECT fre-

quently displayed an aggravating wilfulness. On his third and most recent run of the season, LAST SUSPECT had pulled himself up and this prompted both owner and trainer Captain Tim Forster to withdraw the eleven-year-old from the 'National. Only the persuasive powers of jockey Hywel Davies brought a change of heart, but backers looked upon LAST SUSPECT as something of a rogue and he was readily available at 50/1.

The shocks came thick and fast. At the first fence HALLO DANDY made an early exit and another of the best-fancied horses, LUCKY VANE, came to grief at the tenth. Twenty-seven survivors made their way on towards the Chair, led by DUDIE. There was a moment's anxiety at the big open ditch when both GREASEPAINT and SCOT LANE made terrible mistakes, but their riders were equal to the occasion. CORBIERE, WEST TIP and RUPERTINO went several lengths clear after DUDIE fell at the nineteenth and as they approached Becher's again WEST TIP was going by far the easiest of any. Caught out by the drop at the Brook though, Richard Dunwoody's hopes were dashed at the moment the race appeared to be theirs for the taking and with CORBIERE, RUPERTINO and LAST SUSPECT now disputing the lead, the eventual result was far from certain. GREASEPAINT and MR SNUGFIT, who had made a tremendous amount of ground over the last few fences, were on the heels of the leaders rounding the Canal Turn but as they came across Melling Road for the final time, CORBIERE appeared set for a second victory. Under pressure in second place was GREASEPAINT, strongly pursued by MR SNUGFIT, with LAST SUSPECT being patiently ridden along by Hywel Davies after making a couple of jumping errors at the last two fences. Battling back in his

usual great-hearted manner, CORBIERE forced second-placed Phil Tuck and MR SNUGFIT to fight every yard of the way home but over the last the weight began to tell and the Yorkshire horse landed on the flat looking all over the winner. Some eight lengths in arrears at this point, LAST SUSPECT then ran on brilliantly up the long straight. Passing CORBIERE and wearing down MR SNUGFIT in the final hundred yards, LAST SUSPECT, his tail swishing all the way to the line, won cleverly by a length and a half with CORBIERE third. The triumph was a just reward for the modest jockey Hywel Davies, who only months before had been brought back from the dead by first aid after a crushing racecourse fall. Without his faith in LAST SUSPECT, so amply justified by the horse's first visit to Aintree, this chapter in the great race's history would have been very different.

Above: LAST SUSPECT in mid-division over Becher's first time round

Below: Winning jockey Hywel Davies

1985

With £66,000 added, being £15,000 given by The Horserace Betting Levy Board and £51,000 by Seagram, the latter amount including a trophy value £1,700. For six-year-olds & upwards. The second to receive £14,013, the third £6,876 and the fourth £3,308. The trainer of the Winner to receive a trophy value £400 and the rider of the Winner a trophy value £400

Date: 30th March 1985	Starters: 40	Time: 9 mins 42.7 secs
1st **LAST SUSPECT**	**11.10–5** *(Anne, Duchess of Westminster)*	**H Davies**
2nd **MR SNUGFIT**	**8.10--0** *(Mr A Greenwood)*	**P Tuck**
3rd **CORBIERE**	**10.11–10** *(Mr B R H Burrough)*	**P Scudamore**
4th **GREASEPAINT**	**10.10–13** *(Mr M J Smurfit)*	**T Carmody**
5th **CLASSIFIED**	**9.10–7** *(Mr G A Rogers)*	**J White**
6th **IMPERIAL BLACK**	**9.10–1** *(Mr T Webster)*	**C Hawkins**
7th **RUPERTINO**	**10.10–0** *(Lord Kenyon)*	**R Stronge**
8th **SCOT LANE**	**12.10–1** *(Mr T H Isherwood)*	**C Smith**
9th **GLENFOX**	**8.10–0** *(Mr P R Dickson & Mr R Bowes)*	**Mr D Gray**
10th **BLACKRATH PRINCE**	**9.10–0** *(Mr R Dowsett)*	**B Reilly**
11th **CAPTAIN PARKHILL**	**12.10–0** *(Mr B McLean)*	**C Grant**

Also Ran:

DRUMLARGAN 11.11–8 (Mrs G Webb Bronfman) **J Francome** *Pulled-up; LUCKY VANE 10.10–13* (Miss B Swire) **J Burke** *Pulled-up; HALLO DANDY 11.10–12* (Mr R Shaw) **G Bradley** *Fell; BROOMY BANK 10.10–7* (Capt J M G Lumsden & Viscountess Boyne) **Mr A J Wilson** *Refused; FETHARD FRIEND 10.10–7* (H H K Al-Said & Y Idliby) **P Barton** *Pulled-up; TACROY 11.10–3* (Mr A J Duffield) **A Stringer** *Fell; WEST TIP 8.10–1* (Mr P Luff) **R Dunwoody** *Fell; KUMBI 10.10–0* (Mr D A Lunt) **K Doolan** *Fell; MUSSO 9.10–0* (R E A Bott (Wigmore St) Ltd) **Mr S Sherwood** *Pulled-up; DUDIE 7.10–0* (Mr M B Moore) **A Mullins** *Fell; SHADY DEAL 12.10–3* (Mr G A Hubbard) **R Rowe** *Fell; TUBBERTELLY 8.10–1* (Mr F T McCann) **T J Taaffe** *Refused; TALON 10.10–0* (Mr B Munro-Wilson) **A Webber** *Fell; ONAPROMISE 9.10–5* (Mr J J Greenwood & Mr T Webster) **A Brown** *Pulled-up; KNOCKAWAD 8.10–0* (Mr M L Wilmott) **K F O'Brien** *Fell; HILL OF SLANE 9.10–2* (Mrs M A Jarvis & Mrs R J Kaplan) **S Smith Eccles** *Fell; ROYAL APPOINTMENT 10.10–0* (Mrs J L White) **P Gill** *Fell; SOLIHULL SPORT 11.10–0* (Solihull Sports Services) **S Morshead** *Fell; CLONTHTURTIN 11.10–5* (Mrs F P Rawnsley & Mr D C Rawnsley) **Mr T Thomson Jones** *Pulled-up; FAULOON 10.10–2* (Mr R H Kieckhefer) **K Mooney** *Fell; BASHFUL LAD 10.10–3* (Mrs F H Parkes & Mr M Oliver) **G McCourt** *Fell; CROSA 10.10–0* (Mr S C Jones) **S Moore** *Fell; NEVER TAMPER 10.10–3* (J J Saunders Ltd) **C Brown** *Pulled-up; ROMAN BISTRO 9.10–3* (Mr D Martin-Betts) **P Nicholls** *Refused; LENEY DUAL 10.10–8* (Mr D F Pitcher) **Mr D Pitcher** *Fell; OUR CLOUD 9.10–0* (Mr T D Strong) **Mr J Queally** *Refused; IMMIGRATE 12.10–0* (Mr W Stevenson-Taylor) **J Hansen** *Fell; GREENHILL HALL 9.10–0* (Miss Betty Duxbury) **D Wilkinson** *Pulled-up; NORTHERN BAY 9.10–1* (Twycross Frozen Food Centre) **P Hobbs** *Fell*

The Betting: *13/2 Greasepaint & West Tip; 8/1 Drumlargan; 9/1 Corbiere; 10/1 Lucky Vane; 12/1 Mr Snugfit; 14/1 Hallo Dandy; 16/1 Fethard Friend; 20/1 Classified; 25/1 Hill of Slane & Kumbi; 28/1 Scot Lane; 33/1 Broomy Bank, Rupertino, Tacroy & Talon; 50/1 Last Suspect, Bashful Lad, Clonthturtin, Dudie, Glenfox, Musso, Shady Deal & Tubbertelly; 66/1 Blackrath Prince, Fauloon, Imperial Black, Knockawad, Northern Bay & Royal Appointment; 100/1 Captain Parkhill, Crosa, Immigrate, Leney Dual, Onapromise & Solihull Sport; 150/1 Our Cloud & Roman Bistro; 200/1 Never Tamper & Greenhill Hall.*

Distances: *One and a half lengths; three lengths*

Winner Trained By: *Capt Tim Forster, Letcombe Bassett, Oxfordshire*

Value to Winning Owner: £54,314

1986

For the first time in twenty-five years the Iron Curtain was lifted to allow an eight-year-old entire called ESSEX to make the long overland journey to Aintree in a sporting attempt on the 'National. Accompanied by his trainer Vaclav Chaloupka, who was to ride him in the race, ESSEX became the first Czechoslovakian contender for 'chasing's greatest prize since GYI LOVAM fifty-five years earlier and although he automatically had to carry top weight, his presence certainly added flavour to the event.

Three former winners of the race, LAST SUSPECT, HALLO DANDY and CORBIERE, were bidding again, but first choice of backers was last year's runner-up MR SNUGFIT, now running in the blue and white hoops of Terry Ramsden, though once more partnered by Phil Tuck. Mr Jim Joel's DOOR LATCH, and the representative of Seagram's Major Ivan Straker, THE TSAREVICH, both carried an abundance of public support, while at the other end of the market ANOTHER DUKE presented the possibility of a unique problem for television personality Desmond Lynam. Having leased the outsider to run in the 'National on his behalf, the genial presenter of BBC's *Grandstand* faced the prospect of having to interview himself if the gelding became the surprise winner! Connections of Aintree specialist GREASEPAINT fought a frustrating battle against time to qualify their charge for this year's event, for without a win to his credit since March 1983, the new conditions made it essential that he correct matters before 12th January 1986. He beat the only other finisher in a minor event at Tramore with just days to spare.

There were no such problems for WEST TIP, who shared the same sire, GALA PERFORMANCE, as GREASEPAINT, and who had looked the probable winner last time until being caught out at the second Becher's. Out of the mare ASTRYL, WEST TIP was bred by Thomas J Hayes and changed hands for varying sums before becoming the property of Mr Peter Luff and entering the Droitwich yard of Michael Oliver as an unbroken five-year-old. WEST TIP's career was almost brought to an end before it began, when he suffered serious injuries through a collision with a lorry and it was only the skill of a veterinary surgeon, along with the loving care of the trainer's wife, which pulled him through. WEST TIP was not always the easiest of rides, tending to lose concentration if striking the front too soon, but in Richard Dunwoody he had a most able and stylish jockey. As second rider to Captain Tim Forster, Dunwoody was generously allowed to take the mount on second favourite WEST TIP when the owner of PORT ASKAIG, Lord Chelsea, agreed to release him from his retainer.

Ironically, PORT ASKAIG was the first to fall, quickly followed by highly-fancied DOOR LATCH and after LANTERN LODGE went at the next a greater shock was the uncharacteristic departure of CORBIERE at the fourth. Having jumped well, if in somewhat tearaway fashion, Czechoslovakian challenger ESSEX was pulled up at the thirteenth on account of a broken girth and TACROY and DOUBLEUAGAIN led the twenty-four other survivors over the Water Jump, with KILKILOWEN, THE TSAREVICH and CLASSIFIED heading the main bunch but both LAST SUSPECT and HALLO DANDY were well to the rear. Always well in sight of the leaders, WEST TIP was going well towards the outside in sixth place as he took Becher's for the second time behind CLASSIFIED, KILKILOWEN, THE TSAREVICH, NORTHERN BAY and

YOUNG DRIVER and as SOMMELIER and MON-ANORE moved into contention, the race was still wide open. Coming back from Valentine's these eight had the race to themselves, but as they reached Melling Road, the pace began to tell for all but YOUNG DRIVER, CLASSIFIED and WEST TIP. The Scottish-trained YOUNG DRIVER landed a length in front of WEST TIP over the last, but Richard Dunwoody brought WEST TIP with a smooth run to strike the front nearing the elbow and, resisting the renewed effort of YOUNG DRIVER, stayed on well to win by two lengths. CLASSIFIED was third, twenty lengths further back, just in front of the fast finishing favourite MR SNUGFIT who made up an enormous amount of ground from three out. The heavily backed WEST TIP received a terrific welcome upon returning to scale, as did twenty-two-year-old Richard Dunwoody some little time later when displaying to the crowds the new challenge trophy, a beautiful bronze, commissioned specially by Seagram Distillers, depicting the grace and power of three horses landing after Becher's and sculpted by former Grand National jockey Phil Blacker.

THE GRAND NATIONAL HANDICAP STEEPLECHASE

1986

With £70,000 added, being £15,000 given by The Horserace Betting Levy Board and £55,000 by Seagram, the latter amount including a Trophy value £1,500. For six-year-olds & upwards. The second to receive £14,760, the third £7,235 and the fourth £3,472. The trainer of the Winner to receive a trophy value £500 and the rider of the Winner a trophy value £500

Date: 5th April 1986	Starters: 40	Time: 9 mins 33 secs
1st **WEST TIP**	**9.10–11** *(Mr P Luff)*	R Dunwoody
2nd **YOUNG DRIVER**	**9.10–0** *(Mr J B Russell)*	C Grant
3rd **CLASSIFIED**	**10.10–3** *(Cheveley Park Stud)*	S Smith Eccles
4th **MR SNUGFIT**	**9.10–7** *(Mr T P Ramsden)*	P Tuck
5th **SOMMELIER**	**8.10–0** *(Mr D Wates)*	T J Taaffe
6th **BROOMY BANK**	**11.10–3** *(Capt J M G Lumsden & Viscountess Boyne)*	P Scudamore
7th **THE TSAREVICH**	**10.10–7** *(Major I C Straker)*	J White
8th **MONANORE**	**9.10–0** *(Mr J Meagher)*	T Morgan
9th **LITTLE POLVEIR**	**9.10–3** *(Mr M L Shone)*	C Brown
10th **GREASEPAINT**	**11.10–9** *(Mr M J Smurfit)*	T Carmody
11th **NORTHERN BAY**	**10.10–0** *(Cheveley Park Stud)*	P Hobbs
12th **HALLO DANDY**	**12.10–8** *(Mr R Shaw)*	N Doughty
13th **KILKILOWEN**	**10.11–3** *(exors of the late Mrs S W N Collen)*	K Morgan
14th **IMPERIAL BLACK**	**10.10–0** *(Mr T Webster)*	R Crank
15th **RUPERTINO**	**11.10–0** *(Lord Kenyon)*	G Charles-Jones
16th **WHY FORGET**	**10.10–7** *(Mr P Piller & Mr W A Stephenson)*	R Lamb
17th **GAYLE WARNING**	**12.10–9** *(Mr J G Dudgeon)*	Mr A Dudgeon

Also Ran:

ESSEX 8.12–0 (Czechoslovakia) (Mr J Cuba) **Mr V Chaloupka** *Pulled-up*; *CORBIERE 11.11–7* (Mr B R H Burrough) **B De Haan** *Fell*; *DRUMLARGAN 12.11–6* (Mrs G Webb Bronfman) **T J Ryan** *Fell*; *LAST SUSPECT 12.11–2* (Anne, Duchess of Westminster) **H Davies** *Pulled-up*; *DOOR LATCH 8.11–0* (Mr H J Joel) **R Rowe** *Fell*; *ACARINE 10.10–13* (Mrs P W Harris) **R Stronge** *Brought-down*; *BALLINACURRA LAD 11.10–8* (Mrs A Moynihan) **G Bradley** *Fell*; *LANTERN LODGE 9.10–7* (Mrs M E Farrell) **A Mullins** *Fell*; *TRACYS SPECIAL 9.10–6* (Mr L A H Ames) **S C Knight** *Fell*; *ANOTHER DUKE 13.10–4* (Mr Desmond Lynam) **P Nicholls** *Fell*; *PLUNDERING 9.10–1* (Mrs Miles Valentine) **S Sherwood** *Fell*; *TACROY 12.10–1* (Mr A J Duffield) **A Stringer** *Unseated rider*; *DUDIE 8.10–0* (Mr J Halewood) **K Doolan** *Fell*; *KNOCK HILL 10.10–1* (Mr P S Thompson) **M Dwyer** *Pulled-up*; *BALLYMILAN 9.10–0* (Mr F Sheridan) **C Hawkins** *Unseated rider*; *FETHARD FRIEND 11.10–2* (H H K Al-Said & Y Idliby) **P Barton** *Pulled-up*; *LATE NIGHT EXTRA 10.10–2* (Lt Col E C Phillips & Mrs E C Phillips) **Mr T Thomson Jones** *Pulled-up*; *MASTER TERCEL 10.10–7* (Mr B P Monkhouse) **D Browne** *Fell*; *ST ALEZAN 9.10–2* (Lord Coventry) **C Smith** *Brought-down*; *PORT ASKAIG 11.10–5* (Lord Chelsea) **G McCourt** *Fell*; *DOUBLEUAGAIN 12.10–0* (Mr B Clark & Mr C Holmes) **C Mann** *Brought-down*; *TEN CHERRIES 11.10–0* (Mr M Bell & Capt B W Bell) **A Sharpe** *Fell*; *MOUNT OLIVER 8.10–0* (Mr D A Smith & Mr P D Whitehouse) **J Bryan** *Fell*

The Betting: *13/2 Mr Snugfit; 15/2 West Tip; 9/1 Door Latch; 14/1 Corbiere & Last Suspect; 16/1 The Tsarevich, Greasepaint & Hallo Dandy; 18/1 Knock Hill; 20/1 Broomy Bank; 22/1 Classified, Ballinacurra Lad & Monanore; 25/1 Plundering & Kilkilowen; 33/1 Northern Bay & Acarine; 35/1 Why Forget, Fethard Friend & Port Askaig; 40/1 Drumlargan; 50/1 Ballymilan, Sommelier & Gayle Warning; 66/1 Ten Cherries, Young Driver, Little Polveir, Imperial Black & Rupertino; 100/1 Dudie, Essex & Lantern Lodge; 150/1 Tracys Special, Master Tercel, St Alezan; 200/1 Another Duke & Tacroy; 500/1 Others.*

Distances: *Two lengths; twenty lengths*

Winner Trained By: *Michael E Oliver, Droitwich, Worcestershire*

Value to Winning Owner: *£57,254*

The Czechoslovakian entire ESSEX puts in a bold leap at Becher's first time

1987

In this, the 150th anniversary of the birth of the Grand Liverpool Steeplechase at Maghull, a vain attempt was made by the distillers Jamesons to oust the greatest race of all from its long-held position as the most valuable 'chase in Europe. Their increased prize money for the Fairyhouse Irish 'National was answered swiftly and decisively by Seagram, who made the Aintree spectacular the richest ever with a reward to the winning owner of £64,710.

The late withdrawal of recent Gold Cup winner THE THINKER was disappointing, but trainer Arthur Stephenson had always said it was likely. The long-time ante-post favourite WEST TIP held his place at 5/1, despite a plunge on the attractive grey DARK IVY, ridden by Phil Tuck and prepared by Gordon Richards. Joint top weights were American BEWLEY'S HILL and the Czechoslovakian entry VALENCIO, both at long odds.

The early departure of DOOR LATCH last year, when seemingly offering his elderly owner his finest opportunity of winning the race, now led many to overlook Mr Joel's MAORI VENTURE. Sired by ST COLUMBUS from the mare MOON VENTURE, the sturdy-looking chestnut began showing improved form when joining Andrew Turnell's Marlborough team and on the last day of 1984 produced a good turn of foot to win the Mandarin 'Chase at Newbury. One of those he accounted for that day was DOOR LATCH and upon the death of his owner Major Jack Rubin, MAORI VENTURE was purchased for 17,000 guineas on behalf of Jim Joel. Something of a Lingfield specialist, where he won four times, he was not considered a safe enough jumper to give thirty-two-year-old Steve Knight much chance of winning at Aintree.

On the coldest race day for many years, the vast crowd were delighted by the return of the most emotional winner of the race in recent times. ALDANITI, reuinted with Bob Champion, cantered down the course at the end of his charity walk from Buckingham Palace in aid of the Bob Champion Cancer Trust Fund.

LUCKY REW and SMARTSIDE were the only fallers at the first as LEAN AR AGHAIDH showed the way to INSURE, EAMONS OWEN, CLASSIFIED, NORTHERN BAY and ATTITUDE ADJUSTER. Going comfortably within himself, the grey DARK IVY came to Becher's right on the heels of the leaders, but at his moment of take off he was badly impeded when ATTITUDE ADJUSTER seemed to switch his line of approach. Sandwiched between the Irish horse on his off-side and WHY FORGET on the inner, DARK IVY hit the top of the fence, coming down in the most hideous of fatal falls. BEWLEY'S HILL, immediately behind, was brought down and with the remainder well strung out the race continued under the darkest of clouds. At the Canal Turn front-running LEAN AR AGHAIDH was distracted by the riderless LUCKY REW, but his twenty-year-old rider Guy Landau, taking part in his first 'National, coped well, dropping back to third. With another magnificent leap over the Water, though, LEAN AR AGHAIDH regained the lead. Jumping like a stag, the Stan Mellor-trained chestnut thrilled the crowds lining the railway embankment on the run back to Becher's, but with a group in close pursuit, it seemed impossible that he could win from the front. Tracked all the way back across Melling Road by ATTITUDE ADJUSTER, LEAN AR AGHAIDH still stuck well to his task, though YOU'RE WELCOME, WEST TIP, BIG BROWN BEAR, MAORI VENTURE, THE TSAREVICH and TRACYS SPECIAL were all dangerously close as they jumped the second last. Coming to the final fence THE TSAREVICH clearly had a great chance of providing Major Straker of Seagram with a win for the sponsors. A length to the good over the last, LEAN AR AGHAIDH was at once challenged on the outside by MAORI VENTURE and by THE TSAREVICH against the inside rails. Finally unable to quicken, the long-time leader could only secure third place as, strongly pressed by THE TSAREVICH and ridden out in classic style by Steve Knight, MAORI VENTURE ran on again to win by five lengths. WEST TIP was fourth.

Winning in the third fastest time on record, MAORI VENTURE supplied veteran owner Jim Joel with a Grand National success twenty years after his Derby victory with ROYAL PALACE and thirty years after his first attempt on the Aintree showpiece with GLORIOUS TWELFTH. The trainer's father, Bob Turnell, who sadly died in 1982, would have been immensely proud of his talented son Andrew attaining the prize which he himself had so narrowly missed as a jockey. The owner was flying home from South Africa when the news of his success was broken to him but he was there to congratulate all concerned at Andy Turnell's stables the following day. It was at these celebrations that Jim Joel announced MAORI VENTURE's retirement and, in a characteristic gesture in keeping with the finest traditions of the sport, his intention to leave the horse in his will to the jockey Steve Knight.

Winning jockey Steve Knight

1987

With £80,000 added, being £15,000 given by The Horserace Betting Levy Board and Seagram Limited have made a generous contribution to the prize money, which includes a trophy value £1,650 and a challenge trophy to be returned to the racecourse by 10th March 1988. For seven-year-olds & upwards. The second to receive £16,710, the third £8,210 and the fourth £3,960. The trainer of the Winner to receive a trophy value £600 and the rider of the Winner a trophy value £600

	Date: 4th April 1987		Starters: 40	Time: 9 mins 19.3 secs
1st	**MAORI VENTURE**	11.10–13	*(Mr H J Joel)*	**S C Knight**
2nd	**THE TSAREVICH**	11.10–5	*(Major I C Straker)*	**J White**
3rd	**LEAN AR AGHAIDH**	10.10–0	*(Mrs W Tulloch)*	**G Landau**
4th	**WEST TIP**	10.11–7	*(Mr P Luff)*	**R Dunwoody**
5th	**YOU'RE WELCOME**	11.10–2	*(Mr & Mrs S N J Embiricos)*	**P Hobbs**
6th	**TRACYS SPECIAL**	10.10–0	*(Mr L A H Ames)*	**S McNeill**
7th	**THE ELLIER**	11.10–0	*(Full Circle Thoroughbred Co)*	**F Berry**
8th	**ATTITUDE ADJUSTER**	7.10–6	*(Mrs J Magnier)*	**N Madden**
9th	**NORTHERN BAY**	11.10–1	*(Cheveley Park Stud)*	**R Crank**
10th	**MONANORE**	10.10–3	*(Mr J Meagher)*	**T Morgan**
11th	**SMITH'S MAN**	9.10–0	*(Smith Mansfield Meat Co)*	**M Perrett**
12th	**CORBIERE**	12.10–10	*(Mr B R H Burrough)*	**B De Haan**
13th	**BIG BROWN BEAR**	10.10–2	*(Mr G B Barlow)*	**R Stronge**
14th	**CRANLOME**	9.10–0	*(Mrs P F N Fanning)*	**M Richards**
15th	**COLONEL CHRISTY**	12.10–0	*(Mr R H Hardy & Mr R A Keen)*	**S Moore**
16th	**PLUNDERING**	10.10–11	*(Mrs Miles Valentine)*	**P Scudamore**
17th	**PREBEN FUR**	10.10–0	*(Mr J A Thole)*	**A Stringer**
18th	**BRIGHT DREAM**	11.10–2	*(Mr J F Holmes)*	**R Rowe**
19th	**WHY FORGET**	11.10–0	*(Mr P Piller & Mr W A Stephenson)*	**C Grant**
20th	**GALA PRINCE**	10.10–0	*(Mrs Mary Aston)*	**T Jarvis**
21st	**BRIT**	8.10–1	*(Mr T Jarvis)*	**A Jones**
22nd	**INSURE**	9.10–10	*(Mrs Eileen Turner)*	**Mr C Brooks**

Also Ran:

BEWLEY'S HILL 10.12–0 (USA) (Mrs W B Dixon Stroud, jnr) **Mr W B Dixon Stroud, jnr** *Brought-down*; *VALENCIO 10.12–0* (Czechoslovakia) (Mrs P Seabrook & Miss S Meyer) **R Rowell** *Fell*; *DRUMLARGAN 13.11–2* (Mr G J D Wragg) **Mr G Wragg** *Pulled-up*; *CLASSIFIED 11.10–3* (Cheveley Park Stud) **S Smith Eccles** *Saddle slipped – unseated rider*; *GLENRUE 10.10–3* (Coteville Group) **B Powell** *Fell*; *DARK IVY 11.10–2* (Mrs S Catherwood) **P Tuck** *Hampered – fell*; *DALTMORE 9.10–0* (Mr N Coburn) **A Mullins** *Pulled-up*; *SMARTSIDE 12.10–0* (Mrs E Doyle) **P Gill** *Fell*; *RUN TO ME 12.10–2* (Mr N R Mitchell) **Mr N Mitchell** *Pulled-up*; *HI HARRY 9.10–0* (Mrs M Hefferman) **M Flynn** *Refused*; *MARCOLO 10.10–0* (Mr D Ferguson) **P Leech** *Fell*; *BROWN TRIX 9.10–8* (Mr D F Pitcher) **Mr D F Pitcher** *Unseated rider*; *LITTLE POLVEIR 10.10–2* (Mr M L Shone) **C Brown** *Unseated rider*; *EAMONS OWEN 10.10–0* (Mr W G N Morgan) **Miss Jacqui Oliver** *Unseated rider*; *BROWN VEIL 12.10–1* (Mrs A G Lawe) **Mr M Armytage** *Pulled-up*; *LUCKY REW 12.10–0* (Mrs M S Teversham) **C Mann** *Fell*; *LE BAMBINO 10.10–2* (Mr M Meade) **C Warren** *Pulled-up*; *SPARTAN ORIENT 11.10–0* (Mr H B Geddes & Mr J S King) **L Harvey** *Hampered – knocked-over*

The Betting: *5/1 West Tip; 11/2 Dark Ivy; 9/1 Classified; 12/1 Corbiere; 14/1 Smith's Man & Lean Ar Aghaidh; 16/1 Plundering; 18/1 The Ellier; 20/1 Monanore & The Tsarevich; 25/1 Attitude Adjuster; 28/1 Maori Venture; 33/1 Glenrue & Little Polveir; 40/1 Why Forget; 45/1 Insure; 50/1 Bright Dream, Tracys Special, You're Welcome & Northern Bay; 66/1 Drumlargan, Preben Fur & Marcolo; 100/1 Bewley's Hill, Brown Trix, Daltmore, Hi Harry & Smartside; 150/1 Run to Me; 200/1 Big Brown Bear, Brown Veil & Eamons Owen; 300/1 Colonel Christy; 500/1 Valencio, Gala Prince, Lucky Rew, Cranlome, Le Bambino, Brit & Spartan Orient.*

Distances: *Five lengths; four lengths*

Winner Trained By: *Andrew Turnell, East Hendred, Oxfordshire*

Value to Winning Owner: *£64,710*

1988

With MAORI VENTURE retired after a first successful visit to Aintree, early ante-post betting centred around the three which finished closest to Jim Joel's 'National winner. THE TSAREVICH had gone up five pounds in the handicap, yet owner Major Straker remained convinced the twelve-year-old would be difficult to beat. LEAN AR AGHAIDH followed up his 'National performance with a victory in Sandown's Whitbread Gold Cup. Other well-fancied horses included the Jim Dreaper-trained HARD CASE, the principal hope of the Irish, BUCKO, BORDER BURG and the Peter Scudamore-ridden STRANDS OF GOLD, the ever-popular WEST TIP and the youngster SACRED PATH who – in spite of his 14-month injury – was sent off the 17/2 favourite.

RHYME 'N' REASON was a proven out-and-out stayer by French stallion KEMAL, out of the unraced mare SMOOTH LADY. Bred by Mrs J F C Maxwell at Downpatrick, County Down, he passed into the hands of trainer Michael Dickinson. In only his second season, while handled by David Murray-Smith, RHYME 'N' REASON won a valuable 'chase over Liverpool's Mildmay 'course and just three weeks later became only the second English-trained winner of the Jameson Irish Grand National. By 1988 he had become a member of David Elsworth's team.

A notable prelude to the big race came with HRH the Princess Royal's unveiling Philip Blacker's statue of RED RUM. There was a six-minute delay at the start as the result of REPINGTON and Gee Armytage-ridden GEE-A breaking the tape, but once repaired the field thundered away to a mighty cheer. The customary charge across Melling Road was headed by IN-SURE, LEAN AR AGHAIDH, BIG BROWN BEAR

and LITTLE POLVEIR, but seconds later the favourite SACRED PATH made an early departure at the first fence, joined by two of the least-fancied runners, HETTINGER and TULLAMARINE. SMITH'S MAN was pulled up before reaching the third, at which point YOU'RE WELCOME blundered so badly that his jockey lost his irons and was forced to pull up.

At Becher's, BIG BROWN BEAR held a fractional lead from LEAN AR AGHAIDH. Cruising along comfortably in mid-division, RHYME 'N' REASON met and cleared the mighty fence perfectly but the notorious drop on landing left him sprawling. Incredibly jockey Powell retained his seat, wisely allowed the horse time to make its own recovery and amazingly RHYME 'N' REASON continued, albeit in last place. Less fortunate at the Brook was LUCISIS, brought down by the falling MARCOLO. Still disputing the lead at the Canal Turn, BIG BROWN BEAR and LEAN AR AGHAIDH maintained their position. LEAN AR AGHAIDH showed the way over the Chair, in company with GEE-A and COURSE HUNTER, then came ETON ROUGE, LITTLE POLVEIR and BIG BROWN BEAR and, in the middle of the main bunch of survivors, RHYME 'N' REASON. As both LEAN AR AGHAIDH and BIG BROWN BEAR began to tire shortly after the nineteenth, STRANDS OF GOLD moved strongly to the front, approaching Becher's with a clear advantage. Sadly the nine-year-old clipped the top of the fence, came down too steeply and unseated champion jockey Peter Scudamore. Almost directly behind came COURSE HUNTER who, obviously distracted, slithered for many yards on his nose before recovering. LITTLE POLVEIR was now in front, with RHYME 'N' REASON moving smoothly in second place ahead of WEST TIP, DURHAM EDITION, LAST-

OFTHEBROWNIES and MONANORE. At the plain fence after Valentine's LITTLE POLVEIR unseated his rider and at the next ditch LASTOFTHEBROWNIES fell and GEE-A was pulled up. RHYME 'N' REASON now led the field with WEST TIP, MONANORE and DURHAM EDITION soon getting up to give him the necessary competition. RHYME 'N' REASON came to the final obstacle some three lengths behind DURHAM EDITION, but rallied magnificently. In the final one hundred and fifty yards he passed DURHAM EDITION and running on in spectacular fashion, RHYME 'N' REASON passed the post four lengths in front, with MONANORE in third place and WEST TIP a worthy fourth.

The winning jockey was called before the Stewards to answer their charges of excessive use of the whip in the closing stages of the race. A new Jockey Club Instruction had been issued only sixteen days before, stipulating that anything over ten strokes of the whip could result in disciplinary action from the Stewards. Happily for Brendan Powell, the Liverpool Stewards concluded their investigation by congratulating him on a splendid performance.

RHYME 'N' REASON comes down at Becher's Brook but recovers to win

---

THE GRAND NATIONAL HANDICAP STEEPLECHASE

1988

Guaranteed minimum value £100,000. For seven-year-olds & upwards. Seagram Limited have generously contributed to the prize money, which includes a trophy value £2,000 for the winning owner plus a challenge trophy, to be returned to the racecourse by 9th March 1989. The second to receive £17,661, the third £8,630 and the fourth £4,110. The trainer of the Winner to receive a trophy value £600 and the rider of the Winner a trophy value £600

Date: 9th April 1988	Starters: 40	Time: 9 mins 53.5 secs
1st **RHYME 'N' REASON**	9.11–0 *(Miss Juliet E Reed)*	**B Powell**
2nd **DURHAM EDITION**	10.10–9 *(Mr R Oxley)*	**C Grant**
3rd **MONANORE**	11.10–4 *(Full Circle Thoroughbreds plc)*	**T J Taaffe**
4th **WEST TIP**	11.11–7 *(Mr P Luff)*	**R Dunwoody**
5th **ATTITUDE ADJUSTER**	8.10–6 *(Mrs J Magnier)*	**N Madden**
6th **FRIENDLY HENRY**	8.10–4 *(Mr R V Wright)*	**N Doughty**
7th **THE TSAREVICH**	12.10–10 *(Major I C Straker)*	**J White**
8th **COURSE HUNTER**	10.10–1 *(Mr D Buik)*	**P Croucher**
9th **LEAN AR AGHAIDH**	11.11–0 *(Mrs W Tullouch)*	**G Landau**

Also Ran:

HARD CASE 10.10–12 (Lady Thomson) **K Morgan** *Fell*; *BORDER BURG 11.10–7* (Mr J S Delahooke) **S Sherwood** *Pulled-up*; *LITTLE POLVEIR 11.10–7* (Mr M L Shone) **T Morgan** *Unseated rider*; *LUCISIS 9.10–6* (Mrs H McParland) **Mr J Queally** *Brought-down*; *MIDNIGHT MADNESS 10.10–5* (Mr D Bloomfield) **M Richards** *Pulled-up*; *BUCKO 11.10–5* (Mr J P McManus) **M Dwyer** *Pulled-up*; *STRANDS OF GOLD 9.10–3* (Independent Twine Manufacturing Co Ltd) **P Scudamore** *Fell*; *GEE-A 9.10–3* (Mr G A Hubbard) **Gee Armytage** *Pulled-up*; *YOU'RE WELCOME 12.10–1* (Mr S N J Embiricos & Mrs S N J Embiricos) **P Hobbs** *Pulled-up*; *REPINGTON 10.10–1* (Mr J R Gilman) **C Hawkins** *Refused*; *TRACYS SPECIAL 11.10–0* (Mr L A H Ames) **S Knight** *Pulled-up*; *SACRED PATH 8.10–0* (Mrs Christopher Heath) **C Cox** *Fell*; *MEMBERSON 10.10–3* (Mr P Dufosee) **R J Beggan** *Pulled-up*; *NORTHERN BAY 12.10–4* (Mr R Graham) **H Davies** *Pulled-up*; *SIR JEST 10.10–2* (Mr P Piller) **K Jones** *Refused*; *KUMBI 13.10–0* (Mr D A Lunt) **C Llewellyn** *Fell*; *SMITH'S MAN 10.10–0* (Smith Mansfield Meat Co Ltd) **M Perrett** *Pulled-up*; *BIG BROWN BEAR 11.10–2* (Mr G B Barlow) **R Stronge** *Refused*; *BRIGHT DREAM 12.10–2* (Mr J F Holmes) **R Rowe** *Brought-down*; *INSURE 10.10–0* (Mrs Eileen Turner) **B de Haan** *Unseated rider*; *LASTOFTHEBROWNIES 8.10–0* (Mr M J Smurfit) **T Carmody** *Fell*; *ETON ROUGE 9.10–5* (Mrs Bryan P Jenks) **D Browne** *Pulled-up*; *MARCOLO 11.10–0* (Mr D Ferguson) **Miss V Williams** *Fell*; *POLLY'S PAL 10.10–0* (Mr S G Payne) **J K Kinane** *Jockey knocked from saddle*; *SMARTSIDE 13.10–4* (Mrs Virginia Hambly) **Mr A Hambly** *Fell*; *BRASS CHANGE 10.10–0* (Mr N J Goodliff & Mr J N L Banister) **M Kinane** *Fell*; *PREBEN FUR 11.10–0* (Mr J A Thole) **S J O'Neill** *Pulled-up*; *TULLAMARINE 11.10–0* (Mr P Burfield) **M Bowlby** *Fell*; *SEEANDEM 8.10–0* (Mr B J Caffrey) **P Leech** *Refused*; *OYDE HILLS 9.10–0* (Mrs B N Bletsoe & Mr R C Parker) **M Brennan** *Refused*; *HETTINGER 8.10–0* (Miss Linda Quick) **Penny Ffitch-Heyes** *Fell*.

The Betting: *17/2 Sacred Path; 10/1 Lean Ar Aghaidh & Rhyme 'N' Reason; 11/1 West Tip; 13/1 Hard Case; 16/1 Repington, Bucko & Border Burg; 18/1 The Tsarevich; 20/1 Course Hunter, Durham Edition & Strands of Gold; 22/1 Sir Jest; 25/1 Midnight Madness & Lastofthebrownies; 33/1 You're Welcome, Little Polveir, Tracys Special, Gee-A, Memberson, Attitude Adjuster & Monanore; 40/1 Lucisis; 50/1 Northern Bay & Smith's Man; 66/1 Big Brown Bear & Bright Dream; 80/1 Eton Rouge & Insure; 100/1 Oyde Hills, Friendly Henry, Polly's Pal, Preben Fur, Kumbi, Brass Change, Smartside & Seeandem; 200/1 Marcolo, Hettinger & Tullamarine.*

Distances: *Four lengths; fifteen lengths*

Winner Trained By: *David R C Elsworth, Whitsbury, Hants*

Value to Winning Owner: *£85,881*

1989

National Museums and Galleries on Merseyside opened their doors in March 1989 to an international exhibition celebrating the 150th birthday of the world's greatest steeplechase. It was a resounding success, with over a million visitors in three months.

Aintree's General Manager John Parrett took over as Clerk of the Course, and together with the new Chairman, Peter Greenall, welcomed the increased patronage of Seagram, who for the first time sponsored the entire three days' racing, which carried over £360,000 in added money with the 'National prize money extending to the first six horses.

There were nine fewer entries than the previous year, but some of the expected runners showed considerable quality. Among them were the 1987 Cheltenham Gold Cup winner THE THINKER, and the eight-year-old Welsh 'National hero from Martin Pipe's yard, BONANZA BOY ridden by Peter Scudamore. Another winner of the Welsh 'National was STEARSBY, while proven old stagers such as WEST TIP, DURHAM EDITION, MONANORE and ATTITUDE ADJUSTER appeared again. The rising star MR FRISK was withdrawn on the eve of the race when it became clear that the heavy going would be totally against him. On the strength of his recent Cheltenham triumph, the lightly raced DIXTON HOUSE became a firm 7/1 favourite, while at the considerably longer odds of 100/1, the last-minute purchase of NUMERATE by her father Peter allowed twenty-four-year-old Tarnya Davis to become the only woman in the line-up.

By that prolific sire of jumpers, CANTAB (out of BLUE-SPEEDWELL), LITTLE POLVEIR had originally been bought by Ross-on-Wye trainer, John Edwards for Michael Shone as an unraced four-year-old and had won the Scottish 'National in heavy going. In spite of his splendid performance in the previous year's Aintree marathon, LITTLE POLVEIR was sold for £15,000 just six weeks before the race to Edward Harvey with the sole intention of carrying his son, Captain David Harvey, in Sandown's Grand Military Gold Cup where he finished fourth. His new trainer Toby Balding felt justified in letting him take one final tilt at Aintree providing thirty-year-old stable jockey Jimmy Frost, the son of a Devon farmer, with a first-ever ride in the Liverpool showpiece. Although 50/1 on the morning of the race, those odds were reduced to 28/1 by 'the off'.

Yet again, amid the nerve-stretching tension, there was a hold-up at the start. MEMBERSON had to be re-shod when he spread a plate and then BOB TISDALL added to the chaos by breaking the tape. CERIMAU fell at the first, as did CRANLOME at the next which BOB TISDALL refused. BROWN TRIX and STEARSBY, ahead of WEST TIP and DIXTON HOUSE, made Becher's without any further trouble. But at the first Brook SEEANDEM struck the top of the fence and broke his back in coming down head-first, while at the far end BROWN TRIX completely misjudged his take-off, smashed into the body of the fence and crashed in the ugliest of falls to the ground. Adding to the misery, the favourite DIXTON HOUSE fell, together with HETTINGER and SERGEANT SPRITE; while SIR JEST was brought down and ATTITUDE ADJUSTER was extremely lucky to survive when landing on a fallen horse. STEARSBY and WEST TIP went on, sharing the lead, closely pressed by the outsiders MITHRAS and NEWNHAM, and close on their heels Jenny Pitman's TEAM CHALLENGE. A refusal by STEARSBY at the eleventh left WEST TIP in the lead with NEWNHAM now second and LITTLE POLVEIR behind, closely followed by KERSIL and SMART TAR. At the halfway stage, WEST TIP, LITTLE POLVEIR and MITHRAS jumped the Chair in line abreast. Back at the second Becher's, LITTLE POLVEIR was in front, closely pursued by BONANZA BOY, GALA'S IMAGE, LASTOFTHEBROWNIES and WEST TIP. Crossing the Melling Road for the last time LITTLE POLVEIR appeared to be coming back to his field, now just two lengths ahead of LASTOFTHEBROWNIES, DURHAM EDITION, TEAM CHALLENGE, WEST TIP and BONANZA BOY, with THE THINKER running on superbly after a bad mistake at Becher's. WEST TIP's error at the penultimate fence seemed to have put paid to his chances and as LITTLE POLVEIR cleared the last, the fast-finishing DURHAM EDITION appeared to be the danger. But within half a length of the leader, Chris Grant's mount ran out of steam. There was no stopping the spirited finish of LITTLE POLVEIR, who passed the post seven lengths clear of WEST TIP with the riderless SMART TAR alongside him. THE THINKER was third in front of LASTOFTHEBROWNIES, DURHAM EDITION and MONANORE.

Behind trainer Toby Balding's joy in saddling his second 'National winner, twenty years after HIGHLAND WEDDING, was great sadness. His other runner in the race, the ill-fated BROWN TRIX, had to be put down after breaking his shoulder. He was among those calling for changes to both the fences and conditions of the race. After demands were made in the House of Commons that the race be banned unless it conformed to conditions stipulated by animal rights organisations, the Jockey Club announced it would conduct an intensive review of Grand National safety.

THE GRAND NATIONAL HANDICAP STEEPLECHASE
1989

Guaranteed minimum value £105,000. For seven-year-olds & upwards. Seagram Limited have generously contributed to the prize money, which includes a trophy value £2,620 for the winning owner plus a challenge trophy, to be returned to the racecourse by 7th March 1990. The second to receive £18,859, the third £9,157, the fourth £3,949, the fifth £1,639 and the sixth £809. The trainer of the Winner to receive a trophy value £600 and the rider of the Winner a trophy value £600

Date: 8th April 1989	Starters: 40		Time: 10 mins 6.9 secs
1st **LITTLE POLVEIR**	12.10–3	*(Mr Edward Harvey)*	**J Frost**
2nd **WEST TIP**	12.10–11	*(Mr P Luff)*	**R Dunwoody**
3rd **THE THINKER**	11.11–10	*(T P M McDonagh Ltd)*	**S Sherwood**
4th **LASTOFTHE-BROWNIES**	9.10–0	*(Mrs Anne Daly)*	**T Carmody**
5th **DURHAM EDITION**	11.10–11	*(Mr R Oxley)*	**C Grant**
6th **MONANORE**	12.10–6	*(Full Circle Thoroughbreds plc)*	**G McCourt**
7th **GALA'S IMAGE**	9.10–3	*(Sheikh Ali Abu Khamsin)*	**N Doughty**
8th **BONANZA BOY**	8.11–1	*(Mr S Dunster)*	**P Scudamore**
9th **TEAM CHALLENGE**	7.10–0	*(Mrs Elizabeth Hitchins)*	**M Bowlby**
10th **NEWNHAM**	12.10–5	*(Mr M A Johnson)*	**Mr S Andrews**
11th **THE THIRSTY FARMER**	10.10–2	*(Mrs H M Read)*	**L Kelp**

12th	**ATTITUDE ADJUSTER**	**9.10–6** *(Mrs J Magnier)*	**N Madden**
13th	**SIDBURY HILL**	**13.10–0** *(Mr S Pike)*	**K Mooney**
14th	**MR BAKER**	**11.10–0** *(Mr A C Barrett)*	**M Moran**

Also Ran:

STEARSBY 10.10–9 (Miss Claire Burge & Mr P J Dugdale) **B Powell** *Refused*; *BOB TISDALL 10.10–7* (K Al-Said) **J White** *Refused*; *SMART TAR 8.10–3* (Mrs E R Courage) **C Llewellyn** *Fell*; *DIXTON HOUSE 10.10–3* (Mr P S Hill) **T Morgan** *Fell*; *PERRIS VALLEY 8.10–0* (Mr M J Smurfit) **B Sheridan** *Fell*; *GAINSAY 10.10–6* (Mr Errol Brown) **M Pitman** *Fell*; *MEMBERSON 11.10–2* (Mr P Dufosee) **Mr G Upton** *Pulled-up*; *CRANLOME 11.10–0* (Mrs P F N Fanning) **K F O'Brien** *Fell*; *SIR JEST 11.10–1* (Mr P Piller) **M Hammond** *Brought-down*; *QUEENSWAY BOY 10.10–0* (Queensway Securities Ltd) **A Webb** *Refused*; *BEAMWAM 11.10–6* (Mr D Naylor-Leyland & Mr Mel Morris) **Mr D Naylor-Leyland** *Pulled-up*; *SERGEANT SPRITE 9.10–2* (Mr D Worth) **T J Taaffe** *Fell*; *BARTRES 10.10–3* (Mrs David Buik) **G Bradley** *Pulled-up*; *BROWN TRIX 11.10–5* (Mr D F Pitcher) **Mr D F Pitcher** *Fell*; *SEEANDEM 9.10–0* (Mr B J Caffrey) **L Cusack** *Fell*; *CERIMAU 11.10–0* (Mrs Eva Ellis) **P Hobbs** *Fell*; *RAUSAL 10.10–0* (Mrs K Lloyd & Mr T N Bailey) **D Tegg** *Refused*; *FRIENDLY HENRY 9.10–4* (Mr R V Wright) **H Davies** *Fell*; *MITHRAS 11.10–1* (Mrs H F Richards) **R Stronge** *Pulled-up*; *POLAR NOMAD 8.10–0* (James Stoddart Ltd) **A Merrigan** *Pulled-up*; *NUMERATE 10.10–0* (Mr Peter Davis) **Tarnya Davis** *Pulled-up*; *HETTINGER 9.10–0* (Miss Lynda Quick) **R Goldstein** *Fell*; *KERSIL 12.10–0* (Mr J F. Swiers) **A Orkney** *Pulled-up*; *MEARLIN 10.10–0* (Mr C P House) **S McNeill** *Pulled-up*; *SMARTSIDE 14.10–5* (Mr P Bartley & Mrs Virginia Hambly) **Mr A Hambly** *Refused*; *MR CHRIS 10.10–0* (Mr Chris D Liveras) **B Storey** *Fell*.

The Betting: *7/1 Dixton House; 15/2 Durham Edition; 10/1 Bonanza Boy & The Thinker; 12/1 West Tip; 14/1 Stearsby; 16/1 Lastofthebrownies & Perris Valley; 18/1 Smart Tar & Gala's Image; 20/1 Monanore; 25/1 Bob Tisdall, Gainsay & Attitude Adjuster; 28/1 Little Polveir; 30/1 Team Challenge; 33/1 Memberson & Bartres; 40/1 Sir Jest; 50/1 Rausal, Newnham, Queensway Boy & Sergeant Sprite; 66/1 Friendly Henry, Mithras & Cranlome; 80/1 Polar Nomad & Cerimau; 100/1 Beamwam, The Thirsty Farmer, Numerate, Sidbury Hill, Mr Baker & Seeandem; 200/1 Mr Chris; 300/1 Kersil, Brown Trix, Hettinger, Mearlin & Smartside.*

Distances: *Seven lengths; half a length*

Winner Trained By: *G B Balding, Fyfield, Hants*

Value to Winning Owner: *£66,840*

LITTLE POLVEIR (right) lands a nose ahead of DURHAM EDITION at the last

1990

Interest in the 1990 Grand National was intense. Would the alterations to Becher's achieve the desired effect and could the event survive any more adverse publicity? Public concern was further increased when everyone's favourite racehorse, DESERT ORCHID, was entered for the race. Regarded as the ARKLE of the 'eighties, the striking grey had already won three King George VI 'Chases and the 1989 Cheltenham Gold Cup. However, the horse was withdrawn at the first forfeit stage. Making his sixth and final appearance in the race was WEST TIP. Other old-timers included BONANZA BOY, DURHAM EDITION, LASTOFTHEBROWNIES, TEAM CHALLENGE, MONANORE and the ageing YOUNG DRIVER. Of the newcomers – BIGSUN, RINUS, GHOFAR and the Maryland Hunt Cup winner UNCLE MERLIN – most attention centred on the favourite, BROWN WINDSOR. Also in the line-up was the strongly fancied star of the Hunter 'Chase scene, CALL COLLECT, winner of last season's Liverpool Foxhunters' 'Chase.

A prolonged period of dry weather meant very fast ground. Among those withdrawn at the last minute for this reason were THE THINKER, SACRED PATH and WHY SO HASTY. For the connections of MR FRISK, however, the going couldn't have been better. Bred by Ralph Dalton on the North Yorkshire Moors, his sire, BIVOUAC, stood locally at a mere £100, while the former point-to-point dam, JENNY FRISK, cost the breeder only £150. MR FRISK was bought by Mrs Harry Duffey at the 1986 Doncaster Sales and the chestnut flourished immediately under the care of Upper Lambourn trainer, Kim Bailey. Amateur-ridden by Marcus Armytage, Newmarket correspondent for *The Racing Post*, MR FRISK received late support in the ring which reduced his price from 20's to 16/1.

With hardly any delay, the field was despatched in good order, STAR'S DELIGHT showing prominently at the first fence. The only faller here was GALA'S IMAGE. At the next, UNCLE MERLIN took command from BROWN WINDSOR, GEE-A and MR FRISK. Over the re-vamped Becher's Brook, UNCLE MERLIN set a cracking pace. Nearest to him were STAR'S DELIGHT, MR FRISK, POLYFEMUS, CHARTER HARDWARE and BROWN WINDSOR but LANAVOE at the rear of the field fell at the Brook. Tragedy struck two jumps later when the Scottish 'National winner, ROLL-A-JOINT, died instantly after breaking his neck at the Canal Turn. At a fast and furious pace, UNCLE MERLIN and MR FRISK were well ahead as they returned to the racecourse, clearing the Chair six lengths ahead of POLYFEMUS, BROWN WINDSOR, RINUS and PUKKA MAJOR. With the positions up front unchanged, the Irish challenger HUNGARY HUR broke his leg approaching the nineteenth, at which point JOINT SOVEREIGNTY unseated his rider. UNCLE MERLIN rose at Becher's for the second time a length and a half in front of MR FRISK. Unfortunately UNCLE MERLIN touched down awkwardly at an angle, dislodging jockey Hywel Davies and leaving MR FRISK several lengths ahead.

At this point DURHAM EDITION moved into fourth place just ahead of his stablemate, SIR JEST. After Valentine's, BROWN WINDSOR dropped back to leave RINUS and DURHAM EDITION in pursuit of the frontrunner. At the third from home MR FRISK was ten lengths ahead of DURHAM EDITION but this was cut to six at the second last and to just two at the final fence. In the long stretch to the post, DURHAM EDITION gradually gained as they passed the elbow but MR FRISK held on to win by three quarters of a length. Twenty lengths further back came RINUS in third place.

A combination of the extremely firm going and the modification of three fences resulted in an extraordinary time record for the race. MR FRISK's winning time was 8 minutes 47.8 seconds, an amazing 14.1 seconds faster than RED RUM seventeen years before. MR FRISK chalked up another record just weeks later by becoming the first to win the 'National and the Whitbread Gold Cup in the same season.

THE GRAND NATIONAL HANDICAP STEEPLECHASE
1990

With £90,000 added to stakes. For seven-year-olds & upwards. Seagram Limited have generously contributed to the prize money, which includes a trophy value £3,130 for the winning owner plus a challenge trophy to be returned to the racecourse by 8th March 1991. The second to receive £22,110, the third £10,738, the fourth £4,634, the fifth £1,926 and the sixth £954. The trainer of the Winner to receive a trophy value £600 and the rider of the Winner a trophy value £600

Date: 7th April 1990		Starters: 38	Time: 8 mins 47.8 secs
1st	**MR FRISK**	11.10−6 *(Mrs Harry J Duffey)*	**Mr M Armytage**
2nd	**DURHAM EDITION**	12.10−9 *(Mr R Oxley)*	**C Grant**
3rd	**RINUS**	9.10−4 *(Mr A M Proos)*	**N Doughty**
4th	**BROWN WINDSOR**	8.10−10 *(Mr W Shand Kydd & Mr M Buckley)*	**J White**
5th	**LASTOFTHE-BROWNIES**	10.10−0 *(Mrs Anne Daly)*	**C F Swan**
6th	**BIGSUN**	9.10−2 *(Mr J F Horn)*	**R Dunwoody**
7th	**CALL COLLECT**	9.10−5 *(Mr J Clements)*	**Mr R Martin**
8th	**BARTRES**	11.10−0 *(Mrs David Buik)*	**M Bowlby**
9th	**SIR JEST**	12.10−0 *(Mr P Piller)*	**B Storey**
10th	**WEST TIP**	13.10−11 *(Mr P Luff)*	**P Hobbs**
11th	**TEAM CHALLENGE**	8.10−0 *(Mrs E Hitchins & Mr R Hitchins)*	**B de Haan**
12th	**CHARTER HARDWARE**	8.10−0 *(Charter Racing Ltd)*	**N Williamson**
13th	**GALLIC PRINCE**	11.10−4 *(Iberia Airways)*	**Mr J F Simo**
14th	**GHOFAR**	7.10−0 *(Mr Don Taffner & Sir Hugh Dundas)*	**B Powell**
15th	**COURSE HUNTER**	12.10−0 *(Mr David Buik)*	**G Bradley**
16th	**BONANZA BOY**	9.11−9 *(Mr S Dunster)*	**P Scudamore**
17th	**SOLARES**	10.10−0 *(Mr J L Eyre & Mrs Ann Eyre)*	**Mr P McMahon**
18th	**GEE-A**	11.10−2 *(Mr G A Hubbard)*	**D J Murphy**
19th	**MICK'S STAR**	10.10−1 *(Mr P Scammell)*	**S J O'Neill**
20th	**BOB TISDALL**	11.10−5 *(Mr R Ogden)*	**K Mooney**

Also Ran:

HUNGARY HUR 11.11–2 (Miss D Threadwell) **T Carmody** *Pulled-up*; *PUKKA MAJOR 9.10–4* (Mrs Solna Thomson Jones) **M Richards** *Unseated rider*; *GAINSAY 11.10–7* (Mr Errol Brown) **M Pitman** *Fell*; *JOINT SOVEREIGNTY 10.10–1* (Mr W Braid) **L Wyer** *Unseated rider*; *MONANORE 13.10–5* (Full Circle Thoroughbreds plc) **T J Taaffe** *Carried out*; *STAR'S DELIGHT 8.10–0* (Mr F Barr) **J Lower** *Pulled-up*; *GALA'S IMAGE 10.10–0* (Mr B Thackray) **J Shortt** *Fell*; *TORSIDE 11.10–3* (Mr G C Bisgrove) **J Frost** *Pulled-up*; *ROLL-A-JOINT 12.10–0* (Mr Rhys Thomas Williams) **S McNeill** *Fell*; *POLYFEMUS 8.10–2* (Mr G Johnson) **R Rowe** *Pulled-up*; *CONCLUSIVE 11.10 1* (Mr R Shaw & Mrs R Shaw) **S Smith Eccles** *Fell*; *NAUTICAL JOKE 11.10–0* (Mr P Piller) **Mr K Johnson** *Unseated rider*; *AGAINST THE GRAIN 9.10–0* (Mr J F Mawle) **J Osborne** *Pulled-up*; *YOUNG DRIVER 13.10–4* (Mr M Harker) **J Duggan** *Pulled-up*; *UNCLE MERLIN 9.10–3* (Mrs R V Chapman) **H Davies** *Unseated rider*; *LANAVOE 11.10–0* (Mr F J Lacy) **P Leech** *Fell*; *HUNTWORTH 10.10–9* (Mr W H Walter) **Mr A Walter** *Fell*; *THINKING CAP 9.10–0* (Mr M O'Connor) **P Malone** *Fell*.

The Betting: *7/1 Brown Windsor; 15/2 Bigsun; 9/1 Durham Edition; 13/1 Rinus; 14/1 Call Collect & Ghofar; 16/1 Mr Frisk, Bonanza Boy & Uncle Merlin; 18/1 Polyfemus; 20/1 Lastofthebrownies & West Tip; 25/1 Against The Grain; 28/1 Conclusive & Roll-A-Joint; 50/1 Team Challenge, Joint Sovereignty, Hungary Hur & Star's Delight; 66/1 Sir Jest, Bartres, Charter Hardware, Course Hunter, Gee-A, Mick's Star, Bob Tisdall, Gainsay, Nautical Joke, Gala's Image, Huntworth & Torside; 100/1 Gallic Prince, Thinking Cap, Lanavoe, Pukka Major & Monanore; 150/1 Solarès & Young Driver.*

Distances: *Three quarters of a length; twenty lengths*

Winner Trained By: *K C Bailey, Upper Lambourn, Berkshire*

Value to Winning Owner: *£70,871*

DURHAM EDITION, twice the bridesmaid, closes on the winner, MR FRISK, at the post

1991

A Czechoslovakian runner was among the entries in the form of the eight-year-old mare, FRAZE, who had finished second in the Velka Pardubice Steeplechase. Last year's winner MR FRISK was penalised fully a stone by the handicapper for that victory. Those who finished closest to him, DURHAM EDITION and RINUS, were trying again while BONANZA BOY, BIGSUN and TEAM CHALLENGE made another appearance. Newcomers included DOCKLANDS EXPRESS, MASTER BOB and the French raider, OKLAOMA II. The recent Gold Cup victor, GARRISON SAVANNAH was a surprise winner at Cheltenham and with the trainer's son Mark Pitman again in the saddle, GARRISON SAVANNAH's price fell rapidly as the race approached.

Also fresh from a Cheltenham success in the Ritz Club National Hunt Handicap 'Chase was SEAGRAM. By the English stallion BALAK, out of LLANAH, SEAGRAM was bred by Mrs J A Broome in New Zealand. As an unraced three-year-old, he was purchased by Liverpool businessman Peter Brook whose company, Maincrest, was carrying out some work for Grand National sponsors, Seagram UK. In his very first season, SEAGRAM showed promise and at Aintree in 1985, SEAGRAM gained an impressive victory in the White Satin Hurdle. When Major Straker turned down a second invitation to purchase, SEAGRAM continued to compete under the joint ownership of Sir Eric Parker and trainer David Barons. Twenty-five-year-old Cornishman Nigel Hawke was given a promising first ride in the race, providing the rain held off.

Two days before the race Her Majesty The Queen Mother officially opened the new Grandstand named in her honour.

A demonstration by animal rights activists caused a delay of eight minutes to the start but once the course was cleared, it was the usual dash to the first fence, with the sole departure of the much-fancied DOCKLANDS EXPRESS. RUN AND SKIP came down at the second, by which time GOLDEN FREEZE had taken up the running, followed by OKLAOMA II, GENERAL CHANDOS and OVER THE ROAD with GARRISON SAVANNAH alongside RINUS. Falls were few and far between, Becher's claiming no victims this time, although at the next fence Spanish amateur Jose Simo parted company with SOUTHERNAIR. Just before re-crossing Melling Road, SEAGRAM blundered through the twelfth fence and it was to the jockey's credit that the partnership remained intact. At the Chair TEAM CHALLENGE touched down together with his stablemate GOLDEN FREEZE. With GARRISON SAVANNAH barely two lengths in arrears, Jenny Pitman had three horses in the first five at the halfway stage. RINUS and OKLAOMA II kept up well, closely followed by GENERAL CHANDOS, OVER THE ROAD, NEW HALEN, BALLYHANE, DURHAM EDITION and – although obviously disliking the ground – MR FRISK. SEAGRAM was beginning to make progress after his mishap. RINUS joined GOLDEN FREEZE in the lead at the eighteenth but fell at the twentieth. At Becher's it was the Pitman pair well in command, long-time leader GOLDEN FREEZE just ahead of GARRISON SAVANNAH, with NEW HALEN surviving an error in third place in front of OVER THE ROAD, SEAGRAM and AUNTIE DOT. MR FRISK was wisely pulled up before reaching the Brook. Back on to the racecourse for the final time it was GARRISON SAVANNAH out in front, looking the winner bar a fall and with a brilliant jump at the second last he increased his lead to four lengths over SEAGRAM and the struggling AUNTIE DOT.

SEAGRAM (centre left) takes the second Becher's upsides AUNTIE DOT and behind Jenny Pitman's pair, GOLDEN FREEZE (front centre) and GARRISON SAVANNAH (right)

DURHAM EDITION's late effort now petered out and BONANZA BOY had left himself too much to do. Out-jumping SEAGRAM with another fine leap at the last, GARRISON SAVANNAH increased his advantage to several lengths, setting the crowds cheering home the first horse ever to emulate GOLDEN MILLER's record-breaking double feat of 1934. As so often in the past, however, the 494 yards to the winning post were to prove too demanding, and the blue-blinkered GARRISON SAVANNAH suddenly faltered as he passed the elbow. Unbelievably SEAGRAM was getting closer to the leader with every stride, his jockey Nigel Hawke sensing victory. SEAGRAM passed GARRISON SAVANNAH just 100 yards from the post, increasing his winning margin as he crossed the line to five lengths. A further eight lengths back came AUNTIE DOT in front of OVER THE ROAD, BONANZA BOY and DURHAM EDITION.

1991

With £115,000 added to stakes. For seven-year-olds & upwards. Seagram Limited have generously contributed to the prize money, which includes a trophy value £3,500 for the winning owner plus a challenge trophy to be returned to the racecourse by 7th March 1992. The second to receive £28,370, the third £13,771, the fourth £5,934, the fifth £2,458 and the sixth £1,210. The trainer of the Winner to receive a trophy value £600 and the rider of the Winner a trophy value £600

Date: 6th April 1991		Starters: 40	Time: 9 mins 29.9 secs
1st	**SEAGRAM**	11.10–6 *(Sir Eric Parker & Mr D H Barons)*	**N Hawke**
2nd	**GARRISON SAVANNAH**	8.11–1 *(Autofour Engineering)*	**M Pitman**
3rd	**AUNTIE DOT**	10.10–4 *(Mrs R Wilson)*	**M Dwyer**
4th	**OVER THE ROAD**	10.10–0 *(Mr J R Upson)*	**R Supple**
5th	**BONANZA BOY**	10.11–7 *(Mr S Dunster)*	**P Scudamore**
6th	**DURHAM EDITION**	13.10–13 *(Mr R Oxley)*	**C Grant**
7th	**GOLDEN MINSTREL**	12.10–2 *(Mr W E Gale)*	**T Grantham**
8th	**OLD APPLEJACK**	11.10–1 *(Mr G Tobitt)*	**T Reed**
9th	**LEAGAUNE**	9.10–0 *(Mr Carl Wright)*	**M Richards**
10th	**FOYLE FISHERMAN**	12.10–0 *(Mr J N Hutchinson)*	**E Murphy**
11th	**BALLYHANE**	10.10–3 *(Mr H J Joel)*	**D Murphy**
12th	**HARLEY**	11.10–0 *(Miss Judy Eaton)*	**G Lyons**
13th	**MICK'S STAR**	11.10–0 *(Mrs Anne Daly & Mr Paschal Butler)*	**C Swan**
14th	**TEN OF SPADES**	11.11–1 *(Mr W H Whitbread)*	**J White**
15th	**FOREST RANGER**	9.10–0 *(K Al Said)*	**D Tegg**
16th	**YAHOO**	10.11–1 *(Mr Alan Parker & Mr Howard Parker)*	**N Williamson**
17th	**GOLDEN FREEZE**	9.11–0 *(Mrs Eliz Hitchins & Mr Robert Hitchins)*	**M Bowlby**

Also Ran:

FRAZE 8.11–10 (Statni Statek Benesov) (Czech) **V Chaloupka** *Pulled-up*; *MR FRISK 12.11–6* (Mrs H J Duffey) **Mr M Armytage** *Pulled-up*; *RINUS 10.10–7* (Mr A M Proos) **N Doughty** *Fell*; *OKLAOMA II 11.10–7* (Mr R Mancuso) (France) **R Kleparski** *Pulled-up*; *MASTER BOB 11.10–5* (Mr Ian Wills) **J Osborne** *Pulled-up*; *BIGSUN 10.10–4* (Mr John F Horn) **R Dunwoody** *Pulled-up*; *SOLIDASAROCK 9.10–4* (Mr Les Randall) **G Bradley** *Pulled-up*; *DOCKLANDS EXPRESS 9.10–3* (Mr R H Baines) **A Tory** *Fell*; *HUNTWORTH 11.10–8* (Exors of the late Mr W H Walter) **Mr A Walter** *Pulled-up*; *CRAMMER 11.10–2* (Mr Bill Matthews) **Mr J Durkan** *Unseated rider*; *SOUTHERNAIR 11.10–1* (Mr S Powell) **Mr J Simo** *Fell*; *ENVOPAK TOKEN 10.10–0* (Mr Frank Arthur) **M Perrett** *Pulled-up*; *NEW HALEN 10.10–0* (Mrs Sally Siviter) **S J O'Neill** *Unseated rider*; *RUN AND SKIP 13.10–0* (Mr J L Chamberlain) **D Byrne** *Fell*; *GENERAL CHANDOS 10.10–3* (Lady Harris) **Mr J Bradburne** *Pulled-up*; *THE LANGHOLM DYER 12.10–6* (Edinburgh Woollen Mill Ltd) **G McCourt** *Unseated rider*; *TEAM CHALLENGE 9.10–0* (Mrs E Hitchins & Mr R Hitchins) **B de Haan** *Refused*; *JOINT SOVEREIGNTY 11.10–0* (Mr W Braid) **L O'Hara** *Fell*; *BUMBLES FOLLY 10.10–5* (Mr Colin Lewis) **J Frost** *Pulled-up*; *MISTER CHRISTIAN 10.10–0* (Mr J M T Gaisford & Mr R N Stevens) **S Earle** *Pulled-up*; *HOTPLATE 8.10–2* (W W Bellamy Bakers Ltd) **P Niven** *Pulled-up*; *BLUE DART 11.10–2* (Mr H K Padfield & Mrs D Padfield) **H Davies** *Unseated rider*; *ABBA LAD 9.10–0* (Mrs A Taylor & Miss L H Taylor) **D Gallagher** *Pulled-up*.

The Betting: *13/2 Bonanza Boy; 7/1 Garrison Savannah & Rinus; 9/1 Bigsun; 12/1 Seagram; 15/1 Ten Of Spades; 20/1 Docklands Express & Master Bob; 22/1 Ballyhane; 25/1 Mr Frisk & Durham Edition; 28/1 Crammer & Envopak Token; 33/1 Yahoo; 40/1 Golden Freeze & Foyle Fisherman; 50/1 Golden Minstrel, Team Challenge, Auntie Dot, Over The Road, New Halen, Huntworth & Solidasarock; 66/1 Old Applejack, Run And Skip & Oklaoma II; 80/1 Blue Dart & Hotplate; 100/1 Mister Christian, Fraze, The Langholm Dyer, Southernair, Joint Sovereignty, Forest Ranger & Mick's Star; 150/1 Harley, General Chandos & Bumbles Folly; 200/1 Leagaune; 250/1 Abba Lad.*

Distances: *Five lengths; eight lengths*

Winner Trained By: *D H Barons, Woodleigh, Devon*

Value to Winning Owner: *£90,970*

1992

With a whopping £91,825 contribution towards the prize money for the 'National alone, French brandy producers Martell, Seagram's recently acquired subsidiary, entered the field of British race sponsorship. From Aintree Racecourse Company came the long-awaited news that for the first time in twenty years there would be a second fixture in the autumn.

Following his victory in the Cheltenham Gold Cup, COOL GROUND was pointed at the 'National. After a year on the sidelines through injury, BROWN WINDSOR made a reappearance together with last year's winner SEAGRAM and other notables from that contest such as DOCKLANDS EXPRESS, AUNTIE DOT and OVER THE ROAD. Champion Scudamore teamed up this time with DOCKLANDS EXPRESS leaving Steve Smith Eccles to partner BONANZA BOY. Other newcomers included Neale Doughty's twelve-year-old mount TWIN OAKS who had won six steeplechases at Haydock Park, former Irish 'National winner OMERTA, Jenny Pitman's WILLSFORD, the Irish-trained LAURA'S BEAU and COOL GROUND's stablemate, ROMANY KING.

The most topical tip with the General Election less than a week away also came from the ranks of the newcomers in the giant form of eight-year-old PARTY POLITICS. Bred by his owner, Buckinghamshire farmer David Stoddart, from the stallion POLITICO out of the former 'chase winning mare SPIN AGAIN, PARTY POLITICS was already spoken of at the end of his first season as one of the leading novice 'chasers in the country although an over-ambitious attempt at the Gold Cup ended with his being pulled-up four from home. PARTY POLITICS was still without a win this season. Yet just forty-eight hours before

the race, the tallest horse in training was bought by David Thompson, as a gift for his wife Patricia. The twenty-six-year-old Welshman, Carl Llewellyn, deputised for the injured Andy Adams on PARTY POLITICS and the big horse, trained by Nick Gaselee, went to post at 14/1.

As the forty runners prepared to begin the parade down the course, Neale Doughty hurriedly took TWIN OAKS back to the paddock; apparently the stitching of his saddle had come apart. Back in the line-up TWIN OAKS and the rest were sent off without delay, the veteran GOLDEN MINSTREL setting the pace. RAWHIDE was the only victim at the first, leaving GOLDEN MINSTREL, FOREST RANGER, WILLSFORD, GHOFAR, OVER THE ROAD and BROWN WINDSOR blazing a trail down to Becher's. In this order they rose at the infamous Brook, but even in its modified form it proved too much for the second favourite BROWN WINDSOR. Dunwoody's mount seemed certain to bring down the closely following PARTY POLITICS, yet with surprising agility, the massive animal side-stepped the obstruction without breaking his stride. OMERTA pulled up before reaching the next, HONEYBEER MEAD unseated his rider at the Canal Turn and STEARSBY refused at Valentine's, when WILLSFORD took up the running. After ROWLANDSONS JEWELS parted company with his rider at the Chair, thirty-four runners set off on the second circuit. Still out in front over the nineteenth, WILLSFORD was closely pressed by GOLDEN MINSTREL and HOT-PLATE. Most prominent among the challengers were OVER THE ROAD, GHOFAR, ROMANY KING, FOREST RANGER, COOL GROUND and KARAKTER REFERENCE, while to the rear BONANZA BOY and NEW HALEN found this big ditch the end of their journey. At Becher's, the order was much the same except that PARTY POLITICS had joined those queuing up to tackle the leaders. A fine leap at Valentine's took him into fourth place on the heels of ROMANY KING, HOTPLATE and WILLSFORD. Producing another good jump two fences later, PARTY POLITICS struck the front. His devastatingly long stride never once faltered on that long run home and with the solitary exception of ROMANY KING,

the opposition was routed even before the final fence. PARTY POLITICS crossed the line two and a half lengths in front of ROMANY KING, with LAURA'S BEAU a further fifteen lengths back. DOCKLANDS EXPRESS was fourth, ahead of TWIN OAKS and JUST SO. In all, twenty-two completed the course and there were no injuries to either horses or riders.

A jubilant Carl Llewellyn on the gigantic PARTY POLITICS is led into the winner's enclosure by the traditional escort

1992

With £125,000 added to stakes. For seven-year-olds & upwards. Martell Limited have generously contributed £91,825 to the prize money, which includes a trophy value £4,150 for the winning owner plus a challenge trophy, to be returned to the racecourse by 5th March 1993. The second to receive £31,186, the third £15,151, the fourth £6,543, the fifth £2,726 and the sixth £1,355. The trainer of the Winner to receive a trophy value £750 and the rider of the Winner a trophy value £750. Martell will also award a trophy value £200 to the breeder of the winning horse and a further trophy value £200 (in conjunction with the Thoroughbred Breeders Association) to the breeder of the first British-bred horse to finish in this race.

Date: 4th April 1992	Starters: 40		Time: 9 mins 6.4 secs
1st **PARTY POLITICS**	8.10–7	*(Mrs Patricia Thompson)*	C Llewellyn
2nd **ROMANY KING**	8.10–3	*(Mr L J Garrett)*	R Guest
3rd **LAURA'S BEAU**	8.10–0	*(Mr J P McManus)*	C O'Dwyer
4th **DOCKLANDS EXPRESS**	10.11–2	*(Mr R H Baines)*	P Scudamore
5th **TWIN OAKS**	12.11–7	*(Mr J N G Moreton)*	N Doughty
6th **JUST SO**	9.10–2	*(Mr H T Cole)*	S Burrough
7th **OLD APPLEJACK**	12.10–0	*(Mr George Tobitt)*	A Orkney
8th **OVER THE ROAD**	11.10–0	*(Mr J R Upson)*	R Supple
9th **STAY ON TRACKS**	10.10–0	*(Mr P Piller)*	C Grant
10th **COOL GROUND**	10.11–1	*(Whitcombe Manor Racing Stables Ltd)*	M Lynch
11th **GHOFAR**	9.10–3	*(Sir Hugh Dundas & Mr Don Taffner)*	H Davies
12th **FOREST RANGER**	10.10–0	*(K Al Said)*	D Tegg
13th **WHAT'S THE CRACK**	9.10–0	*(Mr Jerry Wright & Mr J S Rigby)*	J Osborne
14th **RUBIKA**	9.10–2	*(Mr Trevor Hemmings)*	P Niven
15th **GOLDEN MINSTREL**	13.10–0	*(Mr W E Gale)*	E Murphy
16th **AUNTIE DOT**	11.10–7	*(Mrs R Wilson & Mr D Wade-Jones)*	M Dwyer
17th **ROC DE PRINCE**	9.10–9	*(Mrs Patricia Thompson)*	C Swan
18th **MIGHTY FALCON**	7.10–0	*(Mr R J Tory & Mrs V A Tory)*	P Holley
19th **RADICAL LADY**	8.10–0	*(N B Mason Farms Ltd)*	J Callaghan
20th **WILLSFORD**	9.10–0	*(Mr Arnie Kaplan & Mr Rex Johnson)*	M Bowlby
21st **TEAM CHALLENGE**	10.10–0	*(Mrs E Hitchins & Mr R Hitchins)*	B de Haan
22nd **SIRRAH JAY**	12.10–0	*(Mr John Gale)*	R J Beggan

Also Ran:

SEAGRAM 12.11–4 (Sir Eric Parker & Mr D H Barons) **N Hawke** *Pulled-up*; *BONANZA BOY 11.10–11* (News International) **S Smith Eccles** *Unseated rider*; *BROWN WINDSOR 10.10–8* (Mr W Shand Kydd & Mr M Buckley) **R Dunwoody** *Fell*; *OMERTA 12.10–4* (Mrs E McMorrow) **L Wyer** *Pulled-up*; *HUNTWORTH 12.10–0* (Mr Alan Walter & Mr M T Walter) **M Richards** *Pulled-up*; *RAWHIDE 8.10–0* (Mrs Harry McCalmont) **K O'Brien** *Unseated rider*; *KARAKTER REFERENCE 10.10–1* (Mrs R J Doorgachurn) **D O'Sullivan** *Pulled-up*; *ROWLANDSONS JEWELS 11.10–3* (Rowlandsons Ltd) **G Bradley** *Unseated rider*; *CLONEY GRANGE 13.10–0* (Mr E O'Dwyer) **D O'Connor** *Fell*; *NEW HALEN 11.10–0* (Mrs Sally Siviter) **R Bellamy** *Refused*; *HOTPLATE 9.10–5* (W W Bellamy Bakers Ltd) **G McCourt** *Pulled-up*; *MISTER ED 9.10–0* (The Talking Horse Partnership) **D Morris** *Fell*; *ROYAL BATTERY 9.10–0* (Mrs P M Cottle & Mr D H Barons) **R Greene** *Pulled-up*; *GOLDEN FOX 10.10–0* (Mrs Kate Lyons & Mr L Fuller) **S Earle** *Refused*; *STEARSBY 13.10–6* (Mr S Flurry) **S Mackey** *Refused*; *KITTINGER 11.10–0* (Mr J S Lammiman) **I Lawrence** *Refused*; *WHY SO HASTY 11.10–0* (Black Horse Racing) **W Worthington** *Pulled-up*; *HONEYBEER MEAD 10.10–0* (Mr B J M Ryall) **N Mann** *Unseated rider*.

The Betting: *15/2 Docklands Express; 8/1 Brown Windsor; 9/1 Twin Oaks; 10/1 Cool Ground; 12/1 Auntie Dot & Laura's Beau; 14/1 Party Politics; 16/1 Romany King, Stay On Tracks & Willsford; 20/1 What's The Crack; 22/1 Over The Road; 25/1 Ghofar & Bonanza Boy; 28/1 Rubika; 33/1 Omerta & Seagram; 35/1 Old Applejack; 40/1 Roc De Prince; 50/1 Hotplate, Just So, Karakter Reference & Rawhide; 60/1 Rowlandsons Jewels; 66/1 Huntworth & New Halen; 80/1 Mighty Falcon, Radical Lady & Royal Battery; 100/1 Cloney Grange, Honeybeer Mead, Mister Ed, Sirrah Jay & Team Challenge; 150/1 Golden Minstrel; 200/1 Forest Ranger, Golden Fox & Kittinger; 250/1 Stearsby & Why So Hasty.*

Distances: *Two and a half lengths; fifteen lengths*

Winner Trained By: *N A Gaselee, Upper Lambourn, Berkshire*

Value to Winning Owner: *£99,943*

INDEX

393

397

399